THE CONSTITUTIONAL HISTORY OF ENGLAND

Classics of British Historical Literature

JOHN CLIVE, EDITOR

William Stubbs

The Constitutional History of England

ABRIDGED AND WITH AN INTRODUCTION BY

JAMES CORNFORD

The University of Chicago Press
CHICAGO AND LONDON

The University of Chicago Press, Chicago 60637
The University of Chicago Press, Ltd., London

Printed in the United States of America
83 82 81 80 79   987654321
ISBN: 0-226-77834-7
LC: 78-61574

James Cornford, formerly professor of
politics at the University of Edinburgh, is
director of the Outer Circle Policy Unit, London.

Contents

Series Editor's Preface

This series of reprints has one major purpose: to put into the hands of students and other interested readers outstanding—and sometimes neglected—works dealing with British history which have either gone out of print or are obtainable only at a forbiddingly high price.

The phrase Classics of British Historical Literature requires some explanation, in view of the fact that the two companion series published by the University of Chicago Press are entitled Classic European Historians and Classic American Historians. Why, then, introduce the word *literature* into the title of this series?

One reason is obvious. History, if it is to live beyond its own generation, must be memorably written. The greatest British historians—Clarendon, Gibbon, Hume, Carlyle, Macaulay—survive today, not merely because they contributed to the cumulative historical knowledge about their subjects, but because they were masters of style and literary artists as well. And even historians of the second rank, if they deserve to survive, are able to do so only because they can still be read with pleasure. To emphasize this truth at the present time, when much eminently solid and worthy academic history suffers from being almost totally unreadable, seems worth doing.

The other reason for including the word *literature* in the title of the series has to do with its scope. To read history is to learn about the past. But if, in trying to learn about the

British past, one were to restrict oneself to the reading of formal works of history, one would miss a great deal. Often a historical novel, a sociological inquiry, or an account of events and institutions couched in semifictional form teaches us just as much about the past as does the "history" that calls itself by that name. And, not infrequently, these "informal" historical works turn out to be less well known than their merit deserves. By calling this series Classics of British Historical Literature it will be possible to include such books without doing violence to the usual nomenclature.

The writing of constitutional history that is both valid and readable requires qualities of learning, industry, discipline, and artistry rarely found in conjunction. Stubbs possessed those qualities. He also had a marvelously developed sense of the concrete; so that, as Maitland pointed out, "while the institutions grow and decay under our eyes, we are never allowed to forget that this process of evolution and dissolution consists of the acts of human beings." In his perceptive introduction, James Cornford places Stubbs's *Constitutional History* midway between the primarily narrative approach of someone like Macaulay and the primarily analytical approach of twentieth-century constitutional historians. As such, in spite of all the later criticism brought forward against it, the book has maintained its secure place as a classic, the work of an undoubted master.

The *Constitutional History* derives its magisterial character in part from Stubbs's disinclination to do what he condemned in those scholars who had variously theorized about the origins of the English jury system—be misled by superficial coincidences or argue on hypothesis only. Stubbs's legendary caution saved him from these pitfalls. In his case, caution was a positive, not a negative quality; a sense for subtleties, nuances, and distinctions which only the very greatest constitutional historians possess in full measure. They need such a sense because, as Stubbs remarks in his discussion of the Anglo-Saxon system of government, in the early history of institutions there are neither constitutional revolutions nor violent reversals of legislation: "Custom is far more potent than law, and custom is modified infinitesimally every day. An alteration of law is often the mere registration of a custom, when men have recognized its altered character. The names of offices and assemblies are permanent, whilst their character has imperceptibly undergone essential change." To find one's way in the face of such difficulties requires wariness as well as knowledge. Like everything else in history, institutions change. But, as in the instance of the changes brought about in England by the manorial institutions that accompanied the Norman conquest, "new forms displace but do not destroy the old, and old rights remain, although changed in title and forced into symmetry with a new legal and pseudo-historical theory."

The great virtue of Stubbs's caution buttressed by his learning was that it enabled him not only to describe the process of institutional change, but also to weigh the extent of its long-term significance. Thus, having concluded that the new forms of social organization introduced by the Normans did not at first sight seem very oppressive, Stubbs goes on to point out that they actually opened up the way for oppression: "The forms they had introduced tended, under the spirit of Norman legality and feudal selfishness, to become hard realities, and in the profound miseries of Stephen's reign the people learned how completely the new theory left them at the mercy of their lords."

Those who approach Stubbs with a preconception, understandable enough, that all institutional history, however worthy, must of necessity be heavy and dull will be agreeably surprised by the frequent vivid touches which form part of the *History.* "When an English archbishop visited Rome," Stubbs writes, "he spent his time in pilgrimages to holy places: the pope received him with a splendid hospitality, that showed him only what it was desirable that he should see; and he came back rich in relics, but as poor as ever in political experience." As in this instance, the vivid touch is never mere embellishment. Here, for example, it makes concrete the isolation of Anglo-Saxon England from continental European politics; an isolation which, Stubbs goes on to explain with characteristic insight, meant neither lack of civilization nor cultivation.

It would be idle to pretend that Stubbs is easy reading, just as it would be idle to pretend that he has not been severely—and in some instances effectively—challenged by later historians on some important points. Yet one must admire not only his judicious approach to historical evidence and its interpretation, but also, perhaps above all, his unremitting search for historical truth, regardless of his own political and other prejudices. Let the summing up be left to Stubbs himself as, at the end of three volumes and almost two thousand pages, he asks the reader's indulgence to moralize. The author's end will have been gained, he writes, "if he has succeeded in helping to train the judgment of his readers to discern the balance of truth and reality, and, whether they go on to further reading with the aspirations of the advocate or the calmness of the critic, to rest content with nothing less than the attainable maximum of truth, to base their arguments on nothing less sacred than that highest justice which is found in the deepest sympathy with erring and straying men."

JOHN CLIVE

Editor's Introduction

The History of Institutions cannot be mastered—can scarcely be approached—without an effort. It affords little of the romantic incident or of the picturesque grouping which constitute the charm of History in general, and holds out small temptation to the mind that requires to be tempted to the study of truth. But it has a deep value and an abiding interest to those who have courage to work upon it. It presents, in every branch, a regularly developed series of causes and consequences, and abounds in examples of that continuity of life, the realisation of which is necessary to give the reader a personal hold on the past and a right judgment of the present. For the roots of the present lie deep in the past, and nothing in the past is dead to the man who would learn how the present comes to be what it is. It is true Constitutional History has a point of view, an insight, and a language of its own; it reads the exploits and characters of men by a different light from that shed by the false glare of arms, and interprets positions and facts in words that are voiceless to those who have only listened to the trumpet of fame. The world's heroes are no heroes to it, and it has an equitable consideration to give to many whom the verdict of ignorant posterity and the condemning sentence of events have consigned to obscurity or reproach. Without some knowledge of Constitutional History it is absolutely impossible to do justice to the characters and positions of the actors in the great drama; absolutely impossible to understand the origin of parties, the development of principles, the growth of nations in spite of parties and in defiance of

> principles. It alone can teach why it is that in politics good men do not always think alike, that the worst cause has often been illustrated with the most heroic virtue, and that the world owes some of its greatest debts to men from whose very memory it recoils.
>
> In this department of study there is no portion more valuable than the Constitutional History of England.

With this austere warning William Stubbs prefaced the first volume of his *Constitutional History,* published in 1874, and succeeded by second and third volumes in 1875 and 1878.

Stubbs was born at Knaresborough in Yorkshire in 1825, the son of a solicitor who died when Stubbs was seven and left the family in severe poverty. He was educated in Knaresborough and at Ripon grammar school. There he came to the attention of the bishop, who obtained a place for him at Christ Church, Oxford, as a servitor. As an undergraduate he spent much of his time in the college library studying old manuscripts and pursuing his lifelong interest in genealogy, and though timid and reserved and practically excluded from the social life of the college, he gained a reputation for learning. Election to a studentship, the equivalent of a fellowship at Christ Church, was not open to a servitor, and shortly after graduation Stubbs was elected to a fellowship at Trinity College in place of his friend and historical ally Freeman. He was ordained in 1850, and in the same year, he was presented to the college living at Navestock in Essex. There in the next sixteen years he devoted himself to his duties as a country parson, married and raised a family, and used his leisure as Tout puts it "in acquiring such a knowledge of the sources for mediaeval English history as made him the foremost scholar of his generation." He was slow to publish and recognition of his merits came more slowly still. It was not until his appointment as an editor of the Rolls series in 1863 that he really made his mark. In 1866, after several disappointments, he was finally elected to the Professorship of Modern History at Oxford. In these years he blossomed from antiquary to historian on the grand scale as he produced first his work on the Rolls series, then the *Select Charters,* and finally the *Constitutional History.* While his research and writing flourished, Stubbs found himself frustrated by the college system from founding a school of history on the German model. He had to content himself with a handful of devoted pupils whose interest survived the tedium of his obligatory lectures to benefit from his personal advice, encouragement, sympathy, and direction. In 1884 Stubbs was offered by Gladstone the bishopric of Chester and in 1889 he was translated to the bishopric of Oxford. From this time his work as a historian came to an end and he fell increasingly out of touch and out of sympathy with the new trends in historical scholarship. Stubbs seldom entered into public controversy, political, ecclesiastical, or historical, but he held strong views expressed forcefully in private conversation and in letters to his friends, Mandell Creighton, E. A. Freeman and J. R. Green, among others. He died in 1901, full of honors, weary of ecclesiastical office, and pining for his historical studies.

The *Constitutional History,* from which these selections were made, is a book great in its length, its scope, and its impact on the conception of English history and of historical study in England. Each of the volumes runs to some six hundred pages, which cover English constitutional development from Tacitus to the Tudors. No selection can do justice to the whole, more especially since Stubbs was a *pointilliste.* He built up his case by the steady, even relentless, accumulation of detail. Moreover, he separated his treatment into narrative and analytical sections. These relate closely to each other, but are too long to be given in full if any sense of the main lines of development is to be conveyed. I have chosen to concentrate on the constitutional analysis at the expense of political narrative, and thus to assume in the reader a general familiarity with the outline of English medieval history. This is perhaps to give an impression of schematic abstraction which is far from the vivid, concrete, and detailed appreciation of the realities of everyday politics which Stubbs displays in his narrative. It was, however, the combination of exact scholarship with a broad interpretive sweep that gave the *Constitutional History* its great appeal and influence, and in these selections I have tried to represent the essential constitutional doctrine which Stubbs set forth for the admiration and satisfaction of late Victorian England:

> The great characteristic of the English constitutional system, in that view of it which is offered in these pages,—the principle of its growth, the secret of its constitution,—is the continuous development of representative institutions from the first elementary stage, in which they are employed for local purposes and in the simplest form, to that in which the national parliament appears as the concentration of all local and provincial machinery, the depository of the collective powers of the three estates of the realm.[1]

For Stubbs the essential steps in this development had been taken before the middle of the fourteenth century: Anglo-Saxon England was marked by the development of the local and provincial machinery of government, which was subordinated to and then combined with the central and sovereign authority of the Norman system. Under the early Plantagenets came the attempt to reconcile royal authority with local self-government and to suppress the vices of feudalism. In the reigns of Henry III and Edward I the balance was struck and given institutional expression: the next three hundred years are a trial "in which the constitution . . . organized and consolidated under Henry II and Edward I is tested to the utmost, strained and bent and warped, but still survives to remedy the tyranny of the Tudors and overthrow the factitious absolutism of the

1. *Constitutional History*, vol. 1, chapt. 13, p. 544.

Stewarts."[2] Thus Stubbs's doctrine may be summarized as holding that the key to the English constitution was the development of Parliament, that the essential principles of representative government were established early, and that this was emphatically a blessing. As Stubbs put it in his little book on *The Early Plantagenets:*

> This history of England under the early kings of the house of Plantagenet unfolds and traces the growth of that constitution which far more than any other that the world has ever seen, has kept alive the forms and spirit of free government; which has been the discipline that formed the great free republic of the present day; which was for ages the beacon of true social freedom that terrified despots abroad and served as the model for the aspirations of hopeful patriots. It is scarcely too much to say that English history, during these ages, is the history of the birth of true political liberty.[3]

Stubbs's message fell upon receptive ears, and from the weight and quality of the supporting argument his version of the Parliamentary view of the Constitution became within twenty years an historical orthodoxy, propagated through the new history school at Oxford and at other universities where the *Constitutional History* and his book of documents *Select Charters* were adopted as texts.

Like all orthodoxies it has come under attack and Stubbs has been variously assailed for exaggeration, hindsight, anachronism, reliance on inadequate sources, and the imposition of bourgeois ideas upon another age. In considering these criticisms we may gain some measure of understanding of Stubbs as scholar, historian, and constitutional theorist.

There is first a fundamental disagreement between Stubbs and the most trenchant critics of his orthodoxy about the idea of constitutional history itself. As Professor

2. *The Early Plantagenets* (London, 1920), p. 276.
3. Ibid. p. 5.

Sayles puts it, "the whole obligation of the historian is to ascertain what mattered to men living at the time, to men who planned for their own day and not for posterity."[4] Stubbs's search for the origins of important constitutional doctrines and practices distorts understanding of what was actually being done at the time and leads not only to false estimates of the contemporary importance of particular institutions but to the substitution of general trends for the mundane and immediate causes of political action. Before examining the specific criticisms of Stubbs's view of Parliament, it must be said that he was well aware of the temptations of hindsight and says in discussing what he calls the opposed constitutional theories of the national and the royal parties at the end of the fourteenth century:

> It is so much easier, in discussing the causes and stages of a political contest, to generalise from the results than to trace the growth of the principles maintained by the actors, that the historian is in some danger of substituting his own formulated conclusions for the programme of the leaders, and of giving them credit for a far more definite scheme and more conscious political sagacity than they would have claimed for themselves . . .[5]

And yet I do not think that Stubbs's awareness of the dangers of hindsight would have inclined him to the view that the whole obligation of the historian is to understand what was in the mind of men living at the time. Throughout the *Constitutional History* there are scattered reflections on the paradox enunciated in the preface: that institutions grow and take on meanings despite the understandings and the motives of the men who create them. Stubbs saw clearly enough the difference between the significance to contemporaries and to posterity of the same actions, but saw it as the role of the historian to draw out

4. G. O. Sayles *The King's Parliament of England* (London, 1975), p. 136.
5. *Constitutional History,* vol. 2, chap. 17, p. 510.

or discern the lines of development from the muddle of events, precisely, in fact, to understand and illuminate what was at best obscure to the actors themselves. The fact that men stumble upon their principles, discover what they think by doing, pursue those arguments that prove persuasive often to their own surprise, does not mean the principles are unimportant, the men hypocrites, or the arguments "mere rhetoric." Some convenient arguments, some appeals to principle, survive and others do not. Some expedients answer more than a temporary need and from their aptness develop a life independent of the intentions of their authors. The central theme of the *Constitutional History,* "the idea of a growth into political enfranchisement," is one which Stubbs admits may never have occurred to contemporaries: "yet, in the long run, this has been the ideal towards which the healthy development of national life in Europe has constantly tended." Thus while one feels respect for Stubbs's reflections on this paradox because of his technical mastery, his grasp of detail, his disinclination to hasty judgment, and the sense that the pattern which he perceives arises from immersion in the evidence, it is also clear that there is at bottom a difference of historical outlook or assumption between Stubbs and his critics. It is not just a case of Stubbs relying too heavily on particular sources, or of his importing back into the Middle Ages the constitutional controversies of the seventeenth century. Though he was neither rationalist, romantic, nor liberal, Stubbs has a view of the unfolding of an idea in history which is unacceptable to positivist and materialist alike. Stubbs is a puzzle because he combines German historicism with "scientific" historical scholarship, and appears to celebrate the triumph of parliamentary democracy although himself a High Church Tory, and an obstinate and unbending one at that. It is remarkable that his view of English history should so much resemble that of the great Whig historians, and that his view of constitutional development should be so much in tune with

Liberal optimism. But while Stubbs is attached to *Constitutionalism,* shares the sense of a unique and fortunate national experience, believes that the unfolding of liberty is the peculiar and blessed gift of the English, his notion of progress has nothing to do with secular liberalism; history for Stubbs is the work of an ultimately benevolent Divine Providence. As he said in his inaugural lecture as Professor of Modern History in the University of Oxford: ". . . we are coming to see . . . a hand of justice and mercy, a hand of progress and order, a kind and wise disposition, ever leading the world on to the better, but never forcing, and out of the evil of men's working bringing continually that which is good."[6]

Thus, though criticisms of his orthodoxy have much force, it is important, if we are to do justice to Stubbs, to recognize how far his methods and assumptions differ from those of his predecessors and contemporaries. Stubbs, indeed, stands at the watershed between the great political historians whose epic works created, endorsed, and sustained a vision of English history in accord with the hegemony of liberal, progressive, and nationalist attitudes and the generation of professional historians whose imagination was exercised not in the creation of national myths but in recreating the experience of the past through strict interpretation of the sources. He stands, as it were, between the narrative manifestoes of Macaulay and the luminous analyses of Maitland. The *Constitutional History* is at once the last of the epics and the first of the monographs. His peculiar achievement was to have given the fullest, clearest, and most sophisticated expression to the national myth through the application of the strictest canons of modern historical scholarship. And thus he set the terms of historical debate for a generation.

That debate was concerned mainly with the priority

6. Quoted by W. H. Hutton *William Stubbs, Bishop of Oxford, 1825-1901* (London, 1906), p. 61.

which Stubbs gave to the representative principle and the role of Parliament in the Middle Ages. Stubbs is held to have perpetuated the errors of the seventeenth-century controversialists by following their preoccupation with the composition of Parliament, and particularly with popular representation, at the expense of a proper consideration of Parliament's judicial and administrative functions. These were much more important to the contemporary concerns of government than were any ideas of representation and also had important consequences for the development of Parliament in the longer term. He is also held to have exaggerated the degree of importance attached to Parliament's powers in relation to taxation and legislation and thus to have exaggerated the development of Parliament as an established part of the system of government and its importance as a check on royal power. In the view of Stubbs's most persistent and exasperated critic, the principles of the Constitution cannot be supposed to have lain in embryo through two and a half centuries waiting for their practical realization.

Parliament itself at the end of the Middle Ages was no more than an expedient of government, which could be dispensed with or not as the King chose, "a device of government with an uncertain tenure of life, liable like any other such device to be outmoded and superseded or, if circumstance and convenience determined, to be remodelled and revivified."[7]

Henry VII did without Parliament and it was Henry VIII's decision in 1529 to use Parliament as the pliant instrument of his reformation, which led by unexpected and unintended turns to the emergence of the Parliament which Stubbs had seen prefigured in the fourteenth century. A friendly critic has defended Stubbs from the charge of anachronism and exaggeration by citing the richness of the evidence recently printed and available to him in the

7. Sayles, op. cit. p. 135.

form of parliamentary writs, statutes, and rolls, all of which emphasized the importance of the representative side of Parliament: "his hand was forced by the sheer bulk and weight of the printed evidence."[8] There is no doubt something in that argument, as there is in the related point that the very availability of this evidence reflected the interests and preoccupations of the parliamentary historians of the seventeenth and eighteenth centuries. It is also, however, to defend Stubbs on slightly misleading grounds and to suggest that perhaps he did not have an adequate grasp of the realities of medieval politics. But no one reading the political narrative of the *Constitutional History* or the introductions to the Rolls series can doubt Stubbs's grasp of those realities: he had no illusions about the motives or foresight of even those few kings in whom he saw a trace of statesmanship. At the conclusion of his great portrait of Henry II, for example, he marks clearly the contrast between personal failure and historical achievement:

> The most able and successful politician of his time, and thoroughly unscrupulous about using his power for his own ends, he yet died in a position less personally important than any he had occupied during the thirty-five years of his reign, and, on the whole, less powerful than he began. Yet if we could distinguish between the man and the king, between personal selfishness and official or political statesmanship, between the ruin of his personal aims and the real success of his administrative conceptions, we might conclude by saying that altogether he was great and wise and successful.
>
> The constitutional historian, [Stubbs continues] cannot help looking with reverence on one under whose hand the foundations of liberty and national independence were so clearly marked and so deeply laid that in the course of one generation the fabric was safe forever from tyrants or conquerors.

Yet a few pages later this extravagance is followed by the

8. J. G. Edwards *William Stubbs,* The Historical Association (1952), p. 12.

remark that "as governments were in those days, any might be accounted good which was conducted on the principle of law, not on caprice. The notions of constitutional sovereignty and liberty were still locked up in the libraries, or in embryo in the brains of the clergy."[9]

As with the politics so with the social and economic forces: Stubbs deliberately regards them as a background, to be understood but barely acknowledged, to the mainstream of constitutional development. This accent on the importance of institutions must make the student of materialist conceptions of history impatient: Stubbs's influence in the formative period of the teaching of history in the universities certainly contributed to a relative neglect of social and economic factors. Perhaps it is permissible now to regard it as a necessary reminder of the importance of institutions, those devices through which men make their history, devices which develop an inertia of their own and become part of the reality with which successive generations grapple despite the intentions, motives, and conditions of their progenitors. Henry VIII may have been free to choose Parliament as his instrument, but the Parliament he chose was not of his own making and what he found at hand included constraints as well as opportunities, the seeds of opposition as well as the promise of support. Stubbs was always aware of the gap between the motives of political actors and the institutional consequences of their actions, though some he regarded as better endowed than others with the faculty of government, with a sense of how the responsibilities of the State could be properly discharged. He disapproved wholeheartedly of the personal immorality of princes, but his scorn and contempt are reserved for those incapable of any larger sense of their duty than that dictated by personal ambition. Richard I he dismisses as "a mere warrior: he would fight

9. In his introduction to the Peterborough Chronicle: A. Hassall *Historical Introductions to the Rolls Series* by William Stubbs (London, 1902), pp. 92–93, 102.

for anything whatever, but he would sell everything that was worth fighting for."[10] Nor has he much patience with failure. There was no constitutional precedent for the deposition of Edward II, and those who compassed it were beneath contempt: "But on the whole it must be said the success of the revolution constitutes its justification . . . . A King who cannot make a stand against rebellion cannot expect justice either in form or substance."[11]

Stubbs reserves his respect for that handful of kings who like Henry II rose above personal concerns and had the practical imagination to adopt measures that were apt both to the exigencies of the time and to the perennial problems of constitutional government. Stubbs's own emphasis on Parliament tends to divert attention from his more general concern with constitutional government. This emerges most strongly in his treatment of the Anglo-Saxons, William the Conqueror, and Henry II. It may be as well to recall when Stubbs is accused of mistaking administrative reforms for precocious forms of parliamentary democracy, that he was almost equally concerned in the earlier period with the establishment of government under law and with the creation of the administrative machinery to provide for effective central government without which order, stability, and therefore liberty were impossible. In the controversy over the Ancient Constitution Stubbs clearly sides with the believers in Anglo-Saxon liberty and self-government; but he accepts the need for effective central government: "There is much truth, he remarked, though only half the truth, in Mr. Carlyle's observation that the pot-bellied equanimity of the Anglo-Saxon needed the drilling and discipline of a century of Norman tyranny."[12] He accepts the need for the royal prerogative as the reservoir of governmental power but rejects the arbitrary or despotic interpretations of the prerogative by Richard II

10. *Constitutional History,* vol. 1, chap. 12, p. 512.
11. *Constitutional History,* vol. 2, chap. 16, pp. 363–64.
12. Hassall, op. cit., p. 109.

or the Stewarts, whom he equates. What he admires in monarchs are moderation, trust, a willingness to work with their people, a grasp of administrative practicalities, and a sense of duty. He abhors the arbitrary, selfish, and untrustworthy, those who separate themselves from their people, and will not practice restraint. The deposition of Edward II he accepts; he rejoices in Magna Carta, since an even more unsatisfactory king is brought to book but by means which create a constitutional mechanism, adopted to meet the pressing needs of the time, but providing also a precedent to bind future unruly monarchs. The temporary expedient becomes the custom of the constitution. This was the process which interested Stubbs and which he saw repeated and enlarged in the practice of calling parliaments—spasmodic, irregular, and uncertain though it was.

It has also to be remembered that the constitutionalism which Stubbs espoused was rather different from current notions of Parliamentary democracy. The doctrines of the constitution with which Stubbs grew up were those of Blackstone, Paley, and de Lolme: the doctrines of the balanced or mixed constitution, in which popular representation has a remedial and restraining function, rather than providing the motive or source of governmental activity. Bentham, Park, and Austin were eccentric radicals, Dicey unknown, the triumph of utilitarian democracy in the future and our present plebiscitary bureaucracy undreamt of. Stubbs's idea of liberty is both concrete and historical. It involves responsibility, discipline, and training rather than the assertion of interest or of abstract rights. The people's rights are founded in positive law and realized in the practice of self government. Stubbs's view is summed up in this comment on the aftermath of Magna Carta:

> the struggle of eighty years which followed the act of Runnymede not only had to vindicate the substantial liberties involved in that act, but to sharpen and perfect and bring into effective and combined working every weapon which,

> forged at different times and for different purposes, could be made useful for the maintenance of self government. The humble processes by which men made their by-laws in the manorial courts and amerced the offenders; by which they had assessed the estates or presented the report of their neighbours; by which they had learnt to work with the judges of the King's court for the determination of custom, right, justice, and equity, were the training for the higher functions, in which they were to work out the right of taxation, legislation, and political determination on national action.[13]

Thus, while Stubbs's conclusions sit comfortably with Liberal preconceptions he was himself no Liberal. Though his historical friends and allies were Freeman and Green, with whom he shared both a commitment to modern historical method and an almost mystical nationalism, he was if anything hostile to secular liberalism. If he believed in "scientific" history he certainly did not think much of the pretensions of natural science or rather of scientific men to explain the mysteries of the universe. He retained an undisturbed and profound belief in Divine providence untouched by the intellectual currents of doubt around him though well aware of them. He was a devoted Anglican without a touch of the Whig or a hint of Erastianism. During his service on the Royal Commission on Ecclesiastical Courts he made clear his preference for disestablishment rather than that the state meddle further in the affairs of the Church. He expressed in vivid terms his contempt for the parliamentary lawyers who neither knew nor cared for the historical position of the Church. The *Constitutional History* is so balanced, sagacious, and moderate in tone that these convictions rarely peep through; and, as Maitland said, a contemporary could read it without guessing Stubbs's politics. Stubbs in fact cultivated that "attitude of detachment," "that merely historical point of view" which

13. *Constitutional History,* vol. 1, chap. 13, p. 623.

J. B. Bury saw as the characteristic note of the nineteenth century with its "wide diffusion of unobtrusive scepticism among educated people." Stubbs certainly betrays very little of his religious convictions in his historical writing, and yet they inform it and are perhaps the key to his understanding and sympathy for medieval men. And of course he devoted more than half his career to the active service of the Church.

Stubbs's manner is important because it is that perhaps more than anything else which explains his attraction and his influence: it was his quality as a professional historian which elicited the admiration of fellow historians and earned the *Constitutional History* its immediate place as a classic, displacing the partial and inferior works of his predecessors in the field of medieval history. Of the quality of his scholarship I will take leave to quote the opinion of F. W. Maitland on his introductions to the Rolls series:

> No other Englishman has so completely displayed to the world the whole business of the historian from the winning of the raw material to the narrating and generalising. We are taken behind the scenes and shown the ropes and pulleys; we are taken into the laboratory and shown the unanalysed stuff, the retorts and test tubes; or rather we are allowed to see the organic growth of history in an historian's mind and are encouraged to use the microscope. This 'practical demonstration', if we may so call it, of the historian's art and science from the preliminary hunt for manuscripts, through the work of collation and filiation and minute criticism, onward to the perfected tale, the eloquence and the reflections, has been of incalculable benefit to the cause of history in England and far more effective than any abstract discourse on methodology can be.[14]

Thus Stubbs's influence extends beyond the persistence and durability of his interpretation to the methods and

14. F. W. Maitland "William Stubbs, Bishop of Oxford," *English Historical Review,* 16, no. 63 (July 1901): 419.

skills by which his distinguished pupils and critics have sought to modify or overturn his conclusions. A hundred years on the *Constitutional History* is often the starting place for inquiry; and sometimes even the stopping place as well. As a recent writer on the Anglo-Saxon state says of comparisons between English and Carolingian administration: "The best account of them remains that of Stubbs . . . . His conclusion was masterly: it is wiser and safer to allow the coincidences to speak for themselves, and to avoid a positive theory which the first independent investigator may find means of demolishing."[15]

This willingness to suspend judgment, to acknowledge the inadequacies of the evidence, has earned Stubbs the unmerited sobriquet of "the perfect hedger," but as Maitland said what his works contain are "lessons of patient industry, accurate statement, and acute but wary reasoning." Stubbs is not afraid to make up his mind or to come to sweeping conclusions. Indeed, the broad outline of his interpretation has proved very hard to shift. But the abiding pleasure and profit of reading Stubbs is in the detail, the spare and vigorous prose, the occasional vivid aside in which he reveals his familiar understanding of the actors, the continual tension between the great issues of constitutional development and the tawdry ambitions of princes.

These selections are intended to give the main bones of his constitutional theory: they ignore much of great interest, particularly his consideration of the role of the Church, and the political narrative which sustains and gives body to the constitutional interpretation. They stop short with Richard II on the strength of Stubbs's remark that: ". . . if the only object of Constitutional History were the investigation of the origin and powers of parliament, the

15. James Campbell "Observations on English Government from the tenth to the twelfth century", *Transactions of the Royal Historical Society,* fifth series 25 (1975): 43.

study of the subject might be suspended at the deposition of Richard II, to be resumed under the Tudors."[16] Thus the selections are drawn from volumes 1 and 2 only and begin with Stubbs's general remarks on the character of constitutional history, which state his general theme and demonstrate his concern for comparative developments: he studied England with his eye on the Continent about whose history he was notably well informed. Then we skip the earliest chapters where the evidence was least satisfactory and Stubbs's penchant for "the forests of Germania" perhaps betrayed him, and move directly to the seventh chapter of volume 1 in which Stubbs examined the dynamic elements of the Anglo-Saxon constitution before the Conquest, and summed up its salient characteristics and enduring contribution. Thence to chapter 9 and the impact of the Norman Conquest, and on to chapter 13 in which Stubbs surveys constitutional developments up to Magna Carta and assesses the work of Henry II in salvaging the heritage of Saxon and Norman governance from the anarchy of feudalism. I have again ignored the political narrative in the second volume to concentrate on the two chapters of constitutional analysis: chapter 15 on the constitution under Edward I which Stubbs considered the formative period when those principles first found expression which were not to be worked out in practice until the seventeenth century; and chapter 18 in which Stubbs sets out the contrasting theories of Royal prerogative and Parliamentary authority as they emerged from the struggles and fall of Richard II.

The text here reproduced is from the first edition of the *Constitutional History* printed at the Clarendon Press and published in 1874 and 1875. Stubbs made few amendments to later editions and those of no great importance. Of his other writings perhaps the most influential was his *Select Charters,* through which generations of students were

16. *Constitutional History,* vol. 3, chap. 17, p. 2.

introduced for the first time to the materials of medieval history. It became the model for subsequent collections of documents which have been an important tool of historical education in England. The work most admired by fellow historians was his editing of the Chronicles for the Rolls series, on which I have quoted Maitland's opinion above. These introductions have been collected and edited by Arthur Hassall in *Historical Introductions to the Rolls Series* by William Stubbs (London, 1902) and a bibliography of his historical works by W. A. Shaw was published for the Royal Historical Society in 1903. Maitland's appreciation can be found in the *English Historical Review* vol. 16, no. 63, July 1901, in his *Collected Papers* (Cambridge, 1911), and *Select Historical Essays* (Cambridge, 1957). The entry in the *Dictionary of National Biography* which gives an admirable concise life and which echoes Maitland's judgments is by Stubbs's pupil, the great administrative historian T. F. Tout. Other appreciations include J. G. Edwards's *William Stubbs*, Historical Association (1952, reprinted 1968) which is rather solicitous of Stubbs's reputation, and Helen Cam's "Stubbs Seventy Years After," *Cambridge Historical Journal*, 9, (1948) which is rather less so. The work of Stubbs's most formidable critics is summarized in G. O. Sayles's *The King's Parliament of England* (London, 1975), which also contains an excellent bibliography of works on Parliament in the Middle Ages. Many of the articles there cited are conveniently collected in E. B. Fryde and E. Miller's *Historical Studies of the English Parliament* (Cambridge, 1970) 2 vols. The controversy over the early constitution to which Stubbs was heir is explored in J. G. A. Pocock's *The Ancient Constitution and the Feudal Law* (Cambridge 1957). There is unfortunately no comparable work on constitutional theory in the nineteenth century. The shortcomings of the earlier part of the *Constitutional History* were examined in supplementary notes to the French translation by C. Petit-Dutaillis, translated by W. E. Rhodes in 1908 as *Studies and Notes supplementary to Stubbs's Constitutional History, down to the Great Charter.* Stubbs's life and opinions can be followed in W. H. Hutton's *The Letters of William Stubbs, Bishop of Oxford,* London, 1904, or the abridged version *William Stubbs, Bishop of Oxford, 1825-1901,* London, 1906.

Since these selections are presented in facsimile, the only change made has been to provide continuous pagination for this edition. The page numbers in footnotes which refer both to passages in this edition and to others not selected are to the pagination of the original edition.

JAMES CORNFORD

Chapter I

INTRODUCTION.

1. Constitutional History.—2. Its German origin:—in France.—3. In Spain.—4. In Germany.—5. In England.—6. Analogy of Language.—7. Of Religion.—8. Of Law.—9. Result of the comparison.

1. THE growth of the English Constitution, which is the subject of this book, is the resultant of three forces, whose reciprocal influences are constant, subtle, and intricate. These are the national character, the external history, and the institutions of the people. The direct analysis of the combination forms no portion of our task, for it is not until a nation has arrived at a consciousness of its own identity that it can be said to have any constitutional existence, and long before that moment the three forces have become involved inextricably; the national character has been formed by the course of the national history quite as certainly as the national history has been developed by the working of the national character; and the institutions in which the newly conscious nation is clothed may be either the work of the constructive genius of the growing race, or simply the result of the discipline of its external history. It would then be very rash and unsafe to attempt to assign positively to any one of the three forces the causation of any particular movement or the origin of any particular measure, to the exclusion of the other two; or to argue back from result to cause without allowing for the operation of other co-ordinate and reciprocally acting factors. Elements of Constitutional life.

But it does not follow that cautious speculation on questions of interest, which are in themselves prior to the starting point, would be thrown away; and some such must necessarily be discussed in order to complete the examination of the subject in its Preliminary questions.

integrity by a comparison of its development with the corresponding stages and contemporary phenomena of the life of other nations. Of these questions the most important, and perhaps the only necessary ones, for all minor matters may be comprehended under them, are those of nationality and geographical position;—who were our forefathers, whence did they come, what did they bring with them, what did they find on their arrival, how far did the process of migration and settlement affect their own development, and in what measure was it indebted to the character and previous history of the land they colonised?

Germanic origin of the English.

Such a form of stating the questions suggests at least the character of the answer. The English are not aboriginal, that is, they are not identical with the race that occupied their home at the dawn of history. They are a people of German descent in the main constituents of blood, character, and language, but most especially, in connexion with our subject, in the possession of the elements of primitive German civilisation and the common germs of German institutions. This descent is not a matter of inference. It is a recorded fact of history, which those characteristics bear out to the fullest degree of certainty. The consensus of historians, placing the conquest and colonisation of Britain by nations of German origin between the middle of the fifth and the end of the sixth century, is confirmed by the evidence of a continuous series of monuments. These show the unbroken possession of the land thus occupied, and the growth of the language and institutions thus introduced, either in purity and unmolested integrity, or, where it has been modified by antagonism and by the admixture of alien forms, ultimately vindicating itself by eliminating the new and more strongly developing the genius of the old.

Influence of the Germanic races in Europe generally.

2. The four great states of Western Christendom—England, France, Spain, and Germany—owe the leading principles which are worked out in their constitutional history to the same source. In the regions which had been thoroughly incorporated with the Roman empire, every vestige of primitive indigenous cultivation had been crushed out of existence. Roman civilisation in its turn fell before the Germanic races: in Britain it had

perished slowly in the midst of a perishing people, who were able neither to maintain it nor to substitute for it anything of their own. In Gaul and Spain it died a somewhat nobler death, and left more lasting influences. In the greater part of Germany it had never made good its ground. In all four the constructive elements of new life are barbarian or Germanic, though its development is varied by the degrees in which the original stream of influence has been turned aside in its course, or affected in purity and consistency by the infusion of other elements and by the nature of the soil through which it flows.

Constitutional History of France.

The system which has for the last twelve centuries formed the history of France, and in a great measure the character of the French people, of which the present condition of that kingdom is the logical result, was originally little more than a simple adaptation of the old German polity to the government of a conquered race. The long sway of the Romans in Gaul had re-created, on their own principles of administration, the nation which the Franks conquered. The Franks, gradually uniting in religion, blood and language with the Gauls, retained and developed the idea of feudal subordination in the organisation of government unmodified by any tendencies towards popular freedom. In France accordingly feudal government runs its logical career. The royal power, that central force which partly has originated, and partly owes its existence to the conquest, is first limited in its action by the very agencies that are necessary to its continuance; then it is reduced to a shadow. The shadow is still the centre round which the complex system, in spite of itself, revolves: it is recognised by that system as its solitary safeguard against disruption, and its witness of national identity; it survives for ages, notwithstanding the attenuation of its vitality, by its incapacity for mischief. In course of time the system itself loses its original energy, and the central force gradually gathers into itself all the members of the nationality in detail, thus concentrating all the powers which in earlier struggles they had won from it, and incorporating in itself those very forces which the feudatories had imposed as limitations on the sovereign power. So its

Changes in the constitution of France.

character of nominal suzerainty is exchanged for that of absolute sovereignty. The only checks on the royal power had been the feudatories; the crown has outlived them, absorbed and assimilated their functions; but the increase of power is turned not to the strengthening of the central force, but to the personal interest of its possessor. Actual despotism becomes systematic tyranny, and its logical result is the explosion which is called revolution. The constitutional history of France is thus the summation of the series of feudal development in a logical sequence which is indeed unparalleled in the history of any great state, but which is thoroughly in harmony with the national character, forming it and formed by it. We see in it the German system, modified by its work of foreign conquest and deprived of its home safeguards, on a field exceptionally favourable, prepared and levelled by Roman agency under a civil system which was capable of speedy amalgamation, and into whose language most of the feudal forms readily translated themselves.

The working out of feudalism.

Kindred influences of the Goths and other races in Spain.

3. In Spain too the permanency of the Germanic or of the kindred Visigothic influences is a fact of the first historical importance. Here, upon the substratum of an indigenous race conquered, crushed, re-created, remodelled into a Roman province more Roman than Rome itself, is superinduced the conquering race, first to ravage, then to govern, then to legislate, then to unite in religion, and lastly to lead on to deliverance from Moorish tyranny. The rapidity with which Spanish history unfolds itself enables us to detect throughout its course the identity of the ruling, constructive nationality. The Visigothic element is kept to itself at first by its heresy; before the newness of its conversion has given it time to unite with the conquered nation, it is forced into the position of a deliverer. The Moorish conquest compels union, sympathy, amalgamation, but still leaves the apparatus of government in the hands of the Visigothic kings and nobles; the common law, the institutions, the names are Germanic. Although the history of Spain, a crusade of seven centuries, forces into existence forms of civil life and expedients of administration which are peculiar to itself, they are distinctly coloured by the pertinacious freedom of the primitive customs; the con-

stitutional life of Castille is, in close parallel or in marked contrast, never out of direct relation with that of Germany and England, as that of Aragon is with French and Scottish history. To a German race of sovereigns Spain finally owed the subversion of her national system and ancient freedom.

General character of German Constitutional History.

4. In Germany itself, of course, the development of the primitive polity is everywhere traceable. Here there is no alien race, for Germany is never conquered but by Germans; there is much migration, but there is much also that is untouched by migration: where one tribe has conquered or colonised another, there feudal tenure of land and jurisdiction prevails: where the ancient race remains in its old seats, there the alod subsists and the free polity with which the alod is inseparably associated. The imperial system has originated other changes; there are Swabians in Saxony, Saxons in Thuringia: feudal customs in each case follow the tenure, but where the feod is not, there remains the alod, and even the village community and the mark. In the higher ranges of civil order, a mixed imperial and feudal organisation, which like the Spanish has no exact parallel, retains a varying, now substantial, now shadowy existence. The imperial tradition has substituted a fictitious for a true bond of union among the four nations of the German land. To the general reader the constitutional struggle is merely one of nationality against imperialism; of the papal north against the imperial south; but under that surface of turmoil the lower depths of national life and constitutional organism heave constantly. Bavaria, Saxony, Franconia, Swabia have their national policy, and preserve their ancient modifications of the still more ancient customs. The weakness of the imperial centre, the absence of central legislature and judicature, allows the continued existence of the most primitive forms; the want of cohesion prevents at once their development and their extinction. So to deeper study the wonderful fertility and variety of the local institutions of Germany presents a field of work bewildering and even wearying in its abundance: and great as might be the reward of penetrating it, the student strays off to a field more easily amenable to philosophic treatment. The constitutional history of Germany is the

English Constitutional History a development of Germanic principles in comparative purity.

hardest, as that of France is the easiest, subject of historical study. As a study of principles, in continuous and uniform development, it lacks both unity and homogeneousness.

5. England, although less homogeneous in blood and character, is more so in uniform and progressive growth. The very diversity of the elements which are united within the isle of Britain serves to illustrate the strength and vitality of the one which for thirteen hundred years has maintained its position either unrivalled or in victorious supremacy. If its history is not the perfectly pure development of Germanic principles, it is the nearest existing approach to such a development[1]. England gained its sense of unity centuries before Germany: it developed its genius for government under influences more purely indigenous: spared from the curse of the imperial system and the Mezentian union with Italy, and escaping thus the practical abeyance of legislation and judicature, it developed its own common law free from the absolutist tendencies of Roman jurisprudence; and it grew equably, harmoniously, not merely by virtue of local effort and personal privilege.

The smaller states of Europe.

In the four great nationalities the Germanic influence is the dominant principle: in England, Germany and France directly; whilst in Spain all formative power is traceable to the kindred Gothic rule. The smaller states share more or less in the same general characteristics, Portugal with Spain; Scandinavia with Germany and England, with whose institutions it had originally everything in common, and whose development in great things and in small it seems to have followed with few variations, translating their constitutional systems into language of its own.

Italy.

In Italy the confusion of nationalities is most complete, and Roman institutions, owing perhaps to the rapid succession of conquerors and the shortlivedness of their organisations as contrasted with the permanency of the papal-imperial system, subsisted with least change. Yet there also, the Northern States through the German, and the Southern through the Norman connexion, both moreover having gone through the crucible of Lombard

[1] Bethmann-Hollweg, Civilprocess, iv. 10. Konrad Maurer, Kritische Ueberschau, i. 47. Gneist, Self-government, i. 3.

oppression, retain marks of Teutonic impact. The institutions, national and free in one aspect, feudal and absolutist in another, testify, if not to the permanence, at least to the abiding impressions of the association. The republican history of the North and the feudal system of the South, the municipalities of Lombardy and the parliaments of Naples, are much more German than Roman.

Effect of the German and Gothic conquests on language,

6. Nor do the great nationalities return a different answer when interrogated by more convincing tests than that of external history. If language be appealed to, and language is by itself the nearest approach to a perfect test of national extraction, the verdict is in close accordance. The impact of barbarian conquest split up the unity of the Latin tongue as it did that of the Latin empire; it destroyed its uniformity and broke up its constructional forms. But in the breaking it created at least three great languages—the French, the Spanish, and the Italian; each possessing new powers of development which the Latin had lost, and adapting itself to a new literature, fertile in beauty and vivacity, far surpassing the effete inanities that it superseded.

and on new literature.

The breath of the life of the new literatures was Germanic, varied according to the measure of Germanic influence in other things. The poetry of the new nations is that of the leading race: in South France and Spain Visigothic, in North France Norman, even in Italy it owes all its sweetness and light to the freedom which has breathed from beyond the Alps. In these lands the barbarian tongue has yielded to that of the conquered; in Spain and France because the disproportion of the numbers of the two races was very great; both Franks and Visigoths had become Romanised to a certain extent before the conquest; and the struggle with the native peoples assumed in neither case the character of extermination. In Italy the succession of masters was too rapid to allow a change of language to come into question among the greater and more abiding part of the people. Of the Germans of Germany and the English of early times it is scarcely necessary to speak, for whatever may have been the later modifications, the influence of the Latin of the fifth century on the language of either must have been infinitesimal. No European tongue

Analogy of language and polity.

is more thoroughly homogeneous in vocabulary and in structure than that known as the Anglo-Saxon : it is as pure as those of Scandinavia, where no Roman influences ever penetrated, and no earlier race than the German left intelligible traces. Early and medieval German are also alike unadulterated. The analogy between language and institutions is in these cases direct : in Spain and France the outer garb is Roman, the spirit and life is Germanic : one influence preponderates in the language, the other in the polity ; and the amalgamation is complete when the Gaul has learned to call himself a Frenchman, when the Goth, the Suevian, the Alan and the Vandal, are united under the name of Spaniard.

Evidence of religion.

7. The most abiding influence of Rome is that of religion ; the Roman church continues to exist when the old imperial administration has perished. Spain, Gaul and Italy, even Western Britain and Western Germany, retain the Christianity which Roman missions have planted. Yet in this very department the importance of the new spring of life is specially conspicuous. Spain alone of the four nations owes nothing to German Christianity. Her religious history is exactly analogous to that of her language : after a century's struggle the Visigoth and the Suevian become Catholic. In France and Western Germany, which had been Christianised mainly under the imperial influences, and had developed an independent theology during the Roman period, the influx of the Franks and their subsequent conversion produced a complex result. The Christianity which had stood out against Visigothic indifference or intolerance, withered under Frank patronage. The secular tendencies of the imperial religious administration expanded under the Merovingian imitators, and had it not been for the reformation begun by Boniface and worked out under the auspices of the Karolings, the Gallican church might have sunk to the level of the Italian or the Byzantine. But the same Austrasian influences which revivified the composite nationality, breathed new life into the fainting church, drawing from England and the converted North new models of study and devotion. The labours of English missionaries in German Saxony helped to

Germanic influence on the Church.

consolidate and complete in both church and state the Germanic empire of the Karolings. The Austrasian domination was more purely Germanic than the Neustrian which it superseded. Charles the Great, as the reformer of the church and founder of the modern civilisation of France, was a German king who worked chiefly by German instruments.

8. In the domain of Law the comparison is equally clear. The number of possible factors is small: the primitive codes of the conquerors, the Roman law under which the conquered were living, and the feudal customs which were evolved from the relations of the two races. For there remain no original vestiges of the indigenous laws of Spain and Gaul, and it is only from Irish and Welsh remains of comparatively late date that we find that the Celtic tribes had any laws at all. **Influenee of German customs on the common law of the nations.**

The common law of Spain is throughout the medieval period Germanic in its base: although the written law of the Visigoths is founded on the Theodosian code, and the so-called Roman natives lived by Roman law, the *fueros* which contain the customary jurisprudence are distinctly akin to the customs of England and Germany; the wergild and the system of compurgation, the primitive elements of election and representation, are clearly traceable[1]. It is not until the fourteenth century that the civil law of Justinian supersedes the ancient customs, and then with its invariable results. **Spain.**

Medieval France is divided between the feudal customs of the North and the personal law of the South, which last was chiefly based on the Theodosian and earlier Roman jurisprudence. The former territory is more Frank in population, nearer to the German home, and bears more distinct marks of Karolingian legislation; the latter, before the Frank conquest, has borne the successive waves of Visigothic and Burgundian invasion, and has strengthened through them, or imparted to them, its own legal system as developed under the Romans. Of the great expositions of feudal custom, most are from Northern France: the **France.**

[1] Dunham, History of Spain and Portugal, iv. 109–118: from Edinb. Review, No. 61 (an article attributed to Palgrave). Palgrave, Commonwealth, pp. 128–131, &c. Lea, Superstition and Force, p. 65.

libri feudorum were compiled by Lombard lawyers from the acts of the Franconian and Swabian emperors; and the Assizes of Jerusalem are based on the work of a Lotharingian lawgiver. The essence of feudal law is custom, and custom escapes the jealousies and antipathies that assail law imposed by a legislative centre: it grows and extends its area by imitation rather than by authority: and the scientific lawyer can borrow a custom of feudal jurisprudence where he cannot venture to lay down a principle of Roman law. Hence the uncertainty of detail contrasted with the uniformity of principle in feudal law.

Law in Germany.

Germany, except in the few Capitularies of the Frank sovereigns, has no central or common written law; even the Capitularies are many of them only local in their operation: she does not except by way of custom adopt the Roman civil law; her feudal law is, like the feudal law elsewhere, based on the Frank customals. Her common law, whether sought in the jurisprudence of the Alemanni, the Franks and the Saxons, or enunciated in the Sachsenspiegel and the Schwabenspiegel, is primitive, just as all her lower range of institutions may be said to be; it subsists but it does not develop.

English common law based on early Germanic usages.

England has inherited no portion of the Roman legislation except in the form of scientific or professional axioms, introduced at a late period, and through the ecclesiastical or scholastic or international university studies. Her common law is, to a far greater extent than is commonly recognised, based on usages anterior to the influx of feudality, that is, on strictly primitive custom; and what she has that is feudal may be traced through its Frank stage of development to the common Germanic sources[1].

General result.

9. The result of this comparison is to suggest the probability that the polity developed by the German race on British soil is the purest product of their primitive instinct. With the exception of the Gothic Bible of Ulfilas, the Anglo-Saxon remains are the earliest specimens of Germanic language as well as literature, and the development of modern English from the Anglo-Saxon is a

[1] Brunner, in Holtzendorff's Encyclopädie, pp. 226, 227.

fact of science as well as of history. The institutions of the Saxons of Germany long after the conquest of Britain were the most perfect exponent of the system which Tacitus saw and described in the Germania; and the polity of their kinsmen in England, though it may be not older in its monuments than the Lex Salica, is more entirely free from Roman influences. In England the common germs were developed and ripened with the smallest intermixture of foreign elements. Not only were all the successive invasions of Britain, which from the eighth to the eleventh century diversify the history of the island, conducted by nations of common extraction, but, with the exception of ecclesiastical influence, no foreign interference that was not German in origin was admitted at all. Language, law, custom and religion preserve their original conformation and colouring. The German element is the paternal element in our system, natural and political. Analogy, however, is not proof, but illustration: the chain of proof is to be found in the progressive persistent development of English constitutional history from the primeval polity of the common fatherland.

The German element is the paternal element in the English polity.

Chapter II

DEVELOPMENT IN ANGLO-SAXON HISTORY.

69. Development in Anglo-Saxon history from personal to territorial system.—70. Increase of royal power in intension as the kingdom increases in extension.—71. The king becomes lord or patron of the people. — 72. He becomes the source of justice. — 73. Jurisdiction becomes territorial.—74. The tenure of land affected by the territorialising of judicature.—75. Territorialising of military organisation.—76. Legislation; absence of personal law.—77. Influence of the Danes.—78. Influence of Frank legislation.—79. No real growth of unity.—80. Seeds of national life still preserved.—81. National character.

Development in Anglo-Saxon history.

69. ALTHOUGH the framework of Anglo-Saxon society was permanent, and its simple organisation easily adapted itself to the circumstances that fill the five centuries of its history, it was capable of development and liable to much internal modification, according to the variations of the balance of its parts, and the character of its regulative or motive force. The exact chronological sequence of these variations it is difficult to determine, but as to the fact of the development there can be no question. A comparison of the state of affairs represented in Domesday book with the picture that can be drawn from Bede sufficiently proves it. The ages had been ages of struggle and of growth, although the struggle was often fruitless and the growth ended in weariness and vexation. But the transition is more distinctly apparent if we look back further than Bede, and rely on the analogies of the other Germanic nationalities in drawing our initial outline. And this we are justified in doing by the completeness and homogeneousness of the constitution when it first appears to us, and by the general character of the early laws.

Difficulties of treatment.

But the subject is not without its difficulties: the first and last terms of the development are as remote from each other in character as in date. There is a very great difference between the extreme and confusing minuteness of Domesday and the simplicity and elasticity of the ideal German system of the sixth century: whilst on the other hand the scantiness of the latter is compensated by its clearness, and the abundance of the former is deprived of much of its value by the uncertainty of its terminology. For it is unquestionable that great part of the Anglo-Saxon customary law, of which Domesday is the treasury, was unintelligible to the Norman lawyers of the next century, on whose interpretation of it the legal historian is wont to rely. The process of change too was very gradual: it is not marked by distinct steps of legal enactment; the charters only afford incidental illustrations, and the historians were, for the most part, too far removed in time from the events they described to have a distinct idea of it, even if it had been possible for the annalist to realise the working of causes in so slow and so constant action. But all the great changes in the early history of institutions are of this character, and can be realised only by the comparison of sufficiently distant epochs. There are no constitutional revolutions, no violent reversals of legislation; custom is far more potent than law, and custom is modified infinitesimally every day. An alteration of law is often the mere registration of a custom, when men have recognised its altered character. The names of offices and assemblies are permanent, whilst their character has imperceptibly undergone essential change.

General character of the development.

The general tendency of the process may be described as a movement from the personal to the territorial organisation[1]; from a state of things in which personal freedom and political right were the leading ideas, to one in which personal freedom and political right had become so much bound up with the relations created by the possession of land, as to be actually subservient to it: the Angel-cynn of Alfred becomes the Engla-lande of Canute. The main steps also are apparent. In the primitive German

[1] Palgrave, Commonwealth, p. 62.

Progress from personal to territorial system.

constitution the free man of pure blood is the fully qualified political unit[1]; the king is the king of the race; the host is the people in arms; the peace is the national peace; the courts are the people in council; the land is the property of the race, and the free man has a right to his share. In the next stage the possession of land has become the badge of freedom; the freeman is fully free because he possesses land, he does not possess the land because he is free; the host is the body of landowners in arms; the courts are the courts of the landowners. But the personal basis is not lost sight of: the landless may still select his lord; the hide is the provision of the family; the peace implies the maintenance of rights and duties between man and man; the full-free is the equal of the noble in all political respects. In a further stage the land becomes the sacramental tie of all public relations; the poor man depends on the rich, not as his chosen patron, but as the owner of the land that he cultivates, the lord of the court to which he does suit and service, the leader whom he is bound to follow to the host: the administration of law depends on the peace of the land rather than that of the people; the great landowner has his own peace and administers his own justice. The king still calls himself the king of the nation, but he has added to his old title new and cumbersome obligations towards all classes of his subjects, as lord and patron, supreme landowner, the representative of all original, and the fountain of all derived, political right.

The first of these stages was passed when the conquest of

[1] Sohm, Fr. R. G. Verfg. i. 333 sq., maintains that in the Frank dominion it was not the possession of land but personal freedom that entitled or obliged a man to attend in the courts of law, in the host and other assemblies: and that it was only in trials in which land was concerned that the witnesses were required to have a land qualification (ibid. p. 355). In this as in many other points, this writer combats the received view. 'The full freedom of the German law is, in host and in court, given by personal freedom' (ibid. p. 359). Waitz on the other hand holds that 'the hide was the basis of freedom in the full sense of the word,' D. Verfassgs.-Gesch. i. 120; and 'only he who possessed land was fully qualified in the community' (ibid. iv. 450). See above, p. 78. Where there is so much divergence in the application of terms, it is somewhat dangerous to speak positively about stages of development; and in this, as in many other points, the statements of the text must be understood as referring chiefly if not solely to English history.

Britain was completed[1]; and only showed what it had been in the vestiges of the mark system, and in the permanence of the personal nomenclature. The village was the kindred settlement, the hide of land the allotment of the head of the family, the tribal divisions—the hundred, the mægth, the theod,—all personal[2].

The great question of Anglo-Saxon History

The tracing of the process of change under the second and third stages is the problem of Anglo-Saxon Constitutional History. The series is not fully worked out. The Anglo-Saxon king never ceases to be the king of the nation, but he has become its lord and patron rather than its father; and that in a state of society in which all lordship is bound up with landownership: he is the lord of the national land, and needs only one step to become the lord of the people by that title. This step was however taken by the Norman lawyers and not by the English king; and it was only because the transition seemed to them so easy, that they left the ancient local organisation unimpaired, out of which a system was to grow that would ultimately reduce the landownership to its proper dimensions and functions. If the system had in England ripened into feudalism, that feudalism would in all probability have been permanent. Happily the change that produced feudalism for a time, introduced with it the necessity of repulsion. The English, who might never have struggled against native lords, were roused by the fact that their

[1] It may be thought that in granting so much, we are placing the landless Englishman on a lower level than the landless Frank; see the last note. But it is to be remembered that in Gaul and the other Romanised provinces, the fully free Frank was surrounded by a vast servile population, whilst in England the servile class formed a minority comparatively insignificant. The contrast is between full freedom and servitude in the former case; and in the latter between greater and smaller duties and liabilities. But it is quite probable that the rights of attending court and host were burdens rather than privileges to the Anglo-Saxons; and the rule that the landless man must have a lord was a measure rather compelling him to his duty, than depriving him of right. Until that rule was laid down, it is probable that the fully free Englishman, whether he owned land or not, was capable of taking part in the judicial business. Large numbers of landless men must have constantly attended the courts; and mere residence as well as possession of estate must have determined in what court they should attend.

[2] The mægth of Alfred is the provincia of Bede; the theod lande of Alfred is the regio, the theod being the gens. Bede, H. E. ii. 9, iii. 20, v. 12, &c.

lords were strangers as well as oppressors, and the Norman kings realised the certainty that if they would retain the land they must make common cause with the people.

Historical landmarks.

Five historical events mark the periods within which these changes were working: the accretion of the small settlements in heptarchic kingdoms; the union of the heptarchic kingdoms under the house of Cerdic; the first struggle with the Danes; the pacification of England under Edgar; and the introduction of new forms and principles of government by Canute.

Growth of the kingdom.

70. The development of constitutional life depends largely on the historical career of the nation, on the consolidation of its governmental machinery in equality and uniformity over all its area, on the expansion or limitation of the regulative power for the time being: in other words, on the general and external history marked by these eras; on the extension of the kingdom and on the condition of the royal power. England at the period of the Conversion, when for the first time we are able really to grasp an idea of its condition, was composed of a large number of small states or provinces bound in seven or eight kingdoms [1]. The form of government was in each monarchical, and that of the same limited character. By the middle of the tenth century it has become one kingdom, and the royal power is much more extensive in character. During a great part of the intervening period the consolidation of the kingdom and the power of the king have undergone many variations. The tendency towards union has been developed first under one tribal supremacy and then under another, and the royal power, whose growth is of necessity greatly affected by the extension of its territory, and the presence or absence of rival royalties, has fluctuated also. The two of course rise and fall together. But as a rule, at the end of any fixed period, both manifest a decided advance.

It can scarcely be said that the tendency towards territorial

[1] I use the word heptarchy for the sake of brevity and convenience, and of course without vouching either for its accuracy of form or for its exact applicability to the state of things preceding the West Saxon hegemony. During far the greater portion of its duration there were actually seven kingdoms of Germanic origin in the island, and I see nothing in the term that implies any unity of organisation.

Causes of union of the seven kingdoms.

union proceeded from any consciousness of national unity or from any instinct of self-government. Nor can it be attributed solely to the religious unity which rather helped than originated such a tendency. This tendency resulted not so much from the strivings of the peoples as from the ambition of the kings. The task which was accomplished by the West Saxon dynasty had been tried before by the rulers of Kent, Northumbria and Mercia, and the attempt in their hands failed. Nor would it have been more successful under the genius of Athelstan and Edgar, but for the Danish invasions, the extinction of the old royal houses, and the removal, to a certain extent, of the old tribal landmarks.

Maintenance of ancient boundaries, and royal families.

The ancient German spirit showed its tenacity in this. The land had been settled by tribes of kinsmen, under rulers who as kings acquired the headship of the kin as well as the command of the host. Whilst the kin of the kings subsisted, and the original landmarks were preserved, neither religion nor common law, nor even common subjection sufficed to weld the incoherent mass. And it may have been the consciousness of this which hindered the victorious kings from suppressing royalty altogether in the kingdoms they subdued: the vassal kings either became insignificant, sinking into *eorls* and hereditary *ealdormen*, or gradually died out. But, until after the Danish wars, provincial royalty remained, and the cohesion of the mass was maintained only by the necessities of common defence. When Ethelbert of Kent acquired the rule of Essex, when Ethelred of Mercia annexed Hwiccia, when Egbert conquered Mercia, the form of a separate kingdom was preserved; and the royal house still reigned under the authority of the conquerors until it became extinct. Such a system gave of course occasion for frequent rebellions and re-arrangements of territory; when a weak king succeeded a strong one in the sovereign kingdom, or a strong chief succeeded a weak one in the dependent realm. But the continuance of such a system has the effect of gradually eliminating all the weaker elements.

This process of natural selection was in constant working; it is best exemplified in the gradual formation of the seven kingdoms and in their final union under Wessex: the heptarchic king was as much stronger than the tribal king, as the king of united England was stronger than the heptarchic king.

Gradual disappearance of the smaller sovereignties.

The kings of the smaller divisions disappear first, either altogether, or to emerge for a moment when the greater kingdom itself loses its royal house or falls into decrepitude. In the early days of Mercia, kings of Hwiccia, Hecana, Middle Anglia, and Lindsey, still subsisted[1]. Kent in the eighth century broke up into the kingdoms of the East and West Kentings, probably on the lines of the earlier kingdoms which are said to have been united by Ethelbert[2]. In Wessex, besides the kings of Sussex[3] which has a claim to be numbered among the seven great states, were kings of Surrey[4] also. On the death of Kenwalch in A.D. 672, Wessex was divided among the ealdormen (just as the Lombard kingdom broke up on the death of Clephis), and was reunited thirteen years later by Cædwalla[5]: Hampshire was separated

[1] The Hwiccian kings were connected with those of Sussex and Northumbria, and were under the protection of the Mercian kings until they sank into the rank of ealdormen. Bede gives to Osric, one of these princes, the title of king, and the see of Worcester no doubt owes its existence to the fact that their national existence apart from Mercia was still recognised. Hecana or Herefordshire was the kingdom of Merewald, one of Penda's sons (Flor. Wig. M. H. B. p. 638), and has Hereford for its see. Middle Anglia was the kingdom of Peada, another of his sons, and retained its separate organisation long enough to have a see of its own,—Leicester, settled like the other three by Theodore. The pedigree of the kings of Lindsey is preserved by Florence (M. H. B. p. 631), and although none of them are known in history, the territory was in dispute between Mercia and Northumbria in 678, so that they could not have been long extinct; its nationalty also was recognised by the foundation of a see, at Sidnacester.

[2] The existence of the see of Rochester is adduced in proof of the existence of a separate tribal kingdom in Kent, and the same inference is drawn from the fact that double settlements, as in Norfolk and Suffolk (of two fylkis), were common among the German tribes. See Freeman, Norm. Conq. i. 342; Robertson, Essays, p. 120; Kemble, Saxons, i. 148. But the historical mention of the East and West Kentings is later; and where two kings are found reigning together they seem to be of the same family.

[3] Mr. Robertson infers a twofold arrangement in Sussex from the fact that two ealdorman were slain there by Cædwalla (Essays, p. 120), but Sussex as an independent kingdom must have always been united. After its subjection to Wessex it seems to have had two or three kings at a time. (Palgrave, Commonwealth, p. cclxxiv.) They are no longer heard of under Egbert.

[4] Frithewold, subregulus or ealdorman of Surrey, was the founder of Chertsey Abbey. Malmesb. G. P. lib. ii. The name seems sufficient to prove it an independent settlement.

[5] Bede, H. E. iv. 12.

Small provincial kingdoms.

from the body of Wessex in A.D. 755[1], as a provision for the deposed Sigebert. The Isle of Wight had a king of its own[2]. In East Anglia several traditionary kingdoms are commemorated by poetical traditions[3]. Northumbria was in constant division between Bernicia and Deira: and besides the Anglian and Saxon kingdoms, there were in Cornwall, Wales, Cumbria, and on the borders of Yorkshire[4], small states of British origin whose rulers were styled kings. These kings were not merely titular; the kings of Hwiccia, in the endowment of their *comites*, exercised one at least of the most important powers of royalty, and continued to subsist as *subreguli* or ealdormen, ruling their province hereditarily under the sovereignty of Mercia. But they died out, and by their extinction their territory was consolidated permanently with the superior state. And so it probably was in the other cases.

Extinction of the greater kingdoms.

Again when Wessex and Mercia have worked their way to the rival hegemonies, Sussex and Essex do not cease to be numbered among the kingdoms until their royal houses are extinct. When Wessex has conquered Mercia and brought Northumbria on its knees, there are still kings in both Northumbria and Mercia: the royal house of Kent dies out, but the title of king of Kent is bestowed on an *ætheling*, first of the Mercian, then of the West Saxon house[5]. Until the Danish conquest the dependent royalties seem to have been spared; and even afterwards organic union can scarcely be said to exist. Alfred governs Mercia by his brother-in-law as ealdorman, just as Ethelwulf had done by his

1 Chron. Sax. A.D. 755.

2 Bede, H. E. iv. 16.

3 Thorpe's Lappenberg, i. 117.

4 Elmet had a king according to Nennius, M. H. B. p. 76.

5 The succession of the later kings of Kent is extremely obscure, and the chronology as generally received is certainly wrong. It would seem that it had become dynastically connected with Wessex in the latter part of the eighth century. Ealhmund, father of the great Egbert, was king in Kent in the time of Offa; Chron. Sax. A.D. 784: after Offa's death the kingdom was seized by Eadbert Præn; he was overcome by Kenulf of Mercia, who made his brother Cuthred king; after Cuthred's death it was ruled by Kenulf himself; and on his death was seized by Baldred, who in his turn was conquered by Egbert. Ethelwulf son of Egbert ruled Kent during his father's life; when he succeeded to Wessex, his sons Ethelstan and Ethelbert reigned successively in Kent: and on Ethelbert's succession to Wessex, Kent was consolidated with the rest of Southern England.

son-in-law as king[1]: but he himself is king of the West-Saxons; Edward the Elder is king of the Angul-Saxones[2]; some times 'of the Angles'; Athelstan is 'rex Anglorum' king of the English, and 'curagulus' of the whole of Britain[3]. The Danish kingdom still maintains an uncertain existence in Northumbria; Mercia under Edgar sets itself against Wessex under Eadwig. At last Edgar having outlived the Northumbrian royalty and made up his mind to consolidate Dane, Angle and Saxon, receives the crown as king of all England[4] and transmits it to his son. Consolidation under Wessex.

If the extinction of the smaller royalties opened the way for permanent consolidation, the long struggle with the Danes prevented that tendency from being counteracted. The attempts of Ethelwulf to keep central England through the agency of Mercian and East Anglian subject kings signally failed. It was only Wessex, although with a far larger sea-board, that success- Influence of the Danish struggle.

[1] Egbert conquered Mercia and deposed King Wiglaf in A.D. 828; he restored him in 830; in 839 Berhtwulf succeeded him and reigned till 851. Burhred his successor was Ethelwulf's son-in-law, and reigned until 874. Ceolwulf his successor was a puppet of the Danes. As soon as Alfred had made good his hold on Western Mercia he gave it to his sister Ethelfleda, who governed it with her husband Ethelred as ealdorman: Ethelred died in 912, and Ethelfleda in 920. Her daughter Elfwina, after attempting to hold the government, was set aside by Edward the elder, by whom Mercia was for the first time organically united with Wessex.

[2] See Hallam, M. A. ii. 271. Edward is rex 'Angul-Saxonum,' or 'Anglorum et Saxonum,' in charters, Cod. Dipl. cccxxxiii, cccxxxv, mlxxvii, mlxxviii, mlxxx, mlxxxiv, mxc, mxcvi; 'Rex Anglorum' simply in cccxxxvii; and king of the West Saxons in mlxxxv.

[3] A list of the titles assumed by the succeeding kings is given by Mr. Freeman, Norm. Conq. i. 548–551. Athelstan's title of Curagulus or Coregulus is explained as derived from cura, caretaker (ibid. p. 552); and as co-regulus or corregulus in its natural sense seems to be opposed to monarcha, it is probable that the derivation is right; the *cura* representing the *mund* under which all the other princes had placed themselves.

[4] On this subject see Mr. Robertson's remarkable essay, Hist. Essays, pp. 203–216; and Freeman, Norm. Conq. i. 626. The last Danish king of Northumbria was killed in 954. In 959 Edgar succeeded to the kingdom of the West Saxons, Mercians and Northumbrians. Edgar's coronation at Bath took place immediately after Archbishop Oswald's return from Rome, which may be supposed to have been connected with it. Mr. Robertson concludes that Edgar 'would appear to have postponed his coronation until every solemnity could be fulfilled that was considered necessary for the unction and coronation of the elect of all three provinces of England, the first sovereign who in the presence of both archbishops—of the "sacerdotes et principes" of the whole of England,—was crowned and anointed as the sole representative of the threefold sovereignty of the West Saxons, Mercians and Northumbrians.'

Amalgamation of the Danes with the English.

fully resisted conquest. Mercia and Northumbria, though conquered with great slaughter, and divided by the victorious Norsemen, exchanged masters with some equanimity, and the Danes within a very few years were amalgamated in blood and religion with their neighbours. The Danish king of East Anglia accepted the protection of the West Saxon monarch and Mercia was brought back to allegiance. Alfred, by patient laborious resistance as well as by brilliant victories, asserted for Wessex the dominion as his grandfather had the hegemony of the other kingdoms; and his son and grandsons perfected his work.[1]

The king increases in strength as the kingdom increases in area.

It could not fail to result from this long process that the character of royalty itself was strengthened. Continual war gave to the king who was capable of conducting it an unintermitted hold and exercise of military command: the kings of the united territory had no longer to deal alone with the *witan* of their original kingdom, but stood before their subjects as supreme rulers over neighbouring states; the council of their *witan* was composed no longer of men as noble and almost as independent as themselves, *ealdormen* strong in the affection of their tribes and enabled by union to maintain a hold over the kings, but of members of the royal house itself, to whom the kings had deputed the government of kingdoms and who strengthened rather than limited their personal authority[2]. So as the kingdom became united the royal power increased, and this power extending with the extension of the territory, royalty became

[1] The story that Egbert after his coronation at Winchester directed that the whole state should bear the name of England is mythical. It originates in the Monastic Annals of Winchester, MS. Cotton, Dom. A. xiii; extracts from which are printed in the Monasticon Anglicanum, i. 205. 'Edixit illa die rex Egbertus ut insula in posterum vocaretur Anglia, et qui Juti vel Saxones dicebantur omnes communi nomine Angli vocarentur.' On the names England and English, see Freeman, Norm. Conq. i. App. A. The era of Egbert's acquisition of the *ducatus*, by which he dates some of his charters to Winchester (Cod. Dipl. mxxxv, mxxxvi, mxxxviii), must be A.D. 816; and if the ducatus be really a Bretwaldaship, may be marked by his conquest of West Wales or Cornwall which is placed by the Chronicles in A.D. 813, but belongs properly to A.D. 815. At this period however Kenulf of Mercia was still in a more commanding position than Egbert.

[2] See Mr. Robertson's essay on the king's kin; Hist. Essays, pp. 177–189.

territorial also. The consolidated realm enters into continental politics and borrows somewhat of the imperial form and spirit; and this brings on some important changes.

71. The earliest legislation exhibits the king as already in a position in which personal preeminence is secured and fortified by legal provisions. In the laws of Ethelbert the king's *mundbyrd* is fixed at fifty shillings, that of the *eorl* at twelve, and that of the *ceorl* at six; and wrongs done to members of his household are punished in proportion [1]. These laws mention no wergild for the king, but it seems probable that if there were one it also would be calculated on a like scale. A century later the laws of Wihtræd direct that the king is to be prayed for without command, that is, that intercession for him shall be part of the ordinary service of the church; his word without oath is incontrovertible, and even his *thegn* may clear himself by his own oath. The king's *mundbyrd* is still fifty shillings [2]. The laws of Ini king of Wessex, who was contemporary with Wihtræd, show that in that conquering and advancing kingdom the tendency was more strongly developed. If a man fight in the king's house both his life and property lie at the king's mercy; his *geneat* may 'swear for sixty hides'; his *burh-bryce* is a hundred and twenty shillings [3]. But in the reign of Alfred the king's *borh-bryce* or *mundbyrd* was five pounds, his *burh-bryce* a hundred and twenty shillings, whilst that of the *ceorl* was only five [4]. The value of the protection given by the higher classes rises in proportion to that given by the king, whilst that of the simple freeman remains as before, or is actually depressed. It is by the same code that the relation between the king and his subjects is defined as that between lord and dependent; 'if any one plot against the king's life, of himself or by harbouring of exiles, or of his men, let him be liable in his life and in all that he has. If he desire to prove himself true, let him do so according to the king's wergild. So also we ordain for all degrees whether *eorl* or *ceorl*. He who plots against his lord's life let him be liable in his life to him and in all that he has, or let him prove himself true according to his

Earliest status of the Anglo-Saxon king.

Increase in his personal importance.

Law of treason.

[1] Ethelbert, §§ 8, 15, &c.
[2] Wihtræd, §§ 1, 2, 16, 20.
[3] Ini, §§ 6, 19, 45.
[4] Alfred, §§ 3, 40.

Idea of treason.

lord's *wer*[1].' The law of Edward the elder contains an exhortation to the *witan* for the maintenance of the public peace, in which it is proposed that they should 'be in that fellowship in which the king was, and love that which he loved, and shun that which he shunned, both on sea and land[2]:' a clear reference to the relation between the lord and his dependent as expressed in the oath of fealty. The same king, in A.D. 921, received the submission of the East Anglian Danes on the same condition: 'they would observe peace towards all to whom the king should grant his peace, both by sea and land[3]:' and the Cambridgeshire people especially chose him 'to *hlaforde* and to *mundbora*,' so placing themselves under his personal protection. The principle is enunciated with greater clearness in the law of his son Edmund, in which the oath of fealty is generally imposed; all are to swear to be faithful to him as a man ought to be faithful to his lord, loving what he loves, shunning what he shuns[4]. This series of enactments must be regarded as fixing the date of the change of relation, and may perhaps be interpreted as explaining it. The rapid consolidation of the Danish with the Angle and Saxon population involved the necessity of the uniform tie between them and the king: the Danes became the king's men and entered into the public peace; the native English could not be left in a less close connexion with their king: the commendation of the one involved the tightening of the cords that united the latter to their native ruler. Something

The king becomes the lord of his people.

[1] Alfred, § 4. In the introduction to his laws, § 49. 7, he also excepts treason from the list of offences for which a *bot* may be taken: 'in prima culpa pecunialem emendationem capere quam ibi decreverunt, praeter proditionem domini, in qua nullam pietatem ausi sunt intueri, quia Deus omnipotens nullam adjudicavit contemptoribus suis.' This is referred to as a judgment of ancient synods.

[2] Edward, ii. 1, § 1, above p. 149.

[3] Thurferth the eorl and the holds and all the army that owed obedience to Northampton sought him 'to hlaforde and to mundboran;' all who were left in the Huntingdon country sought 'his frith and his mundbyrde;' the East Anglians swore to be one with him, that they would all that he would, and would keep peace with all with whom the king should keep peace either on sea or on land; and the army that owed obedience to Cambridge chose him 'to hlaforde and to mundbora.' Chron. Sax. A.D. 921.

[4] Edmund, iii. § 1.

of the same kind must have taken place as each of the heptarchic kingdoms fell under West Saxon rule, but the principle is most strongly brought out in connexion with the Danish submission.

Imperial titles adopted.

From this time accordingly the personal dignity of royalty becomes more strongly marked. Edmund and his successors take high sounding titles borrowed from the imperial court; to the real dignity of king of the English they add the shadowy claim to the empire of Britain which rested on the commendation of Welsh and Scottish princes [1]. The tradition that Edgar was rowed by eight kings upon the Dee is the expression of this idea which it was left for far distant generations to realise [2].

Religious duty of obedience.

Under Ethelred still higher claims are urged: again and again the witan resolve as a religious duty to adhere to one *cyne-hlaford* [3]: and the king himself is declared to be Christ's vicegerent among Christian people, with the special duty of defending God's church and people, and with the consequent claim on their obedience; 'he who holds an outlaw of God in his power over the term that the king may have appointed, acts, at peril of himself and all his property, against Christ's vicegerent who preserves and holds sway over Christendom and kingdom as long as God grants it [4].' The unity of the kingdom endangered by Sweyn and Canute is now fenced about with sanctions which imply religious duty. Both state and church are in peril; Ethelred is regarded as the representative of both. A few years later Canute had made good his claim to be looked on as a Christian and national king. The first article of his laws, passed with the counsel of his witan to the praise of God, and his own honour and behoof, is this:

[1] Athelstan is 'rex Anglorum, et curagulus totius Britanniae,' or 'primicerius totius Albionis,' or 'rex et rector totius Britanniae.' Edred is 'imperator,' 'cyning and casere totius Britanniae,' 'basileus Anglorum hujusque insulae barbarorum;' Edwy is 'Angulsaxonum basileus &c,' or 'Angulsæxna et Northanhumbrorum imperator, paganorum gubernator, Breotonumque propugnator;' Edgar is 'totius Albionis imperator Augustus;' and so on. See Freeman, Norm. Conq. i. 548 sq.

[2] In A.D. 922 the kings of the North Welsh took Edward for their lord; in 924 he was chosen for father and lord by the king and nation of the Scots, by the Northumbrians, Dane and English, and by the Strathclyde Britons and their king. On the real force of these commendations see Freeman, Norm. Conq. i. 565; and Robertson, Scotland, &c. ii. 384. sq.

[3] Ethelred, v. § 5; viii. §§ 2, 44.

[4] Ibid. viii. § 42.

'that above all other things, they should ever love and worship one God, and unanimously observe one Christianity, and love King Canute with strict fidelity [1].'

The increase of royal assumption not to be attributed to clerical adulation.

It is wrong to regard the influence of the clergy as one of the chief causes of the increase in the personal dignity of the kings. The rite of coronation substituted for the rude ceremony, whatever it may have been, which marked the inauguration of a heathen king, contained a distinct charge as to the nature of royal duties [2], but no words of adulation nor even any statement of the personal sacro-sanctity of the recipient. The enactments of the councils are directed, where they refer to royalty at all, rather to the enforcement of reforms than to the encouragement of despotic claims [3]. The letters of the early Anglo-Saxon bishops are full of complaints of royal misbehaviour: the sins of the kings of the eighth century almost seem to cancel the memory of the benefits received from the nursing fathers of the seventh [4]. Far from maintaining either in theory or in practice the divine right of the anointed, the prelates seem to have joined in, or at least acquiesced in, the rapid series of displacements in Northumbria [5]. Alcuin mourns over the fate of the national rulers, but grants that their crimes deserved all that fell on them. They are like Saul the anointed of the Lord [6], but they have no

[1] Canute, i. § 1.

[2] Above p. 146; where I have protested distinctly against the view of Allen, Prerogative, pp. 18–24.

[3] The canon (12) of the legatine council in A.D. 787 (Councils, &c. iii. 453), attempts to prohibit the murder of kings, so frightfully common at the time, by enforcing regular election and forbidding conspiracy; 'nec christus Domini esse valet et rex totius regni, et heres patriae qui ex legitimo non fuerit connubio generatus,' &c., but the preceding canon (11) is an exhortation to kings; the bishops and others are warned, 'fiducialiter et veraciter absque ullo timore vel adulatione loqui verbum Dei regibus,' the kings are exhorted to obey their bishops, to honour the church, to have prudent counsellors fearing the Lord and honest in conversation, that the people instructed and comforted by the good examples of kings and princes may profit to the praise and glory of Almighty God.

[4] See especially the letter of Boniface to Ethelbald, Councils, &c. iii. 350.

[5] Above p. 137.

[6] See Councils, &c. iii. 476; writing to Ethelred of Northumbria he says, 'vidistis quomodo perierint antecessores vestri reges et principes propter injustitias et rapinas et immunditias . . . timete illorum perditionem . . . p. 491. 'Qui sanctes legit scripturas . . . inveniet pro hujusmodi peccatis reges regna et populos patriam perdidisse.' p. 493.

indefeasible status. In the preaching of peace and good will, the maintenance of obedience to constituted powers is indeed insisted on, but the duty of obeying the powers that be is construed simply and equitably [1]. It is only when, in the presence of the heathen foe, Christendom and kingdom seem for a moment to rest on the support of a single weak hand, that the duty of obedience to the king is made to outweigh the consideration of his demerits. And yet Dunstan had prophesied of Ethelred that the sword should not depart from his house until his kingdom should be transferred to another dominion whose worship and tongue his people knew not [2].

Importance of the religious side of the question.

Nor is it necessary to regard the growth of royal power, as distinct from personal pomp, among the Anglo-Saxons, as affected by the precedents and model of the Frank empire [3]. Although the theory of kingship was in Gaul perhaps scarcely less exalted than at Constantinople, the practice was very different, for the Merovingian puppets were set up and thrown down at pleasure. But during the eighth century the influence of England on the continent was perhaps greater than that of the continent on England. The great missionaries of Germany looked to their native land as the guide and pattern of the country of their adoption. It is only with the Karolingian dynasty that the imitation of foreign custom in England could begin; but even if the fact were far more clearly ascertained than it is, the circumstances that made it possible, the creation of of national unity and the need of united defence, were far more important than a mere tendency to superficial imitation. The causes at work in Gaul and Britain were distinct and the results widely different.

Royal assumption not the result of imitation of Frankish practice.

72. As the personal dignity of the king increased and the character of his relation to his people was modified, his official powers were developed, and his function as fountain of justice

The king becomes the source of justice.

[1] 'The words of the old writer followed by Simeon 'deinde Domini suffragio potitus' clearly show the opinion of the age that the God of battles gave his verdict in victory, and that war was only an appeal to the judgment of God on a large scale.' Robertson, Essays, p. 208. The principle thus expressed might be extended still further; there were no kings *de jure* except the kings *de facto*.

[2] Flor. Wig. ad ann. 1016.

[3] Allen, Prerogative, p. 20.

Growth of the idea.

became more distinctly recognised. The germ of this attribute lay in the idea of royalty itself. The peace, as it was called[1], the primitive alliance for mutual good behaviour, for the performance and enforcement of rights and duties, the voluntary restraint of free society in its earliest form, was from the beginning of monarchy under the protection of the king. Of the three classes of offences that came under the view of the law[2], the minor infraction of right was atoned for by a compensation to the injured, the *bot* with which his individual good will was redeemed, and by a payment of equal amount to the king by which the offender bought back his admission into the public peace[3]. The greater breaches of the peace arising either from refusal to pay the fines, or from the commission of offences for which fines were inadequate, were punished by outlawry; the offender was a public enemy, set outside the law and the peace; his adversary might execute his own vengeance, and even common hospitality towards him was a breach of the law, until the king restored him to his place as a member of society[4]. The third class of offences which seemed beyond the scope of outlawry, and demanded strict, public, and direct rather than casual and private punishment, were yet like the former capable of composition, the acceptance of which to a certain extent depended on the king as representing the people[5]. In all

The king's share in the fines for breach of the peace.

His power of accepting money compensation.

[1] Wilda, Strafrecht, pp. 255 sq., 264 sq. Waitz, D. V. G. i. 391; 'the peace is the relation in which all stand whilst and in so far as all continue in the union and in the right on which the community rests. He who acts against this commits a breach of the peace. The breach of the peace is un-right; the transgression against right is a breach of the peace.' He who sins against one, sins against all; and no man may redress his own wrongs until he has appealed to the guardians of the peace for justice. Hence the peace is the great check on the practice of private war, blood feuds, and the so-called *lex talionis*. I think the German writers take too high a view of the power of the Anglo-Saxon king as guardian of the peace. See Schmid, Gesetze, p. 584; Gneist, Verwaltungsrecht, i. 26.

[2] K. Maurer, Krit. Ueberschau, iii. 26 sq. Bethmann-Hollweg, Civilprocess, iv. 25 sq. Schmid, Gesetze, p. 584. Palgrave, Commonwealth, p. 204. Waitz, D. V. G. i. 392; ii. 40.

[3] K. Maurer, Krit. Ueberschau, iii. 45. Ll. Hloth. and Eadr. §§ 11, 12, 13. Ini, §§ 3, 6, 7, 10. Schmid, Gesetze, p. 679.

[4] Athelstan, ii. § 20, 3. Edgar, i. § 3: 'et sit utlaga, id est exul vel exlex, nisi rex ei patriam concedat.' Ethelred, viii. § 2.

[5] Alfred, § 7, 'sit in arbitrio regis sic vita sic mors, sicut ei condonare voluerit.' Also Ini, § 6; Edmund, ii. § 6; Ethelred, iv. § 4; but compare Alfred, Introd. § 49. 7; as given above, p. 176.

this the king is not only the executor of the peace, but a sharer in its authority and claims. But this position is far from that of the fountain of justice and source of jurisdiction. The king's guarantee was not the sole safeguard of the peace: the hundred had its peace as well as the king[1]: the king too had a distinct peace which like that of the church was not that of the country at large, a special guarantee for those who were under special protection[2].

The king is guardian of the peace.

The *grith*[3], a term which comes into use in the Danish struggle, is a limited or localised peace, under the special guarantee of the individual, and differs little from the protection implied in the *mund* or personal guardianship which appears much earlier[4]; although it may be regarded as another mark of territorial development. When the king becomes the lord, patron and *mundborh* of his whole people, they pass from the ancient national peace of which he is the guardian into the closer personal or territorial relation of which he is the source. The peace is now the king's peace[5]; although the *grith* and the *mund* still retain their limited and local application, they entitle their possessor to no higher rights, they do but involve the transgressor in more special penalties; the *frith* is enforced by

The people pass into the king's peace or protection.

[1] Edmund, iii. § 2. Edgar, i. §§ 2, 3; iii. 7. Ethelred, iii. 3. Canute, ii. §§ 15. 30.

[2] Schmid, Gesetze, p. 584.

[3] Grith [gridh] is properly the *domicile*, Vigfússon (Icelandic Dict. s.v.), and consequently, asylum; then truce or peace limited to place or time. Schmid, Gesetze, pp. 584, 604, So Church-grith is sometimes used for sanctuary; but it really means as much as Church-frith, the peace and security which the law guarantees to those under the church's protection. Schmid arranges the special peaces or several griths under three heads: (1) Place; churches, private houses, the king's palace and precincts; (2) Time; fasts and festivals, coronation days, days of public gemots and courts, special gatherings at drinking parties, sales, markets, guilds, &c., and the times when the fyrd is summoned; (3) Persons; clergy, widows, and nuns. Gesetze, p. 585. Gneist, Verwaltgsr. i. 38, 39. The curious enactment of Ethelred, iii. § 1, distinguishing the grith of the king, that of the ealdorman, that given in the burh-moot, the wapentake and the alehouse, with different fines for breach, is very noteworthy.

[4] Gneist, Verwaltungsrecht, i. 26. The original meaning of *mund* is said to be *hand*, Schmid, Gesetze, p. 634; but it also has the meaning of *word*, sermo; and of *patria potestas*. Waitz, D. V. G. i. 55.

[5] Edward, ii. 1, § 1. 'Inquisivit itaque qui ad emendationem velit redire, et in societate permanere qua ipse sit.' Edmund, ii. § 7. 'Pax regis.' See Gneist, Verwaltungsrecht, i. 26; Self-government, i. 29; K. Maurer, Krit. Ueberschau, iii. 46.

Special peace.

the national officers, the *grith* by the king's personal servants: the one is official, the other personal; the one the business of the country, the other that of the court [1]. The special peace is further extended to places where the national peace is not fully provided for: the great highways, on which questions of local jurisdiction might arise to the delay of justice, are under the king's peace. But the process by which the national peace became the king's peace is almost imperceptible: and it is very gradually that we arrive at the time at which all peace and law are supposed to die with the old king, and rise again at the proclamation of the new [2]. In Anglo-Saxon times the transition is mainly important as touching the organisation of jurisdiction.

The peace is the king's peace.

The national officers now execute their functions as the king's officers, and executors of his peace; the shire and hundred courts, although they still call the peace their own, act in his

[1] The king's hand-grith, in the law of Edward and Guthrum, § 1, must mean the king's mund; the special peace given by the king's hand; see too Ethelred, vi. § 14, the 'pax quam manu sua dederit,' Canute, i. § 2. 2. To this belongs also the chapter on the *Pax regis* in the laws of Edward the Confessor, in which the peace of the coronation-days, that is, a week at Easter, Whitsuntide and Christmas; the peace of the four great highways, Watling-street, Ikenild-street, Ermin-street, and Foss-way, and the peace of the navigable rivers are protected with special fines that distinguish them from the common-law peace of the country, which is also the king's peace. Besides these there is a fourth peace called the king's *hand-sealde grith*, and one given by the king's writ, which answer more closely to the idea of the mund as personal protection; and with this are connected the original pleas of the crown (see below, p. 187). Other offences against the peace, and the protection of other roads and rivers, belong to the view of the local courts, the shire and the sheriff, although not less closely related to the king's peace and jurisdiction. Cf. Glanvill, de Legg. i. 1; Ll. Edw. Conf. § 12; Palgrave, Commonwealth, pp. 284, 285.

[2] 'The Sovereign was the fountain of justice; therefore the stream ceased to flow when the well spring was covered by the tomb. The judicial bench vacant; all tribunals closed. Such was the ancient doctrine—a doctrine still recognised in Anglo-Norman England.' Palgrave, Normandy and England, iii. 193. Speaking of the special protections above referred to, the same writer says: 'Sometime after the Conquest all these special protections were replaced by a general proclamation of the king's peace which was made when the community assented to the accession of the new monarch, and this first proclamation was considered to be in force during the remainder of his life, so as to bring any disturber of the public tranquillity within its penalties. So much importance was attached to the ceremonial that even in the reign of John, offences committed during the interregnum, or period elapsing between the day of the death of the last monarch and the recognition of his successor, were unpunishable in those tribunals whose authority was derived from the Crown.' Commonwealth, p. 285.

name; the idea gains ground and becomes a form of law. Offences against the law become offences against the king, and the crime of disobedience a crime of contempt to be expiated by a special sort of fine, the *oferhyrnesse*[1], to the outraged majesty of the lawgiver and judge. The first mention of the *oferhyrnesse* occurs in the laws of Edward the elder[2], at the era accordingly at which the change of idea seems to have become permanent[3].

Contempt of the king's law is specially punishable.

73. But although it may be convenient to accept this approximation to a date, the influence of the idea may be traced much further back. The administration of the peace is inseparable from the exercise of jurisdiction; those who are in the national peace are subject only to the national courts; those who are in the church's *grith*, are also in the church's *socn;* those who are in the king's *mund*, are under his cognisance; those who are amenable to any jurisdiction, owe suit and service to the courts of the jurisdiction; when all are in the *mund* or *grith* or *frith* of the king, he is the supreme judge of all persons and over all causes, limited however by the counsel and consent of his *witan*.

Growth of the idea of royal jurisdiction.

[1] Ofer-hyrnesse (subauditio, male audire) answers to the later overseunnesse (over-looking, contempt); it is marked by special penalty in the cases of buying outside markets, refusal of justice, accepting another man's dependent without his leave, refusing Peter's pence, sounding the king's coin, neglect of summons to gemot or pursuit of thieves, and disobedience to the king's officers. See Schmid, Gesetze, p. 638.

[2] 'Si quis extra portum barganniet, oferhyrnesse regis culpa est.' Edward, i. § 1.

[3] The concluding chaper of Asser's life of Alfred (M. H. B. p. 497) gives some important data, not only as to the participation of the king in judicature, but as to the composition of the local courts in his day. The nobiles and ignobiles, the eorls and ceorls, were constantly disagreeing in the gemots, 'in concionibus comitum et praepositorum;' a proof that ealdorman and gerefa, eorl and ceorl, had their places in these courts. None of the suitors were willing to allow that what the ealdormen and gerefan determined was true; a proof that although the officers might declare the law the ultimate determination rested in each case with the suitors. This caused a great number of causes to be brought before the king: he summoned the faulty judges before him and carefully examined into each case; or examined them through his messengers: insisting when he found them guilty that they should either resign the offices which he had committed to them, or devote themselves to the study of equity. We learn from this that the appointments to the sheriffdoms and ealdormanships were made by him, not by election of the people; and, as ignorance was the excuse of their sin, equity the object of their enforced study, that it is clearly in the declaration of law not in the determination of suits that they were faulty. The same general conclusion results from the reading of his laws.

Royal jurisdiction over the tenants of folkland.

In regard to the holders of *folkland*, the special royal jurisdiction must have been much older than the time of Alfred; as these tenants were liable to special burdens payable directly to the state, and as the profits of jurisdiction which were counted among these burdens, were inseparable from jurisdiction itself, it is probable that the jurisdiction of these lands was administered by royal officers, not necessarily separate from the business of the hundred courts, but as a part of their work, having special reference to the king's interests[1]. They would be from the first in the peace of the king rather than in that of the hundred. When, however, folklands were turned into booklands in favour of either churches or individuals, and all their obligations save the *trinoda necessitas* transferred with them, the profits of jurisdiction and jurisdiction itself followed too. Such jurisdiction as had been exercised by the king, in or out of the popular courts, was now vested in the recipient of the grant. This may have been a very early innovation. The terms *sac* and *soc*[2], which imply it, are not found until late in the period, but occur almost universally in Norman grants of confirmation, as describing definite immunities which may have been only implied, though necessarily implied, in the grant, and customarily recognised under these names[3]. The

Private jurisdictions.

Sac and soc.

[1] In the Salian Mallus (above, p. 54), the thunginus acted on behalf of the nation, the sacebaro looked after the interests of the king. In the later county court, some such division of duties and interests must have existed between the sheriff and the coroner; and in the Anglo-Saxon time, there may have been a hundred-reeve as well as a hundreds-ealdor (above, p. 101). Yet in the county court the sheriff was nominated by the crown, the coroner chosen by the people; and earlier, the ealdorman was appointed by the king and witan, the sheriff apparently by the king alone. And it is extremely difficult to distinguish between the duties of the sheriff executing the peace as the officer of the nation, and collecting the revenue as steward of the king.

[2] Sac, or sacu, seems to mean litigation, and sôcn to mean jurisdiction; the former from the thing (sacu) in dispute; the latter from the seeking of redress; but the form is an alliterative jingle, which will not bear close analysis. Kemble refers sacu to the preliminary and initiative process, and sôcn to the right of investigation. (Cod. Dipl. i. p. xlv.) Ellis makes *sac* the jurisdiction, and *soc* the territory within which it was exercised. (Introd. i. 273). See also Schmid, Gesetze, p. 654.

[3] Kemble (C. D. i. p. xliv), remarks, that except in one questionable grant of Edgar, sac and soc are never mentioned in charters before the reign of Edward the Confessor; and concludes that 'they were so inherent in the land as not to require particularisation; but that under the Normans, when every right and privilege must be struggled for, and the conse-

idea of jurisdiction accompanying the possession of the soil must be allowed to be thus ancient, although it may be questioned whether, except in the large territorial lordships, it was actually exercised, or whether the proprietor would not as a rule satisfy himself with the profits of jurisdiction, and transact the business of it through the ordinary courts. It is probable that, except in a very few special cases, the *sac* and *soc* thus granted were before the Conquest exemptions from the hundred courts only, and not from those of the shire[1]; and that thus they are the basis of the court-leet, as the mark-system is that of the court baron. There is no evidence of the existence of a domestic tribunal by which the lord tried the offences or settled the disputes of his servants, serfs, or free tenantry; he satisfied himself with arbitrating in the latter case, and producing the criminal in the public courts[2]. But when grants of *sac* and *soc* became common, these questions would swell the business of his private courts, and his jurisdiction would apply as much to those who were under his personal, as to those who were in his territorial protection. By such grants then, indirectly as well as directly, large sections of jurisdiction which had been royal or national, fell into private hands, and as the tendency was for all land ultimately to become bookland, the national courts became more and more the courts of the landowners. The ancient process was retained, but exercised by men who derived their title from the new source of justice. Their juris-

Grants of sac and soc removed the lands from the jurisdiction of the hundred court.

Growth of private courts.

quences of the Norman love of litigation were bitterly felt, it became a matter of necessity to have them not only tacitly recognised but solemnly recorded.' The idea that the manor originates in the gradual acquisition by one family of a hereditary right to the headship of the township and the accumulation in that capacity of lands and jurisdiction, does not seem to have anything to recommend it. In fact, within historic times the headman of the township does not occupy a position of jurisdiction, simply one of police agency.

[1] In Cod. Dipl. dcccxxviii and dccclviii, Edward frees certain estates of Westminster, 'mid sace and mid socne, scotfreo and gavelfreo, *on hundrede and on scire*,' but the exemption is unusual, and even in these passages may not be a full exemption from jurisdiction. However, when in Domesday the sheriff of Worcestershire reports that there are seven hundreds out of the twelve in which he has no authority, is is clear that such jurisdictions must have been already in being.

[2] K. Maurer, Krit. Ueberschau, ii. 56.

Jurisdiction of the thegns.

diction was further modified by enactment: as the *thegn* had *socn* over his own men, the king had *socn* over his *thegns;* none but the king could exercise or have the profits of jurisdiction over a king's *thegn*[1]; none but the king could have the fines arising from the offences of the owner of bookland[2]. And although this might practically be observed by recognising the popular courts as royal courts for the smaller owners of bookland, the king had a '*thening-manna*' court, in which his greater vassals settled their disputes[3]. But the time came when the great local landowner was vested with the right of representing the king as judge and *landrica* in his whole district, and so exercised jurisdiction over minor landowners. This change, the bearing of which on the history of the hundred courts, which also were placed in private hands, is very uncertain, seems to have taken place in the reign of Canute; and may have been a local enactment only[4]. Wherever it prevailed it must have brought the local jurisdictions into close conformity with the feudalism of the continent; and may thus serve to explain some of the anomalies of the system of tenure as it existed in the times reported in Domesday.

Hereditary jurisdictions.

Weakening of the real power of the king.

These immunities, tying the judicature, as it may be said, to the land, and forming one of the most potent causes of the territorial tendency, so far ousted the jurisdiction of the national courts, whether held in the name of the king or of the people, that it might be almost said that the theoretical cha-

[1] Ethelred, iii. § 11: 'Et nemo habeat socnam super taynum regis, nisi solus rex.' Gneist insists that this refers only to thegns who were members of the witenagemot, Verwaltungsrecht, i. 25, 37, 38.

[2] Ethelred, i. §§ 1, 14: 'Et habeat rex forisfacturas omnium eorum qui liberas terras (bôcland) habent, nec componat aliquis pro ulla tyhtla, si non intersit testimonium praepositi regis.' See also Canute, ii. §§ 13, 77.

[3] Kemble, Cod. Dipl. mcclviii; Saxons, ii. 46, 47. In this instance the bishop of Rochester sues the widow of Elfric in the king's 'theningmanna gemot' for certain title deeds alleged to have been stolen: the court adjudged them to the bishop. Afterwards her relations brought the matter before the ealdorman and the folk, who compelled the bishop to restore them. It is a very curious case, and certainly serves to illustrate the principle that the shire could compel recourse to itself in the first instance even where such high interests were concerned. See K. Maurer, Krit. Ueberschau, ii. 57.

[4] Laws of the Northumbrian Priests, § 49; K. Maurer, Krit. Ueberschau, ii. 50.

racter of the sovereign rises as the scope for his action is limited. This, however, was to some extent counteracted by the special retention of royal rights in laws and charters. Accordingly, in the later laws, the king specifies the pleas of criminal justice, which he retains for his own administration and profit; such a list is given in the laws of Canute; breach of the king's protection, house-breaking, assault, neglect of the fyrd, and outlawry[1]. These were the original pleas of the crown, and were determined by the king's officers in the local courts. By a converse process, such small parts of criminal process as still belonged to these courts, arising from the offences of smaller freemen, together with the voluntary and contentious jurisdiction for which the courts of the landowners were not competent, came to be exercised in the king's name. He interfered in suits which had not passed through the earlier stage of the hundred and the shire[2]: and asserted himself as supreme judge in all causes, not in appeals only. All jurisdiction was thus exercised either by the king through his officers, or by landowners who had their title from him. The royal officers acted in the hundred courts with freemen of all classes that still owed suit to them; and the shire courts were composed of all lords of land, *scir-thegns*, and others, including a representation of the humblest landowners.

Pleas of the crown reserved in grants of jurisdiction.

74. The subject of tenure in Anglo-Saxon times is beset with many apparently insuperable difficulties[3]. We have not materials for deciding whether a uniform rule was observed in the several kingdoms or in the legal divisions which continued to represent them down to the Norman Conquest and later: whether the Danish conquest may not have created differences in Mercia, Northumbria, and East Anglia; or whether the variety of nomenclature found in Domesday Book implies a difference of character in the relations described, or merely the variations

Difficulties of Anglo-Saxon tenure.

[1] Canute, ii. § 12; K. Maurer, Krit. Ueberschau, ii. 55. The charter of Alfred, in which these rights are granted away to the abbey of Shaftesbury (Cod. Dipl. cccx), seems to be very doubtful.

[2] Kemble, Saxons, ii. 46; Cod. Dipl. dcxciii, dcclv. In the reign of Ethelred the king sends his insegel or writ to the shiremoot of Berkshire, bidding them arbitrate between Leofwine and Wynflæd; C. D. dcxciii.

[3] Hallam, M. A. ii. 293; Palgrave, Commonwealth, pp. 576 sq.

The Anglo-Saxon system of vassalage grew out of the law not out of the land.

of local and customary terminology; the result of an investigation transacted by different officers, many of whom were Normans, and scarcely understood the meaning of the witnesses whose evidence they were taking. There is, however, no question of any general subversion of the primitive rule before the Norman Conquest. No legislation turned the free owner into the feudal tenant: whatever changes in that direction took place were the result of individual acts, or of very gradual changes of custom arising indirectly from the fact that other relations were assuming a territorial character. Domesday Book attests the existence in the time of Edward the Confessor of a large class of freemen who, by commendation, had placed themselves in the relation of dependence on a superior lord[1]; whether any power of transferring their service still remained, or whether the protection which the commended freeman received from his lord extended so far as to give a feudal character to his tenure of land, cannot be certainly determined; but the very use of the term seems to imply that vassalage had not in these cases attained its full growth: the origin of the relation was in the act of the dependent. On the other hand, the occupation of the land of the greater owners by the tenants or dependents to whom it is granted by the lord prevailed on principles little changed from primitive times and incapable of much development. It would seem, however, wiser to look for the chief cause of change in the alteration of other relations. This tendency with reference to judicature we have just examined. When every man who was not by his own free possession of land a fully qualified member of the commonwealth, had of necessity to find himself a lord, and the king had asserted for himself the position of lord and patron of the whole nation; when every free man had to provide himself with a permanent security for his own appearance in the courts of justice, of which the king was the source, and for the maintenance of the peace, of which the king

[1] Ellis, Introd. to Domesday, i. 64–66. The term is most frequent in Essex and East Anglia; but descriptions that imply the general use of the practice are abundant; such as 'ire cum terra ubi voluerit,' 'quaerere dominum ubi voluerit.' Hallam, M. A. ii. 276, note z.

Growth of the idea of lordship as connected with land.

was the protector; when every owner of bookland had the right of jurisdiction, and the king alone could exercise jurisdiction over the owner of bookland; the relation of the small landowner to the greater or to the king, and the relation of the landless man to his lord, created a perfectly graduated system of jurisdiction, every step of which rested on the possession of land by one or both of the persons by whose relations it was created. The man who had land judged the man who had not, and the constant assimilation going on between the poor landowner and the mere cultivator of his lord's land, had the result of throwing both alike under the courts of the greater proprietors. As soon as a man found himself obliged to suit and service in the court of his stronger neighbour, it needed but a single step to turn the practice into theory, and to regard him as holding his land in consideration of that suit and service[1]. Still more so, when by special grant other royal rights, such as the collection of Danegeld and the enforcement of military service, are made over to the great lords[2]; the occupation, though it still bears the name of alodial, returns to the character of usufruct out of which it sprang, when the national ownership, after first vesting itself in the king as national representative, has been broken up into particulars, every one of which is capable of being alienated in detail.

Military service.

75. In the obligation of military service, may be found a second strong impulse towards a national feudalism. The host was originally the people in arms; the whole free population,

[1] Hence the alodiaries of Domesday are represented as holding their lands of a superior: not because they had received them of him, but because they did suit and service at his court, and followed his banner. Hence, too, Edward the Confessor was able to give to the Abbey of Westminster his own alodiaries; the king being lord of all who had no other lord. They remained alodiaries by title and inheritance, and probably escaped some of the burdens of territorial dependence.

[2] Gneist, who treats this subject from a different point of view, inclines to refer the sinking of the ceorl into dependence generally to three causes: (1) The burden of military service, which led him to commend himself to a lord who would then be answerable for the military service; (2) to the convenience which the poor alodial owners found in seeking justice from a strong neighbour rather than from a distant court; and (3) in the need of military defence during the Danish wars, which drove men into the protection of fortified houses. Verwaltungsrecht, i. 52, 53.

Military service originally a personal obligation.

whether landowners or dependents, their sons, servants, and tenants. Military service was a personal obligation: military organisation depended largely on tribal and family relations: in the process of conquest, land was the reward of service; the service was the obligation of freedom, of which the land was the outward and visible sign. But very early, as soon perhaps as the idea of separate property in land was developed, the military service became, not indeed a burden upon the land, but a personal duty that practically depended on the tenure of land; it may be that every hide had to maintain its warrior; it is certain that every owner of land was obliged to the *fyrd* or expeditio; the owner of bookland as liable to the *trinoda necessitas* alone; the occupier of folkland as subject to that as well as to many other obligations from which bookland was exempted. But although folkland and bookland agreed in this, there was no doubt a fundamental difference in their respective obligations, which was probably expressed in the penalty to which they were severally liable in case of default. The holder of alodial land was subject on the continent to the fine for neglecting the Heerbann [1]; the holder of a beneficium to forfeiture [2]. The same practice would apply in England to bookland and folkland, although from the peculiarly defensive character of English warfare after the consolidation of the kingdom, it might very early be disused. The law of Ini, that the landowning gesithcundman in case of neglecting the fyrd, should forfeit his land as well as pay 120 shillings as fyrdwite [3], may be explained either of the gesith holding an estate of folkland, or of the landowner standing in the relation of gesith to the king: it seems natural however to refer the fine to the betrayal of his character

It becomes connected with land.

Difference of penalty for neglect of the host.

[1] 'Quicumque liber homo in hostem bannitus fuerit et venire contempserit plenum heribannum id est solidos 60 persolvat.' Cap. Bonon. 811, c. 1; Baluze, i. 337; Waitz, D. V. G. iv. 486.

[2] 'Quicumque ex his qui beneficium principis habent parem suum contra hostes in exercitu pergentem dimiserit, et cum eo ire vel stare noluerit, honorem suum et beneficium perdat.' Cap. Bonon. 811, c. 5; Baluze, i. 338; Waitz, D. V. G. iv. 492.

[3] Ini, § 51. 'Si homo sithcundus terrarius expeditionem supersedeat, emendet cxx solidis et perdat terram suam; non habens terram lx solidis; cirliscus xxx solidis pro fyrdwita.'

of free man, his forfeiture to his desertion of his duty as gesith. The later legislation, which directs forfeiture in case of the king's presence with the host, whilst a fine of 120 shillings was sufficient atonement if he were not present, would seem to be the natural result of the change which placed the whole population in dependence on him as lord [1].

The military obligation of the thegn.

It is by no means improbable that the final binding of landownership with military attendance on the king in the form of the thegn's service [2], is connected with the same legislation of Alfred and Edward, which we have already examined in reference to treason and the maintenance of the peace. To their date approximately belong the definitions of the thegn as possessing five hides of his own land, church and kitchen, bell-house and burh-geat-setl, and special service in the king's hall: the thegn of Alfred is the miles of Bede; the history of the year A. D. 894 shows an amount of military organisation on Alfred's part, of which there is no earlier evidence, an army of reserve and a definite term of service [3]. The military policy too of Charles the Great may by this time have affected England; the improvement of organisation involves a more distinct definition of military duties; and it is certain that the increased importance and costliness of equipment must have

[1] Ethelred, v. § 28; vi. § 35. 'Quando rex in hostem pergit, si quis edictu ejus vocatus remanserit, si ita liber homo est ut habeat socam suam et sacam et cum terra sua possit ire quo voluerit, de omni terra sua est in misericordia Regis. Cujuscunque vero alterius domini liber homo si de hoste remanserit, et dominus ejus pro eo alium hominem duxerit, xl solidis domino suo qui vocatus fuit emendabit. Quod si ex toto nullus pro eo abierit ipse quidem domino suo xl sol., dominus autem ejus totidem sol. regi emendabit.' Domesday, i. 172, Worcestershire. In Canute, ii. § 65, neglect of the fyrd involves a fine of 120 shillings, but in § 77, whoever flies from his lord or his companion, in sea or land expedition, is to lose all that he has, and even his bookland is forfeited to the king. His lord enters on the land that he has given him, and his life is forfeit; but this is not the neglect of the fyrd, but the *herisliz* of the continental law, which was punishable by death. Cap. Bonon. 811, c. 4; Baluze, i. 338.

[2] Gneist, Self-government, i. 11: The thegn's service was clearly, (1) personal; (2) at his own cost of equipment; (3) he paid his own expenses during the campaign.

[3] Chron. Sax. A.D. 894. 'The king had divided his forces (fierd) into two, so that one half was constantly at home, half out in the field; besides those men whose duty it was to defend the burhs.'

No exact parallel with Karolingian legislation in Anglo-Saxon times.

confined effective service to the rich [1]. But although the thegn was bound to military service, we have not sufficient warrant for accepting the theory that his service bore to the extent of his land the exact proportion that is laid down in Karolingian legislation or in feudal times [2]. The hide might furnish its man; the thegn might be answerable for five men, or for one warrior five times as well equipped as the ordinary free man: in the reign of Ethelred, eight hides furnished a helm and a coat of mail [3]; in Berkshire in the time of Edward the Confessor, the custom was that every five hides sent one warrior (miles) [4], and each furnished him with four shillings for the provision of two months: if he failed to attend he suffered forfeiture. But we have few more indications of local, and none of general practice, and it is probable that the complete following out of the Frank idea was reserved for Henry II, unless his military reforms are to be understood, as so many of his other measures are, as the revival and strengthening of anti-feudal and prae-feudal custom. Still even these traces are sufficient to show the tendency to bind up special possession with special service, and consequently to substitute some other liability for that of military service in cases where that special qualification did not exist. Whether the simple freeman served as the follower of the lord to whom he had commended himself or to whose court he did service, or as the king's dependent under the banner of the sheriff or other lord to whom the king had deputed the leading, he found himself a member of a host bound together with territorial relations [5]. If he were too poor to provide his arms, or preferred

[1] Gneist, Self-government, i. 10. The stages may be thus marked: (1) the universal obligation; (2) the obligation of the hundred to furnish a hundred warriors; (3) the increased cost of armour restricting effective service. In the seventh century, on the continent, full equipment was worth 33 solidi, that is the price of as many oxen, or of a hide of land: in England, the service was on foot. (4) Although the fully armed warrior might be the king's thegn, all owners of five hides were liable to the same service, and the whole population was still summoned to defensive war, like that against the Danes. Ibid. i. 11–13, 14. Robertson, Hist. Essays, pp. vii–xix, has some very valuable remarks on the whole subject.

[2] Gneist, Self-government, i. 13.

[3] Chron. Sax. A.D. 1008.

[4] Above, p. 117.

[5] Gneist (Self-government, i. 15; Verwaltgsr. i. 15) rightly maintains that the military service was still a personal duty, not a burden on the land;

safe servitude to dangerous employment in warfare, there was no lack of warlike neighbours who, in consideration of his acceptance of their superiority, would undertake the duty that lay upon his land: he was easily tempted to become a socager, paying rent or gavel, instead of a free but overworked and shortlived man-at-arms.

Commutation of military service.

But a further conclusion may be drawn on other grounds. From the time of Alfred the charters contain less and less frequently the clause expressing the counsel and consent of the witan to the grant. It never altogether disappears; but the witan gradually sink into the position of witnesses, and their consent, probably perfunctory enough at the best time, becomes a mere attestation. It would seem to follow from this that the folkland was becoming virtually king's land, from the moment that the West Saxon monarch became sole ruler of the English; a date agreeing nearly with those which we have fixed for the turning point of the system. If then the king was henceforth special lord of the folkland, the folkland itself becomes scarcely distinguishable from the royal demesne; and every estate cut out of it, whether turned into bookland or not, would seem to place the holder in a personal relation to the king which was fulfilled by military service. Every man who was in the king's peace was liable to be summoned to the host at the king's call, but the king's vassals especially; the former for national defence, the latter for all service[1]: but all the English wars of the tenth and eleventh

Change of the folkland to royal demesne.

The duty of national defence.

but the personal duty was at every turn conditioned by the possession of the land.

[1] See Gneist, Self-government, i. 13, 18. In the Karoling period this general armament already bore the name of the *landwehr*. 'Ad defensionem patriae omnes sine ulla excusatione veniant.' Edict. Pistense, A.D. 864, c. 27. 'Et volumus ut cujuscumque nostrum homo, in cujuscunque regno sit, cum seniore suo in hostem vel aliis suis utilitatibus pergat, nisi talis regni invasio, quam lantweri dicunt, quod absit, acciderit, ut omnis populus illius regni ad eam repellendam communiter pergat.' Conv. Marsn. A.D. 847. *adn. Karoli*, § 5. The continuance of the fyrd as a general armament of the people during Anglo-Saxon times was no doubt the result of the defensive character of the warfare with the Danes; otherwise it might have sunk, as on the continent, to the mere *wacta* or police of the country (see above, p. 77); a character which it possessed in England also, and which was called out by the legislation of Edward I. It is important to note this double character of the third obligation of the trinoda necessitas; watch and ward;

centuries were wars of defence, and hence the fyrd system was maintained in its integrity, although the special duty of the thegns, as afterwards that of the knights, subsisted side by side with it. Still, as in the most primitive times, the host contained the free people fighting in their local organisation, and the specially qualified, specially bound, servants and companions of the leaders[1]. The cultivators of Kent might not be bound by the special service[2], might pay gavel, or rent, instead of fighting, be drengs instead of thegns or knights, but they had no right to hold back from the defence of the country.

Composition of the army.

Form of legislation unchanged.

76. In the region of legislation, beside the general tone and tendency which have been illustrated under the heads of justice and land-tenure, the growth of the royal power and the accompanying increase of territorial influences could appear only in the form of enactment, or in the growth or elimination of the principle of personal law. In the former point no change is perceptible. Ethelred and Canute invariably express the counsel and consent of the wise men of the nation to their promulgation of the laws, just as Ini and Alfred had done. The king never legislates by his own ordinance. The codes are in fact not so much the introductions of new principles as the declarations of the customs or common law of the race, dating from far beyond the existence of written record, preserved in the memories of the wise, and kept alive for the most part in constant general experience. It may be that, when the knowledge of law has become professional, or when under new influences indigenous customs are becoming obsolete, they are written down in books; but as a rule it may be said that a publication of laws is the result of some political change or series of changes; so that the very act of legislation implies some crisis in the history of the legislator.

one against malefactors, the other against armed hosts. In the German trinoda necessitas the *wacta* is more important because in more constant requisition than the *lantweri*; in England the fyrd is in more constant requisition, until after the Conquest, than the watch; but the two ideas are never really divorced.

[1] Above, p. 30.

[2] See Robertson, Essays, pp. l–liv. Elton, Tenures of Kent. pp. 45–58. The drengs who held lands under the archbishop were turned into knights by Lanfranc. Epp. Cantuar. p. 225.

The most ancient Germanic code, the Pactus Legis Salicae, seems to mark the period at which the several Frank tribes admitted the sovereignty of the Salian king. The laws of Ethelbert of Kent were the immediate result of the conversion[1]; those of Wihtræd and Ini, of the changes which a century of church organisation made necessary in that kingdom and in Wessex. The codes of Alfred and Edgar are the legislation which the consolidation of the several earlier kingdoms under the West Saxon house demanded, the former for Wessex, Kent and Mercia[2], the latter for the whole of England. Not the least important part of the laws of Alfred and Edward are clothed in the form of treaty with the East Anglian Danes. The laws of Canute are the enunciation, with the confirmation of the conqueror, now the elected king, of the legislation which he had promised to preserve to the people who accepted him. Most of the shorter laws are of the nature of amendments, but serve occasionally to illustrate the growth of a common and uniform jurisprudence which testifies to the increase in strength of the power that could enforce it. Thus the very fact of the issue of a code illustrates the progress of legislative power in assimilating old customs or enacting provisions of general authority. The share of the provincial folkmoots in authorising legislation, though not in originating it, appears as late as the reign of Athelstan; but the single instance that proves it exhibits it in the form of acceptance only. The bishops and thegns of Kent, eorl and ceorl, acquiesce in the enactments of the witenagemot at Greatley[3].

New legislation the result of some national crisis.

The increase of territorial influences might naturally be expected to put an end to the system of personal law wherever it existed, except in the border territories of Wales and Scotland. But in spite of the differences of local custom, it may be

Question of personal law.

[1] Bede, H. E. ii. 5. 'Inter caetera bona quae genti suae consulendo conferebat, etiam decreta illi judiciorum juxta exempla Romanorum cum consilio sapientium constituit.'

[2] 'Nolui multa de meis in scriptura ponere quia dubitamus quid posteris inde placeret; sed quae repperi diebus Inae regis cognati mei, vel Offae Mercenorum regis, vel Æthelbrihtes qui primus in Anglorum gente baptizatus est rex, quae mihi justiora visa sunt, haec collegi et caetera dimisi.' Alfred, Introd. 49, § 9.

[3] See above, p. 115.

questioned whether in England the system of personal law ever prevailed to an extent worth recording. It is true that the tables of wergilds of the different kingdoms differ[1]; but the differences are very superficial, nor is there anything that shows certainly that the wergild of the slain stranger was estimated by the law of his own nation and not by that of the province in which he was slain. But if there ever was a period at which the former was the rule, it must have disappeared as soon as the united kingdom was ranged under the threefold division of West Saxon, Mercian and Danish law, an arrangement which appears to be entirely territorial[2]. The practice of presentment of Englishry in the case of murder which was once attributed to Canute[3] is now generally regarded as one of the innovations of the Norman Conquest. The laws of Edgar however contain an enactment which seems to give to the Danes some privilege of personal law, if not also of actual legislation. In the Supplementum enacted at the Council of Wihtbordesstan, the king and witan enact an ordinance for the whole population of the kingdom, English, Danish and British; but with a sort of saving clause, 'I will that secular rights stand among the Danes with as good laws as they best may choose. But with the English let that stand which I and my witan have added to the dooms of my forefathers for the behoof of all my people. Only let this ordinance be common to all[4].' This is a distinct recognition of the right of the Danes of the Danelaga not only to retain their own customs, but to modify them on occasion: the few customs which they specially retained are enumerated by Canute, and seem to be only nominally at variance with those of their neighbours, whilst of their exercise of the right of separate legislation there seems to be no evidence. And what is true of the Danes,

Tables of wergilds.

Division of the country according to law.

Right of the Danes.

[1] Schmid, Gesetze, pp. 394–400.

[2] See Freeman, Norm. Conq. i. 433.

[3] Ll. Edw. Conf. § 16. Dialogus de Scaccario, I. cap. x (Select Charters, p. 192). A similar measure may possibly have been taken by Canute. If an unknown man was found slain, he was presumed to be a Norman, and the hundred fined accordingly, unless they could prove that he was English. 'Non procedit nec solvatur pro murdro Anglicus sed Francigena; ex quo vero deest qui interfectum hominem comprobet Anglicum esse, Francigena reputatur.' Ll. Henr. I, § 92. 6.

[4] Edgar, iv. § 2. 1.

is equally true of the Mercians and Northumbrians; the variations of custom are verbal rather than real; and where, as in the case of the wergilds, they are real, they are territorial rather than personal. The deeper differences of Briton and Saxon laws on the Western border, or of early Danish and English custom in East Anglia were settled by special treaty, such as those of Alfred and Edward with Guthrum, and the ordinance of the Dunsætas. The subject of personal law then illustrates the Anglo-Saxon development only incidentally; there was no such difference amongst the customs of the English races as existed between Frank, Visigoth and Roman, or even between Frank, Alemannian and Lombard.

Personal law not important in England.

77. Of the influence of the Danes and Norsemen on the constitutional life of England, whether in their character as conquerors generally, or in special relation to the districts which they ravaged, divided and colonised, little that is affirmative can be certainly stated. For nothing is known of their native institutions at the time of their first inroads; and the differences between the customs of the Danelaga and those of the rest of England which follow the Norse occupation, are small in themselves and might almost with equal certainty be ascribed to the distinction between Angle and Saxon. The extent of the Danish occupation southward is marked by the treaty of Alfred and Guthrum, 'upon the Thames, along the Lea to its source, then right to Bedford and then upon the Ouse to Watling Street[1].' To the north they were advanced as far as the Tyne; and their Western boundary was the mountain district of Yorkshire, Westmoreland and Cumberland[2]. Over all this region the traces of their colonisation abound in the villages whose names end in 'by,' the Scandinavian equivalent of the English 'tun,' or 'ham': the division into wapentakes may be Scandinavian more probably than Anglian, and the larger arrangement of the trithings or ridings of Yorkshire and Lincolnshire may be of the same origin. But it is not probable that they introduced any

Effect of Danish invasion.

Limits of Danish occupation.

[1] Alf. and Guthr. § 1.

[2] See Mr. Robertson's Essay on the Dane-law in Scotland, under her Early Kings, ii. 430-444. Freeman, Norm. Conq. i. 644-647.

The infusion of Danish usages was not great, owing to their own condition;

substantial changes into the customs of the common law, for several reasons. In the first place their organisation for the purpose of colonisation was apparently only temporary. It was nearly two centuries before they effected a permanent settlement, during which period they ravaged the coasts in the summer, and in the winter either returned home or remained in camp. Their expeditions were headed by independent chieftains allied, as the old Saxons had been, for the purpose of war, and after the war was over returning to equality and isolation. They were accordingly far more likely to amalgamate with the Anglian population which submitted to them[1] than to create a great and new nation upon lines of their own. The evidence of a popular migration, as distinguished from mere settlement, is wanting, and although the local extermination of the natives must have occasionally made the institution of a new organisation necessary[2], it would appear that such instances were not numerous enough to alter the general complexion of society.

and possibly to their affinity with the Angles.

In the second place, the Angles whom they conquered were, of all the English tribes, the most closely connected with them in their primitive homes: the civilisation which the Danes now possessed was probably about equal to that which the Angles had had three centuries before; they were still heathens, and of their legal system we know no more than that they used the universal customs of compurgation, wergild, and other pecuniary compositions for the breach of the peace[3]. Their heathenism they renounced with scarcely a struggle, and the rest of their jurisprudence needed only to be translated into English. Just as in France the Normans adopted the religion and institutions of the conquered, so in England the Danes sank almost immediately into the mass of the Angles.

It cannot be doubted that the influx of a body of new settlers whose ideas of freedom had not been trained or shackled with

[1] Freeman, Norm. Conq. i. 148.

[2] Such perhaps was the original confederation of the Five Boroughs; above, p. 93.

[3] See the laws of Alfred and Guthrum, and Edward and Guthrum. The lahslit of the Danes is the wite of the Anglo-Saxons; and in many cases, as we have already seen, new names, rather than new customs, date from the Danish occupation: the earl, the hold, the grith, the trithing, the wapentake perhaps, supersede the old names, but with no perceptible difference of meaning.

three centuries of civilisation, must have introduced a strong impulse in favour of the older institutions which were already on the wane. The alodial tenure of the North must have been reinstated in Yorkshire and East Anglia in its full strength[1], even if the subject Angle sank one degree in the scale of liberty. The institutions of the Danish settlements of the Five Boroughs[2] stand out as late as the Conquest, in the possession of a local constitution which, as well as their confederation, seems to date from their foundation in the ninth century. But speculation on such points is scarcely necessary. The amalgamation of the Dane and Angle population began from the moment of the conversion. The peace of Alfred and Guthrum established the social equality of the races: the prowess and policy of Edward and of Ethelfleda reunited the Southern Danes under the West Saxon dynasty, and the royal houses of Northumbria and Wessex intermarried. The attraction of the la rgerand more coherent mass, itself consolidated by the necessity of defence, and the quarrels of the Danish chieftains amongst themselves, led the way to their incorporation. The spasmodic efforts of the Northumbrian Danes were checked by Edmund and Edred; and Edgar, who saw that the time was come to join Dane and Mercian on equality in all respects with the West

Bracing influence of the Danish infusion.

Speedy union of Danes and English.

[1] Robertson, Scotland, &c. ii. 269. 'It will be found that at the date of the Norman Conquest, contrary to the usually received idea, a greater amount of freedom was enjoyed in the Danelage than in England proper, or in other words Wessex and English Mercia. Throughout the latter district, except in the case of the Gavellers of East Kent, military tenure seems to have prevailed with hardly any exception . . . In the Danelage, on the contrary, omitting Yorkshire from the calculation, between a third and a fourth of the entire population were classified either as liberi homines, or as socmen . . . Free socage, the very tenure of which is sometimes supposed to have been peculiarly a relic of Anglo-Saxon liberty, appears to have been absolutely unknown except among the Anglo-Danes.' Whether these conclusions are to be accepted may be questionable, but the argument illustrates remarkably the expression in the text.

[2] It would be hazardous to argue from what is called the 'North People's Law,' Schmid, Gesetze, p. 396; but a reading of it suggests that the Danes estimated their own wer-gilds at twice the value of the Angles, just as in early days the Saxons had valued themselves at twice as much as the wealh. The eorl is worth 15000 thrymsas; the ealdorman 8000; the hold is worth 4000, and the thegn 2000; the king's high-reeve is worth 4000, and there is no counterpart to him, probably because he would always be valued as a Dane. Mr. Robertson dates this earlier than Canute, Scotland, &c. ii. 281.

Ecclesiastics of Danish extraction.

Saxon, consolidated the Northumbrian kingdom with his own. The Danish Odo, Oskytel, and Oswald were archbishops in less than a century after Halfdane had divided Northumbria; and in the struggles of Ethelred, Sweyn and Canute, the national differences can scarcely be traced. The facility with which the Danes of the eleventh century conquered the provinces which their kinsmen had occupied in the ninth can scarcely be referred to this cause with more probability than to the fact that Mercia and East Anglia during the Anglian period had never united with Wessex. The ill-consolidated realm of Edred broke up between Edwy and Edgar, just as that of Ethelred between Edmund and Canute, and that of Canute between Harold and Hardicanute.

The want of cohesion not a result of Danish infusion only.

General conclusion as to the first Danish struggle.

It may be concluded then, that whilst very considerable political modifications and even territorial changes followed the Danish conquest of the ninth century, whilst a rougher, stronger, and perhaps freer element was introduced into the society and even into the blood of the Angles, the institutional history is not largely affected by it. During the conquest the Danes were the *host*, or *here*; when it was over they subsided into the conditions of settled society as they found it; their magistrates, their coins, their local customs, like their dwelling places, retained for a while their old names; but under those names they were substantially identical with the magistrates, coins and customs of the Angles, and in the course of time sank all differences in a common nomenclature.

The second Danish struggle.

Nor again can much of the constitutional change which followed the second Danish domination, that founded by Sweyn and Canute, be attributed to the infusion of new customs from the North[1]. Its chief effects were political, and its constitutional

[1] If the authenticity of the Constitutiones Forestae, ascribed to Canute, were proved, they might be useful as marking the introduction of forest law into England; but they are either spurious, or so much interpolated as to be without value. They are accepted indeed by Kemble and Lappenberg, and with some hesitation by Schmid also (Gesetze, p. lvi), but K. Maurer rejects them as a fabrication of much later date (Krit. Ueberschau, ii. 410). Freeman, Norm. Conq. i. 732, thinks that the code carries its own confutation with it, and Brunner (in Holtzendorff's Encyclopädie, p. 232) detects in it the ring of Norman legal terminology. Besides these laws the institution of the huskarls is the only peculiarity of the Danish régime: on

consequences may be referred to political far more than to ethnical causes. The laws of Canute are but a reproduction of those of Edgar and Ethelred; not a single custom can be assigned to his rule with any certainty that it cannot be found earlier; the language of England is no more affected by that of Denmark in the eleventh century than in the ninth. The changes which are traceable, and which have been adverted to in the general sketch just given of the growth of the royal power, are to be ascribed to the fact that Canute was really a conqueror and the ruler of other far wider if less civilised territories than England. His changes in the forms of charters and writs, if they were really anything more than clerical variations, simply show that he did with a strong hand what Ethelred had done with a weak one. Even the great mark of his policy, the division of England into four great earldoms or duchies, may be paralleled with the state of things under Edgar and his sons.

No new usages introduced by Canute into the laws.

It is however possible to refer the last measure to an idea of reproducing something like the imperial system which Canute saw in Germany. He ruled, nominally at least, a larger European dominion than any English sovereign has ever done; and perhaps also a more homogeneous one. No potentate of the time came near him except the king of Germany, the emperor, with whom he was allied as an equal. The king of the Norwegians, the Danes, and a great part of the Swedes[1], was in a position to found a Scandinavian empire with Britain annexed. Canute's division of his dominions on his death-bed, showed that he saw

Imperial character of Canute.

them see Freeman, Norm. Conq. i. 733. Although they recall very distinctly the features of the primitive comitatus (above, p. 150, n. 2), they do not concern Constitutional History further, and add in no important degree to the elements already existing in English society. The heriot is often regarded as an institution of Canute; but there are many examples of the custom in the charters much earlier, which show that he simply declared the law of an ancient, probably primitive, usage. Kemble, Saxons, ii. 99. The heriots of Theodred, Bishop of Elmham (Cod. Dipl. dccccl vii), Ethelwald the ealdorman (mclxxiii), Elfgar (mccxxiii), Beorhtric (ccccxcii), and many others are known; and they seem to imply an assessment similar to Canute's own. And in this view of the case, where the payment had become a settled amount due from persons of a particular rank, it 'became possible for women to be charged with it.' In other words the heriot was become a burden on the land rather than on the person.

[1] See his letter to the bishops, in Florence of Worcester, A.D. 1031.

Canute's empire not permanent or consolidated.

this to be impossible; Norway, for a century and a half after his strong hand was removed, was broken up amongst an anarchical crew of piratic and bloodthirsty princes, nor could Denmark be regarded as likely to continue united with England. The English nation was too much divided and demoralised to retain hold on Scandinavia, even if the condition of the latter had allowed it. Hence Canute determined that during his life, as after his death, the nations should be governed on their own principles, and as the Saxons, the Bavarians, the Swabians and the Franconians obeyed Conrad the Salic, so the Danes, the Norwegians, the Swedes and the English should obey him. But still further, the four nations of the English, Northumbrians, East Angles, Mercians and West Saxons, might, each under their own national leader, obey a sovereign who was strong enough to enforce peace amongst them. The great earldoms of Canute's reign were perhaps a nearer approach to a feudal division of England than anything which followed the Norman Conquest. That of Mercia was a vast territory in which the earl, an old Mercian noble, united the great territories of the national æthel with the official authority and domain of the ealdorman, and exercised the whole administration of justice, limited only by the king's reeves and the bishops. And the extent to which this creation of the four earldoms affected the history of the next half century cannot be exaggerated. The certain tendency of such an arrangement to become hereditary, and the certain tendency of the hereditary occupation of great fiefs ultimately to overwhelm the royal power, are well exemplified. The process by which, as we have seen, the king concentrates in himself the representation of the nation, as judge, patron, and landlord, reaches its climax only to break up, save where the king's hand is strong enough to hold fast what he has inherited, and the people coherent enough to sustain him. The history of the reign of Edward the Confessor is little more than the variation of the balance of power between the families of Godwin and Leofric; the power of the witenagemot is wielded by the great earls in turn; each has his allies among the Welsh, Irish and Scottish princes, each his friends and refuge on the continent: at their alternate dictation the king receives

Feudal tendency of Canute's government by earls.

Reign of Edward the Confessor.

and dismisses his wife, names and sets aside his bishops. The disruption of the realm is imminent. The work of Godwin is crowned by the exaltation of Harold, who saw the evils of the existing state and attempted at the sacrifice of his own family interests to unite the house of Leofric in the support of a national sovereignty. But the policy of Leofric, followed out by the lukewarm patriotism of Edwin and Morcar, opened the way to the Norman Conquest by disabling the right arm of Harold. The Norman Conquest restored national unity at a tremendous temporary sacrifice, just as the Danish Conquest in other ways, and by a reverse process, had helped to create it.

Policy of Godwin and Leofric.

In all this however there is nothing that would lead to the conclusion of any formal infusion of Scandinavian polity [1]. The measure, so far as it is new, is rather Frank or German, and in advance rather than in the rear of the indigenous development.

78. A glance at the Karolingian legislation of the ninth century suggests the important question whether the legal measures adopted by Alfred and his descendants were to any great extent influenced by continental precedents. The intercourse between the two courts had been close and constant, the social condition of the two nations was far more uniform than a superficial view of their history would lead us to believe, and in the laws of their respective legislative periods there are coincidences which can scarcely be regarded as accidental. During the reign of the Great Charles the Frank court was the home of English exiles, as well as of English scholars [2]. Egbert spent as a banished man in France three years, one of which was marked by Charles's

Question of the infusion of Frank elements in the later Anglo-Saxon system.

[1] Hallam, M. A. ii. 272, comes to the same conclusion. The views of Northern antiquaries, who refer every point of similarity between Scandinavia and England to Norse and Danish influences in Britain, seem to be maintained in ignorance of the body of English history which existed earlier than the Norse invasions, the civilising and Christianising influence of England on Scandinavia, and the common stock of institutions that both nationalities possessed. The temperate and critical treatment of Konrad Maurer is strongly in contrast with this. But even the introduction of the huskarls and the forest law are to a certain extent outside our present subject: the former was no permanent institution, and the latter rests on too weak evidence to be accepted. I have therefore preferred to mention what is important about them under other heads.

[2] See the letters of Offa, Alcuin and Charles, in the Councils and Ecclesiastical Documents; iii. 487, 498, 561–565.

Intercourse of the West Saxon kings with the Karolings;

assumption of the imperial dignity[1]. It is quite possible that there he conceived the desire of establishing a supremacy over the English kingdoms as well as the idea of binding to himself and his dynasty the mother church of the land in alliance for mutual patronage[2]. The character and some part of the history of Ethelwulf are in strict parallel with those of Lewis the Pious, whose correspondent he was in his early years and whose granddaughter he married on his return from his Roman pilgrimage. Alfred drew from the empire some at least of the scholars whose assistance in the restoration of learning repaid to a great extent the debt due to England for the services of Alcuin. Charles the Simple and Otto the Great were married to two of the sisters of Athelstan; and whilst Otto was consolidating the Saxon empire on the continent, his nephew was gathering subject kings at his court and taking to himself the titles of emperor and Augustus.

contemporary policy of the Saxon emperors.

As Otto collected the great duchies of Germany into the hands of his sons and sons-in-law, Edgar placed the great ealdormanships of England in the hands of his own kinsmen. In ecclesiastical legislation at the same time England was largely copying from the manuals of Frank statesmanship. The Anglo-Saxon Canons and Penitentials of the tenth century are in great part

Intercourse of churches.

translations and expansions of the Frank books of discipline which had a hundred years earlier been based on the works of Theodore and Egbert. It would be very rash to affirm that while the bishops, who composed so large a part of the witenagemot, sought foreign models for their canons, they did not seek foreign models for the secular laws. Dunstan had learned monastic discipline where he might also have furnished himself with the knowledge needed for the great office of first adviser to

Periods of Frank and English legislation do not coincide.

the king. But the brilliant period of imperial legislation was over before the time of Alfred; in the disorganisation of the latter period of the Karolings much of the framework of their system had ceased to exist except in the law books; and the parallels between Frank and English law must not be pressed

[1] Chron. Sax. A.D. 836. Brihtric died in A.D. 802: Egbert's stay in France must have covered the date of Charles's coronation.

[2] See Chapter VIII. p. 236.

without allowing for the similarity of the circumstances which prompted them and for the fundamental stock of common principles and customs which underlay them. The law which provided that the landless man must have a lord appears in the Capitularies of Charles the Bald half a century before it appears in the dooms of Athelstan[1]. The judicial investigations made by Alfred through his 'fideles' may remind us of the jurisdiction of the Frank missi[2]: in England, as in the empire, the head of the shire receives a third part of the profits of the law courts[3]: and the great thegn is allowed to swear by the agency of a representative[4]. Yet all these may be merely the results of similar circumstances. In other points, where the coincidences are more striking, difference of circumstances may be fatal to an affirmative theory. It cannot be safely said that Edgar's regulations for the hundred was borrowed from the law of Childebert and Clothair, or that Ethelred's rating of the eight hides to furnish a helm and coat of mail was an imitation of the Frank practice[5], or that the payment of Danegeld in A.D. 991 was consciously adopted on the precedent created by Charles the Bald in A.D. 861, 866 and 877 in Gaul and Lotharingia[6]. Jurists will probably always differ as to the relation between the scabini of Lewis the Pious and the

Coincidences of law and usage.

Uncertainty of connexion.

[1] Above, p. 80.

[2] Asser, M. H. B. 497. 'Nam omnia pene totius suae regionis judicia, quae in absentia sua fiebant sagaciter investigabat qualiter fierent, justa aut etiam injusta; aut vero si aliquam in illis judiciis iniquitatem intelligere posset, leniter advocatos illos ipsos judices aut per se ipsum aut per alios suos fideles quoslibet interrogabat.'

[3] Above, p. 113.

[4] Ranks, § 5. Select Charters, p. 64. Waitz, D.V.G. iv. 228. 'Honorem enim talem nostris vassallis dominicis concedimus, ut ipsi non sicut reliqui manu propria sacramentum jurent, sed melior homo illorum et credibilior illud agere non differat.' Cap. Vern. A.D. 884, c. 11. 'Exceptis nostris vassis dominicis pro quibus illorum homines meliores juramentum persolvent.' Ibid. c. 4. Baluze, ii. 195, 197. But this existed a century before in the Lex Saxonum, where the noble is allowed to swear 'in manu liti sui vel sua armata;' c. 8.

[5] Robertson, Essays, p. x.

[6] See the Capitularies of A.D. 861 (Baluze, ii. 103) and 877. 'Haec constituta est exactio Nortmannis qui erant in Sequana tribuenda ut a regione ejus recederent.' The tax in A.D. 877 is twelve denarii from the mansus indominicatus; from the mansus ingenuilis four from the rent, four from the tenant; from the mansus servilis two from the rent and two from the tenant. Baluze, ii. 175, 176. Waitz, D. V. G. iv. 102. Robertson, Essays, pp. 116, 117. Ann. S. Bertin, A.D. 866.

Parallels not proofs.

assistant thegns of the shiremoot [1]; whether the twelve senior thegns who swear to accuse none falsely are a jury of inquest like the inquisitors of Lewis, or a compurgatory body to determine on the application of the ordeal. The oath imposed by Canute on every one above the age of twelve, that he will not be a thief nor cognisant of theft [2], runs back through the common form to Edmund's oath of allegiance,[3] and finds parallels in the earliest legislation of Charles the Great [4]. In more than one passage the collection of early English usages, known as the Leges Henrici Primi, recalls the exact language of the Capitularies and of still earlier laws [5]. But although we may be inclined to reject the theory that refers all such importations of Frank law to the Norman lawyers, and to claim for the institutions, which like trial by jury came to full growth on English soil, a native or at least a common Germanic origin, it is wiser and safer to allow the coincidences to speak for themselves; and to avoid a positive theory that the first independent investigator may find means of demolishing. It is enough that, although in different lines and in widely contrasted political circumstances, royalty was both in England and on the continent working itself into forms in which the old Germanic

[1] See above, p. 103.

[2] 'Volumus ut omnis homo post duodecimum aetatis suae annum juret quod fur esse nolit nec furi consentaneus.' Canute, ii. § 21. Compare with this the later regulations of Henry II and Richard I. Select Charters, pp. 137, 256.

[3] Select Charters, p. 66. 'Ut nemo concelet hoc in fratre vel proximo suo plus quam in extraneo.'

[4] Waitz, D. V. G. iv. 363. 'Judex unusquisque per civitatem faciat jurare ad Dei judicia homines credentes juxta quantos praeviderit, seu foris per curtes vel vicoras mansuros, ut cui ex ipsis cognitum fuerit, id est homicidia, furta, adulteria et de inlicitas conjunctiones, ut nemo eas concelet.' Capit. Langobard. A.D. 782, c. 8. Cf. Capit. Silvac. A.D. 853; Baluze, ii. 44, 45.

[5] See Schmid, Gesetze, pp. 437, 438, 471, 472, 484, 485; Thorpe, Ancient Laws, pp. 507, 509, 510, &c. The regulations of Athelstan (ii. § 14), Edgar (iii. § 8) and Ethelred (iv. § 6) respecting coin, may be compared with those of Lewis the Pious (Baluze, i. 432, 500), and Charles the Bald (ibid. ii. 120, 121). Cf. both with the Roman Law (Just. Cod. ii. § 24), from which they were doubtless derived. The law against holding gemots on Sundays and festivals (Ethelred, v. 13; Canute, i. 15) also resembles that of Charles the Great (Baluze, i. 183) and Charles the Bald (ibid. ii. 140, 141).

idea of the king is scarcely recognisable, whilst the influence of long-established organisations, of settled homes, and hereditary jurisdictions, was producing a territorial system of government unknown to the race in its early stages. A strong current of similar events will produce coincidences in the history of nations whose whole institutions are distinct; much more will like circumstances force similarly constituted nations into like expedients; nay, great legislators will think together even if the events that suggest the thought be of the most dissimilar character. No amount of analogy between two systems can by itself prove the actual derivation of the one from the other.

Similar tendencies in Frank and English history.

79. Although the progress of the Anglo-Saxon system, from the condition in which its whole organisation depends on personal relations to that in which everything depends on territorial ones, is marked at each step by some change in the royal power, it is better described in this formula than as a progress from democracy to monarchy, or from a democratic to an aristocratic monarchy, or from alodialism to feudalism. The growth of the royal power was theoretical rather than practical; what it gained on one side, it lost on another. The king became the source of justice, the lord and patron of his people, the owner of the public lands; but he had almost immediately to part with the substantial exercise of the powers so appropriated. By the grants of land, constantly increasing in number, the royal demesne was continually diminished, and the diminution of royal demesne made the taxation of the people the only available means of meeting public emergencies. The immunities which by grant or by prescription were vested in the holders of bookland, actually withdrew the profits and powers of jurisdiction from the source from which they themselves emanated. The patronage or lordship which was to unite the king more closely than ever before with the people, was intercepted by a number of mesne lordships and superiorities, which kept them in reality further asunder.

Formula of development.

Diminution of the king's real powers.

Edgar had perfected so far as we can see the theory of royalty. He had collected, we are told, a fleet of not less than 3600 ships, which every summer he reviewed and exercised in circumnavigating Britain, thus providing for present defence and for the

Royalty reached its highest point in Edgar.

Edgar's administration.

maintenance of permanent discipline. The winter and spring he devoted to judicial circuits, in which he traversed all the provinces of the English, and accurately inquired into the observance by the magistrates of the laws of the nation and his own decrees, that the poor might not suffer injury or oppression at the hands of the mighty[1]. Possibly the tradition is brighter than the reality, for the evil times that followed may well have suggested an exaggeration of past blessings. But the spirit of

His legislation.

Edgar's legislation is good. The preamble of his secular laws declares that every man shall be worthy of folkright, poor as well as rich; and the penalties for unrighteous judgment with the promise of redress by the king in the last resort immediately follow[2]. With his death the evil days began at once. The strong men whom he had curbed to his service, took advantage of the youth and weakness of his sons; and internal divisions rendered the kingdom of Ethelred an easy prey to the Danes. The real benefit of the changes of the preceding century fell into the hands of the great ealdormen, and through

Increase of the power of the great lords.

them to the thegns. The local jurisdictions grew: the feeling of national union which had been springing up, was thrown back: the tribal divisions had become territorial, but they were divisions still. The great lords rounded off their estates and consolidated their jurisdictions: each had his own national and ecclesiastical policy. The Mercian Elfhere banished the monks and replaced them with married clerks; the East Anglian Ethelwin, God's friend, and the East-Saxon Brihtnoth, drove out the clerks and replaced the monks[3]. Where ecclesiastical order was settled by the local rulers, notwithstanding the strong hand of Dunstan, it was scarcely to be expected that temporal liberties could be sustained by Ethelred. Another Danish inroad

[1] Florence of Worcester, A.D. 975. Edgar's judicial circuits were copied by Canute; Hist. Ramsey (ap. Gale), p. 441: and they may have been copied from the practice of Alfred; Asser, M. H. B. 497.

[2] Edgar, iii. § 1; 'Volo ut omnis homo sit dignus juris publici, pauper et dives, quicunque sit, et eis justa judicia judicentur; et sit in emendationibus remissio venialis apud Deum et apud saeculum tolerabilis.' The latter clause is re-echoed in the charters of Henry I and John; and may be traced further back in the legislation of Alfred. Ll. Introd. § 49. 7.

[3] Flor. Wig. A.D. 975.

seemed needed to restore the state of things that Edgar had created.

80. One good result attended this apparent retrogression. There had been centralisation without concentration: all rights and duties were ranging themselves round the person of the king, and there was a danger that the old local organisations might become obsolete. Edgar had found it necessary to renew the law of the hundreds and to forbid recourse to the king's audience until the local means of obtaining justice had been exhausted [1]. His fleets and armies may not improbably have been organised on a plan of centralisation. Such a tendency was almost a necessity where the royal authority was becoming recognised as imperial, or as limited only by a witenagemot of royal nominees in which no representation or concentration of local machinery had a place. The fact then that the great lords, by the extension of their own rights and the practical assertion of independence, took to themselves the advantages of the change and maintained their jurisdictions apart, gave a longer tenure of life to the provincial divisions. The national unity was weakened by the sense of provincial unity, and individual liberty was strengthened against the time when the national unity should be, not the centralisation of powers, but the concentration of all organisation; a period long distant and to be reached through strange vicissitudes. In the maintenance of provincial courts and armies was inherent the maintenance of ancient liberty.

Premature centralisation under Edgar.

The events that followed his death had the result of maintaining local divisions and popular institutions.

For notwithstanding the series of developments which have been traced so far, the forms of primitive organisation still generally survived. The warriors of the shire, whether free men of full political right, or the church vassals, or the contingents of the great thegns, fought as men of the shire under the ealdorman or his officer. The local force of Devonshire and Somersetshire was beaten by the Danes at Penho; the East Anglians and the men of Cambridgeshire fought apart at Ringmere; the men of Dorset, Wilts and Devon at Sherstone [2]. Even the

Maintenance of provincial administration in military matters.

[1] Edgar, iii. § 2: 'Nemo requirat regem pro aliqua causa nisi domi negetur ei omne dignum recti vel rectum impetrare non possit.'
[2] Flor. Wig. A.D. 1001, 1010, 1016.

Political independence of the earls.

political attitude of the province was determined by the ealdorman and the thegns. The Northumbrian earl Uhtred and the West Saxon earl Ethelmar make their separate agreements with Sweyn, and in so doing declare their independence of Ethelred[1].

Permanence of old customs.

But still more certainly in the local courts the old spirit of freedom found room. The forms were the same whether the king's gerefa or the lord's steward called them together: the hundred retained its peace, the township its customs: the very disruption of society preserved these things for the better days.

Old customs contain the seed of new liberties.

In the preservation of the old forms,—the compurgation by the kindred of the accused, the responsibility for the wergild, the representation of the township in the court of the hundred, and that of the hundred in the court of the shire; the choice of witnesses; the delegation to chosen committees of the common judicial rights of the suitors of the folkmoot; the need of witness for the transfer of chattels, and the evidence of the hundred or shire to the title to lands; the report of the hundred and shire as to criminals and the duty of enforcing their production and punishment, and the countless diversity of customs in which the several communities went to work to fulfil the general injunctions of the law,—in these remained the seeds of future liberties; themselves perhaps the mere shakings of the olive tree, the scattered grains that royal and noble gleaners had scorned to gather, but destined for a new life after many days of burial. They were the humble discipline by which a downtrodden people were schooled to act together in small things, until the time came when they could act together for great ones.

Growth of national character.

81. The growth of national character under these changes is a matter of further interest. Although the national experience was not enough to produce a strong and thorough feeling of union, it had been equable and general. No part of England was far behind any other in civilisation. The several kingdoms had been Christianised in rapid succession, and the amalgamation of the Danes had been so speedy as little to affect the

[1] Flor. Wig. A.D. 1013.

comparative civilisation of the districts they occupied after it had once fairly begun. Northumbria had indeed never recovered the learning and cultivation of her early days, but Kent and Wessex had retrograded nearly as much during the dark century that preceded Alfred. The depression of national life under Ethelred was much the same everywhere. The free man learned that he had little beyond his own arm and the circle of his friends to trust to. The cohesion of the nation was greatest in the lowest ranges. Family, township, hundred, county held together when ealdorman was struggling with ealdorman and the king was left in isolated dignity. Kent, Devonshire, Northumbria, had a corporate life which England had not, or which she could not bring to action in the greatest emergencies. The witenagemot represented the wisdom, but concentrated neither the power nor the will, of the nation.

Uniform condition of England.

Greatest cohesion in the lowest ranges of organisation.

The individual Englishman must have been formed under circumstances that called forth much self-reliance and little hearty patriotism. His sympathies must have run into very narrow and provincial channels. His own home and parish were much more to him than the house of Cerdic or the safety of the nation. As a Christian, too, he had more real, more appreciable social duties than as an Englishman. He could accept Sweyn or Canute, if he would be his good lord and not change the laws or customs that regulated his daily life. There was a strong sense of social freedom without much care about political power. It was inherent in the blood. Caesar had seen it in the ancient German, and the empire of Charles and Otto strove in vain to remodel it in the medieval aggregation of the German-speaking nationalities; Bavarian, Saxon, Franconian, Swabian, were even less inclined to recognise their unity than were the nations which now called themselves English.

Effect of national history on character.

The form however which this tendency took in the Anglo-Saxon of the eleventh century, is distinct from the corresponding phases of French and German character. The Frenchman can indeed scarcely be said as yet to have developed any national character; or rather the heavy hand of Frank supremacy had not so far relaxed its pressure as to allow the elastic nature of the Gallic element

Contrast with French.

to assert itself; and the historical Frank of the age is still for the most part German. The territory itself scarcely ventures to take a collective name, and resembles the Gallia of Caesar more than that of Honorius. But the new life that is growing up is city life, and the liberties at which it grasps are collective rather than individual privileges. The rural populations of France are, as they were in the latter days of Roman rule, and as they continued to be more or less until the revolution, a people from whom social freedom had so long departed that it was scarcely regretted, scarcely coveted; to whom Christianity had brought little more than the idea of liberty in another life to be waited for and laboured for in the patient endurance of the present. The true life was in the towns, where, in the interests of commerce, or under the favour of some native lord temporal or spiritual, or under the patronage of a king who would fain purchase help on all sides against the overwhelming pressure of his too powerful friends, in the guild and the commune, men were making their puny efforts after free action. But this life had scarcely reached the surface: the acts of kings and councils fill the pages of history. Law was either slowly evolving itself in the shape of feudal custom, or resting on the changeless rock of Roman jurisprudence: the one unconscious of its development and calling forth no active participation in the people, the other subject to no development at all. Even the language has scarcely declared itself, except in the fragments of courtly minstrelsy.

The growing life in France is civic rather than rural.

But it is as yet scarcely conscious.

The contrast between the Englishman and the native German is not so strong. The disruptive tendency in the English state is little connected with primitive national divisions. There is little evidence to show that the people in general felt their nationality as West Saxons or Mercians, however much they might realise their connexion as Yorkshiremen or men of Kent. The Saxon and Bavarian of the continent had each their national policy: their national consciousness was so strong that, like that of the Irish, it constantly impressed itself even upon alien rulers. The Saxon emperor made his nearest kinsman duke of Bavaria only to discover that he had made his son or brother a Bavarian instead of

Contrast with the German.

Absence of a feeling of nationality among the English.

making the Bavarians loyal. The Swabian emperor sent a Swabian duke to Saxony in the idea that the Saxons would cling rather to the emperor than to an alien governor; but the Swabian duke became forthwith a Saxon, and the loyalty that was called forth was devoted entirely to the adopted ruler. And these nations had their political and ecclesiastical aims; the Saxons preferred the pope to any emperor but a Saxon one. The Bavarians were ready to give up the empire altogether if they might have a king of their own. In both there was a singular development of personal loyalty with a distinctly national aim in the politics of the empire. But in the Anglo-Saxon history there is an equally singular lack of personal loyalty, and a very languid appreciation of national action. Such loyalty as really appears is loyalty to the king, not to the provincial rulers whom they saw more closely and knew better. The poetic lamentations of the chronicler over the dead kings, may perhaps express the feeling of the churchmen and the courtiers, but have nothing to answer to them in the case of the provincial rulers. The great earls had not, it would seem, an hereditary hold upon their people; and although they had political aims of their own, these were not such as the people could sympathise with. The popularity of Harold the son of Godwin is only an apparent exception: it was won indeed by his personal gifts and his ubiquitous activity, but carried with it no feeling of loyalty. Much even of that higher sentiment which was bestowed on his kingly career was retrospective; they valued him most when he was lost. Throughout, the connexion between patriotism and loyalty, such patriotism and loyalty as exist, seems to want that basis of personal affection which is so natural and necessary to it. It is not on national glories, but on national miseries that the Chronicler expatiates; and the misery brings out, perhaps more than necessary, the querulous and helpless tone of national feeling; a tone which no doubt is called forth by the oppressions of the Norman regime, but which might, under the same circumstances, in the mouths of other men, have been exchanged for one of very different character: the song of the people emulous of ancient glories, girding itself up

Strength of political provincial feeling among the Germans.

And of personal loyalty.

Languid consciousness of loyalty and patriotism among the English.

for a strong and united effort after liberty. There is no breath of this in the English remains of the eleventh century, and the history of the ill-contrived and worse executed attempts to shake off the yoke of the Conqueror, proves that there was little life of the kind. Yet there was life; although it lay deep now, it would be strong enough when it reached the surface: nor had the Conqueror any wish to break the bruised reed.

Little interest felt in England as to the ecclesiastical quarrels of the continent.

The lack of political aims which might give a stimulus to provincial patriotism, was not compensated by ecclesiastical partisanship, although the struggle between the seculars and regulars does fill a page in English history to the loss it may be feared of more important matter. But the great disputes between the imperial and papal pretensions that moved the continent, found no echo here, and called forth no sympathy. The English, like the continental Saxons, were proud of their faithfulness to Rome; but it was a far distant Rome that interfered very little with them, and that in the minds of their kings and prelates had the aspect of a spiritual city, very different from anything that was really to be found there. The clergy had but a faint notion of the difference between pope and antipope: even in doctrine they had scarcely advanced with the age, and there were points on which they were falling as far behind Roman orthodoxy as the British bishops had been in the Paschal controversy. When an English archbishop visited Rome he spent his time in pilgrimages to holy places: the pope received him with a splendid hospitality, that showed him only what it was desirable that he should see; and he came back rich in relics, but as poor as ever in political experience. The secular world was still farther away from him: Canute, who had certain cosmopolitan and imperial instincts, knew better than to involve England in foreign complications. For a century and a half scarcely one Englishman has left his name on record in the work of any foreign historian.

The reasons of this isolation are apparent. The Englishman had enough to do at home in constant resistance to a persevering foe. But the isolation is not, as might be expected, combined with intenser patriotism. The fire of sympathy burns in a very narrow circle : there is little to call forth or diversify the latent energies.

Development of national life in other forms.

But this is only one aspect of the Englishman. He may be phlegmatic, narrow, languid in political development, but he is neither uncivilised nor uncultivated. The isolation which has been fatal to political growth, has encouraged and concentrated other energies. Since the time of Alfred a national literature has been growing up, of which the very fragments that have survived the revolution of conquest and many centuries of literary neglect, are greater than the native contemporaneous literature of any other people in Europe. No other nation possesses a body of history such as the Anglo-Saxon Bede and the Chronicles. The theological literature, although slight in comparison with that of the Latin-speaking nations, testifies, by the fact that it is in the tongue of the people, to a far more thorough religious sympathy between the teachers and the taught than can be with any degree of probability attributed to the continental churches. In medicine, natural science, grammar, geography, the English of the eleventh century had manuals in their own tongue. They had arts too of their own ; goldsmith's work, embroidery, illumination of manuscripts, flourished as well as the craft of the weaver and the armourer. The domestic civilisation of England, with all its drawbacks, was far beyond that of France. The Norman knights despised, undervalued and destroyed much that they could not comprehend. England was behind Europe in some of the arts which they had in common, but she had much that was her own, and developed what she had in common by her own genius. She might be behind in architecture, although that remains to be proved, for much that we know as the work of Northern architects was imitated from Roman models ; an imitation which, although it later developed into systems far freer and nobler than anything that had existed before, was still only advancing from its rudest stage in France and Germany. England was slow in following the architecture as she was in following the politics of the continent. It is seldom remembered in comparing Norman and Anglo-Saxon in point of civilisation, how very little the Norman

National literature.

National art, and domestic life.

Contrast of Norman and Englishman.

brought in comparison with what he destroyed, and how very little he brought that was his own. His law was Frank or Lombard, his general cultivation that of Lanfranc and Anselm, far more Italian than native: in civilisation—taken in the truer sense of the word,—in the organisation of the social life, in the means of obtaining speedy and equal justice, in the whole domain of national jurisprudence, he was far behind those whom he despised with the insolence of a barbarian; he had forgotten his own language, he had no literature, his art was foreign and purchased. But he was a splendid soldier, he had seen the great world east and west, he knew the balance of power between popes and emperors; and he was a conqueror: he held the rod of discipline which was to school England to the knowledge of her own strength and power of freedom: he was to drag her into the general network of the spiritual and temporal politics of the world, rousing her thereby to a consciousness of unsuspected, undeveloped powers: he was to give a new direction to her energies, to widen and unite and consolidate her sympathies: to train her to loyalty and patriotism; and in the process to impart so much, and to cast away so much, that when the time of awakening came, the conqueror and the conquered, the race of the oppressor and the race of the oppressed were to find themselves one people[1].

[1] 'After the closing scenes of the great drama commenced at Hastings, it ceased to exist as a national character; and the beaten, ruined and demoralised Anglo-Saxon found himself launched in a new career of honour, and rising into all the might and majesty of an Englishman. Let us reflect that the defeats upon the Thames and Avon were probably necessary preliminaries to victories upon the Sutlej.' Kemble, Cod. Dipl. iv. pref. vi. Carlyle, Fred. II., i. 415, taking a different view of the Anglo-Saxon temperament, says, 'without them (i. e. the Normans and Plantagenets) what had it ever been? a gluttonous race of Jutes and Angles, capable of no grand combinations; lumbering about in pot-bellied equanimity; not dreaming of heroic toil, and silence, and endurance, such as leads to the high places of this universe and the golden mountain tops where dwell the spirits of the dawn.'... 'Nothing but collision, intolerable interpressure (as of men not perpendicular), and consequent battle often supervening, could have been appointed those undrilled Anglo-Saxons; their pot-bellied equanimity itself continuing liable to perpetual interruption, as in the heptarchy times.' This recalls the words of earls Ralph and Roger, 'Angli sua solummodo rura colunt, conviviis et potationibus non praeliis intendunt.' Ord. Vit. ap. Maseres, p. 304.

Chapter III

THE NORMAN CONQUEST.

91. Complex results of the Conquest.—92. State of Normandy.—93. Growth of Feudalism.—94. Feudal ideas of the Conquest.—95. National policy of William.—96. Introduction of Feudal usages.—97. Maintenance of old forms.—98. Results of changes of administrators.—99. Subordinate changes in judicature.—100. In taxation.—101. In ecclesiastical affairs.—102. Transitional character of the period.

91. THE effect of the Norman Conquest on the character and constitution of the English was threefold. The Norman rule invigorated the whole national system; it stimulated the growth of freedom and the sense of unity, and it supplied, partly from its own stock of jurisprudence, and partly under the pressure of the circumstances in which the conquerors found themselves, a formative power which helped to develop and concentrate the wasted energies of the native race. In the first place it brought the nation at once and permanently within the circle of European interests, and the Crusades, which followed within a few years, and which were recruited largely from the Normans and the English, prevented a relapse into isolation. The adventurous and highly-strung energy of the ruling race communicated itself to the people whom it ruled; its restless activity and strong political instinct roused the dormant spirit and disciplined even while it oppressed it. For, in the second place, the powers which it called forth were largely exercised in counteracting its own influence. The Normans so far as they became English added nerve and force to the system with which they identified themselves; so far as they continued Norman they provoked and stimulated by opposition and oppression the latent

Complex results of the Conquest.

Its invigorating effect

It calls forth strength in opposition

Formative effect of the Conquest.

energies of the English. The Norman kings fostered, and the Norman nobility forced out the new growth of life. In the third place, however, the importation of new systems of administration, and the development of new expedients, in every department of government, by men who had a genius not only for jurisprudence but for every branch of organisation, furnished a disciplinary and formative machinery in which the new and revived powers might be trained:—a system which through oppression prepared the way for order, and by routine educated men for the dominion of law: law and order which when completed should attest by the pertinacious retention and development of primitive institutions, that the discipline which had called them forth and trained men for them, was a discipline only, not the imposition of a new and adventitious polity. For the Norman polity had very little substantial organism of its own; and what it brought with it to England was soon worn out or merged in that of the nation with which it united. Only the vigour and vitality which it had called forth was permanent.

The Normans in Normandy.

92. Of the constitutional history of the Normans of Normandy we have very little information[1]. A century and a half before the Conquest of England, Rollo had received the province from Charles the Simple: he and his people in becoming Christian had become to a certain extent Frank also. They retained much of the Scandinavian character, but of the Norse customs only those which fell into easy agreement with Frank law; and their native language they entirely forgot. Of Frank law in its early Norman form we have equally scanty evidence. What little is known is learned from later jurisprudence, and that by

[1] See Palgrave, Normandy and England, i. 113. Palgrave enumerates three traditions or legal legends of Rollo: (1) The custom of the *clameur de haro,* by which whoever sustained or feared to sustain any damage of goods or chattels, life or limb, was entitled to raise the country by the cry Haro. (2) The legend of the Roumare, according to which he tried the obedience of his people by hanging his bracelets on a tree, where they remained unguarded for three years and unmolested. (3) The legend of Long-paon, according to which he hanged a husband and wife who had conspired to cheat him. The first two stories are common to England and other countries; the last is in conformity with Scandinavian jurisprudence. Ibid. i. 696–699.

inference rather than historic evidence. Even the existence of the ordinary language of feudalism in Normandy[1] before the Conquest of England has been questioned, unreasonably indeed, but not without such probability as arises from lack of documentary materials of proof. The little that is clearly known seems to be that the Norman duke or count ruled his people as a personal sovereign, and with the advice of a council of great men[2]; that under him were a number of barons, who owed their position to the possession of land for which they were under feudal obligations to him, which they took every opportunity of discarding; who had the status of nobility derived from ancient Norse descent or from connexion with the ducal family, although that nobility neither possessed purity of blood, nor was accompanied by any feeling of honour or loyalty; and who therefore were kept faithful partly by a sense of interest and partly by the strong hand of their master[3]. The population of cultivators lived

Obscurity of their constitutional history.

The nobles

[1] Sismondi's idea that Rollo introduced full-grown feudality into Normandy (Palgrave, Normandy and England, i. 693) is of course quite untenable. Palgrave remarks that 'it remains to be proved whether any system of Norman tenure had been matured into consistency by fiscal talent until after the seventh duke of Normandy won the Anglo-Saxon crown.' Ibid. i. 694. He regards however Richard Sanspeur, the third duke, as the founder of Norman feudalism. Ibid. ii. 534. Waitz agrees with Palgrave as to the comparatively late growth of it; Göttingische Gelehrte Anzeigen, Nachrichten, Feb. 14, 1866; pp. 95, 96.

[2] Freeman, Norm. Conq. iii. 289 sq. Palgrave, Normandy and England, ii. 257, regards William Longsword the son of Rollo as absolute. 'His was the law, his was the state, his was the church.' 'No baronage surrounded his curule chair, no clerk sat at his feet. He spake the law, he gave the law, he made the law, he executed the law.' Ibid. p. 258. 'At no period after the first development of the duchy until it has been united to the crown of France, can we discern any courts or conventions of prelates and nobles equivalent to the Great Councils, States General, or Parliaments of subsequent times.' Ibid. p. 259.

[3] Palgrave, Normandy and England, iii. 28, 29. The Norman counts were at the time of the Conquest, in most cases, younger branches of the ducal house or closely connected with it by affinity. The Counts of Brionne, Evreux, and Eu were descended from sons of Richard I; Count Odo of Aumâle was the Conqueror's brother-in-law; Count Robert of Mortain his half-brother. The three great patriarchs of the other Norman houses were Yvo of Belesme, ancestor of the Montgomery counts of Ponthieu and Alençon, and earls of Shrewsbury; Bernard the Dane, and Osmund de Centville. Ibid. ii. 535, 536; iii. 148. The Beaumonts, whose county of Meulan, or Mellent, was in the French Vexin, and who were the ancestors of the earls of Warwick and Leicester, were descended from a sister of Gunnoris, the wife of Duke Richard I; and the houses of Montgomery,

The cultivators. under this aristocracy, Gallic in extraction, Frank in law and custom, and speaking the language which had been created by their early history. These people were in strict dependence on their Norman lords, although they now and then showed some remembrance of the comparative freedom they had enjoyed under the Frank empire, and retained the local organisation which neither Franks nor Normans were numerous enough to displace[1]; The towns. and commercial prosperity and a strong communal feeling subsisted in the great towns. Nothing but the personal character of the dukes had prevented the territory thus lightly held from dismemberment. Ducal policy. The strong hand had gathered all the great fiefs into the hands of kinsmen whose fidelity was secured by the right of the duke to garrison their castles, and whose tyrannies were limited by the right of the duke to enforce his own peace. Their attempts at independence were checked by ruthless bloodshed. Relation of the duke to the king of France. The duke was himself a vassal by commendation of the king, not so much as king, for the gift to Rollo had left him free, but as duke of the French: Richard of Normandy had commended himself to Hugh the Great, whose descendants had since become kings[2]. But the hold of the royal hand on Normandy was scarcely perceptible; and its constitutional connexion is with the polity of the Karolingian rather than with that of the third race of kings. What little legal system subsisted was derived from the Frank institutions as they were when Normandy was separated from the body of the Frank dominion.

93. Feudalism, the comprehensive idea which includes the whole governmental policy of the French kingdom, was of

Warenne and Giffard, from other sisters of the same famous lady; the house of Breteuil from her brother Herfast. See the pedigrees at the end of Du Chesne's Scriptores Hist. Normannorum.

[1] Palgrave, Normandy and England, iii. 41, 42: 'When we reach the era of written evidence all absolute servitude has become obsolete. The very charter which designates the *Terre-tenant* as a servus guarantees his personal freedom.' Ibid. p. 44.

[2] On the status of the Norman dukes, and the changes of the relation in which they stood to the Karolings, the German kings of the Saxon line, the dukes of the Franks and the kings, see Palgrave, Normandy and England, ii. 125, 227–234, 347, 533; Freeman, Norm. Conq. i. 167, 220, 221, 609; Waitz, Nachrichten (as above), pp. 69–96.

distinctly Frank growth[1]. The principle which underlies it may be universal; but the historic development of it with which the constitutional history of Europe is concerned may be traced step by step under Frank influence, from its first appearance on the conquered soil of Roman Gaul to its full development in the jurisprudence of the Middle Ages[2]. In the form which it

Frank growth of feudalism.

[1] The word *feudum*, fief or fee, is derived from the German word for cattle (Gothic *faihu*; Old High German *fihu*; Old Saxon *fehu*; Anglo-Saxon *feoh*); the secondary meaning being goods, especially money: hence property in general. The letter *d* is perhaps a mere insertion for sound's sake; but it has been interpreted as a part of a second root, *od*, also meaning property, in which case the first syllable has a third meaning, that of fee or reward, and the whole word means property given by way of reward for service. But this is improbable; and the connexion of the word with the Greek ἐμφύτευσις, which is suggested by the similarity of feudal and emphyteutic tenure of land, will not stand the test of criticism. The legal emphyteusis is 'a perpetual right in a piece of land that is the property of another.' This word occurs first in the Digest of Justinian, and the emphyteutic possessor seems generally to be a mere lessee: it appears in the Lombard Capitulary of A.D. 819. The word *feodum* is not found earlier than the close of the ninth century. But neither the etymology of the latter word nor the development of its several meanings can be regarded as certain. See Smith's Dictionary of Antiquities, s. v. *Emphyteusis*; Robertson, Scotland, ii. 454; Du Cange, &c.

[2] As feudalism in both tenure and government was, so far as it existed in England, brought full-grown from France, it is not necessary here to trace in detail its growth in its native country. But it is important to note the change in the opinion of scholars on the subject, which has resulted from the recent investigations of German writers. The view accepted in the last century on the authority of Montesquieu, and generally maintained by the French writers, is that the conquests of the Franks were made by independent nobles, who had a powerful comitatus, and that the lands so acquired were divided amongst the comites, each of whom was bound by a special oath of fidelity to his lord, and held his land by the obligation of military service. Eichhorn, accepting this theory, distinguished the divisions of territory made before Clovis, on the principle of free allotment, from those made by that king and his successors, on a feudal principle: the recipients of the latter grants were supposed to be the *leudes*, and amongst the leudes a narrower class of comites bore the name of *antrustions*. The Merovingian kingdom was, on this hypothesis, a state built up on vassalage: the bond of unity being the connexion of classes in subordination to one another, not the common and immediate subjection to a sovereign government. This theory has been entirely refuted by Waitz, whose authority has been, in this work, regarded as conclusive as to the ancient German system. It was no irregular unorganised fabric, but a complete governmental system. Its conquests were the work of the nations moving in entire order; the comitatus was not the bond of cohesion; the leudes were not comites: all the people were bound to be faithful to the king; the gift of an estate by the king involved no defined obligation of service; all the nation was alike bound to military service; the only comites were the antrustions, and these were few in number; the basis of the Mero-

Condition of feudalism at the time of the Norman Conquest.

has reached at the Norman Conquest, it may be described as a complete organisation of society through the medium of land tenure, in which from the king down to the lowest landowner all are bound together by obligation of service and defence: the lord to protect his vassal, the vassal to do service to his lord; the defence and service being based on and regulated by the nature and extent of the land held by the one of the other. In those states which have reached the territorial stage of development, the rights of defence and service are supplemented by the right of jurisdiction. The lord judges as well as defends his vassal; the vassal does suit as well as service to his lord. In states in which feudal government has reached its utmost growth, the political, financial, judicial, every branch of public administration, is regulated by the same conditions. The central authority is a mere shadow of a name.

Elements of feudalism.

This institution had grown up from two great sources—the beneficium, and the practice of commendation,—and had been specially fostered on Gallic soil by the existence of a subject population which admitted of any amount of extension in the methods of dependence.

The *beneficium.*

The beneficiary system[1] originated partly in gifts of land made by the kings out of their own estates to their kinsmen and servants, with a special under-

vingian polity was not the relation of lord and vassal, but that of the subject to the sovereign. The arguments of Roth (Geschichte des Beneficialwesens, and Feudalität und Unterthanverband) so far coincide with those of Waitz; and the work of Sohm (Altdeutsche Reichs- und Gerichtsverfassung) completes the overthrow of the old theory by reconstructing in a very remarkable manner the old German system in Salian and Merovingian times. It remains now to account for the growth of the feudal system. This is done by Waitz on the theory of a conjunction and interpenetration of the beneficial system and the vassal relation, both being fostered by the growth of immunities; and this is the view adopted in the text. Roth, however, goes further, connecting the antrustionship with the vassal relation, and making the former a link between the primitive comitatus and later feudalism. The infeudation of benefices and transfer of magisterial jurisdictions to the landowners (the seigniorial system), he traces not to any general movement in society, but to the violent innovation of the early Karoling period, which itself resulted from the great secularisations of the eighth century. Waitz's theory is maintained as against Roth, in the points in which the two writers differ, in the last edition of his invaluable work. See also Richter, Annalen der Deutschen Geschichte, pp. 108–111.

[1] Waitz, D. V. G. ii. 226–258.

taking to be faithful [1]; partly in the surrender by landowners of their estates to churches or powerful men, to be received back again and held by them as tenants for rent or service. By the latter arrangement the weaker man obtained the protection of the stronger, and he who felt himself insecure placed his title under the defence of the church. By the practice of commendation [2], on the other hand, the inferior put himself under the personal care of a lord, but without altering his title or divesting himself of his right to his estate; he became a vassal [3] and did homage. The placing of his hands between those of his lord was the typical act by which the connexion was formed. And the oath of fealty was taken at the same time. The union of the beneficiary tie with that of commendation completed the idea of feudal obligation; the two-fold hold on the land, that of the lord and that of the vassal, was supplemented by the two-fold engagement, that of the lord to defend, and that of the vassal to be faithful. A third ingredient was supplied by the grants of immunity by which in the Frank empire, as in England, the possession of land was united with the right of judicature: the dwellers on a feudal property were placed under the tribunal of the lord, and the rights which had belonged to the nation or to its chosen head were devolved upon the receiver of a fief [4]. The rapid spread of the system thus originated, and the assimilation of all other tenures to it, may be regarded as the work of

Commendation.

Twofold nature of vassalage.

Grants of immunity.

[1] Not a promise of definite service but a pledge to continue faithful in the conduct in consideration of which the reward is given, Waitz, D. V. G. ii. 251. Such a condition of course preserved to the giver a hold on or interest in the land, through which he was able to enforce fidelity. See also Roth, Beneficialwesen, p. 385; who points out that even when the possessors of great benefices commended themselves to the kings, they did not in the days of Charles the Bald fall into the class of vassals; 'episcopi, abbates, comites et vassalli dominici . . . beneficia habentes Carolo se commendaverunt, et fidelitatem sacramento firmaverunt.' Ann. Bertin, A.D. 837. But this was a period of transition, and if they did not become vassals in name, they entered into a relation which differed very little from later vassalage.

[2] Waitz, D. V. G. ii. 258–262.

[3] Vassus in the Merovingian period was used, according to Roth, invariably for an unfree person; in the Karolingian period for a freeman commended, or, as he states it, placed in the relation of comitatus, to a lord; Beneficialwesen, p. 367. Waitz, as has been repeatedly mentioned, rejects the idea of connecting the comitatus with commendation.

[4] Waitz, D. V. G. ii. 634–645; iv. 243–273.

Benefices hereditary.

the tenth century; but as early as A.D. 877 Charles the Bald recognised the hereditary character of all benefices[1]; and from that year the growth of strictly feudal jurisprudence may be held to date.

National origin of feudalism.

The system testifies to the country and causes of its birth. The beneficium is partly of Roman, partly of German origin: in the Roman system the usufruct, the occupation of land belonging to another person, involved no diminution of status[2]; in the Germanic system he who tilled land that was not his own was imperfectly free: the reduction of a large Roman population to dependence placed the two classes on a level, and conduced to the wide extension of the institution. Commendation on the other hand may have had a Gallic or Celtic origin[3], and an analogy only with the Roman clientship. The German comitatus, which seems to have ultimately merged its existence in one or other of these developments, is of course to be carefully distinguished in its origin from them. The tie of the benefice or of commendation could be formed between any two persons whatever; none but the king could have antrustions. But the comitatus of Anglo-Saxon history preserved, as we have seen, a more distinct existence[4], and this perhaps was one of the causes that distinguished the later Anglo-Saxon system most definitely from the feudalism of the Frank empire.

Importance of the Anglo-Saxon form of comitatus.

The process by which the machinery of government became feudalised, although rapid, was gradual. The weakness of the Karoling kings[5] and emperors gave room for the speedy develop-

[1] The practice had been growing up for a long period, and the clause of the Capitulary of Kiersi is rather a recognition of a presumptive right than an authoritative enunciation of a principle. See on it Roth, Beneficialwesen, p. 420; Waitz, D. V. G. iv. 693. The hereditary usage was not yet universal, nor did this recognition make it so; the emperor simply makes provision as to what is to be done by his son during his absence, in case of the death of a count or other holder of a benefice. It is, however, a clear proof of the generality of the usage. See Baluze, ii. 179.

[2] See Waitz, D. V. G. ii. 225, 234.

[3] Ibid. iv. 199. The arguments in favour of this theory rest on Breton usages.

[4] See above, p. 153.

[5] The tendency had begun to work during the Merovingian period. It was a regulation of Clothair II, that the count must be a native of the province

ment of disruptive tendencies in a territory so extensive and so little consolidated. The duchies and counties of the eighth and ninth centuries were still official magistracies, the holders of which discharged the functions of imperial judges or generals. Such officers were of course men whom the kings could trust, in most cases Franks, courtiers or kinsmen, who at an earlier date would have been *comites* or *antrustions*, and who were provided for by feudal benefices. The official magistracy had in itself the tendency to become hereditary, and when the benefice was recognised as heritable, the provincial governorship became so too. But the provincial governor had many opportunities of improving his position, especially if he could throw himself into the manners and aspirations of the people he ruled. By marriage or inheritance he might accumulate in his family not only the old alodial estates which, especially on German soil, still continued to subsist, but the traditions and local loyalties which were connected with the possession of them [1]. So in a few years the Frank magistrate could unite in his own person the beneficiary endowment, the imperial deputation, and the headship of the nation over which he presided. And then it was only necessary for the central power to be a little weakened, and the independence of duke or count was limited by his homage and fealty alone, that is by obligations that depended on conscience only for their fulfilment. It is in Germany that the disruptive tendency most distinctly takes the political form; Saxony and Bavaria assert their national independence under

Introduction of feudalism into the machinery of government.

Growth of feudal magistracies into provincial principalities.

over which he was placed. Edict. Cloth. II, c. 12; Baluze, i. 16; Waitz, D. V. G. ii. 377. The intention was that he should have a substantial stake in the well-being of the province, such that compensation could be exacted from him in case of misgovernment.

[1] Abundant proof of this position will be found in German history. The rise of the successive families of Saxon dukes, and the whole history of Bavaria under the Saxon emperors, furnish illustrations. The Saxon dukes of Bavaria carry out the Bavarian policy in opposition to their near kinsmen on the imperial throne. The growth of the Swabian Welfs into perfect identification with the Saxons whom they governed affords another striking instance. In a less degree, but still to some extent, this was the case in France also; but the Gallic populations had lost before the Karoling period most of their national aspirations; nor did the Frank governors identify themselves at any time with the people. Hence the great difference in social results between French and German feudalism.

Disruptive resolutions.

Swabian and Saxon dukes who have identified the interests of their subjects with their own. In France, where the ancient tribal divisions had been long obsolete, and where the existence of the alod involved little or no feeling of loyalty, the process was simpler still; the provincial rulers aimed at practical rather than political sovereignty; the people were too weak to have any aspirations at all: the disruption was due more to the abeyance of central attraction than to any centrifugal force existing in the provinces. But the result was the same; feudal government, a graduated system of jurisdiction based on land tenure, in which every lord judged, taxed, and commanded the class next below him, in which abject slavery formed the lowest, and irresponsible tyranny the highest grade, in which private war, private coinage, private prisons, took the place of the imperial institutions of government.

Opposition between the interest of the Conqueror and that of his barons.

94. This was the social system which William the Conqueror and his barons had been accustomed to see at work in France. One part of it, the feudal tenure of land was perhaps the only description of tenure which they could understand; the king was the original lord, and every title issued mediately or immediately from him. The other part, the governmental system of feudalism, was the point on which sooner or later the duke and his barons were sure to differ; already the incompatibility of the system with the existence of the strong central power had been exemplified in Normandy; the strength of the dukes had been tasked to maintain their hold on the castles and to enforce their own high justice: much more difficult would England be to retain in Norman hands if the new king allowed himself to be fettered by the French system. On the other hand the Norman barons would fain rise a step in the social scale answering to that by which their duke had become a king; and they aspired to the same independence which they had seen enjoyed by the counts of Southern and Eastern France. Nor was the aspiration on their part altogether unreasonable; they had joined in the Conquest rather as sharers in the great adventure than as mere vassals of the duke whose birth they despised as much as they feared his

Feudal tenure of land received without feudal principles of government.

strength[1]. William, however, was wise and wary as well as strong. Hence whilst by the insensible process of custom, or rather by the mere assumption that feudal tenure of land was the only lawful and reasonable one, the Frankish system of tenure was substituted for the Anglo-Saxon, the organisation of government on the same basis was not equally a matter of course. The Conqueror himself was too strong to suffer that organisation to become formidable in his reign, but neither the brutal force of William Rufus, nor the heavy and equal pressure of the government of Henry I, could extinguish the tendency towards it. It was only after it had under Stephen broken out into anarchy and plunged the whole nation in long misery, when the great houses founded by the barons of the Conquest had suffered forfeiture or extinction, when the Normans had become Englishmen under the legal and constitutional reforms of Henry II, that the royal authority in close alliance with the nation was enabled to put an end to the evil.

95. William the Conqueror claimed the crown of England as the chosen heir of Edward the Confessor[2]. It was a claim which

[1] On the descent of the great barons of Normandy see above, p. 249, note 3. Ordericus Vitalis names the chiefs who joined in the deliberation of Lillebonne preparatory to the expedition to England; the Counts Richard of Evreux, Robert of Eu, Robert of Mortain, Ralph de Conches, son of the standard-bearer of Normandy, William Fitz Osbern the steward, William de Warenne and Hugh the butler; Hugh de Grantmesnil and Roger de Mowbray, Roger de Beaumont and Roger de Montgomeri, Baldwin and Richard sons of Count Gilbert of Brionne. Lib. iii. c. 11. At the battle of Hastings, besides most of these, he mentions (iv. c. 14) Count Eustace of Boulogne, Aimer Viscount of Thouars, Hugh de Montfort the constable, and Walter Giffard. The curious, but questionable, list of the contributions to the fleet by the allied barons, is briefly this;—William Fitz Osbern the steward furnished 60 ships; Hugh, afterwards earl of Chester, 60; Hugh de Montfort the constable, 50 ships and 60 knights; Remi, afterwards bishop of Lincoln, a ship with 20 knights; Nicholas, abbot of S. Ouen, 20 ships and 100 knights; Count Robert of Eu, 60 ships; Fulk the lame, 40; Gerald the steward, 40; Count William of Evreux, 80; Roger of Montgomery, 60; Roger of Beaumont, 60; Bishop Odo, 100; Robert of Mortain, 120; Walter Giffard, 30 and 100 knights. Lyttleton, Hist. of Henry II, vol. i. p. 523. These lists are useful as helps in tracing the gradual extinction of the Conquest families during the struggles of the Norman reigns.

[2] Freeman, Norm. Conq. ii. 169; Ord. Vit. iii. 11; Chron. de Bello, p. 2. The Durham charters in which the king states that he is 'Rex Anglorum hereditario jure factus' are forgeries. See Greenwell, Feodary of Durham, pp. lxvii, lxxii. See also p. lxxxii. The king himself on his deathbed declared that he had won the crown by the grace of God, not by hereditary right. Ord. Vit. vii. 15. See Gneist, Verwaltungsr., i. 111.

William tries to reign as an English king. the English did not admit, and of which the Normans themselves saw the fallacy, but which he himself consistently maintained and did his best to justify. In that claim he saw not only the justification of the conquest in the eyes of the Church, but his great safeguard against the jealous and aggressive host by whose aid he had realised it. Accordingly, immediately after the battle of Hastings he proceeded to seek the national recognition. He obtained it from the divided and dismayed witan with no great trouble, and was crowned by the archbishop of York, the most influential and patriotic amongst them, binding himself by the constitutional promises of justice and good laws. **His coronation engagement.** Standing before the altar at Westminster, 'in the presence of the clergy and people he promised with an oath that he would defend God's holy churches and their rulers, that he would moreover rule the whole people subject to him with righteousness and royal providence, would enact and hold fast right law, utterly forbid rapine and unrighteous judgments[1].' The form of election and acceptance was regularly observed and the legal position of the new king completed before he went forth to finish the conquest.

No general division of lands. Had it not been for this the Norman host might have fairly claimed a division of the land such as the Danes had made in the ninth century[2]. But to the people who had recognised William it was but just that the chance should be given them of retaining what was their own. Accordingly, when the lands of all those who had fought for Harold were confiscated[3], those who were willing to acknowledge William were allowed to re-

[1] Flor. Wig. A.D. 1066, W. Pictav. (ed. Maseres, p. 145). See Freeman, Norm. Conq. iii. 559. No doubt the coronation service used was that which had been employed in the case of Ethelred, and the words of Florence represent the coronation engagement: 'Sanctas Dei ecclesias ac rectores illarum defendere, necnon et cunctum populum sibi subjectum juste et regali providentia regere, rectam legem statuere et tenere, rapinas injustaque judicia penitus interdicere.' See above pp. 147, 148.

[2] See above p. 72.

[3] 'The evidence that we have leads us to believe that the whole of the lands of those men, dead or living, who had fought at Senlac, was at once dealt with as land forfeited to the king.' Freeman, Norm. Conq. iv. 24. The evidence consists of references to these confiscations in the Domesday survey. See too Dialogus de Scaccario, i. c. 10.

deem theirs, either paying money at once or giving hostages for the payment[1]. That under this redemption lay the idea of a new title to the lands redeemed may be regarded as questionable. The feudal lawyer might take one view, and the plundered proprietor another. But if charters of confirmation or regrant were generally issued on the occasion to those who were willing to redeem, there can be no doubt that as soon as the feudal law gained general acceptance, these would be regarded as conveying a feudal title. What to the English might be a mere payment of *fyrdwite* or composition for a recognised offence, might to the Normans seem equivalent to forfeiture and restoration. But however this was, the process of confiscation and redistribution of lands under the new title began from the moment of the coronation. The next few years, occupied in the reduction of Western and Northern England, added largely to the stock of divisible estates. The tyranny of Odo of Bayeux and William Fitz Osbern provoked attempts at rebellion in A.D. 1067; the stand made by the house of Godwin in Devonshire in A.D. 1068; the attempts of Mercia and Northumbria to shake off the Normans in A.D. 1069 and 1070; the last struggle for independence in A.D. 1071 in which Edwin and Morcar finally fell; the conspiracy of the Norman earls in A.D. 1074 in consequence of which Waltheof perished, all tended to the same result. After each effort the royal hand was laid on more heavily: more and more land changed owners, and with the change of owners the title changed. The complicated and unintelligible irregularities of the Anglo-Saxon tenures were exchanged for the simple and uniform feudal theory. The fifteen hundred tenants-in-chief of Domesday take the place of the countless landowners of king Edward's time: and the loose unsystematic arrangements which had grown up in the confusion of title, tenure and jurisdiction, were replaced by systematic custom. The change was effected without any legislative act, simply by the process of transfer under circumstances in which simplicity and uniformity

Redemption of lands.

Divisible stock of land increased after each struggle against the Conqueror.

Change of tenure followed with change of owner.

[1] Chron. Sax. A.D. 1066: 'And com to Westmynstre. and Ealdred arcebisceop hine to cynge gehalgode. and menn guldon him gyld. and gislas sealdon. and syththan heora land bohtan.'

Assimilation of all tenures to the feudal tenure.

were an absolute necessity. It was not the change from alodial to feudal so much as from confusion to order. The actual amount of dispossession was no doubt greatest in the higher ranks; the smaller owners may to a large extent have remained in a mediatised position on their estates; but even Domesday with all its fulness and accuracy cannot be supposed to enumerate all the changes of the twenty eventful years that followed the battle of Hastings. It is enough for our purpose to ascertain that a universal assimilation of title followed the general changes of ownership. The king of Domesday is the supreme landlord; all the land of the nation, the old folkland, has become the king's; and all private land is held mediately or immediately of him; all holders are bound to their lords by homage and fealty, either actually demanded or understood to be demandable, in every case of transfer by inheritance or otherwise.

Results.

96. The result of this process is partly legal and partly constitutional or political. The legal result is the introduction of an elaborate system of customs, tenures, rights, duties, profits and jurisdictions. The constitutional result is the creation of several intermediate links between the body of the nation and the king, in the place of or side by side with the duty of allegiance.

Legal changes consequent on the change of tenure.

On the former of these points we have very insufficient data; for we are quite in the dark as to the development of feudal law in Normandy before the invasion, and may be reasonably inclined to refer some at least of the peculiarities of English feudal law to the leaven of the system which it superseded[1]. Nor is it easy to reduce the organisation described in Domesday to strict conformity with feudal law as it appears later, especially with the general prevalence of military tenure. The growth of knighthood is a subject on which the greatest obscurity prevails; and the most probable explanation of its existence in England, the theory that it is a translation into Norman forms of the thegnage of the Anglo-Saxon law, can only be stated as probable. Between the picture drawn in Domesday and the state of affairs which the charter of Henry I was designed to remedy, there is

[1] See more on this question in Chapter XI.

a difference which the short interval of time will not account for, and which testifies to the action of some skilful organising hand working with neither justice nor mercy, hardening and sharpening all lines and points to the perfecting of strong government.

Development between 1086 and 1100.

It is unnecessary to recapitulate here all the points in which the Anglo-Saxon institutions were already approaching the feudal model; it may be assumed that the actual obligation of military service was much the same in both systems, and that even the amount of land which was bound to furnish a mounted warrior was the same, however the conformity may have been produced[1]. The heriot of the English earl or thegn was in close resemblance with the relief of the Norman count or knight. But however close the resemblance, something was now added that made the two identical. The change of the heriot to the relief implies a suspension of ownership, and carries with it the custom of livery of seisin. The heriot was the payment of a debt from the dead man to his lord[2]; his son succeeded him by alodial right. The relief was paid by the heir before he could obtain his father's lands; between the death of the father and livery of seisin to the son the right of the overlord had entered, the ownership was to a certain extent resumed, and the succession of the heir took somewhat of the character of a new grant. The right of wardship also became in the same way a re-entry by the lord on the profits of the estate of the minor, instead of being as before a protection, by the head of the kin, of the indefeasible rights of the heir, which it was the duty of the whole community to maintain.

Resemblance of the thegn and knight.

Difference of heriot and relief.

There can be no doubt that the military tenure, the most prominent feature of historical feudalism, was itself introduced by the same gradual process which we have assumed in the case of the feudal usages in general. We have no light on the point from any original grant made by the Conqueror to a lay follower; but, judging by the grants made to the churches, we cannot suppose it probable that such gifts were made on any expressed condition, or accepted with a distinct pledge to provide a certain contingent of knights for the king's service. The obligation of national defence

Military tenure gradually introduced.

[1] Above, pp. 117, 155, 191. [2] Ibid. pp. 24, 157.

Grants not made conditionally.

was incumbent as of old on all landowners, and the customary service of one fully-armed man for each five hides was probably the rate at which the newly endowed follower of the king would be expected to discharge his duty. The wording of the Domesday survey does not imply that in this respect the new military service differed from the old : the land is marked out not into knights' fees but into hides, and the number of knights to be furnished by a particular feudatory would be ascertained by inquiring the number of hides that he held, without apportioning the particular acres that were to support the particular knight.

Knights' fees gradually introduced.

It would undoubtedly be on the estates of the lay vassals that a more definite usage would first be adopted, and knights bound by feudal obligations to their lords receive a definite estate from them. Our earliest information, however on this as on most points of tenure is derived from the notices of ecclesiastical practice. Lanfranc, we are told, turned the drengs, the rent-paying tenants of his archiepiscopal estates, into knights for the defence of the country[1]: he enfeoffed a certain number of knights who performed the military service due from the archiepiscopal barony. This had been done before the Domesday survey[2], and almost necessarily implies that a like measure had

Case in Kent.

been taken by the lay vassals. Lanfranc likewise maintained ten knights to answer for the military service due from the convent of Christ Church, which made over to him, in consideration of the relief, land worth two hundred pounds annually. The value of the knight's fee must already have been fixed at

Case of Ramsey.

twenty pounds a year. In the reign of William Rufus the abbot of Ramsey obtained a charter which exempted his monastery from the service of ten knights due from it on festivals, substituting

[1] Epp. Cantuar. p. 225. Elton's Tenures of Kent, pp. 68, 69. 'Sed et haec attestantur scripta vetustissima, quae lingua Anglorum *land-bokes*, id est, terrarum libros vocat. Quia vero non erant adhuc tempore regis Willelmi milites in Anglia, sed threnges, praecepit rex ut de eis milites fierent ad terram defendendam. Fecit autem Lanfrancus threngos suos milites ; monachi vero id non fecerunt sed de portione sua ducentas libratas terrae dederunt archiepiscopo, ut per milites suos terras eorum defenderet et omnia negotia eorum apud curiam Romanam suis expensis expediret, unde adhuc in tota terra monachorum nullus miles est, sed in terra archiepiscopi.' As late as 1201 the archbishop obtained a charter for the same purpose ; Houard, Anc. Loix, ii. 352.

[2] Domesday, i. fol. 3.

the obligation to furnish three knights to perform service on the north of the Thames[1]: a proof that the lands of that house had not yet been divided into knights' fees. In the next reign we may infer from the favour granted by the king to the knights who defend their lands 'per loricas,' that is, by the hauberk, that their demesne lands shall be exempt from pecuniary taxation, that the process of definite infeudation had largely advanced. But it was not even yet forced on the clerical or monastic estates. When in 1167 the abbot of Milton in Dorset was questioned as to the number of knights' fees for which he had to account, he replied that all the services due from his monastery were discharged out of the demesne; but he added that in the reign of Henry I, during a vacancy in the abbacy, bishop Roger of Salisbury had enfeoffed two knights out of the abbey lands[2]; he had however subsequently reversed the act and had restored the lands whose tenure had been thus altered to their original condition of rent-paying estate or socage. The very term 'the new feoffment' which was applied to the knights' fees created between the death of Henry I and the year in which the account preserved in the Black Book of the Exchequer was taken, proves that the process was going on for nearly a hundred years[3], and

Case of Milton.

Old and new feoffment.

[1] Ramsey Cartulary, fol. 54 b: in the 29th report of the Deputy Keeper of the Records, app. p. 45. The abbot in 1167 replies to the royal inquiry as to the number of knights enfeoffed in the monastic lands: 'Homines faciunt iiii. milites in communi ad servitium domini regis, ita quod tota terra abbatiae communicata est cum eis per hidas ad praedictum servitium faciendum.' The lands were not yet cut into knights' fees. Liber Niger Scaccarii, ed. Hearne, i. 257. Similarly the bishop of Durham's service for his demesne land was that of ten knights, but it was not cut up into fees. Ibid. 309.

[2] Liber Niger Scaccarii, i. 75: 'Contigit tamen aliquando, ecclesia nostra vacante, Rogerum episcopum Saresberiae illam ex mandato regis Henrici avi vestri in custodiam annis quinque suscepisse. Tunc praedictus episcopus de quodam tenemento quod tenuit R. de Monasteriis feodo censuali, scilicet de duabus hidis, unum fefavit militem. Postmodo vero bonae memoriae R. praedecessore meo constituto abbate, per justitiam regis Henrici et consilio praefati episcopi R. feoda praedicta ad antiquum statum revocata sunt; et quos episcopus constituit milites facti sunt censuarii.'

[3] An objection to this argument may be found in a clause of the so-called Charter of the Conqueror (Ll. Will. iii. § 8), in which the full-grown doctrine of military tenure is expressed thus: 'Omnes comites et barones et milites et servientes, et universi liberi homines totius regni nostri praedicti, habeant et teneant se semper bene in armis et in equis ut decet et oportet; et sint semper prompti et bene parati ad servitium suum integrum

Knights' fees the result of a composition.

that the form in which the knights' fees appear when called on by Henry II for scutage was most probably the result of a series of compositions by which the great vassals relieved their lands from a general burden by carving out particular estates the holders of which performed the services due from the whole; it was a matter of convenience and not of tyrannical pressure.

Number unknown.

The statement of Ordericus Vitalis that the Conqueror 'distributed lands to his knights in such fashion that the kingdom of England should have for ever 60,000 knights and furnish them at the king's command according to the occasion[1]' must be regarded as one of the many numerical exaggerations of the early historians. The officers of the Exchequer in the twelfth century were quite unable to fix the number of existing knights' fees.

No rule as to the extent of a knight's fee.

It cannot even be granted that a definite area of land was necessary to constitute a knight's fee; for although at a later period and in local computations we may find four or five hides adopted as a basis of calculation, where the extent of the particular knight's fee is given exactly, it affords no ground for such a conclusion. In the Liber Niger we find knights' fees of two hides and a half[2], of two hides[3], of four[4], five[5], and six hides[6]. Geoffrey Ridel states that his father held 184 carucates and a virgate, for which the service of fifteen knights was due, but that no knights' fees had been carved out of it, the obligation lying equally on every carucate[7]. The archbishop of York

nobis explendum et peragendum cum opus fuerit, secundum quod nobis debent de feodis et tenementis suis de jure facere; et sicut illis statuimus per commune consilium totius regni nostri praedicti, et illis dedimus et concessimus in feodo jure haereditario.' But this charter is a mere fabrication, and gives no authority whatever to the articles which are not found in the earlier and simpler form. See Hoveden, ii. pref. pp. xxxv, xxxvi. If this clause be genuine, or any part of it, it must be understood to refer only to the cases in which the knights' fees had been actually apportioned.

[1] Ord. Vit. iv. 7. [2] Lib. Nig. i. 64, 75. [3] Ibid. i. 75.

[4] Ibid. i. 79. [5] Ibid. i. 79, 104, 165.

[6] Ibid i. 79; where one hide is reckoned as the sixth part of a knight's fee; and also as a fifth part: the difference being of course accounted for by the quality of the land, or by the tenour of the enfeoffment.

[7] Ibid. i. 210: 'Nullus militum de veteri illo fefamento feofatus fuit nominatim per feodum militis; sed unaquaeque carrucata terrae ad faciendum milites xv. par est alii ad omnia servitia facienda et in exercitibus et in custodiis et ubique.'

had far more knights than his tenure required[1]. It is impossible to avoid the conclusion that the extent of a knight's fee was determined by rent or valuation rather than acreage, and that the common quantity was really expressed in the twenty librates[2], the twenty pounds' worth of annual value which until the reign of Edward I was the qualification for knighthood[3]. It is most probable that no regular account of the knights' fees was ever taken until they became liable to taxation, either in the form of *auxilium militum* under Henry I, or in that of scutage under his grandson. The facts, however, which are here adduced preclude the possibility of referring this portion of the feudal innovations to the direct legislation of the Conqueror. It may be regarded as a secondary question whether the knighthood here referred to was completed by the investiture with knightly arms and the honourable accolade. The ceremonial of knighthood was practised by the Normans, whereas the evidence that the English had retained the primitive practice of investing the youthful warrior is insufficient: yet it would be rash to infer that so early as this, if indeed it ever was the case, every possessor of a knight's fee received formal initiation before he assumed his spurs. But every such analogy would make the process of transition easier and prevent the necessity of any general legislative act of change.

The knight's fee was of the annual value of £20.

Questionable relation of knighthood to knight-service.

It has been maintained that a formal and definitive act, forming the initial point of the feudalisation of England, is to be found in a clause of the laws, as they are called, of the Conqueror; which directs that every free man shall affirm by covenant and oath that 'he will be faithful to King William within England and without, will join him in preserving his

Feudalism not involved in the oath exacted by William.

[1] Lib. Nig. i. 303: 'Sciatis, domine, quod super dominium archiepiscopatus Eboracensis nullum feodum est militis, quoniam tot habemus fefatos milites per quos acquietavimus omne servitium quod vobis debemus, sicut et praecessores nostri fecerunt, et plures etiam habemus quam vobis debeamus. Antecessores enim nostri, non pro necessitate servitii quod deberent, sed quia cognatis et servientibus suis providere volebant, plures quam debebant regi feodaverunt.'

[2] See above, p. 262. In the return of Nigel de Luvetot in the Liber Niger, i. 258, the fractions of the knights' fee are calculated in solidates, or shillings' worths. See also pp. 293, 294.

[3] Select Charters, pp. 446, 447. Cf. Gneist, Verwalt. i. 116, 117.

The general oath of allegiance is not feudal.

lands and honour with all fidelity, and defend him against his enemies[1].' But this injunction is little more than the demand of the oath of allegiance which had been taken to the Anglo-Saxon kings, and is here required not of every feudal dependent of the king, but of every freeman or freeholder whatsoever. In that famous Council of Salisbury of A.D. 1086, which was summoned immediately after the making of the Domesday survey, we learn from the Chronicle that there came to the king 'all his witan, and all the landholders of substance in England whose vassals soever they were, and they all submitted to him, and became his men and swore oaths of allegiance that they would be faithful to him against all others.' In this act has been seen the formal acceptance and date of the introduction of feudalism, but it has a very different meaning. The oath described is the oath of allegiance, combined with the act of homage, and obtained from all landowners whoever their feudal lord might be[2]. It

The oath taken at Salisbury was really anti-feudal.

[1] Ll. Will. I, § 2, below note. See Hoveden, ii. pref. pp. xxv. sq. where I have attempted to prove the spuriousness of the document called the charter of William I printed in the Ancient Laws, ed. Thorpe, p. 211. The way in which the regulation of the Conqueror here referred to, has been misunderstood and misused is curious. Lambarde in the Archaionomia, p. 170, printed the false charter, in which this genuine article is incorporated, as an appendix to the French version of the Conqueror's laws; numbering the clauses 51 to 67; from Lambarde the whole thing was transferred by Wilkins into his collection of Anglo-Saxon laws. Blackstone, Commentaries, ii. 49, suggested that '*perhaps* the very law [which introduced feudal tenures] thus made at the Council of Salisbury, is that which is still extant and couched in these remarkable words,' i. e. the injunction in question; and referred to Wilkins, p. 228. Ellis, in the introduction to Domesday, i. 16, quotes Blackstone, but adds a reference to Wilkins without verifying Blackstone's citation from his Collection of Laws, substituting for that work the *Concilia* in which the law does not occur. Many modern writers have followed him in referring the enactment of the article to the Council of Salisbury.

[2] It is as well to give here the text of both passages. That in the laws runs thus: 'Statuimus etiam ut omnis liber homo foedere et sacramento affirmet quod infra et extra Angliam Willelmo regi fideles esse volunt, terras et honorem illius omni fidelitate cum eo servare et ante eum contra inimicos defendere.' Select Charters, p. 80. The homage done at Salisbury is described by Florence thus: 'Nec multo post mandavit ut archiepiscopi, episcopi, abbates, comites et barones, et vicecomites cum suis militibus die Kalendarum Augustarum sibi occurrerent Saresberiae; quo cum venissent, milites eorum sibi fidelitatem contra omnes homines jurare coegit.' The Chronicle is a little more full, 'Thær him comon to his witan and ealle tha landsittende men the ahtes wæron ofer eall Engleland, wæron thæs mannes men the hi wæron, and ealle hi bugon to him and

is a measure of precaution taken against the disintegrating power of feudalism, providing a direct tie between the sovereign and all freeholders which no inferior relation existing between them and the mesne lords would justify them in breaking. But this may be discussed further on. The real importance of the passage as bearing on the date of the introduction of feudal tenure is merely that it shows the system to have already become consolidated; all the landowners of the kingdom had already become, somehow or other, vassals, either of the king or of some tenant under him. The lesson may be learned from the fact of the Domesday survey.

It shows that the feudal theory was already accepted.

97. The introduction of such a system would necessarily have effects far wider than the mere modification of the law of tenure; it might be regarded as a means of consolidating and concentrating the whole machinery of government; legislation, taxation, judicature, and military defence were all capable of being organised on the feudal principle, and might have been so had the moral and political results been in harmony with the legal. But we have seen that its tendency when applied to governmental machinery is disruptive. The great feature of the Conqueror's policy is his defeat of that tendency. Guarding against it he obtained recognition as the king of the nation and, so far as he could understand them and the attitude of the nation allowed, he maintained the usages of the nation. He kept up the popular institutions of the hundred court and the shire court[1]. He confirmed the laws which had been in use in King's Edward's days with the additions which he himself made for the benefit, as he especially tells us, of the English[2]. We are told, on what seems

The Conqueror's policy was to defeat the disruptive tendency of feudal institutions.

wæron his menn and him hold athas sworon thæt hi woldon ongean ealle othre men him holde beon.' Gneist, Verwalt. i. 116 rightly points out this oath as giving to the English polity a direction very different from that of the continental states.

[1] Statutes of William, § 8: 'Requiratur hundredus et comitatus sicut antecessores nostri statuerunt.'

[2] Ibid. § 7: 'Hoc quoque praecipio et volo ut omnes habeant et teneant legem Edwardi regis in terris et in omnibus rebus, adauctis iis quae constitui ad utilitatem populi Anglorum.' This is re-echoed by Henry I in his Charter, § 13, 'Lagam Edwardi regis vobis reddo cum illis emendationibus quibus pater meus eam emendavit consilio baronum suorum.'

Maintenance of national customs.

to be the highest legal authority of the next century, that he issued in his fourth year a commission of inquiry into the national customs, and obtained from sworn representatives of each county a declaration of the laws under which they wished to live[1]. The compilation that bears his name is very little more than a reissue of the code of Canute. And this proceeding helped greatly to reconcile the English people to his rule. Although the oppressions of his later years were far heavier than the measures taken to secure the immediate success of the Conquest, all the troubles of the kingdom after A.D. 1075, in his son's reigns as well as in his own, proceeded from the insubordination of the Normans, not from the attempts of the English to dethrone the king. Very early they learned that, if their interest was not the king's, at least their enemies were his enemies; hence they are invariably found on the royal side against the feudatories.

William's laws a reissue of the earlier codes.

Maintenance of the national militia.

This accounts for the maintenance of the national force of defence, over and above the feudal army. The *fyrd* of the English, the general armament of the men of the counties and hundreds, was not abolished at the Conquest, but subsisted even through the reigns of William Rufus and Henry I, to be reformed and reconstituted under Henry II; and in each reign it gave proof of its strength and faithfulness. The witenagemot itself retained the ancient form; the bishops and abbots formed a chief part of it, instead of being, as in Normandy, so insignificant an element that their very participation in deliberation has been doubted. The king sat crowned three times in the year in the old royal towns of Westminster, Winchester, and Gloucester[2], hearing

Of the witenagemot.

[1] 'Willelmus rex quarto anno regni sui, consilio baronum suorum fecit summoneri per universos consulatus Angliae Anglos nobiles et sapientes et sua lege eruditos ut eorum et jura et consuetudines ab ipsis audiret. Electi igitur de singulis totius patriae comitatibus viri duodecim jurejurando confirmaverunt primo ut, quoad possent, recto tramite neque ad dextram neque ad sinistram partem devertentes legum suarum consuetudinem et sancita patefacerent nil praetermittentes, nil addentes, nil praevaricando mutantes.' Hoveden, ii. 218. The authority on which the statement is made seems to be that of the justiciar Ranulf Glanvill. See Hoveden, ii. pref. p. xlvii. According to the tradition preserved in the same document the laws ultimately granted by William were those of Edgar. Ibid. p. 235.

[2] Chron. Sax. A.D. 1087. W. Malmesb. G. R. iii. § 279.

the complaints of his people, and executing such justice as his knowledge of their law and language and his own imperious will allowed. In all this there is no violent innovation, only such gradual essential changes as twenty eventful years of new actors and new principles must bring, however insensibly the people, themselves passing away and being replaced by their children, may be educated to endurance.

No violent innovation.

98. It would be wrong to impute to the Conqueror any intention of deceiving the nation by maintaining its official forms whilst introducing new principles and a new race of administrators. What he saw required change he changed with a high hand. But not the less surely did the change of administrators involve a change of custom, both in the church and in the state. The bishops, ealdormen, and sheriffs, of English birth were replaced by Normans: not unreasonably perhaps, considering the necessity of preserving the balance of the state. With the change of officials came a sort of amalgamation or duplication of titles; the ealdorman or earl became the comes or count; the sheriff became the vicecomes[1]; the office in each case receiving the name of that which corresponded most closely with it in Normandy itself. With the amalgamation of titles

Changes resulting from change of administrators.

[1] The correspondence of the offices of count and earl is obvious and need not be discussed further, since *comes* had even before the Conquest been adopted as the Latin word for earl or ealdorman; see above, pp. 112, 156, 158. The identification of the vicecomes with the sheriff requires a little more illustration, for many writers have tried to explain the term as if it were of native growth and have been accordingly puzzled by the fact that the vicecomes is the vicegerent, not of the earl, but of the king. See Madox, Dialogus de Scaccario, pp. 31, 32. Hence also, when it was ascertained that the vicecomes was imported full-grown from Normandy, it was thought probable that the *comes* whom he represented there was the *comes Normannorum*, the duke of Normandy. But the term is really one of Frank origin. The vicecomes is the missus comitis of the Karolings, as distinguished from the vicarius or centenarius, who stands to him in the same subaltern relation in which the vicecomes stands to the comes; but he is the judicial representative of the Karolingian *comes*: the name appears first in Southern France under Lewis the Pious, but never was domesticated in Germany. Sohm, Fr. R. G. Verfg. pp. 508–525. It had been maintained in Normandy by the Normans without any question of verbal correctness, and was in the same loose way transferred to England. The duties of the Norman viscounts very much of course resembled those of the sheriffs both fiscally and judicially, but we know little of their action before the Conquest.

New names bring in new principles.

came an importation of new principles and possibly new functions; for the Norman count and viscount had not exactly the same customs as the earls and sheriffs. And this ran up into the highest grades of organisation; the king's court of counsellors was composed of his feudal tenants; the ownership of land was now the qualification for the witenagemot instead of wisdom; the earldoms became fiefs instead of magistracies, and even the bishops had to accept the status of barons. There was a very certain danger that the mere change of persons might bring in the whole machinery of hereditary magistracies, and that king and people might be edged out of the administration of justice, taxation, and other functions of supreme or local independence. Against this it was most important to guard; as the Conqueror learned from the events of the first year of his reign, when the severe rule of Odo and William Fitz-Osbern had provoked Herefordshire and Kent into hopeless resistance.

Hereditary jurisdictions, a thing to be avoided.

It was no part of William's policy to break up the unity of the royal authority by the creation of great hereditary territorial jurisdictions: but the absolute necessity of measures by which the disruptive tendency should be defeated forced itself upon him probably by degrees; and every opportunity that was furnished by the forfeitures of the first ten years of the reign was turned to progressive advantage. His first earls were merely successors of the earls of Edward the Confessor; William Fitz-Osbern held Herefordshire as it had been held by earl Ralph; Ralph Guader, Roger Montgomery, and Hugh of Avranches filled the places of Edwin and Morcar and the brothers of Harold. But the conspiracy of the earls in A.D. 1074 opened William's eyes to the danger of this proceeding, and from that time onward he governed the provinces through sheriffs immediately dependent on himself, avoiding the foreign plan of appointing hereditary counts, as well as the English custom of ruling by vice-regal ealdormen. He was however very sparing in giving earldoms at all, and inclined to confine the title to those who were already counts in Normandy or in France. To this plan there were some marked exceptions, which may be accounted

William gives very few earldoms.

for either on the ground that the arrangements had been completed before the need of watchfulness was impressed on the king by the treachery of the Normans, or on that of the exigencies of national defence. In these cases he created, or suffered the continuance of, great palatine jurisdictions; earldoms in which the earls were endowed with the superiority of whole counties, so that all the landowners held feudally of them, in which they received the whole profits of the courts and exercised all the regalia or royal rights, nominated the sheriffs, held their own councils and acted as independent princes except in the owing of homage and fealty to the king. Two of these palatinates, the earldom of Chester and the bishopric of Durham, retained much of their character to our own days[1]. A third, the palatinate of bishop Odo in Kent, if it were really a jurisdiction of the same sort, came to an end when Odo forfeited the confidence of his brother and nephew[2]. A fourth, the earldom of Shropshire, which is not commonly counted amongst the palatine jurisdictions, but which possessed under the Montgomery earls all the characteristics of such a dignity, was confiscated after the treason of Robert of Belesme by Henry I[3]. These had been all founded before the conspiracy of A.D. 1074; they were also a part of the national defence; Chester and Shropshire kept the Welsh marches in order, Kent was the frontier exposed to attack from Picardy,

Existence of palatine earldoms.

Their defensive character.

[1] The earldom of Chester has belonged to the eldest son of the sovereign since 1396; the palatinate jurisdiction of Durham was transferred to the crown in 1836 by act of Parliament, 6 Will. IV, c. 19.

[2] The palatine jurisdiction of Odo rests on the authority of Ordericus Vitalis, who speaks as if he understood what he meant by the term; he mentions the gift of Kent three times, (1) in A.D. 1067, 'totam Cantiam fratri suo commendavit'; at that time the archbishop Stigand was a prisoner, and Odo was acting as cojusticiar; (2) under the year 1087 he speaks of him as viceroy, 'in Anglia praeposuit Cantiae regno'; and (3) in 1088, 'palatinus Cantiae comes erat, et plures sub se comites virosque potentes habebat.' This seems distinct enough, but it may be explained perhaps by supposing the writer to have confused Odo's position as justiciar with his territorial endowment in Kent. The overwhelming character of his power may be inferred from the action of the *Placitum apud Pinnendenam*, below, p. 277; in the record of which he is called comes Cantiae; Ang. Sac. i. 335.

[3] Mr. Eyton, in his History of Shropshire, claims it as a palatine earldom for Roger Montgomery, vol. i. 22, 70, 242 sq. See too Nicolas's Historic Peerage, ed. Courthope, p. 434, where Selden is quoted as an authority for the same statement; and see below, Chapter XI.

Palatine earldoms.

and Durham, the patrimony of St. Cuthbert, lay as a sacred boundary between England and Scotland; Northumberland and Cumberland were still a debateable ground between the two kingdoms. Chester was held by its earls as freely by the sword as the king held England by the crown; no lay vassal in the county held of the king, all of the earl. In Shropshire there were only five lay tenants in capite besides Roger Montgomery; in Kent bishop Odo held an enormous proportion of the manors, but the nature of his jurisdiction is not very clear, and its duration is too short to make it of much importance. If William founded any earldoms at all after A.D. 1074, which may be doubted, he did it on a very different scale.

Sheriffdoms occasionally hereditary.

The hereditary sheriffdoms he did not guard against with equal care. The Norman viscounties were hereditary[1], and there was some risk that the English ones would become so too; and with the worst consequences, for the English counties were much larger than the bailiwicks of the Norman viscount, and the authority of the sheriff when he was relieved from the company of the ealdorman, and was soon to lose that of the bishop, would have no check except the direct control of the king. If William perceived this, it was too late to prevent it entirely; some of the sheriffdoms became hereditary, and continued to be so long after the abuse had become constitutionally dangerous[2].

Contiguous territorial accumulations avoided.

The independence of the greater feudatories was still further limited by the principle, which the Conqueror seems to have observed, of avoiding the accumulation in any one hand of a great number of contiguous estates[3]. The rule is not without

[1] See Stapleton, 'Rotuli Scaccarii Normanniae,' i. pp. lviii, lix, &c.

[2] See Chapter XI.

[3] See Thorpe's Lappenberg, iii. 201. The estates of Odo lay in seventeen counties, those of Robert of Mortain in twenty; Eustace of Boulogne had fiefs in twelve counties, and Hugh of Avranches in twenty-one, besides his palatine earldom. Gneist, Self-government, i. 66, 67, gives more details, chiefly from Kelham's Domesday illustrated. There are forty-one great vassals, each of whom has estates in more than six counties: of these five have lands in seven, six in eight, two in nine, four in ten, four in eleven, three in twelve, one in thirteen, two in fourteen, one in twenty, and one in twenty-one; all these are laymen. The greatest number of manors is held by Robert of Mortain, 793; Odo has 439; Alan of Brittany 442.

some important exceptions, and it may have been suggested by the diversity of occasions on which the fiefs were bestowed, but the result is one which William must have foreseen. An insubordinate baron whose strength lay in twelve different counties would have to rouse the suspicions and perhaps to defy the arms of twelve powerful sheriffs, before he could draw his forces to a head. In his manorial courts, scattered and unconnected, he could set up no central tribunal, nor even force a new custom upon his tenants, nor could he attempt oppression on any extensive scale. By such limitation the people were protected and the central power secured.

Distribution of great fiefs in distant counties.

Yet the changes of ownership, even thus guarded, wrought other changes. It is not to be supposed that the Norman baron, when he had received his fief, proceeded to carve it out into demesne and tenants' land as if he were making a new settlement in an uninhabited country. He might indeed build his castle and enclose his chase with very little respect to the rights of his weaker neighbours, but he did not attempt any such radical change as the legal theory of the creation of manors seems to presume. The name 'manor' is of Norman origin, but the estate to which it was given existed, in its essential character, long before the Conquest; it received a new name as the shire also did, but neither the one nor the other was created by this change. The local jurisdictions of the thegns who had grants of sac and soc, or who exercised judicial functions amonst their free neighbours, were identical with the manorial jurisdictions of the new owners. It may be conjectured with great probability that in many cases the weaker freemen, who had either willingly or under constraint attended the courts of their great neighbours, were now, under the general infusion of feudal principle, regarded as holding their lands of them as lords; it is not less probable that in a great number of grants the right to suit and service from small landowners passed from the king to the receiver of the fief as a matter of course; but it is certain that even before the Conquest such a proceeding was not uncommon; Edward the Confessor had transferred to St. Augustine's monastery a number of allodiaries

Legal theory of the origin of manors.

Growth of manorial customs.

in Kent[1], and every such measure in the case of a church must have had its parallel in similar grants to laymen. The manorial system brought in a number of new names; and perhaps a duplication of offices. The gerefa of the old thegn or of the ancient township, was replaced, as president of the courts, by a Norman steward or seneschal; and the bydel of the old system by the bailiff of the new; but the gerefa and bydel still continued to exist in a subordinate capacity as the grave or reeve and the bedell; and when the lord's steward takes his place in the county court, the reeve and four men of the township are there also. The common of the township may be treated as the lord's waste, but the townsmen do not lose their customary share. The changes that take place in the state have their resulting analogies in every village, but no new England is created; new forms displace but do not destroy the old, and old rights remain, although changed in title and forced into symmetry with a new legal and pseudo-historical theory. The changes may not seem at first sight very oppressive, but they opened the way for oppression; the forms they had introduced tended, under the spirit of Norman legality and feudal selfishness, to become hard realities, and in the profound miseries of Stephen's reign the people learned how completely the new theory left them at the mercy of their lords; nor were all the reforms of his successor more stringent or the struggles of the century that followed a whit more impassioned, than were necessary to protect the English yeoman from the men who lived upon his strength.

Manorial institutions.

Estimate of the amount of change.

The new forms oppressive in result.

99. In attempting thus to estimate the real amount of change introduced by the feudalism of the Conquest, many points of further interest have been touched upon, to which it is necessary to recur only so far as to give them their proper place in a more general view of the reformed organisation. The Norman king is still the king of the nation. He has become the supreme landlord; all estates are held of him mediately or immediately, but he still demands the allegiance of all his subjects. The oath which he exacted at Salisbury in A.D. 1086, and which is em-

Position of the Norman king.

[1] Kemble, C. D. iv. 239. See above, p. 189.

bodied in the semi-legal form already quoted, was a modification of the oath taken to Edmund[1], and was intended to set the general obligation of obedience to the king in its proper relation to the new tie of homage and fealty by which the tenant was bound to his lord. All men continued to be primarily the king's men, and the public peace to be his peace. Their lords might demand their service to fulfil their own obligations, but the king could call them to the fyrd, summon them to his courts, and tax them without the intervention of their lords; and to the king they could look for protection against all foes. Accordingly the king could rely on the help of the bulk of the free people in all struggles with his feudatories, and the people, finding that their connexion with their lords would be no excuse for unfaithfulness to the king, had a further inducement to adhere to the more permanent institutions.

Direct relations between king and people.

In the department of law the direct changes introduced by the Conquest were not great. Much that is regarded as peculiarly Norman was developed upon English soil, and although originated and systematised by Norman lawyers, contained elements which would have worked in a very different way in Normandy. Even the vestiges of Karolingian practice which appear in the inquests of the Norman reigns are modified by English usage. The great inquest of all, the Domesday survey, may owe its principle to a foreign source; the oath of the reporters may be Norman, but the machinery that furnishes the jurors is native; 'the king's barons inquire by the oath of the sheriff of the shire, and of all the barons and their Frenchmen, and of the whole hundred, the priest, the reeve, and six ceorls of every township[2].' The institution of the collective Frankpledge, which recent writers incline to treat as a Norman innovation, is so distinctly coloured by English custom that it has been generally regarded as purely indigenous. If it were indeed a precaution taken by the new rulers against the avoidance of justice by the absconding or harbouring of criminals, it fell with ease into the usages and even the legal terms which had been common

Amount of change in jurisprudence uncertain.

Inquests.

Frankpledges.

[1] Above, p. 148.

[2] Domesday of Ely; Domesd. iii. 497.

Trial by battle.

for other similar purposes since the reign of Athelstan[1]. The trial by battle, which on clearer evidence seems to have been brought in by the Normans, is a relic of old Teutonic jurisprudence, the absence of which from the Anglo-Saxon courts is far more curious than its introduction from abroad[2].

Jurisdiction of the sheriff unaltered.

The organisation of jurisdiction required and underwent no great change in these respects. The Norman lord who undertook the office of sheriff had, as we have seen, more unrestricted power than the sheriffs of old. He was the king's representative in all matters judicial, military, and financial in his shire, and had many opportunities of tyrannising in each of those departments: but he introduced no new machinery. From him, or from the courts of which he was the presiding officer, appeal lay to the king alone; but the king was often absent from England and did not understand the language of his subjects.

The justiciar as the king's deputy.

In his absence the administration was entrusted to a justiciar, a regent or lieutenant of the kingdom; and the convenience being once ascertained of having a minister who could in the whole kingdom represent the king, as the sheriff did in the shire, the justiciar became a permanent functionary. This however cannot be certainly affirmed of the reign of the Conqueror who, when present at Christmas, Easter, and Whitsuntide, held great courts of justice as well as for other purposes of state; and the legal importance of the office belongs to a later stage. The royal court, containing the tenants in chief of the crown, both lay and clerical, and entering into all the functions of the witenagemot, was the supreme council of the nation, with the advice and consent of which the king legislated, taxed, and judged.

In the one authentic monument of William's jurisprudence, the act which removed the bishops from the secular courts

1 See above, pp. 87–89.

2 Palgrave argues, from the fact that trial by battle is mentioned in a record of a Worcester shiremoot soon after the Conquest, that the custom may possibly have been of earlier introduction; but it is never mentioned in the laws, and as exemption from it was one of the privileges conferred by charter on towns in the next century, there can be no doubt that it was an innovation, and one which was much disliked. See Palgrave, Commonwealth, p. 225.

and recognised their spiritual jurisdictions, he tells us that he acts 'with the common council and counsel of the archbishops, bishops, abbots, and all the princes of the kingdom[1].' The ancient summary of his laws contained in the Textus Roffensis is entitled, 'What William King of the English with his princes enacted after the conquest of England[2];' and the same form is preserved in the tradition of his confirming the ancient laws reported to him by the representatives of the shires. The Anglo-Saxon Chronicle enumerates the classes of men who attended his great courts: 'there were with him all the great men over all England, archbishops and bishops, abbots and earls, thegns and knights[3].'

The Conqueror legislates with the advice of his council.

The great suit between Lanfranc as archbishop of Canterbury and Odo as earl of Kent, which is perhaps the best reported trial of the reign, was tried in the county court of Kent before the king's representative, Gosfrid bishop of Coutances; whose presence and that of most of the great men of the kingdom seem to have made it a witenagemot. The archbishop pleaded the cause of his church in a session of three days on Pennenden Heath[4]; the aged South-Saxon bishop, Ethelric, was brought by the king's command to declare the ancient customs of the laws,

A trial of the Conqueror's reign.

[1] 'Communi concilio et consilio archiepiscoporum, episcoporum et abbatum et omnium principum regni mei.' Ancient Laws, p. 213; Select Charters, p. 82.

[2] Select Charters, p. 80.

[3] Chron. Sax. A.D. 1087.

[4] It is printed in Anglia Sacra, i. 334–336, from the Textus Roffensis, Wilkins, Concilia, i. 323, 324. The litigation is referred to in Domesday, i. fol. 5. From the same source we have an account of another trial of some interest, between Gundulf bishop of Rochester and Picot sheriff of Cambridgeshire. The suit was brought before the king; he called together the county court of Cambridgeshire, and directed that the right to the disputed land should be decided by their judgment. Bishop Odo presided. The Cambridgeshire men, in fear of the sheriff, decided against Gundulf. Odo thereupon directed that they should choose twelve out of their number to swear to the truth of their report. The twelve swore falsely; and one of them having confessed his perjury to Odo, he ordered the sheriff to send the jurors up to London, and with them twelve of the best men of the county. He also summoned a body of barons. This court of appeal reversed the decision of the shire. The twelve best men tried to deny their complicity with the perjurers, and Odo offered them the ordeal of iron. They failed under the test, and were fined by the rest of the county three hundred pounds, to be paid to the king. Ang. Sac. i. 339; see below, Chap. XI.

Trial at Pennenden.

and with him several other Englishmen skilled in ancient laws and customs. All these good and wise men supported the archbishop's claim, and the decision was agreed on and determined by the whole county. The sentence was laid before the king, and confirmed by him. Here we have probably a good instance of the principle universally adopted; all the lower machinery of the court was retained entire, but the presence of the Norman justiciar and barons gave it an additional authority, a more direct connexion with the king, and the appearance at least of a joint tribunal [1].

Principle of amalgamation.

The principle of amalgamating the two laws and nationalities by superimposing the better consolidated Norman superstructure on the better consolidated English substructure, runs through the whole policy. The English system was strong in the cohesion of its lower organism, the association of individuals in the township, in the hundred and in the shire; the Norman race was strong in its higher ranges, in the close relation to the crown of the tenants in chief whom the king had enriched. On the other hand, the English system was weak in the higher organisation, and the Normans in England had hardly any subordinate organisation at all. The strongest elements of both were brought together.

The same principle carried out in taxation.

100. The same idea of consolidating the royal power by amalgamating the institutions of the two races was probably followed also in the department of finance; although in this point neither party was likely to discern much immediate benefit to any one but the king. William, whose besetting vice was said by his contemporaries to be avarice, retained the revenues of his predecessors and added new imposts of his own. The ordinary revenue of the English king had been derived solely from the royal estates and the produce of what had been the folkland, with such commuted payments of feormfultum, or provision in kind, as represented either the reserved rents from ancient possessions of the crown, or the quasi-voluntary tribute paid by the nation to its chosen head. The Danegeld,

[1] Exactly the same principle was involved in the institution of regular eyres or circuits of the justices by Henry I or Henry II.

that is, the extraordinary revenue arising from the cultivated land, —originally levied as tribute to the Danes, although it had been continued long after the occasion for it had ceased,—had been abolished by Edward the Confessor [1]. The Conqueror not only retained the royal estates, but imposed the Danegeld anew. In A.D. 1084 he demanded a sum of six shillings from every hide of land, three times the old rate [2]. The measure may have been part of the defensive policy which he adopted after discovering the faithlessness of his brother Odo, and which connects itself with the Domesday survey and the Salisbury council two years later; but it became a permanent source of revenue. On the Norman side the supreme landlord was entitled to all the profits of the feudal position, a description of income of which we have no details proper to the reign of the Conqueror, but which becomes prominent immediately after his death. It is needless to observe that the actual burden of the feudal imposts, as well as the older taxation, fell on the English; for the Norman lords had no other way of raising their reliefs, aids, talliages, and the rest, than from the labours of their native dependents. The exaction may have been treated by them as a tyrannical one, but the hardship directly affected the English.

The Danegeld.

Feudal imposts.

The income thus accumulated was no doubt very great. The royal lands are known from Domesday to have produced in the reign of William the Conqueror nearly £20,000 [3]; and the Danegeld of A.D. 1084, if levied from two-thirds of the hidage of the kingdom, would be about as much more. To this must be added the profits of jurisdictions and the other occasional items which we have no means of estimating. Giraldus Cambrensis [4] mentions £40,000 as the amount which in his days

The Conqueror's income.

[1] Edward imagined that he saw the devil sitting on the bags in the treasury. Hoveden, i. 110. The author of the Dialogus de Scaccario says that William turned the Danegeld from a regular into an occasional tax. Lib. i. c. 11.

[2] Chron. Sax. A.D. 1083; Flor. Wig. A.D. 1084; Freeman, Norm. Conq. iv. 685.

[3] Pearson, Early and Middle Ages, i. 385.

[4] De Inst. Princ. iii. c. 30: 'Angliae, regum Anglorum tempore et etiam penultimi Edwardi Westmonasteriensis diebus, annui fiscales redditus, sicut in rotulo Wintoniae reperitur, ad sexaginta millia marcarum summam implebant.'

Income of the Conqueror.

was regarded as representing the income ascribed, on the evidence of Domesday, to Edward the Confessor. Ordericus Vitalis, a well-informed Norman monk of the next century, boldly states William's revenue at £1061 10*s.* 1½*d.* a day, besides the profits of the law courts [1]. If, as has been cleverly conjectured, this circumstantial statement refers properly to the weekly revenue, we arrive at a sum of between fifty and sixty thousand pounds a year. A comparison with the revenue of Henry I, which in his thirty-first year reached a gross amount of £66,000, may show that this is not improbable [2]. But the numerical statements of the early writers are very untrustworthy, and no approach can yet be made to a precise estimate. It is evident, however, that the same general principle was at work in the collection of revenue as in the courts of justice and in the furnishing of military defence. No class was left untaxed; all men had a distinct relation to the king over and above the relation to their lords; and the strongest points of the two national systems are brought into joint working.

Ecclesiastical policy of the Conqueror.

101. The ecclesiastical policy of the Conqueror presents marks of coincidence, and also of contrast, with his secular administration. There is the same change of administrators, but not the same fusion or modification of offices. The change of administrators is gradual in the church as in the state, and nearly as complete: the English church was drawn into the general tide of ecclesiastical politics and lost much of its insular character: it gained in symmetry and definiteness of action, and was started on a new career. But the immediate motives of William's measures are somewhat complex. His attack on England was planned and carried out with the approval of Pope

[1] Ord. Vit. iv. 7: 'Ipsi vero regi, ut fertur, mille et sexaginta librae sterilensis monetae, solidique triginta et tres oboli, ex justis redditibus Angliae per singulos dies redduntur; exceptis muneribus regiis et reatuum redemptionibus, aliisque multiplicibus negotiis quae regis aerarium quotidie adaugent.'

[2] Ben. Pet. ii. pref. xcix. The sum, calculated as carefully as I could do it, is £66,593, but it includes debts and old accounts, and cannot be regarded as an approximation to the true revenue. The treasure in Henry's hands at his death was at least £160,000, of which £100,000 fell to Stephen, Will. Malmesb, Hist. Nov. i. § 14; and £60,000 was in Normandy, Ord. Vit. xiii. 19.

Alexander II, and the hard measure dealt out to the English bishops personally was due quite as much to the desire of satisfying the pope, who had his own jealousies and grudges, as to the belief that the influence of the great ecclesiastics was secretly working against him, or that the support of a strong Norman hierarchy was absolutely necessary for his safety. But William had no intention of following the papal guidance further than was convenient to himself; and in the great adviser whom he chose on his own responsibility he found a very able and conscientious helper. Lanfranc was a statesman as well as a theologian, a lawyer as well as a scholar, and in feeling quite as much an Englishman as a Norman: he was an Italian, too, and, therefore perhaps, not a papalist [1]. Hence whilst attempting the reformation of abuses, which either the national easiness and self-complacency, or the evil influence of the Norman clergy had originated, he adopted no violent or rigorous scheme of discipline, provoked no national antipathies, sacrificed neither the state to the church nor the church to the state. His policy was uniformly in agreement with the king's, and his personal influence kept in harmonious working two systems, which contained elements that after his death were to produce a long and bitter quarrel.

Relations to the pope.

Influence of Lanfranc.

William's own ideas of managing the church were probably developed altogether in England itself. The Norman prelates, with whom as duke he had to do, were either sons of the ruling families [2] or personally insignificant. They had not the position of the English prelates with reference either to the people or to the duke. They were but a small element in his council, and in no close relation with the native population, whilst in

William's church policy worked out in England.

[1] Several letters of Lanfranc and Gregory VII are extant, from which a certain amount of coolness may be inferred to have existed between them. Gregory complains and Lanfranc excuses himself. See Freeman, Norm. Conq. iv. 434–437.

[2] Ordericus names them, lib. iii. c. xi. Odo of Bayeux was the Conqueror's brother; the bishop of Lisieux was brother of the count of Eu, and the bishop of Avranches son of Count Ralph of Bayeux, both cousins of the king; the bishop of Seez belonged to the family of Belesme; Gosfrid of Coutances was a mighty man on both sides the Channel. The archbishop of Rouen and the bishop of Evreux were of less personal importance.

Position of the English bishops.

England they were the most numerous and coherent body in the witenagemot; and although many of Edward's bishops were foreigners, they had inherited the loyalty and traditional support of the districts over which they presided. The ready submission of the witan in A.D. 1066 saved the bishops for the moment: the Conqueror had no wish to make enemies, and they had no champion to take the place of Harold. But when in A.D. 1070 he had found that the influence of the episcopate was so strong that it must be put into safer hands, and when the legates of Alexander II demanded the humiliation of the ignorant supporters of the antipope Benedict and the enforcement of canonical order, he proceeded to displace most of the native bishops. Then Stigand, who occupied two sees, one of which he had taken in the lifetime of a Norman predecessor, and who had received the pall from a schismatic pope, was deposed and imprisoned. With him fell his brother, the bishop of Elmham, and the faultless bishop of Selsey whom he had consecrated, and who might be regarded as sharing his schismatic attitude [1]. The brother bishops of Durham, Ethelwin and Ethelric, had incurred the penalties of treason. York and Lichfield were vacant by death. Dorchester had been filled up by the Norman Remigius since the battle of Hastings [2]. Hereford, Wells, Ramsbury, Exeter, and London were already in the hands of foreigners. It was by no act of extraordinary severity that the change was made; but at the end of A.D. 1070 only two sees retained native bishops, Worcester and Rochester [3]. The way was open for Lanfranc, and his appointment satisfied both king and pope. Henceforth the bishops and most of the abbots were Norman [4];

Deposition of English bishops.

[1] Flor. Wig. A.D. 1070. Remigius, in his profession of obedience to Lanfranc, mentions the mission of legates from the pope with orders that all who had been ordained by Stigand should be deposed or suspended.

[2] He too had been consecrated by Stigand, but the offence was not so fatal in a Norman as in an Englishman; he declares in his profession that he was ignorant of Stigand's uncanonical status. MS. Cotton, Cleopatra, E. I.

[3] Siward of Rochester is said by William of Malmesbury to have died a few days after the Conquest. But he lived several years longer, was present at a council at Winchester in 1072, and died probably in 1075.

[4] The deposition of the abbots was also gradual. See the Chronicle (ed. Earle), pp. 271–275.

Character of the Conqueror's bishops.

but they, like the king, realised their new position as Englishmen by adoption; entering immediately on all the claims of their predecessors and declaring that, so far as their power went, the churches they espoused should suffer no detriment. The Conqueror's bishops were generally good and able men, though not of the English type of character. They were not mere Norman barons, as was the case later on, but scholars and divines chosen under Lanfranc's influence. The abbots were less wisely selected, and had perhaps a more difficult part to play, for the monasteries were still full of English monks, and preserved, and probably concentrated, most of the national aspirations after deliverance which all came to naught.

Ecclesiastical courts.

The most important ecclesiastical measure of the reign, the separation of the church jurisdiction from the secular business of the courts of law, is unfortunately, like all other charters of the time, undated. Its contents however show the influence of the ideas which under the genius of Hildebrand were forming the character of the continental churches. From henceforth the bishops and archdeacons are no longer to hold ecclesiastical pleas in the hundred-court, but to have courts of their own; to try causes by canonical not by customary law, and allow no spiritual questions to come before laymen as judges. In case of contumacy the offender may be excommunicated and the king and sheriff will enforce the punishment. In the same way laymen are forbidden to interfere in spiritual causes[1]. The reform

[1] Ancient Laws, ed. Thorpe, p. 213: 'Ut nullus episcopus vel archidiaconus de legibus episcopalibus amplius in hundret placita teneant, nec causam quae ad regimen animarum pertinet ad judicium secularium hominum adducant, sed quicunque secundum episcopales leges de quacunque causa vel culpa interpellatus fuerit, ad locum quem ad hoc episcopus elegerit vel nominaverit veniat, ibique de causa vel culpa sua respondeat, et, non secundum hundret sed secundum canones et episcopales leges, rectum Deo et episcopo suo faciat. Si vero aliquis per superbiam elatus ad justitiam episcopalem venire contempserit vel noluerit, vocetur semel, secundo et tertio; quod si nec sic ad emendationem venerit, excommunicetur et, si opus fuerit ad hoc vindicandum, fortitudo et justitia regis vel vicecomitis adhibeatur. Ille autem qui vocatus ad justitiam episcopi venire noluerit, pro unaquaque vocatione legem episcopalem emendabit. Hoc etiam defendo et mea auctoritate interdico, ne ullus vicecomes, aut praepositus seu minister regis, nec aliquis laicus homo de legibus quae ad episcopum pertinent se intromittat, nec aliquis laicus homo alium hominem

Consequence of the separation of the spiritual and secular courts.

is one which might very naturally recommend itself to a man like Lanfranc. The system which it superseded was full of anomalies and disadvantages to both justice and religion. But the change involved far more than appeared at first. The growth of the canon law in the succeeding century, from a quantity of detached local or occasional rules to a great body of universal authoritative jurisprudence, arranged and digested by scholars who were beginning to reap the advantages of a revived study of the Roman civil law, gave to the clergy generally a far more distinctive and definite civil status than they had ever possessed before, and drew into church courts a mass of business with which the church had previously had only an indirect connexion. The question of investitures, the marriage of the clergy, and the crying prevalence of simony, within a very few years of the Conqueror's death, forced on the minds of statesmen everywhere the necessity of some uniform system of law. The need of a system of law once felt, the recognition of the supremacy of the papal court as a tribunal of appeal followed of course: and with it the great extension of the legatine administration. The clergy thus found themselves in a position external, if they chose to regard it so, to the common law of the land; able to claim exemption from the temporal tribunals, and by appeals to Rome to paralyse the regular jurisdiction of the diocesans. Disorder followed disorder, and the anarchy of Stephen's reign, in which every secular abuse was paralleled or reflected in an ecclesiastical one, prepared the way for the Constitutions of Clarendon, and the struggle that followed with all its results down to the Reformation itself. The same facility of employing the newly developed jurisprudence of the canonists drew into the ecclesiastical courts the matrimonial and testamentary jurisdiction, and that most mischievous, because most abused, system of enforcing moral discipline by spiritual penalties, at the instance of men whose first object was the accumulation of money.

Growth of the canon law.

sine justitia episcopi ad judicium adducat: judicium vero in nullo loco portetur, nisi in episcopali sede aut in illo loco quem ad hoc episcopus constituerit.'

The foundation of spiritual courts, and the exemption of their proceedings from the common usages of Anglo-Saxon law, had a bearing on the relations of the church to the state in these ways; but it must not be supposed that it was in itself a sign of any disposition in either William or Lanfranc to admit extreme claims on the part of the popes. The results that have been mentioned flowed from a state of things which was now in process of development, and which attained full growth far more rapidly than they could have expected, through circumstances which they could not foresee. Anything like a direct claim on the part of the papacy William repudiated at once. Not only did he distinctly refuse the demand of fealty made by the legate Hubert on behalf of Gregory VII[1], but he seems to have established an understanding with the English church which had the force of a concordat for future times. The arrangement is described by the faithful historian Eademr as a novelty, but it was a novelty necessitated by the newness of the circumstances in which the king found himself. 'He would not suffer that any one in all his dominions should receive the pontiff of the city of Rome as apostolic pope, except at his command, or should on any condition receive his letters if they had not been first shown to himself.' This principle, which was abused by William Rufus, and which could only work well when the chiefs in church and state were in thorough concert, expresses rather than overcomes the difficulty. But it is a difficulty which has

Attitude of William and Lanfranc towards the papacy.

His rules of dealing with Rome.

[1] Freeman, Norm. Conq. iv. 432-431, has traced the history of Gregory's correspondence with the Conqueror. Some time about A.D. 1076, the pope sent a legate to William to ask for a more regular payment of Peter's pence and to demand fealty. The king's answer was this: after the greeting 'salutem cum amicitia,' 'Hubertus legatus tuus, religiose pater, ad me veniens ex tua parte me admonuit, quatenus tibi et successoribus tuis fidelitatem facerem, et de pecunia quam antecessores mei ad Romanam ecclesiam mittere solebant melius cogitarem. Unum admisi, alterum non admisi; fidelitatem facere nolui nec volo; quia nec ego promisi nec antecessores meos antecessoribus tuis id fecisse comperio. Pecunia tribus ferme annis, in Galliis me agente, negligenter collecta est; nunc vero Divina misericordia me in regnum meum reverso, quod collectum est per praesentem legatum mittetur; et quod reliquum est per legatos Lanfranci archiepiscopi fidelis nostri, cum opportunum fuerit, transmittetur. Orate pro nobis et pro statu regni nostri, quia antecessores vestros dileximus et vos prae omnibus sincere diligere et obedienter audire desideramus.' Selden, App. to Eadmer, p. 164; Lanfr. Epp. ed. Giles, No. x.

The Conqueror's rules of dealing with the Church.

never yet been overcome; and it is probable that the Conqueror's rule went as near to the solution as any state theory has ever done. A second rule was this, 'He did not suffer the primate of his kingdom, the archbishop of Canterbury, if he had called together under his presidency an assembly of bishops, to enact or prohibit anything but what was agreeable to his will and had been first ordained by him.' This was a most necessary limitation of the powers given to the newly established courts, nor did it, in an age in which there was no discord of religious opinion, create any of the scandals which might arise under more modern conditions. The two rules together express the principle of the maxim so well known in later times, 'cujus regio, ejus religio' in that early form in which it recommended itself to the great Charles. A third rule was this; 'he did not allow any of his bishops publicly to implead, excommunicate, or constrain by penalty of ecclesiastical rigour, any of his barons or servants, who was informed against either for adultery or for any capital crime, except by his own command.' Of this also it may be said that it might work well when regulated by himself and Lanfranc, but that otherwise it created rather than solved a difficulty [1]. A further usage, which was claimed by Henry I as a precedent, was the prohibition of the exercise of legatine power in England, or even of the legates landing on the soil of the kingdom without royal licence [2].

Simplicity of these rules.

Such precautions as these show little more than an incipient misgiving as to the relations of church and state: a misgiving which might well suggest itself either to the king or to the thoughtful mind of the adviser, who saw himself at the head of a church which had been long at uneasy anchorage apart from these ecclesiastical tumults, into the midst of which it was soon to be hurried. There is something Karolingian in their simplicity, and possibly they may have been suggested by the ger-

[1] Eadmer, Hist. Nov. i. (ed. Selden, p. 6); Select Charters, p. 79.

[2] Eadmer, Hist. Nov. v. p. 118: 'Rex Henricus antiquis Angliae consuetudinibus praejudicium inferri non sustinens, illum ab ingressu Angliae detinebat.' See also Flor. Wig. A.D. 1116. In this case the objection to receive the legate arose from the bishops, abbots, and nobles who discussed the question 'communi consilio.'

minating Gallicanism of the day. They are, however, of great prospective importance and form the basis of that ancient customary law on which throughout the middle ages the English church relied in her struggles with the papacy.

Their importance.

The removal of the episcopal sees from the villages or decayed towns to the cities[1] is another mark of the reign which is significant of change in the ideas of clerical life, but not of important consequence. The Norman prelate preferred Bath to Wells and Chester to Lichfield: he felt that he was more at home in the company of the courtier and warrior than in the monastery. But the change went little further: the monastic rigour was tenacious and aggressive: Lanfranc was himself a monk, and allowed the monastic traditions of the early English church even more than their due weight in his reforms[2]. It is now that the secular clerks finally disappear from those cathedrals which remained monastic until the Reformation. The abuses of the rich foundations by married canons, who would perpetuate a hereditary clerical caste, were glaring; and so strong was their interest in both Normandy and England that neither legal nor ecclesiastical discouragement could avail for a century and a half to extinguish the evil[3]. The cathedrals were divided between the two systems in nearly equal proportions. But the reforming prelates showed no wish to throw in their lot with their churches. The bishop's share of the estates was separated from that of the monks, and the exemptions which had been obtained by the favoured non-cathedral monasteries were grasped at by the conventual cathedrals in order to oust the

Removal of episcopal sees.

Question of monasticism in the cathedrals.

[1] In the council of London, A.D. 1075, it was determined to remove the see of Sherborn to Old Sarum; that of Selsey to Chichester; and that of Lichfield to Chester. The see of Dorchester was removed to Lincoln in 1085; that of Elmham, which had been transferred to Thetford about 1078, was moved to Norwich in 1101. The see of Crediton had been transferred to Exeter in 1050. Bishop John of Wells took up his station at Bath in 1088. See Wilkins, Concilia i. 363.

[2] See Epistolae Cantuarienses, pref. pp. xx-xxvi. Lanfranc seems to have been urged by Alexander II himself to reorganise the cathedral of Canterbury on monastic principles; and the same pope forbade bishop Walkelin of Winchester to expel the monks from his church.

[3] Epp. Cantuar. pref. xxvi. In the reigns of Edward the Confessor and William, the foreign bishops of Wells, Exeter, and York attempted to reduce their canons to rule by ordering them to have a common refectory

Growth of the chapters and convents.

jurisdiction of the bishop in the house and in the property of his chapter. Thus even when the see was transferred to the cities, it was rather the cathedral body than its nominal head that increased in power and pomp. New churches rivalling in beauty and size those of the continent began to be built, and hospitable establishments to be doubled. New orders were instituted in quick succession. The canonical reform failed, but the Augustinian canons grew up out of the failure: every attempt at monastic development took ultimately the form of a new rule, and in England all found a ready and too liberal welcome. In many instances this liberality was exercised at the expense of the parish churches, and an evil precedent was established which outlived in its effects very much of the advantage gained from monastic piety and cultivation. But these results are yet far distant.

New orders of monks.

Transitional character of the Conqueror's reign.

102. A general view of the reign of the Conqueror suggests the conclusion that, notwithstanding the strength of his personal character, and his maintenance of his right as king of the English and patron of the people both in church and in state;—notwithstanding the clearness of his political designs and the definiteness and solidity of his principles of action, there was very much in the state system which he initiated that still lay in solution. So much depended on the personal relations between himself and Lanfranc in church matters, that after their deaths the whole ecclesiastical fabric narrowly escaped destruction; and in temporal matters also, Lanfranc's influence excepted, the king had no constitutional adviser, no personal friend whose authority contained any element of independence. William is his own minister. His policy, so far as it is his own, owes its stability to his will. His witan are of his own creation,—feudatories powerful in enmity, no source of strength even when they are friends and allies, with a policy of their own which he is determined to combat.

and dormitory. They were unable to enforce the command. The institution of Augustinian canons which resulted from the like projects of reform was not adopted in any English cathedral until the see of Carlisle was founded by Henry I, and this continued the only Augustinian cathedral in England until the Reformation. Many of the Scottish cathedrals were, however, made Augustinian in the twelfth and thirteenth centuries.

General character of his government.

His people fear him even when and where they trust him: he is under no real constraint, whether of law or conscience, to rule them well. His rule is despotic therefore, in spite of the old national and constitutional forms which he suffers to exist: it is the rule of a wise and wary, a strong and resolute, not a wanton and arbitrary despot; it avoids the evils of irresponsible tyranny, because he who exercises it has learned to command himself as well as other men. But a change of sovereign can turn the severe and wary rule into savage licence; and the people, who have grown up and have been educated under a loose, disorganised polity, see no difference between discipline and oppression. The constitutional effects of the Conquest are not worked out in William's reign, but in that of Henry I. The moral training of the nation does not as yet go beyond castigation: the lowest depth of humiliation has yet to be reached, but even that yields necessary lessons of its own. It is useless to ask what the result would have been if the first Norman king had been such a man as William Rufus: but it was most fortunate for the English that in the hour of their great peril, when they had neither ruler, counsel, nor system, they fell under the rule of one who was a law to himself, who saw the coincidence of duty and policy, and preferred the forms of ancient royalty to the more ostentatious position of a feudal conqueror. He was a hard man, austere, exacting, oppressive: his heavy hand made the English themselves comprehend their own national unity through a community of suffering. Yet in the suffering they were able to discern that there might be still worse things to bear: one strong master was better than many weak ones, general oppression than actual anarchy. The king made and kept good pe[illegible] The Danegeld and the Forest-law were not too much to pay for the escape from private war and feudal disruption.

Chapter IV

ADMINISTRATIVE AND REPRESENTATIVE INSTITUTIONS.

156. Character of the period, 1155–1215; amalgamation and national unity;—in blood.—157. In language and law.—158. The king.—159. The national Council.—160. Legislation.—161. Taxation.—162. Military organisation.—163. Judicature.—164. The institution of Juries.—165. The Towns.—166. The Clergy.—167. Conclusion.

Distinctive character of the constitution.

156. The great characteristic of the English constitutional system, in that view of it which is offered in these pages,—the principle of its growth, the secret of its construction,—is the continuous development of representative institutions from the first elementary stage, in which they are employed for local purposes and in the simplest form, to that in which the national parliament appears as the concentration of all local and provincial machinery, the depository of the collective powers of the three estates of the realm. We have traced in the Anglo-Saxon history the origin and growth of the local institutions, and in the history of the Norman reigns the creation of a strong administrative system. Not that the Anglo-Saxon rule had no administrative mechanism, or that the Norman polity was wanting in its local and provincial organism, but that the strength of the former was in the lower, and that of the latter in the upper ranges of the social system, and that the stronger parts of each were permanent. In the reigns of the three kings, whose history was sketched in the last chapter, we trace a most important step in advance, the interpenetration, the growing together, of the local machinery and the administrative organism. We have already examined the great crisis by which they were brought together; now we begin

Anglo-Saxon local institutions.

Norman central institutions.

to trace the process by which the administrative order is worked into the common law of the people, and the common institutions of the people are admitted to a share in the administration of the state; the beginning of the process which is completed in national self-government.

Period of interpenetration.

The period is one of amalgamation, of consolidation, of continuous growing together and new development, which distinguishes the process of organic life from that of mere mechanic contrivance, internal law from external order.

Realisation of national unity.

The nation becomes one and realises its oneness; this realisation is necessary before the growth can begin. It is completed under Henry II and his sons. It finds its first distinct expression in Magna Carta. It is a result, not perhaps of the design and purpose of the great king, but of the converging lines of the policy by which he tried to raise the people at large, and to weaken the feudatories and the principle of feudalism in them. Henry is scarcely an English king, but he is still less a French feudatory. In his own eyes he is the creator of an empire. He rules England by Englishmen and for English purposes, Normandy by Normans and for Norman purposes; the end of all his policy being the strengthening of his own power. He recognises the true way of strengthening his power, by strengthening the basis on which it rests, the soundness, the security, the sense of a common interest in the maintenance of peace and order.

The result of Henry's policy.

The national unity is completed in two ways. The English have united; the English and the Norman have united also. The threefold division of the districts, the Dane law, the West-Saxon and the Mercian law, which subsisted so long, disappears after the reign of Stephen. The terms are become archaisms which occur in the pages of the historians in a way that proves them to have become obsolete[1]; the writers themselves are uncertain which shires fall into the several divisions. Traces of slight differences of custom may be discovered in the varying rules of the county courts, which, as Glanvill tells us, are so numerous that it is impossible to put them on record[2];

Union of blood.

Extinction of legal distinctions.

[1] Simeon of Durham, ed. Hinde, i. 220–222.
[2] Glanvill, De Legibus Angliae, lib. xii. c. 6.

but they are now mere local by-laws, no real evidence of permanent divisions of nationality. In the same way Norman and Englishman are one. Frequent intermarriages have so united them, that without a careful investigation of pedigree it cannot be ascertained,—so at least the author of the Dialogus de Scaccario affirms,—who is English and who Norman[1]. If this be considered a loose statement, for scarcely two generations have passed away since the Norman blood was first introduced, it is conclusive evidence as to the common consciousness of union. The earls, the greater barons, the courtiers, might be of pure Norman blood, but they were few in number: the royal race was as much English as it was Norman. The numbers of Norman settlers in England are easily exaggerated; it is not probable that except in the baronial and knightly ranks the infusion was very great, and it is very probable indeed that, where there was such infusion, it gained ground by peaceable settlement and marriage. It is true that Norman lineage was vulgarly regarded as the more honourable, but the very fact that it was vulgarly so regarded would lead to its being claimed far more widely than facts would warrant: the bestowal of Norman baptismal names would thus supplant, and did supplant, the old English ones, and the Norman Christian name would then be alleged as proof of Norman descent. But it is far from improbable, though it may not have been actually proved, that the vast majority of surnames derived from English places are evidence of pure English descent, whilst only those which are derived from Norman places afford even a presumptive evidence of Norman descent. The subject of surnames scarcely rises into prominence before the fourteenth century; but an examination of the indices to the Rolls of the Exchequer and Curia Regis shows a continuous increase in number and importance of persons bearing English names: as early as the reign of Henry I we find among the barons Hugh of Bochland, Rainer

Inter-marriages.

Uncertain infusion of Norman blood.

Value of Norman name and lineage.

Increase of English surnames.

[1] 'Jam cohabitantibus Anglicis et Normannis et alterutrum uxores ducentibus vel nubentibus, sic permixtae sunt nationes ut vix discerni possit hodie, de liberis loquor, quis Anglicus quis Normannus sit genere; exceptis dumtaxat ascriptitiis qui villani dicuntur.' Dialogus, i. c. 10; Select Charters, p. 193.

of Bath, and Alfred of Lincoln, with many other names which show either that Englishmen had taken Norman names in baptism, or that Normans were willing to sink their local surnames in the mass of the national nomenclature.

English names.

157. The union of blood would be naturally expressed in unity of language, a point which is capable of being more strictly tested. Although French is for a long period the language of the palace, there is no break in the continuity of the English as a literary language. It was the tongue, not only of the people of the towns and villages, but of a large proportion of those who could read and enjoy the pursuit of knowledge. The growth of the vernacular literature was perhaps retarded by the influx of Norman lords and clerks, and its character was no doubt modified by foreign influences under Henry II and his sons, as it was in a far greater degree affected by the infusion of French under Henry III and Edward I: but it was never stopped. It was, at its period of slowest growth, as rapid in its development as were most of the other literatures of Europe. Latin was still the language of learning, of law, and of ritual. The English had to struggle with French as well as with Latin for its hold on the sermon and the popular poem: when it had forced its way to light, the books in which it was used had their own perils to undergo from the contempt of the learned and the profane familiarity of the ignorant. But the fact that it survived, and at last prevailed, is sufficient to prove its strength. The last memoranda of the Peterborough Chronicle belong to the year 1154: the last extant English charter can scarcely be earlier than 1155. There are English sermons of the same century, and early in the next we reach the date of Layamon's Brute and the Ormulum. These are fragments of the literature of a language which is passing through rapid stages of growth, and which has not attained a classical standard. Only fragments are left, for the successive stages pass so quickly that the monuments of one generation are only half intelligible to the next. The growth of the language and that of the literature proceed in an inverse ratio. If we were to argue from these fragments, we should infer, that whilst in the department of

Unity and growth of language.

Modifications of vernacular literature.

Continuity, survival, and victory of English.

Fragmentary character accounted for.

Relation of language and literature in the process of development.

law the use of the native tongue was necessarily continuous, it had to rise through the stages of the song and the sermon to that point of development at which those who required history and deeper poetry demanded them in their own language. Such a sequence may imply the increase of education in the English, but it more probably implies the disuse of French in the classes that had a taste for learning: and it is still more probable that the two literatures advanced by equal steps until the crisis came which banished French from popular conversation.

Scraps of English in conversation.

There are traces that seem to show that English was becoming the familiar conversational language of the higher classes. The story of Helewisia de Morville, preserved by William of Canterbury in his life of Becket, exhibits the wife of one of the murderers as using English. 'Huwe of Morvill, war, war, Liulf haveth his sword ydrawen,' was her cry when she invoked the aid of her husband to punish the stubborn virtue of her English favourite [1]. Giraldus Cambrensis, a man of high Norman descent, could not only read but criticise the language of the Chronicles and of Alfred, and compare the dialects of northern and southern England [2]. Hugh of Nunant, a Norman of the Normans, mentions it as a strange thing that William Longchamp the chancellor was ignorant of the language of the people, and regards it in special connexion with his hatred and contempt of the English [3]. Latin was the ordinary language of the monks of Durham, yet they conversed in English with S. Godric, who spoke French only by miracle [4]. The hymn which the blessed virgin taught the same saint was in English [5], and in English it is recorded for the reading of bishop Hugh de Puiset. At Canterbury, in the miraculous history of Dunstan, written by Eadmer, it is the devil that speaks French [6] and corrects the indifferent idiom of an English monk. S. Hugh of Lincoln, who was a Burgundian by birth, did not understand the dialects of Kent

[1] Will. Cant. ap. Giles, ii. 31. [2] Gir. Cam. Opp. vi. 177, 178.

[3] Ben. Pet. ii. 219: 'Ille non respondebat quia linguam Anglicanam prorsus ignorabat.' See also Gir. Camb. V. Galfridi, in Anglia Sacra, ii. 407.

[4] V. S. Godric, pp. 203, 206. [5] Ibid. p. 208.

[6] Eadmer, V. S. Dunstani, p. 236.

and Huntingdonshire, but he was addressed by the natives as if it were naturally to be expected that he would comprehend what they said[1]. Little can be safely inferred from such scattered notices, but that it was not uncommon for educated people to speak both languages. Of any commixture of French and English at this period there is no trace: the language of Chaucer owes its French elements to a later infusion: the structure of our language is affected by the foreign influence as yet in a way which may be called mechanical rather than chemical: it loses its inflexions, but it does not readily accept new grammatical forms, nor does it adopt, to any great extent, a new vocabulary.

English commonly spoken.

No commixture of French with English.

The uniformity of legal system in its application to Norman and Englishman alike, would of necessity follow from a state of society in which Norman was undistinguishable from Englishman: but except in one or two points of transient interest, it is not likely that any great distinctions of legal procedure had ever separated the two races. The Norman character of the Curia Regis and the English character of the shiremoot stand in contrast not so much because the former was Norman and the latter English, but because of the different social principles from which they spring. The Englishman where he is a tenant-in-chief has his claims decided in the Curia Regis; the Norman vavassor and the English ceorl alike are treated in the shiremoot[2]. The trial by battle and the inquest by jury in its several forms are, after the first pressure of the Conquest is over, dealt with by both alike. The last vestige of difference, the presentment of Englishry, loses what significance it ever had. The tenures are the same for all; the Englishman is not disqualified from being a tenant in capite: the Norman may hold land in villenage: the free and common socage of the new system is really the free possession of the old, and the man who holds his acres by suit and service at the county court[3] is as free as if he continued to call his land *ethel* or *bocland*, over

Consolidation of the legal system.

[1] Magna Vita S. Hugonis, pp. 157, 268.
[2] Writ of Henry I, quoted above, p. 390.
[3] 'Per sectam comitatus et de hendemot, unde scutagium dari non debet.' Rot. Pip. 3 Joh.; Madox, Hist. Exch. p. 467.

The villein class.

which none but the king had soken. The one class which is an exception to all these generalisations, that of the *rustici* or *nativi*, is, it would appear, exclusively English: but even these, where they have recognised claims to justice, claim it according to its fullest and newest improvements. The system of recognition is as applicable to the proof or disproof of villein extraction as to the assize of mort-dancester or novel disseisin: nor does the disqualification under which the rustic lies, for ordination or for the judicial work of the jury and assize, arise from his nationality, but from his status. The claims of his lord forbid him to seek emancipation by tonsure; the precarious nature of his tenure forbids him to testify in matters touching the freer and fuller tenure of other men's property.

Englishmen rarely promoted.

Still great promotion in Church and State does not yet commonly fall to the lot of the simple Englishman. Wulfstan of Worcester, the last of the Anglo-Saxon bishops, dies in 1095; Robert, the scholar of Melun, the first English bishop of any note after the Conquest, belongs to the reign of Henry II[1]. The Scot, the Welshman, and the Breton reach episcopal thrones before the Englishman. Archbishop Baldwin, who was promoted to Canterbury by Henry II, seems to have been an Englishman of humble birth; Stephen Langton was also an Englishman, but by this time the term includes men of either descent, and from his time the prelates of foreign extraction form the exceptions rather than the rule. In the service of the State however it is, as we have seen already, by no means improbable that English sheriffs and judges were employed by Henry I: and English scholars and lawyers were rising into distinction in Sicily and even in France.

Character of the union of races.

The union of the races resembles not merely the mechanical union of two bodies bound together by force, or even by mutual attraction, in which, however tight the connexion, each retains its individual mass and consistency: it is more like a chemical commixture in which, although skilled analysis may distin-

[1] Robert is distinctly described by Robert de Monte, as *genere Anglicus* (ed. Pertz, vi. 513); John of Pagham, who was made bishop of Worcester in 1151, may also have been English.

guish the ingredients, they are so united both in bulk and in qualities, that the result of the commixture is something altogether distinct from the elements of which it is composed. The infusion of a little that is Norman affects the whole system of the English, and the mass which results is something different from either the one or the other. True the great proportion of the bulk must be English, but for all that it is not, and nothing will ever make it, as if that foreign element had never been there.

Result of the commixture.

The commixture of institutions is somewhat similar: the new machinery which owes its existence to the new conception of royal power, the Curia Regis and Exchequer, does not remain side by side and unconnected with the shiremoot and the kindred institutions; it becomes just as much a part of the common law as the other: the ancient system of the shire rises to the highest functions of government; the authority of royal justice permeates the lowest regions of the popular organisation. The new consolidating process is one of organism, not of mere mechanism: the child's puzzle, the perfect chronometer, the living creature, symbolise three kinds or stages of creative skill, order, organisation, law; the point that our history reaches at the date of Magna Carta may be fixed as the transition from the second to the third stage.

Commixture of institutions.

Growth of the common law.

In tracing the minute steps of the process by which the commixture of race and institutions was so completed as to produce an organisation which grew into conscious life, we may follow a principle of arrangement different from that used in the eleventh and earlier chapters; and after examining the position of the king, divide the discussion under the four heads of legislation, taxation, the military system, and judicature; closing the history of the period with an attempt to trace the origin and development of that representative principle, which we shall find running through all the changes of administrative policy, and forming as it were the blending influence which enables the other elements to assimilate, or perhaps the breath of life which turns mere organism into living and conscious personality.

Plan of the following Chapter.

158. The very idea of kingship had developed since the age

The king.

Growth of the idea of kingship.

of the Conqueror. This had been one result of the struggle with the Church. The divine origin of royalty had been insisted on as an argument to force on the kings the sense of responsibility. This lesson had been familiar to the ancient English rulers, and its application had been summarily brought home. Edwy, like Rehoboam, had spurned the counsels of the fathers, and the men of the north had left him, and taken Edgar to be king. But the truth was less familiar, and the application less impressive to the Norman. The Conqueror had won England by the sword; and though he tried to rule it as a national king, it was not as one who would be brought to account: William Rufus had defied God and man: Henry I had compelled Anselm to give him a most forcible reminder of the source from which both king and prelate derived their power: Stephen had sinned against God and the people, and the hand of supreme power was traced in his humiliation. The events that were taking place on the Continent conveyed further lessons. In the old struggles between pope and emperor the zeal of righteousness was on the side of the latter: since the reign of Henry IV the balance of moral influence was with the popes; and the importance of that balance had been exemplified both in Germany and in France. The power of the pen was in the hands of the clergy: Hugh of Fleury had elaborately explained to Henry I the duties and rights which his position owed to its being ordained of God[1]. John of Salisbury, following Plutarch and setting up Trajan as the model of princes, had urged the contrast between the tyrant and the king such as he hoped to find in Henry II[2]. Yet these influences were thwarted by another set of ideas, not indeed running counter to them, but directed to a different aim. The clergy had exalted royalty in order to enforce its responsibilities on the conscience of the king; the lawyers exalted it in order to strengthen its authority as the source of law and justice; making the law honourable by magnifying the attributes of the lawgiver. And as the lawyers grew more powerful as a class, the theory of royalty approached more closely to absolutism: their

Moral and religious position of the king.

Scholastic view of kingship.

Legal theory of absolute sovereignty.

[1] See his work in Baluze's Miscellanea, ii. 184 sq.

[2] In the Polycraticus, throughout.

language has a tone, a force, and a consistent logic that is wanting to the exhortations of the churchmen. Yet even to the lawyer this ideal king was not the man who sat on the throne, but the power that would enforce the law. Glanvill cites and applies to Henry II the maxim of the Institutes, 'quod principi placuit, legis habet vigorem,'—a principle which, as Fortescue points out, is absolutely foreign to the ideas of English law[1]; and the author of the Dialogus de Scaccario, who, although himself a priest, represented both in life and in doctrine the ministerial lawyer, lays down that the deeds of kings are not to be discussed or condemned by inferior men, their hearts are in the hands of God, and it is by divine not by human judgment that their cause must stand or fall[2]. Happily a theory of absolutism is compatible with very strong and strict limitations in practice: yet it was probably under the idea that the king is the sovereign lord of his people that Richard I and John forsook the time-honoured practice of issuing a charter of liberties at the coronation. John's idea of his own position was definitely that of an absolute prince: when he heard the demands of the barons he inquired why they had not asked for the kingdom also, and swore that he would never grant them such liberties as would make him himself a slave[3]: yet the liberties they asked were those which his forefathers had been glad to offer to their people. Curiously enough it is in John that the territorial idea of royalty reaches its typical enunciation: all the kings before him had called themselves on their great seals kings of the English: John is the first whose title appears on that solemn and sovereign emblem as *Rex Angliae*.

Influence of the imperial idea.

Practical limitations.

John's idea of his own position.

The growth of real power in the king's hands had advanced in proportion to the theory. Every measure of internal policy by which the great vassals had been repressed, or the people strengthened to keep them in check, had increased the direct influence of the crown; and the whole tendency of the ministerial system had been in the same direction. Hence it was that John was able so long to play the part of a tyrant, and

Growth of real power.

[1] De laudibus Legum Angliae, ch. 9.
[2] Dialogus, praef.; Select Charters, p. 161. [3] M. Paris, p. 254.

that the barons had to enforce the Charter by measures which for the time were an exercise on their part of sovereign power.

Claim of the king to the rule of the British islands.

Somewhat of the greatness of the royal position was owing to the claim, which at this period was successfully urged, to the supreme rule of the British islands; a claim which had been made under the descendants of Alfred, and was regarded by tradition as really established by Edgar. The princes of Wales had acknowledged the suzerainty of the Conqueror, and had been from time to time forced into formal submission by William Rufus and Henry I: but Stephen had been able to do little on that side of the island.

Homage of Wales.

The three Welsh wars of Henry II were not amongst his most successful expeditions, yet by arms or by negotiations he managed to secure the homage of the princes [1], on one of whom he bestowed his own sister in marriage [2]. On Richard's accession the homage was again demanded, and a scutage was raised on the pretext of an expedition to enforce it. Yet when Rhys ap Griffith, the king of South Wales, came to Oxford for the purpose of negotiation, Richard refused to meet him [3], and it does not appear that he ever renewed his homage. On the death of Rhys, the disputed succession to his principality was settled by archbishop Hubert as justiciar [4], and Griffith his successor appeared as a vassal of the English king at the court of John [5]. There seems to have been no reluctance to accept the nominal superiority of England, so long as it was compatible with practical independence.

Ecclesiastical dependence of Wales.

But the fact that their bishops received their consecration at Canterbury, and were, from the reign of Henry I, elected and admitted under the authority of the kings of England, is sufficient to prove that anything like real sovereignty was lost to the so-

[1] Henry's three Welsh wars were in 1157, 1163, and 1165. Homage was performed by the princes at Woodstock July 1, 1163: and they attended his court at Gloucester in 1175. In 1177 they swore fealty at Oxford in May. In 1184 they provoked the king to prepare for another expedition; but when he had reached Worcester, Rhys ap Griffith met him and did homage. The South Welsh were again in arms in 1186. The princes of North Wales, after the marriage of David with the king's sister, were faithful, and adhered to Henry in the rebellion of 1173.

[2] Bened. i. 162. [3] Bened. ii. 97. [4] Hoveden, iv. 21.

[5] Hoveden, iv. 142.

called kings of Wales. They were divided amongst themselves, and the highest object of their political aims was from time to time to throw their weight on the side of the disaffected barons who were their neighbours: creating difficulties in the way of the king of England, which prevented him from meddling with them. But his formal suzerainty was admitted. 'What Christian,' says Matthew Paris, 'knows not that the prince of Wales is a petty vassal (vassalulus) of the king of England[1]?'

Policy of the Welsh princes.

It was very different with Scotland, although Malcolm Canmore had under the spell of the Conqueror's power done formal homage to him, and each of the sons of Margaret had in turn sought support against his competitors at the court of Henry I. The complicated question of the Scottish homage, an obligation based, it is said, on the commendation of the Scots to Edward the Elder, on the grant of Cumberland by Edmund to Malcolm, and on the grant of Lothian by Edgar or Canute to the king of Scots, was one of those diplomatic knots which are kept unsolved by mutual reservations until the time comes when they must be cut by the sword. And to these obscure points a new complication was added when David of Scotland, who had obtained the English earldom of Huntingdon, succeeded to his brother's throne. Henry the son of David received the earldom of Northumberland from Stephen, and his father kept during the whole of Stephen's reign a hold on that county as well as Cumberland and Westmoreland, partly in the alleged interest of his niece the empress, partly perhaps with the intention of claiming those territories as rightfully belonging to his Cumbrian principality. Henry II not only obtained the restoration of the northern counties from Malcolm IV, but compelled him to do homage[2]: William the Lion, who succeeded Malcolm, acted throughout his whole reign as a vassal of England, attending the royal courts and acquiescing for the most part in a superiority which it

Question of the Scottish homage.

Its complications.

[1] M. Paris, p. 626.

[2] Malcolm IV did homage to Henry II at Chester in 1157; he attended him at the siege of Toulouse, and was knighted by him at Tours in 1159. He did homage to the younger Henry at Woodstock in 1163. These homages were apparently due for the county of Huntingdon.

Scottish homage from 1174 to 1189.

would have been folly to dispute[1]. After the unsuccessful attempt in 1174 to assist the rebellious earls, in which he was defeated and captured, Henry II imposed on him the most abject terms of submission: compelling him to surrender the castles of Lothian, and to enforce on his bishops and barons a direct oath of fealty to the English crown. From that obligation Richard released him for the sum of ten thousand marks; but neither Henry's exaction of the homage, nor Richard's renunciation of it, affected the pre-existent claims. With William the Lion it was a far more important object to recover Northumberland, Cumberland, and Westmoreland, than to vindicate his formal independence. The states he ruled or claimed to rule were as yet unconsolidated: he had little authority in the real Scotland that lay beyond the Forth, and from which his royal title was derived. The English-speaking provinces, which he held as lord of Lothian and of Strath Clyde, were as yet no more Scottish than the counties which he wished to add to them. Yet both he and his people aimed at an independence very different from that of Wales. The Scottish bishops, who from the beginning of the twelfth century had struggled against the attempt to reduce them to dependence on York or Canterbury, refused to submit themselves to the English Church, even when they swore fealty to the English king; and actually obtained from Pope Clement III a declaration that they were subject immediately and solely to the apostolic see itself. The

The Scottish church made immediately dependent on Rome.

[1] William succeeded his brother in 1165; in 1166 he followed Henry II to Normandy, according to the Chronicle of Melrose, as a vassal, but returned shortly after. In 1170 he and his brother David did homage to the younger Henry, according to Lord Hailes for Huntingdon, according to Lord Lyttleton for Lothian: there is no decisive evidence on the point. After his release from imprisonment he frequently attended the English court; especially at Northampton in 1176, at Winchester in 1177, at Nottingham in 1179, in Normandy in 1181, at Nottingham in the same year, at London in 1185, at Marlborough in 1186. He attended on Richard at Canterbury in 1189, and was there relieved from the bondage imposed by Henry II; and was again at court in 1194 at Nottingham. In 1200 he did homage to John at Lincoln, 'salvo jure suo.' At this time the county of Huntingdon was in the hands of his brother David; it is therefore difficult to see for what the homage could have been due, unless it were for the traditional claim. Possibly William yielded it in the hope of recovering the northern counties, in which he did not succeed.

Scottish barons, even before they had been released by Richard, refused to be bound by the English undertaking to pay the Saladin tithe[1]. When it is remembered that a large portion of these barons were adventurers of Norman descent, who had obtained estates in the Lowlands, too far from the English court to fear royal interference, it is not difficult to see how the feudal principle gained its footing in Scotland in such strength as to colour all its later history. The Scottish constitution, as it appears under king David, was a copy of the English system as it existed under Henry I, but without the safeguards which the royal strength should have imposed on the great vassals. Hence the internal weakness which so long counteracted the determined efforts of the people for national independence. The anomalous condition of the principality of Galloway, which, as an outlying portion of the Strath Clyde kingdom, clung to English protection to evade incorporation with Scotland, and was from the beginning of the twelfth century subject ecclesiastically to York, gave the English kings another standing-point beyond the border[2]. But although Henry II raised an army for the reduction of Galloway in 1186, and even marched as far northwards as Carlisle, his successors did not regard the question as worthy of a struggle. Alan of Galloway appears amongst the barons, by whose counsel John issued the charter,

Refusal to pay the Saladin tithe.

English influence in Scotland.

Relation of Galloway to England and Scotland.

[1] Bened. ii. 44.

[2] Galloway was under the rule of Fergus, an almost independent prince (princeps), who was connected by marriage with Henry I, until the year 1160, when the country was subdued by Malcolm. Fergus then became a canon and died the next year. On the outbreak of war in 1173, the sons of Fergus expelled the Scottish officers from their country, and in 1174 Henry sent envoys to invite them to become his vassals. They however quarrelled among themselves, and Henry, finding that they intended to make a tool of him, abstained from further negotiations; and William did homage for Galloway as well as Scotland. In 1176 however the king of Scots compelled Gilbert of Galloway, who had murdered his own brother Uhtred, to do homage to Henry, as a Scottish baron, under the terms of the treaty of Falaise. In 1184 Gilbert rebelled against William the Lion, and died before the war was over, in 1185, leaving his heir in Henry's hands. The territory was seized by his nephew, Ronald, against whom Henry marched in 1186. Ronald however met him at Carlisle and did homage: he retained the principality until he died in 1200 at the English court. Alan, his son and successor, married a daughter of David of Huntingdon, and was the father of Dervorguilla Balliol. Galloway furnished a portion of Henry II's mercenary troops.

Galloway dependent ecclesiastically on York.

and the bishops of Whithern received consecration and mission at York, down to the middle of the fourteenth century; but the territory was gradually and completely incorporated with Scotland, as Scotland gradually and completely realised her own national identity: Dervorguilla, the heiress of the princes of Galloway, was the mother of John Balliol, king of Scots.

Claims of the kings on Ireland.

Over Ireland as a whole the claims of the Anglo-Saxon kings were only titular. Edgar however, who had obtained the submission of the Northumbrian Danes, had apparently acted as patron also of the Ostmen in Ireland[1]. Canute may not improbably have done the same; and when those settlers sought and obtained an ecclesiastical organisation in the reign of the Conqueror they received their bishops from Canterbury. But nothing more had been done; and it is uncertain whether in the most extensive claims of the Anglo-Saxon kings to the 'imperium' of all the British isles[2], Ireland was even in thought included. Henry II however, very early in his reign, conceived the notion of conquering the sister island. In his first year he obtained from the English Pope, Adrian IV, the bull *Laudabiliter*, in which, by virtue of a forced construction of the forged donation of Constantine, the pontiff, as lord of all islands, bestowed Ireland on the English king[3]. In the council of Winchester, held the same year, Henry proposed an expedition to conquer the country as a kingdom for his brother William, but was dissuaded by the empress[4]; and the gift remained a dead letter until 1167, when the quarrels of the native princes opened the way for the piratical attempts of Richard of Clare. In 1171 Henry himself, determined to avoid the Roman legation, went, as we have already seen, to Ireland and received the formal

The bull *Laudabiliter*.

Henry proposes a conquest of Ireland.

[1] Coins of Ethelred and Canute, if not also of Edgar, were struck at Dublin; Robertson, Essays, p. 198; Ruding, Annals of the Coinage, i. 262–276; and Nicolas of Worcester in a letter to Eadmer counts the king of Dublin among Edgar's vassals. Cf. Kemble, Cod. Dipl. ii. 404.

[2] 'Ego Aethelred gentis gubernator Angligenae totiusque insulae coregulus Britannicae et caeterarum insularum in circuitu adjacentium.' Kemble, Cod. Dipl. iii. 337; cf. 348, iv. 23.

[3] Giraldus Cambrensis, Opp. v. 316. Cf. Joh. Salisb. Metalogicus, iv. c. 42. John of Salisbury brought an emerald ring from the pope to Henry II by way of investiture.

[4] Robert de Monte, A.D. 1155.

obedience of both kings and prelates, the king of Connaught, who alone resisted, making his submission by treaty in 1175[1]. In 1177 John was made lord of Ireland, and received the homage of some of the barons, amongst whom his father portioned out the country, which was as yet unconquered[2]. In 1185 he was sent over to exercise authority in person, but he signally failed to show any capacity for government, and was recalled in disgrace. Henry seems to have thought that a formal coronation might secure for his son the obedience of the Irish, and obtained from Urban III licence to make him king, and the licence was accompanied by a crown of gold and peacock's feathers[3]. But although a special legate was sent for the purpose in 1187, John was never crowned, and the kings of England remained lords only of Ireland until Henry VIII took the title of king without coronation. John, during the years of the Interdict, made an expedition to Ireland, in which he had some success, bringing the English settlers, who already aimed at independence, into something like order. But the lordship of Ireland was little more than honorary; the native population were driven into semi-barbarism, and the intruding race were scarcely subject even in name to the English crown. The resignation of the kingdom of England to the pope in 1213 was, however, accompanied by the surrender and restoration of Ireland also; and of the annual tribute of a thousand marks, three-tenths were assigned to Ireland, whilst seven-tenths were to be paid for England. The fact that Ireland had in 1151 received a new ecclesiastical constitution from Pope Eugenius probably saved it from annexation to the province of Canterbury, or to the jurisdiction of the primate of England.

The submission of the Irish princes; and the feudal division of Ireland.

John and his successors lords of Ireland.

New ecclesiastical constitution of Ireland.

Whilst the king of England was thus asserting and partially realising imperial claims over his neighbours in the British islands, he was in his continental relations involved in a net of homages and other kindred obligations, which might seem to derogate from the idea of royalty as much as the former magnified it. As duke of Normandy he was a vassal of the king of

Homages paid by the kings for foreign fiefs.

[1] Benedict, i. 101–103. [2] Ib. i. 161, 165. [3] Hoveden, ii. 307.

Homage for Normandy.

France; and as dukes of Aquitaine, counts of Poictou, and counts of Anjou, Henry II and his sons stood in still more complicated feudal connexion. The Norman kings had avoided as much as possible even the semblance of dependence. The Conqueror was not called on after the Conquest to do homage to his suzerain, and William Rufus never was duke of Normandy. Henry I claimed the duchy during the life of Robert, but he avoided the necessity of the ceremony by making his son receive the formal investiture[1]; and Stephen followed the same plan, to secure Normandy for Eustace[2]. In these cases the royal dignity was saved by throwing the duty of homage upon the heir; David king of Scots had allowed his son Henry to take the oath to Stephen, and thus avoided a ceremony which, although it might not have humiliated, would certainly have compromised him[3].

Homage of Henry II for Normandy, Anjou, and Aquitaine.

Henry II had performed all the feudal ceremonies due to Lewis VII before he obtained the English crown[4]; and on the succession of Philip would willingly have devolved the renewal of homage on the sons amongst whom his great foreign dominion was to be divided[5]. When however, after the death of his eldest son, he found himself in 1183 obliged to make a fresh settlement of his estates, with that politic craft which he embodied in his saying that it was easier to repent of words than of deeds, he sacrificed his pride to his security, and did formal homage to his young rival[6]. Richard had done the same before his accession, and was not called on to repeat it[7].

Homage of John.

John, after in vain attempting to avoid it, and after seeing Arthur invested with Normandy and the other paternal fiefs, yielded, as his father had done, to expediency, and performed in

[1] William the Etheling did homage for Normandy in 1119. Cont. F. Wig.; W. Malmesb. G. R. v. § 419.

[2] In 1137; Hen. Hunt. fol. 222; Hoveden, i. 192.

[3] Hen. Hunt. fol. 221, 222; Hoveden, i. 190, 191.

[4] He did homage for Normandy in 1151 to Lewis VII. R. de Monte, (Bouquet, xiii. 292).

[5] The younger Henry acted as seneschal of France at the coronation of Philip II. Bened. i. 242.

[6] Hoveden, ii. 284; Bened. i. 306.

[7] At least no mention is made of the repetition of the ceremony in the account of his interview with Philip immediately after his father's death, Bened. ii. 74.

A.D. 1200 the homage which was a few years later made one of the pleas for his forfeiture[1]. His mother was still alive, and from her he chose to hold Aquitaine, she in her turn doing the homage to the suzerain[2].

Disparagement of the Crown by surrender.

If the royal consecration was supposed to confer such dignity that it was a point of honour to avoid, if possible, the simple ceremonies of homage and fealty for fiefs for which it was justly due, it was only in the greatest emergency and under the most humiliating circumstances that the wearer of the crown could divest himself of his right and receive it again as the gift of his temporary master. Yet this, if we are to believe the historians, happened twice in the short period before us.

Cases of Richard and John.

Richard was compelled to resign the crown of England to Henry VI during his captivity; and John surrendered his kingdom to Innocent III: in both cases it was restored as a fief, subject to tribute: and in the former case the bargain was annulled by the emperor before his death, although Richard was regarded by the electors who chose Otho IV as one of the principal members of the empire[3]. It has been stated that Henry II made a similar surrender, or took a similar oath to the pope on the occasion of his absolution at Avranches:

No such act done by Henry II.

this however was not the case; the fealty which he swore was merely promised to Alexander III as the Catholic pope, not as his feudal lord, and the oath simply bound him not to recognise the antipope[4]. John during his brother's life was said to have undertaken to hold the kingdom as a fief under Philip II if he would help him to win it; but this may have been a mere rumour[5].

View of the pope and emperor.

It can scarcely be thought probable that either Henry VI or Innocent III, although both entertained an idea of universal empire, deliberately contrived the reduction of England to feudal dependence; both took advantage of the opportunity which

[1] Hoveden, iv. 115; R. Coggeshale, p. 172.

[2] Rot. Chart. p. 130; Rigord (Bouquet, xvii. 50); W. Covent. ii. pref. xxxiv.

[3] Hoveden, iii. 202, 203; iv. 37, 38.

[4] It is not clear however that the pope did not intend Henry to bind himself to homage and fealty, and so to hold the kingdom of the papacy. See Robertson's Becket, p. 303.

[5] Hoveden, iii. 204.

Humiliating character of the act.

deprived their victims for the moment of the power of resistance. Richard made his surrender with the advice of his mother, his most experienced counsellor; and John accepted his humiliation with the counsel and consent of all parties, bitterly as they felt it, and strongly as they resented the conduct by which he had made it necessary[1]. In neither case would much heroism have been shown by resistance to the demand: Richard's misfortune and John's misgovernment had left them practically without alternative.

Disuse of the corona-tion-days.

The ceremonial attributes and pomp of royalty changed but little under these sovereigns. The form and matter of the coronation service remained, so far as we have documentary evidence, unaltered: Henry II during his first three years wore his crown in solemn state on the great festivals, though he so far varied the ancient rule as to hold his court on those days at S. Edmund's, Lincoln, and Worcester: but after A.D. 1158 he gave up the custom altogether. Richard only once, after his consecration, wore his crown in state; and John went through the ceremony twice, once on the occasion of his wife's coronation[2]. The venerable practice was distasteful to Henry II, who disliked public ceremonial and grudged needless expense. Richard's constant absence from England, and John's unfriendly relations with Archbishop Langton and the barons, prevented its revival.

The custom obsolete.

The improvement in the legal machinery of the kingdom had deprived it of its former usefulness, and the performance of the grand serjeanties which were due at the coronations might by agreement take place on other occasions, as at the great court held at Guildford in 1186[3].

Pomp of Richard and John.

In other points both Richard and John showed themselves inclined to advance rather than abate the pomp of their position. Richard is the first king who regularly uses the plural 'we' in the granting of charters; John,

[1] Matthew Paris says that the surrender was made by the unanimous consent of all parties (p. 235). The Barnwell canon, copied by Walter of Coventry, allows that the act was politic, although it appeared to many an 'ignominious and enormous yoke of slavery' (ii. 210). In the document itself John states that he acts 'communi consilio baronum suorum.'

[2] Hoveden, iv. 169, 182; above, p. 517.

[3] Benedict, ii. 3; above, p. 489, n. 4.

as we have seen, is the first who formally calls himself the king of the land instead of the king of the people. John is *Rex Angliae.*

Regency in the king's absence.

The long absences of the kings threw additional power, or a firmer tenure of power, into the hands of the justiciars. Yet it may be questioned whether Henry II did not contemplate the institution of a practice according to which either himself or his eldest son should be constantly present in England. The younger Henry is found, both before and after his coronation, acting in his father's place: not only as the centre of courtly pomp, but transacting business, issuing writs, presiding in the Curia, and discharging other functions which seem to belong to regency[1]. During the interregnum which followed Henry's death, his widow acted in her son's name, proclaiming his peace and directing the oaths of fealty to be taken to him; and during his captivity she is found at the head of the administration both in England and Normandy, acting with rather than through the justiciar. John, after the fall of Longchamp in 1191, was recognised by the barons as ruler of the kingdom[2] in his brother's stead. These facts seem to indicate that the viceregal character, which the justiciar certainly possessed, was not without its limits: whilst from the fact that earl Robert of Leicester is found acting together with the justiciar Richard de Lucy[3] during the absence of Henry and his sons, it may be argued that the king avoided trusting even that most loyal servant with a monopoly of ministerial power. But we have not sufficient evidence to define the exact position of either the members of the royal family or the justiciar; and it is very probable that it was not settled even at this time by any other rule than that of temporary convenience.

The younger Henry.

Queen Eleanor.

John.

The justiciar.

159. The national council under Henry II and his sons seems

[1] He was present at Becket's election to the primacy in 1162; R. de Diceto, c. 532: also when Becket received the quittance, in the Exchequer, of his accounts as chancellor; Vita S. T. C., Grim, p. 15; Roger of Pontigny, pp. 107, 108. He must have been quite an infant at the time. After his coronation he had a chancellor and a seal-bearer or vice-chancellor, and that at a time when his father had dispensed with a chancellor.

[2] 'Summus rector totius regni;' R. Devizes, p. 38; above, p. 500.

[3] As for example in 1165, when he refused the kiss of peace to the archbishop of Cologne as a schismatic; R. Diceto, c. 539.

The national council in two aspects; as a feudal court and as a stage towards the representation of estates.

in one aspect to be a realisation of the principle which was introduced at the Conquest, and had been developed and grown into consistency under the Norman kings, that of a complete council of feudal tenants-in-chief. In another aspect it appears to be in a stage of transition towards that combined representation of the three estates and of the several provincial communities which especially marks our constitution, and which perhaps was the ideal, imperfectly grasped and more imperfectly realised, at which the statesmen of the middle ages almost unconsciously aimed. The constituent members of this assembly are the same as under the Norman kings, but greater prominence and a more definite position are assigned to the minor tenants-in-chief; there is a growing recognition of their real constitutional importance, a gradual definition of their title to be represented and of the manner of representation, and a growing tendency to admit not only them, but the whole body of smaller landowners, of whom the minor tenants-in-chief are but an insignificant portion, to the same rights. This latter tendency may be described as directed towards the concentration of the representation of the counties in the national parliament,—the combination of the shiremoots with the witenagemot of the kingdom.

Gradual definition of the position of the feudal tenants.

Possible arrangements of the council.

The royal council, as distinct from the mere assembly and court of the household, might consist of either the magnates, the greater barons, the 'proceres' of the Conqueror's reign; or of the whole body of tenants-in-chief, as was the accepted usage under Henry II; or of the whole body of landowners, whoever their feudal lords might be, which was the case in the great councils of 1086 and 1116, and which, when the representative principle was fully recognised, became the theory of the medieval constitution. These three bodies were divided by certain lines, although those lines were not very definite. The greater barons held a much greater extent of land than the minor tenants-in-chief: they made a separate agreement with the Crown for their reliefs, and probably for their other payments in aid[1]: they had, as we learn from Magna Carta, their several summonses to the great councils, and they led their vassals to the host under their

The greater and lesser barons.

[1] Dialogus de Scaccario, ii. cc. 10, 24.

own banner. The entire body of tenants-in-chief included besides these the minor barons, the knightly body, and the socage tenants of the crown, who paid their reliefs to the sheriff, were summoned to court or council through his writ, and appeared under his banner in the military levy of the county. The general body of freeholders comprised, besides these two bodies, all the feudal tenants of the barons and the freemen of the towns and villages, who had a right or duty of appearing in the county court, who were armed in the fyrd or under the assize of arms, who were bound to the Crown simply by the oath of allegiance taken in the shiremoot, and were qualified to determine by their sworn evidence the rights of their neighbours, the assessment of their goods, and the report of their neighbourhood as to criminals.

The entire body of tenants-in-chief.

The general body of freeholders.

These three possible assemblies may be regarded again as the assembly in its ordinary, extraordinary, and theoretical form: the national council usually contained only the magnates; on great occasions it contained the whole body of the tenants-in-chief; in idea it was the representation of the nation; and on one or two very rare occasions that idea was partially realised. But there were departments of national action in which the uncertainty and indefiniteness of such a theory were inadmissible. For the payment of taxes all men must be brought under contribution, for the efficiency of the national host all men must be brought together in arms. For the first of these purposes they might be visited in detail, for the second they must be assembled in person. Accordingly we find that the military levies in which Henry II brought together the whole kingdom in arms, as for the siege of Bridgnorth in 1155 or for the expedition to Normandy in 1177, may have really been steps towards the assembling of the nation for other purposes; and when, as in the latter case, we find the king acting by the counsel of the assembled host[1], we recur in thought to that ancient time when

Ordinary, extraordinary, and theoretical forms.

Military levies a general assembly of the nation.

[1] Bened. i. 178: 'Venerunt etiam illuc ad eum comites et barones et milites regni per summonitionem suam, parati equis et armis secum transfretare in Normanniam. . . . Congregatis itaque omnibus in urbe Wintoniae rex *per consilium eorum* transfretationem suam distulit.' Immediately after, the 'consiliarii' of the king are mentioned as advising him about the garrisons of the castles.

National concentration in arms.

the only general assembly was that of the nation in arms. But the nation in arms was merely the meeting of the shires in arms: the men who in council or in judgment made up the county court, in arms composed the 'exercitus scirae:' on occasion of taxation or local consultation they were the wise men, the legales homines of the shiremoot. The king's general council is then one day to comprise the collective wisdom of the shires, as his army comprises their collective strength. But it is very rarely as yet that the principle of national concentration, which has been applied to the host, is applied to the council.

Constitution of the national council as stated in the Great Charter.

The point at which the growth of this principle had arrived during the period before us is marked by the fourteenth article of the Great Charter: 'To have the common counsel of the kingdom' for the assessment of extraordinary aids and scutages, 'we will cause to be summoned the archbishops, bishops, abbots, earls, and greater barons singly by our letters; and besides we will cause to be summoned in general by our sheriffs and bailiffs all those who hold of us in chief; to a certain day, that is to say, at a term of forty days at least; and to a certain place; and in all the letters of such summons we will express the cause of the summons; and the summons having been so made, the business shall on the day assigned proceed according to the counsel of those who shall be present, although not all who have been summoned shall have come.' The council is thus no longer limited to the magnates; but it is not extended so as to include the whole nation, it halts at the tenants-in-chief: nor are its functions of advising on all matters recognised, it is simply to be assembled for the imposing of taxation. The provision, that the determination of the members present shall be regarded as the proceeding of the whole body summoned, enunciates in words the principle which had long been acted upon, that absence, like silence, on such occasion implies consent.

A stage of transition.

Writs of summons.

The use of a written summons to call together the council must have been very ancient, but we have no evidence of the date at which it became the rule. The great courts held on the festivals of the Church might not indeed require such a summons, but every special assembly of the sort—and very many such occur from the earliest days of the Norman reigns—must have been convoked by a distinct writ. Such writs were of two kinds: there was first a special summons declaring the cause of meeting, addressed to every man whose presence was absolutely requisite; thus for the sessions of the Exchequer each of the king's debtors was summoned by a writ declaring the sum for which he was called upon to account[1]: and secondly there was a general summons, such as those addressed to the several counties through their sheriffs to bring together the shiremoot to meet the justices or the officers of the forest[2]. The former was delivered directly to the person to whom it was addressed; the latter was proclaimed by the servants of the sheriff in the villages and market towns, and obeyed by those who were generally described in the writ itself, as their business, inclination, or fear of the penalty for non-attendance, might dispose them. On this analogy the writs of summons to the national council were probably of two sorts: those barons who in their military, fiscal, and legal transactions dealt directly with the king were summoned by special writ; those tenants-in-chief who transacted their business with the sheriff were convened, not by a writ in which they were severally named, but by a general summons. Of the greater barons the first person summoned was the archbishop of Canterbury, and it is from the mention by the historians of the offence offered to Becket by neglecting this customary respect that we learn the existence of the double system of summons in the early years of Henry II[3]. The Pipe Rolls however contain very frequent mention of payments made to the summoners, and that in direct connexion with meetings of the council[4]. In 1175 Henry went so far as to forbid those who had been lately in arms against him to appear at his court at all without summons[5]. It is a strange thing that so very few of these early writs are now in existence: the most ancient that we have is one addressed to the bishop of Salisbury

Two sorts of writs of summons: the special,

and the general.

Summons of the greater barons.

Summons of the minor tenants.

Importance of summons.

[1] See the chapters on Summons in the Dialogus de Scaccario, ii. cc. 1, 2.

[2] Such are the 'communes summonitiones' mentioned in Art. 44 of the Great Charter.

[3] See above, p. 467. [4] Ibid. note 3. [5] See above, p. 483.

First extant writ, of 1205.

in 1205, ten years before the granting of the Charter. This document fixes the date of the assembly, which is to be held at London on the Sunday before Ascension Day, and the cause of the meeting, which is to discuss the message brought by the envoys from Philip of France; and it also contains a clause of general summons, directing the bishop to warn the abbots and priors of his diocese to be present on the occasion [1]. Of the general forms of summons addressed to the sheriffs, we have no specimens earlier than the date at which representative institutions had been to a great extent adopted: but if we may judge of their tenour from the like writs issued for military and fiscal purposes, they must have enumerated the classes of persons summoned in much the same way as they were enumerated in the writs ordering the assembly of the county court [2]. Of this however it is impossible to be quite certain. That the county court had a special form of summons for the purpose of taxation we learn from a writ of Henry I, which has been already quoted [3]. It is probable that the clause of Magna Carta represents no more than the recognised theory of the system of summons; a system which was already passing away; for besides that council at S. Alban's in 1213 in which the several townships of royal demesne were represented as in the county court by the reeve and four best men, a council was called at Oxford in the same year in which each county was represented by four discreet men, who were to attend on the king 'to talk with him on the business of the kingdom.' In the writ by which this council is summoned, and which is dated on the 7th of November at Witney, we have the first extant evidence of the representation of the counties in the council [4]; they were already accustomed to elect small numbers of knights for legal and fiscal purposes, and the practice of making such elections to expedite the proceedings of the itinerant justices is confirmed by the Great Charter itself. It is then just possible that the 14th

Summons of the county court.

Summons of four discreet knights in 1213.

[1] Select Charters, p. 274.

[2] Examples, of the reign of Henry III, are in the Select Charters, pp. 334, 349, 365, &c.

[3] Above, p. 393.

[4] Select Charters, p. 279; above, p. 528.

clause may have been intended to cover the practice of county representation which had been used two years before. The further development of the system belongs to a later stage of our inquiries.

Members of the Council.

The character of the persons summoned requires no comment: the archbishops and bishops were the same in number as before, but the abbots and priors were a rapidly increasing body. The number of earls increased very slowly: it may be questioned whether Henry II founded any new earldoms, or whether the two or three ascribed to him were not merely those which, having been created by his mother or Stephen, he vouchsafed to confirm [1]. None were created by Richard; and by John only the earldom of Winchester, which was founded in favour of one of the coheirs of the earldom of Leicester, the latter title being taken by the other coheir. The number of great baronies however was probably on the increase, although we have not sufficient data, either as to the possessors or as to the exact character of such baronies, to warrant a very positive statement. The number of minor tenants-in-chief who attended cannot even be conjectured: but, as the clergy of inferior dignity formed an appreciable part of the council, it is probable that the knights who, without yet possessing a representative character, came up from the shires in consequence of the general summons, were a considerable body: and sometimes they were very numerous. The presence of a large number of deans and archdeacons is mentioned on some special occasions [2], which seem to indicate a plan of assembling the three estates in something like completeness: but we have no reason to suppose that they were ever summoned as a matter of right or as tenants-in-chief.

Earldoms and great baronies.

Minor tenants and clergy.

[1] William of Albini of Arundel was made earl of the county of Sussex by charter in 1155; and Aubrey de Vere about the same time. Henry confirmed the earldoms of Norfolk and Hereford, and the grant to Aubrey de Vere was no doubt a confirmation also. Richard gave charters to William of Arundel and Roger Bigod: John restored the earldom of Hereford in favour of Henry de Bohun, and created that of Winchester for Saer de Quincy. The earldom of Devon is said to have been created by Henry I for Richard of Redvers, and should have been mentioned above, p. 361. See the Fifth Report on the Dignity of a Peer, App. pp. 1–5.

[2] For example on the occasion of the Spanish award in 1177, Bened. i. 145; and at S. Paul's in 1213, M. Paris, p. 240.

Times of holding councils.

The times of assembly were very irregular. In many cases, especially in the early years of Henry II, they coincided with the great festivals, or with the terminal days which were already beginning to be observed by the lawyers. But so great a number of occasional councils were called by Henry, and so few by his sons, that obviously no settled rule can have been observed. And the same remark is true as regards the place of meeting. The festival courts were still frequently kept at Winchester and Westminster; but for the great national gatherings for homage, for proclamation of Crusade, or the like, some central position, such as Northampton or its neighbourhood, was often preferred. Yet some of Henry II's most important acts were done in councils held in the forest palaces, such as Clarendon and Woodstock. Richard's two councils were held in middle England, one at Pipewell in Northamptonshire, the other at Nottingham; both places in which the weariness of state business might be lightened by the royal amusement of the chase.

Name of parliament.

The name given to these sessions of council was often expressed by the Latin *colloquium*[1]: and it is by no means unlikely that the name of parliament, which is used as early as 1175 by Jordan Fantosme[2], may have been in common use. But of this we have no distinct instance in the Latin Chroniclers for some years further, although when the term comes into use it is applied retrospectively; and in a record of the 28th year of Henry III the assembly in which the Great Charter was granted is mentioned as the 'Parliamentum Runimedae.'

Subjects of deliberation.

The subjects on which the kings asked the advice of the body thus constituted were very numerous: it might almost seem that Henry II consulted his court and council on every matter of importance that arose during his reign; all the business that Richard personally transacted was done in his great councils;

[1] e. g. M. Paris, p. 240.

[2] Jordan Fantosme, p. 14. It is used by Otto Morena of the diet or parliament of Roncaglia held by Frederick I in 1154; Leibnitz, Scr. Rer. Brunswic. i. 809. It is first used in England by a contemporary writer in 1246, namely by M. Paris, p. 696; see Hody, History of Convocation, p. 326. It is a word of Italian origin, and may have been introduced either through the Normans, or through intercourse with the French kingdom.

and even John, who acted far more in the manner and spirit of a despot than did his father or brother, did little in the first half of his reign without a formal show of respect towards his constitutional advisers. Nor is there any reason to suppose that such a proceeding was, in the great proportion of instances, merely a matter of form: a sovereign who is practically absolute asks counsel whenever he wants it; and such a sovereign, if he is a man of good sense, with reason for self-confidence, is not trammelled by the jealousies or by the need of self-assertion which are inseparable from the position of a monarch whose prerogatives are constitutionally limited. Hence it was perhaps that these kings, besides constantly laying before their barons all questions touching the state of the kingdom [1],—matters of public policy such as the destruction of the illegal castles and the maintenance of the royal hold on the fortresses, matters relating to legislation, to the administration of justice, to taxation, and to military organisation,—also took their opinion on peace and war, alliances, royal marriages, and even in questions of arbitration between foreign powers which had been specially referred to the king for decision [2]. Of such deliberations abundant instances have been given in the last chapter. It is very rarely that any record is preserved of opposition to or even remonstrance against the royal will. In 1175 Richard de Lucy ventured to remind Henry II, when he was enforcing the law against the destroyers of the forests, that the waste of vert and venison had been authorised by his own writ; but his mediation was summarily set aside [3]: the remonstrances likewise of the one or two counsellors who during the Becket quarrel interposed on behalf of the archbishop, were either tacitly disregarded or resented as an advocacy of the king's

General deliberations.

Miscellaneous matters.

Opposition to the royal will.

[1] Such was the assembly at Bermondsey in 1154 'de statu regni;' Gervase, c. 1377: that 'de statutis regni' at London in 1170, and at Northampton in 1176; Bened. i. 4, 107.

[2] In 1176 Henry II consulted his council before assenting to the marriage of his daughter Johanna; in 1177 he consulted the great assembly of feudal tenants held at Winchester, on the expediency of proceeding with the war. In 1155 he had consulted them on an expedition to Ireland. In 1177 he took their advice on the Spanish arbitration. Benedict, i. 116, 142, 178; R. de Monte, A.D. 1155.

[3] Bened. i. 94.

enemy. Still less are we to look for any power of initiating measures of either public policy or particular reform in any hands but those of the king. The justiciar however probably advised the king on all these matters, and perhaps suggested the administrative changes which he had to work out in their details; in this respect acting as the spokesman of the barons, as the archbishop acted as the spokesman of the Church, and exercising over the king a less overt but more effectual influence than could have been asserted by the barons except at the risk of rebellion. John certainly chafed under the advice of the justiciar, without venturing to dismiss him. In all these matters the regard, even if merely formal, shown by the king to the advice and consent of his barons has a constitutional value, as affording a precedent and suggesting a method for securing the exercise of the right of advising and consenting when the balance of power was changed, and advice and consent meant more than mere helpless acquiescence. The part taken by the national council in legislation, taxation, and judicature may be noticed as we proceed with the examination of those departments of public work.

Position of the justiciar as spokesman of the council.

Position of the Church councils.

The ecclesiastical councils of the period did their work with very little interference from the secular power, and with very little variation from the earlier model. Their privilege of legislating with the royal acquiescence was not disputed, and their right to a voice in the bestowal of their contributions towards the wants of the State came into gradual recognition in the reign of John: but although his expedients for the raising of money may now and then have served as precedents upon which the claim to give or to refuse might be raised on behalf of the several orders in Church and State, no complete system of separate action by the clergy on secular matters was as yet devised, nor was their position as a portion of the common council of the realm defined by the Great Charter apart from that of the other tenants-in-chief. The theory of the Three Estates had yet to be worked into practice; although there were signs of its growing importance.

Legislation.

160. Great as was the legal reputation of Henry II, and greatly

Form of legislation; the Assize.

as the legal system of England advanced under him and his sons, the documentary remains of the legislation of the period are very scanty. The work of Glanvill is not a book of statutes, but a manual of practice; and although it incorporates no doubt the words of ordinances which had the force of laws, it nowhere gives the literal text of such enactments. The formal edicts known under the name of Assizes, the Assizes of Clarendon and Northampton, the Assize of Arms, the Assize of the Forest, and the Assizes of Measures are the only relics of the legislative work of the period. These edicts are chiefly composed of new regulations for the enforcement of royal justice. They are not direct re-enactments or amendments of the ancient customary law, and are not drawn up in the form of perpetual statutes: but they rather enunciate and declare new methods of judicial procedure, which would either work into or supersede the procedure of the common law, whether practised in the popular or in the feudal courts. In this respect they strongly resemble the Capitularies of the Frank kings, or, to go farther back, the edicts of the Roman praetors: they might indeed, as to both form and matter, be called Capitularies. The term Assize, which comes into use in this meaning about the middle of the twelfth century, both on the Continent and in England, appears to be the proper Norman name for such edicts[1]; but it is uncertain

[1] Looking at the word *assisa* simply we might incline to regard it as the *lex assisa* or *sententia assisa*, the settled edict of the king, just as the *redditus assisus* was the fixed or assessed rent of an estate. It is however used so early in the sense of a *session* that the former cannot be regarded as the sole explanation. In the Assize of Jerusalem it simply means a law: and the same in Henry's legislation. Secondarily, it means a form of trial established by the particular law, as the Great Assize, the Assize of Mort d'Ancester; and thirdly, the court held to hold such trials; in which sense it is commonly used at the present day. Yet it occurs in the Norman law books in the twelfth century, and apparently in the Pipe Roll of 2 Henry II, in the sense of a session, and that is taken by many antiquaries as the primary meaning. The formation of assisus from a barbarous use of assido or assideo (instead of assessus) might be paralleled with the derivation of tolta in *malatolta* from tollo, in the sense of taking toll; but the word accido, to tax, may, so far as the *assisus redditus* is concerned, be the true origin of this form, as it is of the modern *excise*. On the other hand, it is impossible not to associate the *assize* of Henry II with the *asetniss* of Ina and Edmund. Possibly the use of the word in so many senses may point to a confusion of three different origins. Cf. the derivation of *taxo*, to tax, from τάσσω, to ordain, or regulate: and the use of the word *tallare* = *accidere, taxare*.

Origin of the Assize.

whether it received this particular application from the mere fact that it was a settlement, like the Anglo-Saxon *asetniss* or the French *établissement*, or from a verbal connexion with the session of the court in which it was passed, or from the fact that it furnished a plan on which sessions of the courts reformed by it should be held. The assize thus differs widely from the charter of liberties, the form which the legislation of Henry I and Stephen had taken, and is peculiar in English history to the period before us, as the form of Provisions marks the legislative period of Henry III, and that of Statute and Ordinance belongs to that of Edward I and his successors. It possesses moreover the characteristic of tentative or temporary enactment, rather than the universal and perpetual character which a law, however superficially, seems to claim[1]: its duration is specified in the form; it is to be in force so long as the king pleases; it may have a retrospective efficacy, to be applied to the determination of suits which have arisen since the king's accession, or since his last visit to England[2]; it is liable to be set aside by the judges where they find it impossible to administer it fairly. But, on the other hand, it is to the assize that the most important legal changes of the period owe their origin: the institution of jury and the whole procedure of the Curia Regis can have come into existence in no other way.

Its character of edict or decree.

In the drawing up of the assize, the king acted by the advice

The form *assisia* suggests further difficulties, but there is no reason to look for an Arabic derivation, as is done in the editions of Du Cange.

[1] The special sanctity of the term law, as used in Holy Scripture and in the Roman jurisprudence, may perhaps account for the variety of expressions, such as those quoted above, by means of which men avoided giving the title of law to their occasional enactments. The Assizes of England, Jerusalem, Sicily, and Romania, the Establishments of S. Lewis, the Recesses of the German diets, and many other like expressions, illustrate this reluctance.

[2] The Assize of Clarendon is to be held good as long as it pleases the king. That of Northampton directs inquiry into disseisins made since the king's last coming to England; and the view of this Assize is to extend from the date of the Assize of Clarendon to the time of its own publication 'atenebit a tempore quo assisa facta fuit apud Clarendonam continue usque ad hoc tempus.' Richard's Assize of Measures was set aside by the justices because the merchants declared it to be impracticable. See Select Charters, pp. 139, 144; Hoveden, iv. 172. John's Assize of Wines was set aside in the same way; ibid. p. 100.

and consent of his national council. This is distinctly stated in the preamble or title of the Assizes of Clarendon and Woodstock: the former is made 'de assensu archiepiscoporum, episcoporum, abbatum, comitum, baronum totius Angliae[1];' the latter 'per consilium et assensum archiepiscoporum, episcoporum et baronum, comitum et nobilium Angliae[2].' The Assize of Northampton was the work, we are told, of the king, made by the counsel of King Henry his son and by the counsel of his earls, barons, knights, and vassals (homines) in a great council, consisting of bishops, earls, barons, and the rest, held 'de statutis regni[3].' The ordinance by which trial by the Great Assize was instituted, was, according to Glanvill, an act of royal beneficence, bestowed on the nation by the clemency of the prince according to the counsel of the nobles[4]. The Assize of Measures was issued in the name of Richard I by the justiciar in 1197, as made by the lord Richard king of England at Westminster, although the king was at the time in France, by the petition and advice of his bishops and all his barons[5]. In this act of legislation the justiciar represented the king. The instructions given to the itinerant justices had likewise the force of laws, and might with justice be termed Assizes. They too were issued by the justiciar in the king's absence, and contained old as well as new regulations for the courts. The Assize of Arms issued in 1181 is not distinctly said to be framed under the advice of the council, and it may possibly have been regarded by the barons with some jealousy as putting arms into the hands of the people; but when John in 1205 summoned the nation to arms in conformity with the principle embodied in his father's assize, he declares that it is so provided with the assent of the 'archbishops, bishops, earls, barons, and all our faithful of England[6].' These instances are sufficient to prove the share taken by the national council in legislation. The duty of proclaiming the law in the country fell upon the sheriffs and the itinerant

Assizes issued with the counsel and consent of the council.

Instances of Assizes.

[1] Select Charters, p. 137. [2] Ibid. p. 150. [3] Ibid. p. 124.

[4] 'Est autem magna assisa regale quoddam beneficium, clementia principis de consilio procerum populis indultum.' Glanvill, ii. c 7.

[5] Hoveden, iv. 33. [6] Select Charters, p. 273.

Proclamation of the new laws in the country.

justices, whose credentials contained perhaps the first general promulgation. The Great Charter was read, by the king's order, publicly in every county, no doubt in the shiremoot and hundred court[1]; duplicates of it were deposited in the cathedral churches.

Importance of constitutional forms.

In all this there was nothing new: it was simply the maintenance of ancient forms, which prove their strength by retaining their vitality under the strongest of our kings. The advice and consent of the council may have been, no doubt in many cases was, a mere formality: the enacting power was regarded as belonging to the king, who could put in respite or dispense with the very measures that he had ordained. Yet in this an advantage may be incidentally traced. If the barons under Henry II had possessed greater legislative power, they might have kept it to themselves, as they did to a certain extent keep to themselves the judicial power of the later parliament; but as it was, legislation was one of the nominal rights that belonged to the whole council as the representative of the nation, and the real exercise of which was not attained until the barons had made common cause with the people, and incorporated their representatives in their own assembly. The period of national as distinct from royal legislation begins when the council has reached its constitutional development as the national parliament. The legislation of the Great Charter was to a certain extent an anticipation, a type, precedent, and a firm step in advance towards that consummation.

Legislative power not really acquired by Parliament until it has become representative.

Taxation; three points.

161. The subject of taxation may be arranged under three heads,—the authority by which the impost is legalised, the description of persons and property on which it is levied, and the determination of the amount for which the individual is liable; in other words, the grant, the incidence, and the assessment.

Norman taxation.

The reticence of historians during the reigns of the Norman kings leaves us in doubt whether the imposts which they levied were or were not exacted simply by their own sovereign will. Two records have been mentioned, however, of the reign of

[1] Select Charters, p. 298: 'quam etiam legi publice praecepimus per totam bailliam vestram.' See above, pp. 115, 116.

Henry I, in one of which the king describes a particular tax as 'the aid which my barons gave me,' whilst in another he speaks of the summoning of the county courts in cases in which his own royal necessities require it[1]. From the two passages it may be inferred that some form was observed, by which the king signified, both to his assembled vassals and to the country at large through the sheriffs, the sums which he wanted, and the plea on which he demanded them. The same method was observed by Henry II and Richard I; and it is only towards the end of the reign of Richard that we can trace anything like a formal grant or discussion of a grant in the national council[2]. It is commonly said that the king took a scutage, an aid, or a carucage; and where the barons are said to have given it, the expression may be interpreted of the mere payment of the money. Of any debate or discussion of such grants in the national council we have rare evidence: the opposition of S. Thomas to the king's manipulation of the Danegeld, and the refusal by S. Hugh of Lincoln to furnish money for Richard's war in France, are however sufficient to prove that the taxation was a subject of deliberation, although not sufficient to prove that the result of such discussion would be the authoritative imposition of the tax[3]. For the shadow of the feudal fiction, that the tax-payer made a voluntary offering to relieve the wants of his ruler, seems to have subsisted throughout the period: and the theory that the promise of the tax bound only the individual who made it, helped to increase the financial complications of the reign of John. Archbishop Theobald had denounced the scutage of 1156, and it is doubtful whether it was

Form of imposing a tax, by signify the king's necessities.

Cases of debate on taxation.

Want of a system of representation.

[1] Above, pp. 371, 393.
[2] In 1159 Henry 'scutagium accepit;' Gerv. c. 1381: in 1194 Richard 'constituit sibi dari' a carucage; Hoveden, iii. 242: in 1198 'cepit . . . quinque solidos de auxilio;' ib. iv. 46. In 1201 we find the word 'expostulans' used of the king's proposition of a tax for the collection of which 'exiit edictum a justitiariis;' R. Coggeshale. In 1203 John 'cepit ab eis septimam partem omnium mobilium suorum;' M. Paris, p. 209. In 1204 'concessa sunt auxilia militaria;' ibid. 209. In 1207 'convenit episcopos et abbates ut permitterent personas dare regi certam summam;' Ann. Waverl. p. 258. A gradual change in the tone of demand may be traceable in this, yet John was really becoming more despotic all the time.
[3] See above, pp. 463, 509.

Opposition to taxation, personal not representative.

raised on his lands. S. Thomas had declared at Woodstock that the lands of his church should not pay a penny to the Danegeld; the opposition of S. Hugh was based not on his right as a member of the national council, but on the immunities of his church; and when Archbishop Geoffrey in 1201 and 1207 forbade the royal officers to collect the carucage on his estates, it was on the ground that he himself had not promised the payment. The pressing necessity of raising the ransom of Richard probably marks an epoch in this as in some other points of financial interest. The gentle terms *donum* or *auxilium* had signified under his father's strong hand as much as Danegeld or tallage; but now not only was the king absent and the kingdom in a critical condition, but the legal reforms in the matter of assessment had raised up in the minds of the people at large a growing sense of their rights. The taxes raised for the ransom were imposed by the justiciar, probably but not certainly, with the advice of the barons[1], and were no doubt collected without any general resistance; but both the amount and the incidence were carefully criticised, and in some cases payment was absolutely refused. The clergy of York, when the king's necessities were laid before them by the archbishop in their chapter, declared that he was infringing their liberties, and closed their church as in the time of interdict[2].

Taxes for Richard's ransom.

Growth of the idea of connecting taxation with representation.

This idea, which is indeed the rudimentary form of the principle that representation should accompany taxation, gained ground after the practice arose of bringing personal property and income under contribution. It was the demand of a quarter of their revenues, not a direct tax upon their land, that provoked the opposition of the canons of York; and although Archbishop Geoffrey is found more than once in trouble for forbidding the collection of a carucage, the next great case in which resistance was offered to the demands of the Crown occurred in reference to the exaction of a thirteenth of move-

[1] Above, p. 501.

[2] Hoveden, iii. 222: 'Vocavit, monuit et rogavit ut quartam partem reddituum suorum ad praefati regis liberationem conferrent; . . . qui renuentes et concanonicos suos in partes suas trahentes, asserebant eum . . . libertates ecclesiae suae velle subvertere.'

able property in 1207. On this occasion it was not an isolated chapter, but a whole estate of the realm that protested. The king in a great council held on January 8 at London proposed to the bishops and abbots that they should permit the parsons and beneficed clerks to give him a certain portion of their revenues. The prelates refused to do so. The matter was debated in an adjourned council at Oxford on February 9, and there the bishops repeated their refusal in still stronger terms. The king therefore gave up that particular mode of procedure, and obtained from the national council a grant of an aid of a thirteenth of all chattels from the laity. That done, having forbidden the clergy to hold a council at S. Alban's, he issued, May 26, a writ to the archdeacons and the rest of the clergy, informing them of the grant of aid, and bidding them follow the good example[1]. Archbishop Geoffrey, who acted as the spokesman of the clergy, now gave up the struggle and went into exile; other circumstances were leading to a crisis: the thirteenth was no doubt generally collected; but early in the following year the interdict was imposed and constitutional law was in abeyance during the remainder of the reign. The twelfth article of the charter, in which the king promises that no scutage or aid, save the three regular aids, should henceforth be imposed without the advice and consent of the national council, does not explicitly mention the imposition of a tax on moveables, nor does it provide for the representation in the council of the great majority of those from whom such a tax would be raised. But in this, as in other points, the progress of events was outstripping and superseding the exact legal definitions of right. The fourteenth article does not provide for the representation of the shires, or for the par-

Protest of the Church against taxation in 1207.

Imposition of the thirteenth.

Exile of Geoffrey.

Growth of the taxative principle, in advance of the Great Charter.

[1] Ann. Waverly, p. 258; M. Paris, p. 221. The writ addressed to the archdeacons, after rehearsing the grant made by the archbishops, bishops, abbots, priors, and magnates, proceeds: 'Verum quia de vobis confidimus quod nos et honorem nostrum diligitis et defensionem regni nostri et recuperationem terrarum nostrarum affectatis, vos rogamus attentius, quatenus tale auxilium nobis, ex parte vestra faciatis ut inde vobis gratias dare debeamus; et quod alii rectores ecclesiarum vicini vestri ad auxilium nobis faciendum exemplo vestro facilius invitentur.' May 26, 1207. Patent Roll, 8 John; ed. Hardy, i. 72.

ticipation of the clergy as an estate of the realm, distinct from their character as feudal freeholders, yet in both respects the succeeding history shows that the right was practically established. So neither is the principle as yet formally laid down that a vote of the supreme council is to bind all the subjects of the realm in matter of taxation without a further consent of the individual. The prevalence of the idea that such consent was necessary brings the subject of the grant into close connexion with that of the assessment. But before approaching that point, the question of incidence requires consideration.

The principle of taxation by the nation itself not yet enunciated.

Indirect taxation of the period.

The indirect taxation of this period is obscure and of no great importance. The prisage of wine, the fines payable by the merchants for leave to import particular sorts of goods, the especial temptation which the stores of wool held out to the king's servants, the whole machinery of the customs, although referred to in the Great Charter as 'antiquae et rectae consuetudines[1],' were, so far as touches constitutional history, still in embryo. The existing practice rested on the ancient right of toll, and not on any historical legislative enactment. Although, then, these sources furnished an appreciable revenue to Richard I and John[2], the general taxation of the country may for our present purpose be regarded as direct taxation only.

Incidence of taxation.

The taxable property may be divided into land and moveables, and again, according to the character of their owners, into lay and clerical; these may be subdivided in the former case according as the layman is a tenant-in-chief, a knight, a freeholder, a burgher, or a villein, in the latter according as the possessor is a prelate, a beneficed clerk, a chapter, or a religious house. Each division of property was brought under contribution at a different period, and for each there was a distinct name and method of taxation.

Realty and personalty, lay and clerical.

All early taxation borne by the land.

All the imposts of the Anglo-Saxon and Norman reigns were, so far as we know, raised on the land, and according to computation by the hide: the exceptions to the rule would be only in the cases of those churches which claimed entire immunity, and those boroughs which paid a composition for their

[1] Article 31.

[2] Madox, Hist. Exch. pp. 529 sq.

taxes in a settled sum, as they paid the composition for the ferm in the shape of an annual rent. This generalisation covers both the national taxes like the Danegeld, and the feudal exactions by way of aid; both were levied on the hide. Henry I had exempted from such payments the lands held in demesne by his knights and barons, in consideration of the expenses of their equipments[1]; but this clause of his charter can have been only partially observed. Henry II, from the very beginning of his reign, seems to have determined on attempting important changes. He brought at once under contribution the lands held by the churches, which had often claimed, but never perhaps had secured immunity.

Taxation of land.

Of Church lands.

In the Assize of Arms in 1181 he took a long step towards taxing rent and chattels, obliging the owner of such property to equip himself with arms according to the amount which he possessed[2]. In the ordinance of the Saladin Tithe personal property is rendered liable to pay its tenth[3]. Under Richard I the rule is extended: for the king's ransom every man pays a fourth part of his moveables[4]: in 1204 John exacted a seventh of the same from the barons[5], and in 1207 a thirteenth from the whole of the laity[6]. This change in the character of taxation serves to illustrate the great development of material wealth in the country which followed the reforms of Henry II. The burdens would not have been transferred from the land to the chattels if the latter had not been found much more productive of revenue than the former.

Taxation of goods introduced.

Sevenths and thirteenths.

But this was not the only change. Henry II adopted the knight's fee instead of the hide as the basis of rating for the knights and barons: and on this basis established a somewhat minute system of distinctions. As early as his second year we find him collecting a scutage, a new form of taxation, at twenty shillings on the 'scutum' or knight's fee, from the knights who held land under the churches[7]. In 1159, for the war of Toulouse, he raised a much larger sum under the same name, from the tenants by knight service; as a commutation for personal

New system of rating land.

The scutage.

[1] Above, p. 305. [2] Ib. p. 488. [3] Ib. p. 489. [4] Ib. p. 501.
[5] Ib. p. 523; M. Paris, p. 209. [6] Above, p. 523. [7] Ib. p. 454.

service he accepted two marks from each, and with the proceeds paid an army of mercenaries[1]. The word scutage, from its use on this occasion, acquired the additional sense of a payment in commutation of personal service, in which it is most frequently used. In 1163, as has been already mentioned[2], the ancient Danegeld disappears from the Rolls; but it is succeeded by a tax which, under the name of donum or auxilium, and probably levied on a new computation of hidage, must have been a reproduction of the old usage. Such a change must indeed have been necessary, the Danegeld having become in the long lapse of years a mere composition paid by the sheriff to the Exchequer, while the balance of the whole sums exacted on that account went to swell his own income. Under Richard the same tax appears under the name of carucage: the normal tax being laid on the carucate instead of the hide, and each carucate containing a fixed extent of one hundred acres[3].

The scutage.

Disappearance of Danegeld.

Its reappearance as carucage.

Class taxation.

Customary amount of scutage and aid.

Each of these names represents the taxation of a particular class: the scutage affects the tenants in chivalry; the donum, hidage or carucage, affects all holders of land; the tenth, seventh, and thirteenth, all people in the realm. Each has its customary amount; the scutage of 1156 was twenty shillings on the fee[4]; those of 1159 and 1161 were two marks; the scutage of Ireland in 1171 was twenty shillings, and that of Galloway in 1186 at the same rate. The scutages of Richard's reign,—one for Wales in the first year and two for Normandy in the sixth and eighth,—were, in the first case ten, in the other cases twenty shillings. John in his first year raised a scutage of two marks; on nine other occasions he demanded the same sum, besides the enormous fines which he extorted from his barons on similar pretexts. Other aids to which the name is not commonly given were raised in the same way and at similar rates. Such were especially the aid pur fille marier, collected by Henry in 1168 at twenty shillings on the fee, and that for the ransom of Richard I at the same amount.

[1] Above, p. 456. [2] Ib. p. 463. [3] Hoveden, iv. 47.

[4] The following particulars are from the Pipe Rolls and Red Book of the Exchequer, as cited by Madox.

The carucage of Richard was probably intended, as the Danegeld had been, to be fixed at two shillings on the carucate. In 1198 however it was raised to five, and John in the first year of his reign fixed it at three shillings[1]. Rate of carucage.

Under the general head of donum, auxilium, and the like, come a long series of imposts, which were theoretically gifts of the nation to the king, and the amount of which was determined by the itinerant justices after separate negotiation with the payers. The most important of these, that which fell upon the towns and demesne lands of the Crown, is known as the tallage. This must have affected other property besides land, but the particular method in which it was to be collected was determined by the community on which it fell[2], or by special arrangement with the justices. The tallages.

It was only on rare occasions that all these methods of raising money were resorted to at once. Such an occasion might be the aid to marry the king's daughter, or to ransom his person; but not the ordinary contributions towards the regular expenses of the Crown. On those great occasions, the knights paid aid or scutage, the freeholders carucage, the towns tallage: the whole and each part bore the name of auxilium. More frequently only one tax was raised at once; a year marked by a scutage was not marked by a donum or a carucage. It was the accumulation and increased rate of these exactions that created the discontent felt under Hubert Walter's administration in the later years of Richard and the early years of John. In this division of burdens, and distinction of class interests, may be traced another step towards the system of three estates: the clergy and laity were divided by profession and peculiar rights and immunities; scutage and carucage drew a line between the tenant in chivalry and the freeholder, which at a later time helped to divide the lords from the commons. The clergy had in their spiritual assemblies a vantage-ground, which they used during the thirteenth century, to vindicate great liberties; and their action led the way to general representative assembling, and made easier for the commons the assertion of their own definite position. Varieties of financial programme. The *Budget* of the year. Growth of system of estates.

[1] Above, p. 516. [2] See below, pp. 585 sq.

Assessment of taxes.

The method of assessment varied according to the incidence of the tax. So long as all the taxation fell on the land, Domesday book continued to be the rate-book of the kingdom[1]; all assessments that could not be arranged directly by it, such as the contributions of the boroughs, were specially adjusted by the sheriffs, or by the officers of the Exchequer in their occasional visitations[2], or were permanently fixed in a definite proportion and at round sums[3]. This system must have proved sufficient so long as the changes of occupation, which had occurred since the Domesday Survey, could be kept in living memory. As soon however as Henry II began to rate the land by the knight's fee, a new expedient was requisite. Hence, when he was preparing to levy the aid pur fille marier, the king issued a writ to all the tenants-in-chief of the Crown, lay and clerical, directing each of them to send in a cartel or report of the number of knights' fees for the service of which he was legally liable[4]. This was done, and the reports so made are still preserved in the Black Book of the Exchequer, to which reference has been more than once made in former chapters. The scutages continued to be exacted on the same assessment, compared from year to year with the Pipe Rolls, until the reign of John, who on several occasions took advantage of the reluctance which his barons showed for foreign war to make arbitrary exactions. A clause of the Great Charter issued by Henry III in 1217 directs that the scutages shall be taken as they were in his grandfather's time. A few years after this, Alexander of Swerford, who compiled the Red Book of the Exchequer, reduced the computation

Domesday the rate-book of land.

The tenants in knight-service are called on to declare their several liability.

[1] Dialogus de Scacc. i. c. 16.

[2] 'Noveris itaque quod plurimum interest si donum vel auxilium civitatis per singula capita commorantium in ea a justitiis constituatur, vel si cives summam aliquam quae principe digna videatur justitiariis offerant et ab eis accipiatur.' Dialogus, ii. c. 13.

[3] See above, p. 382.

[4] One of the answers to this demand probably preserves the exact words of the writ: 'Mihi et aliis comparibus meis per litteras vestras innotuit, ut per fidem et ligantiam quam vobis debemus, vobis per breve nostrum pendens extra sigillum mandaremus quot milites habemus de veteri feodamento de tempore Henrici avi vestri, et quot milites habeamus de novo feodamento post tempus regis Henrici avi vestri, et quot milites habeamus super dominium nostrum.' Liber Niger, i. 148.

of knights' fees to something like order by a careful examination of the Pipe Rolls; but so long as scutages were collected at all, the assessment of the individual depended very much on his own report, which the Exchequer had little means of checking.

Assessment of scutage.

The donum, auxilium, or tallage, which Henry imposed in lieu of the ancient Danegeld, was assessed by the officers of the Exchequer. In 1168 the whole of England was visited by a small commission of judges and clerks, who rated the sums by which the freeholders and the towns were to supplement the contributions of the knights. In 1173 a tallage on the royal demesne was assessed by six detachments of Exchequer officers, and throughout the remainder of the reign the fiscal circuits correspond with those of the justices, or the fiscal business is done by the justices in their judicial circuits. This method of assessment, like that of scutage, failed to secure either party against the other; either the justices had to accept the return of the tax-payer, or the tax-payer had to pay as the judges directed him[1]. Little help could be expected from the sheriff, who indeed was generally an officer of the Exchequer. The assessment of the justices sometimes varied considerably from that of the payer, and in one recorded instance we find the tender of the former accepted in preference to the valuation of the latter. In 1168 the men of Horncastle pay £29 13*s.* 4*d.* for an aid, 'quod ipsi assederunt inter se concessu justitiarum aliter quam justitiae[2].' It is obvious that an exaction, the amount of which was settled as in these two cases by the statement of the payer, was removed by only one step from the character of a voluntary contribution. That step might be a very wide one, and the liberty which it implied might be very limited, but the right of grant and the right of assessment were brought into immediate juxtaposition.

Assessment of tallage by itinerant officers of the Exchequer.

When however, as was the case under the Assize of Arms and the Saladin Tithe, personal property was to be rated, it became clear that no safe assessment could be based either on the taxpayer's statement of his own liability, or on the unin-

Personal property required more careful assessment.

[1] See above, p. 584, note 2.

[2] Pipe Roll, 14 Hen. II; Madox, Hist. Exch. p. 407.

Application of the jury principle to assessment of personal property.

formed opinion of the sheriff and justices. To remedy this, Henry had recourse to his favourite expedient of the jury. He directed that the quantity and character of armour which each man was to provide should be determined by the report of a number of sworn knights and other lawful men of each neighbourhood, who were to draw up a list of the men within their district, with a distinct statement of their liability[1]. In the collection of the Saladin Tithe, in which the king himself took an active part, the same plan was adopted: where suspicion arose that any man was contributing less than his share, four or six lawful men of the parish were chosen to declare on oath what he ought to give[2]. The great precedent for this proceeding was found of course in the plan by which the Domesday Survey had been made, and the occasional recognitions of fiscal liability which had been taken under special writs. The plan was so successful that in 1198 it was applied to the assessment of the carucage, an account of which has been given already[3]. The assessment of the thirteenth in A.D. 1207 was however not made by juries, but by the oath of the individual payer taken before the justices[4]; the contributions of the clergy being a matter of special arrangement made by the archdeacons[5]. The carucage of 1198 is then the land-mark of the progress which the representative principle expressed by the jury had as yet attained in the matter of taxation.

It is applied to the carucage.

Question of collection of tallages.

The further question which arose chiefly in the towns, how the sums agreed to between the special community and the Exchequer were to be adjusted so as to insure the fair treatment of individuals, also came into importance as soon as personal property was liable to assessment. We learn from the story of William Fitz-Osbert, that in London the taxes were raised by capitation or poll-tax, every citizen poor or rich contributing the same amount, the unfairness of the rule being compensated by the lightness of the burden which so many

[1] Bened. i. p. 278; Select Charters, p. 147.
[2] Bened. ii. 31; Select Charters, p. 152.
[3] Above, p. 510.
[4] Patent Rolls, ed. Hardy, i. 72; Select Charters, p. 275.
[5] Above, p. 579, note 1.

joined in bearing. William came forward as the advocate of the poor, and declared that an assessment should be made by which each man should pay in proportion to his wealth : but we are not told by what means he intended to carry out the idea, and his intemperate conduct produced the riot with which our knowledge of the matter terminates [1].

William Fitz-Osbert and graduated taxation.

The whole subject of taxation illustrates the gradual way in which king and people were realising the idea of self-government. The application of a representative scheme to the work of assessment, and the recognition that the liability of the payer was based on his own express consent, either to the grant itself or to the amount of his own contribution, mark a state of things in which the concentration of local interests in one general council was all that was needed to secure the tax-payer from arbitrary treatment on the part of either the sovereign or his ministers. This becomes still more evident as we approach the wider but equally important sphere of judicial action, in which not only the principle, but the actual details of the representative system seem progressively to assert themselves. Before entering upon this, however, some notice must be taken of the military system of Henry II and his sons, which, as exemplified both in the scutage and in the Assize of Arms, may be regarded in close connexion with his expedients of taxation.

Summary of the subject.

162. Henry found on his accession the three kinds of military force, which we have described in a former chapter [2], in full existence, but very incompletely organised, and in consequence of the recent troubles, either burdensome to the nation or thoroughly ineffective. The standing army of mercenaries he was bound by the treaty, which secured him the succession, to disband and banish ; the general body of tenants in chivalry was broken up among the feudatories who had been fighting each for himself; and the national force of the fyrd, which by its very nature was capable of only slight discipline and occasional usefulness, had shared in the general disorder of the country consequent on the paralysis of government. Henry from the very first years of his reign saw that peace was his true interest, but that with so

The military system.

[1] Above, p. 508. [2] Above, p. 431 sq.

Policy of Henry II in military matters.

wide an extent of territory to defend, and so many jealous enemies to keep in check, he could have no peace unless he were strong enough to prevent war. Each then of these three expedients he saw would have its uses, whilst each had its defects. The mercenary force was hateful to the nation; the feudal levy was divided according to the interests of its leaders, was not trustworthy in emergency, and by the strict rules as to the nature and duration of service was incapable of being fully handled: the national militia was either useless for foreign warfare, or could be made useful only by being treated as a mercenary force, an expedient which wasted at once the blood and the treasure of the kingdom. The obvious policy was to use mercenaries for foreign warfare, and to employ the national militia for defence and for the maintenance of peace. The feudal levy, like the rest of the machinery of feudalism which could not be got rid of, might be made occasionally useful in both ways, but would be more useful still, if it could be made to contribute to the support of the crown in ways which would leave the king unembarrassed by the minutiae of feudal custom.

The mercenaries, employed by Henry, Richard, and John.

This policy Henry maintained more or less continuously. He fought his wars on the Continent by means of mercenaries[1]: he had a standing force of 10,000 Brabançons, and a large number of Welsh and Galwegian soldiers. Richard followed the example, and in addition to these embodied a force of Basques and Navarrese, two races whose military malpractices had been condemned by the Lateran Council of 1179, and who with the Brabançons and Catalans enjoy the evil reputation of being the forerunners of the free companies of the next age. Many of these were probably Crusaders who had returned penniless from the East, or mere bandits and brigands who by taking foreign service had escaped the justice of their native lords. John, like his father and brother, maintained a great host of these adventurers, and with them fought the battles and

[1] 'Mavult enim princeps stipendiarios quam domesticos bellicis apponere casibus.' Dialogus, i. c. 9. 'Nolens vexare agrarios milites nec burgensem nec rusticorum multitudinem . . . . . duxit, solidarios vero milites innumeros.' R. de Monte, A.D. 1159.

conducted the cruel ravages which mark the close of his reign. The mercenary force only comes within our view in two points: it was a breach of the compact of Wallingford, in spirit at least, that such a host ever set foot on English soil; and it was only from the revenue of his kingdom that Henry could draw funds to pay its expenses. The king faithfully observed the condition: on one occasion only were his mercenaries brought to England, and then it was to repel invasion, for the purpose of which a force of Flemish soldiers had already landed. They stayed in England for a month, and left with the king on his return to France[1]. Richard had no inclination, as he had indeed no temptation, to break the rule: and John's mercenary army raised to repel the French invasion of 1213, in itself perhaps justified by the emergency, became one of the great occasions of his downfall. The direct question of the payment of the mercenaries only once arises, that is in 1198, when the justiciar proposed that it should be met by a grant for the express purpose of maintaining a body of knights, and was defeated by the resolution of S. Hugh[2]. But in this case the force required was asked rather as a substitute for personal service than as an engine of national defence, and on that ground it was refused.

Mercenaries brought to England only in exceptional cases.

Payment of mercenaries refused.

Henry's manipulation of the feudal host is a more complex matter, for there can be little doubt that he desired to weaken the great feudatories by disarming their vassals, as well as to obtain a more complete command of the resources that lay within his reach. The first expedient to which he had recourse was to break through the net of feudal custom by demanding that every three knights should, instead of serving in person, equip one of their number, probably, for a threefold term of service. This was done in the Welsh war of 1157, and furnished the king with a body of knights, one-third of the whole knightly force of the kingdom, for a space of four months instead of the usual forty days[3]. A similar, if not the same, plan was adopted by Richard, who in the council of Nottingham in 1194

Henry's management of the feudal force.

Joint equipment.

[1] Bened. i. 74. [2] Above, p. 509. [3] R. de Monte, A.D. 1157.

Combination for purpose of equipment.

demanded a third part of the knight-service of the kingdom for his war in Normandy[1]: and John in 1205, by the advice of the council, directed that every nine knights should join to equip a tenth with wages of two shillings a day for the defence of the country[2]. The principle involved in this arrangement is exactly analogous to that adopted by Charles the Great in the capitulary of A.D. 807, in which he directs that when there is war in Spain or with the Avars, every five Saxon warriors are to join to equip a sixth; when the war is in Bohemia, every two are to equip a third; for the direct defence of the country each is to present himself in person[3]. This rule is in direct agreement with the Frank system of armament by which the poorer landowners combined to equip a fully-armed warrior, as was the Berkshire custom recorded in Domesday[4]. The coincidence may be accidental, but it forms one of a great number of small points in which Henry's administrative expedients seem to be borrowed from the Karolingian laws.

Coincidence of the Frank laws.

Scutage as commutation of service.

A second and more comprehensive measure is found in the institution of scutage, which we have already examined under the head of taxation. The transition by which the fyrdwite or penalty for neglecting the summons to arms,—a fine which was provided for also in the most ancient laws of the Germanic races[5],—was so modified as to become an honourable commutation for personal service, was not so great as might appear at first sight. Richard Fitz-Neal distinctly ascribes it to Henry's wish to spare the blood of his subjects[6]; it had however the further merit of providing the king with money to pay an army which he could handle as he pleased; it helped to disarm a dangerous element in the country; and it solved, or rather waived for the time, the already threatening question of the liability to foreign service. That it was used by John, like everything else, as an

[1] Hoveden, iii. 242.
[2] Patent Rolls, i. 55; Select Charters, pp. 273, 274.
[3] Baluze, i. 318.
[4] Baluze, i. 317, 318; above, p. 117; Waitz, D. V. G. iv. 471 sq.
[5] See Waitz, D. V. G. iv. 470; Baluze, i. 299, 300. The heribannum of the Franks, in the sense of a fine for not going to war, corresponds with the Anglo-Saxon fyrdwite.
[6] Above, p. 588, note 1.

engine for extortion, or that in later reigns it was made an excuse for unrighteous exaction, is no argument against its original usefulness. The land-tax of the present day is the link which binds us, directly in this point, with the custom of our forefathers.

Origin of the land-tax.

The Assize of Arms in 1181 was intended to reform and re-arm the national force of the fyrd. It directed that the whole free population, the *communa liberorum hominum*, should furnish themselves with arms. The owner of a knight's fee must possess a coat of mail, a helmet, a shield, and a lance; the freeman possessing sixteen marks of rent or chattels must have the same; the owner of ten marks must possess a hauberk, a head-piece of iron, and a lance; and all burghers and freemen a wambais, head-piece, and lance [1]. Here again we find a strict analogy with the Karolingian system, which no doubt had had in this respect a continuous existence on the Continent; a similar assize was issued by Philip of Flanders and Philip of France at the same time [2]. Every man who possessed twelve mansi was, by the capitulary of A.D. 805, obliged to possess a brunia or coat of mail [3]: by one of A.D. 779 it is forbidden that any should give or sell such arms to a stranger [4]: by that of A.D. 812 he who possesses more than the necessary equipment must employ it, or alienate it, in the royal service [5]: all these are minor points in which the language of the Assize almost exactly coincides.

Assize of Arms, a re-constitution of the fyrd.

The Assize of Arms embodied a principle of perpetual utility, and one the history of which is easily traceable from the first germ of the obligation in the trinoda necessitas, down to the militia armament of the present times: the several questions, all of them important in their day, connected with distraint of knighthood, the commission of array and the like, directly connect themselves with it. It has however in its relation to the maintenance of the peace another important bearing, which connects it directly with the agency of the county courts. The

Importance of the Assize of Arms.

[1] Bened. i. 278. [2] Bened. i. 269, 270.

[3] Baluze, i. 297, 301, &c. The capitulary 'de expeditione Romana,' which directs that each man shall have a brunia for every ten mansi, is a fabrication. Pertz, Legg. ii. App. p. 3.

[4] Baluze, i. 277, 297, 301. [5] Baluze, i. 340.

The Assize of Arms.

'jurati ad arma,' the freemen sworn under the Assize to furnish themselves with arms, were under the special charge of the sheriff, and come into prominence again under Henry III. In the writ of 1205, already referred to, John directs the general armament of the people to resist invasion, but without minute instructions, under the severe penalty of being reduced to perpetual servitude. The duty of watch and ward, of following the hue and cry, and of taking the oath of the peace, prescribed in 1195, serve to connect the several duties of the freeholder with the obligation of the ancient allodial owner; but they come before us in other places.

Maintenance of the feudal force.

Whilst Henry however thus attempted to unite the whole free people under proper discipline for national defence, he maintained the show at least of the feudal force: in 1177 he brought the whole of the knights to Winchester, and made a grand demonstration of the military strength of the kingdom[1]: the plan was followed on several occasions by John, although, as we have already seen, the only result of the assembly, and perhaps the only purpose for which he brought it together, was the extortion of money, by way of fine or in commutation of further service[2].

Naval force of the kingdom.

The naval force of the kingdom during the twelfth century, so far as it can be regarded as a national institution, must have depended for existence on the three principles by which the army was sustained, but in different proportions and combinations. The usage of the reign of Ethelred, according to which each shire furnished its quota of ships[3], had disappeared before the Domesday Survey, although England had continued to be a naval power throughout the reign of the Confessor. Possibly the fleet had become less important as the danger of Danish invasion was less constantly imminent. The great vassals of the Conquest had, it is said, merited their great rewards by their contributions to the Norman fleet[4], but none of them received or held their English lands on the condition of service by sea. The inland counties in some cases reported in

[1] Above, p. 565. [2] Ib. p. 523. [3] Ib. p. 116. [4] Ib. p. 257.

Domesday book special services due when the king went to sea; and Dover held its liberties in return for a provision of twenty ships to be kept for fifteen days annually in the king's service[1]. The fleet however is not a prominent object in the Survey.

Ships of Dover.

Yet the kings, possessing so extensive a sea-board in both England and France, were never at a loss for ships; and the ships when assembled were, like the fyrd, ranged according to the counties from which they came. The crusading expedition of A.D. 1147, by which Lisbon was taken, was to a certain extent a volunteer expedition, and may not be a fair instance of the usual practice: in it however the ships of Norfolk and Suffolk sailed under Hervey Glanvill, a local magnate; those of Kent under Simon of Dover; those of London, Hastings, Southampton, and Bristol under their own captains[2]. The London crusaders of 1188 and 1190 seem to have had an organisation of their own, although in the latter case they formed part of a fleet commanded by royal officers who bore the names of justiciars and constables[3]. Richard made laws for this fleet, with the counsel of his 'probi homines,' and enjoined the observance of them on his own subjects in the strictest terms, compelling them to swear obedience, and commanding them as they cared for their fortunes at home to act in proper submission to their justiciars.

The fleets arranged according to the ports from which they came.

Richard made laws for the fleet.

Even of the fleet of 1190 a large proportion was in no respect national property: the vessels of transport which composed no small part of it were no doubt hired by the king, or possibly impressed for the occasion. Dover and Hastings held their liberties by furnishing twenty ships each for the king's service, and the rest of the Cinque Ports doubtless contributed in proportion. The vessels of war however, the galleys, must have been the property of the king, and it is probably to this crusade that we owe the germ of a permanent navy. Such a navy must have been from remote antiquity an institution among the Mediterranean powers; at this moment the

The beginning of a permanent navy.

[1] Domesd. i. 1. Sandwich owed the same service; and Romney with other ports owed sea-service.

[2] Expugnatio Lyxbonensis, Chron. Rich. I, i. p. cxliv.

[3] Hoveden, iii. 46 sq.; Benedict, ii. 120 sq. The commanders are called constables by Hoveden, iii. 36, justiciars by Bened. ii. 110.

Growth of navies.

Pisans, the Genoese, and the Venetians possessed large fleets of armed transports, which were hired by the French and German Crusaders: the king of Sicily had his 'stolium fortunatum,' for whose commander he borrowed the Arabic title of Emir or Admiral[1]. The Danes and the Flemings likewise possessed naval forces, but these probably belonged to individual adventurers, amongst whom the king or the count might be the first. In England itself Hugh de Puiset, the bishop of Durham, had his own great ship, which became royal property at his death[2]. Except for the distant expeditions to Palestine, the king needed only such a squadron as would carry him and his court from time to time across the Channel[3]: the defence of the coast must have been maintained as of old by local resources.

The permanent fleet a fleet of mercenaries.

The permanent fleet then was from its very origin a fleet of mercenaries, and was maintained from the royal revenue just as a band of Brabançons might have been, although, as the English merchant service was the readiest resource for recruits, the royal fleet was chiefly manned by Englishmen. John's naval armament was organised on this plan; but it is not until after the date of the Charter, which limits our present inquiries, that its importance comes into historical prominence. The legislation of the Admiralty, which is referred to the present period by writers of the fifteenth century, is either antedated, or so modified by translation and adaptation that it is not to be recognised as twelfth-century work.

The king was the paymaster.

It is clear from what has been said that the mercenary force of army and navy was, so far as its maintenance is concerned, dependent on no authority but that of the king, who paid its expenses, as he did all other national and personal expenses, out of the general fund accruing to the Exchequer, over which the national council neither possessed nor as yet asserted any claim.

Judicature.

163. The judicial measures of Henry II constitute a very important part of his general policy. They have been noticed in

[1] Bened. i. 171; ii. 128. [2] Madox, Hist. Exch. p. 493.

[3] Henry II had one ship of his own until Becket ordered three very good ones to be built and equipped; these he presented to his master. W. Fitz-Stephen (V. S. Thom.), i. 193. The full number furnished by the Cinque Ports under Edward III was fifty-seven, twenty-one each by Dover and Hastings, five each by Romney, Hythe, and Sandwich.

their personal and political bearing in the last chapter. We have there seen how the original impulse was given to his reforms by the terms on which the Crown was secured to him, how those reforms were moulded by his peculiar genius or by the influence of well-chosen advisers, the traditions of the Exchequer forming an important element; how the several steps in advance were partly guided by a desire to limit the judicial power of the great feudal vassals, and to protect the people against the misuse by the local magnates of that influence in the county courts which had fallen into their hands. We have accordingly noted the chief occasions on which the sheriffs, and even the royal judges, were brought to special account, and displaced to make way, either for men who had received a better legal training, or for such as were less closely connected with the ruling families of the district, or for those who would bring the shire administration into more thorough concert with the supreme administration, if not completely under its control. We have traced, under the history of Hubert Walter and Geoffrey Fitz-Peter, a growing spirit of legal reform, a rapid invention of new machinery or adaptation of the old machinery to new ends, not indeed free from the imputation that it was chiefly stimulated by financial considerations, but still in its ultimate results conducive to the growth and conscious realisation of the idea of self-government. And we have further inferred that the attitude taken by the clergy, the barons, and the commons at the date of the Great Charter was produced by the altered circumstances in which the kingdom was placed by these changes: that whilst on the one hand they had given to the king an overwhelming power, they had on the other revealed to the Three Estates the unity of their interests, and the possibility of erecting a well-compacted fabric of liberty. We have now to trace the mechanical workings involved in this history.

Recapitulation of the judicial policy of Henry II; and of Richard's ministers.

Henry at his accession found the administrative system in the most attenuated state. Twenty years of misrule had seen the polity of his grandfather broken up rather than suspended, and very few of the old servants of the State survived. Such judicial machinery as existed seems to have been sustained by Richard

Condition of things in 1155.

Reforms of Henry II, his own work.

de Lucy, but the year which had elapsed since the pacification had only given time to attempt the uprooting of the evils of misrule, not to lay the foundations or to rebuild the fabric of a sound government. Hence Henry's reforms, although, so far as he was able to get aid from his grandfather's ministers, they were based upon the older system, owe very much to the king himself, and, from the outset of the reign, exhibit marks of decided growth and difference from the former state of things. The Exchequer was restored under Bishop Nigel as it had existed under Bishop Roger, but the Curia Regis from the first presents a much more definite appearance than before. Still one with the Exchequer in its personal staff, it has much more independent action and a wider sphere; it developes a new and elaborate system of rules and customs. The king's personal tribunal continues to be a supreme and ultimate resort, but the royal judicature from time to time throws off offshoots, which before the end of the period constitute a system of courts and jurisdictions that with some developments and modifications subsist to our own day.

Division of the subject of judicature.

The judicature may be divided into three branches, the central and supreme court or courts, the provincial, popular, or common law tribunals, and the visitatorial jurisdiction by which the first interfered with, regulated, and remodelled the second: and these may be noticed in the order of their authority; first, the king's courts; secondly, the itinerant justices; thirdly, the local tribunals.

The Exchequer and Curia Regis.

The Exchequer and the Curia Regis continue throughout this period to exist in that close union which proves their original identity; but whereas under Henry I the financial character, under Henry II the judicial aspect, of the board is the most prominent. In the former reign the Curia Regis, except when the king takes a personal share in the business, seems to be a judicial session of the Exchequer, an adaptation of Exchequer machinery to judicial purposes; under the latter the Exchequer seems to be rather a financial session of the Curia Regis. The king is ostensibly the head of the one [1], the justiciar the principal

[1] 'Regis Curia, in qua ipse in propria persona jura decernit; . . ex officio principaliter residet [in scaccario] immo et praesidet primus in regno capitalis scilicet justitia.' Dialogus, i. c. 4.

actor in the other; but still the fabric is the same: the judges are the same; the transactions of the Curia frequently take place in the chamber of the Exchequer, and are recorded in its Rolls; and, through all the changes by which the Curia is modelled and divided, the Exchequer forms a rallying-point, or common ground, on which all the members of the supreme judicature seem, as in the Exchequer Chamber at the present day, to meet.

Close union of the two.

Continuity of Exchequer usages.

The financial system of the Exchequer, as it existed under Henry I, has been already described, and illustrated from the single Pipe Roll of the reign as well as from the Dialogus de Scaccario [1]. The latter work describes the practice of the year 1178, in language which shows a substantial agreement with the system presented in the Roll of 1130. This organisation therefore it is unnecessary to recapitulate here. The points in which change and development are traceable are either minute matters of procedure, which scarcely come within the view of constitutional history, or matters of legal interest which belong more strictly to the history of the Curia Regis and itinerant jurisdictions. The Court of Exchequer, taking special cognisance of suits touching the revenue, possessing a different body of judges, and a distinct code of customs, does not as yet exist; but it may be justly presumed that where such suits were entertained, the judges before whom they were tried would be those who were most familiar with the financial work. The fines levied for legal purposes, which were originally the determinate agreements between litigants drawn up and recorded in the king's court, and a source of constant income to the Crown, were regularly concluded 'ad scaccarium [2];' but the judges who witnessed the transaction were not a permanent committee of officers; they were apparently a selection for each occasion from the whole body of the Curia, all of whom were, it is probable, equally eligible and of equal authority. The records of the Exchequer grow during the period in bulk and in number: the

Special legal business in the Exchequer.

[1] Above, p. 377.
[2] See illustrations of business done 'ad scaccarium' in the reign of Henry II in Madox, Hist. Exch. pp. 144, 145.

Increase of Exchequer Records.

Pipe Rolls of Henry II[1] are supplemented under John by Oblate, Liberate, and Mise Rolls[2], in which the particular outgoings on the heads of royal allowances, benefactions, and other payments are circumstantially recorded. The Great Rolls of the Pipe however continue to contain the summaries and authoritative details of the national account.

Growth of the Curia Regis.

The Curia Regis of Henry II attained its ultimate constitution by a long series of somewhat rapid changes. In the early years of the reign it appears to be, as it had been under Henry I, a tribunal of exceptional resort to which appeals, although increasing in number, were still comparatively rare, and the action of which is scarcely distinguishable from that of the national council. The king himself took a leading part in the business, much of which was done in his presence; and even in his absence the action of the justiciar seems to depend on the royal pleasure as indicated by special writs. Such at least is the impression made by the long details of litigation contained in the Chronicle of Battle, and in the account of Richard de Anesty, who has preserved the record of his delays and expenses in a suit which lasted from 1158 to 1163[3]. Yet side by side with this there appears a show of judicial activity among the subordinate members of the household, the court, and the Exchequer. The Chancellor, as we learn from the Lives of S. Thomas, was constantly employed in judicial work, whether in attendance on the king, or, as the Pipe Rolls also testify, in provincial visitations. As early as the second year of the reign,

Personal sessions of the king.

The Chancellor.

[1] Only three Pipe Rolls of Henry II are in print, one of Richard, and one of the reign of John: it is greatly to be desired that the whole series for the two former reigns might be published. They are the only complete series of records for the period, and throw a great deal of light on every department of history, although commonly known only through the medium of Madox's work.

[2] The Fines of the reigns of Richard and John were edited by Hunter among the publications of the Record Commission, in 1835 and 1844; the Rotuli de oblatis of John and the Rotuli 'de Liberate ac de Misis et Praestitis' in 1844 by Sir T. Duffus Hardy; the Rotuli Curiae Regis of Richard and John by Sir F. Palgrave in 1835; and the Close and Patent Rolls of John between 1833 and 1844 by Sir T. D. Hardy.

[3] This important record is only to be found in Sir F. Palgrave's Rise and Progress of the English Commonwealth (vol. ii), where it is illustrated by most interesting notes.

Henry of Essex the Constable, Thomas the Chancellor, and the earl of Leicester the cojusticiar, are found hearing pleas in different counties[1]. The Chancellor, if we may believe the consistent evidence of his biographers, habitually relieved the king of the irksome part of his judicial duties[2]. From the Constitutions of Clarendon again we learn that the Curia Regis possessed the organisation of an established tribunal, the action of which in ecclesiastical cases must be held to prove a still wider action in secular causes. In 1165, the year after the enactment of the Constitutions, we have an agreement between the abbots of Westminster and S. Alban's attested by several of the ministers of the Exchequer under the title of justices[3], and in 1166 we come to the Assize of Clarendon, which marks an epoch in the administration of, at least, the criminal law. During these years—for such is the reasonable inference—the judicial work of the Curia Regis had been growing until it was more than the king and his regular ministers of state could dispatch, and was thus falling, even more completely than it had done under Henry I, into the hands of the officers of the Exchequer. The system of recognitions was, as the Constitutions of Clarendon prove, in full play, and the superior chances of justice which that system afforded was drawing larger business to the court, and at the same time involved a vast 'officina brevium,' with a body of trained clerks[4] and a regular code of practical jurisprudence. Unfortunately we are unable to discover the date at which the Great Assize was issued; if this were known, it would probably be found to coincide with one of the periods at which great changes were made in the judicial staff.

Trials in the country.

The Curia in 1164.

In 1166.

Increase of business.

The first however of these epochs is the year 1166. The

[1] Pipe Rolls of Henry II, pp. 17, 26, 65. An assize of the Chancellor and Henry of Essex is mentioned in Essex, pleas of the Chancellor and the earl of Leicester in Lincolnshire, in the second year. In the fourth year are entered pleas of the Chancellor in Middlesex.

[2] Roger of Pontigny (V. S. Thom. ed. Giles), i. 102; W. Fitz-Stephen, ibid. i. 170, 186.

[3] Madox, Hist. Exch. p. 30; Formulare Angl. p. xix.

[4] Under Becket as Chancellor were fifty-two clerks; some of them however belonged to his private retinue. W. Fitz-Stephen, i. 196.

Itinerant justices in 1166.

changes in the Curia Regis at this date were so great as to call for especial notice from John of Salisbury, even in the height of the Becket controversy [1]; and the Assize of Clarendon, which belongs to the same year, denotes the character of the changes. Yet the Assize of Clarendon was directed to the improvement of provincial justice; and it was carried out, not by a new body of judges, but by two of the king's ministers, the justiciar and the earl of Essex, with the assistance of the sheriffs, who, acting under royal writ as administrators of the new law, still engrossed the title of 'justitiae errantes [2].' The development of the central jurisdiction is traceable by inference from that of the

In 1168.

provincial judicature. The four Exchequer officers [3] who assessed the aid *pur fille marier* in 1168 are found hearing placita and attesting concords shortly after; it follows that they acted not only as taxers but as judges. The six circuits of the tallagers of 1173 were no doubt suggestive of the two circuits of the justices in

In 1176.

1175 and the six circuits of the judges in 1176 [4]. It is then to these years, from 1166 to 1176, that we must refer the creation or development of the large staff of judges in the Curia Regis

Growth of the staff of judges.

which we find acting in 1178. All the eighteen justices of 1176 were officers of the Exchequer; some of them are found in 1175 holding 'placita Curiae Regis' in bodies of three or four judges [5], and not in the same combinations in which they took their judicial journeys. We can scarcely help the conclusion that the new jurisprudence was being administered by

[1] 'Quae autem circa Anglorum curiam innovantur, ubi rerum crebrae mutationes sunt, vobis notiora esse arbitror quam nobis.' John of Salisbury writes thus to Bartholomew bishop of Exeter; Ep. 145.

[2] Above, p. 388, note 1.

[3] Richard of Ilchester, Wido dean of Waltham, Reginald of Warenne, and William Basset, were the four. See Madox, Hist. Exch. pp. 102, 145.

[4] See the lists for 1176, in Bened. i. 107; Madox, Hist. Exch. p. 86; and those for 1173 are in the Pipe Rolls only. In 1175, Ranulf Glanvill and Hugh de Cressi visited the eastern and midland counties, William de Lanvalei and Thomas Basset the south and west. Ibid. p. 85.

[5] For instance, in 1176 William Fitz-Ralph, Bertram de Verdun, and William Basset hear pleas in Curia Regis touching Buckinghamshire and Bedfordshire: yet, on the eyre, these two counties are visited by three other judges; moreover Bertram de Verdun visited Worcestershire, and the other two with Hugh de Gundeville visited seven midland counties. The first placita Curiae Regis mentioned by Madox are in 1175. Hist. Exch. pp. 64, 65.

committees of the general body of justices, who were equally qualified to sit in the Curia and Exchequer and to undertake the fiscal and judicial work of the eyre.

Henry reduces the number in 1178.

The year 1178 furnishes another epoch. Henry finding that the eighteen judges of the Curia were too many, that they caused entanglements in the business of the court, and expense and distress to the suitors, reduced them at once to five[1]. Some were dismissed perhaps for misconduct; but very many of the existing judges reappear again in functions scarcely distinguishable from those which they had discharged before. Yet the statement of the diminution of their number, which is made by a historian singularly well informed as to the affairs of the court, has considerable significance. From this date we may fix the existence of the sittings of the Curia Regis 'in Banco.' Their proceedings are still nominally transacted 'coram rege,' but nominally only. 'The five are to hear all the complaints of the kingdom and to do right, and not to depart from the Curia Regis.' Questions which are too hard for them are to be referred to the king in person, who will decide them with the advice of the wise men of the kingdom.

The Curia Regis 'in banco.'

Changes in 1179.

The year 1179 witnessed another change, possibly however of persons rather than of system. The great justiciar had resigned, and Henry had put the office as it were into commission, employing the bishops of Norwich, Ely, and Winchester as heads of three bodies of itinerant judges, each containing two clerks and three knights. A fourth body, to which the northern counties were assigned, contained Ranulf Glanvill, who was to succeed, the next year, to the justiciarship, with five other judges. This fourth committee, according to the chronicler,

[1] Benedict, i. 207: 'Itaque dominus rex moram faciens in Anglia quaesivit de justitiis quos in Anglia constituerat, si bene et modeste tractaverunt homines regni; et cum didicisset quod terra et homines terrae nimis gravati essent ex tanta justitiarum multitudine, quia octodecim erant numero; per consilium sapientium regni sui quinque tantum elegit, duos scilicet clericos et tres laicos: et erant omnes de privata familia sua. Et statuit quod illi quinque audirent omnes clamores regni, et rectum facerent, et quod a Curia Regis non recederent, sed ibi ad audiendum clamores hominum remanerent, ita ut, si aliqua quaestio inter eos veniret quae per eos ad finem duci non posset, auditui regio praesentaretur et sicut ei et sapientioribus regni placeret terminaretur.'

The Curia in 1179.

entered into the place assigned in 1178 to the five judges retained in the Curia; 'these six are the justices constituted in the Curia Regis to hear the complaints of the people[1]:' why the circuit most remote from the capital was assigned to them we are not told, but as the whole business of the eyre was concluded between April 1 and August 27, there could have been no insuperable difficulty.

This is the last notice of the constitution of the Curia Regis which the historians of Henry's reign have preserved to us: and the modifications which are traceable in records from this point to the date of Magna Carta are of personal rather than legal importance. The work of Glanvill furnishes us with the rules of procedure; the Rotuli Curiae Regis which begin in 1194 afford a record of the actual business done, and the names of the judges employed are discoverable from these and other records.

General conclusion as to the growth of the Curia.

So far then as concerns the framework of the supreme judicature, our conclusion for the present is this: from the year 1179 sessions of 'justitiarii in Banco[2]' are regularly held in the Curia Regis, nominally but not actually 'coram rege.' These justices are a selection from a much larger staff, before whom Exchequer business is done, and who undertake the work of the circuits: and it would appear probable that the selection was altered from time to time, possibly from year to year. Their work was to hear all suits that were brought before the king, not only criminal but civil, cases in which the revenue or rights of the king were touched, and cases of private litigation with which the king, except as supreme judge, had no concern: all the business in fact which came at a later period before the courts of King's Bench, Exchequer, and Common Pleas. Although

[1] Bened. i. 238; R. de Diceto, c. 605.

[2] Glanvill, lib. ii. 6; viii. c. 1; xi. c. 1: 'coram Justitiis Domini Regis in banco residentibus.' Coke's notion that by this session of the judges the Common Bench or Court of Common Pleas is meant, is mentioned by Madox only to refute it; Hist. Exch. p. 546. Foss also argues conclusively against it; Judges of England, ii. 161. See also Hardy's Introduction to the Close Rolls, vol. i. pp. xxv sq. Instances of Final Concords made before the justices of the Curia, answering to those described by Glanvill as made before the justices in Banco, will be found in Madox, Formulare Anglicanum, pp. 217 sq., and in the Fines published by the Record Commission; above, p. 598, note 2.

The later divisions of the courts.

their deliberations were not held in the king's presence, they followed his person, or the justiciar in the king's absence; a rule which must have been most burdensome to ordinary suitors, and which accordingly, so far as touches private civil suits or 'communia placita,' was abolished by Magna Carta. The fixing of the Common Pleas at Westminster broke up the unity of the Curia[1]; but it was not until the end of the reign of Henry III that the general staff was divided into three distinct and permanent bodies of judges, each under its own chief.

The court of royal audience.

But the court or courts thus organised must no longer be regarded as the last resource of suitors. The reservation of knotty cases to be decided by the king with the council of his wise men[2], cases which, as we learn from the Dialogus de Scaccario, included questions of revenue as well as of law in general[3], continues the ancient personal jurisdiction of the sovereign. The very act that seems to give stability and consistency to the ordinary jurisdiction of the Curia, reduces it to a lower rank.

The judicial supremacy of the king.

The judicial supremacy of the king is not limited or fettered by the new rule; it has thrown off an offshoot, or, as the astronomical theorists would say, a nebulous envelope, which has rolled up into a compact body, but the old nucleus of light remains unimpaired. The royal justice, diffused through the close personal council[4], or tempered and adapted by royal grace and equity under the pen of the chancellor[5], or exercised in the national

[1] By the seventeenth article of Magna Carta. The Articuli super Cartas, 28 Edw. I, c. 4, forbid Common Pleas to be holden henceforth in the Exchequer.

[2] Above, p. 601. The same principle is stated in the Articles of the Assize of Northampton: 'Nisi tam grandis sit querela quod non possit deduci sine domino rege, vel talis quam justitiae ei reportent pro dubitatione sua.'

[3] Dialogus, i. c. 8: 'Si . . . fieri contigerit, ut inter ipsos majores dissensionis oriatur occasio . . , horum omnium cognitio ipsi principi reservabitur.'

[4] See Sir Francis Palgrave's Essay on the Jurisdiction of the King's Council, and Dicey's Essay on the Privy Council.

[5] The growth of the Chancellor's jurisdiction does not fall within the present period; but the increased importance of his position is remarkable, and the germ of his future functions was in being already. William Fitz-Stephen, who was one of Becket's clerks, writes thus: 'Cancellarii Angliae est ut secundus a rege in regno habeatur, ut altera parte sigilli regii, quod et ad ejus pertinet custodiam, propria signet mandata; ut capella regis in ipsius sit dispositione et cura, ut vacantes archiepiscopatus, episcopatus, abbatias et baronias cadentes in manu regis ipse suscipiat et conservet; ut

Its continuity.

assembly as in the ancient witenagemote, or concentrated in the hands of an irresponsible executive in the Star Chamber, has for many generations and in many various forms to assert its vitality, unimpaired by its successive emanations.

The growth of the itinerant judicature.

In tracing the history of the central judicature we have had to anticipate the leading points of interest in the development of the visitatorial jurisdiction. The whole may be briefly summed up. The circuits of the royal officers for fiscal and judicial purposes, which we have traced in the reign of Henry I, continue to have the same character under Henry II, the judicial forms following rather than preceding the fiscal. In 1166 the itinerant court receives new and full instructions from the Assize of Clarendon, but it is still the Curia Regis in progress, a great part of the work being done by the sheriffs[1]. In 1176 six circuits are formed, eighteen judges are specially told off in six detachments, as had been done in the fiscal iter of 1173: in 1178, 1179, and 1180 there seem to be four circuits, and the arrangements in the later years vary between two and six. Under Richard we have still further modifications, and the same in the early years of John, none of them however involving a new principle of construction, but all perhaps implying a restriction

Formation and changes of circuits.

omnibus regis adsit consiliis, ut etiam non vocatus accedat; ut omnia sigilliferi regii clerici sui manu signentur, omnia cancellarii consilio disponantur; item ut, suffragantibus ei per Dei gratiam vitae meritis, non moriatur nisi archiepiscopus aut episcopus, si voluerit. Inde est quod cancellaria emenda non est.' V. S. Thom. i. 186. The Dialogus de Scaccario represents the justiciar as 'primus post regem;' the term 'secundus a rege' probably means next after the justiciar; the form is frequently used by Becket's friends. The Dialogus (lib. i. c. 5) confirms most of the statements of the biographer just cited; nothing is done without his consent and advice either in the Curia or in the Exchequer; he has charge of the royal seal, sealing it up into its loculus or purse, which is kept by the treasurer.

The statement that the Chancery is not purchaseable is disproved by some important exceptions. See above, pp. 384, 497. The fact that the chancellor was always in attendance on the king led to the petitions for royal grace and favour being entrusted to him, first for custody, and afterwards for hearing. Hence arose the equitable jurisdiction by which he remedied the 'summum jus' of the common law or promised remedies in cases which were not provided for by the common lawyers.

[1] The action of a justice itinerant at Bedford in 1163 was one of the grounds of the quarrel between the king and Becket; the judge was Simon Fitz-Peter, who had ceased to be sheriff of Bedfordshire two years before. Rog. Pont. S. T. C. i. 114.

Itinerant justices.

of the local jurisdictions of the sheriff and the shire-moot[1]. At last, in the eighteenth clause of Magna Carta, the king undertakes to send two justices four times a year to take the assizes of Mort d'ancester, Novel disseisin, and Darrein presentment. This arrangement proved no doubt far too burdensome to be continued, but the changes indicated in the re-issues of the Charter and carried into effect in septennial iters of the judges lie beyond our present inquiry. The justices of the year 1176 are the first to whom the name *Justitiarii Itinerantes* is given in the Pipe Rolls: the commissioners of 1170 are called *Barones errantes:* 'perlustrantes judices' is the term used by the author of Dialogus; the sheriffs were the 'errantes justitiae' known to John of Salisbury in 1159. The various applications of the terms may mark the growth and consolidation of a system by which the sheriffs were deprived of the most important of their functions.

The courts of these justices are full county courts.

The visits of the itinerant justices form the link between the Curia Regis and the Shire-moot, between royal and popular justice, between the old system and the new. The courts in which they preside are the ancient county courts, under new conditions, but substantially identical with those of the Anglo-Saxon times. The full shire-moot consists, as before, of all the lords of land and their stewards, and the representatives of the townships, the parish priest, the reeve and four men from each; but the times of meeting, the sphere of business, and the nature of procedure during the period before us have undergone great and significant changes, some of which can be minutely traced, whilst others can be accounted for only by conjecture.

Times of holding the county court.

The Anglo-Saxon shire-moot was held twice a year: the county court of Henry I was held as it had been in King Edward's days, that is, according to the 'Leges Henrici I,' twice a year still. Yet in the confirmation of the Great Charter, issued by Henry III in 1217, it is ordered that the county court shall meet not more than once a month, or less frequently where such has been the custom. It is not easy to determine the date or the causes of so great a change. Possibly the sheriffs had

[1] Above, pp. 505 sq.

Increase of small suits in the county courts.

abused their power of summoning special meetings and of fining absentees; a custom which comes into prominence in the reign of Henry III, and which shows that it was the direct interest of the sheriffs to multiply the occasions of summons. Possibly it may have arisen from the increase of business under the new system of writs and assizes, which involved the frequent adjournment of the court for short terms: possibly from an earlier usage by which the practice of the county court was assimilated to that of the hundred with the special object of determining suits between litigants from different hundreds or liberties. Or it may have been caused by the gradual withdrawal of the more important suits from the shire-moot, the natural result of which would be the increase of the number of less important meetings for the convenience of petty suitors.

Limitations of the power of the sheriff.

The power of the sheriff, again, had been very much limited, not only by the course of political events noticed in the last chapter, but by the process of centering the administration of justice in the hands of the itinerant justices and the Curia Regis,—a process the stages of which may be more easily traced. At the beginning of the period the sheriffs were the 'errantes justitiae,' only occasionally superseded and superintended by the itinerant justices. As sheriffs, probably, they presided in the court of the county in which the suitors were the judges, and were answerable for the maintenance of the peace: as royal justices they acted under special writ, managed the pleas of the Crown, and conducted the tourn and leet, or the courts which were afterwards so called. In 1166 they were still in the same position; the itinerant justices by themselves, and the sheriffs by themselves, received and acted on the presentment of the grand juries. But from 1170, after the great inquest into their exactions[1], their authority is more and more limited. In the Assize of Northampton they are rather servants than colleagues of the itinerant justices; in 1194 it is provided that they shall no more be justices in their own counties, and the elective office of coroner is instituted to relieve them from the duty of keeping the pleas of the Crown[2]. In 1195 the duty of receiving the oath

[1] Above, p. 472.

[2] Above, p. 505.

The sheriff forbidden to hold pleas of the Crown.

of the peace is laid, not on the sheriffs, but on knights assigned in each county, the duty of the sheriffs being only to receive and keep the criminals taken by these knights until the coming of the justices. In 1215 the barons propose that the sheriffs shall no longer meddle with the pleas of the Crown, without the coroners[1]; whilst the Great Charter, in the clause founded on that proposal, forbids either sheriff or coroner to hold such pleas at all. We may question whether these regulations were strictly observed, especially as before the year 1258 the sheriffs seem to be as powerful as ever, but they show a distinct policy of substituting the action of the justices for that of the sheriffs, a policy which might have led to judicial absolutism were it not that the growing institution of trial by jury vested in the freemen of the county far more legal power than it took away from the sheriffs. These officers too had long ceased even remotely to represent the local feeling or interest.

The fullest county court held by the itinerant justices.

The shire-moot which assembled to meet the itinerant judges was, however, a much more complete representation of the county than the ordinary county court which assembled from month to month. The great franchises, liberties, and manors which by their tenure were exempted from shire-moot and hundred were, before these visitors, on equal terms with the freeholders of the geldable, as the portion of the county was called, which had not fallen into the franchises. Not even the tenants of a great escheat in the royal hands escaped the obligation to attend their visitation[2]. The representation was thoroughly organised: side by side with the reeve and four men of the rural townships appeared the twelve legal men of each of the chartered boroughs which owed no suit to the ordinary county court[3]. In the formation of the jury of pre-

[1] Articles of the Barons, art. 14; Magna Carta, art. 24.

[2] Assize of Clarendon, art. 9, 11.

[3] Charter of Dunwich, Select Charters, p. 303. Customs of Kent, Statutes of the Realm, i. 223. Instances of this sort of representation taken from the Assize Rolls will be found in Eyton's History of Shropshire in considerable numbers. A writ of Henry III, issued in 1231, directs the summons to the county court to be addressed to 'archbishops, bishops, abbots, priors, earls, barons, knights, and freeholders; four men of each township and twelve burghers of each borough to meet the justices.' Select Charters, p. 349.

Representative juries.

sentment the same principle is as clear; each hundred supplies twelve legal men, and each township four, to make report to the justices under the Assize of Clarendon, and in 1194 twelve knights from each hundred answer for their hundred under all the articles of the eyre, whether criminal, civil, or fiscal[1]. The court thus strengthened and consolidated, is adopted by the royal officers as an instrument to be used for other purposes. All who are bound to attend before the itinerant justices are compelled to attend the forest courts[2]; and they probably form the 'plenus comitatus' which elects, according to Magna Carta, the knights who are to take the assizes, and the twelve knights who are to inquire into the abuses which Magna Carta was designed to reform.

Institution of juries, a step in the growth of a representative system.

164. It is in the new system of recognitions, assizes, and presentments by jury that we find the most distinct traces of the growth of the principle of representation; and this in three ways. In the first place, the institution of the jury was itself based on a representative idea: the jurors, to whatever fact or in whatever capacity they swore, declared the report of the community as to the fact in question. In the second place, the method of inquest was in England brought into close connexion with the procedure of the shire-moot, and thus the inquisitorial process, whether its object was the recognition of a right or the presentment of a criminal, was from the moment of its introduction carried on in association with the previously existing representative institutions, such as were the reeve and four best men, the twelve senior thegns, and the later developments of the same practice which have been just enumerated in our account of the formation of the county court and the usage of legal assessment. In the third place, the particular expedients adopted for the regulation of the inquests paved the way in a remarkable manner for the system of county representation in the parliament as we saw it exemplified on the first occasion of its appearance in the reign of John. The use of election and representation in the courts

[1] Hoveden, iii. 262; above, p. 505.

[2] Assize of Woodstock, art. 11. Cf. Magna Carta, art. 44; Carta de Foresta, art. 2; Assize of Arms, of 1253; Select Charters, p. 365.

of law furnished a precedent for the representation of the county by two sworn knights in the national council. On each of these heads some detail is necessary which may throw light incidentally on some kindred points of interest.

The history of the Jury has been treated by various writers from every possible point of view[1]: its national origin, its historical development, the moral ideas on which it is founded, and the rational analysis of its legal force, have all been discussed many times over with all the apparatus of learning and the acute penetration of philosophical research. Some of these aspects are foreign to our present inquiry. Yet the institution is of so great interest both in itself and in its relations that some notice of it is indispensable.

Trial by jury variously treated.

We have sketched, in an earlier stage of this work, the formation of the primitive German courts: they were tribunals of fully qualified members of the community, a selection it might be from a body of equally competent companions, able to declare the law or custom of the country, and to decide what, according to that custom, should be done in the particular case brought before them. They were not set to decide what was the truth of facts, but to determine what action was to be taken upon proof given. The proof was itself furnished by three means, the oaths of the parties to the suit and their compurgators, the production of witnesses, and the use of the ordeal: the practice of trial by battle being a sort of ultimate expedient to obtain a practical decision, an expedient partly akin to the ordeal as a judgment of God, and partly based on the idea that where legal measures had failed recourse must be had to the primitive law of force,—the feud or right of private war,—only regulated as far as possible by law and regard for the saving of life. For each of these methods of proof there were minute rules and formalities, the infringement or neglect of which put the offender out of court. The complainant addressed his charge to the defendant

Modes of trial among the German races.

Oaths, evidence, ordeal.

[1] See Palgrave, Rise and Progress of the English Commonwealth; Forsyth, History of Trial by Jury; Biener, das Englische Geschwornengericht; Gneist, Self-Government, i. 74 sq.; K. Maurer in the Kritische Ueberschau, v. pp. 180 sq., 332 sq.; and Brunner, Entstehung der Schwurgerichte.

Formalism of the system.

in solemn traditional form; the defendant replied to the complainant by an equally solemn verbal and logical contradiction. The compurgators swore, with joined hands and in one voice, to the purity and honesty of the oath of their principal[1]. Where the oath was inconclusive, the parties brought their witnesses to declare such knowledge as their position as neighbours had given them; the court determined the point to which the witnesses must swear, and they swore to that particular fact[2]. They were not examined or made to testify all they knew; but swore to the fact on which the judges determined that evidence should be taken. If the witnesses also failed the ordeal was used. And where the defeated party ventured to impugn the sentence thus obtained, he might challenge the determination of the court by appealing the members of it to trial by combat. This practice, however common among some branches of the German stock, was by no means universal, and, as has been pointed out, was not practised among the native English.

The germ of the jury not contained in this.

In these most primitive proceedings are found circumstances, which on a superficial view seem analogous to later trial by jury: but on a closer inspection they warrant no distinct impression of the kind. The ancient judges who declare the law and give the sentence—the rachinburgii, or the scabini—are not in any respect the jurors of the modern system, who ascertain the fact by hearing and balancing evidence, leaving the law and sentence to the presiding magistrate: nor are the ancient witnesses who depose to the precise point in dispute, more nearly akin to the jurors who have to inquire the truth and declare the result of the inquiry, than to the modern witnesses who swear to speak not only the truth and nothing but the truth, but the whole truth. The compurgators again swear to confirm the oath of their principal, and have nothing in common with

[1] The Anglo-Saxon forms of oath may be found in the Ancient Laws, ed. Thorpe, pp. 76, 77. The oath of the compurgator runs thus: 'On thone Drihten se ath is clæne and unmæne the N. swor.'

[2] The number of witnesses required varied in the different nations; the Saxon and Lombard laws required two at least: the Bavarian, three or more: the Frank laws, seven or twelve, according to the importance of the matter in question. Brunner, Schwurgericht, p. 51.

the jury but the fact that they swear[1]. Yet although this is distinctly the case, the procedure in question is a step in the history of the jury: the first form in which the jury appears is that of witness, and the principle that gives force to that witness is the idea that it is the testimony of the community: even the idea of the compurgatory oath is not without the same element; the compurgators must be possessed of qualities and legal qualifications which shall secure their credibility.

Yet the oath and evidence are of a representative character.

Beyond this stage, modified it is true here as elsewhere by different circumstances and local usages, the Anglo-Saxon system did not proceed. The compurgation, the sworn witness, and the ordeal supplied the proof; and the sheriff with his fellows, the bishop, the shire-thegns, the judices and juratores, the suitors of the court, declared the law. Only in the law of Ethelred, by which the twelve senior thegns in each wapentake are sworn not to accuse any falsely[2], do we find the germ of a more advanced system, in which the community seems to undertake the duty of prosecution: but the interpretation of the passage is disputed, and its bearing contested, although it seems to imply no more than that the English were far in arrear of the Frank jurisprudence.

Anglo-Saxon system.

The twelve thegns in the shire-moot.

The whole system of recognition by sworn inquest, with the single exception, if it be an exception, which has just been mentioned, was introduced into England by the Normans: the laws of Edward, the Domesday Survey, the fiscal recognitions of the reigns of William Rufus and Henry I[3], are distinctly a novelty, a part of the procedure of the newly-developed system of government. Various theories have been invented for their origin. Many writers of authority have maintained that the entire jury system is indigenous in England, some deriving it from Celtic tradition based on the principles of Roman law and adopted by the Anglo-Saxons and Normans from the

Recognitions introduced into England by the Normans.

[1] Forsyth, Hist. of Jury, p. 83. [2] Above, pp. 115, 396.

[3] Above, pp. 385, 394, 395. To the instances of early recognitions given at p. 395 may be added one described in Thoroton's Nottinghamshire, iii. 77; Henry I in 1106 commissions five barons to ascertain the customs of the church of York by the oath of twelve men, one of whom is Ulviet, lageman of York, father of Thomas the alderman of the Merchant Guild; above, p. 412.

Various opinions on the national origin of jury.

people they had conquered[1]. Others have regarded it as a product of that legal genius of the Anglo-Saxons of which Alfred is the mythic impersonation; or as derived by that nation from the customs of primitive Germany or from their intercourse with the Danes. Nor, even when it is admitted that the system of recognition was introduced from Normandy, have legal writers agreed as to the source from which the Normans themselves derived it. One scholar maintains that it was brought by the Norsemen from Scandinavia; another that it was derived from the processes of the canon law; another that it was developed on Gallic soil from Roman principles; another that it came from Asia through the Crusades, a theory which has little more to recommend it than the still wilder supposition that it is of Slavonic origin, and borrowed by the Angles and Saxons from their neighbours in Northern Europe. But all these theories on examination show that their inventors have either been misled by superficial coincidences, or argue on hypothesis only. The only principle which the systems on which the theories are built have in common is the use of the oath as an instrument of judicial procedure, and this use is universal. The truth seems to be that the inquest by sworn recognitors is directly derived

[1] According to Brunner, pp. 11–19, the origin of the jury among the Welsh, from whom it was borrowed by the Anglo-Saxons, is maintained by Philipps (On Juries) and Probert (On the Ancient Laws of Cambria); Finlason in his introduction to Reeves' History of English Law maintains that it was derived by the Anglo-Saxons, through the Britons, from Rome; Selden, Spelman, Coke, Turner, Phillips, and G. L. von Maurer regard it as a product of Anglo-Saxon genius. Of the authors who hold that it was imported from primitive Germany, Brunner mentions Bacon, Montesquieu, Blackstone, Savigny, and Nicholson in the preface to Wilkins' Anglo-Saxon Laws; Wormius and Worsaae held that it was derived from the Norsemen through the Danes; Hickes, Reeves, and others, that it was derived from the Norsemen through the Normans of the Conquest; and Konrad Maurer, who has investigated the analogous system in use among the Norsemen, argues for a common *North* German origin, from which the principle of jury has been developed in different ways by the several races in which it is found. Of those writers who allow that it is of Norman introduction, Daniels maintained that the Normans found it existing in France; Möhl derives it from the usages of the canon law; Meyer supposed that it came from Asia by way of the Crusades; Maciejowski claimed it for the Slavonic neighbours of the Angles and Saxons. The theory given in the text is mainly that of Palgrave, but corrected and adjusted by the recent writings of Dr. Brunner.

from the Frank Capitularies, into which it may have been adopted from the fiscal regulations of the Theodosian Code[1], and thus own some distant relationship with the Roman jurisprudence. The Karolingian kings issued instructions to their Missi very much as Henry II issued instructions to his itinerant justices, and they gave special commissions of inquiry into fiscal and judicial matters to be answered by the oath of sworn witnesses in the district court[2]. These answers then embodied the belief or knowledge of the local court as representing the community, every qualified member of the community being a member also of the court. The persistence of the inquisitorial system is proved not only by Norman charters and customs, but

The Inquests of the Frank kings.

[1] Palgrave, English Commonwealth, p. 271; Brunner, p. 87. The following passages from the Theodosian Code are cited by Brunner: 'Super vacantibus ac caducis . . . certi etiam dirigantur qui cuncta solerter inquirant et cujus fuerint facultates, et si nemo eas sibi jure nititur retentare. Ac si locum fisco factum esse claruerit occupatis prius bonis et rerum omnium descriptione perfecta . . .' Cod. Theod. x. 10. l. 11. 'Ex privatorum . . . sollicitudine contractuum . . . illis . . . personis a quibus publici muneris injuncta curantur, nullum fomitem calumniae patimur litis accendi. Cur enim continentiam venditionis alienae inquisitio palatina rimetur.' Ibid. l. 29.

[2] The following instances show that this usage was applied primarily to cases in which the royal interests were concerned, and that the witnesses supplied the evidence of the neighbourhood: 'Item volumus ut omnis inquisitio quae de rebus ad jus fisci nostri pertinentibus facienda est, non per testes qui producti fuerint sed per illos qui in eo comitatu meliores et veraciores esse cognoscuntur, per illorum testimonium inquisitio fiat, et juxta quod illi inde testificati fuerint vel contineantur vel reddantur.' Capit. 829. § 2. 'Ut pagenses per sacramentum aliorum hominum causas non inquirantur nisi tantum dominicas.' Capit. 819. § 1; Brunner, p. 88; Baluze, i. p. 409. 'Ut in omni comitatu hi qui meliores et veraciores inveniri possunt eligantur a missis nostris ad inquisitiones faciendas et rei veritatem dicendam et ut adjutores comitum sint ad justitias faciendas.' Baluze, i. 449. The best instances for comparison are the Assizes of Clarendon and Northampton, the Inquest of Sheriffs, and the Capitula of 1194; they may be compared with the capitula data missis in 802, e. g. 'de fidelitate jusjurandum ut omnes repromittant;' Baluze, i. 267. 'Inquiratur qui sunt qui debent domino regi homagium et non fecerunt;' Inquest of Sheriffs, art. xi. 'Item justitiae capiant domini regis fidelitates;' Ass. Northampt. art. 5. Or again on the subject of criminals, fugitives, strangers, forgers, the effects of war, abundant coincidences of the most striking character will be found in the capitularies of 802, 806, 819, 829, 854, 860, 865. The following extract from a capitulary of 868 is in close parallel with the instructions for the Domesday Inquest: 'Inquirant quoque quot (canonici, etc.) tempore avi nostri Karoli et domini genitoris nostri Hludovici unoquoque in loco fuerint et quot modo sint; et ubi loca a Nortmannis sive a quibuslibet aliis destructa et penitus adnullata, quot ibi nunc propter paucitatem rerum et devastationem eorundem constitui vel ordinari possint;' Baluze, ii. 139.

The Inquest perpetuated in Normandy from the Karolingian times.

by the existence of the kindred principle, undeveloped indeed and early forgotten, in the jurisprudence of the rest of France[1]. The order to hold such inquest was a royal, or in Normandy a ducal privilege, although it was executed by the ordinary local officers; primarily it was employed to ascertain the rights and interests of the Crown; by special favour permission was obtained to use it in the concerns of the churches and of private individuals[2]. Even under this system the sworn recognitors were rather witnesses than judges; they swore to facts within their own knowledge; the magistrate to whom the inquiry was entrusted was the inquirer, and he inquired through the oath of men sworn to speak the truth and selected in consequence of their character and local knowledge.

This was the source of trial by jury.

Such was the instrument which, introduced in its rough simplicity at the Conquest, was developed by the lawyers of the Plantagenet period into the modern trial by jury. Henry II expanded and consolidated the system so much that he was not unnaturally regarded as the founder of it in its English character. From being an exceptional favour, it became under his hand a part of the settled law of the land, a resource which was open to

[1] The continuance of the system in France from the Karolingian times and through the Norman period is proved by Dr. Brunner in his work so frequently referred to above. The most curious phaenomena in connexion with it is the fact that it was only on English soil that it gained much development, the Norman lawyers seeing themselves rapidly outstripped by those of England, and the institution withering away in the rest of France until it became extinct.

[2] The coincidences between the practice described by Glanvill and the usages of the Great Coûtumier of Normandy have of course led to two opposite theories; one that the Norman usage was a faulty imitation of the English; the other that the system was transplanted full-grown from Normandy to England. Neither is true; the system of recognition existed in Normandy before it was brought to England, but it was developed in England, and that development probably had a reflex influence on Normandy. It would be wrong to suppose that the Great Coutumier affords an exact picture of the Normandy even of Henry II's reign, much more that the English system developed from a germ which is represented by the Great Coûtumier. There are however in the minute legal peculiarities of the Norman recognitions as described in that work, signs of a primitive character, a simplicity and general applicability which seem to show that it had been naturalised there in a much earlier form than it was in England, and this confirms the historical and documentary evidence. The whole subject is interesting, but it involves a great quantity of minute legal details which have very slight connexion with our present inquiries.

every suitor. The recognitions are mentioned by Ralph Niger[1] as one of his expedients of tyranny; by Ranulf Glanvill as a boon conferred by royal benevolence on the people, and with the counsel and consent of the nobles. John, in a charter granted to the church of Beverley, forbids that the rights of that church should be damaged by assizes or recognitions, and adds that the pleas shall be held in the court of the Provost as they were in the reign of Henry I, before recognitions or assizes had been ordained in the kingdom[2]. So early had Henry II acquired the fame of having instituted the system, which he had indeed remodelled and made a part of the common right of his subjects, but which had certainly existed under his four predecessors.

Recognition by jury said to be an invention of Henry II.

The application of the principle to legal matters—for we have already noticed its fiscal use—may be placed under two heads: the inquest in civil matters exemplified in the Great Assize and in the Assizes of Novel disseisin, Mort d'ancester, Darrein presentment, and others; and the inquest of presentment in criminal matters, which appears in the Assizes of Clarendon and Northampton. The Great Assize was, according to Glanvill, a royal boon by which wholesome provision was made for the lives of men and the integrity of the State, so that in maintaining their right to the possession of their freeholds the suitors may not be exposed to the doubtful issue of trial by battle[3]. This institution proceeds from the highest equity, for the right which after much and long delay can scarcely be said to be proved by battle, is by the beneficial use of this constitution more rapidly and more conveniently demonstrated. It is in fact the most distinct mark of the original equity with which the royal jurisdiction, as civilisation and legal knowledge advanced, was applied to remedy the evils inherent in the rough and indiscriminating formality of the popular tribunals: such the inquest had been under the Karolings, such was the recognition or assize under

His use of it in the assizes.

The Great Assize.

An equitable institution.

[1] Above, p. 492, note 1.

[2] 'Ubi placita inde fuerunt et esse consueverunt tempore regis Henrici patris nostri vel tempore Henrici regis avi patris nostri, antequam recognitiones vel assisae in regno nostro essent constitutae . . . d . . 8° Oct. anno regni nostri quarto.' Houard, Anciennes Loix, ii. 288.

[3] Glanvill, de Legibus, ii. 7; above, p. 575.

Trial by battle disliked.

the Plantagenets. The trial by battle was in England an innovation; it was one from which the English recoiled as an instrument associated with tyranny, if not devised for the purposes of tyrants; and the charters of the boroughs frequently contain a provision, dearly bought no doubt but greatly valued, that the burghers shall not be liable to its use[1]. In the place of this barbarous foreign custom, the following machinery is applied; the possessor of the freehold in dispute applies to the Curia Regis to stop all proceedings in the local courts until a recognition has taken place as to the right of the claimant[2]: and thereupon a writ is issued to the sheriff to that effect. The party in possession is thus said to have placed himself on the assize; and the next step is taken by the claimant, who demands a writ by which four lawful knights of the county or neighbourhood shall be empowered to choose twelve lawful knights of the same neighbourhood, who shall declare on oath which of the two litigants has the greater right to the land in question[3]. The writ accordingly is issued, addressed to the sheriff, directing him to summon four knights to appear at Westminster to choose the twelve. They appear in due course, and under oath nominate the twelve recognitors, who are then summoned to appear before the king or his justices prepared to make their declaration[4]. On the day fixed they present themselves and the suit proceeds; if the twelve are acquainted with the circumstances in dispute and are unanimous, the transaction is complete; they are sworn 'that they will not speak falsehood nor conceal truth' according to knowledge gained by eye-witness or 'by the words of their fathers and by such words as they are bound to have such confidence in as if they were their own[5].' The declaration is made, the sentence is issued. If however the twelve knights or any of them are ignorant, or if they disagree, others are to be called in who have the requisite information; and when the complete number of twelve unanimous witnesses will depose to the fact,

Process of the Great Assize.

Oath of the recognitors.

[1] See the Charter of London, Select Charters, p. 103; Winchester, ib. p. 257; Lincoln, ib. p. 258; above, p. 425, note 1.

[2] Glanvill, ii. 7.

[3] Ibid. c. 10.

[4] Ibid. c. 12.

[5] Ibid. c. 17.

Other assizes.

their verdict is of the same account. The proceedings in the other assizes are of the same kind, save that the twelve recognitors are nominated by the sheriff himself without the intervention of the four knights electors[1].

Recognitions before the itinerant justices.

The date of the original enactment of the Great Assize is unknown; but the use of recognition by twelve sworn witnesses is prescribed in the Constitutions of Clarendon for cases of dispute as to lay or clerical tenure[2]. It there appears as a part of the work of the 'capitalis justitia.' From Glanvill it is clear that all such litigation might be transacted before the itinerant justices; and the Assize of Northampton of 1176 places among the agenda of the eyre recognitions of the seisin of heirs, and of 'disseisin upon the assize,' under which descriptions we may detect the cases of Mort d'ancester and Novel disseisin[3]. In 1194 the grand jury of the hundred are empowered to act on all the business of the session, in which are included all recognitions and assizes ordered by the king's writ, and even recognitions under the Great Assize where the property in dispute is worth five pounds a year or less[4]. In 1198 the sum is raised to ten pounds, and the elections under the Great Assize are to be made before the itinerant justices. The great charter of John likewise retains the three recognitions of Novel disseisin, Mort d'ancester, and Darrein presentment, to be heard in the quarterly county courts by the justices and four chosen knights[5]: and the charter of 1217 orders the same rule to be observed once a year[6], except in cases of Darrein presentment, which are reserved for the justices of the bench. The recognitions have become a permanent and regular part of the county business.

The jury of presentment of criminals.

The development of the jury of presentment is, after its reconstitution or creation by Henry II, marked by corresponding stages of progress. But its origin is less clear. By some jurists it is brought into close connexion with the system of

[1] Glanvill, lib. xiii. cc. 1, 2 sq.
[2] 'Recognitione duodecim legalium hominum.' Art. 9; Select Charters, p. 133.
[3] Art. 5; Select Charters, p. 145.
[4] Articles 2 and 18; Select Charters, pp. 252, 253.
[5] Art. 18. [6] Articles 13 and 15; Select Charters, p. 336.

Theory of the origin of jury in criminal causes.

compurgation, the jurors who present the list of criminals representing the compurgators of the accuser[1], and the jury which at a later period was impannelled to traverse the presentment, representing the compurgators of the accused. Others again connect it with the supposed institution of the collective frankpledge, the corporate responsibility of the tithing, the hundred, and the shire for the production of offenders, which has played so large a part in constitutional theories, but which rests on very slight foundation of fact[2]. The *frithborh* was neither a body of compurgators nor a jury of presentment. As a matter of history it seems lawful to regard the presentment as a part of the duty of the local courts for which an immemorial antiquity may be claimed with at least a strong probability. The leet juries of the small local courts do not draw their origin from any legal enactment, and bear every mark of the utmost antiquity. By them amercements are still made and presentments offered under oath, although their action is restricted and superseded by newer expedients. But their procedure affords some warrant for believing that the twelve senior thegns who swore in the county court to accuse none falsely were a jury of presentment. If such a theory be accepted, the mention of the juratores of the shire and hundred which occurs in the Pipe Roll of Henry I is accounted for, and with it the mention of a criminal jury in the Constitutions of Clarendon[3]. The obscurity of this side of the subject may be regarded as parallel with the scantiness of evidence which we have already noticed as to the recognition. From the year 1166 however the history of the criminal jury is clear. By

Assize of Clarendon.

the Assize of Clarendon inquest is to be made through each county and through each hundred, by twelve lawful men of the hundred and by four lawful men of each township, 'by their oath that they will speak the truth.' By these all persons of evil fame

[1] This is the theory of Rogge, as stated by Brunner, pp. 25, 26. Hickes long ago stated the principle that there is no real connexion between jury and compurgation. The common use of the number twelve is misleading.

[2] The theory of G. L. von Maurer; Brunner, p. 26.

[3] Const. Clar. art. 6: 'Et si tales fuerint qui culpantur quod non velit vel non audeat aliquis eos accusare, vicecomes requisitus ab episcopo faciet jurare duodecim legales homines de vicineto, seu de villa, coram episcopo, quod inde veritatem secundum conscientiam suam manifestabunt.'

are to be presented to the justices, and then to proceed to the ordeal: if they fail in the ordeal they undergo the legal punishment; if they sustain the ordeal, yet as the presentment against them is based on the evidence of the neighbourhood on the score of bad character, they are to abjure the kingdom[1]. The jury of presentment is reduced to a still more definite form, and receives a more distinct representative character in the Assize of Northampton[2], and in the Articles of Visitation of 1194: in the latter capitulary the plan used for nominating the recognitors of the Great Assize is applied to the Grand Jury, for so the body now constituted may be termed:—'In the first place, four knights are to be chosen from the whole county, who by their oath shall choose two lawful knights of each hundred or wapentake, and those two shall choose upon oath ten knights of each hundred or wapentake, or if knights be wanting, legal and free men, so that these twelve may answer under all heads concerning their whole hundred or wapentake[3].' The heads on which they answer include not only the assizes which have been already referred to in connexion with the jury, but all the pleas of the Crown, the trial of malefactors and their receivers as well as a vast amount of fiscal business. The later development of these juries does not fall under our present inquiry, but it may be generally stated thus: at an early period, even before the abolition of ordeal by the Lateran Council of 1215, a petty jury was allowed to disprove the truth of the presentment, and after the abolition of ordeal that expedient came into general use[4]. The further change in the character of the jurors, by which they became judges of fact instead of witnesses, is common to the civil and criminal jury alike. As it became difficult to find juries personally well informed as to the point at issue, the jurors summoned were allowed first to add to their number persons who possessed the requisite knowledge, under the title of afforcement.

Procedure on presentment.

Assize of Northampton, and eyre of 1194.

Later development of the jury.

[1] Assize of Clarendon, art. 1; Select Charters, p. 137.

[2] Assize of Northampton, art. 1; Select Charters, p. 143.

[3] Hoveden, iii. 262; Select Charters, p. 251.

[4] On the subsequent history of criminal jury, see Forsyth, Trial by Jury, pp. 199 sq., where the legal growth of the institution is traced with admirable clearness.

Later character of jury.

After this proceeding had been some time in use, the afforcing jurors were separated from the uninformed jurors and relieved them altogether from their character of witnesses. The verdict of the jury no longer represented their previous knowledge of the case, but the result of the evidence afforded by the witnesses of the fact; and they became accordingly judges of the fact, the law being declared by the presiding officer acting in the king's name.

Judicium parium.

In all these points we see distinctly the growth of a principle of representation, especially applied to the work of the county courts or growing up in them. The 'judicium parium' however, which is mentioned in Magna Carta, has a wider application than this. It covers all cases of amercement in the county, the hundred, and the manorial courts, and exhibits a principle which, rooted in primitive antiquity, is capable of infinite development and beneficial application; and this we have seen exemplified in the assessment processes described above.

Connexion of jury with the representative system.

It remains then briefly to point out the direct connexion between the jury system and county representation. In the earliest existing records of recognitions, the way in which the jurors are to be selected is not clearly laid down[1]. The recognitions of the Norman reigns are regarded as acts of the county court, and the possibility of election by the suitors is not excluded: it is however more probable that the recognitors were selected by the sheriff, possibly by rotation from a general list, possibly according to their nearness to the spot or acquaintance with the business in hand. On the institution of the assizes of Novel disseisin, Mort d'ancester, and Darrein presentment, the sheriff summoned the requisite number of jurors at his discretion, and the plea was held at a place named in the writ of summons, in such a way as to imply that it was to be heard not in the regular county court, but in a special session[2].

[1] In the early instances given by Palgrave, pp. clxxviii sq., we have (1) 'quibus (sc. scyris) congregatis, *eligantur* plures de illis Anglis qui sciunt quomodo terrae jacebant,' &c.; (2) 'Praecipio quod praecipias Hamonem filium Vitalis et probis vicinis de Santwic, *quos Hamo nominabit*, ut dicant veritatem.' See above, p. 395.

[2] Glanvill, xiii. 3: 'Ab initio eligendi sunt duodecim liberi et legales

The Great Assize was differently constituted: there the sheriff nominated four electors to choose the twelve recognitors, and the trial took place before the justices itinerant in the county, or before the court at Westminster[1]. The articles of 1194 place the election of the recognitors, with all the other business of the eyre, in the hands of the grand jury[2]; those of 1198 direct that it shall take place before the justices in the full county court[3]; Magna Carta completes the process, enacting that the assizes shall be taken quarterly in the county court before two justices sent by the king, and four knights of the county, chosen by the county[4].

The Recognitions held in the county court.

The constitution of the grand jury of inquest is similarly developed. The twelve legal knights of the shire, the twelve lawful men of the hundred, and the four men of the township mentioned in the Assize of Clarendon, may have appeared in rotation, or may have been selected by the sheriff or the hundred man or the reeve: but in 1194 they are nominated, through a process of cooptation, by four elected knights[5]. These elected knights may still have been nominated by the sheriff, but it is more probable that they were chosen by the suitors, first, because the appointment of coroners, which is directed in the same document, was made by election of the freeholders, and intended as a check on the power of the sheriff[6]; and, secondly, because the term 'eligendi' may be reasonably interpreted by the clause of Magna Carta just referred to[7]. The mode of nominating the grand jury was modified in later practice, and

Method of electing the Grand Jury.

Probably a free election by the suitors.

homines de vicineto secundum formam in brevi expressam.' The writ merely orders the sheriff to summon and 'imbreviate' twelve recognitors. Even here however there was room for a real election.

[1] Glanvill, ii. 10–12.

[2] Art. 2: 'Item de omnibus recognitionibus,' &c. Above, p. 617.

[3] 'Et capientur coram eis electiones magnae assisae per mandatum domini regis vel ejus capitalis justitiae.' Hoveden, iv. 61.

[4] Art. 18.

[5] 'In primis eligendi sunt quatuor milites de toto comitatu, qui per sacramentum suum eligant duos legales milites de quolibet hundredo vel wapentacco, et illi duo eligant super sacramentum suum x. milites de singulis hundredis vel wapentaccis; vel si milites defuerint, legales et liberos homines, ita quod illi xii. in simul respondeant de omnibus capitulis de toto hundredo vel wapentacco.' Hoveden, iii. 262.

[6] Ibid. p. 263. Art. 20.

[7] 'Cum quatuor militibus cujuslibet comitatus electis per comitatum.' Art. 18.

Elective principle.

the element of popular election was altogether eliminated; in the period before us, however, it furnishes an important illustration of the usage of election which was so soon to be applied to parliamentary representation. In both the systems of judicial jury we have thus the same result, a body of four knights representing the county court for this special purpose, in one case certainly, and in the other probably, chosen by the county court itself. In the fiscal business we have another analogy; the carucage of 1198 is assessed before a knight and a clerk of the Exchequer acting on behalf of the Crown, and the sheriff and lawful knights 'electi ad hoc' acting on behalf of the shire: it was collected by two knights of the hundred, who paid it to the sheriff, and he accounted for it at the Exchequer[1]. We are thus prepared for the great executory measure of 1215, under which the articles of the charter were to be carried out by an inquest of twelve sworn knights in each county, chosen in the county court and of the county itself[2]: and we understand the summons to the council at Oxford of 1213, in which the sheriff of each county is ordered to send four discreet men of his county to speak with the king on the business of the realm[3]. In the four discreet men of the shire we detect the old representative idea of the four good men of the township, who appeared in the shire-moot: now they are summoned to a national assembly which is itself a concentration of the county courts. It is not however yet certain whether the four discreet men, the predecessors of the two discreet knights of later times, were on this occasion elected by the shire. On the analogy of the other elections it might be presumed that they were; but the fact that only a week's notice was given to the sheriffs seems to preclude the possibility of a general election. Nor is it necessary to antedate the growth of an institution, when the later steps

Illustration from fiscal usages.

Magna Carta executed on inquest by twelve chosen knights of each shire.

Council at Oxford in 1213.

[1] Hoveden, iv. 46 sq.; Select Charters, p. 249; above, p. 510.

[2] Art. 48: 'Statim inquirantur per duodecim milites juratos de eodem comitatu, qui debent eligi per probos homines ejusdem comitatus.' See also Patent Rolls, i. 180; Select Charters, p. 298.

[3] Report on the Dignity of a Peer, App. i. p. 2: 'Et quatuor discretos homines de comitatu tuo illuc venire facias ad nos ad eundem terminum ad loquendum nobiscum de negotiis regni nostri.'

of its development are distinctly traceable. Whether or no the fourteenth article of the Great Charter intended to provide for a representation of the minor tenants-in-chief by a body of knights elected in the county court, we see now the three principles involved in such representation already in full working, although not as yet distinctly combined for this purpose. We have a system of representation, we have the practice of election, and we have a concentration of the shires in the great council. The struggle of eighty years which followed the act of Runnymede not only had to vindicate the substantial liberties involved in that act, but to sharpen and perfect and bring into effective and combined working every weapon which, forged at different times and for different purposes, could be made useful for the maintenance of self-government. The humble processes by which men had made their by-laws in the manorial courts and amerced the offenders; by which they had assessed the estates or presented the report of their neighbours; by which they had learned to work with the judges of the king's court for the determination of questions of custom, right, justice, and equity, were the training for the higher functions, in which they were to work out the right of taxation, legislation, and political determination on national action.

The elements of a representative system at work before the Great Charter.

The process of training.

165. The history of the towns presents some points of marked contrast with that of the shires; and these shed light on the later separation of interest between the two classes of communities. The whole period was one of great development in this respect; Henry II and the ministers of his sons encouraged the growth of the mercantile spirit, and reaped the benefit of it in a very great increase of revenue. The privileges of self-government and self-assessment, exemption from the interference of the sheriffs and their arbitrary exactions, the confirmation of guilds, the securing of corporate property, the free election of magistrates, and the maintenance of ancient customs, in many cases to the exclusion of the general reforms, are all of them matters of grant liberally bestowed or sold without reservation. The charters of Richard and John are very numerous; those of Henry II are fewer in number, and do not furnish us with a

Growth of towns.

Their privileges bought by fines.

Charters of towns.

Privileges of towns obtained by fine and charter.

clue to any progressive policy on the king's part, such as might have been inferred from his general practice in other matters. In those few to which an approximate date can be assigned, the privileges granted are not much greater than was the case in the reign of Henry I: but the Pipe Rolls contain great numbers of instances in which the purchase of additional favours is recorded. In some of these, perhaps, the favour is obtained merely for the single occasion, and in such cases no charter need have been drawn up. In others, where a permanent privilege was bought, the charter in which it was contained must have been lost or destroyed, when its importance had been diminished by a new grant of still greater favours. The charters of Richard belong chiefly to his early years, especially to the first year, when he was anxiously raising money for the Crusade. Those

Charters of John.

of John, however, extend throughout the reign, and being enrolled among the royal records[1], have survived in great measure the dangers in which the earlier grants perished. They exhibit the town constitution in almost every stage of development, and in every part of the kingdom. Helston and Hartlepool are alike striving for municipal organisation[2]: one town is rich enough to purchase a constitution like that of Oxford or Winchester, another is too poor or too humble to ask for more than the merchant guild, or the *firma burgi*, or the condition of a free borough[3]. Amongst the more privileged communities great varieties of custom prevail, and provincial laws of considerable antiquity probably underlie the customs of the larger towns. London, Winchester, Oxford, Norwich, and others, appear as typical constitutions on the model of which privileges are granted to the more humble aspirants[4]; and to their

[1] Rotuli Chartarum, edited by Sir T. Duffus Hardy in 1837.

[2] Rot. Chart. pp. 86, 93; Select Charters, pp. 305, 306.

[3] The Hartlepool charter confirms to the *homines* of Hartlepool that they be free burghers; that of Helston begins with a grant that it be a free borough, and have a merchant guild: a second charter to Helston contains the settlement of the ferm. The charter of Kingston lets the ferm to the *homines*; Rot. Chart. p. 52.

[4] Hartlepool is to have the same rights as Newcastle; Beverley as York; Norwich, Lincoln, and Northampton as London; Winchester is the model town for Wallingford, Andover, Salisbury, Ilchester; Oxford for

practice the newly-enfranchised boroughs are referred, in case of a dispute as to the interpretation of the charter. Thus, beside the common instinct which would lead the mercantile communities to act together in cases in which there was no ground for rivalry, and beside the common privilege which exempted them from the jurisdictions to which their country neighbours were amenable, they possessed in common a quantity of peculiar customs, which kept the *burgenses* of the kingdom as a class by themselves, although they never, as was the case in Scotland and in Germany, adopted a confederate bond of union or organised themselves in leagues.

Growth of a burgher spirit.

The boroughs under Henry I had probably, when they obtained any privilege at all, obtained the confirmation of the merchant guild, and by the agreement for the *firma burgi* had limited the exactions of the sheriff so far as regarded the ferm, although the taxes properly so called, especially the tallage, were still collected by him. They had also in some cases obtained a right to have all causes in which they were engaged tried within their own boundaries. If then the sheriff still retained judicial authority over them he must come and hold his court among them. But such a practice, whilst in one respect it saved them from the risks of the county court, in another exposed them to the exactions of the sheriff, who might come and hold 'scotale' at his convenience, and so wring money from his entertainers. It was therefore a great point to exclude the sheriff altogether; and in order to do this, an independent magistracy must be founded, the right of election obtained, and a power to treat on the questions of taxation directly with the royal officers. These then are the points most commonly secured by fine or charter.

The boroughs obtain the right of paying their own ferm and excluding the intermeddling of the sheriff.

The right of excluding the sheriff and having their own pleas decided on their own ground[1] involved their exemption from

Yarmouth and Lynn; Winchester or Oxford for Portsmouth and Marlborough; Winchester or London for Wilton; Launceston for Helston; York for Scarborough; Bristol for Dublin; Northampton for Grimsby; Hastings for Romney.

[1] E. g. in the thirty-first year of Henry II the men of Cambridge pay 300 marks of silver and a mark of gold to have their town at ferm and

They are exempted from the shire-moot and hundred.

the ordinary sessions of the county court; and, as their customs were confirmed by the same act that served to exempt them, they lost the benefit, or escaped the burden, of innovation. The exemption of the citizens of London, Winchester, and other towns from the duellum [1], after it had been introduced into the shire-moot, no doubt arose in some degree from this: when the Assize of Clarendon, by introducing the inquest by presentment into the county court, abolished there the practice of compurgation, sending the accused persons directly to the ordeal, the burghers lost the benefit of the change, and long retained compurgation as the customary mode of defence guaranteed to them by their charters [2].

They are represented in the courts held by the itinerant justices.

From the visitations of the itinerant justices however they were not exempted; but in their courts they obtained special privileges. The burghers of Dunwich and other towns were represented by twelve burghers, just as if they were independent hundreds; and they were amerced by a mixed jury, six men of their own body and six strangers [3].

They obtain a right of electing their magistrates.

These privileges involved almost of necessity a remodelling of the local magistracy: the right of electing their own reeve or praepositus was not the least important of the royal gifts. This does not appear in the charters of Henry II; it is found occasionally in those of Richard [4], and very commonly in those of John. It does not however seem certain that this difference implies an advance towards freedom in the matter; and it is not improbable that whilst the boroughs continued under the management of the sheriff, an office of so little practical import-

'ne vicecomes se inde intromittat;' here *inde* may refer only to the ferm. John's charter (Rot. Chart. p. 83) grants to them 'quod nullus eorum placitet extra muros burgi de Cantebruge de ullo placito praeter placita de tenuris exterioribus, exceptis monetariis et ministris nostris.' The charter to Dunwich grants that the burghers 'nullam sectam faciant comitatus vel hundredorum nisi coram justitiis nostris.' Ib. p. 51.

[1] 'Quod nullus eorum faciat duellum, et quod de placitis ad coronam pertinentibus se possint disrationare secundum consuetudinem civium civitatis Londoniarum.' Charter of Northampton, Rot. Chart. p. 45.

[2] See Palgrave, English Commonwealth, pp. 217, 259.

[3] 'Et cum summoniti fuerint esse coram justitiis, mittant pro se xii legales homines de burgo suo qui sint pro eis omnibus; et si forte amerciari debuerint, per sex probos homines de burgo suo et per sex probos homines extra burgum amercientur.' Rot. Chart. p. 51. See above, p. 607.

[4] 'Et cives Lincolniae faciant praepositum quem voluerint de se per annum, qui sit idoneus nobis et eis.' Foedera, i. 52.

ance as that of the reeve may have been filled up by election. When however the reeve and the probi homines became the governing body, it may well be supposed that the appointment would be a matter of serious question. The citizens of Lincoln are empowered by Richard to make their own reeve, who is however to be a person qualified to serve both them and the king; by John they are directed to choose two, who will be received as their representatives at the Exchequer. Those of Nottingham, according to John's charter, may appoint their reeve annually, but the king reserves the power of removing an unfit person: those of Shrewsbury choose two, of whom the sheriff presents one at the Exchequer: those of Northampton, by the common counsel of the town, are to choose two fit persons and present them to the sheriff, who will present one of them at the Exchequer to pay their own ferm[1]. Both Lincoln and Northampton are to choose four coroners, to keep the pleas of the Crown and be a check on the reeves. Under these magistrates the old local courts retained their organisation, or modified it only by the mixture of the guild customs, which were also of great antiquity[2]. The new borough courts were the old courts[3] of the township, the hundred, and the shire under new names[4].

Election of the *praepositus* or reeve.

Election of borough coroners.

The financial arrangements of the towns have been already mentioned under the head of taxation. From the Pipe Rolls and the Dialogus de Scaccario we learn that they made their separate terms with the justices of the Exchequer. Besides the common payment however, the richer burghers were often

Negotiations of the boroughs with the Exchequer.

[1] The charters will be found in the Rot. Chartarum; that of Shrewsbury, p. 46; Northampton, p. 45; Nottingham, p. 39; Lincoln, p. 56; Gloucester, p. 57; Ipswich, p. 65.

[2] See above, pp. 412 sq. The passages in charters which refer to the men of the merchant guild as distinct from the body of burghers, as at Winchester and Gloucester, probably indicate that in those towns the private jurisdictions of the bishop or other lord remained apart from the general borough organisation, or were not consolidated with the guild.

[3] John grants to the burghers of Leicester that all sales of land of the town that take place in the *portmanmote* shall be valid; Rot. Chart. p. 32. The courts-leet of the Lancashire boroughs are often called *lagh-moots*: and there are many other forms. See above, p. 425.

[4] I have not thought it necessary to recapitulate what was said above, pp. 416, 417, about the clause of enfranchisement: which became probably a part of the common law before the reign of John.

Taxation of the boroughs.

prevailed on, by force or persuasion, to promise additional sums to relieve the king's necessities[1]: as demesne of the Crown, for such most of them continued to be even by the terms of their enfranchisement, they were subject to tallage which, although it might be occasionally mentioned in the national council, was levied by the feudal right of the king as lord. Next to this the 'scotale' seems to have been the most burdensome local custom. The nature of this exaction is very obscure. It was however levied by the sheriff for his own emolument, probably as a reward for his services in maintaining the peace; and was raised by a process similar to that by which the guilds raised their common funds. Whether the sheriff could compel the burghers to make offerings of malt from which a 'scotale' was brewed, the proceeds of which went into his purse; or the name simply means a gathering of the burghers at which they were compelled to promise contributions to the same end, or at which heavy fines for non-attendance were inflicted, it is difficult to say[2]. Whatever it was, however, it was a burden from which the towns were anxious to be relieved, and the relief was either a step towards, or a result of, the exemption from the authority of the sheriffs[3]. Free election of magistrates, independent ex-

The scotale.

[1] Like the benevolences or the compulsory loans of later times: e. g. in the 19th of Henry II, after the citizens of London had paid £666 13*s*. 4*d*. *de novo dono*, Reiner son of Berengar pays 100 marks *de promissione sua*. These promises are however more frequent in the cases of ecclesiastical persons, in which it might be more important to recognise the voluntary character of the payment. See Madox, Hist. Exch. pp. 404, 405.

[2] 'Scotales were abuses put upon the king's people by his officers, who invited them to drink ale, and then made a collection to the intent that they should not vex or inform against them for the crimes they had committed or should commit.' Brady, Boroughs, App. p. 13. The derivation of the word is questionable: Spelman thought that it might be derived from *Scot* and *tallia*, in the sense of a payment: it is possible that the latter syllable may be connected with *hall* (as in Gildhalla); but the connexion with the drinking customs is quite clear, so that the probability is in favour of the more obvious derivation from scot (payment) and ale. The Constitutions of 1236 forbid *scotallae* along with *aliae potationes*. Wilkins, i. 636. The later *church-ale* was a custom of collecting contributions of malt from the parishioners, with which a quantity of ale was brewed, and sold for the payment of church expenses. The custom of fining absentees and drinking the fines may also be connected with it.

[3] E. g. see Richard's charter to Winchester, Select Charters, p. 258. Other officers however could make scotale besides the sheriff, and the prohibition is generally extended to the reeve and other royal officers. Sad

ercise of jurisdiction in their own courts and by their own customs, and the direct negotiation of their taxation with the officers of the Exchequer, were no unimportant steps in the attainment of municipal independence. Nor was any such step retraced; every new charter confirmed, and many of them rehearsed in detail, the customs allowed by the earlier grants which they superseded.

Summary of town privileges.

The city of London still furnishes the type of the most advanced privilege, and the greatest amount of illustrative detail. Yet even the history of London is obscure. We can trace changes in the constitution of the sheriffdom, we have the date of the foundation of the *communa* and the mayoralty; we come upon occasional marks of royal jealousy, and exaggerations of civic independence; we can see two parties at work, the one moved by the court, the other by the municipal instinct; we can discern the points at issue between the rich and the poor. Still these features scarcely blend into a distinct picture, or furnish a consecutive story.

Changes in the constitution of London.

London was represented at the Exchequer, during the first fifteen years of Henry II, by two sheriffs, instead of the four who appeared in 1130, and who reappear in the sixteenth year. In 1174 the smaller number recurs: from 1182 to 1189 only one sheriff acts[1]. At the coronation of Richard I the two sheriffs are Richard Fitz-Reiner and Henry of Cornhell, the latter of whom was Master of the Mint and sheriff of Kent[2], the former the head of a great civic family; his father Reiner had been sheriff from 1155 to 1170, and Berengar his grandfather may not improbably have served before him. In the struggle between John and Longchamp in 1191 these two

The sheriffs of London.

to say, even the archbishop of Canterbury occasionally did it, as is shown by the following passage from Somner on Gavelkind, which further illustrates the nature of the burden: 'Item si dominus archiepiscopus fecerit scotallam infra boscum, quilibet terram tenens dabit ibi pro se et uxore sua 5½ ob. et vidua vel kotarius 1 ob.;' 'memorandum quod predicti tenentes debent de consuetudine inter eos facere scotalium de 16 den. et ob. ita quod de singulis 6 denariis detur unus denarius et obolus ad potandum bedello domini archiepiscopi supra dictum feodum.'

[1] See the thirty-first Report of the Deputy Keeper of the Records, pp. 307, 308; Madox, Firma Burgi, pp. 164, 165.

[2] Madox, Hist. Exch. p. 631; Hoveden, iii. pref. pp. lxxvii, lxxviii.

Two parties among the citizens.

magnates are found on different sides: Richard Fitz-Reiner is the host and supporter of John, Henry, as his duty to the court compelled him, takes the part of the chancellor. When accordingly in the midst of the struggle John took the oath to the communa of London and was followed by the whole body of barons who adhered to him, it is probable that he acted at the suggestion of Richard Fitz-Reiner, and gave completeness to a municipal constitution which had long been struggling for recognition [1]. Immediately after this confirmation of the communa we find Henry the son of Alwyn mayor of London [2]: the sheriffs cease to be the ruling officers, and become merely the financial representatives of the citizens, who are themselves properly the 'fermers' or sheriffs of London and Middlesex [3]. It is a saying among the citizens, that 'come what may, the Londoners should have no king but their mayor.' Henry Fitz-Alwyn is mayor for life: two years after his death, when John, a month before the Great Charter was extorted from him, was buying up help on every side, he granted to the 'barones' of the city of London the right of annually electing the mayor [4]. The privilege was ineffectual so far as it was intended to win the support of the Londoners, for a fortnight after it was granted they received the barons with open arms [5]. The duty of sustaining their privileges fell accordingly on the barons: their customs were guaranteed by the thirteenth article of the Charter, and a clause was added preserving like rights to all the cities, boroughs, towns, and seaports of the realm. Lastly, as one of the twenty-five barons chosen to execute the Charter, appears the Mayor of London.

Establishment of the communa under a mayor.

The mayor annually elected.

Supremacy of the mercantile element.

The establishment of the corporate character of the city under a mayor marks the victory of the communal principle over the more ancient shire organisation which seems to have displaced early in the century the complicated system of guild and franchise. It also marks the triumph of the mercantile over the

[1] Gir. Camb., Ang. Sac. ii. 397. Cf. R. Devizes, p. 38; R. Diceto, p. 664.

[2] Liber de Antiquis Legibus, p. 1. He was one of the treasurers of the sum raised for the king's ransom; Hoveden, iii. 212.

[3] Madox, Firma Burgi, p. 165.

[4] Rot. Chart. p. 207; Select Charters, p. 306. It is dated May 9, 1215.

[5] On the 24th of May. M. Paris.

aristocratic element. Henry Fitz-Alwyn may have been an hereditary baron of London, but his successors, Serlo le Mercer, Ralph Eswy the goldsmith, and others, were clearly tradesmen [1]. It would, doubtless, be unsafe to argue that mercantile pursuits were at this time regarded with anything like contempt in England. That feeling is one of the results of the growth of fictitious and superficial chivalry in the fourteenth century. The men of London had made their pilgrimages to Palestine, and fought their sea fights on the way, in company or in emulation with the noblest of the Norman lords. The story of Gilbert Becket may be fabulous, but Andrew of London and his fellow-citizens in 1147 had done good work for Christendom at the capture of Lisbon, the only real success of the second Crusade [2]; and in 1190 William Fitz-Osbert and Geoffrey the goldsmith of London were among the chief men of the fleet which saved the infant kingdom of Portugal from Moorish conquest [3]. The struggle, so far as we can trace it, was not between nobility and trade, but between the territorial franchise and the mercantile guild. Nor was the victory of the communa to any appreciable degree a victory of the Englishman over the foreigner. The population of London was less English probably than that of the other great towns such as Winchester and York. The names of the leading citizens who are mentioned throughout the twelfth century are with few exceptions, such as Henry Fitz-Alwyn, of alien derivation. Richard the son of Reiner the son of Berengar was very probably a Lombard by descent: the influential family of Bucquinte, Bucca-uncta, which took the lead on many occasions, can hardly have been other than Italian [4]; Gilbert Becket was a Norman. The form of the communa in which the corporate life asserted its independence was itself

Mercantile interests in the city.

Expeditions of the citizens.

Foreign element in the city.

[1] Liber de Antiquis Legibus, pp. 2, 3, sq.

[2] Expugnatio Lyxbonensis, p. cxliv. Henry of Huntingdon specially remarks that this great victory was won not by the nobles, but by men of middle rank.

[3] Hoveden, iii. 42; Bened. ii. 116.

[4] Andrew of London, the leader of the Londoners at Lisbon in 1147, is not improbably the Andrew Bucquinte whose son Richard was the leader of the riotous young nobles of the city who in 1177 furnished a precedent for the Mohawks of the eighteenth century. Benedict, i. 155. Cf. Pipe Roll 31 Henry I, pp. 145, 147.

foreign. From the beginning of its political importance London acts constantly as the purse, sometimes as the brain, never perhaps in its whole history as the heart, of England. The victory of the communa is no guarantee of freedom or fair treatment to the poorer citizens; we no sooner find it in supreme authority than the riot of William Fitz-Osbert occurs to prove that an oligarchy of the purse has as little of tender mercy as an oligarchy of the sword. The real importance of London in this region of history is rather that it affords an example of local independence and close organisation which serves as a model and standard for other towns, than that it leads the way to the attainment of general liberties or peculiarly English objects. Still its position and the action of its citizens give it no small political power, and no insignificant place in history.

A mercantile oligarchy.

Importance of the clergy.

166. The action of the clergy in the great struggles of the period has been already noted, in its proper proportion to the general detail. They by their vindication of their own liberties showed the nation that other liberties might be vindicated as well, and that there are bounds to the power and violence of princes. They had fought the battle of the people in fighting their own. From them too, as subjects and not merely as churchmen, the first movements towards national action had come. They had bound up the wounds of the perishing State at the accession of Henry II; they had furnished the first if not the only champions of freedom in the royal councils, where S. Thomas, S. Hugh, and Archbishop Geoffrey had had courage to speak where the barons were silent. They had, on the other side, not, it may be fairly allowed, without neglecting their spiritual work, laboured hard to reduce the business of government to something like the order which the great ecclesiastical organisation of the West impressed on every branch of its administration. What the Church had borrowed from the Empire in this respect it repaid with tenfold interest to the rising State system of Europe. And this was especially the case in England. We have seen that the Anglo-Saxon Church made possible and opened the way to national unity: it was the common Church which combined Norman and

Their independence.

Their sense of unity.

Englishman in one service, when law and language, land tenure and political influence, would have made them two races of lords and slaves. It was the action of Lanfranc and Anselm that formed the strongest link between the witenagemot of the Confessor and the court and council of the Conqueror and his sons. It was the hard and systematic work of Roger of Salisbury that gave order to the Exchequer and the Curia. The work of Becket as Chancellor is thrown into the shade by his later history, but he certainly was Henry's right hand in the initial reforms of the reign, and the men who carried out those reforms in a direction contrary to the policy which Becket as archbishop adopted, were men who trod in the footsteps of his earlier life. Hubert Walter, the administrator of Henry's system, who under Richard and John had completed the fabric of strong government by means of law, and Stephen Langton, who deserves more than any other person the credit of undoing the mischiefs that arose from that system, maintaining the law by making the national will the basis of the strength of government, were both representative men of the English Church. No doubt there were evils in the secular employments of these great prelates: but if for a time the spiritual work of the Church was neglected, and unspiritual aims fostered within her pale, the State gained immensely by being administered by statesmen whose first ideas of order were based on conscience and law rather than on brute force. Nor was the spiritual part of the work unprovided for. Three archbishops of Canterbury, Anselm, Ralph, and William, all of them belonging to the religious rather than the secular type, had sanctioned the employment of Bishop Roger as justiciar, and without the consent of the Pope, it is said, he refused to bear the title[1]. Innocent III, when he insisted that Hubert Walter should resign the like office, showed that the growing sense of the age forbade what so great a saint as Anselm had connived at; but that growing sense had been educated in great measure by the system which it was soon to discard.

Their systematic routine.

Evil of secular employment,

compensated by usefulness.

It is however in the details of mechanical work that these remarks help to illustrate the subject of this chapter. The

[1] W. Malmesb. G. R. v. § 408; R. Diceto, c. 606.

Bearing of clerical influence on method: systematic order of the growing polity was not a little indebted to the fact that there existed in the Church system a set of models of work. The Church had its ranks and degrees, codes of laws and rules of process, its councils and courts, its central and provincial jurisdictions, its peculiar forms of trial and arbitration, its system of writ and record. In a crisis in which representation and election were growing into importance, and in which all forms were manipulated by clerical administrators, the newer forms must needs be moulded in some degree on the older. on legislation; The legislation of the period, the assizes and constitutions, bear, in common with the Karolingian capitularies, a strong resemblance to ecclesiastical canons, a form which was universal local organisation; and vigorous when the capitulary was forgotten. The local and territorial divisions of the dioceses made indelible the civil boundaries which feudal aggression would have gladly obliterated. The archdeaconries, deaneries, and parishes preserved the local unities in which they had themselves originated, and the exempt jurisdictions of the convents were in their nature an exact parallel with the franchises of the feudal lords, and in the case of great ecclesiastical establishments, possessed both characters. legal practice; The assemblies of the clergy kept up forms that were easily transferred to the local moots: the bishop's visitation was a parallel to that of the sheriff; the metropolitical visitation to that of the Curia or Exchequer; spiritual excommunication was parallel with civil outlawry; clerical procurations with royal purveyance and the payments to the sheriff for his aid; the share of the clergy in determining their assessments suggested the like action on the part of the lay communities, or at least familiarised men with a system of the kind.

on representation. In no particular is this more apparent than in the very important question of election and representation. In the latter point we shall able to trace, as we proceed, very close analogies: the fact that the early representative members in the national council were frequently, if not always, invested with the character of procurators or proxies, bearing letters of credence or ratification that empowered them to act on behalf of their constituents, suggests at once that the custom was borrowed from the ecclesiastical practice of which such procuratorial representation was a familiar part, in negotiation with the Holy See, and in the formation of Church councils at home. The appearance of the proctors of the cathedral and diocesan clergy in the central assemblies of Church and State precedes by a few years the regular incorporation of the knights of the shire in parliament; and Convocation as well as the House of Commons owes its representative character to the great period of definition, the reign of Edward I. In the case of election the connexion is perhaps less close: but there can be little doubt that the struggles for ecclesiastical freedom of election kept in use forms which made the extension of elective liberty possible in other quarters.

Clerical use of representation and election.

The Church recognised three modes of election: the 'via compromissi,' by which the electors deputed to a small committee of their body—an uneven number, three or five—the function of choosing the bishop or abbot; the 'via scrutinii,' in which the several votes were taken in order and the choice determined by the majority; and the 'via inspirationis Spiritus Sancti,' in which at one moment, and in one breath, the whole body uttered the name of the same person, just as in the court of justice the compurgators took their oath. The last-mentioned method in its exact form was of course inapplicable to the cases of popular election; but the acclamations of the crowd of suitors at the county court represents a similar idea, the show of hands corresponds with the 'via scrutinii'; and the 'via compromissi' has its parallel doubtless in the gradual reservation of the choice of members, both in town and shire, to a small deputed body[1], who in the former case finally engrossed the right of election.

Modes of clerical election.

Analogy of lay elections.

The common arrangement of the early medieval courts, by which the king's chapel was made the depository of writs and records, and his clerks or chaplains the framers and writers of such documents, illustrates another side of the same general truth. The ecclesiastical system of writ, summons, and record

System of record.

[1] It is not perhaps too much to say that the election of the sworn knights to nominate the recognitors of the Great Assize was a distinct parallel with elections made 'via compromissi.' The deputies of the convent at Canterbury who carried full powers to the Curia Regis or to Rome were compromissarii, proctors in fact of that church.

Records and Registers.

was probably, in England, derived from the extensive documentary machinery of the Church of Rome, which in its turn was derived from the similar practice of the later Empire [1]. The writs of the Norman Curia may not improbably have been drawn by continuous practice from the formulae of the imperial system of the Franks, great stores of which are to be found in the collections of Marculf and other jurists [2]. The growth of the system is accordingly complex, the written forms of procedure, both lay and clerical, being developed side by side, or in constant entanglement with one another, as might well be the case when they were drawn up by the same writer. It is however interesting to observe that the custom of registering the acts of court, and retaining copies of all letters issued by the king, seems to have been introduced either late in the reign of Henry II or under Richard and John, under whom, as has been already mentioned, the great series of national records begin.

Increase after the accession of John.

William Longchamp, the chancellor and justiciar of Richard, who with all his great faults must have also had a great capacity for business, and who, as we learn from the Red Book of the Exchequer [3], took pains to make himself familiar with its details, must have authorised, perhaps suggested, the enrolment of the acts of the Curia: it was carried out under his vice-chancellor and successor Bishop Eustace. The enrolment of charters and of letters patent and close begins in the chancellorship of Hubert Walter, and is carried out by Walter de Grey, afterwards archbishop of York, who has left in the register of his archiepiscopal acts one of the earliest existing records of the kind. The Lincoln registers begin with the acts of Bishop Hugh of Wells, who had been a deputy of the chancellor from 1200 to 1209 [4].

Episcopal registers.

[1] On the registration of papal letters see the preface to Jaffé's Regesta Pontificum, and also to his Monumenta Gregoriana. Gregory VII, in a letter to Hubert of Terouanne, mentions his own register. The practice existed at Rome from the days of Gregory I or earlier; the most ancient remains however are those of the registers of Gregory I, John VIII, and Gregory VII. The series from Innocent III to Pius V is complete.

[2] Illustrations of this will be found in Brunner, as quoted above, p. 391.

[3] Quoted above, p. 431, note 4.

[4] Of course there may have been episcopal registers, as there may have been royal records, earlier, but with the exception of the Pipe Rolls there is no evidence that such existed. The York and Lincoln registers are

If the episcopal registers were drawn up in imitation of the royal rolls, the latter owed both idea and form to the papal registry, the influence of which was under Innocent III supreme in Europe, and which could trace its method through the 'regesta' of Gregory VII and the earlier popes, to the practice of the ancient republic. In such matters it would not be fair to say that Church and State borrowed from each other; each had a vitality and a development of its own, but each gained strength, versatility, and definiteness from their close union; and that close union was made closer still whilst the business of the two was conducted by the same administrators.

Papal Registers.

167. We have now, however imperfectly, traced the process of events by which the English nation had reached that point of conscious unity and identity which made it necessary for it to act as a self-governing and political body, a self-reliant and self-sustained nation,—a power in Europe, basing its claims for respect not on the accidental position or foreign acquisitions of its kings, but on its own internal strength and cohesion, its growth in good government, and its capacity for a share in the common polity of Christendom. We have also tried to trace the process by which its internal organisation had been so framed, modified, and strengthened, that when the occasion came it was able to answer to the strain: by which, when the need of representative institutions made itself felt, the mere concentration and adaptation of existing machinery supplied all that was required. The century that follows Magna Carta was an age of growth, of luxuriant, even premature, development, the end of which was to strengthen and likewise to define the several constituent parts of the organic whole. The three estates made their way, through this time of training, to a realisation of their distinct identity, and gained such a consciousness of their

Summary of the steps of national growth and organisation.

the most ancient: those of Canterbury begin in 1278; Winchester in 1282; Exeter in 1257; Hereford in 1275; Worcester in 1268; Salisbury in 1297; Lichfield in 1296; Norwich in 1299; Carlisle in 1292; the other sees have records beginning early in the next century. The collection of letters, such as those of Lanfranc, Anselm, and Becket, seems to have been a literary work and not a registration, although in many points it answers the same purpose.

Summary of the points of national growth.

distinct spheres of work as enabled them to act without entanglement of machinery or waste of power. The constitution which reached its formal and definite maturity under Edward I had to learn easy and economic working under his successors. In that lesson it had also severe experiences of struggle, defect, and failure: its representative men lose the grace and simplicity of the earlier times; personal and territorial aims waste the energies of the better and wiser, and divide into permanent factions the ignorant and more selfish. Yet the continuity of life, and the continuity of national purpose, never fails: even the great struggle of all, the long labour that extends from the Reformation to the Revolution, leaves the organisation, the origin of which we have been tracing, unbroken in its conscious identity, stronger in the strength in which it has persevered and grown mightier through trial. The further investigation of this history in its political as well as in its mechanical aspect must begin from Magna Carta, as a new starting-point.

Chapter V

THE SYSTEM OF ESTATES, AND THE CONSTITUTION UNDER EDWARD I.

Ideal of constitutional growth.

183. THE idea of a constitution in which each class of society should, so soon as it was fitted for the trust, be admitted to a share of power and control, and in which national action should

be determined by the balance maintained between the forces thus combined, never perhaps presented itself to the mind of any medieval politician. The shortness of life, and the jealousy inherent in and attendant on power, may account for this in the case of the practical statesman, although a long reign like that of Henry III might have given room for the experiment; and whilst a strong feeling of jealousy subsisted throughout the middle ages between the king and the barons, there was no such strong feeling between the barons and the commons. But even the scholastic writers, amid their calculations of all possible combinations of principles in theology and morals, well aware of the difference between the 'rex politicus' who rules according to law, and the tyrant who rules without it, and of the characteristics of monarchy, aristocracy and democracy, with their respective corruptions, contented themselves for the most part with balancing the spiritual and secular powers, and never broached the idea of a growth into political enfranchisement. Yet, in the long run, this has been the ideal towards which the healthy development of national life in Europe has constantly tended, only the steps towards it have not been taken to suit a preconceived theory. The immediate object in each case has been to draw forth the energy of the united people in some great emergency, to suit the convenience of party or the necessities of kings, to induce the newly admitted classes to give their money, to produce political contentment, or to involve all alike in the consciousness of common responsibility.

Assemblies of Estates summoned in Spain.

The history of the thirteenth century fully illustrates this. Notwithstanding the difference of circumstances and the variety of results, it is to this period that we must refer, in each country of Europe, the introduction, or the consolidation, for the first time since feudal principles had forced their way into the machinery of government, of national assemblies composed of properly arranged and organised Estates. The accepted dates in some instances fall outside the century. The first recorded appearance of town representatives in the Cortes of Aragon is placed in 1162[1], the first in Castile in

[1] In that year queen Petronilla summoned to the Cortes at Huesca 'prelados, ricos hombres, caballeros y procuradores'; and the names of

Representation in Germany and France.

1169[1]. The general courts of Frederick II in Sicily were framed in 1232[2]: in Germany the cities appear by deputies in the diet in 1255, but they only begin to form a distinct part under Henry VII and Lewis of Bavaria[3]; in France the States general are called together first in 1302. Although in each case the special occasions differ, the fact that a similar expedient was tried in all, shows that the class to which recourse was for the first time had was in each country rising in the same or in a proportional degree, or that the classes which had hitherto monopolised power were in each country feeling the need of a reinforcement. The growth of the towns in wealth and strength, and the decline of properly feudal ideas in kings, clergy and barons, tended to the momentary parallelism. The way in which the crisis was met decided in each country the current of its history. In

the towns which sent procuradores to the Cortes at Saragossa in 1163 are known. See Zurita, lib. ii. cc. 20, 24; Schäfer, Spanien iii. 207, 208; Hallam, M. A. ii. 56. The earlier instances, given by Hallam and Robertson (Charles V, vol. i. note 31), are scarcely cases of Cortes.

[1] 'Se sabe que habiendo don Alonso VIII tenido cortes generales en Burgos en el año de 1169, concurrieron a ellas no solamente les condes, ricos hombres, prelados y caballeros sino tambien los ciudadanos y todos los concejos del reino de Castilla'; quoted by Marina, Teoria de las Cortes, c. 14, vol. i. p. 138, from the Cronica General, pt. iv. cap. viii. fo. 387. In 1188 the Cortes of Carrion, attesting the treaty of marriage between Berenguela and Conrad, contained representatives of the towns; 'estos son les nombres de las ciudades y villas cuyos mayores juraron'; ibid. p. 139.

[2] 'Mense Septembris imperator a Melfia venit Forgiam et generales per totum regnum litteras dirigit, ut de qualibet civitate vel castro duo de melioribus accedant ad ipsum pro utilitate regni et commodo generali.' Ric. de S. Germano, A.D. 1232; Frederick's general courts instituted in 1234 are very like the English county courts; 'Statuit etiam ipse imperator apud Messanam, bis in anno in certis regni provinciis generales curias celebrandas . . . et ibi erit pro parte imperatoris nuntius specialis . . . Hiis curiis, bis in anno, ut dictum est, celebrandis, intererunt quatuor de qualibet magna civitate de melioribus terræ, bonæ fidei et bonæ opinionis, et qui non sint de parte; de aliis vero non magnis et de castellis duo intererunt curiis ipsis'; ibid. A.D. 1234.

[3] In the negotiations for the great confederation of Rhenish cities: see Chron. Augustanum and Albert of Stade, A.D. 1255; Datt, de pace publica, c. 4. 20; Zoepfl. Deutsche Rechtsgeschichte, vol. ii. p. 262; and the Essay on the subject by Arnold Busson, Innsbrück, 1874. In 1277 we find the 'communitates civitatum et civium' swearing fealty to Rudolf of Hapsburg; Eberhard. Altah. ap. Canis. Lectt. Antt. iv. 218: in 1309 Henry VII discusses the Italian expedition in a diet at Speyer, 'cum principibus electoribus et aliis principibus et civitatum nunciis,' Alb. Argentin. (ed. Urstisius), p. 116.

England the parliamentary system of the middle ages emerged from the policy of Henry II, Simon de Montfort and Edward I; in France the States General were so managed as to place the whole realm under royal absolutism; in Spain the long struggle ended in the sixteenth century in making the king despotic, but the failure of the constitution arose directly from the fault of its original structure. The Sicilian policy of Frederick passed away with his house. In Germany the disruption of all central government was reflected in the diet; the national paralysis showed itself in a series of abortive attempts, few and far between, at united action, and the real life was diverted into provincial channels and dynastic designs.

Variety of results.

184. The parliamentary constitution of England comprises, as has been remarked already, not only a concentration of local machinery but an assembly of estates[1]. The parliament of the present day, and still more clearly the parliament of Edward I, is a combination of these two theoretically distinct principles. The House of Commons now most distinctly represents the former idea, which is also conspicuous in the constitution of Convocation, and in that system of parliamentary representation of the clergy which was an integral part of Edward's scheme: it is to some extent seen in the present constitution of the House of Lords, in the case of the representative peers of Ireland and Scotland, who may also appeal for precedent to the same reign[2]. It may be distinguished by the term local representation as distinct from class representation; for the two are not necessarily united, as our own history as well as that of foreign countries abundantly testifies. In some systems the local interest predominates over the class interest; in one the character of delegate eclipses the character of senator; in another all local character may disappear as soon as the threshold of the assembly is passed; in one there may be

Double character of the English parliament.

Local representation and class representation.

[1] Vol. i. pp. 45, 564.

[2] Edward's design of having Scotland represented by a parliament to be held in London on the 15th of July 1305, to consist of ten persons, two bishops, two abbots, two earls, two barons, and two for the commune, one from each side of the Forth, chosen by the 'Commune' of Scotland at their assembly, may be seen in Parl. Writs, i. 155, 156, 161–163. These representatives are summoned to the parliament, but rather as envoys than as proper members.

Local representation and class representation.

a direct connexion between the local representation and the rest of the local machinery; in another the central assembly may be constituted by means altogether different from those used for administrative purposes, and the representative system may be used as an expedient to supersede unmanageable local institutions; while lastly, the members of the representative body may in one case draw their powers solely from their delegate or procuratorial character, and in another from that senatorial character which belongs to them as members of a council which possesses sovereignty or a share of it. The States General of the Netherlands under Philip II were a mere congress of ambassadors from the provincial estates; the States General of France under Philip the Fair were a general assembly of clergy, barons, and town communities[1], in no way connected with any system of provincial estates, which indeed can hardly be said to have existed at the time[2]. In Germany the representative elements of the Diet,—the prelates, counts and cities,—had a local arrange-

[1] 'Statim idem dominus rex de baronum ipsorum consilio barones ceteros tunc absentes et nos, videlicet archiepiscopos, episcopos, abbates, priores conventuales, decanos, praepositos, capitula conventus atque collegia ecclesiarum tam cathedralium quam regularium ac secularium, necnon universitates et communitates villarum regni, ad suam mandavit praesentiam evocari; ut praelati, barones, decani, praepositi et duo de peritioribus unius-cujusque cathedralis vel collegiatae ecclesiae personaliter, ceteri vero per oeconomos syndicos et procuratores idoneos cum plenis et sufficientibus mandatis, comparere statuto loco et termino curaremus. Porro nobis ceterisque personis ecclesiasticis supradictis, necnon baronibus, oeconomis, syndicis, et procuratoribus communitatum et villarum et aliis sic vocatis juxta praemissae vocationis formam ad mandatum regium hac die Martis 10ma praesentis mensis Aprilis, in ecclesia beatae Mariae Parisius in praefati regis praesentia constitutis, &c.'—Letter of the French Clergy to Boniface VIII; Dupuy, Proofs of the Liberties, &c., p. 125; Savaron, États Généraux, p. 88.

[2] The very important illustrations of the existence of assemblies of estates in Languedoc given by Palgrave, Commonwealth, ccccxxxv. sq., from Vaissette's Preuves de l'Histoire de Languedoc, show that that territory possessed these institutions, but at a time when it could scarcely be called a part of France. S. Lewis writes to the men of Beaucaire 'congreget senescallus consilium non suspectum, in quo sint aliqui de praelatis baronibus, militibus et hominibus bonarum villarum,' p. ccccxxxviii. In 1271 there is at Beziers 'consilium praelatorum et baronum et aliorum bonorum virorum,' p. ccccxli., and in it the representatives brought procuratorial powers as in England. These instances are the more interesting as coming from the land which had been ruled by the elder Simon de Montfort. Cf. Boutaric, Premiers Etats Gen. p. 5.

ment and system of collective as distinct from independent voting[1]; and in the general cortes of Aragon the provincial estates of Aragon, Catalonia and Valencia, were arranged in three distinct bodies in the same chamber[2]. Nor are these differences confined to the systems which they specially characterise. The functions of a local delegate, a class representative, and a national counsellor, appear more or less conspicuously at the different stages of parliamentary growth, and according as the representative members share more or less completely the full powers of the general body. A detailed examination of these differences however lies outside our subject[3], and in the constitutional history of foreign nations the materials at our command are insufficient to supply a clear answer to many of the questions they suggest.

Different combinations in different constitutions.

185. An assembly of Estates is an organised collection, made by representation or otherwise, of the several orders, states or conditions of men, who are recognised as possessing political power. A national council of clergy and barons is not an assembly of estates, because it does not include the body of the people, 'the plebs,' the simple freemen or commons, who on all constitutional theories have a right to be consulted as to their own taxation if on nothing else. So long as the prelates and barons, the tenants-in-chief of the crown, met to grant an aid, whilst the towns and shires were consulted by special commissions, there was no meeting of estates. A county court, on the other hand, although it never bore in England the title of provincial estates, nor possessed the powers held by the provincial estates

An assembly of estates;

it should contain a representation of all the political factors.

[1] The fully developed diet contained three colleges—I. The Electors; II. the Princes; comprising (1) those voting *sigillatim*, (α) ecclesiastical, (β) temporal; (2) those voting *curiatim*, (α) ecclesiastical; the Prelates on two benches, the Rhine, and Swabia; (β) the Counts, on four benches, Swabia, Wetterau, Franconia, and Westphalia; III. The Imperial Cities voting *curiatim* in two benches, the Rhine and Swabia.

[2] Schäfer, Spanien, iii. 215.

[3] The changes in the form of the States General of France are especially interesting, but are not parallel with anything that went on in England. The introduction of representation into the first and second estate, and the election of the representatives of the three orders by the same constituent body, in 1483, are in very strong contrast with English institutions; see Picot, 'Les Elections aux Etats generaux,' Paris, 1874.

on the continent, was a really exhaustive assembly of this character.

Arrangement of the political factors in estates.

The arrangement of the political factors in three estates is common, with some minor variations, to all the European constitutions, and depends on a principle of almost universal acceptance. This classification differs from the system of caste, and from all divisions based on differences of blood or religion, historical or prehistorical[1]. It is represented by the philosophic division of guardians, auxiliaries, and producers of Plato's Republic. It appears, mixed with the idea of caste, in the *edhi-*

[1] 'Thæt bith thonne cyninges andweorc and his tol mid to ricsianne, thæt he hæbbe his land full mannod, he sceal hæbban *gebedmen* and *fyrdmen* and *weorcmen*'; Alfred's Boetius (ed. Cardale, p. 90). 'Aelc riht cynestol stent on thrim stapelum the fullice ariht stænt; an is *oratores*, and other is *laboratores* and thridde is *bellatores*'; a writer of the tenth century quoted by Wright, Political Songs, p. 365. 'Ther ben in the Chirche thre states that God hathe ordeyned, state of prestis and state of knyghtis and state of comunys;' Wycliffe, English Works (ed. Arnold), iii. 184. Compare 'Piers the Plowman,' Prol. v. 112 sq. ed. Skeat, p. 4. 'Constituitur autem sub te regnum illud in subjectione debita triplicis status principalis: status unus est militantium, alius clericorum, tertius burgensium'; Gerson, 'De considerationibus quas debet habere princeps.' The same writer interprets the three leaves of the fleur de lys (among other explanations) as the three estates, 'statum dico militantium, statum consulentium, statum laborantium;' Gerson, Sermon on S. Lewis, Opp. pt. ii. p. 758. The following passage from Nicolas of Clemangis (De lapsu et reparatione Justorum, c. 16) forms almost a comment on the constitution of Edward I: 'Nulli dubium est omne regnum omnemque politiam recte institutam ex tribus hominum constare generibus, quos usitatiori appellatione tres ordines vel status solemus dicere; ex sacerdotali scilicet ordine, militari et plebeio . . . Perutile immo necessarium mihi videtur ad universalem regni hujus in cunctis suis membris et abusibus reformationem concilium universale trium statuum convocari . . . Congruum nempe esse videtur ut in ruina vel periculo universali universale etiam quaeratur auxilium, et *quod omnes tangit ab omnibus probetur*.' The address of the Commons to Henry IV, in 1401, rehearses 'coment les estates du roialme purroient bien estre resemblez a une Trinite, cest assavoir la persone du Roy, les Seigneurs Espirituelx et Temporelx et les communes;' but, as Hallam remarks, the reference here is to the necessary components of the parliament; see his very valuable note, Middle Ages, iii. 105, 106, where other authorities are given. 'This land standeth, says the Chancellor Stillington, in the 7th of Edward IV, by three states, and above that one principal, that is to wit lords spiritual, lords temporal, and commons, and over that state-royal, as our sovereign lord the king. Rot. Parl. v. 622. Thus too it is declared that the treaty of Staples in 1492 was to be confirmed per tres status regni Angliae rite et debite convocatos, videlicet per praelatos et clerum, nobiles, et communitates ejusdem regni; Rymer, xii. 508.' Ibid.

lingi, *frilingi*, and *lazzi* of the ancient Saxons. In Christendom it has always taken the form of a distinction between clergy and laity, the latter being subdivided according to national custom into noble and non-noble, patrician and plebeian, warriors and traders, landowners and craftsmen. The English form, clergy, lords and commons, has a history of its own which is not quite so simple, and which will be noticed by and by. The variations in this classification when it is applied to politics are numerous. The Aragonese cortes contained four brazos, or arms, the clergy, the great barons or ricos hombres, the minor barons, knights or infanzones, and the towns[1]. The Germanic diet comprised three colleges, the electors, the princes, and the cities, the two former being arranged in distinct benches, lay and clerical[2]. The Neapolitan parliament, unless our authorities were misled by supposed analogies with England, counted the prelates as one estate with the barons[3], and the minor clergy with the towns. The Castilian cortes arranged the clergy, the *ricos hombres*, and the *communidades*, in three estates[4]. The Swedish diet was composed of clergy, barons, burghers and peasants[5]. The Scottish parliament contained three estates, prelates, tenants-in-

Arrangement in three estates,

with minor variations,

in Spain, Germany, and Sweden.

[1] In Aragon proper (1) brazo de ecclesiasticos; (2) brazo de nobles, later, ricos hombres; (3) brazo de caballeros y hijosdalgo, called later infanzones; (4) brazo de universidades. In Catalonia and Valencia there were three, the ecclesiastico, militar, and real, for only royal towns, 'pueblos de realengo,' were represented; Schäfer, iii. 218.

[2] Above, p. 163.

[3] Giannone, History of Naples, Book 20, chap. 4, sect. 1. So too it is said that in Aragon the prelates first appear as a separate brazo in 1301; having before attended simply as barons, henceforth they represent the ecclesiastical estate or interest. Schäfer, Spanien, iii. 217.

[4] The following are the words of the 'Lei fundamental' of the Cortes of 1328–9: 'Porque en los hechos arduos de nuestros reinos es necessario el consejo de nuestros subditos y naturales especialmente de los procuradores de las nuestras cibdades y villas y lugares de nuestros reinos, por ende ordenamos y mandamos que sobre los tales hechos grandes y arduos se hayan de ayuntar cortes y se faga consejo de los tres estados de nuestros reinos, segun lo hicieron los reyes nuestros progenitores'; Recopilacion, L. ii. tit. vii. lib. vi.; quoted by Marina, i. 31.

[5] Universal History, xii. 213. The estates comprised (1) the nobles, represented by one from each family, with whom sat the four chief officers of each regiment of the army; (2) the clergy, represented by the bishops, superintendents, and one deputy from every ten parishes; (3) representatives of the towns, four from Stockholm, two or one from smaller towns; and (4) 250 peasant representatives, chosen one from each district.

In Scotland and France.

chief great and small, and townsmen, until James I, in 1428, in imitation of the English system, instituted commissioners of shires, to supersede the personal appearance of the minor tenants; then the three estates became the lords, lay and clerical, the commissioners of shires, and the burgesses[1]. In France, both in the States General and in the provincial estates, the division is into 'gentz de l'eglise,' 'nobles,' and 'gentz des bonnes villes[2].' In England, after a transitional stage, in which the clergy, the greater and smaller barons, and the cities and boroughs, seemed likely to adopt the system used in Aragon and Scotland, and another in which the county and borough communities continued to assert an essential difference, the three estates of clergy, lords, and commons, finally emerge as the political constituents of the nation, or, in their parliamentary form, as the lords spiritual and temporal and the commons[3]. This familiar formula in either shape bears the impress of history. The term 'commons' is not in itself an appropriate expression for the third estate; it does not signify primarily the simple freemen, the plebs, but the plebs organised and combined in corporate communities, in a particular way for particular purposes. The commons are the 'communitates' or 'universitates,' the organised bodies of freemen of the shires and towns; and the estate of the commons is the 'communitas communitatum,' the general body into which for the purposes of parliament those communities are combined. The term then, as descriptive of the class of men which is neither noble nor clerical, is drawn from the political vocabulary, and does not represent any primary distinction of class. The communities of shires and boroughs are further the collective organisations which pay their taxes in common through the sheriffs or other magistrates, and are represented in

Stages in England.

The estate of the Commons.

Meaning of the 'Commons.'

[1] See the very valuable chapter on the Scottish Constitution in the Lords' Report on the Dignity of a Peer, i. 111 sq.

[2] Savaron, États généraux, p. 74.

[3] The writer of the *Modus tenendi parliamentum*, divides the English parliament into six grades, (1) the king, (2) the prelates, i. e. archbishops, bishops, abbots and priors holding by barony, (3) the proctors of the clergy, (4) the earls, barons and other magnates, (5) the knights of the shire, (6) the citizens and burghers; but this is not a legal or historical arrangement. See Select Charters, p. 498; cf. p. 191, note 2 below.

common by chosen knights or burgesses; they are thus the represented freemen as contrasted with the magnates, who live among them but who are specially summoned to parliament, and make special terms with the Exchequer; and so far forth they are the residue of the body politic, the common people, so called in a sense altogether differing from the former. It is not to be forgotten, however, that the word 'communitas,' 'communauté,' 'la commune,' has different meanings, all of which are used at one time or another in constitutional phraseology. In the coronation oath[1] 'la communauté,' 'vulgus,' or folk, that chooses the laws, can be nothing but the community of the nation, the whole three estates: in the provisions of Oxford 'le commun de la terre' can only be the collective nation as represented by the barons[2], in other words the governing body of the nation, which was not yet represented by chosen deputies; whilst in the Acts of Parliament[3], in which 'la commune' appears with 'Prelatz et Seigneurs' as a third constituent of the legislative body, it can mean only the body of representatives. The inconsistency of usage is the same in the case of the boroughs, where 'communitas' means sometimes the whole body of burghers, sometimes

Uses of the words *Commons* and *Community.*

[1] 'Les queux la communaulte de votre realm aura esluz,' 'quas vulgus elegerit:' Statutes of the Realm, i. 168. It is needless to state at length that the idea of the lex Hortensia, 'ut eo jure quod plebes statuisset omnes Quirites tenerentur,' was never accepted in England except in the days of the Great Rebellion.

[2] 'Ces sunt les vint et quatre ke sunt mis per le commun a treter de aide le rei;' 'Ces sunt les duze ke sunt eslu per les baruns a treter a treis parlemenz per an oveke le cunseil le rei pur tut le commun de la tere de commun bosoine.' Select Charters, p. 381. In the latter passage 'le commun de la tere' seems to mean the nation, in the former the baronage which for the moment represented it.

[3] The words 'le commun' and 'la commune' seem to be used without any apparent difference of meaning in the Revocation of the Ordinances (Statutes i. 189) and elsewhere; and at the period at which the commons were growing into recognition as a third estate of parliament, it is extremely difficult to distinguish the passages in which 'le commun' is used discretively for the commons from those in which it is used comprehensively for the whole body. In the petitions also the word sometimes seems to mean the whole parliament and sometimes only the third estate. But many volumes might be written on this, and indeed every case in which the word occurs from the reign of Henry III to that of Edward III might be commented on at some length. Here I can only refer to the discussions on the word in the Lords' Report on the Dignity of a Peer; Brady's Introduction, pp. 71–84.

the governing body or corporation, sometimes the rest of the freemen, as in the form 'the mayor, aldermen, and commonalty.' As ordinarily employed then the title of 'commons' may claim more than one derivation, besides that which history supplies [1].

Order of the Three Estates.

The commons are the third estate: between the clergy and baronage the question of precedency would scarcely arise, but it is clear from the arrangement of the estates in the common constitutional formulae, both in England and in other countries, that a pious courtesy gave the first place to the clergy. For the term first or second estate there does not seem to be any sufficient early authority [2]. It is scarcely necessary to add that on no medieval theory of government could the king be regarded as an estate of the realm. He was supreme in idea if not in practice; the head, not a limb, of the body politic; the impersonation of the majesty of the kingdom, not one of several co-ordinate constituents.

The system of Estates a product of the thirteenth century.

186. In the earlier chapters of this work we have traced the history of the national council through the several stages of Anglo-Saxon and Norman growth: we have seen in the witenagemot a council composed of the wise men of the nation; in the court of the Conqueror and his sons a similar assembly with a different qualification; and in that of Henry II a complete feudal council of the king's tenants. The thirteenth century turns the feudal council into an assembly of estates, and draws the constitution of the third estate from the ancient local machinery which it concentrates. But the process of change is not quite simple; it is a case of growth quite as much as of political treatment; and before examining the steps by which the representative system was completed we must ask how the other two estates disentangled themselves from one another, and

[1] The fact however of its use on the continent for the *communitates* or *universitates* of the towns is conclusive as to its historical derivation.

[2] 'In England where the clergy have been esteemed one estate, the peers of the realm the second estate and the commons of the realm, represented in parliament by persons chosen by certain electors, a third estate.' Lords' Report, i. 118. So in Scotland the barons were the second estate in parliament; ibid. p. 116. 'Les Etats, soit generaux soit particuliers, sont composez des deputez des trois ordres du royaume, qui sont le clergé, la noblesse et les deputez des communautez;' Ordonn. des Rois, iii. p. xx.

were prepared for the symmetrical arrangement in which they appear permanently; what were the causes of their mutual repulsion or internal cohesion.

The first or spiritual estate comprises the whole body of the clergy, whether endowed with land or tithe, whether dignified or undignified, whether sharing or not sharing the privileges of baronage. It possesses in its spiritual character an internal principle of cohesion, and the chief historical question is to determine the way in which the material ties which united it with the temporal estates were so far loosened as to allow to that principle of cohesion its full liberty. This of course affects mainly the prelates or ecclesiastical lords. Although during both the Anglo-Saxon and the Norman periods the ecclesiastical and temporal magnates possessed a distinct character and special functions, in the character of counsellors it is difficult to distinguish the action of the two. The ealdorman and sheriff would never usurp the function of the bishop, nor would the bishop, as a spiritual person, lead an army into the field; if he did so, or acted as a secular judge over his dependents, he did it as a landlord not as a bishop. In the shiremoot the ealdorman declared the secular law, and the bishop the spiritual; but in the witenagemot no such definite line is drawn between lay and clerical counsellors. Under the Norman kings again the supreme council was not divided into bishops and barons, although, where ecclesiastical questions were raised, the prelates might and would avail themselves of their spiritual organisation, which they possessed over and above their baronial status, to sit and deliberate apart. Even after the system of taxation had been formally arranged, as it was under Henry I and Henry II, the bishops and abbots, as alike tenants-in-chief, sat with the barons to grant aids, took part 'sicut barones ceteri[1]' in the judicial proceedings of the supreme court, and counselled and consented to the king's edicts. They had certainly added the title of 'barones' to that title of 'sapientes,' by which they had originally held, and had never ceased to hold, their seats. This latter title during all the later changes is not forfeited, the

The estate of the clergy.

The prelates in the Anglo-Saxon system;

under the Norman kings;

as barons of the king.

[1] Constitutions of Clarendon, Art. 11.

Union of prelacy and barony.

guardian of the spiritualities of a vacant see, who of course could not pretend to a baronial qualification, received the formal summons [1], and even now, when they no longer hold baronies, the bishops are summoned to the house of lords. The prelates were not the whole clergy; but so long as taxation fell solely on the land, the inferior clergy, who subsisted on tithes and offerings, scarcely came within view of the Exchequer. Thus, although of course the radical distinction between layman and clerk was never obliterated, still in all constitutional action the spiritual character was sunk in the baronial, and the prelates and barons held their places by a common tenure, and as one body.

Causes of the growth of unity in the estate of clergy:—(1) Conciliar action.

Ever since the Conquest, however, there had been causes at work which could not but in the end force upon the clergy the realisation of their constitutional place, and on the prelates a sense of their real union with the clergy [2]. Foremost among these was the growth of conciliar action in the church under Lanfranc and Anselm. The foreign ecclesiastics who sat on English thrones were made by the spirit of the time to take their place in the growing polity of the Western Church, and whatever may have been the later practice of the Anglo-Saxon kings with regard to synods, there is no obscurity about their history under the Normans, or as to their distinctly spiritual character. In these synods the clergy had a common field into which the barons could not enter, and a principle of union second only to that which was inherent in their common spiritual character. In the various synods of the nation, the province, and the diocese, the clergy had a complete constitution; the assemblies contained not only the prelates but the chapters, the archdeacons, and, in the lowest form, the parochial clergy also. Here was an organisation in most respects the counterpart of the national system of court and council.

(2) Growth of Canon law.

A second impulse in the same direction may be found in the introduction and growth of the canon law, the opening for which was made by the Conqueror's act removing the bishop from the

[1] See Hallam, Middle Ages, iii. 5. Abundant proof will be found in the summonses given in the Lords' Report.

[2] Cf. Lords' Report, i. 73.

county court. The ecclesiastical law, which had hitherto been administered either by spiritual men in the popular courts, or, where it touched spiritual matters, by the bishop himself in his diocesan council, now received a recognition as the system by which all ecclesiastical causes and all ecclesiastical persons were to be tried in courts of their own[1]. The clergy were thus removed from the view of the common law, and a double system of judicature sprang up; bishops, archdeacons, and rural deans, had their tribunals as well as their councils. Burchard of Worms, Ivo of Chartres, and after them Gratian, supplied manuals of the new jurisprudence. The persecution of Anselm, the weakness of Stephen, and the Becket controversy, spurred men on in the study of it: the legislative abilities of the archbishops were tasked to the utmost in following the footsteps of Alexander III and Innocent III.

Canon law distinguishing the clerical from the lay estates.

In the third place, the questions of church liberties and immunities, as fought out under Henry I and Henry II, had brought before all men's eyes the increasing differences of status. Appeals to Rome, the action of legates, the increased number of questions which arose between the temporal and spiritual powers in Christendom generally, were impressing a distinct mark on the clergy.

(3) Struggles for clerical immunities.

But it is in a fourth and further point that this distinctive character, so far as concerns our subject, chiefly asserts itself. This is the point of taxation. The taxable property of the clergy was either in land, which, whether held by the usual temporal services or in free alms, shared the liability of the rest of the land, or in tithes and offerings. So long as the land only was taxed, the bishops might constitutionally act with the baronage, paying scutages for their military fiefs and carucages for their lands held by other tenure. When taxation began to affect the spiritual revenue, it touched the clergy generally in a point in which the laity had nothing in common with them. It provoked a professional jealousy which later history abundantly justified. Just as the taxation of moveables led to the

(4) Taxation of clerical property.

[1] 'Non secundum hundret sed secundum canones et episcopales leges rectum Deo et episcopo suo faciat;' Will. I, Select Charters, p. 82.

constitutional action of the commons[1], so the taxation of spirituals developed the constitutional action of the clergy[2].

Growth of the custom of clerical taxation.

The stages of the process may be traced thus. Up to the reign of Stephen it is scarcely apparent. The king seized the castles and estates of the bishops just as he did those of the barons. Under Henry II we first find archbishop Theobald objecting to the payment of scutage by the bishops[3]; and although his objections were overruled by general acquiescence, they seem to point to the idea that previously all ecclesiastical payments to the crown were regarded as free gifts, and that even the lands were held rather on the theory of free alms than of feudal service. But such an idea must have been swept away by Henry II, who called on the bishops as well as the barons to give account of the knights' fees held of them and to pay accordingly[4]. In the ordinance of the Saladin tithe, the first occasion probably on which revenue and moveables were regularly taxed, as the books, vestments, and sacred apparatus of the clergy required special exception[5], it can scarcely be expected that spiritual revenue, tithes and offerings, escaped. But this tax was raised for an ecclesiastical purpose, and was imposed by a council far larger than was usually consulted. In the case, again, of Richard's ransom, there is no mention of spiritual revenue as excepted, indeed seeing that the sacred vessels of the churches were taken, it may be assumed that all branches of such revenue were laid under contribution: this, however, again, was a very exceptional case, and one for which the authority of the saints might be pleaded. In the carucage of 1198 the freeholds of the parish churches are untaxed[6], and during the rest of Hubert Walter's

[1] See vol. i. p. 578 sq.

[2] The French parochial clergy were not summoned either in person or by proctors to the States General, as not possessing 'temporel et justice'; Hervieu, Rev. de Legislation, 1873, p. 381.

[3] Vol. i. pp. 454, 578. Some tradition of this theory must have remained even under Edward I, who in 1276 issued letters patent declaring that the contribution of the archbishop and bishops to the grant of a fifteenth proceeded from the free grace of the bishops, 'et non nomine quintae decimae,' and was not to be construed as a precedent; Parl. Writs, i. p. 5. Cf. p. 14.

[4] Vol. i. p. 472.

[5] Select Charters, p. 152.

[6] 'Libera feoda ecclesiarum parochialium de hoc tallagio excipiebantur.' Hoveden, iv. 46; Select Charters, p. 249.

administration it is not probable that any extraordinary demand was made of the clergy, who, under bishops like Hugh of Lincoln, were prepared to resist any such aggression. The question however arose in its barest form under John, who in his demand of a share of the spiritual revenue showed an idea of legal consistency which only the want of money could have suggested to him. He approached the matter gradually. He began by applying to the Cistercians in 1202[1]. Their wool then, as before and after, afforded a tempting bait to his avarice, a source of profit easily assessed and easily seized. He then demanded a subsidy from the whole clergy of the province of Canterbury for the support of his nephew Otto IV, whose cause was at the moment a holy one under the patronage of Innocent III[2]. The petition was renewed in 1204[3]. Of the result, however, of these demands, we have no account, nor does the demand itself contain distinct reference to the spiritual revenue, or prove more than the wish to obtain a grant from the clergy apart from the laity. After the death of archbishop Hubert this obscurity ceases. On the 8th of January, 1207, the king called together the bishops, and asked them severally to allow the beneficed clergy to pay him a certain proportion of their revenues for the recovery of Normandy[4]. After an adjournment the request was repeated at Oxford on the 9th of February, and was unanimously refused; both provinces replied that such an exaction was unheard of in all preceding ages, and was not to be endured now[5]; and the king had to content himself with a thirteenth of moveables and such voluntary gifts as individual clergy might vouchsafe. The same idea must have occurred about the same time to Innocent III: he demanded a pecuniary aid, and an assembly of bishops, archdeacons and clergy, was convoked on

Increase of taxation under John.

Taxation of spirituals still a novelty.

[1] Rot. Claus. i. 14; Foed. i. 86.

[2] Foed. i. 87; Rot. Pat. i. 18. The letter is directed 'universo clero'; of course the vast majority of the clergy could only contribute from moveables or spiritual revenue.

[3] M. Paris, p. 209.

[4] Ann. Waverl. p. 258.

[5] 'Anglicanam ecclesiam nullo modo sustinere posse quod ab omnibus saeculis fuit prius inauditum;' Ann. Waverl. p. 258. See above, vol. i. p. 579; Select Charters, p. 265.

Taxation of spirituals,

the 26th of May at S. Alban's[1] to grant it, when John, at the instance of the barons, interfered to forbid it. The royal attempt in 1207 was lost sight of in the general oppressions that followed the interdict, and it is probable that until the end of the reign the spiritual revenues escaped direct taxation, simply because they ceased regularly to accrue. As soon, however, as the pope and king were at peace, the long struggle began between the clergy and their united taskmasters, both of whom saw the wisdom of humouring them in their desire to separate their interests from those of the laity. In 1219, in accordance with the decree of the Lateran council of 1215, a twentieth of church revenue was assigned for three years to the crusade[2]; in 1224 the prelates granted a carucage separately from the barons[3]; in 1225, when the nation generally paid a fifteenth, the clergy contributed an additional sum from the property which did not contribute to that tax[4]. In 1226 the beneficed clergy at the pope's request gave the king a sixteenth for his own necessities[5]; in 1229 Gregory IX claimed a tenth for

by the Lateran Council.

and by pope and king.

1 'Conquerente universitate comitum baronum et militum et aliorum fidelium nostrorum audivimus quod, non solum in laicorum gravem perniciem sed etiam in totius regni nostri intolerabile dispendium, super Romscoto praeter consuetudinem solvendo et aliis pluribus inconsuetis exactionibus, auctoritate summi pontificis consilium inire et consilium celebrare decrevistis;' Rot. Pat. i. 72.

2 'Vicesima ecclesiarum,' Ann. Theokesb. p. 64. The tax was paid the same year also in Sicily and France; 'vicesima a personis ecclesiasticis, a laicis vero decima;' R. S. Germ. p. 47. The decree of the Lateran council was 'ex communi approbatione statuimus ut omnes omnino clerici, tam subditi quam praelati, vigesimam partem ecclesiasticorum proventuum usque ad triennium conferant in subsidium Terrae Sanctae;' Labbe and Cossart, xi. 228. See above, p. 36.

3 Above, p. 36.

4 W. Cov. ii. 256, 257; above, p. 38.

5 Probably this was the same contribution as the last-mentioned, see above, p. 39; but it is important as showing the way in which the precedent of 1219 was applied; 'ad petitionem domini papae, ad urgentissimam necessitatem domini regis . . . spontanea voluntate concessa fuit eidem regi Henrico sexta decima pars aestimationis ecclesiarum, secundum taxationem qua taxatae erant ecclesiae in diebus illis quando vicesima pars ecclesiarum collata fuit ad instantiam domini papae in subsidium Terrae Sanctae;' Ann. Osney, p. 68. 'Archiepiscopi, episcopi, abbates, priores et domorum religiosarum magistri per Angliam constituti decimam quintam partem omnium mobilium suorum et feodorum suorum, et clerus inferior aestimato annuo valore singularum ecclesiarum sextam decimam partem inde nobis concesserint;' Royal Letters, i. 299. 'Auxilium de beneficiis suis de quibus quindenam non recepimus impendant;' Wilkins, Conc. i. 620. Probably the grant was made in diocesan synods.

himself[1]. It was from such applications for grants from the spiritualty that the custom arose of assembling the clergy in distinct assemblies for secular business, which so largely influenced the history of both Parliament and Convocation. In 1231 the bishops demurred to a scutage which had been imposed without their consent[2]; in 1240 they refused to consider a demand of the legate because the lower clergy were not represented[3]. Successive valuations of ecclesiastical property, spiritual as well as temporal, were made[4]. The discussion of public questions in ecclesiastical assemblies became more frequent as the constitution of those assemblies took form and consistency under oppression. Innumerable petitions for the redress of grievances illustrate the increased spirit of independence in the clergy, as well as the persistency of the king and the pope in crushing it; and, interpreted by the life of Grosseteste, show a more distinct comprehension by the leaders of the church of their peculiar position as the 'clerus,' the Lord's inheritance. These points will come before us again in reference to the history of Convocation. It is enough

Custom of assembling the clergy for secular business.

Petitions and gravamina.

[1] See above, p. 42; 'decimam reddituum et proventuum clericorum et virorum religiosorum;' Ann. Osney, p. 70.

[2] M. Paris, p. 367; above, p. 42.

[3] M. Paris, p. 534: 'omnes tangit hoc negotium, omnes igitur sunt conveniendi.' Cf. pp. 535, 536.

[4] From the year 1252 onwards a tenth of ecclesiastical revenue was generally taken by the pope's authority: in 1252, 'decimam ecclesiasticorum proventuum in subsidium Terrae Sanctae,' for three years, Foed. i. 280; in 1254 for five years, Ann. Osney, p. 112; Royal Letters, ii. 101; in 1266 for three years, Foed. i. 473: in 1273 for three years; in 1274 a tenth of spirituals for six years; in 1280 and onwards the grants of spirituals to the king in convocation have been noted above. A taxation for the twentieth in 1219 was mentioned in note 5, p. 174. In 1256 Alexander IV ordered a new taxation of benefices to be made 'secundum debitam et justam taxationem,' Foed. i. 345; in consequence of this a taxation was made by Walter Suffield, bishop of Norwich, called the Norwich Taxation; this lasted until the new taxation of 1291; called that of pope Nicolas (see above, pp. 119 sq.), which was in force until the Reformation, and comprised both temporals and spirituals. Curiously enough during Simon de Montfort's administration the spirituals were taxed by the prelates and magnates; 'cum per praelatos et magnates regni nostri provisum sit et unanimiter concessum quod decimae proventuum omnium beneficiorum ecclesiasticorum in regno nostro conferantur ad communem utilitatem ejusdem regni et ecclesiae Anglicanae,' Foed. i. 445: but perhaps this merely means that the tithe collected under the papal authority should be applied to the good of the country instead of the Crusade. The assessment of the lands acquired after the taxation of pope Nicolas was, as we shall see, a subject of difficulty throughout the fourteenth century.

Growth of the clerical estate.

to say here that it was by action on these occasions that the clerical estate worked out its distinct organisation as an estate of the realm, asserting and possessing deliberative, legislative, and taxing powers, and in so doing provided some not unimportant precedents for parliamentary action under like circumstances.

Growth of the estate of baronage.

187. It is less easy to determine, either by date or by political cause, the circumstances that ultimately defined the estate of the baronage, drawing the line between lords and commons. The result indeed is clear: the great land owners, tenants-in-chief, or titled lords, who appeared in person at the parliament, are separated by a broad line from the freeholders, who were represented by the knights of the shire; and legal authority fixes the reigns of Henry III and Edward I as the period of limitation, and recognises the change in the character of qualification, from barony by tenure to barony by writ, as the immediate and formal cause of it. This authority, however, whether based on legal theory or on the historical evidence of custom, rather determines the question of personal and family right than the intrinsic character of baronage, at all events during its present stage of development.

Characteristics of barony.

188. An hereditary baronage may be expected to find its essential characteristic in distinction of blood, or in the extent and tenure of its territory, or in the definitions of law and custom, or in the possession of peculiar privilege bestowed by the sovereign, or in the coincidence of some or all of these.

English nobility as contrasted with foreign.

The great peculiarity of the baronial estate in England as compared with the continent, is the absence of the idea of caste: the English lords do not answer to the nobles of France, or to the princes and counts of Germany, because in our system the theory of nobility of blood as conveying political privilege has no legal recognition. English nobility is merely the nobility of the hereditary counsellors of the crown, the right to give counsel being involved at one time in the tenure of land, at another in the fact of summons, at another in the terms of a patent; it is the result rather than the cause of peerage. The nobleman is the person who for his life holds the hereditary office denoted or implied in his title. The law gives to his children and kinsmen no privilege which it does not give to the ordinary freeman, unless we regard certain acts of courtesy, which the law has recognised, as implying privilege. Such legal nobility does not of course preclude the existence of real nobility, socially privileged and defined by ancient purity of descent, or even by connexion with the legal nobility of the peerage; but the English law does not regard the man of most ancient and purest descent as entitled thereby to any right or privilege which is not shared by every freeman.

English nobility of peerage.

Nobility of blood.

The cause of this difference is a question of no small interest. Nobility of blood, that is, nobility which was shared by the whole kin alike, was a very ancient principle among the Germans, and was clearly recognised by the Anglo-Saxons in the common institution of wergild. The Normans of the Conquest formed a new nobility, which can scarcely be suspected of feeling too little jealousy of the privileges of blood; nor has the line which socially divided the man of ancient race from the 'novus homo,' who rises by wealth or favour, ever been entirely obliterated[1]. The question is not solved by reference to the custom of inheritance by primogeniture, or to the indivisibility of fiefs, so far as it prevailed, because, although these causes may have helped to produce the result, they were at work in countries where the result was different. It is possible that the circumstances of the great houses in the twelfth century, when the noble lines were very much attenuated, when many of them were rich enough to provide several sons with independent fiefs, and those who could not sent their younger sons into holy orders, may have affected the constitutional theory. The truth is, however, that English law recognises simply the right of peerage,

[1] A story told by Trokelow about Johanna of Acre, the daughter of Edward I, who married a simple knight, Ralph of Monthermer, of whose extraction nothing is known, shows how slight was the influence of blood nobility at this time: 'Aderat unus e magnatibus terrae qui in auribus domini regis patris sui intonuit, quod ejus honori adversum foret hujusmodi matrimonium, cum nonnulli nobiles, reges, comites et barones eam adoptabant toro legitimo. Cui illa respondit "non est ignominiosum neque probrosum magno comiti et potenti pauperculam mulierem et tenuem sibi legitimo matrimonio copulare; sic vice versa nec comitissae non est reprehensibile nec difficile juvenem strenuum promovere."' p. 27. The idea of disparagement in marriage must have been on the wane.

Distinction of blood.

not the privilege of nobility as properly understood; it recognises office, dignity, estate, and class, but not caste; for the case of villenage, in which the question of caste does to some extent arise, is far too obscure to be made to illustrate that of nobility, and the disabilities of Jews and aliens rest on another principle. Social opinion and the rules of heraldry, which had perhaps their chief use in determining an international standard of blood, alone recognise the distinction.

Question of land-tenure as touching barony.

189. The nobility of blood then does not furnish the principle of cohesion, or separate the baronage from the other estates. The question of land-tenure has its own difficulties. Upon feudal theory all the king's tenants-in-chief were members of his court and council; and as their estates were hereditary their office of counsellor was hereditary too; but in practice the title and rights of baronage were gradually restricted to the greater tenants who received special summons, when the minor tenants received a general summons, to the council and the host; and the baronage of the thirteenth century was the body of tenants-in-chief holding a fief or a number of fiefs consolidated into a baronial honour or qualification. This qualification was not created by the possession of a certain extent of territory; for although the law defined the obligations of a barony in proportion to those of earldoms and knights' fees, in the ratio of the mark to the pound and the shilling[1], the mere acquisition of thirteen knights' fees and a third[2] did not make the purchaser a baron. Neither was it created by the simple fact of tenancy-in-chief, which the baron shared with the knights and freeholders holding of the crown. The peculiar tenure of barony is recognised in the Constitutions of Clarendon: the relief due for a barony is prescribed by Magna Carta. Whether the baronial honour or qualification was created by the terms of the original grant of the fief, or by subsequent recognition, it is perhaps impossible to determine. As we do not possess anything like an early enfeoffment of a barony, it is safer to confine ourselves to the assertion that, in whatever form the lands were acquired or

Barony not created by extent of tenure;

nor by nature of tenure.

[1] Bracton, lib. ii. c. 36; Magna Carta (Edw. I. A.D. 1297); art. 2.

[2] Forma tenendi Parliamentum, Select Charters, p. 493.

bestowed, the special summons recognised the baronial character of the tenure, or in other words, that estate was a barony which entitled its owner to such special summons.

Tenure of land illustrates the social idea of barony.

But although the extent and nature of tenure of estate in land may not explain the origin of the distinction, they do, more clearly than the theory of nobility, furnish a clue to the causes of the social distinction of the baronage. The twelfth century saw the struggle made by a body of feudatories, thoroughly imbued with the principles of feudalism, for the possession of political power and jurisdiction. Their attempts were defeated by Henry I and Henry II; but the policy of those kings did not require the limitation of the other parts of the feudal theory; on the contrary, it is to their reigns that many of the innovations are ordinarily referred, which by developing the land-laws gave considerable impulse to the growth of the baronage as a separate class. It was the feudal custom or rule that encouraged the introduction of succession by primogeniture, and discouraged the division and alienation of fiefs. In the absence of anything like exact evidence, the general acceptance of these principles is placed at this point. The law by which Geoffrey of Brittany introduced the right of primogeniture into his estates[1] was the work of his father Henry II, who would not have forced on that province a rule which he had not incorporated with his own legal practice. The whole process of the assize of Mort d'ancestor would seem to prove that in estates held by knight-service this was already the rule. In Glanvill's time estates held in socage were equally divided among the sons, the eldest however receiving the capital messuage; the exclusive rights of the eldest born date from the thirteenth century[2]. During the same period of unrecorded change the rule that the tenant must not alienate his land without his lord's consent, a rule which had been formally promulgated in the empire by Lothar II[3], and which was in

Rule of primogeniture.

Restraint on alienation.

[1] See it in Palgrave, Commonwealth, ii. p. ccccxxxv.

[2] Glanvill, vii. c. 3; Digby, Real Property, p. 72.

[3] Hallam, M.A. i. 174, 175. 'Per multas enim interpellationes ad nos factas comperimus milites sua beneficia passim distrahere, ac ita omnibus exhaustis suorum servitia subterfugere; per quod vires imperii maxime attenuatas cognovimus, dum proceres nostri milites suos omnibus beneficiis suis exutos, ad felicissimi nostri numinis expeditionem nullo modo trans-

Restraint on alienation.

general use on the continent, must have been at least partially admitted. The power of alienation, a power which no one would value unless he was debarred from it, had under the Anglo-Saxon law been restricted by the rights of the family only when such rights were specifically mentioned in the title-deeds of the estate; and when Glanvill wrote, this power was subject only to some undefined claims of the heir. First in the Great Charter of 1217 it was limited by the provision that the tenant must not give or sell to any one so much of his estate as to make it incapable of furnishing the due service to his lord[1]. The hold of the lord on the land of his tenant, which a century before had been construed as implying so great rights of jurisdiction, was rapidly being limited to rights of service and escheat: but these rights the tenants-in-chief laboured hard to retain[2]: before the end of the century great obstacles had been put in the way of any such alienation, and were tasking the ingenuity of the lawyers to overcome them. These were devised no doubt to preserve the equitable rights of the lords or the reversionary rights of donors: the latter was the object of the statute *de Donis*, the former was thought to be secured by the statute *Quia emptores*. The principle that a tenant-in-chief of the crown could not alienate without licence had been long admitted[3] before it was exemplified in the statute *de Praerogativa*, the very title of which seems to show that the privileges it contains were not yet shared by the other 'capitales domini[4],' against whom Bracton argues in favour of liberty. But although these

Growth of English law on this point.

ducere valeamus; . . . decernimus, nemini licere beneficia quae a suis senioribus habent sine ipsorum permissione distrahere;' A.D. 1136; Lib. Feudorum, ii. tit. 52. l. 1. Cf. the law of Frederick in tit. 55.

[1] Magna Carta (1217), art. 39.

[2] Bracton, ii. c. 19; 'sed posset aliquis dicere quod ex hoc quod donatorius ulterius dat et transfert rem donatam ad alios, quod hoc facere non potest, quia per hoc amittit dominus servitium suum, quod quidem non est verum, salva pace et reverentia capitalium dominorum.'

[3] In 1225, Thomas of Hoton sold the bailiwick of Plumpton, a serjeanty of the king's forest of Inglewood, with two carucates and four bovates of land to Alan de Capella, 'quam bailliam in manum domini regis cepit (Hugo de Nevilla) eo quod idem Thomas eam dicto Alano vendidit sine licentia domini regis;' Rot. Claus. ii. 38.

[4] Statutes of the Realm, i. 227. The date of the statute is uncertain; it was formerly attributed to 17 Edw. II, but is probably earlier. See on it the Lords' Report, i. p. 400; Cutbill, Petition of Right, p. 12.

measures were justified by legal theory, there are indications that there was, in a section at least of the lords, an inclination to grasp at the ultimate possession of all land not in the royal hands, just as a century before they had grasped at exclusive jurisdiction. The statute of Merton [1], which gives to the lord of the manor the right of enclosing all common land that is not absolutely required by the freeholders, is an early illustration of this. Complaint was made too in the Oxford parliament of 1258, that certain great men bought up mortgages from the Jews and so entered on the lands of the mortgagors [2]. The charge was perhaps directed against the foreign favourites of Henry III, but it was not met adequately by legislation, and possibly it points to an increasing divergency of interest between the barons and the body of knights. But the policy of Edward I and the craft of the lawyers prevented the reduction of the English land system to the feudal model, if it ever were contemplated. The hold which the statutes of 1285 and 1290 gave to the chief lords over their vassals made the king supreme over the chief lords. On the whole, however, restraints on alienation whether general or affecting the tenants-in-chief only, must have tended to the concentration and settlement of great estates and so must have increased the distinction between greater and smaller land owners.

Aggressive instincts of the baronage.

Double effect of Edward's land-laws.

190. The definitions of the law recognise rather than create the character of barony; but the observance of the rule of proportion in the payment of relief, the special provision that the baron must be amerced by his equals or before the royal council, and the rule that by his equals only he should be tried, must have served to mark out who those equals were, and to give additional consistency to a body already limited and beginning to recognise its definite common interest [3].

The definitions of the law as touching barony.

[1] Statutes of the Realm, i. 2.

[2] 'Judaei aliquando debita sua, et terras eis invadiatas, tradunt magnatibus et potentioribus regni, qui terras minorum ingrediuntur ea occasione, et licet ipsi qui debitum debent parati sint ad solvendum praedictum debitum cum usuris, praefati magnates negotium prorogant, ut praedictae terrae et tenementa aliquo modo sibi remanere possint;' Select Charters, p. 377.

[3] Roger of Muntbegon, as 'magnus homo et baro regis,' has the right of

Barony finally created by royal action.

Having, however, all these rights, privileges and interests in common, the baronage was ultimately and essentially defined as an estate of the realm by the royal action in summons, writ, and patent. It was by special summons 'propriis nominibus[1]' that Henry I, Henry II[2], and the barons of Runnymede, separated the greater from the smaller vassals of the crown; and the constitutional change which at last determined the character of peerage was the making of the status of the peers depend on the hereditary reception of the writ, rather than on the tenure which had been the original qualification for summons. We may not suspect the great men who secured the liberties of England of struggling merely for their own privilege: their successes certainly did not result in the vindication of the rights of blood or of those of tenure. The determination of the persons who should be summoned as barons rested finally with the crown[3], limited only on one side by the rule of hereditary right.

The 'majores barones.'

We have already recognised the distinctive character, traceable as early as the reign of Henry I, of a class of vassals who, besides receiving special summons to council[4], had special summons to the host, led their own dependents in battle, and made separate composition with the Exchequer for their pecuniary obligations. Henry III and Edward I either continued or introduced the custom of summoning by special writ to the council a much smaller number of these than were summoned by special writ to perform military service. The diminution was no doubt gratefully admitted both by those who were glad to escape from an irksome duty, and by those who saw their own political strength increased by the disappearance of many who might have been their competitors. There can be little

Diminution in the number summoned to parliament.

swearing by his steward in a court of justice, and of not being personally detained by the county court, in 1220, Royal Letters, i. 102, 104.

[1] See vol. i. p. 567.

[2] 'Barones secundae dignitatis;' W. FitzStephen, S.T.C. i. 235. Hallam (Middle Ages, iii. 8) rightly understands this to refer to the knightly tenants in chief; Lyttelton and Hume refer it to the mesne tenants.

[3] In France the dukes, counts, barons, bannerets, and 'hautes-justiciers' were always summoned; the seigneurs of secondary rank never. Hervieu, Rev. de Legisl. 1873, p. 384.

[4] The form 'majores barones' for the lords specially summoned subsisted as late as the reign of Edward II; see Parl. Writs, II. i. 181.

doubt that the idea of a peerage, a small body of counsellors by whom the exercise of the royal functions could be limited and directed, a royal court of peers like those of France, was familiar to the English politicians of the reign of Henry III; and the influence of such an idea may be traced in the oligarchical policy of the barons in 1258 and 1264. But it never gained general favour: the saying of Peter des Roches, that there were no 'pares' in England, ignorant blunder as it was[1], is sufficient to prove this; and the apprehensions felt that William of Valence would change the English constitution[2], as well as the contemptuous way in which the historians describe the Scottish attempt to create a body of twelve peers[3], show that the scheme, however near realisation, was disliked and ridiculed. The plan of thus limiting the royal power, so frequently brought forward under Henry III, Edward II and his successors, is never once broached in the reign of Edward I. The hereditary summoning of a large proportion of great vassals was a middle course between the very limited peerage which in France coexisted with an enormous mass of privileged nobility, and the unmanageable, ever varying, assembly of the whole mass of feudal tenants as prescribed in Magna Carta. It is to this body of select hereditary barons, joined with the prelates, that the term 'peers of the land' properly belongs; an expression which occurs first, it is said, in the act by which the Despensers were exiled[4], but which before the middle of the fourteenth century had obtained general recognition as descriptive of members of the house of lords.

Growth of the idea of peerage.

Edward's plan a middle course.

It may be doubted whether either Edward I or his ministers contemplated the perpetuity of the restrictions which mark this important change: and it may be not unreasonably held that the practice of the reign owes its legal importance to the fact that it was used by the later lawyers as a period of limitation, and not to any conscious finality in Edward's policy. It is

Edward's reign a date of limitation.

[1] Above, p. 48. [2] Above, p. 53.

[3] 'Ad modum Franciae;' Hemingburgh, ii. 78; Rishanger, p. 151. 'More Francorum;' M. Westm. p. 425.

[4] Statutes of the Realm, i. 181, 184; Lords' Report, i. 281. The word is used so clumsily as to show that it was in this sense a novelty; first 'lui mustrent prelatz, countes, barounes, et les autres piers de la terre, et commune du roiaulme;' then 'nous piers de la terre, countes et barouns.'

In the present period barony implies tenure and summons.

convenient to adopt the year 1295 as the era from which the baron, whose ancestor has been once summoned and has once sat in parliament, can claim an hereditary right to be so summoned[1]. It is unnecessary here to anticipate the further questions of the degrees, the privileges, and the rights of peerage. For the period before us membership of the parliamentary baronage implies both tenure and summons. The political status of the body so constituted is thus defined by their successors: 'the hereditary peers of the realm claim, (i.) in conjunction with the lords spiritual, certain powers as the king's permanent council when not assembled in parliament, (ii.) other powers as lords of parliament when assembled in parliament and acting in a judicial capacity, and (iii.) certain other powers when assembled in parliament together with the commons of the realm appearing by their representatives in parliament, the whole now forming under the king the legislature of the country[2].' The estate of the peerage is identical with the house of lords.

Definition of peerage.

The line drawn between the barons and smaller land-owners.

191. Had it depended upon the barons to draw the line between themselves and the smaller landowners, the latter might in the end have been swamped altogether, or have had to win political power by a separate struggle. The distinction was drawn, on the one hand by the royal power of summons, and on the other by the institution and general acceptance of the principle of shire-representation. For several reasons the minor freeholders might have been expected to throw in their lot with the barons, with whom they shared the character of landowners and the common bonds of chivalry and consanguinity. For a long time they voted their taxes in the same proportion with them, and it was not by any means clear, at the end of the reign of Edward I, that they might not furnish a fourth estate of Parliament. And ultimately perhaps it was rather the force of

[1] Courthope, Hist. Peerage, p. xli., but cf. Hallam, M. A. iii. 124, 125. The question of life peerage need not be considered at the present stage. The importance of 1264 and 1295 arises from the fact that there are no earlier or intermediate writs of summons to a proper parliament extant; if, as is by no means impossible, earlier writs addressed to the ancestors of existing families should be discovered, it might become a critical question how far the rule could be regarded as binding.

[2] Lords' Report, i. 151; cf. p. 14.

the representative system than any strong fellow-feeling with the town populations that made them merge their separate character in the estate of the commons. We have then to account first for their separation from the baronage, and secondly for their incorporation in the third estate: their separation from the baronage was caused not only by the circumstances which drew the baronage away from them, but by other circumstances which gave them a separate interest apart from the baronage; and their union with the town populations was the result of mutual approximation, and not of simple attraction of the smaller to the greater, the weaker to the stronger body.

Effect of representation

192. That portion of the third estate which was represented by the knights of the shire contained not only the residue of the tenants-in-chief but all the freeholders of the county. The chosen knights represented the constituency that met in the county courts. This point admits of much illustration[1], but it is enough now to remark that practically the selection of representatives would depend on the more important land-owners whether they held in chief of the crown or of mesne lords. Formally their bond of union was the common member-ship of the particular shire-moot; but as a political estate they had class interests and affinities[2], and the growth of these in contrast with the interests of the baronial class might form for the investigator of social history an interesting if somewhat perplexing subject. Almost all presumptions based on the principles of nobility and property are common to both bodies; and their political sympathies might be expected to correspond. Yet from the day when the Conqueror exacted the oath of fealty from all the landowners, 'whosoever men they were,' the kings seem to have depended on the provincial knights and freeholders for aid against the great feudatories. The social tyranny of the great barons would fall first on their own vassals; the knights who held single fees in chief of the crown would stand in a position to be coveted by their vassal neighbours, and the two classes would be drawn together by common

The freeholders;

combined in the county courts.

Separation from the great feudatories.

[1] See below, pp. 205 sq.
[2] See Gneist, Verwaltungsrecht, i. 312.

Growth of political sympathy.

dangers. These political sympathies would be turned into a sense of real unity by the measures taken by the kings, and especially by Edward I, to eliminate the political importance of mesne tenure. The obligation to receive knighthood, imposed not only on the tenants-in-chief, not only on all tenants by knight service, but on all who possessed land enough to furnish knightly equipment[1], whether that obligation were enforced or redeemed by fine, consolidated a knightly body irrespective of tenure. The common service in war, which likewise Edward demanded of all freeholders, was another example of the same principle; and although foreign service of the sort was strange to the institutions of England, the very attempt to compel it helped to draw men together. The abolition of subinfeudation in 1290[2] must have increased the number of minor tenants-in-chief whenever the great estates were broken up; and must have diminished the difference, if indeed any such difference still subsisted, between the two classes.

Increase of corporate feeling between minor tenants in chief and mesne freeholders.

Drawn together by common dangers, and assimilated to one another by royal policy, both classes of freeholders had, in the work of the county court, an employment which the technical differences of their tenure did not disturb. Without any regard to tenure, 'discreet and legal' members of these classes acted together in the management of the judicial and financial business, the military work and the police of the shire. The body which, under the name of the 'communitas bacheleriae Angliae[3],' urged on Edward in 1259 the necessity of reforming the laws, was not, however new its designation, a newly formed association; it was a consolidated body of men trained by a century and a half

The county court a common field of work.

[1] See below, pp. 281 sq.

[2] 'In the reign of Edward, provisions were made with respect to tenures, which had the effect of greatly increasing the number of Freeholders, and particularly the statute, "quia emptores terrarum," which prevented all future subinfeudation, making every alienee tenant to the immediate superior of the alienor, which tended gradually to increase very considerably the numbers of the tenants in chief of the crown, as the necessities of the greater tenants in chief and even the necessity of providing for the younger branches of their families, which was generally done by grants of land, compelled them to alienate parcels of land holden by them immediately of the crown;' Lords' Report, i. 129. See also Hallam, Middle Ages, iii. 16.

[3] Above, p. 81.

of common interests and common work. The summons to elect two men to parliament, to grant an aid or to accept a law, was not the first occasion on which the forms of election or the principle of representation came before them. It is quite probable that the idea of a possible antagonism, or a possible equilibrium, between the county court and the baronage, may have suggested to Henry III, as it did to Simon de Montfort, the summoning of such representatives to council. The machinery of the county gave body and form; the common political interest, sympathy and antipathy, gave spirit, to the newly formed 'communitas terrae.'

Cohesion of the freeholders in the county court.

When once made a part of the national council, the knights of the shire would have in their character of delegates or proctors another cause of separation from the barons, which would further react on their constituencies. Men who knew themselves to be delegates, called together primarily to give on behalf of their counties an assent to action already prescribed for them by the magnates, would not only be made to feel themselves a separate class from the magnates, but would be inclined to assume an attitude of opposition. As delegates too, local influences would affect them in a way which must have increased the divergency between them and the barons, who were less identified with local interests and more imbued with the interest of class. The constant changes in the representative members, none of whom would feel that he had a certain tenure of power, would incline the whole body to seek their strength in harmonious action and mutual confidence, not to indulge the personal ambition of particular leaders. And this delegate character, shared with the town representatives, drew the knights to them, and away from the barons. But too much importance must not be attached to these influences: we shall see in the history of the fourteenth century that local and personal interests were strong in all the three estates, and that there was far more to draw them together, or to divide them, so to speak, vertically, than to separate them according to class interests.

The knights draw off from the magnates.

Their representative character draws them to the town representatives.

These points, it is true, illustrate the position of the knights of the shire rather than those of their constituents, but it is to be remembered that it is in the character of 'communitates,' represented by these elected knights, that the landowners of the shires become an estate of the realm.

Approximation of shire and town communities.

193. The causes that drew together the knights of the shire and the burghers in parliament may be similarly stated. The attraction which was not created by like habits of life and thought was supplied by their joint procuratorial character, their common action in the county court, and the common need of social independence in relation to the lords. As time went on, and the two branches of the landed interest became in social matters more entirely separated, no doubt the townsmen were drawn nearer to their country neighbours. The younger sons of the country knight sought wife, occupation, and estate in the towns. The leading men in the towns, such as the De la Poles, formed an urban aristocracy, that had not to wait more than one generation for ample recognition. The practice of knighthood, the custom of bearing coat-armour as a sign of original or achieved gentility, as well as real relationship and affinity, united the superior classes; the small freeholder and the small tradesman met on analogous terms, and the uniform tendency of local and political sympathy more than counteracted the disruptive tendency of class jealousies. Such agencies must be regarded as largely affecting the growth of the third estate into a consciousness of its corporate identity. Probably the proof of their effects will be found more plentifully in the fourteenth century than in the thirteenth. The policy however of raising the trading classes, which is ascribed to Edward III, may be traced in the action of his grandfather, and is far more in harmony with his statesmanship than with that of the founder of the order of the Garter. But notwithstanding the operation of these causes, both under Edward I and during the three succeeding reigns, the glare of a factitious chivalry must, in England as abroad, have rendered the relations of town and country gentry somewhat uneasy.

Peculiarity of the Third Estate in England.

The third estate in England differs from the same estate in the continental constitutions, by including the landowners under baronial rank. In most of those systems it contains the representatives of the towns or chartered communities[1] only. And it was this that constituted the original strength of our representative system: as a concentration of the powers of the county courts, that system contained a phalanx of commoner members, seventy-four knights of the shires[2], who not only helped to link the baronage with the burghers, but formed a compact body which neither the crown nor the sheriff could diminish, as they could diminish the number of barons summoned, or of the representatives of the towns. These knights too were men likely and able to show themselves independent: certainly they could not be treated in the way in which Charles V and Philip II extinguished the action of the Spanish cortes or quelled the spirit of the Netherlands. Their rights were rooted not in royal privilege, which he who gave could take away, but in the most primitive institutions and in those local associations which are to all intents and purposes indelible.

The shire system is the strength of the Third Estate.

194. In the uncertainty which for some half century attended the ultimate form in which the estates would rank themselves, two other classes or subdivisions of estates might have seemed likely to take a more consolidated form and to bid for more direct power than they finally achieved. The lawyers[3] and the merchants occasionally seem as likely to form an estate of the realm as the clergy or the knights. Under a king with the strong legal instincts of Edward I, surrounded by a council of lawyers, the patron of great jurists and the near kinsman of three great legislators, the practice and study of law bid fair for a great constitutional position. Edward would not, like his uncle Frederick II, have closed the high offices of the law to all

Sub-estate of the lawyers.

[1] The Spanish 'poblaciones,' although they contained landowners, were in reality chartered communities, not differing in origin from the town municipalities.

[2] This is a point to be kept carefully in mind when comparisons are drawn between the history of the third estate in Spain and that in England. The shires furnished the only absolutely indestructible part of the parliament.

[3] 'Qu'est il plus farouche que de veoir une nation ou par legitime coustume, la charge de juger se vende, et les jugements soyent payez a purs deniers comptants, et ou legitimement la justice soit refusee a qui n'a de quoy la payer; et ayt cette marchandise si grand credit, qu'il se face en une police un quatriesme estat de gents maniants les proces, pour le joindre aux trois anciens, de l'eglise, de la noblesse, et du peuple.' Montaigne, Essais, liv. i. c. 22. See p. 191, note 1 below.

Foreign classes of lawyers.

but the legal families[1], and so turned the class, as Frederick did the knightly class, into a caste; or, like his brother-in-law Alfonso the Wise, have attempted to supersede the national law by the civil law of Rome; or like Philip the Fair, have suffered the legal members of his council to form themselves into a close corporation almost independent of the rest of the body politic; but where the contemporary influences were so strong we can hardly look to the king alone as supplying the counteracting weight.

Peculiar growth of the profession of law in England.

It is perhaps rather to be ascribed to the fact that the majority of the lawyers were still in profession clerks[2]; that the Chancery, which was increasing in strength and wholesome influence, was administered almost entirely by churchmen, and that the English universities did not furnish for the common law of England any such great school of instruction as Paris and Bologna provided for the canonist or the civilian. Had the scientific lawyers ever obtained full sway in English courts, notwithstanding the strong antipathy felt for the Roman law, the Roman law must ultimately have prevailed, and if it had prevailed it might have changed the course of English history. To substitute the theoretical perfection of a system, which was regarded as less than inspired only because it was not of universal applicability, for one, the very faults of which produced elasticity and stimulated progress and reform whilst it trained the reformers for legislation, would have been to place the development of the constitution under the heel of the king, whose power the scientific lawyer never would curtail but when it comes into collision with his own rules and precedents[3].

[1] See the constitution of Roger, confirmed by Frederick II; Const. Reg. Sic. iii. 39. 1; cf. Giannone, Hist. Naples, i. 535.

[2] On the growth of the professional lawyer class, see Foss's Judges of England, ii. 200; iii. 46 sq. 370–390; iv. 195 sq. 251 sq.; and Gneist, Verwaltungsrecht, i. 341, 350. The frequent legislation of the ecclesiastical councils and the remonstrances of the better prelates of the thirteenth century withdrew the clergy in some measure from legal practice. Edward I in 1292 ordered the judges to provide and ordain seven score attorneys and apprentices to practice in the courts; a certain number to be chosen from the best in each county, and all others excluded; Rot. Parl. i. 84. Fleta mentions several degrees of practising lawyers, servientes, narratores, attornati, and apprentitii.

[3] It is a curious point, which should have been noted in the last chapter, that Bracton, although himself clearly a constitutional thinker, gives the preference in almost all cases to the decisions of Stephen Segrave, the

The action of the Privy Council, which to some extent played the part of a private parliament, was always repulsive to the English mind; had it been a mere council of lawyers the result might have been still more calamitous than it was. The summons of the justices and other legal counsellors to parliament[1], by a writ scarcely distinguishable from that of the barons themselves, shows how nearly this result was reached.

An Estate of Lawyers not acceptable in England.

195. The merchant class, again, possessed in the peculiar nature of their taxable property, and in the cosmopolitan character of their profession, grounds on which, like the clergy, they might have founded a claim for class representation. What the tithe was to the one class, the wool and leather were to the other; both had strong foreign connexions, and the Gilbertine and Cistercian orders, whose chief wealth was in wool, formed a real link between the two. Nor was the wool less coveted than the tithe by kings like Richard and John; the mercantile influence of Flanders and Lombardy might be paralleled with the ecclesiastical influence of Rome. It was perhaps the seizure of the wool of the Cistercians for Richard's ransom that led John to bestow special favour on that order, and then to make the special applications for help in return for those special favours, applications which could scarcely be refused when the taxable fund lay so completely at the king's mercy. So long as the contribution to royal wants was made to bear the character of a free gift severally asked for and severally bestowed, the merchants shared with the clergy the privilege of being specially

Sub-estate of the Merchants.

Their taxable value.

justiciar of Henry III, who supplanted Hubert de Burgh, and was practically a tool of the foreign party. It is clear that Segrave, although a bad minister, was a first-rate lawyer.

[1] 'During the sitting of Parliament the council . . . sat as a house, branch, or estate of Parliament;' Palgrave, King's Council, p. 21. This seems to be a mere rhetorical exaggeration. Yet in 1381 the commons petitioned that 'les prelatz par eux mesmes, les grantz seigneurs temporels par eux mesmes, les chivalers par eux, les justices par eux, et touz autres estatz singulerement,' might debate severally; Rot. Parl. iii. 100. See below, p. 259. In France in the reign of Henry II (1557, 1558) the 'Parliaments' seem to have sat by their deputies as a separate estate of the states general. And in the Rolls of Parliament the judges are sometimes loosely mentioned as one of several 'status' in the general body. The dislike of having practising lawyers in parliament appears as early as the reign of Edward III.

Use made by Edward I of merchant assemblies;

consulted. In 1218 the merchants whose wool was arrested at Bristol granted to Henry III six marks on the sack[1], making perhaps a virtue of necessity, and preferring the form of a grant to that of a fine. Edward I very early in his reign obtained, from the lords and 'communitates' of the kingdom, a grant on the sack at the instance and request of the merchants[2]; possibly the parliament recognised the impost which the merchants by petition or otherwise had declared themselves willing to grant, in order to escape arbitrary seizures or 'prises.' This was in 1275; in 1294 when the king seized the wool, and took the consent of the merchants afterwards to an increased custom during the war, the consent was probably extorted from an assembly of merchants or by distinct commissions[3]. A similar exaction in 1297 was one of the causes of the tumultuous action of earls Bohun and Bigod, and the right of taking the maletote without the common consent and goodwill of the community of the realm was expressly renounced when the charters were confirmed. Still no legal enactment could hinder the merchants from giving or the king from asking. In 1303 Edward summoned an assembly of merchants to the Exchequer at York; ordering two or three burghers from each of forty-two towns to meet them and consider the matter of a grant. The foreign merchants had agreed to increase the custom, but the representatives of towns and cities refused[4]. In this assembly, which

for taxing the wool and other merchandise.

[1] Rot. Claus. i. 351, 353.

[2] 'Cum archiepiscopi, episcopi, et alii praelati regni Angliae, ac comites, barones, et nos et communitates ejusdem regni ad instantiam et rogatum mercatorum . . . concesserimus;' Parl. Writs, i. p. 2; Select Charters, p. 441; below, p. 244.

[3] Above, p. 126.

[4] Select Charters, p. 490; Parl. Writs, i. 134, 135. In this case the king, who on the 1st of February had granted a charter to a large body of foreign merchants, in return for the 'Nova Custuma' (above, p. 157), on the 16th of April ordered the Mayor and Sheriffs of London to send to York two or three merchants from each of the Italian trading companies on the 5th of May. Having secured their assent, he issued on the 8th of May writs to the Sheriffs of the several counties to cause two or three citizens and burghers from each city and borough to meet at York on June 25; on that day the meeting was held and the answer given: 'Dixerunt unanimi consensu et voluntate tam pro se ipsis quam pro communitatibus civitatum et burgorum . . . quod ad incrementum maltolliae nec ad custumas, in praedicto brevi contentas per alienigenas et extraneos mercatores domino regi concessas, nullo modo consentient, nisi ad custumas anti-

Merchant assemblies.

was not a parliament, it is clear that the elected burghers acted as representatives of the mercantile interest rather than of the third estate; and their prompt action no doubt checked in time Edward's scheme of providing himself with additional revenue from denizens, although he carried out the plan of obtaining a new custom from the foreigners. The gatherings of merchants by Edward III, which are sometimes regarded as a marked feature of his policy, are in analogy as well as in contrast with this, and may have been suggested by it. But although in that king's reign the wool was made a sort of circulating medium in which supplies were granted, and the merchants were constantly summoned in large numbers to attend in council and parliament, they wisely chose to throw in their lot with the commons, and sought in union with them an escape from the oppressions to which their stock and staple made them especially liable.

Inexactness of this division.

196. The three estates of the realm were thus divided, but not without subordinate distinctions, cross divisions, and a large residue that lay outside the political body. In the estate of baronage were included most of the prelates, who also had their place in the estate of clergy; the earls more than once took up a position which shewed that they would willingly have claimed a higher political rank than their brother barons[1]; the townsmen who were not included in the local organisations, and the classes of peasants who neither appeared nor were represented in the county courts, formed an outlying division of the estate of the commons. The classification is not either an exact or an exhaustive division of all sorts and conditions of men; such as it is, however, it presents a rough summary of the political constituents of the kingdom, and it was the arrangement on which the theory of the medieval constitution was based. We have now

quitus debitas et consuetas.' The king appointed collectors for the new customs granted by the foreign merchants, April 1st, 1304; ibid. p. 406.

[1] For example, in 1242, the committee of parliament is chosen so as to include four bishops, four earls, and four barons. Many of the lines of distinction which separated the baron from the knight, such as relief and other matters of taxation, might have been made to separate the earls from the barons, but these points become more prominent as the ranks of the lords are marked out by new titles, duke, marquess, viscount.

to trace the process by which the English parliament grew into a symmetrical concentration of the three estates, and to examine the formal steps by which the several powers of the national council were asserted and vindicated, and by which the distinct share of each estate in those several powers was defined and secured, during the period at present before us.

Comparison of the condition of the national council at the close of the twelfth century

197. The national council, as we have traced it through the reigns of Henry II, Richard I, and John, was an assembly of archbishops, bishops, abbots, priors, earls, barons, knights, and freeholders, holding in chief of the crown. Of the latter two classes few could attend the meetings, and they were already separated from the more dignified members by the fact that the latter were summoned by special writ, the former only by a general summons addressed to the sheriffs. In one or two instances before the end of the reign of John the summons to the sheriff had prescribed a form of representation, by which the attendance of elected knights from each shire was substituted for a general summons of the minor tenants-in-chief, which might or might not be obeyed.

with its condition at the close of the thirteenth.

The national council as it existed at the end of the reign of Edward I was a parliamentary assembly consisting of three bodies, the clergy represented by the bishops, deans, archdeacons, and proctors; the baronage spiritual and temporal; the commons of the realm represented by the knights of the shire and the elected citizens and burgesses, and in addition to all these, as attendant on the king and summoned to give counsel, the justices and other members of the continual council.

The various relations of the clergy to the state involve a threefold organisation.

198. The relations of the clergy to the body politic were threefold, and the result of these relations was a threefold organisation for council. The higher clergy, holding their lands as baronies, attended the king's court 'sicut barones ceteri'; the general body of the clergy, as a spiritual organisation, exercised the right of meeting in diocesan, provincial, and national councils, the monastic orders having likewise their provincial and general chapters or councils[1]; and the whole body of bene-

[1] In 1282 Edward commissioned John Kirkby to negotiate with these bodies severally; distinct writs being issued to the Cistercians, who were

ficed clergy, as an estate of the realm possessing taxable property and class interests, was organised by Edward I as a portion of his parliament, by the clause of premunition inserted in the writ of summons addressed to the bishops. This clause, 'the *praemunientes* clause[1],' directs the attendance of proctors for the chapters and parochial clergy with the bishops, heads of cathedral chapters and archdeacons personally, in parliament.

Analogies with the secular assemblies.

It is in the second and third relations that the organisation of the clergy chiefly illustrates our subject. And in each aspect analogies may be traced which illustrate the development of the lay estates. The diocesan synod answers to the county court, the provincial convocation to the occasional divided parliaments, and the national church council to the general parliament. The practice of representation appears nearly at the same time in the church councils and in the parliaments; the same questions may be raised as to the character of the representative members of each, whether they were delegates or independent counsellors; the transition from particular consent to general consent in matters of taxation is marked in both cases; and in both cases the varying share of legislative and consultative authority may be traced according to circumstances, later history furnishing abundant illustration of the process which led to such different results. If the clergy had been content to vote their taxes in parliament instead of convocation, they might have been involved in a perpetual struggle for equality with the commons, which would have left both at the mercy of the crown and baronage. By taking their stand on their spiritual vantage ground they lost much of their direct influence in the parliament itself, but so long as their chiefs sat with the baronage and enjoyed

Persistence of the clergy in granting money in convocation.

to meet at Oxford, the Austin Canons at Northampton, the Benedictines at Reading, the Premonstratensians, all abbots in the province of Canterbury, and the order of Friars preachers; Parl. Writs, i. 385.

[1] 'Praemunientes decanum (vel priorem) et capitulum ecclesiae vestrae, archidiaconos, totumque clerum vestrae diocesis, facientes quod iidem decanus et archidiaconi in propriis personis suis, et dictum capitulum per unum, idemque clerus per duos procuratores idoneos, plenam et sufficientem potestatem ab ipsis capitulo et clero habentes una vobiscum intersint, modis omnibus tunc ibidem ad tractandum, ordinandum et faciendum nobiscum et cum ceteris praelatis et proceribus et aliis in colis regni nostri.' Parl. Writs, i. 30.

a monopoly of the highest offices of state, they retained more than an equitable share of political power. On the other hand, their resolution to grant money in convocation only secured for them a certain right of meeting whenever parliament was called for the same purpose, and that right of meeting involved the right of petitioning and, within certain limits, of legislating for themselves.

The ecclesiastical convocations, councils, and synods.

199. At an earlier period of our inquiries we have seen the clergy united in their special assemblies and in the national council. The developments of the thirteenth century may be briefly stated. The purely ecclesiastical convocations gain strength and consistency under the pressure of royal and papal aggression, especially after the introduction of the taxation of spiritualities; the diocesan synods, being an exhaustive assembly of the clergy, admitted of little modification. Like the cathedral chapters they were separately consulted on taxation, so long as separate consent was required: in 1254 the bishops were directed to summon their chapters, archdeacons, and clergy to consider a grant, and to report to the council at Easter; as late as the year 1280 the diocesan synods of the province of York gave their several consent to the grant of a tenth[1]. In them the representatives sent to the greater assemblies were chosen, and the gravamina drawn up. In some cases even subdivisions of the dioceses acted independently of one another; in 1240 the rectors of Berkshire refused to contribute to the expenses of the papal war against the emperor[2]; and in 1280 each archdeaconry of the diocese of York was separately consulted before the archdeacons and proctors reported to the diocesan synod, and the archdeacon of Richmond did not join in the general grant[3].

Consulted on taxation.

Diocesan and archidiaconal synods.

The provincial synod.

The growth of the provincial synod or convocation is chiefly marked by the institution or development of representation, of which there are few if any traces before the pontificate of Stephen Langton. In 1225 that archbishop directed the attendance of proctors for the cathedral, collegiate and conventual

[1] Prynne, Register, i. p. 3; Hody, Hist. Conv. p. 340; Wilkins, Conc. ii. p. 42; Ann. Lanercost, p. 105; above, p. 113, note 1.
[2] M. Paris, p. 535.
[3] Wilkins, Conc. ii. p. 42.

clergy in addition to the bishops, abbots, priors, deans, and archdeacons[1]. In 1254 the prelates refused to include the secular clergy in a money grant without their consent, and a great council was summoned in consequence[2]. In 1255 the proctors of the parochial clergy of several archdeaconries presented their gravamina in parliament, but it is not clear that the representative principle was regarded as an integral part of the system of convocation[3]. In 1258 archbishop Boniface directed that the archdeacons should be furnished with letters of proxy from the parochial clergy[4], and so empowered they attended the council at Merton which was held preparatory to the Mad Parliament of Oxford. In 1273 archbishop Kilwardby summoned the bishops, with an order to bring with them three or four of their principal clergy[5]. In 1277 the same prelate included in the summons the greater personae of the chapters, the archdeacons, and the proctors of the whole clergy of each diocese, but without prescribing the number or mode of nomination[6]. This deficiency was supplied by archbishop Peckham in 1283[7]. At the council of Northampton held under the king's writ in the January of that year, it was determined to call a convocation at the New Temple three weeks after Easter: and the rule devised on the occasion was expressed in the writ; 'each of the bishops, as was provided in the said congregation, shall about the aforesaid day cause the clergy of his diocese to be assembled in a certain place, and shall there have carefully expounded to them the propositions made on behalf of the king, so that at the said time and place at London, from each diocese two proctors in the name of the clergy; and from each cathedral and collegiate chapter one proctor, shall be sent with sufficient instructions, who shall have full and express power of treating with us and our brethren upon the premisses, and of consenting to such measures as for the honour of the church, the comfort of the king, and the peace of

Growth of representation in the provincial synod.

Rule for representation in convocation.

1 Wilkins, Conc. i. 602; Select Charters, p. 443.
2 Royal Letters, ii. 101; above, p. 67.
3 Ann. Burton, p. 360; Select Charters, p. 322.
4 Select Charters, p. 444; Ann. Burton, p. 411; see above, p. 74, note 3.
5 Wilkins, Conc. ii. 26; Select Charters, p. 444.
6 Wilkins, Conc. ii. 30; Select Charters, p. 445.
7 Wilkins, Conc. ii. 93; Select Charters, p. 456; Parl. Writs, i. 11.

Representation in convocation.

the realm, the community of the clergy shall provide.' This rule was then or soon after accepted as a canon[1]; and the body so constituted, including bishops, abbots, priors, and heads of religious houses, deans of cathedrals and collegiate churches, archdeacons and proctors, was the convocation of the province of Canterbury.

Uses of York and Canterbury.

That of the province of York is somewhat differently constituted, containing two proctors from each archdeaconry, an arrangement which dates at least as early as 1279[2]. It is impossible to fix with any greater certainty the origin of the procuratorial system, but it was probably introduced at a much earlier period, and had long been used in foreign churches[3].

Owing to the unfortunate jealousy which subsisted between the two primates, the assembling of national church councils became, after the independence of York had been vindicated by Thurstan, almost a matter of impossibility. The disputes, amounting often to undignified personal altercation between the archbishops themselves, disturbed the harmony of even the royal courts and national parliaments.

National church councils rarely called.

Only when the authority of a legate superseded for the moment the ordinary authority of both, were any national councils of the church summoned. The most important of these were the councils of 1237 in which the constitutions of Otho were published, and of 1268 in which those of Ottobon were accepted. The comparative rarity of these assemblies, and the fact that the prelates were the only permanent element in them, rob them of any importance they might otherwise have had in the history of our ecclesiastical organisation.

This division between the two provinces was, in secular questions, remedied by the custom of bringing the leading men of both to the national parliaments[4]; but this was felt to be

[1] The canon (so called) is given among the 'Statuta Johannis Peckham' in Wilkins, ii. 49; see also Johnson's Canons, ed. Baron, ii. 268. It is not really a canon; by its reference to the convocation at the Temple, three weeks after Michaelmas, it is shewn to belong to the same year 1283.

[2] Wilkins, Conc. ii. 41.

[3] Compare the account of the legatine council of Bourges held in 1225; W. Covent. ii. 277.

[4] In 1207 John collected the clergy of both provinces to grant an aid; Ann. Waverley, p. 258.

inadequate in cases in which the special rights of the clergy were concerned. Accordingly in 1252 [1] we find the archbishop of York and the bishops of Carlisle and Durham declining to answer a request of the king on the ground that it was a matter which touched the whole English church, and that they did not think it consistent or honourable to depart from the customary procedure in such cases, in which a common debate was usually had between the clergy of the two provinces. But although such communication might in general terms be called customary, the extant evidence points rather to a discussion or arrangement by letter between the archbishops than to any common deliberation of the churches.

Proposals for conference between the two provincial synods.

200. When Edward I in 1295 determined to summon to parliament the whole clergy of the two provinces by their representatives, he probably desired not only to define the relations between the several estates, but to obtain the joint action of the two provinces, and to get rid of the anomalous modes of summons and attendance which had been from time to time adopted in the innumerable councils of the century. There were precedents for summoning to councils, in which no specially ecclesiastical business was discussed, not only the prelates but the archdeacons and deans, as representing the parochial and cathedral clergy. One remarkable assembly of the kind, in 1177 [2] on the occasion of the arbitration between Castille and Navarre, seems to show that Henry II regarded the presence of these 'minor prelates' as necessary to make his court sufficiently impressive to his foreign visitors. The council of 1255 [3] in which the proctors of the beneficed clergy exhibited their gravamina, was a parliament, although it may not be certain that the proctors appeared as members rather than petitioners. Simon de Montfort's parliament of 1265 contained cathedral deans and priors as well as prelates [4]. In 1265 Henry III summoned proctors for the cathedral chapters to the parliament of Winchester [5]. In 1282 the proctors of the chapters were summoned

Parliamentary representation of the clergy.

Early examples.

[1] Royal Letters, ii. 94, 95.
[2] Ben. Pet. i. 145; see above, vol. i. p. 486.
[3] Above, p. 197.
[4] Above, p. 93.
[5] Select Charters, p. 409.

to the two provincial parliaments of York and Northampton [1].

Council or convocation of 1294.

In 1294 Edward called what may be regarded as a clerical parliament at Westminster, apart from the other two estates and at a different time; summoning the clergy of the two provinces by their prelates, chapters, archdeacons and proctors for the 21st of September [2], and the lay estates for the 2nd of November.

Parliament of 1295.

The following year he incorporated the three in one assembly and adopted for the representation of the clergy the method instituted twelve years before for the provincial convocations [3]. But although so closely united in idea the two representative bodies, convocation [4] and the parliamentary representation of the clergy, are kept clearly distinct.

Difference between the convocation and the parliamentary session of the clergy.

The convocations are two provincial councils meeting in their respective provinces, generally at London and York; the parliamentary representatives are one element of the general parliament and meet in the same place. The convocations are called by the writ of the archbishops addressed through their senior suffragans to each bishop of their provinces; the parliamentary proctors are summoned by the king's writ addressed directly to the bishops individually, and directing by the clause 'praemunientes' [5] the attendance of the proctors. The former are two spiritual assemblies; the latter

[1] Parl. Writs, i. 10; Select Charters, p. 456.

[2] Parl. Writs, ii. 25, 26; Select Charters, p. 476.

[3] The 'modus tenendi parliamentum' describes the clerical proctors in parliament, as two from each archdeaconry, not as was really the case, two from each diocese; Select Charters, p. 493. This is but one of the many misstatements of that document, but it may shew that even when it was written, the question of clerical representation was becoming obscure.

[4] The word *convocation* had not yet acquired its later technical meaning. The prior and convent of Bath, 1295, elect their proctor under the praemunientes clause, to appear in the 'generalis convocatio;' Parl. Writs, i. 34; in 1297 the writ of the archbishop for the spiritual assembly is entitled 'Citatio pro convocatione'; ibid. p. 53.

[5] See above, p. 195, note. Philip the Fair seems to have had an intention in 1297 of summoning the whole of the French clergy to Paris to make a grant; but, warned perhaps by the events of 1296 in England, he did not venture to do it, and wrung the money he wanted from provincial councils; Boutaric, Premiers États gen. p. 6. The parochial clergy, the rectors or curés of parishes, were systematically excluded from the states general (Hervieu, Rev. de Legislation, 1873, p. 380), inasmuch as they did not possess temporalities or jurisdiction. Nor were the clergy assembled according to their ecclesiastical divisions; not in dioceses and provinces, but in bailliages and senechaussées, like the laity; ibid. 396.

one temporal representation of the spiritual estate; and it is, as we shall see, only owing to the absolute defeasance of the latter institution that the convocations have any connexion with parliamentary history. Every step of the development of the two has however a bearing on the growth of the idea of representation, both in the nation at large and in the mind of the great organiser and definer of parliamentary action, Edward I[1].

Later relation of convocation to parliament.

201. The baronial estate underwent during this period the great change in respect to its conciliar form from qualification by tenure to qualification by writ, from which the hereditary peerage emerges. This change affected however only the simple barons[2]. As a rule all the earls and all the bishops were constantly summoned, the only exceptions being made when the individual omitted was in personal disgrace. The list of abbots and priors however varies largely from time to time; more than a hundred were summoned by Simon de Montfort in 1264[3]; nearly seventy by Edward I to the great parliament of 1295[4]; in the reign of Edward III the regular number fell to twenty-seven[5]; the majority being glad to escape the burden of attendance and, by the plea that their lands were held in free alms and not by barony, to avoid the expenses by which their richer brethren maintained their high dignity[6]. The modifica-

Development of the baronage.

All bishops and earls summoned.

Diminished number of abbots and priors.

[1] I need hardly remark here that although the procuratorial system as used in clerical assemblies has a certain bearing on the representative system in England, it is much less important here than in those countries in which there were no vestiges of representative lay institutions left, and where the representation of communities in the states general must have been borrowed from the ecclesiastical system. In England the two forms grow side by side, the lay representation is not formed on the model of the clerical.

[2] Occasionally bishops, abbots, and barons were allowed to appear by proxy; thus in the parliament of Carlisle (Parl. Writs, i. 185, 186) a great number of proxies or attorneys were present; and some even of the elected proctors of the clergy substituted others as their proxies. Abbesses and peeresses who had suits to prosecute or services to perform also sent proctors, but not as members of the parliament, simply as suitors of the high court.

[3] Ten abbots, nine priors, and one dean of the province of York, fifty-five abbots, twenty-six priors, and four deans of the province of Canterbury; and the heads of the military orders.

[4] Sixty-seven abbots and three heads of orders; Parl. Writs, i. 30.

[5] See the tables given by Gneist, Verwalt. i. 382–387.

[6] See Prynne, Register, i. pp. 141 sq. The position of the abbots and priors as distinguished from the bishops is historically important, in relation

Diminished number of barons.

tion in the character of the lay baronage is a matter of greater significance. This question has been made the subject of what may be called a great body of historical literature, out of which, observing the due proportion of general treatment, we can state here only a few conclusions.

Qualification for summons as a baron.

The 'majores barones' of the reigns of Henry II, Richard and John, were, as has been several times stated, distinguished from their fellows, by the reception of special summons to council, special summons to the army, the right of making special arrangements with the exchequer for reliefs and taxes, of leading their own vassals in battle, and of being amerced by their equals. The coincidence of these points enables us to describe if not to define what tenure by barony must have been; it may, as some legal writers have maintained, have comprehended the duties of grand serjeanty, it may have been connected originally with the possession of a certain quantity of land; but it certainly possessed the characteristics just enumerated. The number of these barons was very considerable: in 1263, a hundred and eighteen were specially summoned to the Welsh war [1]; a hundred and sixty-five in 1276 [2]; a hundred and twenty-two in 1297 [3]; and correspondingly large numbers on other occasions. That the occurrence of a particular name in the list proves the bearer to have held his estates *per baroniam* may be disputed, but it can scarcely be doubted that all who were summoned would rank among the *majores barones* of the charter. The extant writs of summons to parliament are much more rare, and these contain far fewer names than the writs of military

Great number of barons summoned for military service.

to council and also to tenure. Before the Conquest all the bishops attended the witenagemot, and only a few of the abbots. When the practice of homage was introduced, the bishops, we are told by Glanvill and Bracton, did no homage after consecration, but only fealty: whilst according to the latter writer, abbots 'ad homagium non teneantur de jure, faciunt tamen tota die de consuetudine:' lib. ii. c. 35. The reduction in the number of parliamentary abbots was probably owing to their dislike of attendance at secular courts, which suggested the excuse alleging their peculiar tenure.

[1] Lords' Report, iii. 30.

[2] Parl. Writs, i. 193–195.

[3] Parl. Writs, i. 282. Not less than 174 were summoned for the defence against Scotland in the autumn of the same year, but many of these were addressed as knights; ibid. pp. 302-304.

service. Only eighteen barons were summoned by Simon de Montfort; only forty-one were summoned by Edward I to the parliament of 1295[1]; thirty-seven in 1296[2]. Occasionally the number increases; especially when a number of counsellors is also summoned. To the parliament of March 6, 1300, ninety-eight lords and thirty-eight counsellors were called[3]; and the letter addressed by the parliament of Lincoln to the pope was sealed by ninety-six lay lords, eighty of whom had been summoned by special writ[4]. It is clear from these facts, all of which belong to the parliaments properly so called in which the three estates were assembled, that very large discretionary power remained in the royal hands; and that, unless he was warranted by earlier custom, the existence of which we can only conjecture[5], Edward I must, in the selection of a smaller number to be constant recipients of special summons, have introduced a constitutional change scarcely inferior to that by which he incorporated the representatives of the commons in the national council: in other words, that he created the house of lords as much as he created the house of commons. The alteration or variation in the number of the barons summoned implied also an alteration in the qualification for summons; if the king were at liberty to select even a permanent number of lords of parliament from the body of tenants in chief or barons, the qualification

Smaller numbers summoned to parliament.

Importance of the principle established by Edward I.

[1] Parl. Writs, i. 31.

[2] Parl. Writs, i. 48.

[3] Parl. Writs, i. 82, 83; seventy-two abbots, &c., were also summoned.

[4] Parl. Writs, i. 90. The whole list summoned to Lincoln contained two archbishops, eighteen bishops, eighty abbots, three masters of orders, ten earls, and eighty specially summoned barons and knights; the letter (ibid. pp. 102–104) is sealed by seven earls and ninety-six other lords. See the 4th Report of the Lords' Committee, pp. 325–341; where it is maintained that the occurrence of a name among these ninety-six signataries does not by itself imply a peerage.

[5] The famous quotation of Camden, Britannia (ed. 1600), p. 137, has never been, I believe, verified; it runs as follows: 'Ille enim' (sc. Henricus III), 'ex satis antiquo scriptore loquor, post magnas perturbationes et enormes vexationes inter ipsum regem, Simonem de Monteforti et alios barones, motas et sopitas, statuit et ordinavit quod omnes illi comites et barones regni Angliae quibus ipse rex dignatus est brevia summonitionis dirigere, venirent ad parlamentum suum et non alii, nisi forte dominus rex alia consimilia brevia eis dirigere voluisset.' Cf. Brady, Intr. p. 145; Hallam, M.A. iii. 7.

Institution of hereditary writs.

of tenure ceased to be the sole qualification for summons. But it is probable that the change went still further, and that of the diminished number some at least did not possess the qualification by baronial tenure, but became barons simply by virtue of the special writ, and conveyed to their heirs a dignity attested by the hereditary reception of the summons. If this be true, and it is supported by considerable evidence [1], the tenure *per baroniam* must have ceased to have any political importance, and we have in the act, or in the policy suggesting it, a crowning proof of Edward's political design of eliminating the doctrine of tenure from the region of government. The later variations, in number and qualification, of the house of lords, may be noted when we reach the time at which that house obtained a separate existence.

Continuance of baronial assemblies, in the *magnum concilium.*

The baronage spiritual and temporal did not, however modified, merge its independent existence in the newly constituted parliament of Edward I. It had been in possession of the functions of a common council of the realm far too long not to have acquired powers with which it could not part. Under the title of 'magnum concilium regis et regni' it retained, like the convocation of the clergy, distinct methods of assembly, and certain powers which ultimately fell to the house of lords. But these must be considered in another part of our work.

Representation of the commons.

202. The great mark which the century and the reign of Edward I leave on our constitutional history is the representation of the commons: the collecting in parliament of the representatives of the communities of both shires and boroughs, the concentration of the powers which had been previously exercised in local assemblies or altogether superseded by the action of the barons, and the admission of such representatives to a share in

[1] See Courthope's edition of Nicolas's Historic Peerage, pp. xxv. sq.; Third Lords' Report, p. 235 sq. An example is Thomas de Furnival, of whom it was found in the 19th Edw. II that he did not hold his estates per baroniam, who yet was summoned from 1295 to 1332; nine other persons summoned in 1295 are 'not anywhere stated to have been previously barons of the realm.' The last statement is I think somewhat arbitrary; all the nine had had special military summons repeatedly.

the supreme work of government. In order to avoid needless repetition it will be desirable to examine this part of our subject under the several heads, of (1) the constitution of the local courts and communities, (2) their powers and functions, and (3) the periods and causes of the introduction of their representatives into the national parliament. So much however has been already said on the first and second points in the earlier chapters of this work, that it will be enough briefly to recapitulate our chief conclusions about them and to account for the modifications which affected them in the century before us.

Arrangement of the following pages.

203. (1) The county court in its full session, that is, as it attended the itinerant justices on their visitation, contained the archbishops, bishops, abbots, priors, earls, barons, knights, and freeholders, and from each township four men and the reeve, and from each borough twelve burghers[1]. It was still the folkmoot, the general assembly of the people, and in case of any class or person being regarded as outside the above enumeration, the sheriff was directed to summon to the meeting all others who by right or custom appeared before the justices. It contained thus all the elements of a local parliament—all the members of the body politic in as full representation as the three estates afterwards enjoyed in the general parliament.

I. Constitution of the county court.

The county court, according to the 42nd article of the charter of 1217[2], sat once a month; but it is not to be supposed that on each occasion it was attended by all the qualified members; the prelates and barons were generally freed from the obligation of attendance by the charters under which they held their estates; every freeman might by the statute of Merton appear by attorney[3], and by the statute of Marlborough all above the

Its times of meeting.

[1] The writ of 1217 for the promulgation of the Charter orders the sheriff to publish it, 'in pleno comitatu tuo convocatis baronibus, militibus et omnibus libere tenentibus ejusdem comitatus.' Brady, App. 166. The Writs containing the list of names given in the text, begin in 1217, Rot. Claus. i. 380: there is one of 1231 in the Select Charters, p. 349. See too Bracton, lib. iii. tr. i. c. 11.

[2] Select Charters, p. 337.

[3] Statutes of the Realm, i. 4: 'provisum insuper quod quilibet liber homo qui sectam debet ad Comitatum, Trithingam, Hundredum et Wapentachium, vel ad curiam domini sui, libere possit facere attornatum suum ad sectas illas pro eo faciendum.' Such an appointment of a proxy, by Thomas

Persons excused attendance.

rank of knight were exempted from attendance on the sheriff's tourn[1], unless specially summoned: the charters of the boroughs implied and sometimes expressed a condition that it was only when the court was called to meet the justices that their representatives need attend[2]; in some cases the barons and knights compounded for attendance by a payment to the sheriff[3]; and the custom of relieving the simple knights, by special licence issued by the king, prevailed to such an extent that the deficiency of lawful knights to hold the assizes in the county court was a constant subject of complaint[4]. The monthly sessions then were only attended by persons who had special business, and by the officers of the townships with their lawful men qualified to serve on the juries. For the holding of a full county court, for extraordinary business, a special summons was in all cases issued; our knowledge of its composition is derived from such special writs.

Ordinary monthly sessions.

Special sessions.

History of the sheriffs.

204. The sheriff is still the president and constituting officer of the county court; to him is directed the writ ordering the general summons, and through him is made the answer of the county to the question or demand contained in the writ. Successive limitations on his judicial power have been imposed from the reign of Henry II to the date of Magna Carta, but have scarcely diminished his social importance[5]; and although the general contributions of the country, the fifteenths, thirtieths and the like, no longer pass necessarily through his hands, he retains the collection of scutages and other prescriptive imposts, and considerable power of amercement for non-attendance on his summons. The king retains the power of nominating the

de Burgh, to appear in the shiremoot of Staffordshire in 1223, is given in the Close Rolls, i. 537.

[1] Statutes of the Realm, i. 22: 'de turnis vicecomitum provisum est quod necesse non habeant ibi venire archiepiscopi, episcopi, abbates, priores, comites, barones nec aliqui viri religiosi seu mulieres nisi eorum praesentia specialiter exigatur.'

[2] Select Charters, p. 303.

[3] As in the honour of Aquila in Sussex; see vol. i. p. 102.

[4] See the 28th article of the petition of the barons in 1258; Select Charters, p. 378. An instance will be found as early as 1224, Rot. Claus. i. 627.

[5] Vol. i. pp. 606, 607; see Gneist, Verwalt. i. 320.

sheriffs, but not without a struggle; the right of nomination being at one time claimed for the baronage in parliament, and at another for the county court itself. By the provisions of Oxford in 1258 it was ordered that the sheriff should be a vavasour of the county in which he was to reside and should retain office for a year only[1]. In 1259, it was provided that for the current year appointment should be made by the chief justice, treasurer and barons of the exchequer, absolutely; and in future from a list of four good men chosen in the county court[2]. The efforts made by Henry III to get rid of the provisionary council involved in each case an attempt to remove their sheriffs and to nominate his own. In 1261, at the Mise of Merton concluded in December, a committee of arbitration was named to determine the question of right; the six arbitrators referred it to Richard of Cornwall as umpire, and he decided in favour of the king, though he attempted to introduce the principle of election[3]: and the decision was confirmed by the award of S. Lewis. After this no attempt was made by the barons to renew the quarrel; but under Edward I the question of a free election by the shires was mooted. Such free election had long been the right of the citizens of London; the freeholders of Cornwall and Devon had purchased the like privilege from John and Henry III[4]; and the lawyers of Edward I seem to have held, and foisted into the copies of the laws of the Confessor an article declaring that such election was an ancient popular right[5]. It was possibly in concession to this opinion that in 1300, by one of the *Articuli super Cartas*, Edward granted the election of the sheriffs to the people of the shire where they desired to have it, and where the office was not

Struggles to change the mode of appointing the sheriffs.

Election of sheriffs.

[1] Select Charters, p. 382.

[2] Ann. Burton, p. 478; above, p. 82. The securing a sheriff from among the inhabitants of the county was probably as material a point as the obtaining the right of election; see Ann. Dunst. p. 279: 'eodem anno, 1278, amovit rex omnes vicecomites Angliae clericos scilicet et extraneos, et substituit loco eorum milites de propriis comitatibus.'

[3] Above, pp. 85, 86.

[4] Madox, Hist. Exch. pp. 283, 288; Rot. Claus. i. 457; ii. 25, 169, 184.

[5] 'Per singulos comitatus in pleno folcmote, sicut et vicecomites provinciarum et comitatuum eligi debent;' Thorpe, Ancient Laws, p. 197.

Final settlement of the question.

'of fee' or hereditary[1]. But the privilege was sparingly exercised if it were exercised at all, and was withdrawn by the Ordinances of 1311[2]. In 1338 Edward III ordered the sheriffs to be elected by the counties, but in his fourteenth year it was finally provided that no sheriff should continue in office for more than a year, the appointment remaining, as prescribed by the Ordinances, in the hands of the officers of the exchequer[3]. It would seem that during this period it was more important to the king and to the barons to secure the right of appointment, than to limit the powers of the sheriff; and consequently his position and influence underwent less change than they had done under the legislation of Henry II. The real loss of his ancient importance resulted from the limitation of his period of office.

II. Business of the county transacted in the county court.

205. (II) In the county courts and under the guidance of the sheriffs was transacted all the business of the shire: and the act of the county court was the act of the shire in matters judicial, military, and fiscal, in the details of police management, and in questions, where such questions occurred, connected with the general administration of the country. It is unnecessary to repeat what has been said on these points in a former chapter; but some illustration may be given of the completeness of the county administration for each purpose; of the use, in each department, of representation; and of the practice of electing representatives, who thus act on behalf of the whole community of the shire. The ideas of representation and election are not inseparable; at certain stages the sheriff in the county, or the reeve in the township, might nominate, from a fixed list, by choice, or in rotation; but the tendency of the two ideas is

[1] Statutes of the Realm, i. 139; 'le roi ad grante a soen poeple qil eient esleccion de leur viscontes en chescun conte, ou visconte ne est mie de fee, sil voelent.' An examination of the lists of sheriffs shows that the privilege could only have been slightly valued; the changes in 1300 and 1301 are few.

[2] Statutes of the Realm, i. 160.

[3] Foed. ii. 1049, 1090; the Act passed in 1340 ordered that the appointment should be made in the Exchequer by the Chancellor, Treasurer, and Chief Baron, with the justices, if present; Statutes, i. 283. In 1376 the commons again petitioned for elective sheriffs; Rot. Parl. ii. 355.

to unite and the historic evidence shows their joint-use generally at this time. The custom of electing representatives in the county court was in full operation before such representatives were summoned to parliament.

(1) The judicial work of the county court.

The judicial work of the county was done in the county court: except in the county court even the itinerant justices could not discharge their functions; and the county was the sphere of jurisdiction of the justices of assize and justices of the peace. The county was the *patria* whose report was presented by the juries; and a process by assize was 'per judicium et consilium totius comitatus[1].' The uses of representation and election have already been illustrated sufficiently in our discussion of the origin of juries.

(2) The conservation of the peace.

206. The conservation of the peace, or police, a department that links the judicial with the military administration of the shire, was fully organised on the same principles. For each necessary measure the county was an organic whole; the action was taken in the county court; and in the execution of the law the sheriff was assisted or superseded by elected representatives. The writs for the conservation of the peace, directing the taking of the oath, the pursuit of malefactors, and the observance of watch and ward, are proclaimed in full county court; attachments are made in obedience to them in the county court before the coroners, and when the institution is modified, as in 1253, the sheriffs are ordered to summon all the knights and freeholders of their counties, four men with the reeve from each township, and twelve burghers from each borough, to receive and execute the royal mandate[2]. The coroners, whose duty was to watch the interests of the crown in this region of work as well as in the fiscal and judicial business, were always elected by the full county court[3]. In the fifth year of Edward I, an officer called 'custos pacis,' whose functions form a stage in the growth of the office of justice of the peace, was

[1] 'Nihil fecimus in facto memorato nisi per consilium et judicium totius comitatus . . . ex recordo dictae assisae quod de communi consensu et testimonio totius comitatus fideliter conscriptum vobis transmittimus.' Royal Letters, i. 21. On the general subject, see Gneist, Verwaltungsrecht, i. 317 sq.

[2] Select Charters, p. 365.

[3] See below, p. 227.

Election of conservators.

elected by the sheriff and community of each county in the full county court; and the conservators who carried out the provisions of the statute of Winchester, although no mention of the mode of appointment occurs in the act itself, were after the first vacancy elected in the same way[1]. In this instance the principle was extended to the election of constables for the hundreds.

(3) The military business of the shire.

207. The military administration of the county, except so far as it was connected with the conservation of the peace, was less capable of being conducted on a symmetrical plan of representation. It furnishes, however, illustrations of the completeness of the local agencies, and of the concentration of those agencies for national purposes, which are of the first importance: for both the feudal military system and the system of the national defence have their exact analogies in the system of the national council; and if the parliament is not the host in council as it was in primitive times, the national force is the presentment in arms of those elements which in the parliament meet for council. The national force, as a whole, falls into three divisions; the armed vassals of the tenants in chief who served under their own lords, each of those lords receiving a special summons to arms; the minor tenants in chief who served under the sheriff; and the body of freeholders sworn under the assize of arms. Of the second and third divisions the sheriff was the proper leader; they were the men who served on assizes and juries, and who in other matters acted constitutionally with him. In every change of military organisation, and there were several such changes in the course of the thirteenth century[2], the sheriff retains his place. In 1205 John warned the sheriffs that by assent of the national council every nine knights throughout all England were to furnish a tenth[3]. In 1231 Henry III ordered them to furnish a fixed contingent of men at arms to be provided by the men of the county sworn under the assize of arms[4]. On the great occa-

The minor tenants in chief and the *jurati ad arma* commanded by the sheriff.

[1] See below, pp. 227, 272; Gneist, Verwalt. i. 320 sq.; Stat. i. 98.
[2] See below, pp. 278 sq.; Gneist, Verwalt. i. 313-317.
[3] Select Charters, p. 273.
[4] Ibid. p. 350.

sions during the troubled period of the reign of Henry III, or in the wars of Edward I, when writs of military summons are directed to the barons, the sheriffs are directed to bring up the force of the freeholders, and when the system of commissions of array is adopted, the letters investing the commissioners with their powers are addressed to the sheriffs [1]. But over and above the authority they possessed over the minor freeholders, they exercised a sort of vigilant superintendence over the forces of the barons, under the king's writ. Thus in 1217 Henry III directed them to bring to Oxford the whole military force of the shire, whether due from prelates, barons, and tenants in chief, or from the 'jurati ad arma [2].' In 1223 he ordered them to summon all the tenants in chief by knight-service, whether archbishops, bishops, abbots, priors, earls, barons, knights or others [3]; and this plan was followed in later years as if the agency of the sheriff were more to be trusted than that of the special messengers. The writs for distraint of knighthood were also directed to the sheriffs. The writs of Edward I, being more peremptory, are also more full, and exhibit his design of consolidating the national force without distinction of tenure; they reach the climax when in 1297 he orders the sheriffs to give notice to all who possess twenty librates of land or more, whether holding in chief or not, whether within or without franchises, to prepare at once with horses and arms to follow the king whenever he shall demand their service [4]. The military progress of the period must however be traced in a separate section.

Military work of the sheriff; summoning the entire force; compelling knighthood.

The military orders of the sheriff were published in the county court; of this practice the year 1295 furnishes a good instance; Edward, having appointed the bishop of Durham and the earl of Warenne to provide for the defence of the northern shires, ordered the sheriffs to assemble before them all the knights of their shires and two good men of each township, to hear and execute the orders of the newly appointed officers [5].

His orders published in the county court.

[1] See below, p. 284. [2] Rot. Claus. i. 336; Lords' Report, App. p. 2.
[3] Lords' Report, App. p. 3.
[4] Parl. Writs, i. 281; Lords' Report, App. p. 79; below, pp. 281, 282.
[5] Parl. Writs, i. 270.

For all questions touching the character of tenure, and the extent of obligation, the juries employed in other matters would be necessarily employed by the sheriff in this department likewise.

(4) The remedial measures executed by the county court.

208. In the execution of the remedial measures which form so large a part of the political history of the century, the agency of the counties is employed, generally by means of elected representatives. In 1215, immediately after the charter of Runnymede, John directed twelve lawful knights to be chosen in each shire, at the first county court held after the receipt of the writ, to enquire into the evil customs which were to be abolished[1]. The same plan was followed at each renewal of the charters. In 1222 two knights were sent up from Wiltshire to lay the forest liberties before the king[2]. In 1226 and 1227, on occasion of a dispute as to the administration of the counties, Henry III ordered the sheriffs in the next county court to bid the knights and good men of the counties to choose from among themselves four lawful and discreet knights to appear at Lincoln and at Westminster to allege the grounds of complaint[3]. In 1258 four knights brought up the complaints of the shires to the October parliament[4]. By the articles of 1259 four such officers were appointed to watch the action of the sheriffs in each shire[5]. The close connexion of this occasional work with the general government is shown by the fact that in 1297 the knights of the shire were summoned to the parliament expressly to receive copies of the confirmation of charters[6], and that in 1301 the great object for which the parliament of Lincoln was summoned was to receive the report of the perambulations made under the new forest articles[7].

(5) The fiscal business of the county.

209. But the fiscal business is that in which the shire system most closely approached, before it actually touched, the

[1] Select Charters, p. 298.
[2] Rot. Claus. i. 498.
[3] Select Charters, p. 348; Rot. Claus. ii. 153, 212.
[4] Foed. i. 375; Brady, Intr. p. 141. See above, p. 79.
[5] Ann. Burton, p. 477.
[6] Parl. Writs, i. 56. See above, p. 141.
[7] Parl. Writs, i. 88–90; above, p. 150.

national council; and in it therefore the special action of the shire has the greatest constitutional interest. The practice of assessing and collecting taxes by chosen juries, and the practice of obtaining money grants by special and several negotiation, ultimately brought the crown and the tax-payer into very close communication. Many instances of this tendency have been already given [1], and they may be multiplied. In 1219 two knights are appointed in each county to collect the amercements [2]. In 1220 the sheriffs are ordered to cause two lawful knights to be chosen in full county court, by the will and counsel of all men of the county, to take part in the assessment and collection of the carucage [3]. In 1225, when the management of the fifteenth was taken out of the hands of the sheriff, committed to special justices and audited by special commission, the collection and assessment were entrusted to four elected knights of each hundred, who inquired by jury into all disputed cases [4]. In 1232 the fortieth was assessed in each township by the reeve and four chosen men of the township, in the presence of knights assigned [5]; a similar mode was adopted in 1237 [6]. The precise regulation of the method of assessment becomes less important when the grants are made in duly constituted assemblies; but the practice of choosing four knights to assess, tax, levy, and collect a money grant in each shire was continued under Edward I [7], and the directions for the purpose were promulgated in the county court [8]. The Customs were under like management: in 1275 the sheriffs of London and Gloucestershire were ordered to cause two lawful men to be chosen in London, Bristol, and other parts, as sub-collectors of the custom on wool [9].

Assessment by juries.

Special negotiations for grants of money.

Election of assessors and collectors.

Assessment in the townships.

Election of collectors of customs.

[1] Vol. i. pp. 577–587.
[2] Royal Letters, i. 28; Rot. Claus. i. 398.
[3] Select Charters, p. 343.
[4] Foed. i. 177; Select Charters, p. 346; and see Rot. Claus. ii. 40, 45, 71, 95, and p. 38, note 1, above.
[5] Select Charters, p. 351.
[6] Select Charters, p. 357.
[7] Parl. Writs, i. 106; the fifteenth granted in 1301 was thus collected. The king even furnished a speech which was to be delivered by the royal commissioners to the knights and good people of the county assembled to prevail on them to furnish supplies in kind, to be paid for by the fifteenth; ibid. p. 401; cf. pp. 404 sq.
[8] Parl. Writs, i. 403.
[9] Parl. Writs, i. 2.

Important illustration of the position of the county court in taxation.

But the reign of Henry III supplies at least one clear proof that not merely the assessment but the concession of a grant was regarded as falling within the lawful power of a local assembly. We have seen how Henry I, when directing the customary assembling of the shiremoots, declared his intention of laying before them his sovereign necessities whenever he required an aid; and although we do not find a grant made during the twelfth century in the county courts, we have abundant evidence of the transactions of the justices of the Exchequer in the matter of taxation, which took place in those sessions. The business of setting the tallage, when despatched between the justices or barons of the exchequer and the payers, and when the payers ascertained their liability and apportioned their quota by jury, approached within one step a formal consent to taxation. So when the fourteenth article of the charter mentions, as a part of the process of holding the 'commune consilium,' that the minor tenants in chief should be summoned by the general writ addressed to the sheriff, it is at least possible that the business announced in that general writ would be discussed in the assembly, which was the proper audience of the sheriff. In the year 1220 we have an important illustration which must be compared with the cases of grants, before adduced, by ecclesiastical assemblies of diocese and archdeaconry.

Case of the shiremoot of Yorkshire in 1220.

Geoffrey Neville, the king's chamberlain, was sheriff of Yorkshire, and had to collect the carucage, already mentioned as the occasion on which two knights of the shire were elected to make the assessment. The writ declaring the grant to have been made by the 'magnates et fideles' in the 'commune consilium,' was dated on the 9th of August[1]. In the month of September, the chamberlain writes to the justiciar[2]: he had received the writ on the 2nd, and had summoned the earls, barons, and freeholders, to hear it on the 14th. On that day the earls and barons had sent their stewards, as was usual, and did not attend in person. The writ was read: to the disgust of the sheriff the stewards replied with one accord, that their lords

[1] Select Charters, p. 343.

[2] Royal Letters, i. 151.

had never been asked for the aid and knew nothing of it; without consulting them, they dared not assent to the tax; they insisted that the lords of Yorkshire, like those of the southern shires, ought to have been asked for the grant by the king either by word of mouth or by letter. The sheriff attempted to answer them, but was obliged to grant a postponement until the next county court, that in the meantime they might lay the king's command before their lords. He learned, however, that if Henry, in a visit which he was shortly to make to York, should call together the magnates, and make the proposal in form, it would be accepted; if the justiciar recommended compulsion he was ready to employ it.

The stewards of the lords refuse to pay a tax.

The matter referred to the county court.

The case is perhaps exceptional: the Yorkshire barons would ordinarily have been consulted before the question of collection could arise; but the event clearly proves that the county court claimed a right to examine the authority under which the tax was demanded, and to withhold payment until the question was answered. The county court of Worcester thus declined to pay the illegal exaction of the eighth in 1297[1]. The knights who were summoned in 1254 to the parliament could scarcely have done more. It is however certain that the sovereign authority had been given to the grant before the writ was issued. The county court therefore, in its greatest force, was far from the independent position of an assembly of provincial estates.

Worcestershire refuses in 1297.

210. It might be inferred, as a corollary from these facts, that the several county courts had the power of directly approaching the king as communities from a very early period. As the crown recognised their corporate character by consulting

(6) Access of the counties to the king.

[1] See above, p. 136. The passage is curious and important; 'Sexto kalendas Octobris, cum ministri regis exigerent sextam partem infra burgum bonorum omnium et octavam extra burgum, responsum fuit eis per comitatum, "rex Henricus aliquando promisit communitati regni quod libertates magnae cartae et forestae concederet et confirmaret si daretur ei quinta decima quam tunc petebat, sed pecunia accepta libertates tradidit oblivioni. Ideo quando habuerimus libertatum saisinam gratis dabimus pecuniam nominatam."' Ann. Wigorn. p. 534. In 1302 the sheriff of Lincoln is ordered to assemble the taxors and collectors of the fifteenth, and the knights and others of his county, 'quos praemuniendos esse videris,' to the next county court, to meet the king's officers; Parl. Writs, i. 403.

Direct negotiation of the counties with the king.

them through inquests, and taxing them as consolidated bodies, they must have had through their sheriffs or through chosen representatives the right of approaching the crown by petition or of negotiating for privileges by way of fine. There is sufficient proof that they did so from time to time, just as the several town communities and the ecclesiastical bodies did. When the men of Cornwall agreed by fine with John, that their county should be disafforested and they should elect their own sheriff[1]; when the men of Devon, Dorset, and Somerset, treated for the same or the like privileges with John and Henry III, the negotiation may or may not have been carried on through the sheriff; it must have been initiated and authorised by the county court. So likewise with petitions: in the parliament of 1278 the county of Cheshire petitions, as 'la commune de Cestresire,' for the usages which it enjoyed before it fell into the king's hands[2]. After the consolidation of the parliamentary system such memorials became more frequent, and were no doubt presented by the knights of the shire.

Analogy of the town communities with the shires.

211. The communities of cities and boroughs, the organisations which in foreign constitutions composed the whole estate of the commons, present points of analogy and contrast with the county communities, under both of the heads just noticed. Being in their origin sections of the shire, and lying locally within the area of the shire, they retain for the most part the same constituent elements and the same administrative functions which were common to them and the shire before their separation. Trained throughout their subsequent history on a plan of privilege and exemption, exposed far more than the shires to the intrusion of foreign elements and foreign sympathies, and open to the influx of the political ideas which came in along with the trade of the foreign merchants, they were subject to internal jealousies and class divisions, of which there are fewer traces in the counties, where the local interests of the great lords were

[1] Above, p. 207.

[2] Rot. Parl. i. 6. In 1300 Edward summoned seven knights from each of the ridings of Yorkshire to meet the barons of the Exchequer at York, 'super quibusdam negotiis nos et communitatem comitatus praedicti specialiter tangentibus tractaturi.' Parl. Writs, i. 86.

the chief dividing causes. Any complete generalisation upon the constitutional history of the towns is impossible for this reason, that this history does not start from one point or proceed by the same stages. At the time at which they began to take a share in the national counsels through their representatives, the class of towns contained communities in every stage of development, and in each stage of development constituted on different principles. Hence, by the way, arose the anomalies and obscurities as to the nature of the constituencies, which furnished matter of deliberation to the House of Commons for many centuries, and only ended with the Reform Act of 1832. The varieties of later usage were based on the condition in which the borough found itself when it began to be represented, according as the local constitution was for the moment guided by the court leet, the burgage holders, the general body of householders, the local magistrates or landlords, the merchant guild, or the like. Of these points something may be said when we reach the subject of the suffrage; it is noticed here in order to show that the obscurity of the subject is not a mere result of our ignorance or of the deficiency of record, but of a confusion of usages which was felt at the time to be capable of no general treatment; a confusion which, like that arising from the connexion between tenure and representation, prevailed from the very first, and occasioned actual disputes ages before it began to puzzle the constitutional lawyers.

Difficulty of generalisation on this head.

Actual obscurity of the question.

212. I. We look in vain then for any uniform type of city or borough court which answers to the county court[1]: in one town the town-meeting included all householders, in another all who paid scot and lot—analogous to the modern ratepayers—in another the owners of burgages, in another the members of the merchant guild or trade guilds: every local history supplies evidence of the existence of a variety of such courts, with conflicting and co-ordinate jurisdictions. Roughly, however, we may divide them into two classes, those in which the local administration was carried on by a ruling body of magistrates or magnates, and

I. Constitution of the towns and their courts.

(a) One class under close corporations:

[1] This was the case in France also, where similar questions arise as to the elections to the States General; Boutaric, pp. 20, 21.

(b) another with simpler and freer organisation.

those in which it remained in the hands of the townspeople in general; the former being the type of the larger and more ancient municipalities, the latter that of the smaller towns and of those whose corporate character was simpler and newer[1]. In London and the other great towns which in the reign of Edward I much more nearly rivalled London than they do now, there was a doubt whether the jurisdiction of the magistrates were not, so far as it touched questions of finance and general politics, a usurped jurisdiction. And this division of opinion caused the tumults which arose in the capital, on the right of the magistrates to determine the incidence of taxation, and to elect the mayor, to the exclusion of the general body of the citizens. Of these disputes the reign of Henry III furnishes a continuous record, the divisions being complicated by the political affinities of their leaders as royalists or as members of the baronial party[2]. And this feeling could not be confined to London; something of the kind was felt everywhere except in those small towns where the more ancient type of moot and court still retained its efficiency.

Political struggles of the governing bodies with the general body of inhabitants.

II. Variety of powers and functions in towns.

213. II. As there were many types of town constitution existing at the same time, so too there were many degrees of completeness of functions. Some were almost independent republics,

[1] Thus in 1245, the magnates elected one person as sheriff, 'quidam de vulgo' chose another; Lib. de Antt. Legg. p. 11; in 1249, when the justices wished to negotiate with the mayor and aldermen, 'universus populus contradixit non permittens illos sine tota communa inde aliquid tractare,' ibid. p. 16; in 1254 the whole communa passed several bye-laws, p. 20; in 1255 the citizens refused to pay queen-gold, p. 23; in 1257 the alderman and four men of each ward met the council in the Exchequer, and discussed the question whether the assessment of tallage ought to be made by the mayor and other officers, or 'per viros ad hoc per totam communam electos et juratos,' p. 33. In 1263 a popular mayor 'ita nutrierat populum civitatis, quod vocantes se communam civitatis habuerant primam vocem in civitate;' on all matters of business he said to them 'vultis vos ut ita fiat,' they replied 'Ya, ya,' and it was done, the aldermen and magnates not being consulted, p. 55. In 1272 there was a struggle between the magnates and 'ille populus vocans se communem civitatis,' about the election of mayor, p. 152.

[2] So it is remarked by the French writers referred to above, Boutaric and Picot, that the universal suffrage prevailed more in the *villes prêvotales* than in the *communes*; the former being the towns administered by a royal bailiff or praepositus, the latter being independent corporations, where the suffrage was exercised by the magistrates.

some mere country townships that had reached the stage at which they compounded severally for their ferm, but were in all other respects under the influence of the sheriff and the county court. There were, however, some points in which—London with sheriffs and a shire constitution of its own being perhaps the only exception—the sheriff and the county court still reviewed or incorporated the town constitution.

Functions of the sheriffs in the towns.

In matters of jurisdiction: the towns, however completely organised, could not exclude the itinerant justices, whose court being the shiremoot involved the recognition of the sheriff. Hence in the general summons of the county court before those officers the boroughs were ordered to send twelve burghers to represent the general body[1].

(1) Attendance before the justices in eyre.

In the measures for the conservation of the peace, the sheriff had orders to enforce the observance of watch and ward, to forbid tournaments and other occasions of riot, and to examine into the observance of the Assize of arms, not only in the geldable or open townships of the shire but in the cities and boroughs as well[2]. The details of the system were carried out by the local officers; the great towns elected their own coroners, mayors, bailiffs and constables, but they were under view of the sheriff.

(2) View of the arms under the Assize, watch and ward.

The military contingents of the towns, composed of the men sworn under the Assize of arms, were also led by the sheriffs: these contributions to the national force being, except in the case of a few large towns, too small to form a separate organised body.

(3) The armed force of the towns was under the sheriff.

In point of direct dealing with the crown, whether in the executive measures resulting from reform, in fiscal negotiations, or in the transactions which took the form of fine or petition, every town, as indeed every individual, had a distinct and recognised right to act; and these points, which serve in regard to the counties to show the corporate unity of the community, and therefore require illustration in relation to that point, need no further treatment here.

(4, 5, 6) Direct negotiation of the towns with the crown.

[1] Select Charters, p. 349.

[2] Select Charters, pp. 353, 362; 'vicecomites . . . circumeant comitatus suos de hundredo in hundredum, et civitates et burgos;' p. 363.

Were the towns to be treated as parts of the shire?

Under these circumstances, we can well imagine that Simon de Montfort and Edward I, when they determined to call the town communities to their parliaments, may have hesitated whether to treat them as part of the shire communities or as independent bodies. Earl Simon adopted the latter course which was perhaps necessary under the local divisions of the moment: as he summoned out of the body of the baronage only those on whom he could rely, so he selected the towns which were to be represented and addressed his summons directly to the magistrates of those towns[1]. And this plan was adopted by Edward I on one of the first occasions on which he called the borough representatives together[2]. But when the constitution took its final form, a form which was in thorough accordance with the growth of the national spirit and system, it was found more convenient to treat them as portions of the counties; the writ for the election was directed to the sheriff, and the formal election of the borough members, as well as that of knights of the shire, took place in the county court. Thus the inclusion of the boroughs in the national system was finally completed in and through the same process by which the general representation of the three estates was insured.

Writs for borough elections directed to the sheriffs.

The English boroughs had no collective organisation.

The towns of England, neither by themselves nor in conjunction with the shires, ever attempted before the seventeenth century to act alone in convention like the Scottish boroughs, or in confederation like the German leagues. The commons had no separate assembly, answering to the convocation of the clergy or the great council of the baronage. In 1296, however, Edward summoned representative burghers from the chief towns to meet first at Bury and afterwards at Berwick to advise on the new constitution of the latter town; and this plan may have been occasionally adopted for other purposes[3].

III. Early cases of representation.

214. III. We have now to link together very succinctly the several cases in which, before the year 1295, the representative principle entered into the composition of the parliaments; the

[1] Select Charters, p. 406.
[2] In 1283; above, p. 116; Select Charters, p. 458.
[3] Parl. Writs, i. 49, 51. Cf. p. 156 above

political causes and other phenomena of which have been treated in the last chapter. From the year 1215 onwards, in the total deficiency of historical evidence, we can only conjecture that the national council, when it contained members over and above those who were summoned by special writ as barons, comprised such minor members of the body of tenants in chief as found it convenient or necessary to obey the general summons which was prescribed, for the purpose of granting special aids, by the fourteenth article of the charter. These would be more or less numerous on occasion, but would have no right or title to represent the commons; they attended simply by virtue of their tenure.

Obscurity during the years 1215 to 1254.

The year 1254 then is the first date at which the royal writs direct the election and attendance in parliament of two knights from each shire: the occasion being the granting of an aid in money to be sent to the king in Gascony, and the parliament being called by the queen and the earl of Cornwall in the belief that, as the bishops had refused to grant money without consulting the beneficed clergy, the surest way to obtain it from the laity was to call an assembly on which the promise of a renewal of the charters would be likely to produce the effect desired[1]. There is no reason to suppose that the counties were represented in the Oxford parliament of 1258, or that the knights who brought up the complaints of the shires to the October parliament were elected as representatives to take part in that parliament, or that the 'bacheleria,' which in 1259 took Edward for its spokesman, was the collective representation of the shires. The provisionary government which lasted from 1258 to 1264 restricted rather than extended the limits of the taxing and deliberative council. In the intervening struggle however both parties had recourse to the system of representation: in 1261 the baronial leaders summoned three knights of each shire to a conference at S. Alban's, and the king

Summons of knights of the shire in 1254.

No representation in 1258 or 1259.

King and barons adopt it in 1261.

[1] Above, pp. 67, 68. That the knights of the shire assembled on this occasion represented the minor tenants in chief seems to be too lightly admitted by Hallam, Middle Ages, iii. 19; apparently on the argument of the Lords' Committee, i. 95. There is nothing in the writ that so limits their character; Select Charters, p. 367.

retaliated by directing the same knights to attend his parliament at Windsor[1]. In 1264, immediately after the battle of Lewes, Simon summoned two knights of each shire to a parliament at London[2], and in the December of the same year he called together the more famous assembly, to which not only knights of the shire were summoned by writs addressed to the sheriffs, but two discreet and lawful representatives from the cities and boroughs were summoned by writs addressed to the magistrates of the several communities[3]. It is not impossible that Henry III after the victory at Evesham, when he summoned proctors for the cathedral chapters[4], summoned also representatives of the commons to the parliament of Winchester. The preamble to the statute of Marlborough in 1267 states that the king had called to parliament the more discreet men of the realm, 'tam de majoribus quam de minoribus[5],'—the discretion, which was the peculiar qualification of the knights of the shire, affording a presumption that they were present. In 1269, at the great court held for the translation of S. Edward the Confessor, attended by all the magnates, were present also the more powerful men of the cities and boroughs; but when the ceremony was over, the king proceeded to hold a parliament with the barons[6], and the citizens and burghers can only be supposed to have been invited guests such as attended, by nomination of the sheriffs,

Two parliaments of Simon de Montfort.

Possible cases of representation in 1265 and 1267.

Attendance of representatives in 1269, not in parliament.

[1] Above, p. 85.

[2] Above, p. 90.

[3] Above, p. 92. The fact that the peculiar constitution of this parliament did not attract the notice of the historians has led to the conclusion that borough representation was not such a novelty as to call for much remark at the time; see Edinb. Rev. vol. xxxv. p. 38. As however there is no real evidence of any summons of the boroughs before this time, there seems little reason to question that this was the first occasion. The case of S. Alban's, in which in the reign of Edward II the burghers claimed a right of sending two members to parliament in discharge of all service due to the crown, as customary in the days of Edward I and his progenitors (see Brady, Introduction, p. 38; Hallam, Middle Ages, iii. 29), and that of Barnstaple (see Hallam, iii. 32), where, in the 18th of Edward III, the burghers alleged a lost charter of Athelstan to support their claim to representation, need not be discussed. They were both cases of imposture, got up with the intention of escaping from the services due to the lords of the towns, the abbot of S. Alban's and the lord Audley; and the S. Alban's claim was part of a great effort, which lasted for more than half a century, to throw off the authority of the abbey; see Vitæ Abb. S. Alb. (ed. Riley), ii. 156 sq.

[4] Select Charters, p. 409.

[5] Statutes, p. 19.

[6] Ann. Wykes, pp. 226, 227.

at the coronations and other great occasions [1]. In 1273 we find a more important illustration of the growth of the custom: at Hilary-tide a great convocation of the whole realm was held to take the oath of fealty to Edward I, and to maintain the peace of the realm: 'thither came archbishops and bishops, earls and barons, abbots and priors, and from each shire four knights and from each city four citizens [2].' This assembly was, in its essence if not in its form, a parliament, and acted as the common council of the kingdom. The preamble of the statute of Westminster of 1275 declares the assent of archbishops, bishops, abbots, priors, earls, barons and the community of the land thereto summoned [3]; an assertion which distinctly implies, besides the magnates, the attendance, of a body which can hardly have been other than the knights, though not necessarily elected representatives. In 1278 the statute of Gloucester was enacted with the assent of the most discreet, 'ausi bien les greindres cum les meindres [4].' In 1282 the two provincial councils of Northampton and York contained four knights of each shire and two representatives of each city and borough [5]. In 1283 the parliament of Shrewsbury comprised representatives of twenty-one selected towns separately summoned as in 1265, and two knights of each shire [6]. In 1290 two knights of each shire attended the Westminster parliament [7]: in 1294 four [8]; and in 1295 two knights from each shire, two citizens from each city, and two burghers from each borough [9].

Great convention in 1273.

Parliament of 1275.

Parliament of Gloucester.

Councils of 1282 and 1283.

Parliaments of 1290, 1294, and 1295.

The last date, 1295, may be accepted as fixing finally the right of shire and town representation, although for a few years the system admits of some modifications. The great councils of the baronage, are sometimes, until the writs of summons are examined, almost indistinguishable from the parliaments; they are in fact a permanent survival from the earlier system. But

Later variations of parliamentary constitution.

[1] Thus for the coronation o Edward II, the sheriffs were ordered, 'et milites, cives, burgenses ac alios de comitatu praedicto, quos fore videris invitandos, ut dictis die et loco solempnizationi praedictae personaliter intersint, ex parte nostra facias invitari;' Foed. ii. 28.

[2] Ann. Winton, p. 113. [3] Statutes, i. 26. [4] Statutes, i. 45.

[5] Above, p. 114. [6] Above, p. 116. [7] Above, p. 122.

[8] Above, p. 127. [9] Above, p. 129.

even in the parliaments proper there were, as we shall see, a variety of minute irregularities, such for instance as the summoning to the parliament of Lincoln of the representatives who had sat in the preceding parliament, and in 1306 of one representative from the smaller boroughs; but such anomalies only illustrate the still tender growth of the new system. The parliament of 1295 differed, so far as we know, from all that had preceded it, and was a precedent for all time to come, worthy of the principle which the king had enunciated in the writ of summons. The writs for assembling the representatives are addressed to the sheriffs; they direct the election not only of the knights but of citizens and burghers; the return to the writ is not merely as in 1265 and 1283 the reply of the separate towns but of the county courts, in which the elective process is transacted; and the parliament that results contains a concentration of the persons and powers of the shiremoot. In that assembly, on great occasions, the towns had appeared by their twelve burghers, now they appear to make their return to the sheriff, who thereupon makes his report to the government.

The parliament of 1295 a model parliament.

The name of parliament not restricted to representative assemblies.

215. In thus tracing the several links which connect the parliament of 1295 with those of 1265 and 1254, we must be content to understand by the name of parliament all meetings of the national council called together in the form that was usual at the particular time. We must not take our definition from the later legal practice and refuse the name to those assemblies which do not in all points answer to that definition. After 1295 it is otherwise; that year established the precedent, and although, in the early years that follow, exceptional practices may be found, it may be fairly questioned whether any assembly afterwards held is entitled to the name and authority of parliament, which does not in the minutest particulars of summons, constitution, and formal despatch of business, answer to the model then established. This rule, however, was not at once recognised, and for many years both the terminal sessions of the king's ordinary council, and the occasional assemblies of the magnum concilium of prelates, barons and councillors, which we

have noticed as a great survival of the older system, share with the constitutional assembly of estates the name of parliament[1].

216. Before proceeding to inquire into the powers of the body thus composed, we have to meet the natural question, who were the electors of the representative members. On any equitable theory of representation, the elected representatives represent those members of the body politic who have not the right of appearing personally in the assembly, and they are elected by the persons whom they represent. The knights of the shire represented the community of the shire which was intermediately represented by the county court; the representatives of the towns represented the community of the several towns intermediately represented by their agents in the county court. The two cases must be considered separately.

By whom were the representatives elected?

It is most probable, on the evidence of records, on the analogies of representative usage, and on the testimony of later facts, that the knights of the shire were elected by the full county court. The institution of electing representative knights for local purposes was in active operation for nearly eighty years before such representatives were summoned to parliament; those earlier elections were made by the full county court; and in the writs ordering the parliamentary elections no words are contained which restrict the liberty heretofore exercised. The four knights elected under the eighteenth article of Magna Carta, to assist the itinerant justices in taking recognitions, are elected *per comitatum*[2]: the county court which attended the itinerant justices was, as we have seen, of the fullest possible character[3]. The twelve knights chosen to inquire into the forest abuses, under the forty-eighth article[4],

Election of knights of the shire.

Knights elected by the shire for local purposes.

[1] For example, the summons to the council called for Sept. 30, 1297, is entitled 'de parliamento tenendo:' in 1299 a writ 'de parliamento tenendo,' dated Sept. 21, is addressed only to the archbishop of Canterbury, five bishops, four earls, and five others, barons of the council. Lords' Report, App. pp. 87, 111. On the other hand the great council of the barons called at Salisbury, Feb. 5, 1297, is entitled 'de parliamento tenendo apud Sarisburiam;' Ibid. p. 77.

[2] Select Charters, p. 291.

[3] Above, p. 205.

[4] Select Charters, p. 294; 'qui debent eligi per probos homines ejusdem comitatus.'

Cases of election in the shire-moot for local purposes.

are chosen 'per probos homines comitatus,' and in the first county court after the issue of the writ[1]. The two knights, collectors of the carucage of 1220, are elected 'de voluntate et consilio omnium de comitatu in pleno comitatu[2].' The four knights of the shire summoned to meet the sheriffs in 1226 are to be chosen in the county court by the knights and good men of the county[3]. In 1254 the knights summoned to grant an aid are described as 'four lawful and discreet knights of the aforesaid counties, that is to say, two of the one county and two of the other, whom the same counties shall choose for the purpose to represent all and singular of the same counties[4].' The knights summoned to the first parliament of Simon de Montfort are chosen 'per assensum ejusdem comitatus[5].' In 1282 the sheriff is ordered to send four knights from each county 'having full power to act for the communities of the same counties[6].' In 1283 he is directed to cause two knights to be chosen in each county, to attend the king on behalf of the community of the same county[7]. In 1290 the knights are described as elected from the more discreet and able, and as having full power for themselves and the whole community of the counties[8]. In 1294 and 1295 the qualification and authorisation are stated in the same words[9].

These are elections by the full county.

No restriction implied in the writs of summons to parliament.

There is then no restriction on the common and prescriptive usage of the county court. Nor does any such restriction appear in the extant returns of the sheriffs in 1290 and 1295[10]. In 1290 the knights are described as elected 'per assensum totius comitatus,' or 'per totam communitatem,' or 'in pleno comitatu;' in 1295 the knights for Lancashire are elected 'per

[1] 'Qui eligentur de ipso comitatu, in primo comitatu qui tenebitur post susceptionem litterarum istarum;' Select Charters, p. 298.

[2] Select Charters, p. 343.

[3] 'In proximo comitatu dicas militibus et probis hominibus bailliae tuae, quod quatuor de legalioribus et discretioribus militibus ex se ipsis eligant;' Select Charters, p. 348.

[4] Select Charters, p. 367.

[5] Select Charters, p. 403.

[6] Select Charters, p. 455.

[7] Select Charters, p. 458.

[8] Select Charters, p. 467.

[9] Select Charters, pp. 471, 476. Compare the writs of the 28th and 34th years; Parl. Writs, i. 84, 167.

[10] Parl. Writs, i. 21–24, 38, 40, 41.

consensum totius comitatus;' those for Oxfordshire and Berkshire 'per assensum communitatis;' those for Dorset and Somerset, 'per communitatem' and 'in plenis comitatibus.' In 1298 the knights for Cornwall are elected 'per totam communitatem;' those for Dorset, Somerset and Hertford 'in pleno comitatu per totam communitatem[1];' the diversity of form in the several returns serving to prove the uniformity of the usage.

Nor in the wording of the returns.

Analogous examples may be taken from the election of coroner and conservator, and from the practice of the ecclesiastical assemblies, in which the representative theory is introduced shortly before it finds its way into parliament; and these instances are the more convincing because the continuity and uniformity of practice has never been questioned. The writ for the election of coroners orders it to be done 'in pleno comitatu per assensum totius comitatus[2];' the election of verderers is made 'convocato toto comitatu,' 'pereundem comitatum[3];' the election of conservator is made 'in pleno comitatu de assensu ejusdem comitatus[4].' The election of proctors for the clergy is made, as it is hardly necessary to say, by the whole of the beneficed clergy of each archdeaconry.

Analogy of the election of coroners, verderers, and conservators.

The later modifications of the right of election belong to a further stage of our inquiries; but we may adduce now the answer made by Edward III in 1376 to a petition that the knights should be elected by common choice of the best men of the county, and not certified by the sheriff alone without due election. The king replied that they should be elected by

Royal decisions in favour of the full county court.

[1] Parl. Writs, i. 70, 74.

[2] 'Praecipimus tibi quod in pleno comitatu Wigorniae per assensum totius comitatus eligi facias de fidelioribus et discretioribus militibus de comitatu . . . duos coronatores.' Rot Claus. i. 414; cf. pp. 419, 463, 506, 622.

[3] 'Praecipimus tibi quod sine dilatione convocato comitatu tuo statim per eundem comitatum eligi facias unum de legalioribus et discretioribus militibus . . . qui melius esse possit viridarius;' Rot. Claus. i. 409; cf. pp. 410, 493, 497.

[4] 'Tunc in pleno comitatu suo de assensu ejusdem comitatus et de consilio Simonis de Wintonia . . . eligi facias unum alium de fidelibus regis;' 8th March, 1287; Parl. Writs, i. 390.

Royal decisions.

the common assent of the whole county[1]: in 1372, when a proposition was made to prevent the choice of lawyers, he ordered that the election should be made in full county court[2]. These replies, made within eighty years of the introduction of the usage, seem to be conclusive as to the theory of election.

We must not, however, suppose that this theory was universally understood, or generally accepted, or that it was not in practice limited by some very strong restrictions.

Theory that the knights of the shire represented the minor tenants in chief.

It seems almost unquestioned that the national assemblies between 1215 and 1295 were composed on the principle stated in the fourteenth article of the charter, and thus contained a considerable number of minor tenants-in-chief attending in obedience to the general summons; it might then not unreasonably be contended that the new element of the representative knights was a substitute for those minor tenants, and so that the knights of the shire represented not the body of the county but simply the tenants-in-chief below the rank of baron. If this were the case, the assembly by which the election was made would not be the full county court; the electors would be the tenants-in-chief, not the whole body of suitors; and the new system, instead of being an expedient by which the co-operation of all elements of the people might be secured for common objects, would simply place the power of legislation and taxation in the hands of a body constituted on the principle of tenure[3]. It has been accordingly supposed that the court summoned for the election was not the court leet of the county, at which all residents were obliged to attend, but the court baron, composed of persons owing suit and service to the king, and excluding the tenants of mesne

[1] Rot. Parl. ii. 355: 'le roi voet q'ils soient esluz par commune assent de tout le Contee.' [2] Rot. Parl. ii. 310.

[3] This appears to be the theory of the Lords' Report on the Dignity of a Peer, to which only a general reference need here be given. The Lords however confess that it is involved in very great obscurity. It was the theory of Blackstone, Brady, and Carte; Prynne on the other hand maintained that the knights were elected in full county by and for the whole county; Regist. ii. p. 50; and this view is followed by Hallam, Middle Ages, iii. 19, 216–219. But the further question who were the suitors of the county court that made the election, the freeholders only or the court in general, may be discussed further on, in connexion with the general subject of the suffrage.

lords[1]. To this must be objected that there is no authority for drawing at this period any such distinction between the two theoretical characters of the county court[2], and that it is impossible that an election known to be made by a mere fraction could be said to be the act of the whole community, or to be transacted 'in pleno comitatu.' If such, moreover, were the case, the whole body of mesne tenants who were not included in the town population would be represented in parliament by their feudal lords, or, if their lords were below the degree of barony, would be unrepresented altogether. But it was certainly opposed to the policy of the crown, from the very date of the conquest, that the feudal lords should stand in such a relation to their vassals, although from time to time they had assumed it, and the assumption had been tacitly admitted. And it is impossible to suppose that Edward I, who in so many other ways showed his determination to place the whole body of freeholders on a basis of equality, exclusive of the question of tenure, should have instituted a system which would draw the line more hardly and sharply than ever between the two classes. These considerations would seem to be conclusive as to the original principle on which the institution was founded. But the facts that questions did arise very early on the point, that the doctrines of tenure more and more influenced the opinions of constitutional lawyers, and that there was always a class among the barons who would gladly have seen the commons reduced to entire dependence on the lords, have led to much discussion, and perhaps the question may never be quite satisfactorily decided.

This theory is wanting in authority; is opposed to the policy of the crown; and irreconcileable with the other measures of Edward I. Yet questions arose very early upon this.

As the knights of the shire received wages during their attendance in parliament, it was fair that those persons who were excluded from the election should be exempt from contri-

How far does the question of wages paid to the knights of

[1] Lords' Report, i. 149, 150. This view, which need not be here re-argued, was by anticipation refuted by Mr. Allen in the Edinburgh Review, vol. xxvi. pp. 341–347; on the ground that the vavassores of the barons, the mesne tenants, are spoken of as attending the courts, both in the charters of Henry I (above, vol. i. p. 390), and in the 'Extenta Manerii' of the reign of Edward I; Statutes, i. 242.

[2] Hallam, M.A. iii. 217.

the shire illustrate the question?

bution to the wages. To many of the smaller freeholders the exemption from payment would be far more valuable than the privilege of voting; and the theory that the knights represented only the tenants-in-chief would be recommended by a strong argument of self-interest. The claim of exemption was urged on behalf of the mesne tenants in general, on behalf of the tenants in socage in the county of Kent as against the tenants by knight service, and on behalf of the tenants of land in ancient demesne of the crown[1]. In the last of these three cases the exemption was admitted, for as the crown retained the power of tallaging such tenants without consulting parliament, they were without share in the representation[2]. As to the two former cases, opinions were divided at a very early period, and petitions for a legal decision were presented in many parliaments from the reign of Edward III to that of Henry VIII. The petitions of the commons generally express their desire that the expenses should be levied from the whole of the commons of the county, a desire which is in itself sufficient to show that no exemption could be urged on the ground of non-representation[3]. The reiteration of the petition shows that it met with some opposition, which must have proceeded from those lords who retained the idea that they represented their tenants, and were anxious to maintain the hold upon them which that idea implied. The crown as constantly avoids a judicial decision, and orders that the usage customary in the particular case shall be maintained. This hesitation on the part of the government in several successive reigns may have arisen from a desire to avoid a quarrel with either estate, but more probably proceeded from the recognised obscurity of the question, the theory having been from the first subject to the doubts which we have noted. In consequence of the au-

Exemption claimed for tenants in socage, for mesne tenants, and for tenants in ancient demesne.

Petitions of the commons opposed to such exemptions.

The crown decides in favour of custom.

[1] See Hallam, Middle Ages, iii. 114–116.

[2] Lords' Report, i. 58, 232.

[3] Lords' Report, i. 330, 331, 366, 369. Cases might be pleaded that would lead to almost any conclusion: e.g. in 1307 the sheriff of Cambridgeshire is forbidden to tax the villein tenants of John de la Mare for the wages of the knights, because he had attended personally in parliament; Parl. Writs, i. 191.

thority of custom thus recognised, the Kentish socagers secured their exemption[1], but between the general body of freeholders and the tenants-in-chief the dispute was never judicially settled; as the awakening political sense showed men the importance of electoral power, the exemption ceased to be courted, and the laws which defined the suffrage must have practically settled the question of contribution[2]. The discussion of the matter, in which the belief of the commons was uniformly on one side, and in which no adverse decision by the crown was ever attempted, tends to confirm the impression that, although there was real obscurity and conflict of opinion, both the right of election and the burden of contribution belonged to the whole of the suitors of the county court. Had the counter pleas been successful, had the tenants in ancient demesne, the mesne tenants, and the tenants in socage, been exempted, the county constituencies would have been reduced to a handful of knights, who might as easily have attended parliament in person, as their compeers did for many ages in Aragon and Scotland.

The dispute never decided on its merits.

General conclusion.

217. Yet it is almost equally improbable that, in an age in which political intelligence was very scanty, the whole county court on each summons for an election, was fully attended, carefully identified the qualified members, and, free from all suspicion of undue influence, formally endeavoured to discover the most discreet, or most apt, or most able, among the knights of the shire. Unquestionably the tenants-in-chief of the crown, men who still received their summons to the host, or held their lands by barony, the knightly body too, who had interests of their own more akin to those of the baron than to those of the socager, would possess an influence in the assembly, and a will to exercise it. The chief lord of a great manor would have

Theory and practice may not have coincided.

Influence of the greater men in the shire-moot.

[1] Lords' Report, i. 364.

[2] 'We are of opinion that no conclusion whatever can be drawn from the disputes concerning the payment of wages.' 'Villeins contributed.' Allen, Edinb. Rev. xxxv. 27. Brady (Introd. p. 141) points out that the payment of wages to knights appointed for county business was not a novelty. In 1258 the knights appointed, four in each shire to present before the council at Michaelmas the complaints against the sheriffs, had writs for their expenses 'de communitate;' Rot. Claus. 42 Hen. III. m. 1 dors.

Early traces of undue influence in elections.

authority with his tenants, freeholders as they might be, which would make their theoretical equality a mere shadow, and would moreover be exercised all the more easily because the right which it usurped was one which the tenant neither understood nor cared for. Early in the fourteenth century undue influence in elections becomes a matter of complaint. But it is long before we have sufficient data to determine how far the suitors of the county court really exerted the power which we cannot but believe the theory of the constitution to have given them: when we do reach that point, the power often seems to be engrossed by the great men of the shire. The office of representative was not coveted, and we can imagine cases in which the sheriff would have to nominate and compel the service of an unwilling member. But by whomsoever the right was actually used, the theory of the election was that it was the act of the shire-moot, that is of all the suitors of the county court assembled in the county court, irrespective of the question of whom or by what tenure their lands were held.

No competition for the office of knight of the shire.

General conclusion.

Elections in boroughs.

218. With regard to the boroughs analogous questions arise. It may be asked whether the towns which were directed to return representatives were the demesne boroughs of the crown only[1], or all the town communities which the sheriff regarded as qualified under the terms of the writ. The former theory has been maintained, on the same principle of the all-importance of tenure which suggested the limitation of the county constituencies to the tenants-in-chief[2]; and there may have been

[1] In favour of the restriction is Brady; in favour of the more liberal view, Prynne, Hallam, Allen. The Lords' Report seems to halt between the two. The question is however practically decided by the cases mentioned in the text and in the note on the next page.

[2] On this point we may look for illustration from the elections of representatives of the third estate in the States General. M. Boutaric gives the data for the States General of Tours, in 1308; he concludes that the municipal magistrates were not representatives except when specially elected and commissioned, but that the representatives were generally chosen from among the magistrates; that sometimes a town entrusted the commission to a clergyman, and the clergy to a layman; that in the communes the deputies were chosen in the regular general assembly; and in the districts which had no communal organisation, in similar general gatherings, where all inhabitants had an equal voice; Premiers États Généraux, p. 21. M. Hervieu, Rev. de Legislation, 1873, pp. 410 sq.,

periods at which it was acted upon, for the number of borough representatives long and greatly fluctuated. But the evidence of fact seems decisive in favour of the more liberal interpretation, so far at least as concerns the reign of Edward I to which we must naturally look as the fairest and first source of precedent. In the great parliament of 1295 many towns which were held in demesne by other lords than the crown, were represented: such were Downton a borough of the bishop of Winchester, Ripon and Beverley, two towns which until recent times were dependent on the archbishop of York; and in 1298 North-Allerton a borough of the bishop of Durham; no doubt the instances might be multiplied[1]. Yet the matter is not so clear, but that in the writs for collecting money granted in these assemblies, whether from confusion of idea, or the observance of routine forms, expressions are found that might lead to a different conclusion. The writ in 1295 asserts that the citizens and burghers and good men of the demesne cities and boroughs had courteously granted a subsidy[2]. If this expression be understood as a statement of fact, then the term 'dominicae civitates et burgi' must be made to include all boroughs whether held in chief or through mesne lords: if it be understood to state a theory, then the mesne boroughs which had sent members had gone beyond their duty in doing so. It is perhaps more

The towns returning members were not merely the demesne towns of the crown.

Yet there were early doubts on this.

Writs of 1295.

limits this conclusion very materially; 'Tantôt, en effet, c'est le suffrage à deux degrés qui est la base de ces elections, et tantôt le suffrage universel;' an immense variety of usages prevailed, many of them exactly analogous to the later usages in England, when the various classes of burghers, the corporations, the householders, the freemen, the scot and lot payers, claimed the right. The subject has been still further illustrated by M. Picot in his paper on 'Les elections aux États généraux,' Paris, 1874.

[1] The following boroughs represented in the parliaments of Edward I were of the same class; Lynn belonged to the see of Norwich, Salisbury to the bishop, S. Alban's to the abbot; Evesham to the abbot; Tunbridge and Bletchingley to the earl of Gloucester; Arundel and Midhurst to the earl of Arundel; Farnham to the see of Winchester; Edinb. Rev. xxxv. pp. 36, 37. Compare the returns given in the Parliamentary Writs, i. 34 sq.

[2] Parl. Writs, i. 45: 'cum . . . cives, burgenses et alii probi homines de dominicis nostris civitatibus et burgis ejusdem regni septimam de omnibus bonis suis mobilibus . . . nobis curialiter concesserint et gratanter;' here 'curialiter' simply means courteously, not as the Lords' Committee understood it, as a formal act of a court.

The form in 1296 is distinct enough.

likely to be an old form applied without much definiteness on a new occasion, and the form used in 1296[1] must be taken to express both theory and fact. In this the grant is distinctly said to be made by the citizens, burghers, and other good men of all and singular the cities and boroughs of the kingdom of whatsoever tenures or liberties they were, and of all the royal demesnes. But again, the fact that neither of the counties palatine, Chester or Durham, furnished either knights of the shire, citizens, or burghers, until the reigns of Henry VIII and Charles II, respectively, shows that the doctrine of demesne, qualified by the possession of peculiar privileges, created early anomalies and with them obscurities which nothing will explain but the convenient, almost superstitious, respect shown to ancient usage. The third of the great palatinates, Lancaster, is constantly represented, although for many years in the reign of Edward III the towns of the county were too much impoverished to send members to parliament.

Inconsistency in practice.

Example of city elections only in London.

Of the elections of city and borough members we have, except in the case of London, no details proper to the present period. In the capital, in 1296, all the aldermen and four men of each ward met on the 26th of September, and chose Stephen Aschewy and William Herford to go to the parliament of S. Edmunds; and on the 8th of October the 'communitas' was called together, namely six of the best and most discreet men of each ward, by whom the election was repeated and probably confirmed[2]. Whether these two gatherings in the case of London correspond with the two processes which must have taken place in the election of borough members, it would be rash to determine. In the latter case it must be supposed that the members were nominated in the borough assembly, or that

[1] Parl. Writs, i. 51: 'cives, burgenses et alii probi homines de omnibus et singulis civitatibus et burgis regni nostri de quorumcunque tenuris aut libertatibus fuerint et de omnibus dominicis nostris . . . curialiter concesserint et gratanter.' So too in France in 1308, not merely the demesne towns but all the 'insignes communitates' were represented in the states general. Boutaric, pp. 16, 20, 28–35.

[2] Parl. Writs, i. 49. A similar plan was used for the election of the sheriffs of London, who were chosen 'per assensum duodecim proborum hominum singularum wardarum;' in the 29th and 31st parliaments of Edward I; Brady, Boroughs, p. 22.

delegates were appointed in that assembly to elect them, and a return thereon made to the sheriff before the election was made in the county court[1]. The proceedings before the sheriff seem to be the election, or report of nomination, by the citizens and burghers, the manucaption or production of two sureties for each of the elected persons, and the deliverance by act or letter of the full powers to act on behalf of the community which elected them. The difficulty of determining who the real electors were need not be re-stated.

Proceedings before the sheriff relating to borough elections.

All the representatives of the commons received wages to defray their necessary expenses: these were fixed in the 16th of Edward II at four shillings a day for a knight and two shillings for a citizen or burgher; and they were due for the whole time of his service, his journey to and fro, and his stay in parliament[2]. The notices of these payments are as early as the attendance of representative members; on the 10th of February 1265 Henry III orders the sheriffs to assess by a jury of four lawful knights the expenses of the journey, so that the county be not aggrieved[3], the community of the county being clearly both electors and payers. The writ reads so much as a matter of course as to suggest that the practice was not new[4].

Wages of the representative members.

219. The number of cities and boroughs represented in the reign of Edward I was 166; the number of counties 37: as each returned two members[5], the whole body at its maximum would number 406; but the towns almost always varied, and no doubt this number is very far ahead of the truth.

Number of representative members.

[1] The return for the town of Oxford in 1295 is thus recorded: 'Nulla civitas neque burgus est in comitatu Oxoniensi nisi villa Oxoniensis; et breve quod michi venit returnatum fuit ballivis libertatis villae praedictae, qui habent returnum omnimodorum brevium, et ipsi mihi responderunt quod ex assensu communitatis villae Oxoniensis electi sunt secundum formam brevis duo burgenses subscripti.' But in Somersetshire the return is general: 'In plenis comitatibus Somerset et Dorset per communitatem eorundem eligere feci quatuor milites et de qualibet civitate duos cives et de quolibet burgo duos burgenses;' Parl. Writs, i. 41.

[2] Hallam, Middle Ages, iii. 114; Prynne, Register, iv. p. 53.

[3] Lords' Report, i. 489.

[4] See above, p. 231, note 2.

[5] To the parliament or Great Council of 1306 the sheriffs were directed to send two members for the larger, one for the smaller boroughs; several of the latter availed themselves of the relief. But this assembly was in other respects anomalous; see Parl. Writs, i. 72, note. Cf. Hallam, iii. 117.

Further questions as to the powers of the parliament.

Such in its constituent parts was the ideal parliament of 1295. The growth and extent of its powers is a further question of equal interest. We have in former chapters examined the powers of the national council under the Norman and Plantagenet kings, and in the last chapter have watched the constant attempts made by personal and political parties to extend them. We have seen too how those attempts coincide in time with an irregular but continuous enlargement of the constitution of the national council. The next question is to determine how far and by what degrees the new elements of parliament were admitted to an equal share with the older elements in the powers which were already obtained or asserted; how far and by what steps were the commons placed on a constitutional level with the other two estates during the period of definition.

Powers of parliament under John.

(1) In taxation.

220. The great council of the nation[1], before the end of the reign of John, had obtained the acknowledgment and enjoyed the exercise of the following rights. In respect of taxation, the theoretical assent, which had been taken for granted under the Norman kings, had been exchanged for a real consultation; the *commune concilium* had first discussed the finance of the year under Henry II, had next demurred to the nature of the exaction under Richard, and under John had obtained in the Great Charter the concession that without their consent given in a duly convoked assembly no tax should be levied beyond the three prescriptive feudal aids. They had further, by the practice of the king's ministers in the exchequer, been consulted as to the mode of assessment and had given counsel and consent to the form in which the taxes were collected.

(2) In legislation.

In respect of legislation they had received similar formal recognition of their right to advise and consent, and had, as it would appear from the preamble of some of the assizes, exercised a power of initiating amendments of the law by means of petition.

(3) In judicature.

As a high court of justice they had heard the complaints of the king against individuals, and had accepted and ratified his judgments against high offenders. And lastly

[1] On the exact relations of the several powers of the parliament, whilst it consisted of prelates and barons only, see Gneist, Verwalt. i. 366 sq.

as a supreme deliberative council they had been consulted on questions of foreign policy, of internal police and national defence; in the absence of the king from England they had practically exercised the right of regulating the regency, at all events in the case of the deposition of Longchamp; and by a series of acts of election, acknowledgment, and acceptance of the kings at their accession, had obtained a recognition of their right to regulate the succession also.

(4) In general business.

Progress during the minority of Henry III.

During the minority and in the troubled years of Henry III they had fully vindicated and practically enlarged these rights. In matters of taxation they had frequently refused aid to the king, and when they granted it they had carefully prescribed the mode of collection and assessment; in legislation they had not only taken the initiative by petitions, such as those which led to the Provisions of Oxford, and by articles of complaint presented by the whole or a portion of their body, but they had, as in the famous act of the council of Merton touching the legitimising of bastards by the subsequent marriage of their parents, refused their consent to a change in the law, by words which were accepted by the jurists as the statement of a constitutional fact[1]. Their judicial power was abridged in practice by the strengthened organisation of the royal courts, but it remained in full force in reference to high offenders, and causes between great men; the growth of the privileges of baronage gave to the national council, as an assembly of barons, the character of a court of peers for the trial and amercement of their fellows; and even where a cause was brought against the king himself, although it must begin with a petition of right and not as in causes between subjects with a writ, the lawyers recognised the *universitas regni* as the source of remedy, and

(1) In taxation.

(2) In legislation.

(3) As to judicature.

[1] 'Nolumus leges Angliae mutari;' Bracton states the principle; 'leges Anglicanae . . . quae quidem cum fuerint approbatae consensu utentium, et sacramento regum confirmatae, mutari non possunt nec destrui sine communi consilio et consensu eorum omnium quorum consilio et consensu fuerunt promulgatae. In melius tamen converti possunt etiam sine illorum consensu;' lib. i. c. 2. Thus we have seen Edward I refusing to annul the statute de Religiosis; 'illud statutum de consilio magnatum suorum fuerat editum et ordinatum et ideo absque eorum consilio non erat revocandum;' Hemingb. ii. 57; above, p. 126.

the king's court as one of the three powers which are above the king himself[1]. Their general political power was greatly increased; they had determined the policy of the crown in foreign affairs; they had not only displaced the king's ministers but had placed the royal power itself in commission; they had drawn up a new constitution for the country and imposed new oaths on the king and his heir. It is true that the most important of these were party measures, carried out in exceptional times and by unconstitutional means, but it was as representing the supreme council of the kingdom that the baronial party acted, and the rights they enforced were enforced in the name of the nation.

(4) As to general deliberation.

Further claims made by the parliament.

But the claims of the same body had gone further, and had in some respects run far in advance of the success which was actually achieved at the time or for ages later; nay in one or two points they had claimed powers which have never yet been formally conceded. The principles that the grant of money should depend on the redress of grievances, and that the parliament should determine the destination of a grant by making conditions as to expenditure[2], were admitted by the royal advisers, although the king contrived to evade the concession. The right of electing the ministers, a premature and imperfect realisation of the

Grants should depend on redress, and supplies should be appropriated to special purposes.

[1] In 1223 the pope declared Henry III of age, 'quantum ad liberam dispositionem de castris et terris et gwardiis suis, non autem quoad hoc ut in placito posset ab aliquo communiri;' Ann. Dunst. p. 83. If the last word be read *conveniri* or *summoneri*, it is conclusive as to the fact that the king might be sued at law; and we thus have a passage proving the method in which he could be compelled to give redress before the form of petition of right was instituted. The statement of Chief Justice Wilby (Year Book, 24 Edw. III. fo. 55), that he had seen a writ 'Praecipe Henrico regi Angliae,' &c., would thus become more probable than it has been generally regarded. Bracton, however, writes so that we must suppose the practice to have been changed before his time; 'contra ipsum [regem] non habebitur remedium per assisam, immo tantum locus erit supplicationi ut factum suum corrigat et emendet, quod si non fecerit, sufficiat ei pro poena quod Dominum expectet ultorem . . . nisi sit qui dicat quod universitas regni et baronagium suum hoc facere debeat et possit in curia ipsius regis;' lib. iii. tract. i. c. 10. The passages quoted by Prynne, Plea for the Lords, p. 97, stating that the king might be *sued*, are scarcely relevant, for they belong to the year 1259, and are apparently misconstrued. See however Mr. Cutbill's pamphlet on Petition of Right (London, 1874), and Allen on the Prerogative, pp. 94 sq, 190, 191.

[2] Above, pp. 53, 54.

doctrine of a limited monarchy, was likewise demanded as authorised by ancient practice[1]. The right of controlling the king's action by a resident elective council also was asserted; but though Henry was constrained to accept these terms, he steadily refused to admit them as a matter of right and they were ultimately rejected with the acquiescence of the nation[2].

Right of electing ministers and council.

The early years of Edward I saw all the privileges which had been really used or acquired under Henry III fully exercised. The parliament of prelates and barons had been asked for, and had granted aids[3], had given counsel and consent to legislation, had acted as a supreme court of justice[4], and had discussed questions of foreign policy and internal administration[5]. The further steps gained by the constitutional assembly in this reign were gained by it in its new and complete organisation.

Rights exercised in the early years of Edward I.

Two drawbacks materially affected the value of these rights: the recognition of certain power on the king's part, to do by his own authority acts of the same class as those for which he asked counsel and consent; and the recognition of certain undefined rights of individual members to concede or refuse consent to the determinations of the whole body; the latter being seriously increased by the incompleteness of the national representation before the 23rd of Edward I.

Two drawbacks:—(1) The king's prerogative.

(2) The right of the individual.

221. Although the national council had made out its right to be heard on all four points of administrative policy, it had not obtained an exclusive right to determine that policy. The taxes might be granted in parliament, but the king could still take the customary aids without reference to parliament; he could tallage his demesnes and could interpret the title of demesne so as to bring the chartered towns, or a large portion of them, under contribution; he could increase the customs by separate negotiations with the merchants, and at any time raise money by gifts negotiated with individual payers, and assessed by the officers of the exchequer. The laws again were issued with counsel and consent of the parliament, but legal enactments might, as before,

(1) The parliament did not yet exclude the power of the crown to tax, and legislate.

[1] Above, pp. 41, 62, 63 sq.
[2] Above, pp. 53, 63, 77 sq.
[3] Above, pp. 109, 105, 121.
[4] Above, pp. 109.
[5] Above, pp. 123, 124.

Legislation by ordinance

in the shape of assizes or ordinances, be issued without any such assistance; and the theory of the enacting power of the king, as supreme legislator, grew rather than diminished during the period, probably in consequence of the legislative activity of Frederick II, Lewis IX, and Alfonso the Wise. The king's court, the curia regis, might be influenced and used to defeat the right of the barons to be judged by their peers, and there was not in the article of the charter anything that so fixed the method of such judgment as to make it necessary to transact it in full council; and the political action of the crown, in matters both foreign and domestic, could, as it always can, be determined without reference to anything but the royal will. Nor, as we shall see, was the failure of the national council to secure exclusive enjoyment of these rights owing to their own weakness: both Henry III and Edward I possessed in their personal inner council, a body of advisers organised so as to maintain the royal authority on these points, a council by whose advice they acted, judged, legislated, and taxed when they could, and the abuse of which was not yet prevented by any constitutional check. The opposition between the royal and the national councils, between the privy council and the parliament, is an important element in later national history.

Jurisdiction of the king's court.

The king's council.

(2) Difficulty arising from individual right to consent or dissent.

222. The second, however, of these points, the uncertainty of the line dividing corporate and individual consent, and the consequent difficulty of adjusting national action with incomplete representation, bears more directly on the subject before us. The first question has already arisen[1]: did the consent of a baron in council to grant a tax bind him individually only, or did it form part of such a general consent as would be held to bind those who refused consent? When Geoffrey of York, or Ranulf of Chester, refused to agree to a grant, was the refusal final or was it overborne by the consent of the majority? Did the baron who promised aid make a private promise or authorise a general tax? Was taxation the fulfilment of individual voluntary engagements or the legal result of a sovereign act?

[1] Vol. i. pp. 578, 579.

The unrepresented classes.

Secondly, how far could the consent, even if it were unanimous, of a national council composed of barons and superior clergy, bind the unrepresented classes, the commons, and the parochial clergy? The latter question is practically answered by the contrivances used to reconcile compulsion with equity. The writ of Edward I for the collection of the aid *pur fille marier* rehearses that it was granted in full parliament by certain bishops and barons, for themselves and for the community of the whole realm, so far as in them lay[1]. As a parliamentary assembly, legally summoned, they authorised a tax which would bind all tenants of the crown, but they did it with an express limitation, a conscious hesitation, and the king did not at the time venture to collect it. This was on the very eve of the contest for the confirmation of the charters. The documentary history of the reign of Henry III illustrates the difficulty at an earlier stage. In 1224 the prelates granted a carucage of half a mark on their demesne lands and those of their immediate tenants[2], and two shillings on the lands of the under tenants of those tenants: the feudal lord thus represented all who held directly or mediately under him. In 1232 the writ for collecting the fortieth states that it was granted by the archbishops, bishops, abbots, priors, clergy, earls, barons, knights, freeholders, and villeins[3], implying that not only the national council but the county courts had been dealt with: but in 1237 a similar writ rehearses the consent of the prelates, barons, knights and freeholders for themselves and their villeins[4]. Yet it is certain that in neither of the parliaments in which these taxes were granted were the villeins

Difficulty of reconciling theory with practice.

[1] Above, p. 121: Select Charters, p. 466.

[2] Above, p. 36, note 1.

[3] Select Charters, p. 351; 'Sciatis quod archiepiscopi, episcopi, abbates, priores, et clerici terras habentes quae ad ecclesias suas non pertinent, comites, barones, milites, liberi homines et villani de regno nostro concesserunt nobis,' &c.

[4] Select Charters, p. 357; 'Scias quod cum in octavis sancti Hilarii . . . ad mandatum nostrum convenirent apud Westmonasterium archiepiscopi, episcopi, abbates, priores, comites et barones totius regni nostri et tractatum haberent nobiscum de statu nostro et regni nostri, iidem archiepiscopi, episcopi, abbates, priores et clerici terras habentes quae ad ecclesias suas non pertinent, comites, barones, milites et liberi homines pro se et suis villanis, nobis concesserunt,' &c.

represented, and almost as certain that the commons were unrepresented also. The consent thus rehearsed must have been a simple fabrication, a legal fiction, on a theoretical view of parliament, or else the exacting process of the central assembly must have been supplemented by the consent of the county courts, in which alone, at the time, the liberi homines and villani assembled, that consent being either taken by the itinerant judges or presumed to follow on a proclamation by the sheriff. The expressions, however used, show a misgiving, and warrant the conclusion that the line between corporate and individual, general and local, consent was lightly drawn: the theory that the lord represented his vassal was too dangerous to be unreservedly admitted when all men were the king's vassals; the need of representation was felt. But the line continued uncertain until 1295; and even after that the variety of proportion in which the several estates taxed themselves shows that the distinction between a voluntary gift and an exacted tax was imperfectly realised.

Possible action of the county courts.

Refusal of individuals;

The idea that the refusal of an individual baron to grant the tax absolved him from the necessity of paying it, although now and then broached by a too powerful subject, could be easily overborne by force: ordinarily the king would seize the lands of the contumacious, and take by way of fine or ransom what could not be extracted by way of gift. The claim of a particular community to refuse a tax which had not been assented to by its own representatives, such as was claimed by Ghent in the sixteenth century, was based on the same idea, and would be overcome in the same way. Such a hypothesis, however, could only arise in a community which had not realised the nature of sovereign rights or of national identity. The refusal of an estate of the realm to submit to taxation imposed in an assembly at which it had not been represented, or to which its representatives had not been summoned, rested on a different basis. Such was the plea of the clergy in 1254[1], and it was recognised by the spirit of the constitution.

of communities;

of an estate of the realm.

[1] Above, pp. 67, 68, 197.

The practice had long been to take the consent of the communities by special commission. The year 1295 marks the date at which the special commissions, as a rule, cease, and the communities appear by their representatives to join in the act of the sovereign body. The process of transition belongs to the years 1282 to 1295, and the transition implies the admission of the commons to a share of taxing power, together with the clergy and the baronage.

Cessation of special commissions to raise money.

223. The dates may be more precisely marked. In 1282 the king's treasurer negotiated with the several shires and boroughs for a subsidy, just as might have been done under Henry II: the money so collected being insufficient, the king at Rhuddlan summoned the clergy and commons to two provincial councils, in one of which the commons granted a thirtieth on condition that the barons should do the same[1]. In 1289 a special negotiation was proposed, but not carried into effect[2]. In 1290 the barons granted an aid *pur fille marier*, the knights of the shire were subsequently summoned to join in a grant of a fifteenth, and the clergy in a separate assembly voted a tenth of spirituals; the boroughs probably and the city of London certainly paid the fifteenth without having been represented in the assembly that voted it, except as parts of the shires represented by the knights[3]. In 1294 the clergy in September granted a moiety of their entire revenue in a parliamentary assembly of the two provinces held at Westminster[4]; the earls, barons, and knights granted a tenth in November[5], and commissioners were sent out in the same month to request a sixth from the cities and boroughs[6]; the three estates, roughly divided, thus granting their money at different dates, in different proportions, and in different ways. In 1295 the special negotiation disappears; the three estates, although making their grants in different measure and by separate vote, are fully represented, and act in this, as in other respects, in the character of a consolidated parliament.

Chronological summary.

[1] Above, pp. 114, 115; Parl. Writs, i. 12.
[2] Above, p. 120.
[3] Above, pp. 121, 122. Cf. Brady, Boroughs, p. 27.
[4] Above, p. 126.
[5] Above, p. 127.
[6] Above, p. 127; Brady, Boroughs, pp. 31, 32.

The right to grant customs claimed by the parliament,

Nor was the recognition of this right of taxation confined to direct money grants. The impost on wool, woolfells and leather, has a similar history, although the steps of reform are different and the immediate burden fell not on an estate but on individual merchants. In 1275 we are told that the prelates, magnates, and communities, at the request of the merchants granted a custom on these commodities[1]: in 1294 a large increase of custom was imposed by the king's decree, rehearsing however the consent of the merchants[2], not that of the parliament. In the articles of 1297 the royal right of taxing wool was placed under the same restrictions as the right of direct taxation[3]; but the idea was still maintained that an increase of the impost might be legalised by the consent of the payers, and an attempt[4] to substitute the action of a 'colloquium' of merchants for that of the national parliament was defeated by the representatives of the boroughs in 1303.

and recognised in 1297.

The confirmation of charters in 1297 recognised on the king's part the exclusive right of the parliament to authorise taxation: 'for no occasion from henceforth will we take such manner of aids, tasks, or prises, but by the common assent of the realm and for the common profit thereof, saving the ancient aids and prises due and accustomed[5].' Already the right of the commons to a share in the taxing power of parliament was admitted.

Share of the estates in legislation.

224. The right of the three estates to share in legislation was established by a different process and on a different theory; it was a result rather than a cause of the recognition of their character as a supreme council. The consent of individuals

[1] Above, pp. 109, 192; Select Charters, p. 441; Parl. Writs, i. 2. Yet the language of the several writs on this subject is scarcely consistent; the earl of Pembroke describes the custom as granted by the archbishops, bishops, and other prelates, the earls, barons, and communities of the realm at the instance and request of the merchants; the king describes it as 'de communi assensu magnatum et voluntate mercatorum;' and as 'grante par touz les granz del realme e par la priere des communes de marchanz de tot Engleterre.'

[2] Above, p. 126, note 3; Hale, Concerning the Customs, p. 155; and ch. xvii. below.

[3] Above, p. 142; Select Charters, p. 485.

[4] Above, pp. 156, 192.

[5] Select Charters, pp. 485, 486. On this a good resumé will be found in Gneist, Verw. i. 393-396.

Different conditions of legislation and taxation.

was much less important in the enacting or improving of the law than in the payment of a tax; the power of counsel in the one case might fairly be supposed to belong to one of the three estates in larger proportion than to the others; and the enacting, if not also the initiative, power belonged to the king. The nation granted the tax, the king enacted the law: the nation might consent to the tax in various ways, severally by estates, communities, or individuals, or corporately in parliament; but the law was enacted once for all by the king with the advice and consent of parliament; it was no longer in the power of the individual, the community, or the estate to withhold its obedience with impunity. In very early times it is possible that the local assemblies were required to give assent to the legal changes made by the central authority, that a publication of the new law in the shiremoot was regarded as denoting the acceptance of it by the people in general, and that it would be contrary to natural equity to enforce a law which had not been so published[1]. But from the existing remains of legislation we are forced to conclude that whilst customary law was recorded in the memories of the people, legislative action belonged only to the wise, that is to the royal or national council. That council in the twelfth century contained only the magnates; at the end of the thirteenth it contained also the inferior clergy and the commons: the latter, fully competent as they were to discuss a tax, were not equally competent to frame a law; and such right of initiation as the right of petition involved could be set in motion outside as easily as inside parliament. Yet the right of the nation to determine by what laws it would be governed was fully admitted. Canute and the Conqueror had heard the people accept and swear to the laws of Edgar and Edward. The Great Charter and the Provisions of Oxford were promulgated in the county courts, and all men were bound by oath to obey them, as if without such acceptance they

Early cases of acceptance of legislation in local assemblies.

Legislation proper to the king's council;

but the right of the people admitted.

[1] See the passage quoted from Bracton, above, p. 237, where the 'consensus utentium' is reckoned with the oath of the king, among the authorisations of legislation. In France the royal ordinances had no force in the territories of the barons until approved by them; Ordonnances des Rois, i. 54, 93; Boutaric, Premiers États généraux, p. 4.

In the coronation oath, lacked somewhat of legal force. Bracton enumerates the 'consensus utentium' as well as the king's oath among the bases of law. It is to the conservation of the laws which the folk, vulgus, communauté, shall have chosen, that the later coronation oath binds the king. The enactment of Edward II in 1322, that matters to be established touching the estate of the king and his heirs, the realm and the people, shall be treated, accorded, and established in parliaments by the king and by the assent of the prelates, earls, and barons and the commonalty of the realm, is but an amplification of the principle laid down by his father in 1295.

Sidenote: and by the statute of 1322.

Sidenote: Legislation by baronial parliaments.

The legislation, however, of the reign of Henry III, and most of that of Edward I, was the work of assemblies to which the commons were not summoned. It has been well remarked that whereas for his political work Edward found himself obliged to obtain the cooperation of the three estates[1], his legislative work was done without the cooperation of the commons, until in the question of taxation they had enforced their right to be heard. By whatever process the consent of the 'communaulté' to the statute of Westminster the first was signified, and whatever were the force of the summons by virtue of which the 'communaulté' was supposed to be present, it is certain that in 1290 the statute 'quia emptores' was passed in a council at which no representatives of the commons attended, and as certain that the statute of Carlisle was published after deliberation not only with the magnates but with the 'communitates' of the realm[2]. The statute 'quia emptores' was not improbably the last case in which the assent of the commons was taken for granted in legislation: for in the later enactments by ordinance it is not the commons only but the parliament itself that is set aside; and although some few statutes made after 1290 do not declare expressly the participation of the three estates, it is possible, by comparing the dates of those acts with the extant

Sidenote: The statute of Quia Emptores.

[1] Shirley, Royal Letters, ii. pref. xxii.

[2] Above, p. 156. 'Dominus rex post deliberationem plenariam et tractatum cum comitibus, baronibus, proceribus et aliis nobilibus ac communitatibus regni sui, habitum in praemissis, de consensu eorum unanimi et concordi ordinavit et statuit;' Statutes, i. 152.

writs of summons, to show that all such acts as were really laws were enacted in full parliaments to which the words of the statute of Carlisle are equally applicable[1]. The commons had now a share of the 'commune consilium regni' which was indispensable to the abrogation or amendment of a law[2].

The statute of Carlisle.

225. But neither this conclusion nor even the principle stated by Edward II in 1322, implies the absolute equality of the share of each estate. Counsel and consent are ascribed to the magnates, but it is a long time before more is allowed generally to the commons than petition, instance, or request: and the right of petition the commons possessed even when not called together to parliament; the community of a county might declare a grievance, just as the grand jury presented a criminal. Further, so long as the enacting power was exercised by the king, with the counsel and consent of the magnates only, a statute might be founded on a petition of the clergy; and it may be questioned whether, according to the legal idea of Edward I, an act so initiated and authorised would not be a law without consent of the commons, just as an act framed on the petition of the commons would if agreed to by the magnates become law without consent of the clergy either in convocation or in parliament. The determination of this point belongs to the history of the following century. We conclude that, for the period before us, it would be true to say, that, although in theory legislation was the work of the king in full parliament,

The share of the several estates in legislation not necessarily an equal share.

Right of petition.

[1] 'Si quae statuta fuerint contraria dictis cartis vel alicui articulo in eisdem cartis contento, ea de communi consilio regni nostri modo debito emendentur vel etiam adnullentur.' Edward I. Feb. 14, 1301; Statutes (Charters), i. 44. See on these points Gneist, Verwalt. i. 399 sq.

[2] Yet some of the most important acts of parliament are dated several days after the writs were issued for the payment of the wages of the knights and burghers, e.g. in 1300 the Articuli Super Cartas are published April 15, the writs for wages are issued March 20; Foed. i. 920; Parl. Writs, i. 85; in 1301 the letters to the pope are dated Feb. 12: the writs, Jan. 30; in 1307 the writs for expenses are issued the very day the parliament met: not much can be argued however from this, for the final form which the law took would be settled at the end of the parliament; the representatives might leave as soon as the important business of petition and consultation was over. There could be no reason why they should stay until the charters were actually sealed or the copies of the statutes written out for circulation.

Imperfect definition of powers.

he exercised the power of legislating without a full parliament, and that in the full parliament itself the functions of the three estates were in this respect imperfectly defined. It is certain however, from the action of the king in reference to mortmain, that a statute passed with the counsel and consent of parliament, however constituted, could not be abrogated without the same counsel and consent[1].

The commons did not share the judicial power of parliament.

226. The third attribute of the old national council, that of a supreme tribunal of justice, for the trial of great offenders, and the determination of great causes, was never shared by the commons[2]. The nearest approach to such a participation was made when in 1283 they were summoned to Shrewsbury, on the trial of David of Wales: but they attended merely as witnesses; he was tried by the king's judges and only in the presence, not by a tribunal, of his peers. It is true that the abundant facilities which the system of jury gave for the trial of commoners by their peers superseded any necessity for criminal jurisdiction to be exercised by the assembly of the commons; but it is not quite so clear why the right of hearing appeals in civil cases was restricted to the lords, or why they should continue to form a council for the hearing of petitions to the king, when the commons did not join in their deliberations. This resulted however from the fact that the system of petition to the king in council had been perfected before the commons were called to parliament; and thus the whole subject of judicature belongs to the history of the royal council rather than to that of parliament strictly so called. But it is noteworthy in connexion with the fact that the estate which retained the judicial power of the national council retained also the special right of counsel and consent in legislation, these rights being a survival of the time when the magnates were the whole parliament; and on the other hand the smaller council which, as the king's special advisers, exercised judicial authority in Chancery, or in Privy Council and Starchamber, claimed also the right of legislating by ordinance.

[1] Above, p. 116.

[2] 'Les juggementz du parlement appertiegnent soulement au roy et as seigneurs, et nient as communes;' Rot. Parl. iii. 427.

227. The general deliberative functions of parliament, and the right of the representatives of the commons to share with the magnates in discussing foreign affairs or internal administration, scarcely come before us during this period with sufficient distinctness to enable us to mark any steps of progress. On the one hand the right of deliberation had been exercised by the great men long before the time of the Great Charter, and abundant evidence shows that they retained the right. The stories of the debate on the 'Quo Warranto' and the action of the earls in 1297 fully illustrate this. The action of the commons is distinctly traceable in the presentation of the Bill of twelve articles at the parliament of Lincoln in 1301; but their representatives had left before the barons drew up their letter to the pope[1]. Here again it is probable that the theory of the constitution was somewhat in advance of its actual progress. The principle declared by Edward I in 1295 would seem to touch this function of the national council more directly even than taxation or legislation; but in practice, as had been done long ago, silence was construed as assent and counsel taken for granted from the absent as well as the present.

Obscurity of delibera-tions on points of general policy.

228. The forms of the writs of summons furnish illustrations if not conclusive evidence on the general question. The special writs addressed to the magnates usually define their function in council by the word *tractare*. In 1205 the bishop of Salisbury is summoned to treat on the common interest of the realm[2]; in 1241 the bishops and barons are summoned *ad tractandum*[3]; in 1253 to hear the king's pleasure and to treat with his council[4]; in Simon de Montfort's writ for 1265 the

Illustration, from the forms of writ, of the share of the several es-tates in de-liberation.

[1] The proceedings of Edward in the parliament of Lincoln, as touching the papacy, may be compared with those taken by Philip the Fair in 1302 and 1303. The latter king, having in 1302 called together the states general, in which each estate remonstrated by letter with the pope, in 1303 called a council of barons, in which he appealed against the pope, obtaining a separate consent to the appeal, from the provincial estates of Languedoc, and from the several communities singly throughout the rest of France. See Boutaric, Premiers États généraux, pp. 12–15.

[2] Lords' Report, App. p. 1; Select Charters, p. 274; see Hallam, Middle Ages, iii. 36, 37.

[3] Lords' Report, App. p. 7.

[4] Lords' Report, App. p. 12.

Forms of writ, for magnates.

words are *tractaturi et consilium vestrum impensuri*[1]; to the first parliament of Edward I, the archbishop of Canterbury is invited *ad tractandum et ordinandum*[2]; to the parliament of Shrewsbury in 1283 the barons are summoned *nobiscum locuturi*[3]; in 1294 the king declares his wish to hold *colloquium et tractatum*[4]; in 1295 earls, barons, and prelates are summoned *ad tractandum, ordinandum et faciendum nobiscum et cum praelatis et caeteris proceribus et aliis incolis regni nostri*[5]; in 1297 the barons only, *colloquium et tractatum specialiter habituri vestrumque consilium impensuri*[6]; in 1298 the form is *tractatum et colloquium habituri*[7], and from 1299 generally *tractaturi vestrumque consilium impensuri*[8]. In this last formula we have the fullest statement of the powers which, on Edward's theory of government, were exercised by those constituents of the national council that had for the longest time been summoned: and these functions must be understood as being shared by the judges and other councillors who are summoned in almost exactly the same terms[9].

Writs for knights of the shire.

The writs ordering the return of representative knights run as follows; in 1213 John summons them *ad loquendum nobiscum de negotiis regni nostri*[10]; in 1254 the special purpose is expressed *ad providendum . . . quale auxilium . . . impendere velint*[11]; in 1261 the words are *colloquium habituros*[12]; in 1264 *nobiscum tractaturi*[13]; under Simon de Montfort in 1265 all the

[1] Lords' Report, App. p. 33; Select Charters, p. 406.
[2] Parl. Writs, i. p. 1; Lords' Report, App. p. 36.
[3] Parl. Writs, i. p. 15; Lords' Report, App. p. 49.
[4] Parl. Writs, i. p. 25; Lords' Report, App. p. 56.
[5] Parl. Writs, i. p. 31; Lords' Report, App. p. 67.
[6] Parl. Writs, i. p. 51; Lords' Report, App. p. 77.
[7] Parl. Writs, i. p. 65.
[8] Parl. Writs, i. p. 82; Lords' Report, App. p. 102.
[9] The differences are slight; the barons are summoned *in fide et homagio*, the prelates *in fide et dilectione*, the judges and councillors without any such adjuration. The barons and prelates are summoned 'quod . . . personaliter intersitis nobiscum ac cum ceteris praelatis, magnatibus et proceribus,' or 'magnatibus' simply; the judges and councillors 'ac cum ceteris de consilio nostro,' all alike 'tractaturi vestrumque in praemissis consilium impensuri.'
[10] Lords' Report, App. p. 2; Select Charters, p. 279.
[11] Lords' Report, App. p. 13; Select Charters, p. 367.
[12] Lords' Report, App. p. 23; Select Charters, p. 396.
[13] Foedera, i. 442; Select Charters. p. 403.

Form of *full powers.*

representatives are summoned in the same form as the magnates[1]; in 1282 the character of the full power which they receive from their constituencies is expressed, *ad audiendum et faciendum ea quae sibi ex parte nostra faciemus ostendi*[2]; in 1283 the words are *super hiis et aliis locuturi*[3]; in 1290 the full powers are described, *ad consulendum et consentiendum pro se et communitate illa hiis quae comites, barones et proceres praedicti tunc duxerint concordanda*[4]; in 1294 *ad consulendum et consentiendum*[5]; in 1295 both knights of the shire and representatives of the towns are to be chosen *ad faciendum quod tunc de communi consilio ordinabitur*[6]; and this form is retained until under Edward II the words *ad consentiendum* are added[7].

Form in the case of representatives generally.

General inference from these forms.

The variations of expression may safely be interpreted as showing some uncertainty as to the functions of the representatives, although as in the case of the barons, it may often merely show the difference of the occasion for which they were summoned. But it would be wrong to infer from the words in which their full representative powers were described that their functions were ever limited to mere consent to the resolutions of the magnates. Certainly this was not the case in questions of taxation, in which the several bodies deliberated and determined apart. The fact that the representative or delegate powers are so carefully described in the later writs shows the care taken, at the time of transition from taxation by local consent to taxation by general enactment, that no community should escape contribution by alleging the incomplete-

[1] Lords' Report, App. p. 33; Select Charters, p. 406.

[2] Parl. Writs, i. 10; Select Charters, p. 455.

[3] Parl. Writs, i. 16; Select Charters, p. 458.

[4] Parl. Writs, i. 21; Select Charters, p. 467.

[5] Parl. Writs, i. 26; Select Charters, p. 471.

[6] Parl. Writs, i. 29; Select Charters, p. 476. The summons to the parliament of Lincoln orders the representatives to be sent 'cum plena potestate audiendi et faciendi ea quae ibidem in praemissis ordinari contigerint pro communi commodo dicti regni;' Parl. Writs, i. 90.

[7] The form in which the third estate was called to the States general at Tours in 1308 is thus given by M. Boutaric, p. 18: 'Pour entendre, recevoir, approuver et faire tout ce qu'il serait commandé par le roi, sans exciper du recours a leurs commettants.'

ness of the powers with which it had invested its delegates; *ita quod pro defectu hujus potestatis negotium praedictum infectum non remaneat quoquo modo*[1]. The delegates had full procuratorial power both to advise and to execute. The fact however remains that, although the assembly was called for advice and cooperation, it was cooperation rather than advice that was expected from the commons: counsel is distinctly mentioned in the invitation to the magnates, action and consent in the invitation to representatives. Similar variations are to be found in the writs directing the parliamentary representation of the clergy; in 1295 the proctors as well as the prelates are summoned *ad tractandum, ordinandum et faciendum*[2]; in 1299 the form is *ad faciendum et consentiendum*[3]. Under Edward III *faciendum* is frequently omitted, and in the reign of Richard II their function is reduced to simple consent.

Relation of the commons to the lords.

No light as yet on the method of voting.

History has thrown no light, as yet, on the way in which the powers of the representatives, whether procuratorial or senatorial, were exercised; and when in the long political discussions of the fourteenth century some vestiges of personal independent action can be traced amongst the commons, it is difficult to see that the constitutional position of the representatives in their house differed at all from that of the peers in theirs. It is of course possible that some change for the better followed the division of parliament into two houses. In fact so long as the whole body sat together the discussion would be monopolised by those members who, by skill in business, greatness of personal position, or fluency in French or Latin, were accustomed to make themselves heard. Few of these would be found amongst the knights, citizens, and burghers. The obscurity of details does not stop here. No authentic record has yet been found of the way in which the general assent of the assembly was taken, or the result of a division ascertained. We might infer from the procuratorial character of the powers of the representatives, that on some questions, taxation in particular, the two members for each community would have only a joint vote. The so-called 'Modus

[1] See the Writs of 1294 and 1295.

[2] Parl. Writs, i.30.

[3] Parl. Writs, i. 83.

tenendi parliamentum' might be thought likely to illustrate this[1]. But that curious sketch of the parliamentary constitution, which may possibly have been drawn up in the reign of Edward III, contains, in so many places, statements that seem to describe an ideal of the writer rather than the existing condition of things, that it can nowhere be relied on as applicable to the machinery of parliament under the rule of Edward I.

The 'modus tenendi parliamentum' not to be trusted.

229. To this point then had the parliamentary constitution grown under the hand of this great king. The assembly definitely constituted in 1295,—at once a representation of the three estates and a concentration of the local institutions,—the clergy, the barons and the communities, associated for financial, legislative, and political action—achieved in 1297 the fullest recognition of its rights as representing the whole nation. It had come into existence by a growth peculiar to itself, although coinciding in time with the corresponding developments in other nations, and was destined to have a different history. Of this representative body the king was at once the hand and the head, and for foreign affairs the complete impersonation. He called together the assembly when and where he chose; the result of the deliberations was realised as his act; the laws became valid by his expressed consent, and were enforced under his commission and by his writ; his refusal stayed all proceedings whether legislative or executive. It was no part of the policy of Edward to diminish royal power and dignity; probably for every concession which patriotism or statesmanship led him to make, he retained a check by which the substance of power would be kept in the hand of a sovereign wise enough to use it rightly. The parliamentary constitution was by no means the whole of the English system: there still remained, in varying but not exhausted strength, by no means obsolete, the several institutions royal and popular, central and local, administrative and executive, out of which the parliamentary constitution itself

Relation of the events of 1295 to those of 1297;

and of the king to the new parliament.

Checks on the system.

[1] Select Charters, p. 501. There all the laity appear to vote together, and with equal votes; two knights, we are told, could outweigh one earl; and in the house of clergy two proctors could outvote a bishop. But nothing can be really inferred from this.

sprang, whose powers it concentrated and regulated but did not extinguish, and whose functions it exercised without superseding them. The general reforms in law, army and finance, which were completed by Edward I, bear the same mark of definiteness and completeness which he so clearly impressed on parliament; a mark which those departments continued to bear for at least two centuries and a half, and which in some respects they bear to the present day. The permanent and definite character thus impressed gave strength to the system, although it perhaps diminished its elasticity and in some points made the occasion for future difficulties.

Edward's character as a definer.

Continuity of the king's personal influence.

The high court of parliament had for one of its historical antecedents the ancient court and council of the king, which was as certainly the parent of the house of lords, as the shire system was of the house of commons. The king's court had in its judicial capacity been the germ of the whole higher judicial system of the country, as well as of the parliamentary and financial machinery. But so far from having lost strength by dividing and subdividing its functions, the magical circle that surrounded the king remained as much as ever a nucleus of strength and light. Such strength and light Edward was well able to appreciate; and in it he found his royal as contrasted with his constitutional position; in other words he organised the powers of his prerogative, the residuum of that royal omnipotence which, since the days of the Conquest, had been on all sides limited by the national growth and by the restrictions imposed by routine, law, policy, and patriotic statesmanship. The primitive constitution, local, popular, self-regulating, had received a new element from the organising power of the Normans. The royal central justice had come to remedy the evils of the popular law; the curia regis was a court of equity in relation to the common law of the county court. Now, the curia regis had incorporated itself with the common law system of the country, just as parliament had become a permanent institution. The royal chancery was now regarded as a resource for equitable remedy against the hardships of the courts of Westminster, as the courts of Westminster had been a remedy against the inequalities of the shiremoot. The vital and prolific power remained unimpaired, and side by side with the growth of the power of parliament, grew also the power of the crown exercised in and through the council[1].

Origin of the king's council.

230. The special circle of *sapientes*, councillors, and judges, to which Henry II reserved the decision of knotty cases of finance and law[2], was perhaps the first germ of the later council, as the little circle of household officers may have formed the nucleus of the Exchequer and the Curia Regis. But, beyond the short mention of it in the Gesta Henrici and the Dialogus de Scaccario, we have no traces of its action. Richard I had his staff of personal counsellors, his clerks and secretaries such as Philip of Poictiers, but they were rather a personal than a royal retinue, and as he was constantly absent from England his personal council had no constitutional status as apart from that of his justiciar. John however had a large body of advisers, many of them foreigners, who, except as his servants, could have had no legal position in the country, and for whom he obtained such a position by appointing them to definite offices, sheriffdoms and the like. But although it may fairly be granted that the king's private advisers had thus early gained definite recognition, and together with the officers of the household, court, and exchequer, may have been known as the royal council, it is to the minority of Henry III that the real importance of this body must be traced. Notwithstanding the indefiniteness of the word *concilium*, it is clear that there was then a staff of officers at work, not identical with the *commune consilium regni*. The *supernum* or *supremum concilium*[3], to which jointly with the king[4] letters and petitions are addressed,

The early council of Henry III.

[1] On the History of the Council, see Sir F. Palgrave's Essay on the King's Council, Dicey's Essay on the Privy Council, and Gneist, Verwalt. i. 352 sq. In the last of these the history of the council is given with too little regard to historical sequence or development, but the subject is one of exceedingly great difficulty.

[2] Vol. i. 603.

[3] 'Quoniam in praesentia domini legati et superni concilii domini regis estis;' F. de Breauté to Hubert de Burgh, Royal Letters, i. 5.

[4] Royal Letters, i. 37, 43.

The titles of the council.

clearly comprised the great men of the regency, William Marshall the *rector regis et regni*, Gualo the legate and Pandulf after him, Peter des Roches, the justiciar, chancellor, vice-chancellor and treasurer[1]. It is addressed as *nobile consilium*[2], *nobile et prudens consilium*[3]; its members are *majores* or *magnates de consilio*[4], *consiliarii* and *consiliatores*[5]. Its action during the minority is traceable in every department of work, and it worked in the king's name. It may indeed be inferred from the mention made in the treaty of Lambeth of the *consilium* of Lewis, that such a body was generally regarded as a part of the royal establishment, and the institution may have been borrowed from France, where in consequence of the dismemberment of the monarchy there was nothing answering to the *commune consilium regni*.

Its composition under Henry III.

But however this may have been, from the accession of Henry III a council comes into prominence which seems to contain the officers of state and of the household, the whole judicial staff, a number of bishops[6] and barons, and other members who in default of any other official qualification are simply counsellors; these formed a permanent, continual[7] or resident council, which might transact business from day to day, ready to hold special sessions for special business, to attend the king in parliament and act for him[8]; but the dis-

1 Royal Letters, i. 44; addressed to Henry, Pandulf, Peter des Roches, 'ceterisque consiliatoribus domini regis.' The archbishop of Dublin writes to Ralph Neville asking him to excuse him 'apud concilium domini regis;' ibid. 89.

2 Royal Letters, i. 94.

3 Royal Letters, i. 123.

4 Royal Letters, i. 60, 70; Foedera, i. 400.

5 Royal Letters, i. 13, 32, 44, 129, &c.

6 Letters of the pope allowing the bishops to be members of the council are in the Royal Letters, i. 549.

7 'Son continuel conseil;' Rot. Parl. iii. 16, 349; Nicolas, Proceedings of the Privy Council, i. p. 3. 'Familiare consilium,' M. Paris, p. 923; 'secretum concilium,' Hemingb. ii. 20.

8 The several sorts of business transacted before the council in the early years of Henry III are given by Sir T. Hardy from the Close Rolls, in his preface to the first volume; 'it had a direct jurisdiction over all the proceedings of the courts below, with the power of reversing any judgment of those courts founded in error;' 'whenever the council thought it expedient to have the advice and assistance of any particular persons, whether barons, bishops, or others, the chancellor by order of the council issued writs of summons to such persons, according to circumstances; and if any information was required, writs and commissions emanating from the council

tinguishing feature of which was its permanent employment in the business of the court. The historians now and then inform us of the addition and removal of members[1]. The foreign favourites of Henry acted as members of this council and provoked the hatred of the nation by their opposition to the king's constitutional advisers, whose functions they usurped and whose influence in the council they were sufficiently numerous to overpower.

Council under Henry III.

Among the many schemes of reform which we have seen brought forward between 1237, 1244[2], and 1258, were plans for imposing a constitutional oath on the counsellors, and for introducing special nominees of the baronage into the body; thus making the permanent council a sort of committee of the commune concilium; and, when in the provisionary schemes of 1258[3] and 1264 the royal power was in the hands of the barons, a regularly constituted council, of limited number

Plans for having an elective council.

were dispatched out of Chancery, and the inquisitions made by virtue of such writs being presented to the Council, instructions upon the matter at issue were thereupon delivered as the case required. Conventions, recognisances, bails, and agreements were also made before the Council. Oaths, vouchers, and protestations were also made before it. Orders for payments of money were issued from it. Judgment was given in matters tried before it upon petition. Persons were ordered to appear before the Council to show why they opposed the execution of the king's precepts; and so also persons aggrieved, to state their complaints; and the aggressors were commanded to appear and answer the charges preferred against them.' 'It was declared by the king that earls and barons should only be amerced before the Council,' &c.

[1] Thus friar Agnellus was a counsellor of Henry III in 1233; M. Paris, 391; the king called friar John of S. Giles to his council in 1239; ibid. 518; Simon the Norman and Geoffrey the Templar were expelled from the council; ibid. 519; Paulin Piper and John Mansell in 1244 were appointed by the king to be his principal counsellors; and Lawrence of S. Martin 'consiliorum regalium moderatorem; ibid. 616. William Perepound, an astrologer, was in the council in 1226; ibid. 331. In 1237 William, bishop elect of Valence, 'factus est consiliarius regis principalis, cum aliis undecim, qui super sacrosancta juraverunt quod fidele consilium regi praestarent; et ipse similiter juravit quod eorum consilio obediret;' Ann. Dunst. p. 146. In 1255 Sir John de Gray retired from the Council, M. Paris, p. 914; in 1256 John Darlington was called to it, ibid. 923; in 1257 Hurtaldus, a royal counsellor, special clerk, and treasurer of the king's chamber, died; ibid. 957. In 1253, the king wished the bishop of Salisbury to attend the council, 'et praebuit se difficilem propter quod ad praesens nolumus habere alios consiliarios quam ordinavimus,' Prynne, Reg. i. 390.

[2] Above, pp. 56, 63.

[3] Above, p. 77.

and definite qualifications, was appointed to attend and act for the king. The obscurity which hangs over the council during Henry's reign is not altogether dispelled in that of his son. Henry had retained a special council as long as he lived, and Edward's absence from England at his accession, left the power in the hands of his father's advisers. He seems thus to have accepted the institution of a council as a part of the general system of government, and, whatever had been the stages of its growth, to have given it definiteness and consistency. It is still uncertain whether the baronage generally were not, if they chose to attend, members ex officio, but it is quite clear that where no such qualification existed, members were qualified by oath and summons. We find among the writs of summons many addressed to these sworn councillors, the deans and clerks sworn of the council[3], and others; and we may fairly conclude that it now contained all the judges and officers of the household, although the former at least would not be able to keep continual residence. At any rate it was as members of the royal council that the judges were from the year 1295 summoned to the parliaments and great councils of the kingdom[4].

Council under Edward I,

Qualification of councillors, by oath.

[1] The Annals of Burton, p, 395, give the oath taken by the king's councillors in 1257; they bind themselves to give faithful counsel, to keep secrecy, to prevent alienation of ancient demesne, to procure justice for rich and poor, and to allow justice to be done on themselves and their friends, to abstain from gifts and misuse of patronage and influence, and to be faithful to the queen and to the heir. The oath taken under Edward I is in the Foedera, i. 1009. It contains twelve articles, the last of which is to be sworn by the judges also: these are to give, expedite, and execute faithful counsel; to maintain, recover, increase, and prevent the diminution of, royal rights; to do justice, honestly and unsparingly, and to join in no engagements which may prevent the counsellor from fulfilling his promise; and lastly, to take no gifts in the administration of justice, save meat and drink for the day. See also Parl. Writs, II. ii. 3.

[2] Thus on the day after Henry's death the great seal was delivered to the archbishop of York and R. Aguillun 'et caeteris consiliariis domini regis in praesentia eorundem consiliariorum;' Foed. i. 497.

[3] Select Charters, p. 474. See the oath taken by the bishop of London, 'quem rex vult esse de consilio regis,' in 1307; Foed. i. 1009.

[4] 'For ages past the members of the concilium ordinarium who are not also members of Parliament have been reduced to the humble station of assistants to the House of Lords.' Edinb. Rev. xxxv. 15. On this subject see Prynne's Register, i. pp. 341 sq. 361 sq. He argues that as they are not uniformly summoned, as they are not mentioned in the writs to the magnates, but apparently summoned at the will of the king, and simply

Although a large proportion of its members, would, as earls, barons, and bishops, be members of the *commune concilium*, the judges and special counsellors, who owed their place there simply to the royal summons, or to royal nomination independent of feudal or prescriptive right, were not necessarily parts of that constitutional body; and the *commune concilium*, after it had taken its ultimate form and incorporated representative members, contained a very large number who were not members of the permanent council. Nor were the relations of the two bodies to the king of the same sort; he acted with the counsel and consent of the commune concilium, but in and through the permanent council; the functions of the latter were primarily executive, and it derived such legislative, political, taxative and judicial authority as it had from the person of the king, although many of its members would have a constitutional share of those powers as bishops and barons. Thus the permanent council might claim a share in those branches of administration which emanated directly from the king rather than in those which emanated from the subject; in legislation and judicature rather than in constitutional taxation. In the latter department each member of the council would either as a baron tax himself personally, or as a commoner tax himself through his representative. Hence the mere counsellor would not as such have a voice in taxation; and hence probably arose the custom of regarding the judges and other summoned counsellors as rather assistants than members of the parliament or great council; and thus perhaps the judges and the lawyers with them lost their chance of becoming a fourth estate.

Place of the council and its members in parliament.

It would be dangerous to decide by conjecture on a point which has been discussed with so much learning and with such discordant views by many generations of lawyers, when the terms used are in themselves ambiguous and at different periods mean very different things. The fact that the word council implies both an organised body of advisers, and the assembly in which

Variety of opinions on the council.

as counsellors, cum caeteris de consilio nostro, and as they could not appear by proxy, they are assistants only, not essential members of the parliament. See Gneist, Verwalt. i. 389.

General conclusions as to the character of the king's council.

that organised body meets; that it means several differently organised bodies, and the several occasions of their meeting; that those several bodies have themselves different organisations in different reigns although retaining a corporate identity; and that they have frequently been discussed by writers who have been unable to agree on a common vocabulary or proper definitions, has loaded the subject with difficulty. We may however generalise thus: (1) there was a permanent council attendant on the king, and advising him in all his sovereign acts, composed of bishops, barons, judges and others, all sworn as counsellors; and this council sitting in terminal courts assisted the king in hearing suits and receiving petitions. (2) In the parliaments of the three estates from the year 1295 onwards, the judges and other legal members of this permanent body, who did not possess the rights of baronage, were summoned to advise the king. (3) In conjunction with the rest of the prelates and baronage, and excluding the commons and the minor clergy, the permanent council acted sometimes under the title of *magnum concilium*; and this name was, occasionally, given to assemblies in which the council and the Estates met, which are only distinguishable in small technical points from proper parliaments. Many of the assemblies of the reign of Henry III, the constitutions of which we have regarded as steps towards the realisation of the idea of parliament, may be regarded, in the light reflected from the fourteenth century, as examples of the *magnum concilium*; but in point of fact the *magnum concilium* under Edward II and Edward III was only a form of the general national assembly which had survived for certain purposes, when for other practical uses of administration it had been superseded by the parliament of the three estates as framed by Edward I. The privy council, from the reign of Richard II onwards, although it inherited and amplified the functions of the permanent council of Edward I, differed widely in its organisation, and the steps by which the difference grew must be discussed later on.

The *Magnum Concilium*.

The Privy Council.

The name of parliament, the king's parliament, belonged to the sessions of each of the three bodies thus distinguished, the terminal session of the select council, the session of the great council, and the session of the commune concilium of the three estates[1]. The historians distinguish between general and special parliaments, the former[2] being the full assembly of the *commune concilium* in the completeness recognised at the moment; the latter the royal session for the dispatch of business[3]. In the Rolls of Parliament the confusion of name and distinction of functions are still more conspicuous, for most of the early documents preserved under that name belong to the sessions of the council for judicial business, held, as the Provisions of Oxford had ordered, at fixed times of the year, and resembling in idea, if not in fact, the crown-wearing days of the Norman kings[4].

General and special parliaments.

Confusion of name.

Whilst the constitutional reforms of Edward I were gradually taking their final shape, it is not surprising that some confusion should arise between the functions of the king's council and those of the national council. In both we find the king legislating, judging, deliberating, and taxing, or attempting to tax. If in the one he enacted laws and in the other issued ordinances, if in the one he asked for an aid and in the other imposed a tallage or negotiated the concession of a custom, the ordinance and the statute differed little in application, the voluntary contribution and the arbitrary tallage were demanded with equal cogency from the taxpayer. Some few facts, if not rules or principles may, notwithstanding the rapid changes of the times, be determined, but in general it may be affirmed that for all business, whether it were such as could be done by the king alone, or such as required the co-operation of the nation, the action of the smaller circle of advisers was continually employed. The most important points, however, are those connected with judicature and legislation.

The king acts both in Council and in Parliament.

231. The petitions, addressed to the king or to the king

I. Petitions.

[1] See above, p. 213, note; Prynne, Reg. i. 397.

[2] 'Magnum parliamentum;' Ann. Winton. p. 119; Ann. Waverl. p. 390. 'Parliament general'; Stat. Westm. i; Select Charters, p. 440. The writs for the first parliament of 1275 call it a 'generale parliamentum;' Parl. Writs, i. 1.

[3] 'Singulare non generale tenuit parliamentum;' Ann. Osney, p. 299.

Petitions in council.

and his council, which are preserved in the early rolls of parliament, furnished abundant work to the permanent council, and the special parliaments were probably the solemn occasions on which they were presented and discussed. These stated sessions[1] were held by Edward I at Hilarytide, Easter, and Michaelmas, or at other times by adjournment. At them were heard also the great placita, or suits which, arising between great men or in unprecedented cases, required the judgment of the king himself; and the general parliaments, which were of course much less frequent, were for the sake of convenience and economy usually called at times when the council was in session; a fact which has increased the difficulty of distinguishing the acts of the two bodies. The placita on these occasions were either relegated to small bodies of auditors who reported their opinion to the council, or were heard in the full council itself. Of the former sort were the suits between the abbot of S. Augustine and the barons of Sandwich in 1280, and between the men of Yarmouth and the Cinque Ports in 1290, in which a small number of councillors were assigned as auditors[2]; of the latter was the claim of Gilbert of Clare to the castle and town of Bristol[3], and the king's demand of a sentence against Llewelyn, at Michaelmas, 1276[4], both of which were heard and decided in full council, composed of magnates, justices, and others, whose names are recorded. The hearing of petitions was much more laborious work, and required more minute regulation. In the eighth year of Edward I it was ordered that all petitions should be examined by the judges of the court to which the matter in

Placita in council.

Committees of council.

Hearing of Petitions.

[1] The provisions of Oxford ordered three parliaments in the year, October 7, February 2, and June 1; Select Charters, pp. 381, 383. Edward I is said to have held four, at Christmas, Hilarytide, Easter, and Michaelmas; Lords' Report, i. 169; but these were not by any means regular. They frequently were held on the octaves of the festivals, and thus the Christmas Court would run on into the Hilarytide Council.

[2] Parl. Writs, i. 8, 19, 20; B. Cotton, p. 175.

[3] Parl. Writs, i. 6; two foreigners, Francesco Accursi and the bishop of Verdun were present, besides the magnates, 'plurimorum magnatum terrae in pleno consilio regis.' The list comprises the archbishop of Canterbury, four bishops, three earls, eleven barons, seventeen judges and clerks, Francesco Accursi, and G. de Haspal.

[4] Parl. Writs, i. 5.

question properly belonged, so that only important questions should be brought before the king and council, especially such as were matters of grace and favour which could not be answered without reference to the king[1]. A further order of the twenty-first year provided that these petitions should be divided by the persons assigned to receive them, into five bundles, containing severally the documents to be referred to the Chancery, the Exchequer, the judges, the king and council, and those which had been already answered, so that matters referred to the king himself might be laid before him before he proceeded to transact business[2]. For the hearing as well as the reception of these petitions provision was made in the parliament, or by the king before the parliament opened; and from the records of 1305 we find that they were now presented in the full parliament of the estates[3], for in that year Edward named special commissions of judges and barons to receive the petitions touching Scotland, Gascony, Ireland, and the Channel Islands. Those which could not be answered without reference to the king formed a special branch of business[4], and it was

Arrangement and answering of petitions, in Parliament.

[1] 'Pur ceo ke la gent ke venent al parlement le Roy sunt sovent deslaez et desturbez a grant grevance de eus e de la curt par la multitudine des peticions ke sunt botez devant le Rey, de queus le plus porroient estre espleytez par Chanceler e par justices, purveu est ke tutes les peticions ke tuchent le sel veynent primes al chanceler, e ceus ke tuchent le Escheker veynent al Escheker, e ceus ke tuchent justices u ley de terre veinent a justices, e ceus ke tuchent Juerie veynent a justices de la Juerie. Et si les bosoigns seent si grantz u si de grace ke le chanceler e ces autres ne le pussent fere sanz le rey, dunk il les porterunt par lur meins demeine devant le rey pur saver ent sa volente; ensi qe nule peticion ne veigne devaunt le roy e son conseil fors par les mains des avauntditz chaunceller e les autres chef ministres; ensi ke le rey e sun consail pussent sanz charge de autre busoignes entendre a grosses busoignes de sun reaume e de ses foreines terres;' Rot. Claus. 8 Edward I, m. 6, dorso; Ryley, Pleadings, &c., p. 442.

[2] 'Le roy voet et ordeine qe totes les petycions qe de si en avant serrunt liveres as parlemens a ceaus qil assignera a recevoir les, qe totes les peticions seient tot a primer, apres ce qe eles serrunt receves, bien examinees; et qe celes qe touchent la Chancelerie seient mises en un lyaz severaument, e les autres qe touchent le Escheker en autre liaz; et ausi seit fet de celes qe touchent les justices; et puis celes qe serront devant le rey e son consail severaument en autre liaz; et ausi celes qe aver ont este respondues devant en several liaz; et ensi seient les choses reportees devant le rey devant ceo qe il les comence a deliverer;' Rot. Claus. 21 Edward I, m. 7; Ryley, Pleadings, p. 459.

[3] Parl. Writs, i. 155; Ryley, p. 508.

[4] See Hardy's Preface to the Close Rolls, i. p. xxviii.

Receivers and triers of petitions.

from the share taken by the Chancellor in examining and reporting on the bills of grace and favour that his equitable jurisdiction in the fourteenth century grew up. The nomination of receivers and triers became a part of the opening business of every parliament, and the ultimate division of the work, in the reign of Richard II, was into three portions, one for the king, one for the council, and one for the parliament itself.

II. Share of the king's council in legislation.

232. Edward I, in the preamble of several of his statutes, some of which were distinctly the result of deliberation in the general parliament, mentions the participation of the council as well as that of the assembled estates. The first statute of Westminster was enacted by the king *par son conseil*, and by the assent of the magnates and community[1]: the statute *de religiosis* is made *de consilio praelatorum comitum et aliorum fidelium regni nostri de consilio nostro existentium*[2]; the statute of Acton Burnell is an enactment by the king, *par luy e par sun conseil a sun parlement*[3]. In such cases it seems impossible to understand by the *conseil* merely the advice of the persons who are afterwards said to have consented. In other cases, however, the king enacts, or ordains by his council, when the action of parliament is altogether unnoticed. The statute of Rageman is 'accorded by the king and by his council[4];' the statute 'de Bigamis' rehearses the names of a sort of committee of councillors, in whose presence the draught of it was read before it was confirmed by the king and the entire council[5]. It would seem certain from this that the king in his council made ordinances[6], as by the advice of his council he enacted laws with consent of parliament. All Edward's legislation may be received as of

[1] Statutes, i. 26. [2] Ibid. i. 51. [3] Ibid. i. 53, 54. [4] Ibid. i. 44.

[5] Statutes, i. 42. This statute gives the names of the councillors, of whom Francesco Accursi was one; it was approved by 'omnes de consilio, justitiarii et alii;' the councillors named are two bishops, one dean, three archdeacons, five magistri, and nine others, who were employed at various times as itinerant justices and in like offices. The constitution is said to be made in parliament after Michaelmas, 1276; the assembly that gave sentence against Llewelyn, and decided the cause of the earl of Gloucester, mentioned above, p. 262.

[6] The statute 'de falsa moneta,' Statutes, i. 131, is quoted in the Wardrobe accounts as 'ordinatio facta per ipsum regem et consilium suum in parliamento tento apud Stebenhethe'; p. 5.

full and equal authority, but we have to look forward to days in which the distinction between statute and ordinance will be closely scrutinised.

Comparison with the institutions of France under Philip the Fair.

For this part of Edward's system a parallel may be sought in the practice of the French court under Philip the Fair. The parliament of Paris may be generally compared with the special judicial session or parliament of the council[1]. The somewhat later bed of justice, in which the king, with his court of peers and prelates, officers and judges, solemnly attested the decisions or the legislation put in form by parliament, loosely resembles the magnum concilium; and the States General answer to the parliament of the three estates. How far Edward I adopted from French usage the form of legal council which he seems to have definitely established, and the practice of giving to its legal members a place in parliament, and how far Philip the Fair borrowed from England the idea of the States General, need not be discussed, for it cannot be determined on existing evidence. But the parallel, superficial as it may be, marks out the end of the reign of Edward in England and the period of Philip the Fair in France, as the point at which the two constitutions approximated more nearly than at any other in the middle ages. The divergences which followed arose not merely from the absolutist innovations in France, but from the working of more ancient causes, which had for the moment drawn together to develop stronger differences hereafter. In England the several bodies maintained more or less a right of co-operating in each branch of administration; in France the states general, although in the first instance called for the purpose of political deliberation, were soon limited to the subject of taxation and declaration of grievances, and lost their political weight with their deliberative power; whilst the judicial work, and the duty of registering rather than of joining in legislation, fell to the parliament of Paris. In England the jurisdiction of the House of Lords was co-ordinate with that of the council; the legislative power of the parliament did not exclude the ordaining power

[1] One of the best illustrations of this analogy is the Statute de Bigamis; see above, p. 264. [2] Compare Boutaric, les Premiers États généraux, p. 3.

of the council; the council acted exclusively in all political matters on which the parliament deliberated, and if in taxation the sole authorising body was the assembly of the three estates in parliament, the exclusion of the king's right of tallaging, and of the action of his ministers in obtaining loans and benevolences, was not completely secured until a comparatively late period.

Edward's changes in the judicial system.

233. The judicial machinery of the kingdom received during the period before us, and finally under Edward I, the form which with a few changes it still retains; the measures by which this was done may be briefly enumerated here, although from henceforth they cease to have any special bearing on our main subject. The evolution of the several courts of supreme judicature from the personal jurisdiction of the king, first in the Curia Regis and Exchequer, we have already examined. We have traced to the arrangements made by Henry II in 1178 for the constant session of a limited number of judges in the Curia, the probable origin of the King's Bench as a distinct tribunal, and we have seen, in the 17th article of Magna Carta, the Common Pleas separated from the other suits that came before this court. At the beginning of the reign of Henry III the three courts are distinguished; first, as to the class of causes entertained, the Exchequer hearing cases touching the king's revenue; the Court of Common Pleas the private suits of subjects; and the King's Bench, under the head of *placita coram rege*, all other suits, whether heard before the king, or before the justiciar, or the limited staff of judges. They are distinguished, further, as to the place of session, the Common Pleas being fixed at Westminster, the other two following the king, although the Exchequer, in its proper character, was as a rule held at Westminster. The justiciar, however, was still the head of the whole system, and the body of judges was not yet divided into three distinct benches or colleges, each exclusively devoted to one branch. This final step is understood to have been taken shortly before the end of the reign of Henry III, but no legislative act has been found on which it was based, and

Division of the courts:

under Henry III.

[1] On this see Gneist, Verwalt. i. 317-320 sq.; 337-352.

it may have been originally a mere voluntary regulation adopted for convenience. The multiplication of suits, the increasing spirit of litigation, and the great development of legal ingenuity at this period, will account for the growth of distinct systems of rules, forms of pleading, and the like, in the three courts. The increasing difficulty of administering justice under three forms, by the same judges, would cause the gradual apportioning of particular individuals to particular courts; and as the office of great justiciar, after the fall of Hubert de Burgh, lost its importance, and may be said to have become practically extinct, the tendency to division was strengthened by the acephalous condition of the courts. This was remedied by the appointment of a head or capital member to each body. From the beginning of the reign of Edward I we find a series of Chief Justices of Common Pleas [1], as well as of the King's Bench, and from the middle of the next reign a regular succession of Chief Barons of the Exchequer. The tendency to specialisation was, however, somewhat neutralised by the exertions of the professional lawyers to attract business into the courts in which they practised. In 1282 the king had to prohibit the treasurer and barons of the Exchequer from hearing common pleas, as contrary to the custom of the kingdom, except in cases which touched the king or the ministers of the Exchequer [2]. This custom was embodied in a statute in 1300; and although the pertinacity of the lawyers contrived to evade it by the means of fictitious pleadings, it served to show the king's intention of completely defining the business of the tribunals. The same process is traceable in the division of the petitions presented to the king and council in 1280 and 1293, those referred to the justices being separated from those referred to the Exchequer [3]. The common law jurisdiction of the Chancellor was perhaps

Further separation.

Extinction of the justiciarship.

Three chief judges.

Coordinate jurisdictions.

[1] See Foss's Tabulae Curiales. In 1278, at Gloucester, the king in council re-nominated a chief justice and two others, 'Justitiae de Banco ad placita regis;' a chief and four others, 'justitiae de Banco Westmonasterii;' six justices in eyre for the north, and six for the south; with fixed sums, 'nomine feodi ad sustentationem,' varying from sixty to forty marks. Parl. Writs, i. 382.

[2] Foedera, i. 618.

[3] Above, p. 263.

The Chancellor as judge.

comprehended in the same scheme of specialisation: in 1280, after Epiphany, the king went to hunt in the New Forest, but the Chancellor returned to London as to a certain place where all who sought writs, and were prosecuting their rights, might find a ready remedy [1]. But if this were so, the plan was found impracticable for the present; Edward could not do without his Chancellor, who accompanied him in his long visit to France; and in the Articuli super Cartas the clause which forbade the hearing of Common Pleas in the Exchequer, directed that the King's Bench and the Chancery should still follow the king's person; implying further that the Exchequer, which in 1277 had been taken to Shrewsbury, and in 1299 to York [2], should remain at Westminster.

Equitable jurisdiction of the Chancellor.

234. The origin of the equitable jurisdiction of the Chancellor is connected directly with the history of the king's council. The Chancellor had long been, as a baron of the Exchequer and as a leading member of the Curia, in possession of judicial functions. To him, as well as to the justices of the land and the Exchequer, the ordinance of 1280 referred a distinct class of petitions. But as yet the king was the chief judge in equity, or 'matters of grace and favour.' And 'matters which were so great, or of grace, that the Chancellor and others could not dispatch them without the king,' were ordered to be brought before the king, and except by the hands of the Chancellor and other chief ministers, no petition was to come before the king and his council. At this period, then, the Chancellor, although employed in equity, had ministerial functions only [3]. When early

[1] Ann. Waverl. p. 393.

[2] In 1210 the Exchequer was taken to Northampton, Madox, p. 131; in 1266 the Exchequer and King's Bench were at S. Paul's; Lib. de Antt. Legg. p. 84; in 1277 the Exchequer and in 1282 the Bench went to Shrewsbury; in 1290 the Exchequer was held at the Hustings in London; in 1299, both Exchequer and Bench went to York. See Madox, Hist. Exch. pp. 552, 553; Ryley's Pleadings, p. 225; Parl. Writs, i. 86; Ann. Winton, p. 124; Ann. Dunst. p. 278.

[3] Neither Glanvill, the Mirror, Bracton, Briton, Fleta, nor the 'Diversité des Courtes,' ever allude to the Chancery as a court of Equity; Hardy, Close Rolls, i. pref. p. xxiii. Yet the distinction was recognised between law and equity as early as the time of Glanvill, and was inherent in the double character of the judicature; and Fleta (ii. 13) mentions the hearing of petitions as one of the principal duties of the chancellor and his

in the reign of Edward III the Chancellor ceased to be a part of the king's personal retinue and to follow the court, his tribunal acquired a more distinct and substantive character, as those of the other courts had done under the like circumstances; petitions for grace and favour began to be addressed primarily to him, instead of being simply referred to him by the king, or passed on through his hands. In the 22nd year of that king such transactions are recognised as the proper province of the Chancellor[1], and from that time his separate and independent equitable jurisdiction began to grow into the possession of that powerful and complicated machinery which belongs to later history. Since the fall of the great justiciar, the Chancellor was in dignity, as well as in power and influence, second to the king. Robert Burnell was the first great chancellor, as Hubert de Burgh was the last great justiciar.

The chancellor ceases to follow the king.

Court of chancery.

235. The provincial jurisdiction exercised by itinerant justices, has a conspicuous place among the institutions reformed by Edward I, and contributes an important element to the social and political history of his father's reign also. The 18th article of the Charter of John directed that for the purpose of taking assizes of mort d'ancestor, novel disseisin, and darrein presentment, two justices should visit each county four times a year. This regulation was confirmed in the Charter of 1216, but materially altered by that of 1217[3] which placed the assize of darrein presentment under the view of the justices of the bench and directed the other two to be taken only once a year. These itinerant justices were however properly justices for these

Edward's reforms in itinerant judicature.

clerks, 'quorum officium sit supplicationes et querelas conquerentium audire et examinare, et eis super qualitatibus injuriarum ostensarum debitum remedium exhibere per brevia regis.'

[1] 'Quia circa diversa negotia nos et statum regni nostri Angliae concernentia sumus indies multipliciter occupati, volumus quod quilibet negotia tam communem legem regni nostri Angliae quam gratiam nostram specialem concernentia penes nosmet ipsos habens ex nunc prosequenda, eadem negotia, videlicet negotia ad communem legem penes venerabilem virum electum Cantuariensem confirmatum cancellarium nostrum per ipsum expedienda, et alia negotia de gratia nostra concedenda penes eundem cancellarium seu dilectum clericum nostrum custodem sigilli nostri privati, prosequantur;' Rot. Claus. 38 Edw. III; Hardy, Close Rolls, i. pref. xxviii.

[2] Select Charters, p. 283. [3] Ibid. p. 336.

Earlier itinerant justices.

assizes merely; and their sessions do not appear to have taken the place or have superseded the necessity of the more important visitations for the purpose of gaol delivery and amercements which had been continued since 1166. These visitations seem to have been held at irregular intervals and under special articles of instruction; some of the justices being, as Bracton tells us, commissioned to hear all sorts of pleas [1], and some restricted to particular classes of causes. Throughout the reign of Henry III these courts are found everywhere in great activity, their judicial work being still combined with financial work, the amercement of shires and hundreds, of contumacious and negligent suitors, and the raising of money from the communities not represented in the *commune concilium.* Their exertions in one form or another brought a large revenue to the crown, and whilst they enabled Henry to resist the reasonable demands for reform, they turned a measure which had been both welcome and beneficial into a means of oppression. Hence both the barons and the people generally looked on them with great jealousy. The petition that led to the Provisions of Oxford contains complaints of mal-administration and extortion [2]: the monastic annalists register long details of expensive litigation, and under the protection of their great neighbours the stronger towns refused to receive the itinerant judges unconditionally. In 1261 Worcester declined to admit them on the ground that seven years had not elapsed since the last visit [3], and Hereford did the same, pleading that their proceedings were contrary to the Provisions of Oxford [4]. That constitution however contained no regulation as to a septennial eyre, and the annals of Dunstable, Worcester, Winchester, and Waverley, furnish abundant evidence that the visitations were much more frequent. No fixed rule can be inferred from these notices, and it is most probable that the irregular system of earlier times was continued. If this be so, Edward I has the credit of reducing to definite rules the characteristic procedure of his great-grandfather, when he substituted regular visitations of judges of

Eyres under Henry III.

Unpopularity of these courts.

Frequency of their sessions.

[1] Bracton, Lib. iii. tr. i. c. 11.
[2] See articles 13, 14.
[3] Ann. Wigorn. p. 446.
[4] Cont. M. Paris, p. 990.

assize, for the irregular circuits of the justices itinerant. The first measure of the reign, taken by his ministers before his arrival, was to stop the work of the itinerant justices[1]. In his fourth year by the statute of Rageman[2] he ordered a general visitation for hearing complaints of trespass and offences against statutes committed during the last twenty-five years; but this seems to have been no more than a proceeding under special commission. The newer system is referred by the legal historians to the 30th article of the second statute of Westminster, A.D. 1285[3]; by which two sworn justices are to be assigned, before whom, in conjunction with one or two knights of the shire, all assizes of mort d'ancestor, novel disseisin and attaints, are to be taken, thrice a year, in July, September, and January. From the form of writ ordering the trial of questions of fact before the justices at Westminster, unless the sworn justices hold their visitation before a fixed day, these latter received the name of justices of Nisi Prius. The statute 21 Edward I, divided the kingdom into four circuits, each of which had two justices assigned to it[4]: these were to take the assizes as before, but without a restriction of terms, and were to be on duty throughout the year. By a further act of the 27th year, the justices of assize were ordered to act as justices of gaol delivery[5]; and thus obtained all the judicial authority which had belonged to their predecessors, although special commissions for criminal cases, such as that of the justices of Trailbaston appointed in 1305[6], were now and then appointed. The system of division of business, now established in the courts of Westminster, so far affected the provincial jurisdiction, that it was necessary to provide that assizes and inquests might be taken before any one judge of the court in which the plea was brought and one knight of the shire[7]; and it was not until the 14th of Edward III that inquests of nisi prius were allowed to be heard by the justices of Nisi Prius, altogether irrespective of

Statute of Rageman.

Institution of justices of *nisi prius*,

and circuits of assizes;

of gaol delivery.

Modifications.

[1] Ann. Winton. p. 113.
[2] Statutes of the Realm, i. 44; in 1278 two bodies of six itinerant judges were appointed by the king and council; Parl. Writs, i. 382.
[3] Statutes, i. 86.
[4] Statutes, i. 112.
[5] Statutes, i. 129.
[6] Parl. Writs, i. 408.
[7] Statutes, i. 130.

Various commissions of judges.

the court to which the justices belonged[1]. The commission of oyer and terminer dates from the 2nd of Edward III[2]; and the commission of the peace completed the five several authorities possessed by the judges on circuit.

Conservation of the peace.

236. Intermediate between the provincial administration of the supreme courts and the ancient local administration of shire and hundred come the offices connected with the maintenance of peace and police, derived from the higher source, and co-ordinate with the justitiary, as distinct from the popular, jurisdiction of the sheriff. Knights assigned to enforce the oath of peace and the hue and cry, appear as early as the year 1195[3].

Knights assigned.

Their designation as *assigned* seems to prove that they were royal nominees and not elected officers, but their early history is obscure. To this class may be referred also the appointment by Henry III in 1230, of three[4], and in 1252 of two, knights assigned in each county to enforce the assize of arms[5], and the nomination of constables of hundreds and townships, to secure the conservation of the peace. In 1264 a single 'custos

Custodes pacis.

pacis' was assigned in each shire to conserve the peace and possibly to watch, possibly to supersede, the sheriff, but with instructions not to interfere with his functions so as to diminish the revenue[6]. In the 5th of Edward I, it appears that this *custos pacis* had become an elective officer, chosen by the sheriff and the community of the county, in the county court and under the instructions of the king conveyed by the sheriff[7]. We are not however able to discover whether the office was a permanent or an occasional one. In 1282 the earl of Cornwall was assigned by the king to conserve the peace in Middlesex and

[1] Statutes, i. 286.
[2] Statutes, i. 258.
[3] Select Charters, p. 256; see vol. i. p. 507.
[4] Royal Letters, i. 371 sq. This is probably the first institution of the office of constable in the township and hundred.
[5] Select Charters, pp. 362, 366.
[6] Select Charters, p. 403. 'Nolumus autem quod praetextu hujus mandati nostri de aliquibus quae ad officium vicecomitis pertinent, vos intromittatis quominus vicecomes de exitibus ejusdem comitatus nobis plene respondere valeat;' Lambarde, Eirenarcha, p. 19.
[7] 'Cum vicecomes noster Norfolk, et communitas ejusdem comitatus elegerit vos in custodem pacis nostrae ibidem,' &c. Rot. Pat. 5; Edw. I. Lambarde, Eirenarcha, p. 17.

several other counties, with power to appoint deputies [1]. After the passing of the statute of Winchester, the office of conservator of the peace, whose work was to carry out the provisions of that enactment, was filled by election in the shiremoot [2]. The act of the 1st Edward III, c. 16 [3], which orders the appointment, in each county, of good men and loyal to guard the peace, connects itself more naturally with the statute of Winchester and through it with the *milites assignati* of Henry III and Richard I, than with the chosen *custodes* of Edward I. These nominated conservators, two or three in number, were commissioned by the 18th Edward III, stat. 2, c. 2 [4], to hear and determine felonies, and by 34 Edward III, c. 1 [5], were regularly empowered to do so. The office thus became a permanent part of the county machinery in the hands of the Justices of the Peace.

Conservators of the peace.

Justices of the peace.

The changes and improvements in the general judicial system inevitably tended to diminish the consequence of the ancient popular courts, withdrawing from them the more important suits and allowing the absence of the more important members. The changes which affected the position of the sheriff have been already noted. It is to the thirteenth century that the ancient machinery of the county court and hundred court owes its final form. The second charter of Henry III determines the times of meeting: the shiremoot is henceforth to be held from month to month; the sheriff's tourn twice a year, after Easter and after Michaelmas; and view of frankpledge is to be taken at the Michaelmas tourn [6]. By a supplementary edict in 1234 Henry allowed the courts of the hundred, the wapentake, and the franchises of the magnates to be held every three weeks, and excused the attendance of all but those who were bound to special service, or who were concerned in suits [7]. These courts,

Courts of the shire and hundred.

Times of meeting.

[1] Parl. Writs, i. 384.
[2] See above, p. 210. Probably the conservators were in the first instance appointed by the crown; the vacancies being filled by election; see Parl. Writs, i. 389–391. An enumeration of the duties of these officers may be found in the Commissions issued by Edward II, Parl. Writs, II. ii. 8, 11, 12.
[3] Statutes, i. 257.
[4] Statutes, i. 301.
[5] Statutes, i. 364.
[6] Select Charters, p. 337.
[7] Ann. Dunst. pp. 140, 141; Royal Letters, i. 450; Brady, Hist. vol. i. App. p. 254.

Continuity of the popular courts.

the continuance of which is based, according to this edict, on the fact that under Henry II they were held every fortnight, are thus shown to be still substantially the same as in Anglo-Saxon times, when the shiremoot was held twice a year and the hundred-moot once a month. The statute of Merton allowed all freemen to appear by attorney in the local courts; the attendance of the magnates of the county at the sheriff's tourn was dispensed with by the Provisions of Westminster in 1259 and by the Statute of Marlborough in 1267[1].

The manorial courts.

The smaller manorial courts gradually adopted the improvements of the larger and popular courts, but great diversities of custom still prevailed, and the distinction between court leet and court baron, the jurisdiction derived from royal grant and that inherent in the lordship, whether derived from the original grant or from the absorption of the township jurisdiction, becomes more prominent. How much of the organisation which characterised these courts, and of which we have abundant illustration in the court rolls of every manor, was devised by the ingenuity of lawyers, and how much is of primitive origin, it would be hard to say. The whole jurisprudence of these courts rests on custom and is rarely touched by statute: custom is capable of much elaboration and modification; its antiquity can only be shown by record or by generalising from a large number of particulars. On the whole, however, the structure of these courts bears, as we have seen[2], so many marks of antiquity, that we may fairly suppose the later lawyers to have merely systematised rules which they found prevailing. The increased importance of the minuter local franchises, as sources of revenue to the lords, after the passing of the statute Quia Emptores, will account for the large increase of local records. The Court Rolls of manors generally begin in the reign of Edward I; the necessity of keeping a formal record would have the effect of giving regularity and fixed formality to the proceedings.

Court rolls.

Regulation of juries.

The regulations for juries occupy a prominent place among the minuter acts of Edward's legislation. The determination

[1] Above, p. 206. [2] Vol. i. pp. 88, 89, 399, 606.

of the qualification of a juror, which had no doubt some bearing in the later question of the electoral suffrage, belongs to this reign. In 1285, for the relief of the poorer suitors who felt the burden of attendance at the courts very heavily, it was ordained that a reasonable number of jurors only should be summoned, and that none should be put on assizes within their own shire who could not spend twenty shillings a year, or out of their shire who could not spend forty [1]. In 1293 the qualification for the former was raised to forty shillings, and for the latter to a hundred; saving however the customs observed in boroughs and before the itinerant justices [2].

Qualification of jurors.

Every branch of judicature thus received consistency, consolidation and definition under the hands of Edward and his ministers.

237. The disappearance of the great justiciar, which left the Chancellor at the head of the royal council and broke into three the general body of judges, had its results in the Exchequer also. There the treasurer stepped into the place of the justiciar, and became, from the middle of the reign of Henry III, one of the chief officers of the crown [3]. In the same reign was created the office of Chancellor of the Exchequer, to whom the Exchequer seal was entrusted, and who with the Treasurer [4] took part in the equitable jurisdiction of the Exchequer, although not in the common law jurisdiction of the barons which extended itself as the legal fictions of pleading brought common pleas into this court [5]. But the financial business of the Exchequer underwent other great modifications. The official work of that great department was broken up into sections. Large branches of expenditure were reckoned among

Changes in the exchequer.

Treasurer and chancellor of the exchequer.

Jurisdiction in common pleas and equity.

[1] Statutes, i. 86, 89. There is an order to remove ignorant jurors in a particular case, and substitute nearer neighbours and better informed men, in the Close Rolls of Henry III, vol. ii. p. 124.

[2] Statutes, i. 113.

[3] Madox, Hist. Exch. p. 564; the title of the Treasurer is sometimes Treasurer of the Exchequer, sometimes the king's Treasurer; in 1307 Walter Langton is called Treasurer of England; ibid. p. 579.

[4] Thomas, Hist. Exch. pp. 94, 95. Blackstone, Comm. iii. 44.

[5] John Mansel is regarded by Madox as filling this office in the 18th of Henry III; but the first person who is known to have borne the title is Ralph of Leicester, in the 32nd year; Madox, Hist. Exch. pp. 580, 581.

Changes in the financial work of the exchequer.

the private accounts of the king kept in the Wardrobe[1]. The grants of money in parliament, the fifteenths, thirtieths and the like were collected by special justices and no longer accounted for by the sheriffs or recorded in the Great Rolls of the Pipe[2]. The constant complaints which were made in the reigns of Edward III and Richard II of the difficulty of auditing the national accounts, show that the real value of the old system of administration was much impaired. In fact the king's household accounts were no longer the national accounts, and yet the machinery for managing the two was not definitely separated. Edward II paid his father's debts to the amount of £118,000. The debts of Edward II were not paid late in the reign of his son[3]. The banishment of the Jews, the employment of foreign merchants to farm the revenues, the alterations in the methods of taxation, and the varying use of gold, bills of exchange, and raw material as a circulating medium for international transactions, furnished an amount of work to which the old machinery was unequal, and which accounts for some of the embarrassments which the following century, ignorant of the principles of political economy, failed to overcome. Of the details of taxation as a part of the financial work enough has been already said.

Decline in the fiscal system.

Military system in the thirteenth century.

238. In the development of military organisation the thirteenth century is not less fertile than it is in other respects[4], nor is the defining and distinctive policy of Edward I less con-

[1] The receipts at the Wardrobe begin as early as 1223; Rot. Claus. i. 628; Madox, p. 184. A Wardrobe account of 1282-1285 is printed as an Appendix to Ellis's John of Oxenedes; it contains the expenses of the Welsh war, amounting to £102,621 0s. 4*d.*; pp. 308, 311. The whole wardrobe account of 1299-1300, accounting for expenses to the amount of £64,105, was published by the Society of Antiquaries in 1787; other accounts of the same kind are printed in the Archæologia, vols. 15, 16, 17, 28, 31.

[2] Thus the fifteenth raised in 1225 was assessed and collected under the superintendence of justices assigned, and called 'justitiarii quintae decimae;' and audited by the bishop of Carlisle, Michael Belet and William de Castellis; Rot. Claus. ii. 40, 45, 71, 95; Foedera, i. 177.

[3] Archbishop Islip (1349-1366) writes to Edward III: 'utinam . . . scires debita tua et debita patris tui et intelligeres, id est, pericula animae tuae et periculum animae patris tui propter debita multimoda creditoribus non soluta . . . sed Deus propitietur animae ejus . . . forte filius tuus pro te non solvet;' MS. Bodl. 624.

[4] On this see Gneist, Verwalt. i. 313-317.

spicuous. Henry III, it is true, engaged in no such great war as demanded any concentration of the national strength. The attempt made by John to hold the kingdom by a mercenary force was not repeated under his son, although during the struggle with the barons it was opportunity rather than will that was lacking, and England was in danger of being invaded by a foreign army under the queen and the refugees after the battle of Lewes. The impossibility of maintaining a force of mercenaries precluded the existence of a standing army; the loss of the foreign dominions of the crown took away the pretext which Henry II or Richard might have alleged; the small territory left to the king in the south of France was the only field for his warlike energies or military skill. Henry III, then, so far as he had need of an army, and Edward I after him, could only use and develop the materials already in existence, that is, the feudal service which was due from the tenants-in-chief, and the national militia organised by Henry II under the assize of arms [1]. The military measures of these two reigns have, however, considerable interest, both in analogy with other branches of the royal policy and in their permanent effects on our military history. The armed force of the nation was divided by the same lines of separation which divided it in matters of land tenure, judicature, council, and finance. It was the fixed and persistent policy of the kings, fully developed under Edward I, to unite the whole people for administrative purposes, whether by eliminating the feudal distinctions or by utilising them for the general objects of government; that, as the parliament should be the whole nation in council, and the revenue the joint contributions of the several estates, the national defence and its power for aggressive warfare should be concentrated, simplified, and defined; and thus the host should be again the whole nation in arms. Such a consummation would be perfect only when the king could demand immediately, and on the same plea, the services of all classes of his subjects; but the doctrine of feudal obligation was nowhere so strong as in the matter of military service, and Edward's design, so far as it failed to

Mercenaries abandoned.

Divisions of the national force.

Edward I tries to get rid of the feudal influence in military affairs.

[1] Vol. i. pp. 587–592.

His policy somewhat premature.

eliminate the importance of tenure from this branch of the national system, remained imperfect. It may be questioned, however, whether, with existing materials, he could have entirely dispensed with the feudal machinery, and whether the wars of the next century and a half were not needed to prove its weakness and to supply a substitute in the form of a regular military system.

(1) Military levy of the feudal body.

The military levy of the feudal tenants-in-chief presents a close analogy with the assembly of the *commune concilium* as described in Magna Carta. The great barons were summoned by special writ to appear on a certain day, prepared with their due number of knights, with horses and arms, to go on the king's service for a certain time, according to the king's orders[1]. At the same time the sheriff of each county had a writ directing

Action of the sheriff.

him to warn all the tenants-in-chief of his bailiwick to obey the general summons to the same effect; under the general term tenants-in-chief were included not only the minor tenants, but the archbishops, bishops, abbots, earls, barons, and knights who had also received the special summons, the double warning being intended no doubt to secure the complete representation of the outlying estates of the baronage. But the chief business of the sheriff in this department would be to collect and see to the

Nature of the summons.

proper equipment of the minor tenants in chivalry. When the summons was issued for a purpose which fell within the exact terms of feudal obligation, as understood at the time, the vassals were enjoined 'in fide qua nobis tenemini,' or 'sub debito fidelitatis,' or 'sicut ipsum regem et honorem suum diligunt necnon et terras et tenementa quae de rege tenent,' or finally, 'in fide et

Term of service.

homagio et dilectione.' If the service demanded were likely to be prolonged beyond the customary period of forty days, or were in any other way exceptional, the summons took a less

Service of courtesy.

imperative form; thus in 1277 Edward I uses the words 'affectuose rogamus' in requesting the barons to continue their service against the Welsh, and engages that no prejudice should accrue to them by reason of their courtesy in complying[2]: and

[1] Countless examples of these summonses will be found, for the reign of Henry III and onwards, in the Appendix to the Lords' Report on the Dignity of a Peer; and for the reigns of Edward I and Edward II, in Palgrave's Parliamentary Writs.

[2] Parl. Writs, i. 213.

we have already seen how in 1297 the use of this form was made by the constable and marshall an excuse for disobeying the royal order[1]. In such cases letters of thanks were issued at the close of the campaign[2], with a promise that such compliance should not be construed as a precedent. For expeditions on which it was unnecessary to bring up the whole force of the tenants-in-chief, the king sometimes orders a definite quota to be furnished by each, in proportion to his obligation; thus in 1234 Henry de Trubleville is ordered to attend 'te quinto militum[3],' that is, with four other knights, and Walter de Godarville 'te altero,' that is, with one. This plan was perhaps identical with the muster of a third or fourth part of the usual service, of which there are instances under Henry II and Richard[4]. We have already noticed the fact that the number of tenants who were specially summoned to the army was much larger than that of the barons so summoned to the council; and it is by no means improbable that the force so specially summoned constituted the largest part, if not the whole, of the available feudal army, many of the minor tenants being poor men, willing to serve under the greater lords, and certainly requiring the utmost pressure before they would undertake the expenses and other liabilities of knighthood.

Letters of thanks.

Service by a quota.

Great number of tenants in chief.

From the statement contained in the writ of summons as to the purpose of the armament we gather a somewhat indistinct idea of the limits of feudal obligation. John, in 1205,

[1] Above, p. 135. Still more urgent language is used in 1302; Parl. Writs, i. 366: 'mandamus in fide et homagio . . . quod sitis ad nos . . . cum toto servitio quod nobis debetis . . . et, ut fidelitatis vestrae constantia sibi famae laudem adaugeat, vos requirimus quatinus praeter servitium vestrum sic armatorum suffulti potentia pro communi praefati regni utilitate . . . veniatis.'

[2] Parl. Writs, i. 196; 'cum milites et alii de communitate comitatus Sallopiae curialitatem et subsidium de equis et armis et alio posse suo, non ratione alicujus servitii nobis ad praesens debiti, sed sponte et graciose . . . fecerint . . . concedimus . . . quod occasione hujusmodi curialitatis et subsidii hac vice nobis gratiose facti . . . nichil novi juris nobis vel heredibus nostris accrescere, nec eidem communitati aliquid decrescere possit,' &c., cf. pp. 252.

[3] Lords' Report, App. pp. 6, 7.

[4] Vol. i. pp. 589, 590.

Extent of service required.

summons his barons 'ad movendum inde cum corpore nostro et standum nobiscum ad minus per duas quadragesimas[1];' in 1213, 'ad eundum nobiscum[2];' and in 1215, 'ad transfretandum cum corpore nostro[3],' the destination being Gascony. Notwithstanding the refusal of the baronage to undertake service in Gascony as a duty of their tenure, Henry III continued his father's policy in this point, not only by summoning the tenants-in-chief to cross the seas with him, but in one instance, at least, by ordering them to join the Count of Brittany and to serve under his orders[4]. Edward I then, both in 1294 and 1297, had precedents for demanding foreign service from the barons, although the language in which he, at least in 1297, couched the request, showed that he had misgivings which were warranted by the result. This last case, however, opened a still wider question.

Foreign service demanded of the feudal force.

(II) Military service due as a matter of allegiance.

The second branch of the national force comprehended all those who were bound, not by homage but by allegiance, to attend the king in arms; in other words, the whole population capable of providing and wearing arms, who were embodied under the assize of arms, and in strict connexion with the shire administration. The measures taken for the efficiency of this force were very numerous. Henry III, in 1230 and 1252, issued stringent edicts for the purpose[5], and in 1285 Edward I still further improved the system by the statute of Winchester[6]. In these acts the maintenance of the 'jurati ad arma' is closely connected with the conservation of the peace, according to the idea that this force was primarily a weapon of defence, not of aggression. But as the Welsh and Scottish wars had in a great measure the character of defensive warfare, the service of the national militia, the qualified fighting men of the counties, was called into requisition; and in great emergencies Henry III and Edward I conceived themselves justified in using them as William Rufus had done, for foreign warfare. In 1255 Henry,

Assize of arms.

Foreign service demanded.

[1] Lords' Report, App. p. 1.
[2] Lords' Report, App. p. 1.
[3] Lords' Report, App. p. 2.
[4] Lords' Report, App. pp. 5, 7.
[5] Royal Letters, i. 371; Select Charters, p. 362.
[6] Statutes, i. 96–98; Select Charters, p. 459.

in the general summons to the sheriffs for his expedition to Scotland, includes not only the tenants-in-chief, but other vavassours and knights who do not hold of the king in chief, and who are to attend 'as they love the king and their own honour, and as they wish to earn his grace and favour[1].' In this writ we have an early indication of the policy which tended, by the creation of a knightly class not necessarily composed of tenants-in-chief, to raise a counterpoise to the over-weight of feudal tenure in matters of military service. And we are thus enabled to explain the frequent orders for the distraint of knighthood as arising from something above and besides the mere desire of extorting money.

Distraint of knighthood.

239. The distraint of knighthood was both in its origin and in its effects a link between the two branches of the national force. The tenure of twenty librates of land by knight service properly involved the acceptance of knighthood; the assize of arms made the possession of arms obligatory on every one according to his wealth in land or chattels. Whoever possessed twenty librates of land, of whomsoever he held it or by whatsoever tenure, might on analogy be fairly required to undertake the responsibility of a knight. The measures for the enforcement of this duty began early in the reign of Henry III. In 1224 the king ordered the sheriffs to compel all laymen of full age who held a knight's fee or more, to get themselves knighted[2]: it may be doubted whether this applied to mesne tenants, for in 1234 the same order is given with reference to tenants-in-chief only[3]; but probably it was intended to be universal. The chroniclers under the year 1254 tell us that all who held land of ten or fifteen pounds annual value, were ordered to receive knighthood, but in this case there is possibly some confusion

[1] Foed. i. 326; 'Mandatum est singulis vicecomitibus Angliae, quod cum omni festinatione clamari faciant publice per totam balliam suam quod omnes illi qui de rege tenent in capite et servitium ei debent, quod omni dilatione et occasione postpositis, veniant ad regem cum equis et armis et toto posse suo, profecturi cum eo ad partes Scotiae, sicut ipsum regem et honorem suum necnon et terras et tenementa quae de rege tenent diligunt; et alios vavasores et milites qui de rege non tenent in capite, similiter veniant cum equis et armis, sicut ipsum regem et honorem suum diligunt, et gratiam et favorem regis perpetuum promereri voluerint.'

[2] Rot. Claus. ii. 69.

[3] Royal Letters, i. 456.

Distraint of knighthood.

between the acceptance of knighthood and the provision of a full equipment [1]. In 1274 inquiry is made into the abuse, by the sheriffs and others, of the power of compelling knighthood [2]; in 1278 Edward imposes the obligation on all who possess the requisite estate, of whomsoever held, and whether in chivalry or not [3]; in 1285 owners of less than £100 per annum are excused [4]; in 1292 all holding £40 a year in fee are to be distrained [5]. In some cases the knighthood is waived and the military service alone demanded; thus in 1282 owners of £20 annual value are ordered to provide themselves with horses and arms, and to appear in the provincial councils at York and Northampton [6]: in 1297 the same class are called on for military service together with the barons [7]. There can be no doubt that this practice was one of the influences which blended the minor tenants-in-chief with the general body of the freeholders; possibly it led also to the development of the military spirit which in the following century sustained the extravagant designs of Edward III and was glorified under the name of chivalry.

Infantry force.

240. The barons, knights, and freeholders liable to knighthood furnished the cavalry of Edward's armies, and were arranged for active service under bannerets, attended by a small number of knights and squires or *scutiferi* [8]. The less wealthy men of the shires and towns, sworn under the assize, furnished the

[1] 'Qui redditus (sc. uniuscujusque libere tenentis) si decem librarum constiterit, gladio cingatur militari et una cum magnatibus Angliae Londoniam citra clausum Paschae veniant prompti et parati cum dictis magnatibus transfretare;' Ann. Theokesb. p. 154. The summons however mentions only freeholders of £20 value, and does not specify knighthood; Select Charters, p. 367. In 1256, Matthew Paris and Bartholomew Cotton repeat the story 'ut quilibet qui haberet xv libratas terrae et supra cingulo militiae donaretur,' the latter adding 'vel per annum unam marcam auri regi numeraret;' M. Paris, p. 926, 935; B. Cotton, p. 136; Joh. Oxenedes, p. 187. The fines under Edward I varied in amount; Parl. Writs, i. 221.

[2] Foedera, i. 517.

[3] Select Charters, p. 446; Parl. Writs, i. 214, 219; Foed. i. 567; 'de quocunque teneant.'

[4] Foed. i. 653; Parl. Writs, i. 249.

[5] Foed. i. 758; Parl. Writs, i. 258.

[6] Parl. Writs, i. 10; Select Charters, p. 455.

[7] Parl. Writs, i. 285 sq.; Foedera, i. 864.

[8] The banneret received 3*s*., the knights 2*s*., and the squire 12*d*. a day, in 1300; Wardrobe Accounts, p. 195. This was in time of war; in peace the bannerets and knights received a fee of ten or five marks in lieu of wages; ib. p. 188.

infantry, the archers, the machinists, the carpenters, the miners, the ditchers and other workmen[1]. Of these the men at arms, according to their substance, provided their own equipment, from the fully armed owner of fifteen librates who appeared with his hauberk, helmet, sword, dagger, and horse, to the owner of less than forty shillingsworth of chattels, who could provide only a bow and arrows. These were under the regular inspection of the sheriffs and knights assigned to examine into their efficiency, and the force would if assembled in arms have included the whole adult male population. Such a levy was never even formally called for; it would have been quite unmanageable, would have robbed the land of its cultivators, and left the country undefended except at headquarters. In 1205[2] and again in 1213[3], when John was in dread of invasion, he ordered that all men should on the rumour of the enemy's landing assemble to resist him, on pain of forfeiture and perpetual slavery. Henry III in 1220, in 1224, and again in 1267, called up the posse comitatus of the neighbouring counties only, for the sieges of Rockingham, Bedford, and Kenilworth[4]. In 1264 when Simon de Montfort found it necessary to make the utmost efforts to repel the invasion threatened by the queen, he called out a proportion only of this force; eight, six, or four men from each township armed at the discretion of the sheriff and provided with forty days' provision at the expense of the community that furnished them[5]. And this plan was followed in less pressing emergencies. Thus in 1231 the sheriff of Gloucestershire was ordered to send two hundred men with axes, furnished with forty days' provision at the expense of the men of the shire who were sworn to provide small arms, and at the same time to send to the king's camp all the carpenters of the county[6].

Equipment of the ordinary men at arms.

Only a portion of this force ever actually employed.

[1] Copiatores, Parl. Writs, i. 252; fossatores, ibid.

[2] Rot. Pat. i. 55; Select Charters, p. 273.

[3] Foed. i. 110.

[4] Royal Letters, i. 56; Rot. Claus. i. 639; Foed. i. 467. In 1224 the posse comitatus of Devon was called up to watch or besiege Plympton castle; the knights of the county 'responderunt unanimiter se nec posse nec debere hujusmodi custodiam facere cum domini sui sint in exercitu vestro, quibus sua debent servitia.'

[5] Foed. i. 437.

[6] Foed, i. 200; Select Charters, p. 350.

Commissions of array.

241. Under Edward I this arrangement was extended, and developed by means of Commissions of array. In 1282, on the 30th of July, he commissioned William le Butiller of Warrington to 'elect,' that is to press or pick a thousand men in Lancashire; on the 6th of December[1] writing from Rhuddlan, and at several other dates during the same winter, he informed the counties that he had commissioned certain of his servants to choose a fixed number of able-bodied men and to bring them to head-quarters to serve on foot: the commission for Nottingham and Derby fixes 300, that for Stafford and Salop 1000, that for Lancashire 200, that for Hereford and the Marches 2360. In 1294 the commissioners are not limited to fixed numbers[2]. In 1295 the counties of Hants, Dorset, and Wilts are ordered to provide 3000 archers and balistarii to man the fleet[3]; in 1297 large commissions are issued for the collection of Welshmen and men of the marches to join in the expedition to Gascony[4]. Under Edward I the forces raised in this way were paid by the king; very large levies were thus made in 1297 and onwards to serve *ad vadia nostra*[5]. These and the county force generally were placed under the superintendence of a *capitaneus*[6] or *cheve-*

The king was paymaster of force raised by these commissions.

[1] Parl. Writs, i. 228, 245 sq.

[2] Parl. Writs, i. 266.

[3] Parl. Writs, i. 270; at the same time Surrey and Sussex are ordered to find 4000, Essex and Herts 4000, Norfolk, Suffolk, Cambridge and Hants 8000, Kent 4000, Oxon and Berks 2000.

[4] Parl. Writs, i. 295, 296. Wales had furnished soldiers to Henry II, whose mercenaries are called by Ralph de Diceto, Marchiones, as well as Walenses. In the commissions to raise a force in 1297 Edward instructs the commissioners to explain the business to the Welsh, 'en la plus amiable manere e la plus curteise que vous saverez!' a mild form certainly of impressment. Ibid. 283.

[5] Parl. Writs, i. 224.

[6] See Parl. Writs, i. 193, 222, &c. These *capitanei* appear first in the Marches; in 1276 Roger Mortimer was made captain for Salop, Stafford, and Hereford, and William Beauchamp for Chester and Lancashire; and similar commissions were issued in 1282. In 1287 the earl of Gloucester was made 'capitaneus expeditionis regis in partibus de Brecknock'; Parl. Writs, i. 252: Edmund Mortimer and the earl of Hereford in Cardiganshire, ibid. p. 254. In 1296 Robert de la Ferete and William of Carlisle are named *capitanei et custodes pacis* for Cumberland, ibid. 278; in 1297, *capitanei munitionis* are appointed in Northumberland and Cumberland, ibid. 294; also 'capitanei custodiae partium Marchiae,' ibid. 301. At last in 1298 officers are generally appointed as 'Cheveteignes des gentz d'Armes;' William Latimer being named 'notre lieutenant e soverein cheventeine de vous e tutes les gentz de armes a cheval e a pie' for the northern counties, with a captain under him in each; ibid. p. 319. In 1315 Edward II allowed the Yorkshire and northern *lieges* to choose their own custodes et capitanei; ibid. II. i. 435.

teigne in each shire, who must have been the prototype of the later lord-lieutenant. The abuse of the system which threw the expense of additional arms and maintenance on the townships and counties began under Edward II, although down to his last year his writs make arrangement for the payment of wages. The second statute of 1 Edward III, c. 5, was directed to the limitation of the power of compelling military service; and after a series of strong complaints by the commons, who were greatly aggrieved by the burden of maintaining the force so raised, it was enacted in 1349 that no man should be constrained to find men at arms, hobblers, or archers, other than those who held by such services, if it be not by the common assent and grant made in parliament. The maritime counties however even under Edward I were liable for the charges of defending the coast, and found the wages of the coast guard.

Abuse of the system.

Restriction of commissions of array under Edward III.

242. The arrangement and classification of the last-mentioned force furnishes a good illustration of the internal organisation of the army generally[1]. The coast guard of each county was under the command of a knight as 'major custos,' constable, or chief warden; under him was an 'eques supervisor' who managed the force of one, two, three, or more hundreds, with a 'vintenarius' and a 'decenarius' under him. The wages of the custos were two shillings a day, those of the supervisor sixpence, the two inferior officers each threepence, and each footman twopence. The general force of infantry and archers was arranged in bodies of a hundred, each under a mounted constable or *centenarius*, and sub-divided into twenties, each under a *vintenarius*: the constable had a shilling, the vintenarius fourpence, and the common soldier twopence a day[2]. The final arrangement of the men was the work of the king's constable, who claimed twopence in the pound on the wages of stipendiaries[3]. It would only be when assembled for local defence that the infantry could retain their local organisation.

Internal arrangement of the army.

Wages of infantry and archers.

The military action of the general population, who were not

[1] See Parl. Writs, i. 268, 272, 274 sq.; Foed. i. 826.

[2] Wardrobe Accounts, p. 241; Parl. Writs, II. i. 472. The payments varied; cf. p. 710.

[3] Foed. i. 615.

bound by tenure to serve in the field, sometimes wears the appearance of volunteer service, and as such is rewarded, like the extra service of the feudal tenantry, with the king's thanks. In 1277 Edward wrote to thank the county of Shropshire for their courtesy in furnishing aid to which they were not bound by tenure, and such cases were not uncommon on the border, where military zeal and skill were quickened by the instinct of self-preservation [1].

Voluntary service.

Employment of the whole force in 1297.

The great exigency of 1297 furnishes a complete illustration of the use of all these means of military defence and aggression: on the 5th of May [2] the king ordered all the freeholders of the kingdom possessing £20 a year in land, whether holding of the king in chief or of other lords, to provide themselves with horse and arms to accompany him in defence of the kingdom whenever he should ask it. Ten days later [3] he called on the sheriffs to ask, require, and firmly enjoin upon the persons before described, to meet him at London prepared to cross the sea with him in person to the honour of God and themselves for the salvation and common benefit of the realm: the same day he ordered all ecclesiastics and widows holding in chief to furnish their due service [4]; and further addressed to the earls and barons the letter of earnest request which furnished the marshall and constable with the ground of excuse when the crisis came. On the 24th of May he wrote to the sheriffs requiring a list of the freeholders and knights who were generally included in the summons of the 15th [5]. On the 16th of September the prince of Wales issued commissions for the selection in each county of knights and valetti to be retained in his service during his father's absence with a special view towards defence against the Scots [6]; on the 23rd of October commissions of array were issued for a force of 23,000 men, to be chosen in eleven northern and western counties, and 6400 more in Wales and Cheshire [7].

System of the navy.

243. The measures taken by Edward for the defence of the coast, which have been already mentioned, were a part of the

[1] Above, p. 279. [2] Parl. Writs, i. 281. [3] Ibid. i. 282.
[4] Ibid. i. 281. [5] Ibid. i. 285. [6] Ibid. i. 299, 300. [7] Ibid. i. 304.

system on which he laid the foundations of the later navy. The attempt made successfully by John to create a fleet of mercenaries which, combined with the naval force furnished by the ports, would be a match for any other fleet in Europe, had not been renewed under Henry III. Probably the force of the ports was by itself sufficient to repel any fleet that Philip Augustus or Lewis could have mustered after the death of John. Throughout the reign of Henry III, when ships were required, the necessary number were impressed by the sheriffs of the maritime counties or the barons of the Cinque Ports[1]. If they were wanted for transport, the ports were summoned to furnish a proportion of proper size and strength. If it was desirable to take the offensive the barons of the ports might be empowered to ravage the French coasts, and indemnify themselves with spoil; this was done by Henry III in 1242[2], and, if rumour is to be trusted, by Simon de Montfort in 1264[3]. The shores of England were never seriously threatened with invasion except in 1213, 1217, and 1264, and the invasion was prevented in the former years by John's fleet, in the latter by the contrary winds assisting the efforts of Simon de Montfort. But in 1294 Edward saw the necessity of giving a more definite organisation to this the most natural means of defence. The piratic habits which the old system had produced in the seaport towns had led to a series of provincial quarrels which occasionally ended in a seafight; and they likewise imperilled the observance of treaties with foreign powers. The Cinque Ports went to war with the men of Yarmouth, or with the Flemings, with little regard to the king's peace or international obligations[4].

Growth of the fleet, under John.

Under Henry III.

Edward organises the defence of the coast by the shipping,

[1] In 1207 the barons of the Cinque Ports were ordered to impress all ships, Foed. i. 96; and a like order is given by Edward in 1298; Parl. Writs, i. 308. In 1253, 300 great ships were pressed; M. Paris, p. 868. In less urgent circumstances a particular quota is asked for; ten ships are demanded of the ports of Norfolk and Suffolk to convey the king's sister in 1236; Foed. i. 225; and eight ports provide ships carrying sixteen horses to convey the queen to France in 1254; ibid. 295. Philip the Fair got together a fleet by the same means; B. Cotton, p. 282.

[2] Foed. i. 246, 250; M. Paris, p. 589.

[3] Lib. de Antt. Legg. pp. 69, 73.

[4] See B. Cotton, 171, 174, 227; Royal Letters, ii. 244; Parl. Writs, i. 115.

Naval institutions.

It is uncertain whether the superintendence of naval affairs had been as yet in the hands of any permanent official; or whether the king, or the justiciar in his place, were not admiral as well as general in chief. In 1217 the victory which saved England from the last attempt of Lewis was won by the fleet nominally under the command of the justiciar, Hubert de Burgh, but Philip of Albini and John Marshall, to whom Henry's council had entrusted the guardianship of the coast, were the responsible commanders [1]. In 1264 Thomas de Multon and John de la Haye were appointed by Simon de Montfort, 'custodes partium maritimarum' with the charge of victualling and commanding the fleet [2]. In the earlier years of Edward I the officers of the Cinque Ports seem to have exercised the chief administrative power; and no attempt had yet been made to unite the defence of the coasts, the maintenance of a fleet of war or transport, and the general regulation of the shipping, under one department. In 1294 however, when the constitutional storm was rising, when the Welsh, the Scots, and the French were all threatening him, Edward instituted a permanent staff of officials. He appointed William Leyburne captain of all the portmen and mariners of the king's dominions, and under him John de Bottetourt warden of all from the Thames to Scotland [3]. For the manning of the fleet he issued orders to the sheriffs to collect the outlaws of their shires with the promise of wages and pardon [4]: besides these the chief captain was empowered to impress men, vessels, victuals, and arms, paying however reasonable prices [5]. It is not surprising that a force so raised signalised itself by a cruel devastation of Normandy in the following year: or that whilst they were so employed the French mariners who had been brought together on the same plan made a half-successful raid upon Dover, and shortly after threatened Winchelsea. It was

Custodes partium maritimarum.

Admirals appointed.

Impressment.

[1] M. Paris, p. 298.

[2] Foed. i. 447. See Selden, Mare Clausum; Opp. ii. 1327 sq.

[3] B. Cotton, p. 234. Walsingham (i. 47, and Rishanger, p. 143) gives these officers the title of Admiral, which was new in England, although common in Southern Europe, where it was derived from the Arabic Emir (Amyrail = Comes, Trokelowe, p. 30) and had been used for some centuries.

[4] B. Cotton, p. 235.

[5] B. Cotton, p. 237. Here again the Wardrobe Accounts afford abundant information.

in fear of such reprisals that the king instituted the system of coast guard already described, and agisted or rated the land-owners of the maritime counties for its support[1]. In 1298 the orders for the superintendence of the fleet are given to Robert de Burghersh as lieutenant-warden of the Cinque Ports, and John le Sauvage as lieutenant-captain of the mariners[2]. The negotiation of peace with France probably made further proceedings unnecessary for a time. In 1302 Robert Burghersh is still warden of the Cinque Ports and answerable for the service of fifty-seven ships due from them[3]; in 1304 he with Robert le Sauvage and Peter of Dunwich has the charge of victualling the twenty ships furnished by the city of London[4]. In 1306 we find a further step taken; Gervas Alard appears as captain and admiral of the fleet of the ships of the Cinque Ports and all other ports from Dover to Cornwall[5]; and Edward Charles captain and admiral from the Thames to Berwick: a third officer of the same rank probably commanded on the coast of the Irish sea, and thus the maritime jurisdiction was arranged until the appointment of a single high admiral in 1360. The history of the jurisdiction of these officers is as yet obscure, both from the apocryphal character of all the early records of the Admiralty and from the nature of their authority, which was the result of a tacit compromise between the king as sovereign and lord of the sea, entitled to demand for offence or defence the services of all his subjects, the privileged corporations of the sea-port towns with their peculiar customs and great local independence, and the private adventure of individuals, merchants, and mariners, whose proceedings seem to be scarcely one degree removed from piracy. Some organisation however must have been created before Edward II could claim for himself and his predecessors the dominion of the sea, or his son collect and arm the navy with which he won the battle of Sluys. As a matter of administration however the navy was yet in its earliest stage.

Appointment of naval commanders;

three admirals.

Obscurity of the history of the Admiralty.

In a general summary like the foregoing, it is impossible

[1] B. Cotton, p. 312.
[2] Parl. Writs, i. 308.
[3] Foedera, i. 936, 945.
[4] Foedera, i. 961, 962.
[5] Foedera, i. 990.

to do more than point out the chief departments in which Edward's energy and special sort of ability are prominent. Other points will arise as we pursue the history of his descendants. These, however, may help us to understand both the spirit and method which he displayed in definitely concentrating the national strength, and by which he turned to the advantage of the crown and realm, the interests of which he had made identical, the results of the victory that had been won through the struggles of the preceding century.

Attempt to adjust the credit of constitutional progress.

244. On a review of the circumstances of the great struggle which forms the history of England during the thirteenth century, and after realising as well as we can the constitution that emerges when the struggle is over, a question naturally arises as to the comparative desert of the actors, their responsibility for the issue, and the character of their motives. It is not easy to assign to the several combatants, or the several workers, their due share in the result. The king occupies the first place in the annals; the clergy appear best in the documentary evidence, for they could tell their own tale; the barons take the lead in action; the people are chiefly conspicuous in suffering. Yet we cannot suppose either that the well proportioned and well defined system which we find in existence at the death of Edward I grew up without a conscious and intelligent design on the part of its creators, or that the many plans which, under his father, had been tried and failed, failed merely because of the political weakness or accidental ill success of their promoters. Comparing the history of the following ages with that of the past, we can scarcely doubt that Edward had a definite idea of government before his eyes, or that that idea was successful because it approved itself to the genius and grew out of the habits of the people. Edward saw, in fact, what the nation was capable of, and adapted his constitutional reforms to that capacity. But although we may not refuse him the credit of design, it may still be questioned whether the design was altogether voluntary, whether it was not forced upon him by circumstances and developed by a series of successful experiments. And in the same way we may question whether the clerical and

baronial policy was a class policy, the result of selfish personal designs, or a great, benevolent, statesmanlike plan, directed towards securing the greatness of the country and the happiness of the people.

Edward's action partly designed, partly the result of compulsion.

First, then, as to the king: and we may here state the conclusions before we recapitulate the premisses, which are in fact contained in the last two chapters. The result of the royal action upon the constitution during the thirteenth century was to some extent the work of design, to some extent an undesigned development of the material which the design attempted to mould and of the objects to which it was directed; to some extent the result of compulsion such as forced the author of the design to carry out his own principles of design even when they told against his momentary policy and threatened to thwart his own object in the maintenance of his design. Each of these factors may be illustrated by a date; the design of a national parliament is perfected in 1295; the period of development is the period of the organic laws, from 1275 to 1290; the date of the compulsion is 1297. The complete result appears in the joint action of the parliaments of Lincoln in 1301 and of Carlisle in 1307.

The design.

The design, as interpreted by the result, was the creation of a national parliament, composed of the three estates, organised on the principle of concentrating local agency and machinery in such a manner as to produce unity of national action, and thus to strengthen the hand of the king, who personified the nation.

Its character as the consummation of a growing policy.

This design was perfected in 1295. It was not the result of compulsion, but the consummation of a growing policy. Edward did not call his parliament, as Philip the Fair called the States General, on the spur of a momentary necessity, or as a new machinery invented for the occasion and to be thrown aside when the occasion was over, but as a perfected organisation, the growth of which he had for twenty years been doing his best to guide. Granted that he had in view the strengthening of the royal power, it was the royal power in and through the united nation, not as against it, that he designed to strengthen. In the face of France, before the eyes of Christendom, for the prosecution

Edward's clear perception of the needs of the people.

of an occasional war with Philip, for the annexation of Wales and Scotland, or for the recovery of the Holy Sepulchre, a strong king must be the king of a united people. And a people, to be united, must possess a balanced constitution, in which no class possesses absolute and independent power, none is powerful enough to oppress without remedy. The necessary check on an aspiring priesthood and an aggressive baronage, the hope and support of a rising people, must be in a king too powerful to yield to any one class, not powerful enough to act in despite of all, and fully powerful only in the combined support of all. Up to the year 1295 Edward had these ends steadily in view; his laws were directed to the limitation of baronial pretensions, to the definition of ecclesiastical claims, to the remedy of popular wrongs and sufferings. The peculiar line of his reforms, the ever perceptible intention of placing each member of the body politic in direct and immediate relation with the royal power, in justice, in war, and in taxation, seems to reach its fulfilment in the creation of the parliament of 1295, containing clergy and people by symmetrical representation, and a baronage limited and defined on a distinct system of summons.

Growth of his policy.

But the design was not the ideal of a doctrinaire, or even of a philosopher. It was not imposed on an unwilling or unprepared people. It was the result of a growing policy exercised on a growing subject matter. There is no reason to suppose that at the beginning of his reign Edward had conceived the design which he completed in 1295, or that in 1295 he contemplated the results that arose in 1297 and 1301. There was a development co-operating with the unfolding design. The nation, on whom and by whom he was working, had now become a consolidated people, aroused by the lessons of his father's reign to the intelligent appreciation of their own condition, and attached to their own laws and customs with a steady though not unreasoning affection, jealous of their privileges, their charters, their local customs, unwilling that the laws of England should be changed. The reign of Henry III, and the first twenty years of Edward, prove the increasing capacity for self-government, as well as the increased desire and understanding of the idea of self-government. The writs, the laws, the councils, the negotiations of these years have been discussed in this and the preceding chapter: they prove that the nation was becoming capable and desirous of constitutional action; the capacity being proved by the success of the king's design in using it, the conscious desire by the constant aspiration for rights new or old.

Progressive plans.

The adaptability of his people to the execution of his design may well have revealed to Edward the further steps towards the perfection of his ideal. The national strength was tried against Wales, before Scotland opened a scene of new triumphs, and the submission of Scotland encouraged the nation to resist Wales, Scotland, and France at once. In the same way the successful management of the councils of 1283 and 1294 led to the completion of the parliament in 1295. In each case the development of national action had led to the increase of the royal power. Edward could not but see that he had struck the very line that must henceforth guide the national life. The symmetrical constitution, and the authoritative promulgation of its principle, mark the point at which the national development and the fullest development of Edward's policy for his people met. He was successful because he built on the habits and wishes and strength of the nation, whose habits, wishes, and strength he had learned to interpret.

Power of resistance to royal power increased.

But the close union of 1295 was followed by the compulsion of 1297: out of the organic completeness of the constitution sprang the power of resistance, and out of the resistance the victory of the principles, which Edward might guide, but which he failed to coerce. With the former date then the period closes during which the royal design and the national development work in parallel lines or in combination; henceforth the progress, so far as it lies within the compass of the reign, is the resultant of two forces differing in direction, forces which under Edward's successors became stronger and more distinctly divergent in aim and character. It seems almost a profanation to compare the history of Edward I with that of John; yet the circumstances of 1297 bear a strong resemblance to those of 1215:

Exceptional character of the crisis of 1297.

if the proceedings of 1297 had been a fair example of Edward's general dealings with his people, our judgment of his whole life must have been reversed. They were, however, as we have seen, exceptional; the coincidence of war at home and abroad, the violent aggression of Boniface VIII, and the bold attempt at feudal independence, for which the earls found their opportunity in the king's difficulties, formed together an exigency, or a complication of exigencies, that suggested a practical dictatorship: that practical dictatorship Edward attempted to grasp; failing, he yielded gracefully, and kept the terms on which he yielded.

Edward inherited some sound institutions.

In an attempt to ascertain how far Edward really comprehended the constitutional material on which he was working, and formed his idea according to the capacity of that material, we can scarcely avoid crediting him with measures which he may have inherited, or which may have been the work of his ministers. Little as can be said for Henry III himself, there was much vitality and even administrative genius in the system of government during his reign. Local institutions flourished, although the central government languished under him. Some of his bad ministers were among the best lawyers of the age. Stephen Segrave, the successor of Hubert de Burgh, was regarded by Bracton as a judge of consummate authority; Robert Burnell and Walter de Merton, old servants of Henry, left names scarcely less remarkable in their own line of work than those of Grosseteste and Cantilupe. No doubt these men had much to do with Edward's early reforms. We can trace the removal of Burnell's influence in the more peremptory attitude which the king assumed after his death, and the statesmanship of the latter years of the reign is coloured by the faithful but less enlightened policy of Walter Langton. But, notwithstanding all this, the marks of Edward's constitutional policy are so distinct as to be accounted for only by his own continual intelligent supervision. If his policy had been only Burnell's, it must have changed when circumstances changed after Burnell's death, as that of Henry VIII changed when Cromwell succeeded Wolsey; but the removal of the minister only sharpens the edge of the king's zeal. His policy, whoever were his advisers, is uniform

Edward's ministers.

and progressive. That he was both well acquainted with the machinery of administration, and possessed of constructive ability, is shown by the constitutions which he drew up for Wales and Scotland: both bear the impress of his own hand. The statute of Wales not only shows a determination closely to assimilate that country to England in its institutions, to extend with no grudging hand the benefits of good government to the conquered province, but furnishes an admirable view of the local administration to which it was intended to adapt it. The constitution devised for Scotland is an original attempt at blending the Scottish national system as it then existed with the general administration of the empire, an attempt which in some points anticipates the scheme of the union which was completed four centuries later. A similar conclusion may be drawn from Edward's legislation: it is not the mere registration of unconnected amendments forced on by the improvement of legal knowledge, nor the innovating design of a man who imagines himself to have a genius for law, but an intelligent development of well ascertained and accepted principles, timed and formed by a policy of general government. So far, certainly, Edward seems qualified to originate a policy of design.

Personal share of the king in administration.

But was the design which he may be supposed to have originated the same as that which he finally carried out? Was the design which he actually carried out the result of an unimpeded constructive policy, or the resultant of forces which he could combine but could not thwart? Was it a policy of genius or of expediency? It may be fairly granted that the constitution, as it ultimately emerged, may not have been that which Edward would have chosen. Strong in will, self-reliant, confident of his own good will towards his people, he would have no doubt preferred to retain in his own hands, and in those of his council, the work of legislation, and probably that of political deliberation, while his sense of justice would have left the ordinary voting of taxation to the parliament as he constructed it in 1295 out of the three estates. Such a constitution might have been more like that adopted by Philip the Fair in 1302 than like that embodied by the statement of parliament in 1322, or enunciated

Policy of genius or of expediency.

How far Edward's policy was spontaneous.

by Edward himself in his answer to the pope. The importance actually retained by the council in all the branches of administration proves that a simple parliamentary constitution would not have recommended itself to Edward's own mind. On the other hand, his policy was far more than one of expediency. It was diverted from its original line no doubt by unforeseen difficulties. Edward intended to be wholly and fully a king, and he struggled for power. For twenty years he acted in the spirit of a supreme lawgiver, admitting only the council and the baronage to give their advice and consent. Then political troubles arose and financial troubles. The financial exigencies suggested rather than forced a new step, and the commons were called to parliament. In calling them he not only enunciated the great principle of national solidarity, but based the new measure on the most ancient local institutions. He did not choose the occasion, but he chose the best means of meeting the occasion consonant with the habits of the people. And when he had taken the step he did not retrace it. He regarded it as a part of a new compact that faith and honour forbad him to retract. And so on in the rest of his work. He kept his word and strengthened every part of the new fabric by his own adhesion to its plan, not only from the sense of honour but because he felt that he had done the best thing. Thus his work was crowned with the success that patience, wisdom, and faith amply deserve, and his share in the result is that of the direction of national growth and adaptation of the means and design of government to the consolidation and conscious exercise of national strength. He saw what was best for his age and people; he led the way and kept faith.

Contrast with other kings of the time.

Thus he appears to great advantage even by the side of the great kings of his own century. Alfonso the Wise is a speculator and a dreamer by the side of his practical wisdom; Frederick II a powerful and enlightened self-seeker in contrast with Edward's laborious self-constraint for the good of his people. S. Lewis, who alone stands on his level as a patriot prince, falls below him in power and opportunity of greatness. Philip the Fair may be as great in constructive power but he constructs only a fabric of absolutism. The legislation of Alfonso is the work of an innovator who, having laid hold on what seems absolute perfection of law, accepts it without examining how far it is fit for his people and finds it thrown back on his hands. Frederick legislates for the occasion; in Germany to balance opposing factions, in Italy to crush the liberty of his enemies or to raise the privileges of his friends: S. Lewis legislates for the love of his people and for the love of justice, but neither he nor his people see the way to reconcile freedom with authority. These contrasts are true if applied to the Mainzer-recht or the Constitutions of Peter de Vineis, the Establishments of S. Lewis or the Siete Partidas. Not one of these men both saw and did the best thing in the best way: and not one of them founded or consolidated a great power.

Alfonso.

Frederick and Lewis.

In estimating the share of the baronage in the great work there is the difficulty, at the outset, of determining the amount of action which is to be ascribed to persons and parties. In Henry III's reign we compare without being able to weigh the distinct policies of the Marshalls, of the earls of Chester and Gloucester, Bohun and Bigod. Even the great earl of Leicester appears in different aspects at different parts of his career, and the great merit of his statesmanship is adaptative rather than originative: what he originates perishes, what he adapts survives. In the earlier period the younger Marshalls lead the opposition to the crown partly from personal fears and jealousies, but mainly on the principles of Runnymede; they perish however before the battle. The earl of Chester, the strongest bulwark of the royal power, is also its sharpest critic, and, when his own rights are infringed, its most independent opponent; his policy is not that of the nation but of the great feudal prince of past times. The earls of Gloucester, father and son, neither of them gifted with genius, try to play a part that genius only could make successful: like Chester, conscious of their feudal pretensions, like the Marshalls, ready to avail themselves of constitutional principle to thwart the king or to overthrow his favourites. In their eyes the constitutional struggle was a party contest: should the English baronage or the foreign

Distinctive policy of the baronial families.

The earls of Gloucester.

The earls of Gloucester.

courtiers direct the royal councils. There was no politic or patriotic zeal to create in the national parliament a properly-balanced counterpoise to royal power. Hence when the favourites were banished, the Gloucesters took the king's side; when the foreigners returned, they were in opposition. They may have credit for an unenlightened but true idea that England was for the English, but on condition that the English should follow their lead. They have the credit of mediating between the English parties and taking care that neither entirely crushed the other. Further it would seem absurd to ascribe to the Gloucesters any statesmanlike ability corresponding to their great position. The younger earl, the Gilbert of Edward I's reign, is bold and honest, but erratic and self-confident, interesting rather personally than politically.

Simon de Montfort.

To Leicester alone of the barons can any constructive genius be ascribed; and as we have seen, owing to the difficulty of determining where his uncontrolled action begins and ends, we cannot define his share in the successive schemes which he helped to sustain. That he possessed both constructive power and a true zeal for justice cannot be denied. That with all his popularity he understood the nation, or they him, is much more questionable: and hence his greatest work, the parliament of 1265, wants that direct relation to the national system which the constitution of 1295 possesses. In the aspect of a popular champion, the favourite of the people and the clergy, Simon loses sight of the balance of the constitution; an alien, he is the foe of aliens; owing his real importance to his English earldom he all but banishes the baronage from his councils. He is the genius, the hero of romance, saved by his good faith and righteous zeal.

Bohun and Bigod.

Bohun and Bigod, the heroes of 1297, are but degenerate sons of mighty fathers; greater in their opportunity than in their patriotism; but their action testifies to a traditional alliance between barons and people and recalls the resistance made with better reason and in better company by their forefathers to the tyranny of John. We cannot form a just and general judgment on the baronage without making these distinctions. On the whole, however, it must be granted that while the mainspring of their opposition to Henry and

Edward must often be sought in their own class interests, they betray no jealousy of popular liberty, they do not object to share with the commons the advantages that their resistance has gained, they aspire to lead rather than to drive the nation; they see, if they do not fully realise, the unity of the national interest whenever and wherever it is threatened by the crown.

Share of the clergy in the constitutional growth.

It is in the ranks of the clergy that we should naturally look, considering the great men of the time, for a moderate, constructive policy. The thirteenth century is the golden age of English churchmanship. The age that produced one Simon among the earls, produced among the bishops Stephen Langton, S. Edmund, Grosseteste, and the Cantilupes. The Charter of Runnymede was drawn under Langton's eye; Grosseteste was the friend and adviser of the constitutional opposition. Berksted, the episcopal member of the electoral triumvirate, was the pupil of S. Richard of Chichester: S. Edmund of Canterbury was the adviser who compelled the first banishment of the aliens; S. Thomas of Cantilupe, the last canonised Englishman, was the chancellor of the baronial regency.

How they are to be judged.

These men are not to be judged by a standard framed on the experience of ages that were then future. It is an easy and a false generalisation that tells us that their resistance to royal tyranny and the aid that they gave to constitutional growth were alike owing to their desire to erect a spiritual sovereignty and to depress all dominion that infringed upon their own liberty of tyrannising. The student of the history of the thirteenth century will not deny that the idea of a spiritual sovereignty was an accepted principle with both clerk and layman. The policy of the papal court had not yet reduced to an absurdity the claims put forth by Gregory VII and Innocent III. It was still regarded as an axiom that the priesthood which guided men to eternal life was a higher thing than the royalty which guided the helm of the temporal state: that the two swords were to help each other, and the greatest privilege of the state was to help the church. Religious liberty, as they understood it, consisted largely in clerical immunity.

But granting that principle,—and until the following century, when the teaching of Ockham and the Minorites, the claims of Boniface VIII and their practical refutation, the quarrel of Lewis of Bavaria and John XXII, the schism in the papacy, and the teaching of Wycliffe, had opened the eyes of Christendom, that principle was accepted,—it is impossible not to see, and ungenerous to refuse to acknowledge the debt due to men like Grosseteste. Grosseteste the most learned, the most acute, the most holy man of his time, the most devoted to his spiritual work, the most trusted teacher and confidant of princes, was at the same time a most faithful servant of the Roman Church [1]. If he is to be judged by his letters, his leading principle was the defence of his flock. The forced intrusion of foreign priests, who had no sympathy with his people and knew neither their ways nor their language, leads him to resist king and pope alike; the depression of the priesthood, whether by the placing of clergymen in secular office, or by the impoverishment of ecclesiastical estates, or by the appointment of unqualified clerks to the cure of souls, is the destruction of religion among the laity. Taxes and tallages might be paid to Rome when the pope needed it, but the destruction of the flock by foreign pastors was not to be endured. It may seem strange that the eyes of Grosseteste were not opened by the proceedings of Innocent IV to the impossibility of reconciling the Roman claims with his own dearest principles: possibly the idea that Frederick II represented one of the heads of the Apocalyptic Beast, or the belief that he was an infidel plotting against Christendom, influenced his mental perspicacity. Certainly as he grew older his attitude towards the pope became more hostile. But he had seen during a great part of his career the papal influence employed on the side of justice in the hands of Innocent III and Honorius III. Grosseteste's attitude towards the papacy however was not one of unintelligent submission.

Grosseteste.

His characteristic views.

His attitude towards Rome.

[1] Grosseteste's belief that the bishop receives his power from the pope and the pope receives his from Christ, a doctrine which in its consequences is fatal to the doctrine of episcopacy and the existence of national churches, is clear from his letter No. 127; ed. Luard, p. 369. But that he did not see to what it would lead, is clear from the whole tenour of his life.

The words in which he expresses his idea of papal authority bear a singular resemblance to those in which Bracton maintains the idea of royal authority [1]. The pope could do no wrong, for if wrong were done by him he was not acting as pope. So the king as a minister of God can only do right; if he do wrong, he is acting not as a king but as a minister of the devil [2]. In each case the verbal quibble contains a virtual negation: and the writer admits without identifying a higher principle than authority. But it is not as a merely ecclesiastical politician that he should be regarded. He was the confidential friend of Simon de Montfort, and the tutor of his children. He was more than once the spokesman of the constitutional party in parliament and he was the patron of the friars who at the time represented learning and piety as well as the doctrines of civil independence in the Universities and country at large [3]. Bolder and more persevering than S. Edmund, he endured the same trials, but was a less conspicuous object of attack and gained greater success. Grosseteste represents a school of which

His views of the papacy.

His political position.

[1] 'Praesidentes huic sedi sacratissimae principalissime inter mortales personam Christi induuntur, et ideo oportet quod in eis maxime sint et reluceant Christi opera, et nulla sint in eis Christi operibus contraria; et propter idem, sicut Domino Jesu Christo in omnibus est obediendum, sic et praesidentibus huic sedi sacratissimae in quantum indutis Christum et in quantum vere praesidentibus in omnibus est obtemperandum; sin autem quis eorum, quod absit, superinduat amictum cognationis et carnis aut mundi aut alicujus alterius praeter quam Christi, et ex hujusmodi amore quicquam Christi praeceptis et voluntati contrarium, obtemperans ei in hujusmodi manifeste se separat a Christo et a corpore ejus quod est ecclesia, et a praesidente huic sedi in quantum induto personam Christi et in tantum vere praesidente; et cum communiter in hujusmodi obtemperatur vera et perfecta advenit discessio et in januis est revelatio filii perditionis' (2 Thess. ii. 3); Grosseteste's sermon before the Council of Lyons; Brown s Fasciculus, ii. 256.

[2] 'Exercere igitur debet rex potestatem juris, sicut Dei vicarius et minister in terra, quia illa potestas solius Dei est, potestas autem injuriae diaboli et non Dei, et cujus horum opera fecerit rex, ejus minister est cujus opera fecerit. Igitur dum facit justitiam vicarius est Dei aeterni, minister autem diaboli dum declinet ad injuriam.' Bracton, Lib. iii. de Actionibus, c. 9.

[3] The sentiments not of the people but of the Universities, and incidentally of the Franciscans also, are exemplified in the long Latin poem printed in Wright's Political Songs, pp. 72-121. I have not quoted this curious document as an illustration of the belief of the people, who could not have read it or understood it; but it was clearly a manifesto, amongst themselves, of the men whose preaching guided the people.

S. Richard of Chichester and his disciple Berksted, with archbishops Kilwardby and Peckham, were representatives; a school part of whose teaching descended through the Franciscans to Ockham and the Nominalists, and through them to Wycliffe. The baronial prelate was of another type. Walter of Cantilupe no doubt had his sympathies with the English baronage as well as with the clergy and was as hostile to the alien favourites of the court as to the alien nominees of Rome. A man like Thomas of Cantilupe united in a strong degree the leading principles of both schools; he was a saint like Edmund, a politician like his uncle, and a bishop like Grosseteste. Another class, the ministerial prelate, such as was bishop Raleigh of Winchester, was forced into opposition to the crown rather by his personal ambitions or personal experiences than by high principle: the intrusion of the foreigner into the court and council was to him not merely the introduction of foreign or lawless procedure, but the exclusion from the rewards that faithful service had merited; and his feeling, as that of Becket had been, was composed, to a large extent, of a sense of injury amounting to vindictiveness. Yet even such men contributed to the cause of freedom if it were only by the legal skill, the love of system, and ability for organisation which they infused into the party to which they adhered. The opposition of the English clergy to the illegal aggressions of the crown in his father's reign taught Edward I a great lesson of policy. He at all events contrived to secure the services of the best of the prelates on the side of his government, and chose for his confidential servants men who were fit to be rewarded with high spiritual preferment. The career of Walter de Merton proves this: another of his great ministers, bishop William of March, was in popular esteem a candidate for canonisation and a faithful prime minister of the crown. Walter de Langton the minister of his later years, earned the gratitude of the nation by his faithful attempts to keep the prince of Wales in obedience to his father, and to prevent him taking the line which finally destroyed him. Of archbishop Winchelsey we have already seen reason to believe that he was an exceptional man in a position the excep-

The baronial prelate.

The secular prelate.

Opposition of the clergy to Edward I.

Winchelsey.

tional character of which must affect our judgments of both himself and the king. If the necessities of the case excuse the one, they excuse the other. He also was a man of learning, industry, and piety, and if he did not play the part of a patriot as well as Langton had done, it must be remembered that he had Edward and not John for his opponent, Boniface and not Innocent for his pope. But on the whole perhaps the feeling of the English clergy in the great struggle should be estimated rather by the behaviour of the mass of the body than by the character of their leaders. The remonstrances of the diocesan and provincial councils are more outspoken than the letters of the bishops, and the faithfulness of the body of the clergy to the principles of freedom is more distinctly conspicuous than that of the episcopal politicians: the growing life of the Universities, which towards the end of the century were casting off the rule of the mendicant orders and influencing every class of the clergy both regular and secular, tended to the same end; and, although, in tracing the history of the following century, we shall have in many respects to acknowledge decline and retrogression, we cannot but see that in the quarrels between the crown and the papacy, and between the nation and the crown, the clergy for the most part took the right side. Archbishops Stratford and Arundel scarcely ever claim entire sympathy, but they gained no small advantages to the nation, and few kings had better ministers or more honest advisers than William of Wykeham.

The body of the clergy.

They take the side of freedom.

If we ask, lastly, what was the share of the people, of the commons, of their leading members in town and shire, our review of the history furnishes a distinct if not very circumstantial answer. The action of the people is to some extent traceable in the acts of the popular leader. Simon de Montfort possessed the confidence of the commons: the knightly body threw itself into the arms of Edward in 1259 when it was necessary to counteract the oligarchic policy of the barons: the Londoners, the men of the Cinque Ports, the citizens of the great towns, the Universities under the guidance of the friars, were consistently on the side of liberty. But history has preserved

Sympathy of the people with the reforms.

No great names preserved.

no great names or programmes of great design proceeding from the third estate. Sir Robert Thwenge the leader of the anti-Roman league in 1232, and Thomas son of Thomas who led the plebeians of London against the magnates, scarcely rise beyond the reputation of local politicians. Brighter names, like that of Richard Sward, the follower of Richard Marshall, are eclipsed by the brilliance of their leaders. It was well that the barons and the bishops should furnish the schemes of reform, and most fortunate that barons and bishops were found to furnish such schemes as the people could safely accept. The jealousy of class privilege was avoided and personal influences helped to promote a general sympathy. The real share of the commons in the reformed and remodelled constitution is proved by the success of its working, by the growth of the third estate into power and capacity for political action through the discipline of the parliamentary system; and the growth of the parliamentary system itself is due to the faithful adhesion and the growing intelligence of the third estate.

Concluding award.

Let then the honour be given where it is due. If the result is a compromise, it is one made between parties which by honesty and patriotism are entitled to make with one another terms which do not give to each all that he might ask; and justly so, for the subjects on which the compromise turns, the relations of Church and State, land and commerce, tenure and citizenship, homage and allegiance, social freedom and civil obligation, are matters on which different ages and different nations have differed in theory, and on which even statesmen and philosophers have failed to come to a general conclusion alike applicable to all ages and nations as the ideal of good government.

Chapter VI

ROYAL PREROGATIVE AND PARLIAMENTARY AUTHORITY.

271. Question of the existence of a political scheme.—272. The burden borne by the knights of the shire.—273. Antagonistic growth of royal assumption and popular claims.—274. The king should live of his own.—275. Limitation of his right of tallage.—276. Limitation of his right to exact Custom.—277. Origin and growth of the Customs.—278. The king's power of borrowing, and system of loans.—279. Limitation of the right of Purveyance.—280. Limitation of the abuse of commissions of array.—281. Coinage.—282. Estimate of the king's revenue.—283. Attempts to limit the household expenses.—284. Restraints on the alienation of crown lands.—285. Compulsory economy at court.—286. Parliamentary checks on ministers; oaths, election, and account.—287. Appropriation of supplies.—288. Audit of accounts.—289. Restraint on the king's power of legislation.—290. Treatment of petitions.—291. Suspension of Statutes.—292. Legislation by ordinance.—293. Right of initiation, debate and consent.—294. General power of deliberation exercised by the commons.—295. Interference with justice forbidden.—296. The king's power in the constitution of parliament.—297. Minor prerogatives.—298. Influence of the period on the character of the nation.

Material, formal, and progressive elements of constitutional life.

271. The material elements of constitutional life are inherent in the nation itself, in its primitive institutions and early history. The regulative and formative influences have proceeded mainly from the authority of the kings, the great organisers of the Norman and early Plantagenet lines. The impulse and character of constitutional progress have been the result of the struggles of what may be termed the constitutional opposition.

Scheme of progress.

It is so much easier, in discussing the causes and stages of a political contest, to generalise from the results than to trace the growth of the principles maintained by the actors, that the historian is in some danger of substituting his own formulated conclusions for the programme of the leaders, and of giving them credit for a far more definite scheme and more conscious political sagacity than they would ever have claimed for themselves. This is especially true with regard to the period which we have just traversed, a period of violent faction struggles, graced by no heroes or unselfish statesmen, yet at its close marked by very significant results. It is true, more or less, of the whole of our early history; the march of constitutional progress is so steady and definite as to suggest everywhere the idea that it was guided by some great creative genius or some great directive tradition. Yet it is scarcely ever possible to distinguish the creative genius; it is impossible to assign the work to any single mind or series of minds, and scarcely easier to trace the growth of the guiding tradition in any one of the particulars which it embodies. As in the training of human life, so in national history, opportunity is as powerful as purpose; and the new prospects, that open as the nation advances in political consciousness and culture, reveal occasions and modes of progress which, as soon as they are tried, are found to be more exactly the course for which earlier training has prepared it than any plan that might have been consciously formed.

Difficulty of detecting any definite scheme of constitutional progress.

As this is clear upon any reading of history, it must be allowed that some generalisation from results is indispensable: without it we could never reach the principles that underlie the varied progress, and history would be reduced to a mere chapter of accidents. But the questions remain unanswered how far the men who wrought out the great results knew what they were doing; had they a regular plan? was that plan the conception of any one brain? who were the depositaries of the tradition? had the tradition any accepted formula? The history of political design is not less interesting than the registration of results. We have seen that the great champions of the thirteenth century directed their efforts to the attainment of an ideal which they failed to realise, and that the overt struggles of the fourteenth century had their source and object in factious aims and factious divisions; that in the former the constitution grew rather according to the spirit of the liberators than on the lines which they had tried to trace; and in the latter its development was due to the conviction, common to all factions, that the nation in parliament was a convenient arbiter, if not the ultimate judge of their quarrels. There is this difference between the two: the

How far were the actors in the drama conscious of their part.

Contrast between the thirteenth and fourteenth centuries.

former witnessed a real growth of national life, the latter a recognition of formal principles of government—principles which all parties recognised, or pretended, when it was convenient, to recognise. The thirteenth century had the spirit without the letter of the constitutional programme; the fourteenth had the letter with little of the spirit. Many of the principles that appear in the programme of the fourteenth existed in the minds of the heroes of the thirteenth: the idea of limiting royal power by parliaments, of controlling royal expenditure, of binding royal officials, of directing royal policy, was in the mind of the barons who worked with Simon de Montfort; very little of the spirit of the deliverer was in Thomas of Lancaster or Thomas of Woodstock. The peculiar work of Edward I had introduced into the national life the elements that gave form and attitude to political principle. By completing the constitution of parliament he perfected the instrument which had been wanting to Simon de Montfort; by completing administrative machinery he gave a tangible and visible reality to the system for the control of which the king and the parliament were henceforward to struggle. The effect of this on the design of the constitution was to substitute for the negative restrictions, by which the provisions of Oxford had limited the royal authority, the directive principles which guided the national advance in the following century; and thus to set clearly before men's minds royal prerogative on the one hand and constitutional government on the other. Thus distinctly presented, the political formula was less dependent than it had been before upon individual championship; but it was more liable to be abused for personal and party ends.

The spirit and the letter.

Place of Edward I between the two.

Important bearing of his reign on constitutional consciousness.

The battle of the commons fought by the knights of the shire.

272. If we ask who were the men or the classes of men who believed in as well as took advantage of the formula, now made intelligible and practical, the whole history of the fourteenth century supplies a harmonious answer. It was not men like Thomas of Lancaster; he used it because it had already become an influence which he could employ for his own purposes. It was not the clerical body generally, for they, although they supplied many supporters and workers, were hampered by their relations

to the papacy, and were now losing that intimate sympathy with the nation which had given them their great position in the days of Langton. It was not the town communities, in which, beyond an occasional local tumult, the history of the age finds little to record; nor the great merchants who, for good or for evil, are found chiefly on the side of that royal authority which seemed to furnish the most certain guarantees of mercantile security and privilege. Both historical evidence and the nature of the case lead to the conviction that the victory of the constitution was won by the knights of the shires[1]; they were the leaders of parliamentary debate; they were the link between the good peers and the good towns; they were the indestructible element of the house of commons; they were the representatives of those local divisions of the realm which were coeval with the historical existence of the people of England, and the interests of which were most directly attacked by the abuses of royal prerogative. The history bears evidence of their weakness as well as of their strength, their shortcomings as well as their deserts; the manipulation of the county courts by the sheriffs could change the policy of parliament from year to year; the interest of the landowner predominates every now and then over the rights of the labourer and artisan. Yet on the whole there is a striking uniformity and continuity in the policy of the knights; even the packed parliaments are not without courage to remonstrate, and, when uninfluenced by leaders of faction, their voice is invariably on the side of freedom. They are very distinctly the depositaries of the constitutional tradition; and this fact is one of the most distinctive features of our political history, as compared with most of other nations in which representative institutions have been tried with less success.

Historical prominence of the knights.

273. The growth of constitutional life is stimulated by the growth of royal assumption. Royal prerogative during this century is put upon its defence and compelled to formulate its claims, reserving however a salvo of its own indefeasible omni-

Antagonistic growth of prerogative.

[1] 'It is pretty manifest that the knights, though doubtless with some support from the representatives of towns, sustained the chief brunt of battle against the crown;' Hallam, Middle Ages, iii. 118.

Mutual action of prerogative and popular pretension.

potence that will enable it to justify any amount of statecraft. If popular claims are now and then outrageously aggressive, it must be confessed that the history of prerogative is one long story of assumption and evasion: every concession is made an opportunity for asserting pretensions that may cover new usurpations, and the acceptance of such a concession is craftily turned into an assumed acquiescence in the supreme right which might withhold as easily as it gives. The history of the national growth is thus inseparable from the history of the royal prerogative, in the widest sense of that undefinable term; and for every assertion of national right there is a counter assertion of royal autocracy. On the one side every advantage gained by the parliament is regarded as one of a very limited number of privileges; on the other every concession made by the crown is made out of an unlimited and unimpaired potentiality of sovereignty. Thus it sometimes strikes the student that the theory and practice of the constitution vary inversely, and that royalty becomes in theory more absolute as in practice it is limited more and more by the national will: as the jealousy of parliamentary or ministerial interference becomes more distinctly felt, the claims of the king are asserted more loudly, the indefinite margin of his prerogative is extended more indefinitely as restraint increases; the sense of restraint compels the exaggeration of all royal attributes. The theory of sovereignty held by Henry III is far more definite than that of Henry II, and that of Richard II than that of Edward I.

Programme of constitutional development.

The principles of constitutional growth, as enunciated by the party opposed to royal assumption, may be arranged under a small number of heads; and the counter principles of prerogative may be ranged side by side with them; it being always understood that the prerogative is not limited by these assertions, but still possesses an inexhaustible treasury of evasion. That the king should 'live of his own,' supporting royal state and ordinary national administrative machinery out of ordinary revenue; that the laws should not be changed without the national consent; that the great charter should be kept inviolate and inviolable, not merely in the letter, but as a pregnant source of rights and principles;

that the king's ministers are accountable to the nation for their disposal of national contributions, and for their general good behaviour; that grievances should be redressed before the money granted becomes payable; that the king should act by the counsel of his parliament, should not go to war, or attempt any great enterprise without its consent; and if he withdraw himself from its advice and influence, may be constrained to do his duty;—such were some of the fundamental convictions of the national party. That the nation must provide for the royal necessities irrespective of the king's good behaviour, that the most binding part of the royal oath was to secure the indefeasibility of the king's authority, that the king being the supreme landowner had a heritable right over the kingdom, corresponding with that of the private landowner over his own estate; that as supreme lawgiver he could dispense with the observance of a statute, suspend its operation, pardon the offenders against it, alter its wording and annul it altogether; that in fact he might do everything but what he was bound not to do, and even repudiate any obligation which he conceived to militate against his theory of sovereign right;—such were the principles in which Richard II was educated, or such was his reading of the lessons taught by the reign of his grandfather.

Principles of the constitutional party.

Principles of the supporters of Prerogative.

Yet royal prerogative was not in its origin a figment of theorists. It grew out of certain conditions of the national life, some of which existed before the Norman Conquest, others were the products of that great change, and others resulted from the peculiar course of the reigns of Henry II and his descendants. The general results of the history of the fourteenth century may be best arranged with reference to this consideration. We must look at the original basis of each great claim made on behalf of the crown, the design adopted for its remedy and the steps by which this remedy was obtained; but, we must remember always that, beyond the definite claims, there extends the region of undefined prerogative, which exists in theory without doing harm to any but the kings themselves, but which, the moment they attempt to act upon it, involves suffering to the nation and certain if not speedy retribution to the rulers.

The theory of prerogative must be judged by history.

The king should live of his own.

274. The principle that the king should live of his own[1] had a double application: the sovereign who could dispense with taxation could dispense likewise with advice and co-operation; if his income were so large that he could conveniently live within it, his administration must be so strong as to override all opposition; if his economy were compulsory, his power would be strictly confined within limits, whether territorial or constitutional, which would make him, what many of the continental sovereigns had become in the decay of feudality, only the first among the many almost equal potentates who nominally acknowledged him as lord. The former alternative would have left him free to become a despot; the latter, although perhaps it was the ideal of a party among the feudal lords of the thirteenth century, was made impossible by circumstances, by the personal character and policy of nearly all the Plantagenet kings, by the absolute necessity of a consolidated and united national executive for purposes of aggression and defence, and by the existence in the nation itself of a spirit which would probably have preferred even a despotic monarch to the rule of a territorial oligarchy. No king of the race of Plantagenet ever attempted to make his expenditure tally with his ordinary income, and no patriotic statesman dreamed of dispensing altogether with the taxation, which gave to the nation an unvarying hold on the king whether he were good or bad. But the adjustment and limitation of taxation, the securing of the nation against the hardships which could not but follow from the impoverishment of the crown, and the enforcing of honest dealing in the raising and expenditure of money, formed a body of constitutional questions the answer of which had to be worked out in the political struggles of two centuries.

Difficulties in the way of enforcement.

The source of constitutional struggles.

Legislation of *Magna Carta* on taxation.

The great charter had seemed to give a firm basis on which a structure of limited monarchy might be raised, in the rule that the king might not impose any general tax without the consent of the nation, expressed by the common council of the tenants

[1] The words of the 4th Ordinance of 1311, Statutes, i. 158, constantly recurring; e.g. 'Que notre seigneur le roi vive de soen,' Rot. Parl. 6 Edw. III. vol. ii. p. 166; 'viver deinz les revenues de votre roialme,' ibid. iii. 139.

in chief; but that article had been allowed to drop out of the charter at its successive confirmations; and the real restraint of the taxing power of the crown was imposed by other means. The honesty of the early ministers of Henry III, and the weakness of his own personal administration, had made it impossible for him to act without the national consent; and under Edward I the power of consent was lodged in the hands of a parliament far more national in its character than the 'commune consilium' of the charter. Yet even the 'confirmatio cartarum' had left some loopholes which the king was far too astute to overlook, and which the barons must have known to be dangerous when they compelled him to renounce the general salvo in 1299[1]. These were too tempting even for the good faith of Edward I; and his son and grandson took ample advantage both of the laxity of the law and of the precedents which he had created. One of the results of the reign of Richard II was the final closing of the more obvious ways of evading the constitutional restrictions, but the entire prevention of financial over-reaching on the part of the crown was not attained for many centuries; and successive generations of administrators developed a series of expedients which from age to age gave new name and form to the old evil.

Incompleteness of the limitations on the royal power of taxing.

The financial evasions of the period now before us may be referred to the heads of direct taxation, customs, and the incurring of royal or national debt; closely connected with these as engines of oppression are the abuses of the royal right to purveyance, to pressed service of men and material, and to the ordering of commissions of array. The origin, the abuse, and the remedying of the abuse, of these devices form an interesting portion of our national history, and as such they have been noticed as they arose in the foregoing pages. A brief recapitulation of the main points is however necessary from the higher ground which we have now reached.

Division of the subject.

275. The right of the king to tallage his demesnes, whether cities, boroughs, or rural townships, was not abolished by the 'confirmatio cartarum' in terms so distinct as to leave no room for evasion. The word 'tallagium' was not used in the document

The right to tallage demesne.

[1] See above, p. 148.

Tallage due properly from lands in demesne.

itself, and the 'aides, mises et prises,' which were renounced, were in the king's view the contributions raised from the kingdom generally without lawful consent, not the exactions made by demesne right from the crown lands[1]. It might be pleaded on Edward's behalf that in that act he intended only to renounce that general and sovereign power of taxing the commons which he had attempted to exercise in 1297, and which was one cause of the rising to which he was compelled to yield; not to surrender the ordinary right which as a landlord he possessed over his demesne, or over those communities which had purchased the right of being called his demesne in order to avoid more irksome obligations[2]. And probably this view was shared by the magnates. When then, on the 6th of February, 1304, Edward ordered a tallage to be collected from his cities, boroughs, and lands in

[1] This is not the view of Hallam, who argues as if the act 'de tallagio' were the authentic form of the concession, and as if the king had never tallaged any lands except demesne lands, so that only this right was now renounced. He thinks then that the right of tallage was expressly surrendered, and accuses the three Edwards of acting illegally in exacting it; Middle Ages, iii. 43. Unconstitutional the exaction certainly was, but not contrary to the letter of the law. He writes too as if he thought that these tallages were common, whereas there is but one instance in each reign. But Hallam's view of Edward I was, as he allows, influenced by that of Hume.

[2] The ancient demesne of the crown contributed to general taxation, together with the towns, in a larger proportion than the counties; paying a tenth, for instance, when the knights of the shires voted a fifteenth. Hence it was of some importance to the little country towns which enjoyed no particular privileges, to be taxed 'cum communitate comitatus,' and not with the towns; and even London itself did not despise the privilege, which it obtained by special charter from Edward III and Richard II; Liber Albus, i. 147, 167, 168. In the 19th of Edward II the men of Sevenhampton, Stratton, and Heyworth, in Wiltshire, proved to the king that, as they were not tenants in ancient demesne by Domesday, they ought not to be tallaged; Madox, Firma Burgi, p. 6. This record proves that Edward I and Edward II thought themselves justified in tallaging ancient demesne only. A very large portion of the boroughs were however in ancient demesne, and the sheriffs and judges probably gave the king the benefit of the doubt in all doubtful cases, e.g. 'in carta dicti prioris non fit aliqua mentio de tallagio; videtur consultius esse pro statu domini regis in hac parte quod supradicti tenentes dicti prioris remaneant onerati versus dominum regem;' Madox, Firma, p. 248. The represented towns of course paid the larger rate in all cases, unless, like London, they could obtain special exception. Thus then the obligation to pay tallage, or the value of corporate privilege which was coincident with it, was the foundation of the difference of rate between the towns and the counties; and this will account for the general dislike of the small towns to send members to parliament.

demesne, assessed, according to the historian, at a sixth of moveables, it is by no means clear that he acted in contravention of the letter of the law[1]. In the parliament of 1305 no complaint was made against the measure, but the king, at the petition of the archbishops, bishops, prelates, earls, barons, and other good men of the land, granted them leave to tallage their own ancient demesnes as he had tallaged his[2]. The circumstances of the case are obscure; the accounts of Edward II show that in 1303 a scutage for the Scottish war was due, for which no parliamentary authority is producible, but against which no complaint was made. Possibly the tallage of 1304 was a supplementary measure to the scutage of 1303, both of them being the result of some deliberation, the history of which is lost.

Tallage of Edward I in 1304.

This tallage however of Edward I was an unfortunate precedent. In the sixth year of Edward II the example was followed; on the 16th of December, 1312, the very day on which the letters of safe conduct were issued to the earl of Lancaster after Gaveston's murder, the king published an order for the collection of a fifteenth of moveables and a tenth of rent in his cities, boroughs, and demesne lands. The fact that the ordinances of 1311 had made no provision against such a tax, and that the writs for collection, which were issued on the last day of a parliament[3], make no mention of the authorisation of the parliament, points to the conclusion that the tallage was not regarded as unlawful. But the lesson of the ordinances had already begun its work: the citizens of London and the burghers of Bristol resisted the impost. The latter, who refused to pay because some of their fellows were imprisoned in the Tower of London, were engaged in an internal quarrel which left them very much at the king's mercy; the former however made a firm stand. They granted that the king might at his will tallage his demesnes, cities, and boroughs, but they maintained that the

Tallage of Edward II in 1312.

It is resisted by London and Bristol.

[1] Hemingb. ii. 233; Rot. Parl. i. 266; Record Report, ii. app. ii. 141. From the extant rolls of this tallage it is clear that demesne only was tallaged. See too Morant, Hist. Colchester, p. 47.
[2] Rot. Parl. i. 161, 162; above, p. 157.
[3] Parl. Writs, II. ii. 59, 60, 61, 83–85; Liber Albus, i. 428.

Resistance of the Londoners to tallage in 1312.

citizens of London were not to be so tallaged, appealing to the clause of Magna Carta which guaranteed to them their ancient privileges. The chancellor had stated that the tallage was imposed by the king in the right of his crown, a distinct assertion of prerogative which the citizens did not contradict, and against which they would have cited the 'confirmatio cartarum,' if that act had been understood to apply to their case. Neither party however was in a position to take extreme measures, and the citizens by two loans, one of £1000 and one of £400, purchased a respite until the parliament of 1315; the loans were to be allowed in the collection of the next general aid, and the tallage was thus merged in the twentieth granted in the next parliament. Many other towns procured exemption[1] on the ground that they were not of ancient demesne; the scheme no doubt proved unprofitable, and no other tax of the kind was attempted during the remainder of the reign; Edward III however revived, in 1332, the impost in exactly the same form. The letters for the collection were issued on the 25th of June[2]; the parliament, which met on the 9th of September, immediately took up the matter, and the king, in accepting a grant of a fifteenth and tenth, recalled the commissions for the tallage, promising that henceforth he would levy such tallages only as had been done in the time of his ancestors and as he had a right to do[3]. This was probably the last occasion on which this ancient form of exaction was employed[4]. The second statute of 1340[5] contained a clause providing that the nation should be 'no more charged or grieved to make any common aid or sustain charge, except by the common assent of the prelates, earls, barons, and other magnates and commons of the realm, and that in parliament.'

Tallage under Edward III in 1332.

[1] Madox, Firma Burgi, pp. 6 sq., 248. [2] Foed. ii. 840.

[3] 'Le roi a la requeste des ditz prelatz, countes, barouns, et les chivalers des countes, en esement de son dit poeple, ad grante que les commissions nadgaires faites a ceux qui sont assignez de asseer taillage en les cités, burghs, et demeynes par toute Engleterre soient de tot repellez quant a ore ; et que sur ce briefs soient mandez en due forme et que pur temps a venir il ne ferra asseer tiel taillage fors que en manere come ad este fait en temps de ses autres auncestres et come il devera par reson;' Rot. Parl. ii. 66.

[4] See Hallam, Middle Ages, iii. 112, 113, where the beginning of Edward III's reign is fixed as the point of time when tenants in ancient demesne were confounded with ordinary burgesses. [5] Statutes, i. 290.

Of the scope of this enactment there can be no doubt; it must have been intended to cover every species of tax not authorised by parliament, and although in other points Edward systematically defied it, it seems to have had the effect of abolishing the royal prerogative of tallaging demesne. But public confidence was not yet assured; in 1348 the commons made it one condition of their grant that no tallage or similar exaction should be imposed by the Privy Council[1]. In 1352 the king declared that it was not his intention or that of the lords that tallage should be again imposed[2], but the petition of the parliament in 1377[3], almost in the words of the statute of 1340, was answered by Edward with a promise that only a great necessity should induce him to disregard it. Another ancient impost was now becoming obsolete. The scutages so frequent under John and Henry III had ceased to be remunerative. The few taxes of the kind raised by Edward I seem to have been collected almost as an afterthought, or by a recurrence to the old idea of scutage as commutation for personal service. The scutage for the Welsh war of 1282, for instance, appears in the accounts of 1288, and the scutages of the 28th, 31st, and 34th years of the reign appear so late in the reign of Edward II as to seem nothing better than a lame expedient for pecuniary exaction[4]. Yet it occasionally emerges again as a tax payable when the king went to war in person; as so due it was remitted by Richard II after his Scottish expedition in 1385; and henceforth it sinks into insignificance[5]. The three customary aids however continued to be collected, although the nation expected them to be abolished by the statute of 1340. In 1346 Edward, on the occasion of the knighthood of the Black Prince, levied the aid in an unconstitutional way and in illegal amount, not however without a strong remonstrance from the parliament[6].

Abolition of the power of tallage.

Scutage become obsolete.

Continuance of the three customary aids.

[1] Rot. Parl. ii. 201, [2] Rot. Parl. ii. 238. [3] Rot. Parl. ii. 365.

[4] Rot. Parl. i. 292; Parl. Writs, II. i. 442 sq. So also the scutage for 4 Edw. II. collected in 1319; Parl. Writs, II. i. 517. The counties were amerced by Edward II in 1321 for not sending their force to Cirencester; Parl. Writs, II. i. 543.

[5] Rot. Parl. iii. 213. In 1377 a tax of a pound on the knight's fee was proposed and rejected; above, p. 437. According to Coke no scutage was levied after the eighth year of Edward II; the impost was expressly abolished by statute 12 Charles II; Blackstone, Comm. ii. 75. [6] Above, p. 383.

The newer forms of taxation.

276. The disappearance of these ancient taxes is not to be attributed either to the opposition of the parliament or to the good faith of the king so much as to the fact that they were being superseded by other methods of exaction, which were at once more productive and more easily manipulated, the subsidies on moveables and the customs on import and export. In the former no new exercise of prerogative was possible; the tallage, in fact, which we have just examined, was simply an unauthorised exaction on moveables, which disappears with the feudal obligations of demesne. The history of the customs is more interesting and important.

Freedom of trade established by *Magna Carta.*

The forty-first article of the great charter empowered all merchants to transact their business freely within the kingdom without any 'maletote' or unjust exaction, but subject to certain ancient and right customs, except in the time of war, when the merchants of the hostile nation were disqualified. The mention of a maletote seems to show that such an impost was not unusual, and the ancient and right customs were sufficiently well ascertained. The taxable commodities were of three sorts: wine, general merchandise, and wool. On wine the ancient custom was 'the prisage,' the royal right of taking from each wine-ship, when it landed, one cask for every ten which the vessel contained, at the price of twenty shillings the cask[1]. The customs on general merchandise were collected in the shape of a fifteenth or other sum levied very much as a toll or licence to trade[2]. The wool was especially liable to be arrested and redeemed from the king's hands by a ransom, for which even the name maletote is too mild a term. Great irregularity prevailed in the whole management of the customs until the accession of Edward I: the merchants, except where they were secured by royal charter or by the strength of their own confederations, lying very much at the mercy of the king's servants, and the prices of their commodities being enormously enhanced by the risk of trading. The wine trade was probably the most secure

Ancient and right customs or prises.

Edward I regulates the customs.

[1] Madox, Hist. Exch. p. 525; Hale, on the Customs, printed in Hargrave's Tracts, i. 116 sq.; Liber Albus, i. 247, 248.

[2] Madox, Hist. Exch. p. 529 sq.

in consequence of the necessity of keeping Gascony in good temper. The negotiations of Henry III with the merchants have been already noted.

Origin of the customs on wool: grant in 1275.

The vote of the parliament of 1275[1], which gave to Edward I a custom of half a mark on the sack and 300 woolfells, and a mark on the last of leather, is the legal and historical foundation of the custom on wool. It was levied on all exports, and became at once an important part of the ordinary revenue, not as a maletote and therefore not transgressing the terms of the great charter. In the summer of 1294, under the immediate pressure of a war with France, the king obtained the consent of the merchants to a great increase of the custom; the rate on the sack of broken wool was raised to five marks, other wool paid three marks on the sack, the woolfells passed at three marks for the 300, and leather at ten marks on the last[2]. The rate was reduced the same year, probably in consequence of a parliamentary remonstrance, the wool and woolfells paying three marks and the leather five. The seizure of the wool in 1297[3] was clearly an exceptional measure, like the prohibition of export under Edward III, adopted probably to secure an immediate payment of the custom, for the rate fixed in 1294 is mentioned in the 'confirmatio cartarum' as the regular impost which, with all similar maletotes the king promises to release; on the abolition of the maletote the custom fell to the rate fixed in 1275.

Increase in 1294 by the merchants.

Seizure of wool in 1297.

277. The exigencies of the year 1303 suggested to the king a

[1] Above, pp. 109, 192, 244; Hale, Customs, pp. 147, 154.

[2] Above, p. 126. 'Custumam anno xxii mercatores regni in subsidium guerrae, quam rex pro recuperatione Vasconiae contra Gallicos intendebat, de lanis et coriis exeuntibus regnum regi gratanter concesserunt, videlicet de quolibet sacco lanae fractae quinque marcas, de quolibet sacco alterius lanae vel pellium lanatarum tres marcas, de quolibet lasto coriorum decem [B. Cotton, p. 246, reads *quinque*] marcas; quod quidem subsidium rex postmodum gratiose mitigavit, videlicet concessit xv° die Novembris eodem anno xxii° finiente, incipiente xxiii°, quod omnes mercatores tam regni quam aliunde, mercatoribus regni Franciae duntaxat exceptis, . . . regi de quolibet lasto tam lanae fractae quam alterius et etiam pellium lanatarum tres marcas, de quolibet lasto coriorum ducendorum ad easdem partes quinque marcas persolverent, a 29° Julii anno xxii° Edw. I. et usque festum sancti Michaelis tunc proxime sequentem, et ab eodem festo usque festum natalis Domini anno xxv° incipiente;' Account of 28 Edw. I; cited by Hale, p. 135.

[3] Above, p. 134.

Imposition of custom on foreign merchants by the 'Carta mercatoria.'

new method of dealing with the wool; and, by a grant of large privileges to the foreign merchants, he obtained from them the promise to pay, among other duties, a sum of forty pence on the sack, the same on 300 woolfells, and half a mark on the last. In this act, which was no doubt negotiated between the royal council and the merchants, and which took the form, not of statute or ordinance, but of royal charter[1], the king avoided a direct transgression of the 'confirmatio cartarum'; the persons who undertook to pay were aliens, and not included among the classes to whom the 'confirmatio' was granted, and the impost was purchased by some very substantial concessions on the king's part. But although the money came through the foreign merchants it was really drawn from the king's own subjects; the price of imports was enhanced, the price of exports was lowered by it. Accordingly the English burghers assembled at York the same year, refused to join in the bargain, and Edward did not attempt to coerce them. The increment fixed in 1303 was known as the 'nova' or 'parva custuma,' in opposition to the 'magna et antiqua custuma' of 1275, and its history from this point is shared by the other custom duties which had a somewhat different origin.

'Parva custuma' on wool.

Customs on wine and other merchandise, under the 'Carta mercatoria' of 1303.

The customs paid by the foreign merchants included, as has been mentioned, not only exports of wool and cloth, but wine and all other imported commodities, on which the king had by ancient prescription a right of prisage regulated by separate arrangement with the several bodies of foreign traders, each of which had its agency at the great ports. The charter of 1303[2] reduced the irregularities of these imposts to a fixed scale;—exported cloth was charged at two shillings, eighteen pence, and one shilling on the piece, according to its quality; wax at a shilling on the quintal; imported wine paid, besides the ancient prisage, two shillings on the cask, and all other imports threepence on the pound sterling of value; the same sum of threepence in the pound was levied on all goods and money exported; with these was accorded the increment on wool just described. The opposition of the English

[1] Above, pp. 156, 192, 244; Hale, p. 157; Foed. ii. 747.
[2] Hale, pp. 157 sq.; Foed. ii. 747.

merchants to these exactions continued to be manifested[1]; although they were not contrary to the 'confirmatio,' they contravened the article of the Great Charter which secured the freedom of trade, and were the subject of a petition presented by the parliament in 1309[2]. In reply to that petition Edward II suspended the collection of the new customs on wine and merchandise[3], to see, as he said, whether prices were really affected by them; after a year's trial he determined to reimpose them, but after the lapse of another year they were declared illegal by the ordainers, and ceased to be collected in October 1311. During the whole time of the rule of the ordinances the new customs were in abeyance; the new increment of 1317 was of the nature of a loan not an unauthorised general impost[4]; when Edward had gained his great victory in 1322 he restored the new customs, and for one year added an increment on wool, doubling the old custom payable by denizens and charging aliens double of that[5]. The re-established customs of 1322 were confirmed by Edward III in 1328[6], and became from that time a part of the ordinary income of the crown, receiving legal sanction in the Statute of Staples in 1353[7]. The latter variations of tariff are beyond the scope of our inquiries.

Petitions against the new customs.

Suspended by the ordainers.

Restored by Edward II.

Become a part of the ordinary revenue.

These details are sufficient to show that up to the accession of Edward III the regulation of the customs was quietly contested between the crown and the nation; the latter pleading the terms of the charter and the authority of the ordainers, the former acting on the prerogative right and issuing regulations

Character of this struggle.

[1] In 1309, June 27, Edward appointed the Friscobaldi to receive the new customs from the foreign merchants, and from the native merchants who were willing to pay them; Parl. Writs, II. ii. 20. Two months after this they were suspended.

[2] Rot. Parl. i. 443; above, p. 324.

[3] Above, p. 325, note 1. The additional custom on wool continued to be collected; Parl. Writs, II. ii. 25.

[4] Above, p. 341. See Parl. Writs, II, ii. 116–121; it was a heavy sum, on cloth, 6*s*. 8*d*., 4*s*., and 13*s*. 4*d*., according to value and dye; 5*s*. on the tun of wine, and 2*s*. on the pound of value; on woolfells and leather 10*s*.

[5] Parl. Writs, II. ii. 193, 230. An impost of 3*d*. in the pound on the German merchants, by Edward II, is petitioned against in 1339; Rot. Parl. ii. 46.

[6] Foed. ii. 747, 748.

[7] Statutes, i. 333. The custom paid by aliens according to this statute is ten shillings on the sack and 300 woolfells, and twenty shillings on the last (art. i.); the poundage (3*d*. in the pound sterling) is authorised by the 26th article, p. 342; cf. Hale, p. 161.

Use of the staples.

in council. The contest continues during a great part of the next reign, especially with regard to wool, the institution of the staples making this source of income peculiarly easy to be tampered with.

Unconstitutional taxation of wool by Edward III, through his dealings with the merchants.

In 1332, the year that witnessed Edward's unsuccessful attempt to tallage demesne, he issued an ordinance for the collection of a subsidy on the wool of denizens, at the rate of half a mark on the sack and 300 woolfells, and a pound on the last. This was done by the advice of the magnates, and was recalled the next year[1]. In 1333 the merchants granted ten shillings on the sack and woolfells and a pound on the last, but this also was regarded as illegal and superseded by royal ordinance[2]. The history of these attempts is not illustrated by the Rolls of the Parliament, so that it is impossible to say how far the issue or withdrawal of the order received the national sanction. The national enthusiasm for the war however put a more formidable weapon in the king's hands. In August 1336 the export of wool was forbidden by royal letters, and the parliament which met in the following month at Nottingham granted a subsidy of two pounds on the sack from denizens, three pounds from aliens[3].

Variety of negotiations.

In 1337 the process was reversed; in March the export of wool was forbidden by statute until the king and council should determine how it was to be dealt with[4], and the king and council thus authorised imposed a custom of two pounds on the sack and woolfells, and reeth on the last, doubling the charge in the case of aliens[5]. This exaction, although imposed under the shadow of parliamentary authority, had distinctly the character of a maletote, and as such the estates in 1339 petitioned against it, praying that it might be abolished by statute;

Petitions against the maletote.

the commons added that so far as they were informed it had been imposed without assent given either by them or by the lords[6]. The popular excitement had risen so high in consequence that a revolt was threatened, and the king had been compelled in 1338 to use the mediation of the archbishop to

[1] June 30, 1333; Hale, p. 162.
[2] Sept. 21, 1334; Hale, p. 163.
[3] See above, pp. 379, 380; cf. Rot. Parl. ii. 122, 143.
[4] Statutes, i. 280.
[5] Hale, p. 263.
[6] Rot. Parl. ii. 104, 105; above, p. 381.

prevent a rising[1]. The financial measures of 1339 and 1340 resulted, as we have seen[2], in a grant of the tenth fleece, sheaf and lamb in the former year, and of the ninth in the latter. In consideration of the urgency of the case, the king having consented to abolish the maletote, the parliament granted an additional subsidy of forty shillings on the sack, the 300 woolfells and the last[3]. This was intended to continue for a year and a half[4], but on the expiration of the term was continued by agreement with the merchants, and again became matter of petition in 1343[5]. To the petition the king replied that as the price of wool was now fixed by statute it could not be affected by the maletote, and the increased rate was continued for three years longer with parliamentary authority. In 1346 the commons again[6] petitioned for its removal, but it was already pledged to the payment of the king's debts. The process is repeated each time the impost expires; the merchants continue the grant and the parliament renew the authorisation, notwithstanding the petitions against it[7]. The commons apparently consent to the renewal instead of insisting on their remedy, knowing that if they did not the king and council would collect it in virtue of their bargain with the merchants. The dates of these renewals have been given in the last chapter. On several of these occasions the king undertook that it should be done no more, and that after the expiration of the present grant the old rate should be restored. The statute of 1340 was appealed to as the time from which the innovation was forbidden[8]. The exaction although felt to be heavy was agreed to by the parliament as a matter of necessity, the commons clearly thinking that if their right to impose it were now fully recognised, their claim to

Financial importance of the wool.

Grants renewed by arrangement with the merchants, against the will of parliament.

The commons have to submit.

[1] Hale, p. 163; Foed. ii. 1025. [2] Above, pp. 380, 382.
[3] Stat. 14 Edw. III. st. 2, c. 4; vol. i. p. 291.
[4] Rot. Parl. ii. 114; Stat. 14 Edw. III. st. 1, c. 21; vol. i. p. 289.
[5] Rot. Parl. ii. 138, 140. [6] Rot. Parl. ii. 161.
[7] 'Certeinz marchantz par confederacie faite entre eux, en coverte et coloure manere de usure, bargainez ove le roi, et cheviz sur meismes les biens a trop grant damage de lui et grant empoverissement de son poeple;' Rot. Parl. ii. 170.
[8] Rot. Parl. ii. 365. In 1377, 'ne nul imposition mys sur les leynes, pealx lanutz, quirs, si non le aunciene coustume . . . tant soulement, solonc l'estatut fait l'an de votre roialme quatorzisme;' to this the king replies, 'il y a estatut ent fait quele le roi voet q'il estoise en sa force.'

Unauthorised customs made illegal in 1362 and 1371.

withdraw it could not be resisted when the time came. The result proved their wisdom; Edward would never refuse to grant a perpetual privilege in return for a momentary advantage; so without any critical struggle the principle was yielded in 1340; but as in the case of the tallage, the commons did not trust the king; in 1348 they insisted that the merchants should not again make grants on the wool. Finally in 1362 and again in 1371 it was enacted by statute that neither the merchants nor any other body should henceforth set any subsidy or charge upon wool without the consent of the parliament[1]. The wearisome contest so long continued for the maintenance of this branch of prerogative comes thus to an end.

Origin of tunnage and poundage.

The process by which denizens as well as aliens became subject to custom on wine and merchandise is in exact analogy with the history of the wool. In 1308 Edward II persuaded a considerable number of English merchants to buy off the right of prisage by paying two shillings a tun on wine[2]. In 1347 the council under Lionel of Antwerp imposed a tax of two shillings on the tun and sixpence on the pound by agreement with the merchants[3]. This was continued from term to term by similar negotiations: the same rate was granted by the representatives of the towns under the influence of the Black Prince in 1372[4], and in 1373 it was formally granted in parliament for two years; from that time, under the name of tunnage and poundage it became a regular parliamentary grant[5]. The exactions on manufactured cloth exported, after a short struggle on the king's part, were also subjected to the control of parliament.

Importance of these details.

The history of the customs illustrates the pertinacity of the commons as well as the evasive policy of the supporters of prerogative; and it has a constitutional importance altogether out of proportion to its interest among the more picturesque objects of history. If the king had not been induced or compelled finally to surrender his claim, and to abide both in letter and spirit by the terms of the 'confirmatio cartarum,' it would have

[1] Statutes, i. 374, 393; Rot. Parl. ii. 308. [2] Parl. Writs, II. ii. 18.
[3] Rot. Parl. ii. 166, 229; above, p. 397; Sinclair, Hist. of Revenue, i. 122.
[4] Above, p. 424; Rot. Parl. ii. 310,
[5] Above, p. 426; Rot. Parl. ii. 317; Hale, p. 173.

been in his power either by allying himself with the magnates entirely to crush the trade and independent spirit of the towns, or by allying himself with the merchants to tax the body of the nation at his discretion. The commons showed, by their determination to make no difference between direct and indirect taxation, a much more distinct perception of the circumstances than appears in other parts of their policy. The king might be requested to live of his own, and so far they would relax the hold which royal necessities might give them over him; but, if he could not live of his own, they would not allow him either to sacrifice one half of the nation to the other, or to purchase a relief from direct imposts by conniving at unfair manipulation of indirect taxation. No attempt at unauthorised taxation of merchandise was made after the accession of Richard II.

No difference to be made between direct and indirect taxation.

278. The financial science of the fourteenth century had devised no scheme for avoiding a national debt; nor indeed was the idea of national debt in its barest form presented to it. The king was both in theory and practice the financier of the nation; all its expenditure was entered in the king's accounts; the outlay on the army and navy was registered in the rolls of the Wardrobe of Edward I; and if the king had to provide security for a loan he did it upon his own personal credit, by pledging his jewels, or the customs, or occasionally the persons of his friends for the payment. The system of borrowing, both from foreigners and denizens, had been largely developed by Henry III, whose engagement of the credit of the kingdom to the pope was a stroke of financial genius that rebounded with overwhelming force against himself and nearly cost him his crown. It was however only one example of a systematic practice.

The king's power of borrowing money.

Throughout his reign and onwards to the year 1290 the Jews afforded the most convenient means of raising money. This was done frequently, as had been usual under the earlier kings, by directly taxing them; they were exempted from the general taxation of the country to be tallaged by themselves; for the Jews, like the forests, were the special property of the king[1], and,

The Jews as a source of Revenue.

[1] By the statute 'De la Jeuerie,' Statutes, i. 221, 222, of the reign of Edward I, every Jew over twelve years old paid threepence annually at

Condition of the Jews in England.

as a property worth careful cultivation, they had peculiar privileges and a very dangerous protection; like the foreign merchants they had their own tribunals, a legal and financial organisation of their own, which, whilst it gave them security against popular dislike, enabled the king at any moment to lay hand upon their money. Not being, like the natives, liable to the ecclesiastical penalties for usury, the Jews were able to trade freely in money, and their profits, if they bore any proportion to their risks, must have been extremely large. As a result they were disliked by the people at large and heavily taxed by the crown. Henry II in 1187 exacted a fourth part of the chattels of the Jews; John in 1210 took 66,000 marks by way of ransom; Henry III in the form of tallage exacted at various periods sums varying between 10,000 and 60,000 marks, and in the year 1230 took a third of their chattels; in 1255 he assigned over the whole body of the Jews to earl Richard as security for a loan. The enormous sums raised by way of fine and amercement show how largely they must have engrossed the available capital of the country[1]. As the profits of the Jewish money trade came out of the pockets of the king's native subjects, and as their hazardous position made them somewhat audacious speculators, and at the same time ready tools of oppression, the better sense of the country coincided with the religious prejudice in urging their banishment. S. Lewis in 1252 expelled them from France; in England Simon de Montfort persecuted them. Grosseteste advised their banishment for the relief of the English whom they oppressed, but declared that the guilt of their usury was shared by the princes who favoured them, and did not spare the highest persons in the realm in his animadversions[2]. The con-

Exactions from them.

Their exile demanded

Easter, 'de taillage au roy ky serf il est'; and every one over seven years old wore a yellow badge, 'en fourme de deus tables joyntes.' According to Sinclair, i. 107, quoting Stevens, p. 79, the tallage in the third year of Edward I was threepence a head, in the fourth year fourpence. The statute probably belongs to the year 1275. See Madox, Exch. p. 177, note r.

[1] Madox, Hist. Exch. pp. 150–178.

[2] He writes to the countess of Winchester thus: 'Intimatum namque est mihi quod Judaeos quos dominus Leircestriensis de municipio suo expulit, ne Christianos in eodem manentes amplius usuris immisericorditer opprimerent, vestra disposuit excellentia super terram vestram recolligere. . . . Principes quoque, qui de usuris quas Judaei a Christianis extorserunt ali-

dition of the Jews was felt to be discreditable to the nation; the queen Eleanor of Provence was their steady enemy, and her son Edward I shared her antipathy. An early statute of his reign[1] forbade usury with special reference to the Jews, and in 1290 they were banished. This act of course was an exercise of considerable self-denial on the part of the crown, and the drain of money which resulted was no doubt one cause of Edward's pecuniary difficulties which occurred in 1294, but their expulsion was felt as a great relief by the nation at large, and it cut off one of the most convenient means by which the king could indirectly tax his people. It does not appear, however, that Edward himself had to any great extent used the Jews as his bankers.

Usury forbidden.

Banishment of the Jews.

The employment of foreign bankers for the purpose of raising money by loan, anticipating revenue, or collecting taxes, had been usual under Henry III, and possibly had begun as early as the reign of John, who had constantly furnished his envoys at Rome with letters of credit for the large sums which they required for travelling expenses and bribes. It is unnecessary for our present purpose to trace these negotiations farther back; but the extent of the foreign dominions of Henry II, and the adventurous policy of Richard I, had opened England to the foreign speculators, and laid the foundation for a system of international banking[2]. Under Henry III, however, the system had expanded, one chief cause being the exactions of the court of Rome, which involved the maintenance of a body of collectors and exchangers. Like the Jews, these money dealers readily lent themselves to the oppressions of the alien favourites; and the Caorsini and their fellows share the popular hatred with the Poictevins and Savoyards, whose agents they frequently were. From the beginning of the reign of Edward I we find the Italian bankers regularly engaged in the royal service. Edward was encumbered with his father's debts, and his

The employment of foreign bankers.

Expansion of the system under Henry III.

quid accipiunt, de rapina vivunt et sanguinem eorum quos tueri deberent sine misericordia comedunt, bibunt et induunt;' Epistt. ed. Luard, pp. 33, 36.

[1] Usury was forbidden them by the statute 'de la Jeuerie'; Statutes, i. 221; cf. Madox, p. 177; Pike, Hist. of Crime, i. 462 sq.

[2] On the whole of this subject see Mr. Bond's valuable article and collection of documents in the 28th volume of the Archaeologia.

Italian bankers employed by Edward I.

own initiatory expenses were increased by the cost of his crusade and his long detention in France in 1274. His first financial measure, the introduction of the great custom on wool, was carried out with the assistance of the Lucca bankers, who acted as receivers of the customs from 1276 to 1292[1]. The new source of income was in fact pledged to them before it became due. In 1280 merchants of Lucca and Oudenarde received the fifteenth granted by the estates[2]. Ten different companies of Florentine and Lucchese merchants were engaged in the wool transactions of 1294[3]. In 1304 the Frescobaldi of Florence were employed to receive the new customs granted by the foreign merchants, and throughout the reign of Edward II the Frescobaldi and Bardi share the king's unpopularity. The national records of these two reigns are filled with notices of payments made on account of sums bestowed by way of indemnity for loss incurred in the royal service. Under Edward III these notices are rarer, partly because that king negotiated more easily with Flemish and English merchants, but chiefly perhaps because he did not pay his debts. The bankruptcy of the Florentine bankers in 1345 went a long way towards closing this way of procuring money, and must have damaged the credit of Edward all over the continent; in 1352 the commons complained that the Lombard merchants had suddenly quitted the country with their money, and without paying their debts[4]. The Flemish merchants however showed more astuteness than the Italians; they obtained from Edward III and his great lords tangible security for their debts; the crown of England and the royal jewels were more than once pawned[5]. The earl of Derby was detained in prison for the debts of Edward III, as Aymer de Valence had been for those of Edward II; the merchants of Brabant in 1340 insisted, according to the story, on arresting the archbishop of Canterbury as surety for payment[6]; and the king himself declared that he was detained very much like a prisoner at Brussels. The English merchants, who succeeded to the ungrateful task

The Frescobaldi.

Flemish merchants.

[1] Hale, p. 154; Parl. Writs, i. 381; Madox, Hist. Exch. pp. 536, 537.
[2] Bond, p. 280. [3] Ibid. pp. 284, 285. [4] Rot. Parl. ii. 240.
[5] Foed. ii. 1213, 1229; iii. 7, 12. [6] Above, p. 385.

of satisfying the king's necessities, fared no better than the aliens; the commons in 1382 told the king that 'utter destruction' had been the common fate of those who, like William de la Pole, Walter Chiryton and others, had negotiated the king's loans[1].

These negotiations were not confined to professional agents: the princes of the Netherlands were ready and able to lend, the great feudatories of the French crown were among the royal creditors, and more than one of the popes lent to the king not only the credit of his name but sums of money told down, the payment of which was secured by a charge on the revenue of royal estates.

Loans from princes and popes.

All these transactions have one common element: to whomsoever the king became indebted the nation was the ultimate paymaster; either the parliament was asked for additional grants which could not be refused, or the treasury became insolvent, all the ordinary revenue being devoted to pay the creditors, and the administration of the country itself was carried on by means of tallies. The great mischief that would have arisen from repudiation compelled the parliaments to submit, but this necessity called forth more strongly than before the determination to examine into royal economies and especially into the application of the national contributions.

The nation was expected to pay and paid.

Besides these, however, moneys were largely borrowed from individuals and communities at home. We have seen Henry III personally canvassing his prelates and barons for contributions of the kind. The special negotiations with the several communities for grants of money may even under Edward I have taken the form of loan, but after the concessions of 1297 they could take no other. If it was necessary for any reason to anticipate the revenue, the clergy or the towns could be compelled to lend. Thus in 1311[2] Edward II borrowed largely from the towns and monasteries; in 1313 he borrowed nearly ten thousand pounds from the

Loans from the prelates, towns, and monasteries.

[1] Rot. Parl. iii. 123.

[2] In 1311 Edward II obtained a subsidy from certain 'fideles' and 'probi homines' of Norfolk and Suffolk, for which he issues letters undertaking that the payment shall not prejudice them; Parl. Writs, II. ii. 34. This may have been of the nature of a loan; and the instructions given to the townsmen of Oxford, Canterbury, &c., and to the religious houses of the neighbourhood, to listen to what Ingelard de Warle shall tell them on

Loans to Edward II to be repaid from the taxes.

bishops, chapters, and religious houses, to be repaid out of the next grant made in parliament or in convocation; in 1314, 1315, and 1316 similar sums were raised in this way[1], and the plan was followed by Edward III and Richard II. As the money was already paid, the lenders, when they met in council, had really no alternative but to release the king from payment. The raising of money by a vote of the clerical estate in convocation does not seem to have been considered as a breach of the letter of the 'Confirmatio Cartarum.' Yet it appears, at first sight, more distinctly in contravention of that act than the exaction of tallage and custom. Nor can it be asserted that the grants made in convocation were reported in parliament, so that they became in that way a part of the parliamentary grant; the clergy met generally at a different time and place from the parliament; they were very jealous of any attempt made by the parliament to control or even to suggest the amount of their vote, and they declined as much as they could to accept the character of a secular court even for the most secular part of national business. The idea that the clerical aids were free gifts made by the clergy out of their liberality to the king's needs or for national defence was probably found so convenient that no one insisted on maintaining the letter of the law; on the one hand it saved the clergy from the penalties of disobedience to the canon law as expressed in the bull of Boniface VIII; on the other it enabled the king to dispense with or to diminish the pressure of parliamentary negotiation; nor did the laity in parliament ever propose to relieve the clergy if they were willing to give. As the clergy moreover paid in common with the towns the higher rate of contribution on their estimated revenue they really gave little occasion for jealousy. The value of taxable property during the fourteenth century did not vary very much; the annual sum of £20,000 which was the amount of a clerical tenth was a very

Votes of money in Convocation.

the king's behalf (ibid. p. 31) probably referred to a similar negotiation, either for men or money; see below, p. 540. Other loans were raised from towns; Parl. Writs, II. ii. 35, 36.

[1] For the loans of 1313 see Parl. Writs, II. ii. 64 sq.; for those of 1314, ibid. pp. 78 sq.; for those of 1315, ibid. pp. 87 sq., 97 sq.; for those of Edward III, Foed. ii. 1040, 1064, 1107, 1116, 1206, 1214, iii. 68, 233, &c. &c.; and for the attempts of Richard II, Rot. Parl. iii. 62, 64, 82, &c.

important item in a royal revenue which did not perhaps ordinarily exceed £80,000; it was easily collected, and paid, if not willingly, at least unresistingly. The clergy however were as we have seen not less alive than were the laity to the opportunity of making their own conditions and of securing some check on the application of their grants.

Importance of the clerical grant.

279. Next in importance to the unconstitutional practice of raising money by tallage, custom, and loan, without the co-operation of parliament, may be ranked the prerogative right of purveyance[1], and its accompanying demands of service to be paid for at the lowest rate and at the purchaser's convenience,—often not to be paid for at all. There can be little doubt that this practice, which was general throughout Europe, was a very old privilege of the crown, that, wherever the court moved or the king had an establishment, he and his servants had a recognised right to buy provisions at the lowest rate, to compel the owners to sell, and to pay at their own time. It was not like the *feorm-fultum* of the Anglo-Saxon kings or the *firma* recorded in Domesday, a fixed charge on distinct estates and communities, but rather akin to the ancient right of *fodrum* or *annona militaris* exercised by the Frankish kings, who when engaged in an expedition took victuals and provender for their horses, or to the procurations levied by prelates on visitation[2]. It had also much in common with the prerogative of prisage exercised on the owners of wine and other merchandise for the relief of the king's necessities. The early history of the practice in England is obscure; the abuse of it may have been of comparatively late origin, or its early traces may be lost in the general oppressions, so that it comes to light only when men begin to formulate their grounds of complaint. Archbishop Islip, whose letter on the subject addressed to Edward III has been already quoted[3],

The right of purveyance.

Archbishop Islip's letter

[1] Hallam, Middle Ages, iii. 148.

[2] The right of purveyance implied payment, and is thus distinguished from the procurations; see Waitz, Deutsche Verfassungs-geschichte, iv. 14. But except in the matter of payment it is almost identical with the *fodrum*, which had its analogies in Anglo-Saxon institutions. Of such a kind was the custom of billeting the king's servants, his hawks and hounds, on the religious houses, which is often mentioned in the charters.

[3] Above, pp. 375, 403.

refers the initiation of the abuse to Edward II and his courtiers; forty years before he wrote, it had, he says, begun to be burdensome[1]; and as he became archbishop in 1349 the traditionary era coincides with the parliament of 1309, in which purveyance was the first subject of complaint. It had however been touched by legislation much earlier, in the great charter of 1215 and in the statute of Westminster in 1275. In the former we find that the right was claimed by the constables of the royal castles[2], who are forbidden to exact it; the latter, in its first clause, limits and provides a remedy for the common abuse. It was not expressly renounced in the confirmation of the charters[3], but legislation was again attempted in the second of the *Articuli super Cartas* of 1300. According to the rehearsal of this statute the king and his servants wherever they went took the goods of clerks and laymen without payment, or paying much less than the value; it is ordered that henceforth such purveyance shall be made only for the king's house, that it shall not be taken without agreement with the owner, in due proportion to the needs of the house and for due payments; the taking of undue purveyance is punishable with dismissal and imprisonment, and, if done without warrant, is to be treated as felony. Notwithstanding this enactment, and the demand for its execution, made in the parliament of Lincoln in 1301, in 1309 purveyance is the first of the gravamina presented to the parliament, and, by a promise that the law should be carried out, Edward obtained a grant of a twenty-fifth[4]. But the following year the complaints were

Early legislation on the subject of purveyance.

Restraint imposed in 1300.

Petitions in 1309,

and 1310.

[1] 'Illud enim maledictum praerogativum tuae curiae, videlicet capere res aliquas pro minori pretio quam venditor velit dare, coram Deo est dampnabile. Sed modo est tantum induratum et usitatum in tua curia et tempore patris tui et avi tui, quod jam duravit per XL annos et sic tibi videtur praescriptum illud maledictum praerogativum;' Speculum Regis, c. 4.

[2] Articles 28–31.

[3] In 1297, on the 26th of August, immediately after the king had sailed (above, p. 140), the judges at the Guildhall proclaimed on behalf of the king and his son, that for the future no prise should be taken of bread, beer, meat, fish, carts, horses, corn, or anything else, by land or by water, in the city or without, without the consent of the owner. This was before the Charters were formally confirmed, and may have been a special boon to the Londoners; Lib. Cust. p. 72.

[4] Writs for the trial of officers who had acted dishonestly in regard to prisage were issued Dec. 18, 1309; Parl. Writs, II. ii. 24.

renewed in the petition which led to the appointment of the ordainers[1]; the state had been so much impoverished by the king's follies that he had no means of maintaining his household but by extortions which his servants practised on the goods of Holy Church and of the poor people without paying anything, contrary to the great charter. The practice was forbidden by the tenth of the ordinances[2], and Edward, when he revoked the ordinances, confirmed the statute made in 1300 by his father[3]. No legislation however seems to have been strong enough to check it; it fills the petitions addressed to the parliament; not only the king but his sons and servants everywhere claim the right; it is the frequent theme of the chroniclers; and it is the subject of ten statutes in the reign of Edward III, by the last of which, passed in 1362, the king declares that of his own will he abolishes both the name and the practice itself; only for the personal wants of the king and queen is purveyance in future to be suffered, and the hateful name of purveyors is changed for that of buyers[4]. It is probable that this statute really effected a reform; legislation however, though less frequently required, was occasionally called for; in the times of civil war purveyance was revived as a terrible instrument of oppression, and was not finally abolished until Charles II resigned it along with the other antiquated rights of the crown.

Forbidden by the Ordinances; and in the revocation in 1322.

Legislation of 1362.

Tyranny of forced labour.

The prerogative of purveyance included, besides the right of preemption of victuals, the compulsory use of horses and carts and even the enforcement of personal labour[5]. In the midst of ploughing or harvest the husbandman was liable to be called on to work and to lend his horses for the service of the court,

[1] Liber Custumarum, p. 199; above, p. 326. [2] Above, p. 330.
[3] Rot. Parl, i. 456. [4] Statutes, i. 371.
[5] See above, p. 404, note 1. 'Item aliquando contingit quod aliqui de familia tua volunt habere homines, equos et carectas in una parochia; illi de parochia conveniunt cum eis pro dimidia marca vel plus vel minus ut possint domi remanere et non laborare in tuo servitio; die sequenti veniunt alii de familia tua et capiunt homines equos et carectas in eadem parochia, quamvis illi qui dederunt dimidium marcae crediderunt securitium habuisse; et ideo cave tibi!' Islip, Spec. Reg. c. 3. One of the charges against William Longchamp in 1190 was that he exacted the service of horses from the monasteries; see Ben. Pet. ii. The impressment of carts and horses is forbidden by the 30th article of the Charter of 1215; Select Charters, p. 292.

Exaction of labour in connexion with purveyance.

or of any servant of the king who had sufficient personal influence to enable him to use the king's name. It is difficult to conceive an idea of any custom which could make royalty more unpopular, for it brought the most irritating details of despotic sovereignty to bear upon the humblest subject. Nor can the maintenance of such a right be defended as a matter of policy or expediency; it might be advisable, under the pressure of circumstances, in case of a hurried march or on great occasions of ceremony, that the king's household should be protected against the extortion of high prices for the necessaries of life; but the systematic use of what at the best should only have been an occasional expedient betrays either a deliberate purpose of oppression or a neglect of the welfare of the people which was as imprudent as it was criminal. The abuse of purveyance accounts for the national hatred of Edward II, and for the failure of Edward III to conciliate the affection of the people, and helps us to understand why even Edward I was not a popular king. But it was unconstitutional as well as unwise. The goods and services extorted by the king's servants were paid for, if they were paid for at all, with tallies, on the production of which the unfortunate owner, at the next taxing, was relieved to the amount of his claims. He was therefore taxed beforehand not only against his will but in the most vexatious way.

A great cause of unpopularity.

Supplies levied on the counties.

280. Nor did the abuse end here; not only individuals but whole counties were harassed by the same means: on one occasion the sheriff is ordered to furnish supplies, beef, pork, corn, for the coronation festival or for the meeting of parliament; on another he is directed to levy a supply of corn to victual the army[1]; the supply is to be allowed from the issues of the shires

[1] These instances are in close analogy with the annona militaris or fodrum. In 1301 the sheriffs are ordered to furnish corn to be paid for out of the fifteenth; Parl. Writs, i. 402; in 1306 purveyance of corn for the army seems to be allowed to the sheriffs in passing their accounts; ibid. p. 374. So in 1297 supplies of meat were levied; above, p. 134. Under Edward II in 1307 the sheriffs are ordered to pay for the provisions taken for the coronation, out of the funds in their hands, 'absque injuria cuiquam inferenda, propter quod si super illo clamor ad nos perveniat, nos ad te punitione gravissima capiemus;' Foed. ii. 26. In 1312, 1313, and 1314, purveyance is ordered for the meeting of parliament, the payments to be made at the Exchequer; Parl. Writs, II. ii. 54, 55, 63 sq., 82 sq. In 1330 the counties of Dorset and Somerset complain of the purveyance of corn and

or in the collection of the next aid. Enforced labour at the king's wages is extended even to military service; the commission of array becomes little else than a purveyance of soldiers, arms, and provisions, and the ancient duty and institution of training under the assize of arms is confounded, in popular belief and in the system of ministerial oppression, with the hateful work of impressment. The commission of array affords a good instance of the growth of a distinct abuse from a gradual confusion of rights and duties into a tyrannical and unconstitutional exaction,—a growth so gradual that it is almost impossible to say when and where the unconstitutional element comes in. The duty of every man to arm himself for the purpose of defence and for the maintenance of the public peace, a duty which in the form of the fyrd lay upon every landowner, and under the assize of arms and statute of Winchester on the whole 'communa liberorum'; the duty of the sheriff to examine into the efficiency of equipment as a part of the available strength of the shire; the right of the king to accept a quota from each community to be maintained by the contributions of those who were left at home, an acceptance which had been welcomed by the nation as a relief from general obligation; such duties and rights were of indisputable antiquity and legality. The right of the king to demand the service of labourers and machinists at fair wages was a part of the system of purveyance, and the impressment adopted by Edward I was probably a reform rather than an abuse of that right. Yet out of the combination of these three, the assize of arms, the custom of furnishing a quota, and the royal right of impressment, sprang the unconstitutional commission of array. This existed in full force only in the worst times of the reigns of Edward II and Edward III, but in its origin it dates much farther back, even to the days when William Rufus could call out the fyrd and rob the men of the money with which their counties had supplied them for travelling expenses. Nor

Commissions of Array.

Growth of the system of Commissions.

bacon taken by the sheriff; Rot. Parl. ii. 40. In 1339 commissions of purveyance were issued and hastily recalled; ibid. ii. 106. The petitions on the subject are very numerous: purveyance for Calais is a matter of complaint in 1351 and 1352; ibid. ii. 227, 240.

Grants of men in council.

was the practice of making a grant of men, like a grant of money, altogether strange to the *commune concilium;* Henry III had accepted a grant of one labourer from each township to work the engines at the siege of Bedford. What the council could grant, the king could take without a grant; the same king could impress by one writ all the carpenters of a whole county. Such expedients were however under Henry III only a part of the general policy of administration; after Edward I had infused the spirit of law and order they became exceptional, and, as an exception to his general system, the demand of service in arms from the whole nation at home and abroad caused the loud complaints of his subjects in 1297; only as exceptional can it be justified on the plea of necessity. No such plea could be alleged under Edward II. Edward I moreover had always paid the wages of his forced levies; under Edward II the counties and even the townships were called upon to pay them; they were required to provide arms not prescribed by the statute of Winchester, to pay the wages of the men outside of their own area, and even outside of the kingdom itself. In 1311[1], whilst the ordainers were employed in drawing up the Ordinances, Edward II, without consulting parliament, applied to the several counties for the grant of an armed man from each township to be paid for seven weeks at the expense of the township; on consulting the barons however, and perhaps after a remonstrance from them, he withdrew the request. In 1314, after the battle of Bannockburn, commissions of array were issued for the election of soldiers to be paid by the townships[2], and in 1315 a full armament according to the statute of Winchester was ordered; all men capable of bearing arms were to prepare themselves for forty days' service[3]: and there was a similar levy in 1316[4]. It seems

Payment of wages.

Edward II tries to levy a force at the cost of townships.

[1] May 20: 'hominibus illis peditibus vadia sua pro septem septimanis sumptibus dictarum villarum ministrari;' possibly this was done by a separate negotiation with the county courts similar to that by which Edward was raising money at the time; see above, p. 532. He wrote on the same day to the earl of Lancaster and other great lords, asking their consent to the aid; but on the 5th of July the commissioners were withdrawn and the money spent was repaid; Parl. Writs, II. i. 408, 414.

[2] Parl. Writs, II. i. 431. [3] Ibid. 457. [4] Ibid. 479.

to have made little difference whether the king was acting with or against the authority of the Ordinances. On two occasions, in 1316[1] and 1322[2], the parliament granted a vote of men to be provided by the communities of the shires, when the towns made a grant of money; but each time, in a subsequent assembly of the knights of the shire, the grant of men was commuted for a contribution in money. But if the parliament could authoritatively make such a grant, the king could ask it as a favour of the communities without consulting parliament. In 1318[3] he requested the citizens of London and other large towns to furnish armed men at their own cost, undertaking that it should not prejudice them in future; in 1322[4] both before and after the battle of Boroughbridge he made the same request and took money in commutation. In 1324 however the king, or the Despensers in his name, ventured without consulting parliament to demand a similar aid: on the 6th of August, in alarm at the threat of invasion, Edward issued letters patent in which he declared that the array of arms under the statute of Winchester was unsuitable and insufficient for national defence, and that therefore 'de consilio nostro' it was ordained that in each county a certain number of men should be equipped with sufficient armour at the expense of the county[5]. This 'purveyance of armour' tempted the avarice of the king's

Votes in parliament to the same effect.

Grants of men commuted for money.

Purveyance of armour in 1324.

[1] The service required in 1316 was for sixty days; it was redeemed by a grant of a sixteenth; see above, p. 340; Parl. Writs, II. i. 157, 464; Sinclair, Hist. of Revenue, i. 119.

[2] The service in 1322 was for forty days; Parl. Writs, II. i. 573, ii. 186.

[3] Parl. Writs, II. i. 505, 510.

[4] Parl. Writs, II. i. 556, 557, 566. Even after the parliamentary grant of 1322 Edward continued his 'earnest requests' for additional grants of men from the towns; ibid. 579; and for increased force, the wages of which he would pay; ibid. 578, 597.

[5] Parl. Writs, II. i. 668: 'considerantes etiam quod dictum statutum tempore domini Edwardi quondam regis Angliae patris nostri pro conservatione pacis, tempore pacis etiam, periculo extero non ingruente, ordinatum fuit, et quod pro prompta defensione nostra et dicti regni contra subitos et inopinatos aggressus dicti regis (Franciae) praeter formas proclamationis et statuti praedictorum majorem et fortiorem potentiam aliorum hominum peditum armatorum oportet necessario nos habere, de consilio nostro . . . ordinavimus.' The particular sorts of armour are then prescribed; the armour is to be kept in the towns until the levies are ready, and after the campaign it is to be carefully preserved and used for training under a new form to be afterwards issued.

servants, and the demand shortly afterwards was considerably reduced, the conduct of the purveyors being subjected to severe scrutiny[1]. The failure of the expedient in 1311 and 1314, and its commutation even when fortified with parliamentary authority in 1316 and 1322, show that it was viewed with repulsion and alarm. The principle on which it rested was called in question by the first parliament of Edward III. A petition was presented that the 'gentz de commune' might not be distrained to arm themselves at their own cost contrary to the statute of Winchester, or to serve beyond the limits of their counties except at the king's cost[2]. This was established by statute in a modified form, and it was enacted that except in case of invasion it should not be done[3]. Another petition states the abuse of the commissions of array: such commissions had been issued to certain persons in the several counties to array men-at-arms and to pay them and convey them to Scotland or Gascony at the cost of the commons, arrayers and conveyers, without receiving anything from the king; whereat the commons, the arrayers and the conveyers were greatly aggrieved: the king's answer recorded in the statute was that it should be done so no more[4]. One of the charges brought against Mortimer in 1330 was that he had obtained from the knights at the parliament of Winchester a grant of men to serve in Gascony at the cost of the townships[5]. No sooner however was the pressure of war felt than the practice was resorted to again.

Dislike of the system.

Statutes passed under Edward III.

Practice resumed.

[1] On the 19th of November (Parl. Writs, II. i. 677) the king ordered that the purveyance of haubergeons and plate armour should cease, but that the men required should be armed with aketons, bacinets, gauntlets, and other infantry arms.

[2] Rot. Parl. ii. 10, art. 9.

[3] Statutes, i. 255; 1 Edw. III. st. 2, c. 5.

[4] Rot. Parl. ii. 8; 'ensement pur ceo que commissiouns sunt este mandez as certeinz persones del ditz countes de araier gentz d'armes et a paier, de eux mener in Escoce, et en Gascoyne, as custages de la commune et des araiours et menours, sauntz rien prendre de roy, dount la commune et les araiours et menours ount est greve grantment; dount ils prient remedie, issint que quant le roy envoit ses commissiouns pur choses que luy touchent, que le execucion ceo face a custages le roy, et que nul ne soit destreint de aler en Escoce ne en Gascoyne, nule part hors de realme, ne de autre service faire que a ses tenementz ne devient de droit a faire.' 'Quant al point tochante la commission des arraiours et des menours des gentz, il semble au conseil, qe mes ne soit foit;' ibid. p. 11. It was ordered by statute; 1 Edw. III. st. 2. c. 7; Statutes, i. 256.

[5] Rot. Parl. ii. 52.

In 1339 the men provided for the Scottish war were directed by the parliament to be paid by their counties until they reached the frontier, and from thence onwards by the king[1]. The statute of 1327 was contravened, by competent authority perhaps, but without being repealed. As a natural consequence the king regarded himself as freed from his obligation. In 1344 and 1346 the commons urged loudly the breach of faith involved in this; notwithstanding their liberal grants and the king's equally liberal promises, there were issued from day to day commissions to array all over England men-at-arms, hobelours, and archers; the weapons were charged to the commons; victuals were levied from the commons without any payment, and the horses of the king and prince were in several places lodged at the heavy cost of the commons. Edward in reply urged the authority of parliament, the necessity of the case, and the existence of a remedy in case of oppression[2]. Warned by this answer the commons in the next parliament declined to advise the king as to the maintenance of the war and petitioned again; the king promised redress 'sauvee totefoiz la prerogative[3].' The commissions take their place with the maletote and purveyance among the standing grievances; and the remedy is equally long in coming. In 1352 it was prayed that no one who was not bound by his tenure should be compelled to furnish armed men, unless by common assent and grant made in parliament[4]. The petition was granted and incorporated in a statute[5], which was confirmed in the 4th year of Henry IV[6]. Neither royal promise nor legislation however was sufficiently powerful to restrain abuses, although during the latter years of Edward III and the comparatively peaceful reign of Richard the complaints are less loud than before.

Persistence of the commons in petitioning against it.

Insufficiency of legislation to restrain the abuse.

281. Besides the contrivances just enumerated, by which the royal prerogative enabled the king, indirectly or directly, contrary to the law and spirit of the constitution to tax his subjects, there were other means of doing the same thing in a more circuitous

Minor sources of income.

[1] Rot. Parl. ii. 110. [2] Rot. Parl. ii. 159, 160. See above, p. 396.
[3] Rot. Parl. ii. 165, 166; petition 16. See also Rot. Parl. ii. 170, 171.
[4] Petition 13; Rot. Parl. ii. 239.
[5] Statutes, i. 328. [6] Statutes, ii. 137.

Profits on coinage.

way: the management of the coinage for instance, which was on the continent a most fertile expedient of tyranny. This is a matter of considerable interest, but its history does not furnish data sufficiently distinct to be calculated along with the more direct means of oppression. We have noted the early severities of Henry I against the fraudulent moneyers, the accusation of connivance brought against Stephen, the changes of coinage under Henry II. That king has the credit of restoring the silver coinage to its standard of purity, which, except in the latter years of Henry VIII and in the reign of Edward VI, was never afterwards impaired. Under Henry III and Edward I the introduction of foreign coin and the mutilation of the English currency shook the national confidence, and the edicts of the latter king as well as those of Edward II seem to have been insufficient to restore it. The parliament of 1307[1] however, by authorising the existing currency, asserted the right of the nation to ascertain the purity of the coinage; in the thirtieth of the ordinances the king is forbidden to make an exchange or alteration of the currency except by the common counsel of the baronage and in parliament[2]; and frequent legislation in the course of the century shows that the right was maintained so far as the legislature could bind the executive power. None of the kings however need be suspected of conniving at any direct abuse in this matter[3].

Coinage regulated by parliament.

Difficulty of estimating the royal income.

282. It would greatly assist us in forming a judgment as to the amount of justification or excuse that could be alleged on behalf of the kings in their exercise of prerogative, if we could calculate what the amount of their regular income really was; and probably materials are in existence which might furnish the laborious student with trustworthy conclusions on the point. But the labour of working through these materials would be stupendous, and the results of such investigation can scarcely be looked for in this generation. We have however several detached

[1] Above, p. 316, note 1.

[2] Statutes, i. 165.

[3] See Ruding, Annals of the Coinage. i. 17, 18. The petitions on the subject are very numerous, but the abuses are owing to the currency of foreign coins, or to the want of a new issue of English silver; the old money was clipped, not debased.

volumes of accounts and occasional estimates which on particular items leave little to be desired. The royal income from the crown lands, escheats, and ordinary revenue, is the most difficult to calculate because of its perpetual variations. The produce of the customs has been estimated with some approach to exactness; the grants from the clergy can be exactly determined; and the Rolls of Parliament contain several estimates, not always to be relied on, of the amount of the lay grants. In the Wardrobe Accounts and Issue Rolls of the Exchequer we have records of expenditure, the usefulness of which is diminished by the fact that we cannot separate ordinary from occasional outlay and must therefore leave a very large margin in all conclusions. The general statements of contemporary historians are, it is believed, utterly unworthy of credit; they are estimates founded on the merest gossip of the times, and in many instances the results of calculations that seem in the last degree chimerical: in common with all medieval generalisations as to numbers they partake of the primitive indistinctness which has been remarked in the Homeric computations, and are in singular contrast with the scrupulous accuracy in matters of names and dates which the most critical judgment will not refuse to acknowledge in the annalists of this period. **Existing materials.**

The Wardrobe Account of the year 1300 certifies the amount of royal receipts and expenditure during that year: the sum of receipts is £58,155 16*s.* 2*d.*; the sum of expenditure £64,105 0*s.* 5*d.*[1] This was a year of active but not costly hostilities with Scotland, and was not marked by any extraordinary taxation. The account seems to be very exact, but no doubt some margin must be allowed for the supplies received in kind from the royal estates. **Accounts of the year 1300.**

The Issue Roll of the year 1370 exhibits an expenditure of £155,715 12*s.* 1½*d.*[2], and that of 1346 is described as con- **Accounts of 1370 and 1346.**

[1] Wardrobe Account, or Liber Quotidianus Contrarotulatoris Garderobae; ed. Topham, 1787; pp. 15, 360.

[2] Issue Roll of Thomas de Brantingham, bishop of Exeter, for the forty-fourth year of Edward III. The sum of the first half of the year is given in the roll itself, £78,516 13*s.* 8½*d.*; the second half, which I have added up, amounts to £77,198 18*s.* 5*d.*, but I cannot certify its exact accuracy.

taining an account of £154,139 17*s.* 5*d.*[1] Both of these were years of great military preparation and extravagant expenditure; taxation also was extremely heavy. The estimated expenditure of Edward III between July 20, 1338, and May 25, 1340, a period of unexampled outlay, was £337,104 9*s.* 4*d.*[2] The Wardrobe Accounts of Edward II vary in a most extraordinary manner; the expenditure of 1316–1317 is £61,032 9*s.* 11¾*d.*; that of 1317–1318 is £36,866 16*s.* 3½*d.*; and that of 1320–1321 is £15,343 11*s.* 11¾*d.*[3] The variation may be accounted for probably by the fact that, whilst in the first of these years the kingdom was comparatively peaceful and under the management of the council of the ordainers, it was in a very disturbed state during the second in consequence of the war between the earls of Warenne and Lancaster, and in the third owing to the attack on the Despensers. The revenue was probably collected with some difficulty and the accounts ill kept.

Estimate of 1338–1340.

Accounts of Edward II.

Later estimates.

Of the income of Richard II we have no accessible computation, but that of Henry IV, Henry V, and Henry VI has been carefully estimated, and may be referred to now so far as it illustrates that of the earlier reigns. The income of Henry IV is reckoned at £48,000[4]; that of Henry V appears from an official record to have been estimated at £55,754 10*s.* 10½*d.*[5], and that of Henry VI at £64,946 16*s.* 4*d.*[6] But these sums are not the result of an exact account kept in any one year; it is impossible to suppose that the revenue of Henry IV, swelled as it was by the enormous estates of the duchy of Lancaster, was less than that of Edward II, and the curious approximation of the revenue

[1] Forster on the Customs, Intr. p. 31; quoted by Sinclair, i. 128. Forster found the sum recorded on the Pell or Issue Roll of the year.

[2] Ordinances and Regulations of the Household (ed. Soc. Antiq. 1790), pp. 3–12.

[3] Archaeologia, xxvi. pp. 318, 319; from an article by Mr. T. Stapleton.

[4] Sinclair, i. 144.

[5] Foed. x. 113. The revenue of the ninth year of Henry V consists of the customs and subsidies on wool, merchandise, tunnage, and poundage, amounting to £40,687 19*s.* 9¼*d.*; the casual revenue paid at the exchequer £15,066 11*s.* 1*d.*; altogether £55,754 10*s.* 10¼*d.* To these Sir John Sinclair adds the sum of the revenue derived from the other estates of the king, the duchies of Cornwall, Lancaster, Aquitaine, &c., making the whole £76,643 1*s.* 8¾*d.*; Hist. Rev. i. 147.

[6] Rot. Parl. iv. 433; Sinclair, i. 153. The gross income of the crown, exclusive of the customs and subsidies on wool, &c., was in 1443

of Henry VI to that of Edward I may suggest a natural doubt. But allowing for this, we may perhaps infer from the other data that the sum of £65,000 may be taken to represent the ordinary revenue in time of peace, and that of £155,000, the expenditure in time of war, when the nation was exerting itself to the utmost. The variations of prices and fluctuations in the value of the current coinage during the century and a half to which these figures belong cannot be exactly estimated, but the like variations affect all the accounts from year to year, and the differences at the beginning and end of a century are not greater or more determinate than those which mark the beginning and end of a decade. Any calculation must be accepted subject to these variations, which necessarily affect its exact accuracy, but which it is, if not impossible, exceedingly difficult, to adjust.

Amount of revenue in time of war and peace.

If these figures be accepted as an approximation to the truth, the difference between ordinary and extraordinary expenditure would seem to be from £90,000 to £100,000, which sum would represent the contributions of the country at large, including the vote of additional customs and subsidies from clergy and laity. And a rough computation of the sums derived from these sources leads to the same conclusion. The greatest variation is found in the sums raised by the customs on wool. The regular or ancient custom of half a mark on the sack ought to be accounted in the ordinary revenue, but it may be used as a basis for calculating the extraordinary contribution. The 'magna custuma' during the reign of Edward I produced about £10,000 a year[1]; when, then, in 1294 that king demanded

Difference between ordinary and extraordinary expenditure.

Produce of the 'magna custuma.'

£34,224 10*s*. 8½*d*.; which was reduced by establishment charges and the like to £8,990 17*s*. 6*d*., exclusive of the duchy of Lancaster. The customs and subsidies on an average of three years amounted to £30,722 5*s*. 7¾*d*.

[1] Hale, p. 154:—

					£	s.	d.
'A festo S. Dunstani anno	7	ad idem festum anno	8	Edw. I	8,108	13	5
	8	,, ,,	9	,,	8,688	19	
	9	,, ,,	10	,,	8,694	19	
	10	,, ,,	11	,,	10,271	13	3
	11	,, ,,	12	,,	9,098	7	0
	12	,, ,,	13	,,	8,094	13	6
	14	,, ,,	15	,,	8,023	6	10
	15	,, ,,	16	,,	8,860	6	1
	16	,, ,,	17	,,	9,974	6	1

In 1421 the whole customs on wool produced £6,414 10*s*. 3¼*d*.; Rymer, x.

Various estimates of the subsidy of wool.

five marks on the sack, the exaction, if it had been collected, would have amounted to £100,000. As however five marks was not far from being the full value of the wool, and as the exaction was on the whole a failure, the sum of £80,000 may be perhaps an extravagant estimate. In 1338 a grant of half the wool of the country was reckoned at 20,000 sacks[1]; a subsidy then of 45*s.* on the sack would produce £90,000, and the ordinary grant of 43*s.* 4*d.* would produce £86,666 13*s.* 4*d.*; if on the other hand the vote of 30,000 sacks granted in 1340[2] be regarded as indicating the taxable amount more truly, the revenue from it would amount to £65,000. In 1348 the annual subsidy on wool was valued at £60,000[3]. Again, the vote of the tenth fleece, sheaf, and lamb, given in 1339[4], was estimated by reference to the spiritual revenue of the church, as valued for the papal taxation in 1291; it was in fact the tithe of the kingdom; the spiritual revenue under that taxation amounted in the gross to about £132,000, including however all the glebe-lands of the parish churches and the estimated income from offerings, which must be calculated at at least a third of the sum. Neither the grant of the tenth fleece nor that of the ninth, which was conceded in 1340, produced anything like the amount of the taxation of 1291, and this principle of assessment was therefore given up, but we may infer from these circumstances that it had been calculated to bring in about £100,000, a sum considerably in advance of that arising from the increased custom or subsidy on wool.

Further, we possess an account of the imports and exports of the kingdom in the 28th year of Edward III, 1354; the number of sacks exported was 31,651½, and the custom paid on

113. The produce of the customs on wool in the 9th of Henry VI was £7,780 3*s.* 1*d.*; in the 10th, £6,996 16*s.* 0¾*d.*; in the 11th, £6,048 0*s.* 8*d.*; Rot. Parl. iv. 435; Hale, p. 154.

[1] Above, p. 380. [2] Above, p. 382. [3] Rot. Parl. ii. 200.

[4] Above, p. 380. The editors of the Nonae Rolls, i. e. the account of the ninth sheaf, fleece, and lamb granted in 1340, remark that the commissioners in 1340 'were to consider the ninth of corn, wool, and lambs in 1340 worth as much in a parish as the tenth of corn, wool, and lambs, and all other titheable commodities and the glebe lands were, when the valuation was made of them in 1292.' The commons in 1410 state that the subsidy and custom on wool in 1390-1391 amounted to £160,000; Rot. Parl. iii. 625: this seems impossible.

them and on 3,665 woolfells was £81,624 1*s.* 1*d.*; the authority for the calculation is not very good, but the result is in accordance with our other data [1].

Greatest amount raised.

Lastly, we may infer from the general tenour of the financial statements on the Rolls of Parliament that the sum which under the greatest pressure the country could furnish was about £120,000. The parliaments of Richard II declared that to raise £160,000 [2] was altogether beyond their power, and that of 1380 reckoned the grant of 100,000 marks as a fair contribution from the laity.

Produce of tenths and fifteenths.

Of the produce of a vote of tenths and fifteenths we have no computation after the reign of Henry III that is trustworthy [3]; but as the amount of the clerical grant was commonly estimated at a third of the whole subsidy, and as the clerical tenth amounted to a little less than £20,000, we arrive at the sum of £60,000 as an approximation to the total sum. A single tenth and fifteenth seldom proved sufficient for a year when the subsidy on wool was not granted; a fifteenth and a half and a tenth and a half would produce £90,000, which is a little more than the calculated subsidy on wool. The variations of the budgets during those years of Edward III in which the greatest pressure was felt, would thus seem to have been caused rather by a wish to avoid alarming the people with the prospect of fixed and regular imposts than by any desire or indeed any possibility of altering the incidence of taxation.

Revenue of the clergy.

The revenue of the clergy, not including the baronies of the bishops, which were taxed with the property of the laity, amounted, spirituals and temporals together, to £199,311

[1] This calculation is given by Campbell in the Lives of the Admirals, i. 250, 251, and from Campbell by the authors of the parliamentary history. The original authority is Misselden's Circle of Commerce, published in 1633, pp. 119, 120. There is an important misprint of 130,651, for 31,651; but in other respects the estimate seems to be trustworthy.

[2] See above, p. 449.

[3] In 1224 a fifteenth produced £57,838 13*s.* 6*d.*; in 1233 a fortieth produced £16,475 0*s.* 9*d.*; in 1237 a thirtieth produced £22,594 2*s.* 1*d.* Liber Ruber Scaccarii; Hunter, Three Catalogues, p. 22. The English envoys at Lyons in 1245 estimated the whole revenue of Henry III at less than £40,000; and Matthew Paris in 1252 says that the 'reditus regis merus' was less than a third of 70,000 marks; M. Paris, pp. 667, 859. In 1347 the men of Ledbury estimated the subsidy of wool as double, and the men of Weobley as treble the amount of the fifteenths; but these are local valuations.

Taxation of the clergy.

5*s.* 0¾*d.*[1], under the taxation of 1291; heavy deductions have to be made on account of the devastation of the northern province by the Scots, which compelled a new taxation in 1318, and which considerably reduced the entire sum. On this valuation all the grants of the clergy in parliament and convocation were based, the lands acquired since 1291 being after some discussion in parliament taxed with those of the laity[2]. When Edward I in 1294 took a moiety of this, or £99,000[3], the exaction bore to the sum usually demanded about the same proportion as the tax on wool bore to the usual custom, but the demand was fully paid by the clergy, whilst the wool to a great extent escaped. In 1371 the clergy voted a sum equal to that granted by the laity, £50,000[4]; and in 1380 half as much as the lay grant, 50,000 marks[5]. The fact then that their assessment had been made once for all, whilst the laity were re-assessed from year to year, did not, as might be supposed, enable the clergy to elude taxation. They had no inducement to conceal their wealth, the record of which was in the king's keeping; and if at any time their grants failed to produce a sum proportionate to that given by the laity, the matter was at once readjusted by raising the rate of the tax instead of re-assessing individuals.

General estimate.

From these data we may conclude that when the king would live of his own and in time of peace he had a revenue of about £65,000; that for a national object, or for a popular king, grants would be readily obtained to the amount of £80,000; and that under great pressure and by bringing every source of income at once into account, as much as £120,000 might be raised, in addition to the ordinary revenue.

[1] These figures are given subject to correction by competent authority. They are the result of a painful calculation from the *Taxatio* itself. In the province of Canterbury the sum of spirituals is £106,053 11*s.* 2½*d.*; that of temporals £51,637. The spirituals of York come to £24,309 11*s.* 11¾*d.*, and the temporals to £11,969 6*s.* 7½*d.*; in both cases exclusive of the archdeaconry of Richmond, the temporals and spirituals of which amounted together to £5,341 15*s.* 3*d.*

[2] See above, pp. 396, 423. [3] Above, p. 126. [4] Above, p. 423.

[5] Rot. Parl. iii. 90; above, p. 449. A petition of the year 1346 that the fifteenths might be collected 'saunz rien encrestre' seems to show that the commons wished to avoid new valuations; Rot. Parl. ii. 161.

Ordinary revenue.

The ordinary revenue is however what was meant by the king's own; a sum of about £65,000, of which about £10,000 proceeded from the customs; these, with the other proceeds of the exchequer, the ferms of the counties, and other sources of ancient revenue, which had amounted to £48,781[1] under Richard I, were received at the exchequer to the sum of nearly £50,000 under Edward I[2]; casual windfalls in the shape of escheats and small profits on coinage and the like brought in about £10,000[3], and the revenue of the next year was generally anticipated in some small degree until a general grant wiped away the king's debts.

Estimate of outlay.

Obscure as these calculations of income now seem, the calculations of expenditure are much more difficult, and the student of to-day shares the bewildered sensations of the taxpayer of the fourteenth century as he approaches them. Certain records of outlay we possess, but they are very imperfect and irregular, and no doubt they were known to be so when the nation both in and out of parliament was clamouring in vain for an audit of the royal accounts; the blame of all extravagance was thrown upon the royal household, and no wonder when the whole accounts of army, navy, and judicial establishments appeared in the computus of the wardrobe along with the expenses of the royal table, jewel chests, and nursery. The Wardrobe Account of the 28th of Edward I assigns the several items of expenditure thus: Alms, £1,166 14*s.* 6*d.*[4]; necessaries, horses bought, messengers, wages, and shoes, £3,249 16*s.* 2*d.*[5]; victualling, stores, and provisions for the royal castles, £18,638 1*s.* 8*d.*[6]; the maintenance of the royal stud, £4,386 4*s.* 5*d.*[7]; the wages of military officers, artillerymen, infantry, and mariners, £9,796 9*s.* 2½*d.*[8]; the proper expenses of the wardrobe, including the purchases made for the queen and the chancery, £15,575 18*s.* 5½*d.*[9]; the difference between

Expenses of Edward I.

[1] Bened. Petr. ii. pref. p. xcix.

[2] Wardrobe Account, p. 1; 'Summa totalis receptae per scaccarium anno praesenti 28°, £49,048 19*s.* 10*d.*'

[3] Wardrobe Account, p. 15; 'Summa totalis receptae praeter scaccarium £9,106 16*s.* 2½*d.*'

[4] Wardrobe Account, p. 47.

[5] Wardrobe Account, p. 100.

[6] Wardrobe Account, p. 154.

[7] Wardrobe Account, p. 187.

[8] Wardrobe Account, pp. 210, 240, 270, 279.

[9] Wardrobe Account, p. 360.

Wardrobe accounts.

the sum of the Wardrobe Account and the entire outlay of the king, £10,946 5*s.* 4*d.*, is put down to the expense of the household and probably accounted for in another roll[1]. Far the largest portion of the expenditure is however seen to be devoted to the public service, considerably more than half being assigned to the garrisons and to the payment of the troops. The household expenses, properly so called, form a minor item. On this head we have some other data. The roll of the household expenses of the 44th year of Henry III exhibits an outlay of £7,500[2], but this was at the time at which his freedom was very much limited by the government established under the Provisions of Oxford; in 1255 he is found complaining that the income of his eldest son amounts to more than 15,000 marks[3]. In the first year of Edward I the household expenses from Easter to August amount to £4,086 0*s.* 4½*d.*; and in the 21st year the expenditure of the prince of Wales for the year is £3,896 7*s.* 6½*d.*[4]. The household expenditure of Henry IV varied between £10,000 and £16,000 annually[5]. Like Edward III he had a large family and establishment, and the expenditure of his magnificent grandfather can scarcely be computed at less.

Household expenses.

283. These figures do not make it at all easier to understand the constant irritation caused by the expenses of the household, so long as those expenses are regarded as mere personal extravagance. The sum of £12,000 or £15,000 could scarcely be considered enormous for a court which was expected by the nation to be at least as splendid as the courts of the great continental kings, at a time too when the king had no private revenue; for from the Conquest until the accession of Henry IV the king's estate was simply the estate of the crown, his foreign dominions being a cause of expense rather than a

[1] Wardrobe Account, p. 360.
[2] Devon's preface to Pell Roll of Edw. III, p. xvii.
[3] Sinclair, History of the Revenue, i. 103; M. Paris, p. 902; Hume, ii. 57.
[4] Devon, Preface to the Pell Roll of 44 Edw. III, pp. xvi, xvii.
[5] £10,000 in 1404; £16,000 anno 11 Henry IV; Sincl. i. 144, from Noy, p. 5; see Rot. Parl. iii. 528; in 1433 the estimate was £13,678 12*s.* 11*d.*

source of revenue. We may safely conclude that the murmurs against the prodigality of the kings were produced rather by the fact that they failed to make the ordinary revenue meet the ordinary expenditure, and that the nation having no way of auditing either receipts or outlay readily laid hold of the expenses of the court as the cause of increased taxation. It was the greediness of the courtiers, as they thought, which brought the evil of purveyance to every man's door, which increased general taxation, and threw on the several communities, in the shape of provision of men, arms, and victuals, the maintenance of the public burdens. To some extent the instinct was a true one; the maintenance of an enormous household and stud[1], for which provisions were collected at the lowest possible prices, just when the nation was suffering from bad harvests or plague and famine, shows an absence of the proper feeling which the king should have had for his people, and condemns such a king as Edward III. A little self-denial might have proved at least a wish to show sympathy; to maintain the splendour of the court during the prevalence of the plague was a folly as well as a sin. But the complaints are far louder against Edward II and Richard II than against Edward III. In their case we see how necessary it was for a powerful king to be a warrior. Their inactivity may have spared the pockets of the people, but the lightness of taxation did not make them popular. From anything that appears, the English would rather have been heavily taxed for war than see the king spend his time in hunting and feasting at his own cost. True, when the burden of war became intolerable, they wished for peace; possibly the sins of the warrior kings were visited on the next generation who tried in vain to pay their debts and were called to account for everything they spent, every friend they promoted, every minister they trusted.

Want of a proper audit.

Popular feeling on the expense of the household.

[1] The number of horses kept at the king's expense is one important item in archbishop Islip's remonstrance; the cost of a horse is calculated at £6 1*s*. 4*d*. per annum; Speculum Regis, c. 8. The great cost of the stud appears also from the Wardrobe Accounts; and the exercise of the right of purveyance for horses is a frequent matter of complaint; Rot. Parl. ii. 169, 229, 270.

National discontent at the royal expenses.

But it remains a most puzzling fact that the household outlay of the sovereign was the point which, in some measure from the minority of Henry III, and more distinctly from the accession of Edward II, formed the subject of national outcry and discontent. It was the easiest point to attack; it was also the most difficult to defend, and the hardest so to reform as to make it defensible. To make the king a mere stipendiary officer, or to place over him, as over an infant or lunatic, a commission for the management of his income, presented insurmountable difficulties under the actual conditions as well as on the theory of royalty.

Attempt to limit the king's power of giving.

284. The most plausible means of making and keeping the king rich enough to pay his own way was doubtless to prevent him from alienating the property of the crown; and the attempts to secure this object come into historical importance earlier than the direct restraints on expenditure. The outcry against foreign favourites, which had been raised at intervals ever since the Conquest, was the first expression of this feeling. The crown was very rich; so the nation was fully persuaded. The Conqueror had had an enormous income, William Rufus and Henry I had maintained and increased it. Stephen had begun the process of impoverishment, from which the crown had never recovered. His fiscal earldoms had been endowed out of crown revenue, royal demesne had been lavished on natives and aliens. Henry II had resumed, or tried to resume, what Stephen had alienated, and had been economical in private as well as in public, but Richard sold all that he could sell, and John wasted all that he could waste. The early years of Henry III were spent in attempts made by his ministers to restore the equilibrium of the administration; again there had been a resumption of alienated estates and a contraction of expenses. But Henry, when he came of age, was as lavish as his father had been, and the crown was poorer than ever. And now there was less excuse than before, for the great families of the Conquest were dying out; the vast escheats that fell to the king might have sufficed for the expenses of government, but instead of keeping them in his own hands he lavished them

Lavish bestowal of escheated lands.

on his foreign friends and kinsmen. It may be questioned whether, if the administration had been sound and economical, the king could have attempted to enrich himself by retaining the great fiefs, as the duchy of Lancaster, and to some extent the earldoms of Cornwall and Chester, were afterwards retained. The barons would have probably been jealous of any attempt to alter the balance existing between the crown and their own body. Owing to this feeling, which, when the crown was adequately endowed, was a just one, the early emperors had been expected at their election to divest themselves of such fiefs as they had held before. But on the other hand there was an equally well founded jealousy of a king who heaped upon his own sons and brothers all the fiefs that escheated during his reign, just as against a bishop who reserved all preferment for his own nephews. The king of the Romans was forced to swear that he would not alienate the property of the crown, and the like promise appears in one form of the English coronation oath[1]. The barons were amply justified in urging on Henry III the banishment of the aliens and the recovery of royal demesne; at the beginning of the reign they had compelled him to make proper provision for his brother, at the end of the reign they begrudged every acre that he bestowed on his sons[2]. In a penitential proclamation issued in 1271 he declared that he would retain all escheats for the payment of his debts[3]. The bestowal of the earldom of Cornwall on Piers Gaveston by Edward II was offensive, not merely as the promotion of an insolent favourite, but as a piece of impolitic extravagance. The national instinct was aroused by it; when the barons got the upper hand their first act was to limit the royal power of giving; the third article of the ordinances directed that no gift of land, franchise, escheat, wardship, marriage, or bailiwick should be made to any one without consent of the ordainers[4]; the clergy, in 1315, granted their money on condition that all grants made during the reign should be resumed[5]. The same principle was maintained under Richard II; Edward III in this, as in many other points, had

Resumptions of royal demesne.

[1] See above, p. 105. [2] See above, p. 41.
[3] Foed. i. 488; see p. 556 below. [4] Statutes, i. 158; see above, p. 329.
[5] Parl. Writs, II. ii. 92; see above, p. 339.

Policy of Edward III.

been either crafty enough to evade, or strong enough to break down, the rule; but by promoting his friends and kinsmen in the presence, and with the approval of, parliament, he had made the nation sharers in his imprudence. Yet in 1343 the commons petitioned that he would not part with the property of the crown; and Archbishop Islip urged in vain that he should pay his debts before he alienated his escheats[1]. Edward III had gone a long way towards building up a new nobility; the Montacutes, Percies, Latimers, Nevilles, and other great houses of the later baronage, owed their promotion to his policy or bounty. These adopted the prejudices or principles of the elder baronage. What Edward had done for them Richard attempted to do for Michael de la Pole and Robert de Vere, and was as speedily arrested in his design, as if he had really hoped to supplant them by his new creations. Again the cry was raised against alienation; a stringent oath against the acceptance of gifts was imposed on the ministers; and the friends of the king were sacrificed on the ground that contrary to oath and public policy they had received such gifts[2]. The principle was not conceded when the struggle ended in the king's destruction.

Enforced economy of the court.

285. Still less effective were the attempts made to limit the expenses of the household by direct rules. In this object the nation had help from the practice of some at least of the kings. The expenditure of the court had been regulated by Henry II in the curious ordinance which prescribes the allowances of the great officers of state and servants of the kitchen in the same page[3]. Henry III had been seized with qualms of conscience more than once, and had reduced his expenditure very materially. In 1250 he had cut down the luxuries and amusements of the court, diminished his charities, and even reduced the number of lights in his chapel; the historian remarks that his economy verged on avarice: he paid his debts and plundered the Jews[4]. In 1271, when on recovery from sickness he had taken a new vow of crusade, he had made over the whole revenue to his council for the payment of his debts, reserving

[1] Rot. Parl. ii. 141; Speculum Regis, cc. 7, 8.
[2] Rot. Parl. iii. 15, 16, 115, 213, etc.
[3] See above, vol. i. p. 345.
[4] See above, p. 66.

to himself only six score pounds to spend before he should start for Palestine[1]. The orderly accounts of Edward I, so often quoted above, show that he was careful although not parsimonious. But Edward II could not be trusted to manage his own. Accordingly with his reign began the attempts of the barons, in and out of parliament, to direct the administration of the household. The ordinances of 1311 were based on a proposition for the regulation of the household; the ordainers were empowered 'ordener l'estat de nostre hostel et de nostre realme[2]'; and in 1315 the king was put on an allowance of ten pounds a day[3], little more than he had when prince of Wales. In 1318, on the reconciliation of Lancaster, another commission of reform was appointed[4]. The repeal of the ordinances left Edward free to hasten his own fall; and no limit was attempted during the reign of Edward III, until in the good parliament the elected counsellors were directed to attempt the general amendment of the administration. Although this project was abandoned when John of Gaunt recovered his power, it was revived immediately on the accession of Richard II. Year after year we have seen commissions appointed in parliament to make the reforms needed, and the constant renewal of the commissions shows that the reforms were not made. When the king had at last emancipated himself from tutelage, he gave free reins to his prodigality. The bill of Thomas Haxey, in which the expenses of the ladies and bishops about the court were complained of, touched only a portion of the evil. Popular rumour alleged that not less than 10,000 people were daily entertained at the king's expense, and although this is incredible, and even a tithe of the number must have been in excess of the truth, the evil was not imaginary. The court was extravagant; it was also unpopular; its unpopularity made prodigality a greater sin. Richard's fall initiated a long reign of economical administration; Henry IV and the Lancastrian kings generally avoided offence in this respect, but the restraint was imposed by policy rather than by necessity. The parlia-

Commissions to reform the king's household.

Under Edward II,

and Richard II.

Haxey's bill.

[1] Foed. i. 488. [2] Foed. ii. 105; Liber Custumarum, pp. 198, 199.
[3] Above, pp. 338. [4] Above, p. 343.

ment had claimed and exercised the right of interference, but it had likewise become apparent that no such restrictions as they had sought to impose on Edward II and Richard II were applicable to a strong king; that the extravagance of the court was really only a minor cause of public distress, a colourable ground of complaint against an otherwise intolerable administration; and that such abuses were only a part of a wider system of misgovernment, the correction of which demanded other more stringent and less petty contrivances.

Responsibility of ministers insisted on.

286. The idea of controlling expenditure and securing the redress of all administrative abuses by maintaining a hold upon the king's ministers, and even upon the king himself, appears in our history as soon as the nation begins to assert its constitutional rights in the executory clauses of the great charter. Three methods of attaining the end proposed recommended themselves at different times: these are analogous, in the case of the ministers, to the different methods by which, under various systems, the nation has attempted to restrain the exercise of royal power, the rule of election, the tie of the coronation oath, and the threats of deposition; and they are liable to the same abuses. The scheme of limiting the irresponsible power of the king by the election of the great officers of state in parliament has been already referred to, as one of the results of the long minority of Henry III[1]. It was in close analogy with the practice of election to bishoprics and abbacies, and to the theory of royal election itself. When, in 1244 and several succeeding years, the barons claimed the right of choosing the justiciar, chancellor and treasurer, they probably intended that the most capable man should be chosen, and that his appointment should be, if not for life, at least revocable only by the consent of the nation in parliament. The king saw more clearly perhaps than the barons that his power thus limited would be a burden rather than a dignity, and that no king worthy of the name could consent to be deprived of all freedom of action. Henry III pertinaciously resisted the proposal, and it was never even made to Edward I, although in one instance he was requested to dis-

Three ways of doing it.

Claim to elect ministers.

[1] See above, pp. 40, 41, 62 sq.

miss an unpopular treasurer[1]. Revived under Edward II, in the thirteenth and following articles of the ordinances, and exercised by the ordainers when they were in power[2], it was defeated or dropped under Edward III, and again brought forward in the minority of Richard II. The commons petitioned in his first parliament, that the chancellor, treasurer, chief justices and chief baron, the steward and treasurer of the household, the chamberlain, privy seal, and wardens of the forests on each side of the Trent, might be appointed in parliament; and the petition was granted and embodied in an ordinance for the period of the king's minority[3]. In 1380 the commons again urged that the five principal ministers, the chancellor, treasurer, privy seal, chamberlain and steward of the household, should be elected in parliament, and that the five chosen in the present parliament might not be removed before the next session; the king replied by reference to the ordinance made in 1377[4]. In 1381 they prayed that the king would appoint as chancellor the most sufficient person he could find, whether spiritual or temporal[5]; in 1383 that he would employ sage, honest, and discreet counsellors[6]; and in 1385 he had to decline summarily to name the officers whom he intended to employ 'for the comfort of the commons[7].' But it may be questioned whether under the most favourable circumstances the right claimed was really exercised; the commons seem generally to have been satisfied when the king announced his nomination in parliament, and to have approved it without question. The appointments made by Edward II in opposition to the ordainers, when he removed their nominees and appointed his own, were acts of declared hostility, and equivalent to a declaration of independence. The ultimate failure of a pretension, maintained on every opportunity for a century and a half, would seem to prove that however in theory it may have been compatible with the idea of a limited monarchy, it was found practically impossible to maintain it; the

Officers of state elected.

Petitions on the subject.

[1] See above, p. 150.

[2] See above, pp. 330, 333, note 4, 343 sq. In 1341 the commons demanded that the nomination should be made in parliament; Edward agreed, but repudiated the concession; above, p. 390.

[3] Rot. Parl. iii. 16.

[4] Rot. Parl. iii. 82.

[5] Rot. Parl. iii. 101.

[6] Rot. Parl. iii. 147.

[7] Rot. Parl. iii. 213.

personal influence of the king would overbear the authority of any ordinary minister, and the minister who could overawe the king would be too dangerous for the peace of the realm. The privy council records of Richard II show that even with ministers of his own selection the king did not always get his own way.

Attempts to bind the ministers by oaths.

A second expedient was tried in the oath of office, an attempt to bind the conscience of the minister which belongs especially to the age of clerical officials. The forms of oath prescribed by the Provisions of Oxford illustrate this method [1], but there is no reason to suppose that it was then first adopted. The oath of the sheriffs and of the king's counsellors is probably much more ancient, and the king's own oath much older still. The system is open to the obvious objection which lies against all such obligations, that they are not requisite to bind a good minister or strong enough to bind a bad one; but they had a certain directive force, and in ages in which the reception of money gifts, whether as bribes or thank-offerings, was common and little opposed to the moral sense of the time, it was an advantage that the public servants should know that they could not without breach of faith use their official position for the purpose of avarice or self-aggrandisement. But when we find the best of our kings believing themselves relieved from the obligation of an oath by absolution, we can scarcely think that such a bond was likely to secure good faith in a minister trained in ministerial habits, ill paid for his services, and anxious to make his position a stepping-stone to higher and safer preferment [2]. It is seldom that the oath of the minister appears as an effective pledge: the lay ministers of Edward III in 1341 [2] allowed their master to make use of their sworn obligation to invalidate the legislation of parliament and to enable him to excuse his own repudiation of his word. Generally the oath only appears as an item among the charges against a fallen or falling minister, against whom perjury seems a convenient allegation [3].

Futility of the device.

[1] Above, p. 78. [2] Above, p. 391.

[3] On the oaths demanded from ministers, see Rot. Parl. ii. 128, for the year 1341; ibid. 132, for 1343; and under Richard II, ibid. iii. 115, etc., etc.

The third method was rather an expedient for punishment and warning than a scheme for enforcing ministerial good behaviour; it was the calling of the public servant to account for his conduct whilst in office. In this point the parliament reaped the benefit of the experience of the kings; and did it easily, for as the whole of the administrative system of the government sprang out of the fiscal action of the Norman court, a strict routine of account and acquittance had been immemorially maintained. The annual audits of the Exchequer had produced the utmost minuteness in the public accounts, such as have been quoted as illustrating the financial condition of England under Edward I. Minute book-keeping however does not secure official honesty, as the Norman kings were well aware; the sale of the great offices of state, common under Henry I and tolerated even under Henry II, shows that the kings were determined that their ministers should have a considerable stake in their own good conduct; a chancellor who had paid £10,000 for the seals was not likely to forfeit them for the sake of a petty malversation which many rivals would be ready to detect. On the other hand the kings possessed, in the custom of mulcting a discharged official,—a custom which was not peculiar to the Oriental monarchies,—an expedient which could be applied to more than one purpose. Henry II had used the accounts of the Chancery as one of the means by which he revenged himself on Becket. Richard I had compelled his father's servants to repurchase their offices, and the greatest of them, Ranulf Glanvill, he had forced to ransom himself with an enormous fine. The minister who had worn out the king's patience, or had restrained his arbitrary will, could be treated in the same way. Hubert de Burgh had been a good servant to Henry III, but the king could not resist the temptation to plunder him. Edward I again seems to have considered that the judges whom he displaced in 1290 were rehabilitated by the payment of a fine, a fact which shows that the line was not very sharply drawn between the lawful and unlawful profits of office. Edward II revenged himself on Walter Langton, Edward III vented his irritation on the Stratfords, John of

Annual audit in the Exchequer.

How this was affected by the sale of offices.

The mulcting or 'ransoming' of ministers.

Disgraced ministers restored on payment of fines.

Gaunt attacked William of Wykeham with much the same weapons; and in each case the minister assailed neither incurred deep disgrace nor precluded himself from a return to favour.

The ministers of Edward II held accountable by the people.

Such examples taught the nation the first lessons of the doctrine of ministerial responsibility. Great as were the offences of Edward II, Stapledon the treasurer and Baldock the chancellor were the more immediate and direct objects of national indignation; they were scarcely less hated than the Despensers, and shared their fate. The Kentish rioters or revolutionists of 1381 avenged their wrongs on the chancellor and treasurer, even whilst they administered to the Londoners generally the oath of fealty to king Richard and the commons. But it is in the transactions of the Good Parliament that this principle first takes its constitutional form; kings and barons had used it as a cloak of their vindictive or aggressive hostility, the commons first applied it to the remedy of public evils. The impeachment of lord Latimer, lord Neville, Richard Lyons, Alice Perrers, and the rest of the dishonest courtiers of Edward III, is thus a most significant historical landmark. The cases of Latimer and Neville are the most important, for they, as chamberlain and steward, filled two of the chief offices of the household, but the association of the other agents and courtiers in their condemnation shows that the commons were already prepared to apply the newly found weapon in a still more trenchant way, not merely to secure official honesty but to remedy all public abuses even when and where they touched the person of the king, and moreover to secure that public servants once found guilty of dishonest conduct should not be employed again[1]. As the grand jury of the nation, the sworn recognitors of national rights and grievances, they thus entered on the most painful but not least needful of their functions. The impeachment of Michael de la Pole in 1386 and of Sir Simon Burley and his companions in 1388, was the work of the commons. It is to be distinguished carefully from the proceedings of the lords appellant, which were indefensible on moral or political grounds; for there the guilt

The victims of 1381.

Impeachments by the Commons in 1376.

Impeachments in 1386 and 1388.

[1] See Rot. Parl. ii. 333, 355, iii. 160, 249.

of the accused was not proved, and the form of proceeding against them was not sanctioned either by law or equity. But the lesson which it conveyed was full of instruction and warning. The condemnation of Michael de la Pole especially showed that the great officers of state must henceforth regard themselves as responsible to the nation, not to the king only. The condemnation of the favourites proved that no devotion to the person of the king could justify the subject in disobeying the law of the land, or even in disregarding the principles of the constitution as they were now asserting themselves. The cruelty and vindictiveness of these prosecutions must be charged against the lords appellant who prompted the commons to institute them : the commons however were taught their own strength even by its misuse. And still more terribly was the lesson impressed upon them when Richard's hour of vengeance came, and they were employed to impeach archbishop Arundel, ostensibly for his conduct as chancellor and for his participation in the cruelties of which their predecessors in the house of commons had been the willing instruments, but really that they might in alliance with the king complete the reprisals due for the work in which they had shared with the appellants. The dangerous facility with which the power of impeachment might be wielded seems to have daunted the advocates of national right; the commons as an estate of the realm joyfully acquiesced in the change of dynasty, but, by subsequently protesting that the judgments of parliament belonged to the king and lords only, they attempted to avoid responsibility for the judicial proceedings taken against the unhappy Richard.

Importance of these as precedents.

The question of expenditure undertaken by the parliament.

287. If the king could not be made 'to live of his own, and no hold which the nation could obtain over his ministers could secure honesty and economy in administration, it would seem a necessary inference that the national council should take into its own hands the expenditure of the grants by which it was obliged to supplement the royal income. The functions of the legislature and the executive were not yet so clearly distinguished as to preclude the attempt : the consent of the nation was indeed necessary for taxation, but the king was the supreme

judge of his own necessities; he was still the supreme administrator in practice as well as in theory, an administrator who must be trusted whether or no he were worthy, and whom it was impossible to bring to a strict account. The men who had not hesitated to claim a right to interfere with the household expenditure, were not likely to be restrained by any theoretical scruples from interference with the outlay of money which they themselves had contributed. In this, as in so many other ways, the barons of the thirteenth century set the example to the commons of the fourteenth. Strangely enough the first idea of the kind came from the king's ministers. From the beginning of the reign of Henry III we have seen the special grants of the parliament entrusted for collection and custody to officers specially appointed for the purpose; frequently the form of taxation, including provision for the custody as well as the assessment of the grant, is issued by the advice and consent of the national council, and the audit withdrawn from the ordinary view of the court of Exchequer, where the king might be supposed to have too much influence[1]. In 1237 William of Raleigh, as the king's minister, proposed that the national council should not only draw up the form of taxation but elect a committee in whose hands the money collected should be deposited, and by whom it should be expended[2]. Although on that occasion the barons do not seem to have realised the importance of the concession, they are found a few years later complaining that no account had been rendered of this very grant, and intimating a suspicion that the proceeds were in the king's hands at the time that he was asking for more[3]. In 1244 the scheme of reform contained a proposal for the election of three or four counsellors, one part of whose work would be to secure the proper expenditure of the aids[4]. Throughout the baronial struggle the attempt was made to take out of the king's hands the power of expending public money. The time was not ripe for this. Edward I was too strong for any such restriction. Under Edward II the attempt to impose it was but one part of

Proposal in 1237 that special officers should take charge of the grant.

Proposal to elect treasurers.

[1] Select Charters, pp. 343, 352, 357; cf. pp. 38, 276.
[2] Above p. 53. [3] Above, p. 59. [4] Above, p. 63.

a project which took all real power out of the king's hands; the proposal enforced in 1310 and 1311, that all the proceeds of the taxes and customs should be brought into the Exchequer[1], shows that that court had become a sort of national court of audit; but its efficiency depended too much on the power or goodwill of the king to be trusted implicitly, and the hold which the ordainers kept upon it superseded rather than restricted the king's authority. From the time however at which the wars of Edward III began to be burdensome, the parliament showed a strong wish both to determine the way in which the grants should be applied, and to secure an efficient audit of accounts by the appointment of responsible treasurers for each subsidy. The first of these points the king readily yielded: the ministers were accustomed, at the opening of parliament, to declare the special need of the moment, and although the form frequently degenerated into mere verbiage, the hearers seem to have understood it as a recognition of their right to discriminate. Sometimes then the subsidy of the year is given for the defence of the coast, sometimes to enable the king to maintain his quarrel with his adversary of France, sometimes for the restoration of the navy, sometimes for the defence of Gascony; in 1346 and 1348 the money raised from the northern counties is applied to the defence against the Scots[2]; in 1353 the whole grant is appropriated to the prosecution of the war[3]; in 1346, 1373, and 1380, the continuance of the aid is made contingent on the continuance of the war. In 1380 the commons prayed that the aid might be spent on the defence of the kingdom, especially in the reinforcement of the earl of Buckingham's army in Brittany: the king replied that it should be spent for this purpose subject to the advice of the council and the lords[4]. In 1390 the custom on wool was appropriated partly to the expenses of the king, partly to the war, in a way which

Order for all taxes to be brought into the Exchequer.

Increased desire for an audit under Edward III.

Appropriation of grants.

[1] Above, pp. 329, 330. [2] Rot. Parl. ii. 161, art. 15; 202 art. 7.

[3] 'Que les subsides a ore grantez, ensemblement ove les quinzismes et dismes sont a lever, soient sauvement gardez sanz estre despendues ou mys en autre oeps nul fors que tant soulement en la maintenance de ses guerres solonc sa bone disposition;' Rot. Parl. ii. 252. Cf. pp. 160, 317; and see below, p. 568, note 1. [4] Rot. Parl. iii. 90, 93, 94.

anticipates the modern distinction between the civil list and public expenditure [1].

Audit of accounts attempted.

288. The efficient audit of the accounts was a much more difficult point, and it was not finally secured so long as Edward III lived. In 1340, however, William de la Pole was required by a committee of lords and commons to render an account of his receipts [2], and in 1341 the demand was distinctly made by both lords and commons, that certain persons should be appointed by commission to audit the accounts of those who had received the subsidy of wool and other aids granted to the king, and likewise of those who had received and expended his money on both sides of the sea since the beginning of the war; all the accounts to be enrolled in chancery as had been aforetime the custom [3]. The king yielded the point, as we have seen; undertook that the accounts should be presented for audit to lords elected in parliament, assisted by the treasurer and chief baron of the Exchequer. Whether the promise was better kept than the other engagements entered into at this parliament, we cannot distinctly discover; notwithstanding many just grounds of complaint, this particular point does not again come into prominence until the last year of the reign, when in the Good Parliament Peter de la Mare demanded an audit of accounts. In the last parliament of Edward III the commons petitioned that two earls and two barons might be appointed as treasurers to secure the proper expenditure of the subsidy [4]. Immediately on the accession of Richard II, when the difficult position of John of Gaunt and the prevailing mistrust of the court seemed to give an opportunity, the claim, which had been

Election of auditors.

Audit demanded in 1376 and 1377.

[1] 'Concessum est autem regi in hoc parliamento, ut habeat de quolibet sacco lanæ xl. solidos, de quibus xls. decem applicarentur in præsenti regis usibus, et xxx servarentur in futurum in manibus thesaurariorum constituendorum per parliamentum non expendendi nisi cum werræ necessitas instare videretur. Similiter rex habebit de libra sex denarios, quatuor servandos ad usum præfatum per dictos thesaurarios et duos jam percipiendos et expendendos ad voluntatem regis;' Wals. ii. 196. The same plan was adopted under Henry IV in 1404; Annales Henrici IV (ed. Riley), pp. 379, 380. In 1327 the petition that no minister might be replaced in office until he had rendered a final account was summarily negatived. Rot. Parl. ii. 9, 11.

[2] Rot. Parl. ii. 114.

[3] Above, p. 390; Rot. Parl. ii. 128, 130.

[4] Rot. Parl. ii. 364.

frustrated in 1376, was again made[1]. In the grant of aid made in October 1377 the lords and commons prayed that certain sufficient persons might be assigned on the part of the king to be treasurers or guardians of the money raised, 'to such effect that that money might be applied entirely to the expenses of the war and no part of it in any other way[2].' William Walworth and John Philipot were accordingly appointed, and swore in parliament to perform their duty loyally, and to give account of receipt and issue according to a form to be devised by the king and his council. The expedient was not altogether successful. John of Gaunt was suspected and openly accused of getting the money out of the hands of the treasurers for his own purposes, and when, at the next parliament, the commons, through Sir James Pickering their Speaker, demanded the account, the chancellor, Sir Richard le Scrope, demurred. Yielding however to the urgency of the commons, he laid the statement before them and they proceeded to examine and criticise it. The result was the bestowal of another grant with a humble prayer that it might be spent on the defence and salvation of the country and on nothing else, and that certain sufficient persons might be assigned as treasurers[3]. The warning thus given was taken: in the parliament of 1379 the king without being asked ordered the accounts of the subsidy to be presented by the treasurers[4]; and among the petitions of the commons appears a prayer that the treasurers of the war may be discharged of their office and the treasurer of the king of England appointed to receive all the money and all the grants to be made henceforth for war, as had been usual aforetime[5]; and this was followed up in 1381, when the commons proposed and the king directed a searching reform of the whole procedure of the Exchequer[6]. The particular point is again, as in the reign of Edward II, merged in the general mass of constitutional difficulties which fill the rest of the reign of Richard, but it furnished an example to the following parliaments, and from thenceforward, except during times of civil discord, treasurers of the subsidies

Failure of the experiment.

The principle is yielded in 1379.

Regular appointment of Treasurers of the war.

[1] Above, p. 444.
[2] Rot. Parl. iii. 7.
[3] Rot. Parl. iii. 35, 36.
[4] Rot. Parl. iii. 56, 57.
[5] Rot. Parl. iii. 66, art. 27.
[6] Rot. Parl. iii. 118, 119.

were regularly appointed, to account at the next parliament for both receipts and issues[1]. The commons had thus secured the right which the barons in 1237 had failed to understand, and they had advanced a very important step towards a direct control of one branch of administration as well as towards the enforcing of ministerial responsibility. This point is however interesting in connexion with the subject of general politics, rather than as one of the details of financial administration.

Great importance of the financial limitation thus set.

289. The command of the national purse was the point on which the claims of the nation and the prerogative of the king came most frequently into collision both directly and indirectly; the demand that the king should live of his own was the most summary and comprehensive of the watchwords by which the constitutional struggle was guided, and the ingenuity of successive kings and ministers was tasked to the utmost in contriving evasions of a rule which recommended itself to the common sense of the nation. But it must not be supposed that either the nation or its leaders, when once awakened, looked with less jealousy on the royal pretensions to legislate, to resist all reforms of administrative procedure, to interfere with the ordinary process of law, or to determine by the fiat of the king alone the course of national policy. On these points perhaps they had an easier victory, because the special struggles turned generally on the question of money; but though easier it was not the less valuable. There is indeed this distinction, that whilst some of the kings set a higher value than others on these powers and on the prerogatives that were connected with them, money was indispensable to all. The admission

The royal pretensions to legislate, to administer and to determine public policy.

[1] In 1382 tunnage and poundage were granted for two years, 'issint toutes voies que les deniers ent provenantz soient entierment appliez sur la salve garde de la meer, et nulle part aillours. Et a la requeste de la commune le roi voet que Mons[r]. Johan Philipot, Chivaler, soit resceivour et gardein de les deniers,' &c.; Rot. Parl. iii. 124. The same year in October the grant of a tenth and fifteenth was made 'entierment sur le defens du roialme;' ibid. 134. In 1383 the fifteenth is to be delivered to the admirals for the safe keeping of the sea; ibid. p. 151. In 1385 the receivers of the fifteenth were appointed in parliament, and ordered to pay nothing except by warrant from the king, and under the supervision of two lords appointed as supervisors; ibid. 204, 213; for the neglect of this order the chancellor was called to account in 1386; see above, p. 474. In 1390 a treasurer and controller were appointed; Rot. Parl. iii. 262, 263.

of the right of parliament to legislate, to inquire into abuses, and to share in the guidance of national policy was practically purchased by the money granted to Edward I and Edward III; although Edward I had a just theory of national unity, and Edward III exercised little more political foresight than prompted him to seek the acquiescence of the nation in his own schemes. It has been well said that although the English people have never been slow to shed their blood in defence of liberty, most of the limitations by which at different times they have succeeded in binding the royal power have been purchased with money[1]; many of them by stipulated payments, in the offering and accepting of which neither party saw anything to be ashamed of. The confirmation of the charters in 1225 by Henry III contains a straightforward admission of the fact: 'for this concession and for the gift of these liberties and those contained in the charter of the forests, the archbishops, bishops, abbots, priors, earls, barons, knights, freeholders and all men of the realm granted us a fifteenth part of all their moveable goods[2].' The charter of the national liberties was in fact drawn up just like the charter of a privileged town. In 1297 Edward I in equally plain terms recognised the price which he had taken for renewal of the charter of his father[3]. In 1301 at Lincoln the barons on behalf of the whole community told the king that if their demands were granted they would increase their gift from a twentieth to a fifteenth[4]; in 1310 they told Edward II that they had by the gift of a twentieth purchased relief from prises and other grievances[5]; in 1339

The share of Parliament in these points vindicated.

Purchase of liberties and rights.

Bargain and sale of privilege.

[1] Hallam, Middle Ages, iii. 162.

[2] 'Pro hac autem concessione . . . dederunt nobis quintam decimam partem omnium mobilium suorum;' Select Charters, p. 345.

[3] 'Quintam partem omnium bonorum suorum mobilium . . . concesserint pro confirmatione Magnae Cartae;' Parl. Writs, i. 53.

[4] 'Le pueple du reaume ensi ke totes les choses suzdites se facent e seent establement afermez e accompliz ly grante le xvme en luy del xxme einz ces houres graunte, issint ke tote les choses suzdites entre sy e la Seint Michel prochein suant se facent, autrement que rien ne seit levee;' Parl. Writs, i. 105.

[5] 'La communaute de vostre terre vous donerent le vintisme dener de lour biens, en ayde de vostre guerre de Escoce, e le vintisme quint pur estre deporte des prises et grevances;' Lib. Cust. p. 199. Similar expres-

Purchase of privileges.

the king informed the commons, by way of inducing them to be liberal, that the chancellor was empowered to grant some favours to the nation in general, 'as grantz et as petitz de la commune; to which they replied in the next session that if their conditions were not fulfilled they would not be bound to grant the aid[1].' The rehearsal, in the statutes of 1340 and later years, of the conditions on which the money grants of those years were bestowed, shows that the idea was familiar. It furnished in fact a practical solution of difficult questions which in theory were insoluble. The king had rights as lord of his people, the people had rights as freemen and as the estates of the realm which the king personified: the definition of the rights of each, in theory most difficult, became practically easy when it was reduced to a question of bargain and sale.

Presentation of gravamina.

As year by year the royal necessities became greater, more complete provision was made for the declaration of the national demands. The presentation of gravamina was made an invariable preliminary to the discussion of a grant, the redress of grievances was the condition of the grant, and the actual remedy, the execution of the conditions, the fulfilment of the promises, the actual delivery of the purchased right, became the point on which the crisis of constitutional progress turned. Except in cases of great and just irritation, an aid was never refused. When it was made conditional on redress of grievances the royal promise was almost necessarily accepted as conclusive on the one side; the money was paid, the promise might or might not be kept. Especially where the grievance was caused by maladministration rather than by the fault of the law, it was impossible to exact the remedy before the price was paid. Even under Henry IV the claim made by the commons that the petitions should be answered before the subsidy was granted, was refused as contrary to the practice of parliament. Thus the only security for

Promises of redress.

The demand of redress before supply.

sions are found in the reign of Edward III; see for example, Rot. Parl. ii. 273.

[1] 'Furent monstrez ascunes lettres patentes par les queles monseigneur l'ercevesque avoit poair de granter ascunes graces as grantz et as petitz de la commune;' Rot. Parl. ii. 104; cf. p. 107.

redress was the power of refusing money when it was next asked, a power which might again be met by insincere promises or by obstinate persistence in misgovernment which would ultimately lead to civil war. The idea of making supply depend upon the actual redress could only be realised under a system of government for which the nations of Europe were not yet prepared, under that system of limited monarchy secured by ministerial responsibility, towards which England at least was feeling her way.

Offer of the king to receive petitions.

290. It was under Edward III that it became a regular form at the opening of parliament for the chancellor to declare the king's willingness to hear the petitions of his people[1]: all who had grievances were to bring them to the foot of the throne that the king with the advice of his council or of the lords might redress them; but the machinery for receiving and considering such petitions as came from private individuals or separate communities was perfected, as we have seen, by Edward I. Petitions however for the redress of national grievances run back to earlier precedents, and became, almost immediately on the completion of the parliamentary system in 1295, the most important part of the work of the session. The articles of the barons of 1215, the petition of 1258, the bill of articles presented at Lincoln in 1301, the petitions of 1309 and 1310, were the precedents for the long lists of petitions, sometimes offered by the estates together or in pairs, but most frequently by the commons alone. These petitions fill the greatest part of the Rolls of Parliament; they include all personal and political complaints, they form the basis of the conditions of money grants, and of nearly all administrative and statutory reforms. They are however still petitions, prayers for something which the king will on consultation with the lords or with the council give or withhold, and on which his answer is definitive, whether he gives it as the supreme legislator or as the supreme administrator, by reference to the courts

Precedents of petitions offered in behalf of the community.

Multitude of petitions presented.

[1] For example in 1352; 'que s'ils avoient nulles petitions des grevances faites a commune poeple, ou pur amendement de la ley, les baillassent avant en parlement: et aussint fut dit a les prelatz et seigneurs que chescun entendreit entour la triere des petitions des singuleres persones, es places ou ils furent assignez;' Rot. Parl. ii. 237; cf. ii. 309; iii. 56, 71 sq.

of law, or by an ordinance framed to meet the particular case brought before him, or by the making of a new law.

Machinery for judicial action on petitions.

The first of these cases, the reference of petitions addressed to the king, to the special tribunal to which they should be submitted, need not be further discussed at this point[1]. It has, as has been pointed out in an earlier chapter, a bearing on the history of the judicature, the development of the chancery, and the jurisdiction of the king in council; but, except when the commons take an opportunity of reminding the king of the incompleteness of the arrangements for hearing petitions, or when they suggest improvements in the proceedings, it does not much concern parliamentary history: although the commons make it a part of their business to see that the private petitions are duly considered, the judicial power of the lords is not shared by the commons nor is action upon the petitions which require judicial redress ever made a condition of a money grant.

Legislation on petitions, by statute or ordinance.

The other two cases are directly and supremely important. Whether the king redresses grievances by ordinance or by statute he is really acting as a legislator[2]. Although in one case he acts with the advice of his council and in the other by the counsel and consent of the estates of the realm, the enacting power is his: no advice or consent of parliament can make a statute without him; even if the law is his superior, and he has sworn to maintain the law which his people shall have chosen, there is no constitutional machinery which compels him to obey the law or to observe his oath.

Office of the king.

More particularly, he is the framer of the law which the advice or consent of the nation have urged or assisted him to make; he turns the petitions of the commons into statutes or satisfies them by ordinance; he interprets the petitions and interprets the statutes formed upon them. By his power too of making ordinances in council he claims the power not only to supply the imperfections of the statute law, but to suspend its general operation, to make particular exceptions to its application, to abolish it altogether where it is contrary to his prerogative right. Many of these powers and claims are so

[1] See above, pp. 262–264.

[2] See below, p. 584.

intimately bound up with the accepted theory of legislation that they cannot be disentangled without great difficulty, and in some points the struggle necessarily ends in a compromise.

Legislation based on petition of the estates.

Nearly the whole of the legislation of the fourteenth century is based upon the petitions of parliament. Some important developments of administrative process grew out of the constructive legislation of Edward I, and were embodied in acts of parliament as well as in ordinances; but a comparison of the Rolls of Parliament with the Statute Book proves that the great bulk of the new laws were initiated by the estates and chiefly by the commons. Hence the importance of the right of petition and of freedom of speech in the declaration of gravamina, asserted by the invaluable precedents of 1301 and 1309. As the petitions of the commons were urged in connexion with the discussion of money grants, it was very difficult to refuse them peremptorily without losing the chance of a grant. They were also, it may be fairly allowed, stated almost invariably in reasonable and respectful language. Thus, although, when it was necessary to refuse them, the refusal is frequently stated very distinctly; in most cases it was advisable either to agree or to pretend to agree, or if not, to declare that the matter in question should be duly considered; the form 'le roi s'avisera' did not certainly in its original use involve a downright rejection. But the king's consent to the prayer of a petition did not turn it into a statute; it might be forgotten in the hurry of business, or in the interval between two parliaments; and, as the house of commons seldom consisted of the same members two years together, it might thus drop out of sight altogether, or it might purposely be left incomplete. If it were turned into a statute, the statute might contain provisions which were not contained in the petition and which robbed the concession of its true value; or, if it were honestly drawn up, it might contain no provisions for execution and so remain a dead letter. And when formally drawn, sealed, and enrolled, it was liable to be suspended either generally or in particular cases by the will of the king, possibly, as was the case in 1341, to be revoked altogether. The constant complaints, recorded in the petitions

Petition gives the power of initiation.

Chances of defeat after the petition is answered.

Evasions of the answers.

on the Rolls of Parliament, show that resort was had to each of these means of evading the fulfilment of the royal promises even when the grants of money were made conditional upon their performance; and the examination of these evasions is not the least valuable of the many lessons which the history of the prerogative affords.

The Commons insist on clear and formal answers.

The first point to be won was the right to insist on clear and formal answers to the petitions: and this was itself a common subject of petition: in several of the parliaments of Edward III, for instance in 1332[1], the proceedings of the session were so much hurried that there was no time to discuss the petitions, and the king was requested to summon another parliament. In 1373 the king urged that the question of supplies should be settled before the petitions were entertained; the commons met the demand with a prayer that they should be heard at once[2]. Occasionally the delay was so suspicious that it had to be directly met with a proposition such as was made in 1383[3], that the parliament should not break up until the business of the petitions had been completed. If the answer thus extorted were not satisfactory, means must be taken to make it so: in 1341, when the king had answered the petitions, the lords and commons were advised that 'the said answers were not so full and sufficient as the occasion required,' and the clergy were likewise informed that they were not 'so pleasant as reason demanded.' The several estates accordingly asked to have the answers in writing; they were then discussed and modified[4]. If the answers were satisfactory, it was necessary next to make them secure; to this end were addressed the petitions that the answers should be reduced into form and sealed before the parliament separated; thus in 1344 and 1362 the commons prayed that the petitions might be examined and redress ordered before the end of the parliament 'pur salvetee du poeple[5];' in 1352 that all the reasonable petitions of their estate might be granted, confirmed and sealed before the departure of the parliament[6]; and

[1] Rot. Parl. ii. 65, 66, 67, 68.
[2] Rot. Parl. ii. 316, 318.
[3] Rot. Parl. iii. 147.
[4] Rot. Parl. ii. 129, 130, 133.
[5] Rot. Parl. ii. 149, 272.
[6] Rot. Parl. ii. 238.

in 1379 the same request was made with an additional prayer that a statute might be made to the same effect; the king granted the first point, but said nothing about the statute, and no such statute was enacted [1]. As a rule however this was the practice: either the petitions were answered at once, or the private and less important were left to the council, or once or twice perhaps, as in 1388, were deferred to be settled by a committee which remained at work after the parliament broke up [2].

Petitions answered at once.

A more damaging charge than that of delaying the answers to petitions is involved in the complaint that the purport of the answers was changed during the process of transmutation into statute. To avoid this the commons petitioned from time to time that the statutes or ordinances of reform should be read before the house previously to being engrossed or sealed. Thus in 1341 it was made one of the conditions of a grant, that the petitions showed by the great men and the commons should be affirmed according as they were granted by the king, by statute, charter, or patent [3]; in 1344 the commons prayed that the petitions might be viewed and examined by the magnates and other persons assigned [4]; in 1347 the commons prayed that all the petitions presented by their body for the common profit and amendment of mischiefs might be answered and endorsed in parliament before the commons, that they might know the endorsements and have remedy thereon according to the ordinance of parliament [5]; in 1348 they asked that the petitions to be introduced in the present session might be heard by a committee of prelates, lords, and judges, in the presence of four or six members of the commons, so that they might be reasonably answered in the present parliament, and when they were answered in full, the answers might remain in force without

Petitions altered in the process of being turned into statutes.

Attempts of the commons to prevent this.

[1] Rot. Parl. iii. 61.

[2] In 1344 the commons petitioned 'que vous pleise ordener par assent des prelatz et grantz certeynes gentz qui voillent demorer tan que les petitions mys avant en parlement soient terminez avant lour departir, issint qe la commune ne soit saunz remedie;' Rot. Parl. ii. 149. See above, p. 497; and compare the proceedings in 1371, Rot. Parl. ii. 304.

[3] Rot. Parl. ii. 133; Statutes, i. 298.

[4] Rot. Parl. ii. 149, 150.

[5] Rot. Parl. ii. 165.

Demands of the Commons for the honest handling of their granted petitions.

being changed[1]. In 1377 it was necessary to maintain that the petitions themselves should be read before the lords and commons, that they might be debated amicably and in good faith and reason, and so determined [2]: and in the same parliament the commons demanded that, as the petitions to which Edward III in the last parliament but one had replied 'le roi le veut' ought to be made into statutes, the ordinances framed on these petitions should be read and rehearsed before them with a view to such enactment [3]; in 1381 they demanded that the ordinance for the royal household, made in consequence of their petition might be laid before them that they might know the persons and manner of the said ordinance before it was engrossed and confirmed [4]; in 1385 as in 1341 it was made one of the conditions of a grant, that the points contained in certain special bills should be endorsed in the same manner as they had been granted by the king [5]. Many expedients were adopted to ensure this; in 1327 it was proposed that the points conceded by the king should be put in writing, sealed and delivered to the knights of the shire to be published in their counties [6]; in 1339 the commons prayed the king to show them what security he would give them for the performance of their demands [7]; in 1340 a joint committee of the lords and commons was named to embody in a statute the points of petition which were to be made perpetual, those which were of temporary importance being published as ordinances in letters patent [8]; in 1341 the prayer was that the petitions of the magnates and of the commons be affirmed accordingly as they had been granted by the king, the perpetual points in statutes, the temporary ones in letters patent or charters[9]; and in 1344 the conditions of the money grant were embodied in letters patent 'pur reconforter le poeple,' and so enrolled on the statute roll [10]. This form of record recommended itself to the clergy also; they demanded that their grant and the conditions on which it was made should be recorded in a charter [11].

[1] Rot. Parl. ii. 201.
[2] Rot. Parl. iii. 14.
[3] Rot. Parl. iii. 17.
[4] Rot. Parl. iii. 102.
[5] Rot. Parl. iii. 204.
[6] Rot. Parl. ii. 10.
[7] Rot. Parl. ii. 105.
[8] Rot. Parl. ii. 113.
[9] Rot. Parl. ii. 133.
[10] Rot. Parl. ii. 150.
[11] Rot. Parl. ii. 152.

Variation of petitions.

We have not, it is true, any clear instances[1] in which unfair manipulation of the petitions was detected and corrected, but the prayers of the petitions here enumerated can scarcely admit of other interpretation; unless some such attempts had been made, such perpetual misgivings would not have arisen. There was no doubt a strong temptation, in case of any promise wrung by compulsion from the king, to insert in the enactment which embodied it a saving clause, which would rob it of much of its value. The mischief wrought by these saving clauses was duly appreciated. By a 'salvo ordine meo,' or 'saving the rights of the church,' the great prelates of the twelfth century had tried to escape from the obligations under which royal urgency had placed them[2], and had perpetuated if they had not originated the struggles between the crown and the clergy. Henry II, himself an adept in diplomatic craft, had been provoked beyond endurance by the use of this weapon in the hands of Becket. Edward I had in vain attempted in 1299[3] to loosen the bonds in which his own promise had involved him, by the insertion of a proviso of the kind; and again in 1300[4] the articles additional to the charters had contained an ample reservation of the rights of his prerogative. The instances, however, given above, which are found scattered through the whole records of the century, show that the weak point of the position of the commons was their attitude of petition. The remedy for this was the adoption

Introduction of saving clauses.

[1] One instance, quoted by Ruffhead in his preface to the statutes, is this. In 1362 the commons petitioned against the use of French in the courts of law; the king answered the petition with an assent that legal proceedings should be henceforth in English; but when this answer became a statute, it contained a provision that the records should be kept in Latin. This however is scarcely an instance in point. See Rot. Parl. ii. 273; Statutes, i. 375; Ruffhead, i. pref. p. xv.

[2] 'Nam sicut nostri majores formulas juris suspectissimas habebant in jure, sic rex semper in verbis archiepiscopi, conscientiam habentis purissimam, quasdam clausulas causabatur, scilicet nunc "salvo ordine meo," nunc "salvo honore Dei," nunc "salva fide Dei";' R. de Diceto, i. 339.

[3] Above, p. 148.

[4] 'En totes les choses desusdites et chescune de eles, voet le rei e entent, il e soen consail et touz ceus qui a cest ordenement furent, que le droit et la seignurie de sa coroune savez lui soient par tout;' Art. super Cartas, Stat. i. 141. The importance of this clause came into discussion in the debates on the Petition of Rights in 1628 and is especially treated in Glanvill's speech printed in Rushworth's Collections, vol. i. p. 374.

Remedy for this abuse, the introduction of *Bills* in the form of statutes.

of a new form of initiation; the form of bill was substituted for that of petition; the statute was brought forward in the shape which it was intended ultimately to take, and every modification in the original draught passed under the eyes of the promoters[1]. This change took place about the end of the reign of Henry VI.

Undertaking of Henry V with regard to petitions.

Henry V had been obliged to reply to a petition, in which the commons had insisted that no statutes should be enacted without their consent, that from henceforth nothing should 'be enacted to the petitions of his commune that be contrarie of their asking, whereby they should be bound without their assent[2].' This concession involves, it is true, the larger question of the position of the commons in legislation, but it amounts to a confession of the evil for the remedy of which so many prayers had been addressed in vain.

Petitions for the enforcing of statutes actually passed.

The frequent disregard of petitions ostensibly granted, but not embodied in statutes, is proved by the constant repetition of the same requests in successive parliaments, such for instance as the complaints about purveyance and the unconstitutional dealings with the customs which we have already detailed. The difficulty of securing the execution of those which had become statutes is shown by the constant recurrence of petitions that the laws in general, and particular statutes, may be enforced: even the fundamental statutes of the constitution, the great charter, and the charter of the forests, are not executed in a way that satisfies

General petition.

the commons, and the prayer is repeated so often as to show that little reliance was placed on the most solemn promises for the proper administration of the most solemn laws[3]. It became a rule during the reign of Edward III for the first petition on the roll to contain a prayer for the observance of the great charter, and this may have been to some extent a mere for-

Petition for particular statutes to be observed.

mality. But the repeated complaints of the inefficiency of particular statutes are not capable of being so explained. Two examples may suffice: in 1355 the commons pray specially that

[1] Ruffhead, Statutes, i. pref. p. xv: the form being 'quaedam petitio exhibita fuit in hoc parliamento formam actus in se continens.'
[2] Rot. Parl. iv. 22; Hallam, iii. 91.
[3] See for example Rot. Parl. ii. 139, 160, 165, 203, 227.

the statute of the staple, the statute of 1340 on sheriffs, the statute of purveyance, the statute of weights and measures, and the statute of Westminster the First may be kept; in each case the king assents[1]. The annual appointment of sheriffs which was enacted by statute in 1340 is a constantly recurring subject of petitions of this sort. It would seem that the king tacitly overruled the operation of the act and prolonged the period of office as and when he pleased; the answer to the petition generally is affirmative, but Edward III in granting it made a curious reservation which seems equivalent to a refusal: 'in case a good sheriff should be found, his commission might be renewed and he himself sworn afresh[2].' Richard II in 1384 deigned to argue the point with the commons: it was inexpedient, he said, that the king should be forbidden to reappoint a man who had for a year discharged loyally his duty to both king and people[3]. In 1383 he had consented that commissions granting a longer tenure of the sheriffdom should be repealed, saving always to the king his prerogative in this case and in all others[4]; but now he declared simply that he would do what should seem best for his own profit and that of the people. He stated his reasons still more fully in 1397[5].

Argument of the king on the statutes touching sheriffs.

291. If it were within the terms of the king's prerogative not merely to allow a statute to become inefficient for want of administrative industry, but actually to override an enactment like that fixing the duration of the sheriff's term of office, it was clearly not forbidden him to interfere by direct and active measures with the observance of laws which he disliked. It is unnecessary to remark further on the cases of financial illegality in which the plain terms of statutes were transgressed, and which have been already noticed. These infractions of the

Interference of the king with the execution of statutes.

[1] Rot. Parl. ii. 265, 266.

[2] Rot. Parl. ii. 168. A very similar answer was given in 1334; ibid. p. 376; cf. Rot. Parl. iii. 44.

[3] 'Le responce du chanceller fuist tiell, q'il serroit trop prejudiciel au roi et a sa corone d'estre ensi restreint, que quant un Viscont s'ad bien et loialment porte en son office au roi et au poeple par un an que le roi par avys de son conseill ne purroit re-eslir et faire tiell bon officier Viscont pur l'an ensuant. Et pur ce le roi voet faire en tiell cas come meultz semblera pur profit de lui et de son poeple;' Rot. Parl. iii. 201.

[4] Rot. Parl. iii. 159.

[5] Rot. Parl. iii. 39.

constitution cannot be palliated by showing that an equal straining of prerogative was admitted in other departments, but the examples that prove the latter show that finance was not the only branch of administration in which the line between legislative and executive machinery was very faintly drawn. The case of a king revoking a statute properly passed, sealed, and published, as Edward III did in 1341, is happily unique[1]; that most arbitrary proceeding must have been at the time regarded as shameful, and was long remembered as a warning. Edward himself, by procuring the repeal of the obnoxious clauses in the parliament of 1343, acknowledged the illegality of his own conduct. The only event which can be compared with it is the summary annulment by John of Gaunt of the measures of the Good Parliament, an act which the commons in the first parliament of Richard II remarked on in general but unmistakeable terms of censure[2]; but the resolutions of the Good Parliament had not taken the form of statute, and so far as they were judicial might be set aside by the exercise of the royal prerogative of mercy. The royal power however of suspending the operation of a statute was not so determinately proscribed. The suspension of the constitutional clauses of the charter of Runnymede, which William Marshall, acting as regent, omitted in the reissue of the charter of liberties in 1216, shows that under certain circumstances such a power was regarded as necessary; and the assumption by Edward I, in 1297, of the attitude of a dictator, was excused as it is partly justified, by the exigency of the moment. There are not however many instances in which

Revocation of statutes in 1341.

John of Gaunt annuls the acts of the Good Parliament.

Suspension of the execution of statutes.

[1] Above, p. 391.

[2] 'Item que la commune loy et auxint les especialx loys, estatutz et ordinances de la terre, faitz devant ces heures, pur commune profit et bone governance du roialme, lour feussent entierement tenuz, ratifiez et confermez, et que par ycelles ils fussent droiturelement governez; qar la commune soy ent ad sentuz moelt grevez cea en ariere que ce ne lour ad my este fait toutes partz einz qe par maistrie et singulertees d'aucuns entour le roy, qui Dieux assoille, ont este plusours de la dite commune malmesnez . . . Requerante as seigneurs du parlement, que quan que y feust ordenez en ce parlement, ne fust repellez sanz parlement;' Rot. Parl. iii. 6. Here the commons themselves added the saving clause, 'salvant en toutes choses la regalie et dignitee nostre seigneur le roi avaunt dit, a la quelle les communes ne veullient que par lours demandes chose prejudiciele y fust faite par aucune voie;' ibid.

so dangerous a weapon was resorted to[1]. The most significant are those in which the king was acting diplomatically and trying to satisfy at once the pope and the parliament. Thus in 1307 Edward I, almost as soon as he had passed the statute of Carlisle, which ordered that no money raised by the taxation of ecclesiastical property should be carried beyond sea, was compelled by the urgent entreaty of the papal envoy to suspend the operation of the law in favour of the pope: in letters patent he announced to his people that he had allowed the papal agents to collect the firstfruits of vacant benefices, notwithstanding the prohibitions enacted in parliament[2]. The whole history of the statute of provisors is one long story of similar tactics, a compromise between the statute law and the religious obedience which was thought due to the apostolic see; by regarding the transgression of the law simply as an infraction of the royal right of patronage, to be condoned by the royal licence, the royal administration virtually conceded all that the popes demanded; the persons promoted by the popes renounced all words prejudicial to the royal authority which occurred in the bulls of appointment, and when the king wished to promote a servant he availed himself of the papal machinery to evade the rights of the cathedral chapters. This compromise was viewed with great dislike by the parliaments; in 1391 the knights of the shire threw out a proposal to repeal the statute of provisors, which had lately been made more rigorous, although the proposal was supported by the king and the duke of Lancaster; but they allowed the king until the next parliament to overrule the operation of the statute[3].

Edward I suspends the operation of the statute of Carlisle.

Exceptions from the statute of provisors.

Evasion of the statute of provisors.

[1] In 1385 Richard II suspended the execution of the act of 1384 touching justices and barons of the Exchequer until it could be explained by parliament; Rot. Parl. iii. 210; but his suspension was itself enrolled as part of a statute, so that it is really a case of initiation by the king, not of arbitrary suspension; Statutes, ii. 38.

[2] Rot. Parl. i. 222; above, p. 156.

[3] 'Fait a remembrier touchant l'estatut de provisours, que les communes pur la grant affiance qu'ils ont en la persone nostre seigneur le roy et en son tres excellent sen, et en la grant tendresse qu'il ad a sa corone et les droitz d'icelle, et auxint en les nobles et hautes discretions des seigneurs, s'assenterent en plein parlement que nostre dit seigneur le roy par advys et assent des ditz seigneurs purra faire tielle soefferance tochant le dit estatut come luy semblera resonable et profitable tan qu'al proschein

Petitions against grants of pardon and protection.

The more common plan of dispensing by special licence with the operation of a statute in the way of pardons and grants of impunity, was less dangerous to the constitution and less clearly opposed to the theory of the monarchy as accepted in the middle ages. Yet against the lavish exercise of this prerogative the commons are found remonstrating from time to time in tones sufficiently peremptory. The power was restricted by the statute of Northampton passed in 1328; but in 1330 and 1347 the king was told that the facilities for obtaining pardons were so great that murders and all sorts of felonies were committed without restraint; the commons in the latter year prayed that no such pardons might be issued without consent of parliament, and the king, in his answer, undertook that no such charters should thenceforth be issued unless for the honour and profit of himself and his people[1]. A similar petition was presented in 1351[2], and instances might be multiplied which would seem to show that this evil was not merely an abuse of the royal attribute of mercy or a defeat of the ordinary processes of justice, but a regularly systematised perversion of prerogative, by the manipulation of which the great people of the realm, whether as maintainers or otherwise, attempted to secure for their retainers, and those who could purchase their support, an exemption from the operation of the law. Even thus viewed however it belongs rather to the subject of judicature than to legislation.

The king undertakes to use it moderately.

Contrivances for the repeal of statutes.

These were the direct ways of thwarting the legal enactments to which the king had given an unwilling consent. Indirectly the same end was obtained by means which, if not less distinctly unconstitutional, were less distinctly illegal; that is, by obtaining petitions for the reversal of recent legislation, or by influencing the elections in order to obtain a subservient majority. For both of these the short duration of the parliaments afforded great facilities; and under Edward III and Richard II both were adopted. In 1377 for instance the awards of the Good Parlia-

parlement, par issint que le dit estatut ne soit repellez en null article d'icell.' Rot. Parl. iii. 285; cf. pp. 301, 317, 340; Walsingham, ii. 203.

1 Statutes, i. 264; Rot. Parl. ii. 172. See also pp. 242, 253; iii. 268, &c.

2 Rot. Parl. ii. 229.

ment were annulled on the petition of a packed house of commons[1]. In 1351 the commons prayed that no statute might be changed in consequence of a bill presented by any single person[2]; in 1348 that for no bill delivered in this parliament in the name of the commons or of any one else might the answers already given to their petitions be altered[3]. The king in the former case asked an explanation of the request, but in the latter he replied more at length: 'Already the king had by advice of the magnates replied to the petitions of the commons touching the law of the land, that the laws had and used in times past and the process thereon formerly used could not be changed without making a new statute on the matter, which the king neither then nor since had for certain causes been able to undertake; but as soon as he could undertake it he would take the great men and the wise men of the council and would ordain upon these articles and others touching the amendment of the law, by their advice and counsel, in such manner that reason and equity should be done to all his lieges and subjects and to each one of them.' This answer is in full accord with the policy of the king; it is a plausible profession of good intentions, but an evasive answer to the question put to him.

Evasive answer of the king.

292. The theory that the laws were made or enacted by the king with the consent of the lords and at the petition of the commons implies of course that without the consent of the king no statute could be enacted at all: and so far as the rolls of parliament show, no proposed legislation except the ordinances of 1311 reached the stage at which it took the form of statute without having been approved by the king. The legislation of the ordainers was altogether exceptional. As a rule, it was the petition not the drafted statute which received the royal consent or was refused it. Hence the king retained considerable power of discussing the subject of petition before giving his final answer, and many of the recorded answers furnish the reasons for granting, modifying or refusing the request made. These cases of course differ widely from the examples given above, in

The king's power of answering petitions otherwise than by granting or rejecting them.

[1] Above, p. 438. [2] Rot. Parl. ii. 230; art. 29. [3] Ibid. ii. 203.

which, after the prayer was granted, the language of the statute was made to express something else. But although they illustrate very remarkably the political history of the period at which they occur, they need not here be considered as instances of the king's admitted power or prerogative in legislation, and the examples which we have already given are enough to show the danger of abuse to which the accepted theory was liable. Two further points may however be summarily noticed in this place, rather as completing our survey of the subject than as directly connected with the history of prerogative: these are the king's power of issuing ordinances, and the exact position occupied by the separate estates in parliamentary legislation[1].

Distinction between statutes and ordinances.

The difficulty of determining the essential difference between a statute and an ordinance has been already remarked more than once. Many attempts have been made to furnish a definition which would be applicable to the ordinance at all periods of its use, but most frequently it is described by enumerating the points in which it differs from a statute[2]: the statute is a law or an amendment of law, enacted by the king in parliament, and enrolled in the statute roll, not to be altered, repealed, or suspended without the authority of the parliament, and valid in all particulars until it has been so revoked; the ordinance is a regulation made by the king, by himself, or in his council or with the advice of his council, promulgated in letters patent or in charter, and liable to be recalled by the same authority. Moreover the statute claims perpetuity; it pretends to the sacred character of law, and is not supposed to have been admitted to the statute roll except in the full belief that it is established for ever. The ordinance is rather a tentative act which, if it be insufficient to secure its object or if it operate mischievously, may be easily recalled, and, if it be successful, may

Recognised distinctions.

[1] This point must be discussed further on in connexion with other questions bearing on the change of the balance of power between the crown, lords, and commons; but some facts are indispensable at the point which we have now reached. [2] See Hallam, Middle Ages, iii. 49, 50.

[3] In 1373 the commons complained that the clergy had ignored an ordinance, made in the recent great council at Winchester, touching tithe of underwood, because it had not been made a statute: 'les persones de seint Eglise, entendantz qe cel ordinance ne restreint mye lour aunciene accrochement surmettantz qe ceo ne fust mye afferme pur estatut;' Rot. Parl. ii. 319.

by a subsequent act be made a statute. But these generalisations do not cover all the instances of the use of ordinance. The fundamental distinction appears to lie far deeper than anything here stated, while in actual use the statute and the ordinance come more closely together. The statute is primarily a legislative act, the ordinance is primarily an executive one; the statute stands to the ordinance in the same relation as the law of the Twelve Tables stands to the prætor's edict; the enacting process incorporates the statute into the body of the national law, the royal notification of the ordinance simply asserts that the process enunciated in the ordinance will be observed from henceforth. But although thus distinguished in origin, they have practically very much in common: the assizes of Henry II, viewed in their relation to the common law of the nation, are ordinances, although they have received the assent of the magnates; their subject matter is the same, the perpetuity of their operation is the same, and in time they themselves become a part of the common law. Magna Carta is in its form an ordinance rather than a statute, but it becomes one of the fundamental laws of the realm almost immediately after its promulgation. Throughout the thirteenth century, during which the functions of the legislative were being only very gradually separated from those of the executive, the king still regarded himself as sovereign lawgiver as well as sovereign administrator. Hence even under Edward I the ordinance is scarcely distinguishable from the statute, and several of the laws which were afterwards implicitly accepted, as statutes of his enacting, were really ordinances,—ordinances which, like the Extravagants of the popes or the *Novellæ* of the Byzantine emperors, only required to be formally incorporated with the Corpus juris, to become laws to all intents and purposes. When however, in consequence of Edward's consolidating and defining work, the functions of the parliament as sharing sovereign legislative power gained recognition, and the province of the executive both in taxation and legislation was more clearly ascertained, it was not possible at once to disentangle the action of the king in his two capacities; matters which might have well been treated by

Primary distinction.

Reason for the confusion between them.

Statutes and ordinances under Edward I.

Confusion between the two.

ordinance, such as the banishment of the Despensers, were established by statute, and matters which were worthy of statutable enactment were left to the ordinance. Nor was this indistinctness solely due to the double function of the king; the magnates also as members of the royal council, or a large proportion of them, had double duties as well; and thus although the form of statute differed from that of ordinance, the two were now and then issued by the same powers and occupied the same ground. Hence even in the parliament itself little fundamental difference was recognised: the ordinances of the great council of 1353 were not allowed to be enrolled as statutes until they had received fresh authority from the parliament of 1354; but on the other hand the answers to the petitions in 1340 were divided into two classes[1], to be embodied respectively in statutes and ordinances, the latter as well as the former being published with the full authority of the parliament, but not regarded as perpetual or incorporated with the statute law.

The obscurity cleared up in the reign of Edward III.

As, however, the growth of the constitution in the reign of Edward III cleared up very considerably what was obscure in the relations of crown and parliament, as the ordaining power of the crown in council became distinguishable by very definite marks from the enacting power of the crown in parliament, and as further the jealousy between the crown and parliament increased, the maintenance and extension of the ordaining power became with the supporters of high prerogative a leading principle, and the curbing of that ordaining power became to the constitutional party a point to be consistently aimed at. It had long been found that the form of charter or letters patent was capable of being used to defeat, rather than to openly

[1] 'Lesqueux Ercevesque, Evesques, et les autres ensi assignez, oies et tries les ditz requestes, par commune assent et accord de touz firent mettre en estatut les pointz et les articles qui sont perpetuel. Le quel nostre seignur le roi, par assent des touz en dit parlement esteantz, comanda de engrosser et ensealer et fermement garder par tut le roialme d'Engleterre, et lequel estatut comence, "A l'honur de Dieu," &c. Et sur les pointz et articles qui ne sont mye perpetuels, einz pur un temps, si ad nostre seignur le roi, par assent des grantz et communes, fait faire et ensealer ses lettres patentes qui commencent en ceste manere, "Edward, &c. Sachetz que come prelatz, countes,"' &c. Rot. Parl. ii. 113; cf. p. 280. quoted above, p. 407.

contravene, the operation of a law which limited the power of the crown. The Charter granted by Edward I to the foreign merchants was an ordinance which evaded the intention of the Confirmatio Cartarum; and as we have seen in our brief summary of the history of the Customs, the precedent was followed as long as the kings were strong enough to enforce compliance. With the reign of Richard II this dishonest policy was largely extended: the chronicles complain that whatever good acts the parliaments passed were invalidated by the king and his council[1]. That this was done in the overt way in which in 1341 and 1377 Edward III and John of Gaunt had repudiated constitutional right, we have no evidence. There is however a petition of the commons, presented in 1389, in which they pray that the chancellor and the council may not, after the close of parliament, make any ordinance contrary to the common law or the ancient customs of the land and the statutes aforetime ordained or to be ordained in the present parliament: the king replies that what had hitherto been done should be done still, saving the prerogative of the king[2]. This petition and the answer seem to cover the whole grievance. The commons define and the king claims the abused prerogative; and the saving words dictated by Richard 'issint que la regalie du roi soit sauve,' embody the principle, which in the condemning charges brought against him in 1399 he was declared to have maintained, that the laws were in the mouth and breast of the king, and that he by himself could change and frame the laws of the kingdom[3].

Jealousy felt of the ordaining power of the council.

Petition in 1389.

Claim of prerogative.

The subject, as it is needless to debate here, has its own difficulties, which are not peculiar to any stage or form of government. The executive power in the state must have certain powers to act in cases for which legislation has not provided, and modern legislation has not got beyond the expedient of

Right of the executive to act in unforeseen emergencies.

[1] It is said of the parliament of 1382, 'multa sunt et alia quae statuta sunt ibidem. Sed quid juvant statuta parliamentorum cum penitus expost nullum sortiantur effectum. Rex nempe cum privato consilio cuncta vel mutare vel delere solebat quae in parliamentis antehabitis tota regni non solum Communitas sed et ipsa nobilitas statuebat;' Wals. ii. 48; Chr. Angl. p. 333.

[2] Rot. Parl. iii. 266.

[3] Above, p. 505.

investing the executive with authority to meet such critical occasions. The crown is able on several matters to legislate by orders in council at the present day, but by a deputed not a prerogative power; but there are conceivable occasions on which during an interval of parliament, the ministers of the crown might be called upon to act provisionally with such authority as would require an act of indemnity to justify it. The idea of regulating the ordaining power of the crown by recognising it within certain limits was in embryo in the fourteenth century[1], but it appears distinctly in the rules laid down in 1391 and 1394 for the 'sufferances' or exceptions which the king was allowed to make from the operations of the statute of provisors. The statute of proclamations passed in 1539[2], the 'lex regia' of English history, which gave to the proclamations of Henry VIII the force of laws, is one of the most curious phenomena of our constitutional life: for it employs the legislative machinery which by centuries of careful and cautious policy the parliament had perfected in its own hands, to authorise a proceeding which was a virtual resignation of the essential character of parliament as a legislative body; the legislative power won for the parliament from the king was used to authorise the king to legislate without a parliament.

Parliament authorises the king to make ordinances in particular cases.

Statute of proclamations.

How the king and estates shared the work of legislation.

293. The second point referred to above as necessary to complete our view of this subject is the part taken by the several factors employed in legislation; the king, the parliament, and the separate estates of parliament; the powers of initiation, consultation, consent, and enactment, as they are modified during the course of the fourteenth century, and illustrated by the

[1] In 1337 the export of wool was forbidden by statute 'until by the king and his council it be thereof otherwise provided;' Statutes, i. 280: that is, the king and council were empowered to settle the terms on which the wool should be set free; see above, p. 526. In 1385 similar power was given to settle the staples by ordinance; 'ordinatum est de assensu parliamenti et plenius concordatum quod stapula teneatur in Anglia; sed in quibus erit locis, et quando incipiet, ac de modo et forma regiminis et gubernationis ejusdem, ordinabitur postmodum per consilium domini regis, auctoritate parliamenti: et quod id quod per dictum consilium in hac parte fuerit ordinatum, virtutem parliamenti habeat et vigorem;' Rot. Parl. iii. 204.

[2] 31 Henry VIII, c. 8.

documentary evidence already adduced in relation to other parts of the subject. And it is by no means the least of the constitutional results of the century, that whereas at the beginning almost all legislation is originated by the king, at the close of it the petitions of the commons seem almost to engross the power of initiation.

Initiative power of the king and council.

The fact that the king and council could at any time initiate legislation in parliament is of course beyond question; and there can be little doubt that until the reign of Edward II almost all modifications of the existing laws were formally introduced by the king, and, where the consent of the parliament was deemed necessary, were laid before the assembled estates for the purpose of consultation. Edward II is said to have claimed for the crown an exclusive power of amending the law, in a declaration that England was not governed by written law but by ancient customs, which when they were insufficient he was bound to amend and reduce to certainty by the advice of the magnates and on the complaint of the people[1]. But, if this saying were intended as an assertion of prerogative, it contains a most distinct admission of the royal duty and responsibility, the 'querimonia vulgi' was a not less powerful weapon than the 'quas vulgus elegerit' of the coronation oath. The enacting clause of the statute of 1362 on purveyance is perhaps the best instance of the continuity of the king's right of initiation: 'for the grievous complaint which hath been made of purveyors,' 'the king of his own will, without motion of the great men or commons, hath granted and ordained in ease of his people[2]' that the abuses shall cease. The clause however is prefaced by a statement that the king is legislating at the petition of the commons and by the assent of the magnates, and his claim to initiate is stated rather as an additional sanction to the act than as a special feature of the process of legislation.

The royal right of initiating reform in legislation.

The magnates had a right of initiation.

That a similar power of introducing new laws belonged to the great council of the nation before the completion of the parliamentary system is equally unquestioned. Not to adduce again

[1] See above, p. 337, note 3.
[2] Statutes, i. 371; Rot. Parl. ii. 270. See above pp. 414, 415.

The magnates initiate legislation.

the articles of Runnymede or the petitions of 1258, we may quote as a sufficient proof the proposal made by the bishops in the council of Merton in 1235; 'all the bishops asked the magnates to consent that children born before marriage should be legitimate as well as they that be born after marriage, as touching succession of inheritance, because the church holds such for legitimate: and all the earls and barons with one voice answered that they would not change the laws of England which have been hitherto used and approved[1].' Here it is clear that the bishops had introduced a proposal for a new law. The statute 'Quia emptores' was passed 'ad instantiam magnatum[2],' as was also the statute 'de malefactoribus' in 1293[3]. The *articuli super cartas* in 1300 were enacted at the request of the prelates, earls, and barons[4]. Throughout the fourteenth century petitions presented by the magnates either by themselves or in conjunction with the commons are sufficiently frequent to show that the right was not allowed to remain unexercised[5]. The fact that such origination is not mentioned in the wording of the statutes may be accounted for by the fact that the commons almost invariably included in their petitions the points demanded by the magnates, and thus the petition of the latter was merged in the more general statement of counsel and consent. A single instance will suffice: in 1341 the lords petitioned for a declaration that the peers of the land should not be tried except in parliament: that declaration was embodied in a statute enacted 'by the assent of the prelates, earls, barons, and other great men, and of all the commonalty of the realm of England[6],' a form sufficiently exceptional to prove that legislation on the petition of the magnates was less usual than legislation on petition of the commons.

Examples.

Statute framed on the petition of the magnates.

Petitions of the whole parliament.

The bills of articles presented by the barons, on behalf of the whole community of the realm, to Edward I at Lincoln in 1301[7],

[1] Statutes, i. 4.
[2] Statutes, i. 106.
[3] Statutes, i. 111.
[4] Statutes, i. 136.
[5] In 1339 the magnates petitioned alone on the subject of wardship and the rights of lords of manors; Rot. Parl. ii. 104; in 1341 the lords and commons petitioned together; ibid. 118.
[6] Statutes, i. 295.
[7] Parl. Writs, i. 104: 'Billa praelatorum et procerum regni liberata domino regi ex parte totius communitatis in parliamento Lincolniæ.'

and the petitions of 1309[1] and 1310[2] were rather petitions of the parliament than petitions of the commons: but they were important precedents for the separate action of the third estate. The statute of Stamford, the result of the petitions of 1309, mentions more than once the supplications of the commonalty as the moving cause of the legislation[3]; in 1320 again the supplication of the commonalty is referred to in the preamble to the statute of Westminster the Fourth[4]. It is however the second statute of 1327 that introduces the form which was afterwards generally adopted, of specifying the petition of the commons in contradistinction to the assent of the magnates[5]; and thus the right of initiation is distinctly and unmistakeably recognised. This form continues to be generally used until the twenty-third year of Henry VI, when the words 'by authority of parliament' were added; from the first year of Henry VII the mention of petition is dropped and the older form of assent substituted, a change which was probably connected with the adoption of the form of an act or draughted statute in preference to that of petition.

Petitions of the commonalty.

Petitions of the commons.

The power of initiation by petition belonged to the estate of the clergy assembled in parliament; and upon their representations statutes were occasionally founded, the enacting words of which imply the co-operation of the lords and commons by way of assent: thus in 1344, on the grant made by the prelates and proctors of the clergy, and, as we know from the rolls of parliament, as the result of their petition, the king, by assent of the magnates and of all the commonalty, does of his good grace grant the privileges demanded[6]. As the right of petition belonged to every subject it is scarcely necessary to adduce these illustrations of the practice; legislation however, properly so called, does not seem to have ever followed on the petition of private individuals.

Initiation by the clergy.

Statute of 1344 founded on a petition of the clergy.

[1] Rot. Parl. i. 443: 'Les articles souz escritz furent baillez a nostre seigneur le roy par la communalte de son roialme a son parlement.'
[2] Lib. Cust. p. 199: 'Ceo est la petition des Prelats, contes et barons.'
[3] Statutes, i. 154–156.
[4] Statutes, i. 180.
[5] Statutes, i. 253.
[6] Statutes, i. 302; Rot. Parl. ii. 150.

Right of discussion in parliament.

The right of debating on the subjects which were either laid by the king before the parliaments, or introduced by means of petition, was recognised in the widest way as belonging to each of the estates separately and to all together: there seems indeed to have been no restriction as to the intercourse of the two houses or individual members; the king's directions at the opening of parliament that the several estates, or portions of them, should deliberate apart being simply a recommendation or direction for the speedy dispatch of business. Late in the reign of Edward III, long after the final separation of the two houses, we have seen a custom arising by which a number of the lords either selected by their own house or chosen by the commons were assigned to confer with the whole body of the commons on the answer to be given to the king's request for money[1]; but long before this, and in fact almost as soon as the parliament definitely divided into two houses, it is clear that the closest communication existed between the two. The commons were expected, after debating on the questions laid before them, to report their opinion to the lords[2]: the lords and commons in 1341 joined in petitions[3], and in every case of a money grant not only conference but agreement must have been the rule. The attempt made by Richard II in 1383[4] to nominate the committee of lords who were to confer with the commons was the only occasion on which the king tried to disturb this right of consultation; but on one or two occasions the lords by adopting a sullen tone towards the commons endangered the free exercise of it; in 1378 for instance they objected to a conference of select lords with the house of commons as a novelty introduced of late years, and stated that the proper and usual plan was for both houses to depute a small number of their members to discuss

Communication between the lords and commons.

[1] In 1373; see above p. 426.

[2] In 1347 they are expressly directed to do this; Rot. Parl. ii. 165; in 1348 they are ordered to report to the king and his council; in 1351 to report to the king on a day fixed; in 1352 to report by means of a chosen committee; Rot. Parl. ii. 200, 226, 237. In the last year the lords sent their advice to the commons; in 1362 the knights were examined before the lords; in 1368 the two houses had full deliberation together; Rot. Parl. ii. 269, 295; and in 1376 the king directed them to report to one another on each point; ibid. p. 322.

[3] See above, p. 588.

[4] See above, p. 465, note 2.

matters quietly together, after which each of the two committees reported to its own house[1]. In 1381 they declared, in answer to a request from the commons to know the mind of the prelates, barons, and judges separately, that the practice of parliament was that the commons should lay their advice before the lords and not the lords before the commons[2]. The consultative voice belonging to the estate of clergy would seem to have been equally free, but the traces of it are more rare, partly because of the uncertainty of the attendance of the proctors of the clergy under the præmunientes clause, partly because that voice when exercised at all would generally be exercised by the bishops, and it is difficult to distinguish between their action as members of the house of lords and as the leaders of the clerical estate. If we suppose Thomas Haxey, the famous petitioner of 1397, to have been a clerical proctor, his history affords a proof, not only of the session of the estate of clergy in that parliament, but of its actual co-operation and consultation with the house of commons. But this is not quite clear[3]. We shall however find reason to believe that the proceedings of parliament in the fourteenth century were not bound by any very strict rules. The 'Modus tenendi parliamentum,' which, if it describes anything that ever existed, must be understood to describe the state of parliament under Richard II, gives an account of the way in which disputed questions between the several estates of parliament were settled: the steward, constable, and marshall or two of them chose five-and-twenty members from the whole body, two bishops, three clerical proctors, two earls and three barons, five knights of the

Freedom of intercourse between the lords and commons.

Communication of the clergy with the commons.

Account given in the 'Modus tenendi parliamentum.'

[1] Rot. Parl. iii. 36.

[2] Rot. Parl. iii. 100: 'et priast outre la dite commune que les prelatz par eux mesmes, les grantz seigneurs temporelx par eux mesmes, les chivalers par eux mesmes, les justices par eux et touz autres estatz singulerement fussent chargez de treter et communer sur ceste lour charge, et que lour advis fust reportez a la commune, a fyn que bon remede fust ordenez. A quoi fust dit et responduz, qe le roi ad fait charger les seigneurs et autres sages de communer et treter diligeaument sur les dites matires, mais l'anciene custume et forme de parlement a este tout dys, que la commune reporteroit leur advis sur les matires a eux donez au roi nostre seigneur et as seigneurs du parlement primerement, et non pas e contra.'

[3] See above, p. 492.

shire, and five citizens and burghers; these twenty-five reduced their number either by pairing off or by electing a smaller number among themselves, and the process was repeated until the representation of the whole parliament was lodged in the hands of a committee that found itself unanimous [1]. There is no instance on the rolls of parliament in which this plan was followed, but the method adopted in 1397, when the clerical estate delegated its functions to a single proctor, and in 1398, when the committee to which the parliament delegated its full powers was chosen in something like the same proportion from the several estates, may show that such an expedient may have recommended itself to the statesmen of the day.

Committee of the whole parliament.

Right of assent belonging to the several estates.

The question of assent is of greater importance, but is also more clear. The theory of Edward I, that that which touches all should be approved of all, was borne out by his own practice and by the proceedings of his son's reign. The statutes of Edward II are almost invariably declared to be enacted with the assent of prelates, barons, and whole community, which in this collocation can scarcely be understood to mean anything but the commons. The mention of the petition of the commons which is introduced under Edward III does not merely describe a lower position taken up by the third estate, but must be regarded a fortiori as implying assent;—that for which they have prayed they can hardly need to assent to;—it would further seem proved by the fact that in the statutes of the clergy, which were not passed at the petition of the commons, the assent of the commons is declared as it had been under Edward II [2]. It may however be questioned whether the assent of the commons was necessary to such statutes framed on the petitions of the clergy, whether the assent of the clerical estate was necessary to statutes framed on petition of the commons, and whether there was not some jealousy felt by the commons of any legislation that was not founded on their own petitions.

Two subordinate questions.

Was the assent of the commons

The first of these points has been referred to already; and it cannot be very certainly decided [3]. If Edward I, as his prac-

[1] Select Charters, p. 496.
[2] Statutes, i. 293, 302.
[3] Above, p. 247.

tice seems to show, regarded the enacting power as belonging to the crown advised by the magnates, it is very possible that he looked on the other two estates as being in somewhat the same position with respect to himself and the lords, and required the assent of each in those measures only which concerned them separately. But if this were the case, the practice had as early as 1307 outgrown the theory, for the statute of Carlisle[1], which closely concerns the clergy, does not express the consent even of the prelates, and no doubt was passed without their overt co-operation, which would have exposed them to excommunication. It is not however surprising that, when the commons under Edward III contented themselves with the title of petitioners, the clergy should imagine themselves entitled to the same rights, or that the kings should favour an assumption that tended to exalt their own claims to legislate. Thus, although in 1340, 1344, and 1352 the statutes passed at the petition of the clergy received the assent of the commons[2], it seems almost certain that from time to time statutes or ordinances were passed by the king at their request without such assent. The articuli cleri of 1316, which were the answers of the king and council to certain questions propounded by the clerical estate in parliament, were enrolled as a statute without having received the consent of the commons[3]. In some instances the results of the deliberations of convocation, in the form of canons and constitutions, would require royal assent, or a promise to abstain from interference, before the church could demand the aid of the secular arm in their execution or repel the prohibitions of the civil courts; in such cases it might well be questioned whether the enactments would come before parliament at all, and the letters of warning addressed by

necessary to statutes passed on petition of the clergy?

Statutes passed on petition of the clergy, by assent of lords and commons.

[1] Statutes, i. 150-152.

[2] The statute of 1340 is enacted at the request of the prelates and clergy 'par accord et assent des ditz peres et de toutz autres somons et esteantz en notre dit parlement;' Statutes, i. 293; Rot. Parl. ii. 113. The statute of 1344 is in the form of a charter granted 'par assent des grantz et des communes;' Statutes, i. 302. That of 1352 is 'de l'assent de son dit parlement;' ibid. i. 325.

[3] Statutes, i. 175, 176. The questions were presented in the parliament of Lincoln in January; the answers were given, after a clerical grant of money, at York in the following November.

The commons petition that statutes may not be made on petition of the clergy, without examination.

Edward I to the ecclesiastical councils of his reign, forbidding them to attempt any measure prejudicial to the crown or kingdom, show that some suspicions of their aggressive character were felt at that time. In 1344 the commons petitioned that no 'petition made by the clergy to the disadvantage or damage of the magnates or commons should be granted without being examined by the king and his council, so that it might hold good without damage to the lords and commons.' This somewhat self-contradictory request seems certainly to imply that such legislation had been allowed, and that the commons did not at the moment see their way to resist it by declaring that no such statute should be enacted without their consent. But after all it is not quite clear that the petition refers to statutes at all, and not rather to ordinances, for which the assent of the commons was not required [1]. In the parliament of 1377, however, it was definitely demanded that neither statute nor ordinance should without the consent of the commons be framed on a petition of the clergy: the clergy refused to be bound by statutes made without their consent, the commons would not be bound by constitutions which the clergy made for their own profit. The king answered by a request for more definite information, which was equivalent to delay; and the commons afterwards took the matter into their own hands [2]. The statute of 1382 against the heretic preachers, which was repealed in the next parliament at the petition of the commons, as having

[1] The petition of 1344 may have had a general application, but the particular circumstances under which it was presented were these: in 1343 archbishop Stratford in a council of bishops issued a series of constitutions, by one of which ecclesiastical censures were decreed against all who detained tithe of underwood or 'sylva caedua.' The commons immediately seized on this as a grievance, petitioned as stated in the text, and further prayed that prohibitions might issue in cases where suits for tithe of wood were instituted; Rot. Parl. ii. 149. In 1347 they accused the clergy of claiming tithe of timber under the same constitution, and the bishops denied the charge; Rot. Parl. ii. 170; but it was renewed in 1352; ibid 241. In 1371 a statute was passed at the request of the commons forbidding the clergy to demand tithe for wood of more than twenty years' growth; Statutes, i. 393; Rot. Parl. ii. 301; but the clergy persisted in regarding this as an ordinance and as not binding: and there can be little doubt that the petition of 1377 had this point in view. The question of tithe of underwood occupies far more space in the Rolls of Parliament than that of heresy.

[2] Rot. Parl. ii. 368.

been made without their consent, forms one clause of a statute which declares itself to have been made by the king, the prelates, lords and commons in parliament[1]. It may or may not have received the assent of the commons, but it bears no certain evidence of having been framed on a petition of the clergy, nor do the commons allege that it has. It almost certainly was suggested by the bishops, whose functions it was intended to amplify, but there is nothing to connect it specially with the parliamentary estate of the clergy, nor was the dread of heresy at all peculiar to that body.

Statute of 1382 against heretic preachers.

That the consent of the estate of clergy was necessary to legislation approved by the lords and commons has never been maintained as a principle, or even as a fact of constitutional government. It is therefore sufficient to cite the declaration of the statute of York in 1322, in which no mention is made of the clergy among the estates of parliament whose consent is necessary for the establishment of any measure touching the king and the realm[2]. If there had been any intention on the part of Edward I to make the clerical estate a permanent check on the commons, that intention was defeated by the abstention of the clergy themselves, their dislike to attend in obedience to a secular summons, and their determination to vote their taxes in convocation. But it seems to have been regarded as a piece of necessary caution that in critical cases their right to participate in the action of parliament should not be overlooked. On more than one occasion, as in 1321, their presence is insisted on, in order that the proceedings of parliament may not be subsequently annulled on the ground of their absence; and the delegation of their powers to Sir Thomas Percy in the parliament of 1397 shows that Richard II carefully avoided even the chance of any such flaw invalidating his proceedings. Yet the protests of the clergy must now and then have defeated proposed legislation. In 1380 the prelates and clergy protested against the extension of the functions of the justices of the peace: the king declared that he would persist in doing

The consent of the estate of clergy not required for legislation.

Abstention of the clergy from parliament.

Their presence required.

[1] Statutes, ii. 23, 26; Rot. Parl. ii. 124.
[2] Statutes, i. 189; see above, p. 352.

Protests of the clergy.

justice, but the resolution did not become a statute[1]. Sometimes the clerical protests were formal; in 1351, probably, they withheld their assent to the statute of Provisors; at all events it contains no statement of the assent of the prelates[2]; and in 1365, in particular reference to the statute of Præmunire, they declared that they would not assent to anything that

Protests by the prelates.

might injure the church of England[3]. A similar protest was made by the two archbishops in the name of the clergy in 1390[4], and in 1393 archbishop Courtenay put on record a schedule of explanatory protests intended to avoid offending the pope, whilst he supported the national legislation against his usurpations[5]. These protests can be scarcely regarded as more than diplomatic subterfuges: in each case the law is enacted in spite of them.

Reasonable jealousy of the commons about legislation.

The jealousy of the commons with regard to any statute which was initiated by any other means than by their petition was not unreasonable, if we consider the attitude of the king in council, and the legislative powers claimed for the magnates and clergy. The illustrations already given of the manipulation of petitions prove that there was ground enough for apprehension, and the case of the repealed statute of 1382 just referred to is strictly in point here. Strange to say, the same influence which had obtained the passing of that statute prevented the record of its repeal from being entered on the Statute Roll. Possibly the lords refused their consent to the petition; at any rate the repeal was inoperative.

Dissent of the lords defeats legislation.

We have not yet reached the point at which recorded discussions in parliament enable us to say how the dissent of the lords to a petition of the commons or the dissent of the commons to a proposal of the lords was expressed: so far as we have gone it was announced by the king in his answer to the petitions. Where the lords had refused to consent the king states the fact and the reasons of the refusal. Such for instance is

The lords oppose a proposal of the commons.

the case in 1377, when the commons had proposed special measures for the education of the boy king, to which the lords demurred, thinking that all that was needed could be done in other ways[6]. From similar examples it would appear that

[1] Rot. Parl. iii. 83. [2] Statutes, i. 317. [3] Rot. Parl. ii. 285.
[4] Rot. Parl. iii. 264. [5] Ibid. 304. [6] Above, p. 444.

although the lords and commons had ample opportunities of conference, their conclusions were stated to the king separately. But it is in many instances impossible to distinguish whether the lords are acting as a portion of the royal council or as an estate of the realm : sometimes they join in the prayer of the commons, sometimes they join in the answers of the king[1].

Importance of the point now examined.

In following up the points that have arisen touching the legislative rights of the commons we may seem to have wandered far from the main question of the chapter, the contest between prerogative and parliamentary authority. The digression is however not foreign to the purpose; the period has two great characteristic features, the growth of the power of the commons, and the growth of the pretensions of prerogative. Whatever conduces to the former is also a check on the latter; and every vindication of the rights of parliament is a limitation of the claims of prerogative. Thus viewed, each of the several steps by which the commons claimed and obtained their right takes away from the crown a weapon of aggression or cuts off a means of evasion : and the full recovery of the right of initiating, consulting on and assenting to or dissenting from legislation, destroys the king's power of managing the powers and functions of council, and indirectly affecting the balance of power among the estates, so as to keep in his own hands the virtual direction of legislation. When all is done he possesses, in his right to say 'le roi le veut,' or 'le roi s'avisera,' more power than can be wisely entrusted to an irresponsible officer.

The decisive power of the king in legislation.

General deliberation.

294. The ninth article of the ordinances of 1311 prescribed that 'the king henceforth shall not go out of his realm nor undertake against any one deed of war without the common assent of his baronage, and that in parliament.'[2] This claim, made on behalf of the baronage, was exercised, from the beginning of the reign of Edward III, and more or less efficiently from the date of the ordinances themselves, by the whole body of the parlia-

Claim of the parliament to decide on peace and war

[1] See for example, Rot. Parl. ii. 130; and cf. Rot. Parl. ii. 152; 'au queux fu respondu par notre seigneur le roi et par les grantz en dit parlement.'

[2] Statutes, i. 159.

ment. The importance of the point thus claimed would seem to be one of the results of the loss of Normandy and Anjou by John. That king, so long as he stood, as his brother and father had stood, at the head of a body of vassals whose interests on the continent were almost identical with his own, had had no need to consult his baronage or ask permission of his people before making an expedition to France: when he did consult the 'commune consilium' on such questions it was simply with a view to taxation or the collection of forces. His own will seems to have been supreme as to the making of war or peace: he persisted in his expedition of 1205[1], in spite of the most earnest intreaties of the archbishop, his chief constitutional adviser, and in the later years of his reign the barons, who could not disobey his summons to arms, could fetter his action only by refusing to follow him to Aquitaine, a refusal which he construed as rebellion.

Henry III asked advice on these subjects.

Under Henry III it was very different; he could not have stirred a step without the baronage, and accordingly in his few expeditions he acted with the advice and support of the parliament. He carried the semblance of consultation still further; for if we are to believe the London annalists, he not only took but asked leave of the citizens of the capital before starting on his journeys. In Easter week, 1242, at Paul's Cross, he asked leave to cross over to Gascony; the same form was observed in 1253, 1259, and 1262[2], and would almost seem to have been a customary ceremony in which the citizens of London represented the community of the realm. The acceptance of the Sicilian crown for his son Edmund, an act to which the magnates, if they had been duly consulted, could not be supposed to have assented, was a rash and fatal assumption of prerogative on Henry's part which brought its own punishment and afforded a warning to his successors.

Edward I discussed peace and war in parliament.

Edward I engaged in no war without obtaining both advice and substantial aid from his parliaments, and when the barons in 1297 refused to go to Flanders at his command, they sought their justification in tech-

[1] M. Paris, p. 212.

[2] Liber de Antt. Legg. p. 9; 'petiit licentiam'; p. 19 'cepit licentiam'; cf. pp. 42, 50, where 'capere licentiam' may merely mean 'to take leave.'

nical points of law [1], not in the statement that the war had been begun without their consent.

The language of the ordinance of 1311 seems then unnecessarily stringent if it be understood as limiting an exercise of arbitrary power on this point. Read in connexion with the weak and halting policy of Edward II, it seems almost an insult to limit the military power of a king, one of whose great faults was his neglect of the pursuits of war. If it were not intended as a declaration of public policy, in which case it assumes, much more than the other ordinances, the character of a political principle, it must have been meant to prevent Edward from raising forces, on the pretext of foreign war, which might be used to crush the hostile baronage at home. However this may have been, both during the domination of the ordainers and during his own short periods of independent rule, the subject was kept before the king's eyes. In 1314 the earls refused to follow him to Bannockburn because the expedition had not been arranged in parliament [2]; in 1319 he had to announce the day of muster as fixed by assent of the magnates in parliament [3]; he asked by letter their consent to the issue of commissions of array [4], and in the latter years of his reign the contemplated expedition to France was the chief object for which he brought the parliaments together. Although during this reign the commons as well as the magnates, when they were called on to furnish money, arms, and men, had opportunity of showing willingness or unwillingness to join in the wars, the complete recognition of their right to advise, a right which they were somewhat reluctant to assume, belongs to the reign of Edward III.

The ordinance of 1311.

Refusal of the earls to go to Scotland without order of parliament.

The commons acquire the right to deliberate on war and peace.

From the very first transactions of the reign the commons were appealed to as having a voice in questions of war and peace. Isabella and Mortimer were anxious to fortify their foreign policy with the consent of the commons; and when Edward himself started on his great military career, he started with the conviction, which every subsequent year of his life must have deepened, that he could only sustain his armaments and his

Advice of the commons asked, on war and peace.

[1] See above, p. 132.
[2] See above, p. 337.
[3] See Parl. Writs, I. ii. 518, 519.
[4] Above, p. 540.

credit by drawing the nation into full and sympathetic complicity with his aims. In 1328 it was with the counsel and consent of the prelates and 'proceres,' earls, barons, and commons that Edward resigned his claims on Scotland[1]; in 1332 the lords by themselves, and the knights of the shire by themselves, debated on the existing relations with Scotland and Ireland, and joined in recommending that the king should continue in the north watching the Scots, but not quitting the realm[2]. From the beginning of the French war onwards, to enumerate the several occasions on which the commons were distinctly asked for advice would be to recapitulate a great part of the history discussed in the last chapter. We have there seen how their zeal kept pace with the king's successes, how in his necessities they welcomed the opportunity of making conditions before they granted money, how when the war flagged they inclined to throw the responsibility of continuing it upon the lords, and how when they were thoroughly wearied they made no scruple of declaring themselves unanimously desirous of peace[3]. But on the whole they seem to have been awake to the king's policy, and to have been very cautious in admitting that peace and war were within their province at all. And the same feeling appears in the following reign; in 1380 the commons petitioned against the plurality of wars[4]; from time to time we have seen them vigorously endeavouring to limit, direct, and audit the expenditure on the wars, and even attempting to draw distinctions between the national and royal interests in the maintenance of the fortresses of Gascony and Brittany; but when the question is put barely before them they avoid committing themselves. In 1382 they declare that it is for the king and the lords to determine whether he shall go in person to the war or undertake any great expedition[5], but by their reluctance to pro-

The importance of this in the reign of Edward III.

Under Richard II.

The commons are cautious in accepting the place of counsellors.

[1] Rot. Parl. ii. 442.

[2] Rot. Parl. ii. 66, 67

[3] In 1339 the commons declare that they are not bound to give advice on matters of which they have no knowledge; Rot. Parl. ii. 105; in 1348 they say much the same; ibid. ii. 165. See above, pp. 381, 397.

[4] Rot. Parl. iii. 93.

[5] Rot. Parl. iii. 145: 'ne l'ordinance de son voiage, ou de nul autre grant viage a faire soleit ne doit appertenir a la commune einz au roi mesmes et as seigneurs du roialme.'

vide funds they showed conclusively that their wish was, not perhaps that the king should waste his youth in idleness, but that he should not gain experience and military education at their cost. In 1384, when consulted on the negotiations for peace, they replied that they could not, in the sight of existing dangers, advise the king either way; it seemed to them that the king might and should act in this behalf as it should seem best to his noble lordship, as concerning a matter which was his own proper inheritance that by right of royal lineage has descended to his noble person, and not as appertaining to the kingdom or crown of England [1]. Such a response, implying that Richard should enforce his claims on France without the assistance of England, provoked a sharp rejoinder; the commons were charged on the part of the king to declare on the spot their choice of war or peace; there was, he told them, no middle course, for the French would agree to truces only on terms most favourable to themselves. They answered that they wished for peace, but were not able to understand clearly the terms on which peace was possible, and that they did not think that the English conquests in France should be held under the king of France in the same way as the royal inheritance in Gascony was held. The king, having told them that peace could not be made on such terms, asked them how 'if the said commons were king of the realm, or in the state in which the king is,' they would act under the circumstances. They answered that, as the magnates had said that if they were in the position of the king they would choose peace, so they, the commons, protesting that they should not henceforth be charged as counsellors in this case, nor be understood to advise either one way or the other, agreed to return the answer which the prelates and magnates had given; 'such answer and no other they give to their liege lord.' Under these circumstances, had the occasion ever arisen for the commons to demand a peremptory voice in the determination of peace or war, they might have been silenced by their own confession.

Richard II forces them to answer directly.

Caution of the commons.

So far then the king could in this point have made no claim

[1] Rot. Parl. iii. 170, 171.

The royal usurpations in this matter were indirect.

on the part of his prerogative, which the commons could have contested. As it was, however, no such assertion was necessary, and the dangerous exercise of sovereign power in this department consisted in unwarranted acts of executive tyranny, the raising of provisions and munitions by way of purveyance, and the levying of forces by commissions of array, both which subjects we have already examined. The commons preferred, in questions of peace and war, an indirect to a direct control over the king's actions; the king would have preferred more substantial power with a less complete acknowledgment of his absolute right to determine national policy. Royal prerogative and parliamentary control seem to change places. The king is eager to recognise the authority that he may secure a hold on the purse of the commons; the commons, as soon as they feel confident in the possession of the purse, do not hesitate to repudiate the character of advisers, and leave to the king the sole responsibility for enterprises which they know that he cannot undertake alone. Hence the interchange of compliments, the flattering recognition of the prerogative power and personal wisdom of the prince, the condescending acknowledgment that in all matters of so high concern the prince must have the advice of his faithful commons.

Attitude of king and parliament.

Advice asked on the public peace.

295. The speeches of the chancellors at the opening of parliament very frequently contained, besides a request for advice on war or peace and a petition for money, a demand of counsel from the several estates of the realm on the best means of securing the public peace[1]; and it is in this clause, coupled with the general offer to receive petitions and gravamina, that the fullest recognition is found of the right of the commons to review the administrative system, and recommend executive reforms as well as new statutes. They were thus justified in pressing on the king's notice the misconduct of the sheriffs, their continuance in office for more than a year contrary to the statutes, the evils

Participation of the commons in the review of judicial matters.

[1] For example, see Rot. Parl. ii. 103: 'furent trois causes purposes, dount la primere fu, que chescun grant et petit endroit soi penseroit la manere coment la pees deinz le roialme purroit mieutz et se deveroit plus seurement estre gardee.' Cf. ibid. pp. 136, 142, 161, 166,

which attended the unsettled jurisdiction of the justices of the peace, the abuses of the Exchequer, the usurpations of the courts of the steward and marshall, and in general those mischiefs which arose from the interference with the ordinary course of justice by the exercise of royal prerogative. Thus the commons, although not pretending to be a court of justice, attempted to keep under review the general administration of justice, and to compel the king to observe the promises of the coronation oath and the emphatic declaration of the great charter. No words of that famous document were better known or more frequently brought forward than the fortieth clause 'nulli vendemus, nulli negabimus aut differemus rectum et justitiam[1];' and none probably were more necessarily pressed on the unwilling ear of the dishonest or negligent administrator. The frequent petitions of the commons on this point show the prevalence of the abuses and the determination of the nation not to rest until they were abated. The sale of writs in chancery was made a matter of complaint in 1334, 1352, 1354, 1371, 1376, and 1381; the words of the great charter being in each case quoted against the king[2]: the complaints are variously answered, in 1334 and 1352 the king charges the chancellor to be gracious; in 1371 he is directed to be reasonable; but in each case the answer implies that the royal right to exact heavy fees cannot be touched; 'the profit of the king that has customarily been given aforetime for writs of grace cannot be taken away,' is the reply of Edward III in 1352:[3] 'our lord the king does not intend,' says Richard II, 'to divest himself of so great an advantage, which has been continually in use in chancery as well before as after the making of the said charter, in the time of all his noble progenitors who have been kings of England[4].' The prescriptive right thus pleaded in the king's favour as the source of equity could not be allowed in the case of the clearer infractions of common right, even when they proceeded from the highest authority. In 1351 begins a series of petitions against the usurped jurisdiction of the council; the commons pray that no man be put to answer

The great charter a watchword in matters of justice.

Profits on writs.

Petitions for the due administration of justice.

[1] E.g. Rot. Parl. ii. 313, iii. 116, and the passages referred to below.
[2] Rot. Parl. ii. 376, 241, 261, 305, 376.
[3] Rot. Parl. ii. 241.
[4] Rot. Parl. iii. 116.

Petitions against the jurisdiction of the privy council.

for his freehold, or for anything touching life or limb, fine or ransom[1], before the council of the king or any minister whatsoever, save by the process of law thereinbefore used. The king replies that the law shall be kept, and no man shall be bound to answer for his freehold but by process of law; as for cases touching life and limb, contempt or excess, it shall be done as was customary. The next year, 1352, the complaint is stated more definitely; the petitioners appeal to the thirty-ninth article of the charter, and insist that except on indictment or presentment of a jury no man shall be ousted of his freehold by petition to the king or council; the king grants the request[2]. Ten years after, in 1362 and 1363, the complaint is renewed; false accusations have been laid against divers persons before the king himself; the commons pray that such false accusers be forced to find security to prosecute their charges, or incur the punishment of false accusers, that no one may be taken or imprisoned contrary to the great charter; the petition was granted, and the answer incorporated in a statute[3]. The royal council was the tribunal before which these false suggestions were made, and before which the accused were summoned to appear: the punishment of the accusers did not tend to limit the powers of the council; in 1368 the prayer is again presented and granted, but, like all administrative abuses, it was not remedied by the mere promise of redress[4]; and as the council grew in power the hope of redress was further delayed. In 1390 Richard included this jurisdiction of the council among the rights of the prerogative: the commons prayed that no one might be summoned by the writ 'quibusdam de causis' before the chancellor or the council to answer any case in which a remedy was given by the common law; the king 'is willing to save his prerogative as his progenitors have done before him[5].' It is scarcely a matter of wonder that with such a system of prevarication in the highest quarters there should be oppression wherever oppression was possible. In the disorder of the times there are traces

The jurisdiction of council a prerogative right.

[1] Rot. Parl. ii. 228.
[2] Rot. Parl. ii. 239.
[3] Rot. Parl. ii. 270, 280, 283; Statutes, i. 382, 384.
[4] Rot. Parl. ii. 295; cf. also the petitions in 1377, ibid. iii. 21; in 1378, ibid. iii. 44; and in 1394, ibid. 323.
[5] Rot. Parl. iii. 267.

of attempts made on the part of the great lords to revive the feudal jurisdictions which had been limited by Henry II, and to entertain in their courts suits which were entirely beyond their competence. The complaint made to Edward III in 1376, against those who accroached royal power by new impositions [1], may possibly be explained in this way; but under Richard II the evil is manifest. In 1391 the commons grievously complained that the king's subjects were caused to come before the councils of divers lords and ladies to answer for their freeholds, and other things real and personal, contrary to the king's right and the common law [2]: a remedy was granted by statute, [3] but in 1393 the complaint was renewed and the king had to promise that the statute should be kept.[4] It is not improbable that the foundation of the great palatine jurisdiction of the duke of Lancaster may have afforded an inviting example for this species of abuse.

Mischief of this in times of disorder.

Private jurisdictions.

Such prerogative or prescriptive right as could be claimed for the jurisdiction of the royal council, within lawful limits, might also be pleaded for the courts of the steward, the constable, the marshall, and other half private, half public tribunals, which had survived the enactments of the great charter, and which throughout the whole period before us were felt as a great grievance. The necessity of maintaining these courts for certain specific purposes, and the instinctive policy, inherent in such institutions, of extending their jurisdiction wherever it was possible, together with the vitality fostered by the possessors of the vested interests, gave them a long-continued existence. The Articuli super Cartas in 1300 had defined their jurisdiction [5]: notwithstanding much intermediate legislation, they were found in 1390 to be drawing to themselves cases of contracts, covenants, debts, and other actions pleadable at common law. The king again defines the sphere of their work, but even here he draws in the question of prerogative; the jurisdiction of the constable of Dover touches the king's inheritance, before doing anything

Courts of the king's officers.

Petitions against the jurisdictions of steward and marshall.

[1] Above, p. 434.
[2] Rot. Parl. iii. 285.
[3] Statutes, ii. 82.
[4] Rot. Parl. iii. 305.
[5] Statutes, i. 138, art. 3: for petitions on the subject, see Rot. Parl. ii. 140, 201, 228, 240, 336, 368; iii. 65, 202.

there he will inquire into the ancient custom and frame his remedy thereupon[1].

Innumerable petitions on matters of judicature.

It would be vain to attempt, even by giving single examples, to illustrate all the plans suggested by the indefatigable commons to meet the abuses prevalent in the administration of justice, very many of which were quite unconnected with the doctrine of prerogative, except that, where the king gave a precedent of illegality and defended it by his prerogative right, he was sure to find imitators. Justice was delayed, not only in compliance with royal writ, contrary to the charter, but by the solicitations of great men, lords and ladies, who maintained the causes not merely of their own bona fide dependents, but of all who were rich enough to make it worth their while[2]. The evil of maintenance was apparently too strong for the statutes; the very judges of the land condescended to accept fees and robes from the great lords[3], as the king out of compliment wore the livery of the duke of Lancaster. The justices of assize were allowed to act in their own counties, in which they were so closely allied with the magnates, that abuses prevailed of which it was not honest or decent to speak particularly: that especial mischief was abolished by statute in 1384[4]. The inefficacy of appeals was a crying evil; the judges heard appeals against their own decisions. The choice of the justices of assize was a frequent matter of discussion, and the functions as well as the nomination of the justices of the peace was a subject both of petition and statute, of peculiar interest to the knights of the shire, who were, as we have remarked, the most energetic part of the parliament[5]. Enough, however, has been said on this point to illustrate the question before us, the unwillingness of the king to grant a single prayer that might be interpreted as limiting his 'regalie[6],' and the determination of the

Evil of maintenance and livery.

Claims of the commons to regulate the choice of justices.

[1] Rot. Parl. iii. 265, 267.

[2] See the petititions against maintenance; e.g. Rot. Parl. ii. 10, 62, 166, 201, 228, 368.

[3] Rot. Parl. iii. 200.

[4] Rot. Parl. ii. 334, iii. 139, 200; Statutes, ii. 36.

[5] In 1363 the commons petitioned for power to elect justices of labourers and artisans and guardians of the peace, but the king directed them to nominate fit persons out of whom he would choose; Rot. Parl. ii. 277. The same proposal was made in the good parliament; ibid. 333.

[6] The constant allegation of the *regalie* appears in the very first years of

commons to control the power which they believed themselves competent to regulate, and fully justified in restricting where restriction was necessary.

Possibility that the house of commons might become a court of justice.

It is curious perhaps that the house of commons, whilst it thus attempted, and exercised in an indirect way, a control over every department of justice, should not have taken upon itself to act judicially, but have left to the house of lords the task of trying both the causes and the persons that were amenable to no common-law tribunal. If they ever were tempted to act as judges it must have been during the period before us, when the division of the two houses was still new and when many members of the lower house might fairly have considered themselves to be the peers of the magnates, who were distinguished only by the special summons. The king or the influential minister—Edward II at York in 1322, Mortimer at Winchester in 1330, or Edward III in the destruction of Mortimer—would perhaps have welcomed the assistance of the commons in judgment as well as in legislation. But it was a happy thing on the whole that the commons preferred the part of accuser to that of judge, and were content to accept the award of the magnates against the objects of their indignation. The events of the closing years of Richard's reign show that the third estate, notwithstanding its general character of patriotic independence, was only too susceptible of royal manipulation; that the right of impeachment was a weapon which might be turned two ways. The fact that most of the great malefactors on whom the power of impeachment was exercised were magnates, gave them as a matter of course the right to be tried by their peers, and the lords, new in their judicial work, thought it necessary in 1330 to disavow any intention of trying any who were not their peers[1]. But the commons wisely chose their attitude on the occasion of the deposition of Richard, and declared that they

The commons content themselves with the power of impeachment.

They decline to be judges.

Richard II, and continues throughout the reign. Many instances have been already given; see also Rot. Parl. iii. 15, 71, 73, 99, 267, 268, 279, 286, 321, 347.

[1] Rot. Parl. ii. 53, 54: they had tried Sir Simon Bereford, John Maltravers, Thomas Gurney, and William de Ocle for the murder of Edward II. Thomas Berkeley was tried by a jury of knights in the parliament; ibid. p. 57.

were not and had not acted as judges[1]. The fact that they had in 1384 heard the complaint of John Cavendish against Michael de la Pole, and the other occasions on which the petitions of individuals were laid before them, show how nearly they were willing to undertake the functions of a court of law[2].

Confusion between legislative and executive functions.

The indistinctness of the line drawn between the executive and legislative powers in the kingdom, and between the executive and legislative functions of the king, accounts to some extent, not indeed for the theoretical assumptions of high prerogative, but certainly for the difficulty of securing proper control over the administration in the hands of the parliament. Nor is the indistinctness all on one side. A king who inherited traditions of despotism, or who like Richard II had formed a definite plan of absolute sovereignty, saw little difference between the enacting and enforcing of a law, between the exaction and the outlay of a pecuniary impost, between the raising and the command of an army: he inherited his crown from kings, many of whom had exercised all these powers with little restraint from the counsel or consent or dissent of their parliaments. With the barons of the thirteenth century and the parliaments of the fourteenth it was the substance of power not the theoretical limitation of executive functions that was the object of contention. The claims made in 1258 for the direct election of the king's council and ministers, the resuscitation of the same projects in 1311 and 1386, were nearly as much opposed to the ultimate idea of the constitution as were the abuses of power which they were intended to rectify. When the parliament under the leadership of the barons proceeded to make regulations for the household, to fix the days and places of muster, to determine beforehand the times for their own sessions, to nominate justices of the peace and other subordinate ministers of justice, they were clearly intruding into the

It explains the attitude of the more despotic kings.

Intrusions of the parliament into executive matters.

[1] Rot. Parl. iii. 427.

[2] Rot. Parl. iii. 168: 'un Johan Cavendish de Londres pessoner soi pleignast en ce parlement, primerement devant la commune d'Engleterre en lour assemble en presence d'autres prelatz et seigneurs temporels illoeques lors esteantz, et puis apres devant touz les prelatz et seigneurs esteantz en ce parlement.' The chancellor answered the complaint first before the lords, then before the lords and commons together; ibid.

province of the executive. That their designs were beneficial to the nation, that their attempts even when frustrated conduced to the growth of liberty, that they were dictated by a true sense of national sympathy, is far more than enough to acquit them of presumption in the eyes of the posterity which they so largely benefited. But the same facts did not present themselves in the same light to the kings who had in the person of Richard II perfected the idea of territorial monarchy. And this must be allowed to mitigate in some degree the censure that is visited on those sovereigns who were the most ardent maintainers of prerogative. They had inherited their crown with duties to both predecessors and successors: they were none of them, unless it were Edward II, men of mean ability, or consciously regardless of their duties towards their people: they looked on the realm too much as a property to be managed, not indeed without regard to the welfare of the inhabitants, but with the ultimate end and aim of benefiting its owner; a family perhaps, but one in which the patria protestas was the supreme rule,—a rule to which there was no check, against which there was no appeal. The constitutional historian has not to acquit or condemn, but he must recognise the truth of circumstances in which entire acquittal and entire condemnation alike would be unjust.

Some excuse for the high theory of prerogative.

Equitable judgment necessary.

296. In no part of the constitutional fabric was more authority left to the king, and in none was less interference attempted by the parliament, than in the constitution of the parliament itself. It would almost seem as if the edifice crowned by Edward I in 1295 was already deemed too sacred to be rashly touched. The king retained the right of summoning the estates whenever and wherever he chose; he could, without consulting the magnates, add such persons as he pleased to the permanent number of peers, and he might no doubt, with very little trouble and with no sacrifice of popularity, have increased or diminished the number of members of the house of commons by dealing with the sheriffs. On these three points occasional contests turned, but they scarcely ever, as was the case in later reigns, came into the foreground as leading constitutional questions.

Power of the king in the constitution of parliament.

The frequent session of parliament was felt as a burden by

Sentiment of the king and the nation as to frequent sessions of parliament.

the nation at large far more than as a privilege; the counties and boroughs alike murmured at the cost of representation; the borough representatives in the lower house and the monastic members of the upper house avoided attending whenever they could; and frequent parliaments were generally regarded as synonymous with frequent taxation. On the other hand the more active politicians saw in the regular session of the estates the most trustworthy check upon the arbitrary power of the king, who was thus obliged to hear the complaints of the people, and might, if they dealt judiciously in the matter of money, be obliged to redress their grievances. With the king the feeling was reversed in each case; as a means of raising money, he might have welcomed frequent and regular sessions; as a time for compulsory legislation and involuntary receiving of advice, he must have been inclined to call them as seldom as possible. Accordingly when political feeling was high there was a demand for annual parliaments; when the king's necessities were great and the sympathy of the nation inert or exhausted, there was a manifest reluctance to attend parliament at all. Thus in 1258 the barons under the provisions of Oxford directed the calling of three parliaments every year, and Edward I observed the rule so far as it involved annual sessions for judicial purposes; but neither of these precedents applied exactly to the parliaments when completely constituted. Three times in the year was clearly too often for the country to be called on to send representatives either to legislate or to tax. The completion of the parliamentary constitution having rendered the necessity less pressing, the latter years of Edward I and the early years of Edward II saw these assemblies called only on urgent occasions, and this no doubt, as well as the wish to imitate the barons of 1258, led the lords ordainers[1] of 1311 to direct annual parliaments; the same question arose in 1330[2] and 1362, and in both those years it was ordered by statute that parliaments should be held once a year and oftener if necessary[3]. The same demand was

Three parliaments in the year.

Annual parliaments, ordered by the ordainers, and by statute.

[1] Statutes, i. 165, art. 29.

[2] Statutes, i. 265.

[3] Statutes, i. 374; on the subject of annual parliaments, see especially the article by Mr. Allen in the 28th volume of the Edinburgh Review; no. 55, pp. 126 sq.

made in the Good Parliament and was answered by a reference to existing statutes[1]. The question and answer were repeated in the first parliament of Richard II[2], and in 1378 the chancellor in his opening speech referred to the rule now established as one of the causes of the summons of parliament[3]. In 1388 the commons even went so far as to fix by petition the time for summoning the next parliament[4]. Examples of a contrary feeling may be found: thus in 1380 both lords and commons petition that they may not be called together for another year[5]. Other instances show that the need of money occasionally influenced the king more strongly than the fear of receiving unwelcome advice; in 1328 four parliaments were held, in 1340 three, and in many of the later years of Edward III and of the early years of Richard II the estates were called together twice within a period of twelve months. In those years again for which supplies had been provided by biennial or triennial grants made beforehand no parliament was called at all. The result was to leave matters very much as they were; annual parliaments were the rule; it was only in unquiet times that the commons found it necessary or advisable to insist on the observance of the rule; but when they found Richard II proposing to dispense altogether with parliament and reduce the assembly of the estates to a permanent committee, they were at once roused to the enormity of the offence against their rights.

Irregularity of sessions accounted for.

The determination of the place of parliament and of the length of the session rested with the king. Occasionally the place was fixed with a view of avoiding the interference of the London mob with the freedom of debate; Winchester and Salisbury were chosen by Mortimer, and Gloucester by John of Gaunt for this reason; most of the deviations from the rule of meeting at Westminster were however caused by the Welsh and Scottish wars. The power of prorogation either before or after the day of meeting rested with the king, and although in a vast majority of instances

Place of session fixed by the king.

Power of prorogation.

[1] Rot. Parl. ii. 355, art. 186. [2] Rot. Parl. iii. 23, art. 54.
[3] Rot. Parl. iii. 32. [4] Rot. Parl. iii. 246.
[5] Rot. Parl. iii. 75: 'en priantz a nostre seignur le roi que nul parlement soit tenuz deinz le dit roialme pur pluis charger sa poevre commune par entre cy et le dit feste de S. Michael proschein venant en un an.'

the parliaments were newly summoned and the representative members chosen afresh for each session, the few exceptional cases of prorogation are sufficient to prove that the royal right was exercised without hesitation and without producing any irritation[1]. Occasionally as in 1339 the commons expressed a wish for a new election[2], being unwilling perhaps to extend their delegated powers to purposes which were not contemplated when they were first chosen. Neither king nor parliament liked long sessions; the king would gladly dispense with the attendance of his advisers as soon as money was granted; and the advisers were eager to depart as soon as their petitions were answered. In 1386, on the occasion of the impeachment of Michael de la Pole, it is doubtful whether the parliament resisted the king's intention to dismiss them or compelled him, by a threat of dissolution, to attend against his will. But generally it seems to have been more difficult to keep the members together than to shorten, for any reason, the duration of the session.

New election asked for.

Long sessions disliked.

Creation of earls by advice and consent of the parliament.

The king exercised without any direct check the power of adding to the numbers of the house of lords by special summons, in virtue of which the recipient took his seat as a hereditary counsellor. Edward III however introduced the custom of creating great dignities of peerage, earldoms and dukedoms, in parliament and with the consent of that body. By doing this he probably hoped to avoid the odium which his father had incurred in the promotion of Gaveston, and to obtain parliamentary authorisation for the gifts of land or other provision, made out of the property at his disposal, for the maintenance of the new dignity. Thus in 1328 at the Salisbury parliament he made three earls, those of Cornwall, March, and Ormond[3]; in the parliament held in February, 1337, he made seven earls[4], three by the definite advice and four with the counsel and consent of parliament, one of whom, William Montacute earl of Salisbury, had some years before received a considerable endowment at the

[1] The principal cases of prorogation up to this point were in 1311, above, p. 331; in 1333, p. 377; in 1381, p. 460; in 1388, p. 479, and in 1397-8. Mr. Allen (Edinb. Rev. xxviii. 135-137) gives some other instances which are not prorogations; e.g. the great council at Winchester in 1371, and the supplementary sessions at Lincoln in the reign of Edward II.

[2] Above, p. 381.

[3] A. Murimuth, p. 58.

[4] Ibid. p. 81.

request of the parliament as a reward for his assistance rendered to the king against Mortimer[1]. The promotions made by Richard II were likewise announced or made in parliament, although not always with a statement of counsel or consent. But this practice did not extend to simple baronies, which continued to be created by the act of summons until in 1387 Richard created Sir John Beauchamp of Holt, lord Beauchamp and baron of Kidderminster by letters patent[2]. These examples therefore do not affect the general truth of the proposition that the determination of the numbers of the house of lords practically rested with the king, controlled, and that very inadequately, by the attempts made in parliament to prevent him from alienating the estates of the crown by the gift of which his new nobility would be provided for. As has been already observed, the number of barons summoned during the fourteenth century gradually decreased: the new creations or new summonses did not really fill up the vacancies caused by the extinction of great families or the accumulation of their baronies in the hands of individual magnates. The institution of dukedoms and marquessates by Edward III and Richard II, and the creation of viscounts by Henry VI, increased the splendour of the house of lords and perhaps

Creation of a baron by patent.

Power of the king in forming the house of lords.

New titles.

[1] Rot. Parl. ii. 56; William Montacute was made earl of Salisbury by the request of parliament; Henry of Lancaster earl of Derby, and Hugh of Audley earl of Gloucester 'de diffinito dicti parliamenti nostri consilio,' Lords' Report, vol. v. pp. 27, 31, 32. William Clinton earl of Huntingdon, ibid. p. 28; William Bohun earl of Northampton, ibid. p. 30; Robert Ufford earl of Suffolk, ibid. p. 31; by the counsel and consent of parliament. So also the marquess of Juliers in 1340 was made earl of Cambridge, the king's eldest son was created prince of Wales by advice of parliament; Ralph Stafford earl of Stafford, and Henry duke of Lancaster in 1351, with the consent of the lords. Richard II did not uniformly follow his grandfather's precedents; but it was occasionally done down to the year 1414; see Sir Harris Nicolas on the proceedings in the case of the earldom of Devon, app. ix. p. clxxviii.

[2] 'Sciatis quod pro bonis et gratuitis serviciis quae dilectus et fidelis miles noster Johannes de Beauchamp de Holt senescallus hospitii nostri nobis impendit, ac loco per ipsum tempore coronationis nostrae hucusque nobis impenso, et quem pro nobis tenere poterit in futuro in nostris consiliis et parliamentis, necnon pro nobili et fideli genere unde descendit, ac pro suis magnificis sensu et circumspectione, ipsum Johannem in unum parium ac baronum regni nostri Angliae praefecimus; volentes quod idem Johannes et heredes masculi de corpore suo exeuntes statum baronis optineant ac domini de Beauchamp et barones de Kydermynster nuncupentur;' Lords' Report, v. 81. The example was not followed until 1443.

contributed to set it wider apart from the body of Englishmen, but did not in any way strengthen either the royal power or the actual importance of the baronage. It was copied from the customs of France and the empire, and may even have produced, in the multiplication of petty jealousies and personal assumptions, evils which, however rife abroad, had not yet penetrated deep into English society.

No attempt to alter the numerical proportion of the house of commons.

No attempt seems to have been made during the first century of its existence to alter the numerical proportions of the house of commons, either on the part of the king or on the part of parliament. The number of counties being fixed, and the number of representatives from each being determined by a custom older than the constitution of parliament itself, there was no colourable pretext on any account to vary it. The exceptional cases of 1352, 1353, and 1371, in which one representative was summoned from each county, were not regarded as full and proper parliaments, but as great councils only, the action of which required subsequent ratification from the proper assembly of the estates. The number of town representatives might no doubt easily have been tampered with. Summoned as they were by the general writ addressed to the sheriff, and not individually specified in that writ, they might, either by the indulgence or by the political agency of the sheriff, have been deprived of the right or allowed to escape the burden of representation. That this was to some extent allowed, would seem to be proved by the statute of 1382, which forbids the sheriff to be negligent in making his returns, or to leave out of them any cities or boroughs that were bound and of old time were wont to come to the parliament[1]. But the borough element of parliament was, during the greatest part of the fourteenth century, of very secondary importance; the action of the town representatives is scarcely ever mentioned apart from that of the knights of the shire, and seldom noted in conjunction with it; it is only from the subservient and illiberal action of Richard's later parliaments that we can infer that they occupied a somewhat more influential place at the close of the reign than at the beginning; and it would seem

Number of knights of the shire unvaried.

Variation in the number of borough members.

[1] Statutes, ii. 25; Rot. Parl. iii. 124.

to have been scarcely worth while for either the royal or the anti-royal party to have attempted important action through their means.

Attempts to influence the elections.

It was not then by altering the balance of numbers in the house of commons that the rival parties, in the infancy of representative institutions, attempted to increase their own power; but by the far more simple plan of influencing the elections and, if the use of the term is not premature, by modifying or trying to modify the franchise. The former seems to have been the policy of the king, who could deal immediately with the sheriffs or who could overawe the county court by an armed force; the latter was attempted on one occasion at least by the opposition. In 1377 John of Gaunt procured the return of a body of knights of the shire which enabled him to reverse the acts of the parliament of 1376[1]; in 1387 Richard by directing the sheriffs to return knights who had not taken part in the recent quarrels, 'magis indifferentes in modernis debatis' was held to have interfered unconstitutionally with the rights of the commons[2]; and the parliament of 1397 was elected and assembled under intimidation[3]. The despairing cry of the earl of Arundel when put on his trial, 'The faithful commons are not here,' and his persistent declaration that the house of commons did not express the real sense of the country, can bear no other interpretation. It was moreover one of the charges on which the judicial sentence against Richard was founded that 'although by statute and the custom of his realm, at the convoking of every parliament, his people in every county ought to be free to choose and depute knights for such counties to be present in parliament and exhibit their grievances and to prosecute for remedies thereupon as it should seem to them expedient; the king, in order that he might in his parliaments obtain more freely effect for his arbi-

The king employs the sheriffs to return his candidates.

Attempts of the king to influence the elections.

Alleged against Richard II.

[1] Chron. Angl. p. 122; 'milites vero comitatus, quos dux pro arbitrio surrogaverat; nam omnes qui in ultimo parliamento steterant procuravit pro viribus amoveri, ita quod non fuerunt ex illis in hoc parliamento praeter duodecim, quos dux amovere non potuit, eo quod comitatus de quibus electi fuerant alios eligere noluerunt.'

See above, p. 479.

[3] Ann. Ricardi, p. 209; 'militibus parliamenti qui non fuerunt electi per communitatem, prout mos exigit, sed per regiam voluntatem.' Cf. Political Poems, ed. Wright, i. 413.

trary will, frequently directed his mandates to the sheriffs directing them to return to his parliaments certain persons named by the king himself as knights of the shires; which knights, being favourable to the king, he was able to induce, sometimes by various threats and terrors, sometimes by gifts, to consent to things which were prejudicial to the realm and very burdensome to the people, especially the grant of the custom of wool for the king's life[1]'. The charge was no doubt true and the evil practice itself may have been a regular part of Richard's deliberate attempt on the national liberties.

A part of Richard's scheme.

Attempts made by the commons to alter the mode of election.

The commons, however jealous of the king's interference with the elections, were not themselves disposed to acquiesce in the unsatisfactory condition of the electoral body,—the county court, which was peculiarly amenable to manipulation, not only by the king but by the great lords of the shire. The petition presented in 1376 might tell two ways; in it the commons prayed that the knights of the shire for these parliaments might be chosen by common election of the best people of the counties, and not certified by the sheriff alone without due election, on certain penalties[2]: it might mean that the mixed crowd of the county courts was unfit to choose a good representative, or that the sheriff took advantage of the unruly character of the gathering, sometimes perhaps to return the member without show of election, sometimes to interpret the will of the electors in favour of his own candidate. Instances were not unknown in which the sheriff returned his own knights when the county had elected others[3]. The attempt made by the commons in 1372[4] to prevent the election of lawyers as knights of the shire is another illustration of the wish to purge the assembly of a class of members who were supposed to be more devoted to private gain than to public good[5]. On both occasions the king refused

[1] Above, p. 504. Rot. Parl. iii. 420. [2] Rot. Parl. ii. 355.

[3] In 1319 the sheriff of Devon returned members not elected by the commons of the county, and Matthew Crauthorne, who had been duly elected, petitioned against the return; Parl. Writs, II. ii. 138.

[4] Rot. Parl. ii. 310; Statutes, i. 395.

[5] In 1330 Edward III had been obliged to order that more care should be taken in the county elections: 'pur ce que avant ces heures acuns des chivalers, que sunt venuz as parlementz pur les communautes des countes,

the petition, deciding in favour of the liberty of the constituencies on the ground of custom. Whether the liberty or the custom was in reality so important an object in the royal mind as the retention of the power exercised by the government through the sheriffs in the county court, the events of the reign of Richard enable us to decide.

The king refuses to alter the custom.

297. It is unnecessary to discuss the further points of royal prerogative in this place. Numerous as they are, they are not matters in which the crown came into conflict either with the parliament when full grown or with that constitutional spirit which was the life-breath of parliamentary growth. We have examined in detail the struggle between prerogative, in the sense of undefined royal authority, and parliamentary control, under the three chief heads of taxation, legislation, and executive functions, in council, courts of justice and military affairs. The minor points, to which properly belongs the definition of prerogative, as 'that which is law in respect to the king which is not law in respect to the subject,' are matters of privilege rather than of authority. Some of these points touch tenure, as the peculiar rights and customs enumerated in the statute *de Prerogativa Regis*[1]; such are the right of wardship, marriage and dower of the heirs of tenants in chief, the restraints on alienation of lands held in chief and serjeanties, the presentation to vacant churches after lapse, the custody of the lands of lunatics and idiots, the right to wreck, whales and sturgeons, the escheats of the land falling by descent to aliens, and other like customs. These are distinctly defined by law or prescription. Of another class, those concerning trade, such as have up to our present point a practical importance, have been noted in connexion with our discussion on the revenue; others, such as the power of creating monopolies, have an

Technical points of prerogative.

Statute *de Prerogativa Regis.*

Powers of the king with reference to trade,

ount este gentz de coveigne et maintenours de fauses quereles, et n'ount mie soeffret que les bones gentz poient monstrer les grevaunces du comun people, ne les choses que deussent aver este redresses en parlement a grant damage de nous et de nostre people, vous mandoms et chargeoms que vous facez eslire par commun assent de vostre countee deux des plus leaux et plus suffisauns chivalers ou serjauntz a meisme le countee, qui soient mie suspecionous de male conveigne,' &c.; Rot. Parl. ii. 443.

[1] Statutes, i. 226.

and to the clergy.

importance which lies far ahead of the present inquiry. The special prerogatives of the king with regard to the church and clergy must be examined in another part of our work.

The revolution of 1399 not a final determination of the whole question.

The examination however of the former points, so far as it has gone, leads to the same conclusions as those which are drawn from the direct and continuous narrative of the history of the fourteenth century. The struggle between royal prerogative and parliamentary authority does not work out its own issue in the fate of Richard II; the decision is taken for the moment on a side issue,—the wrongs of Henry of Lancaster; the judicial condemnation of Richard is a statement not of the actual causes of his deposition, but of the offences by which such a measure was justified. Prematurely Richard had challenged the rights of the nation, and the victory of the nation was premature. The royal position was founded on assumptions that had not even prescription in their favour, the victory of the house of Lancaster was won by the maintenance of rights which were claimed rather than established. The growth of the commons, and of the parliament itself in that constitution of which the commons were becoming the strongest part, must not be estimated by the rights which they had actually secured, but by those which they were strong enough to claim, and wise enough to appreciate. If the course of history had run otherwise, England might possibly have been spared three centuries of political difficulties; for the most superficial reading of history is sufficient to show that the series of events which form the crises of the Great Rebellion and the Revolution might link themselves on to the theory of Richard II as readily as to that of James I. In that case we might have seen the forces of liberty growing by regular stages as the pretensions of tyranny took higher and higher flights, until the struggle was fought out in favour of a nation uneducated and untrained for the use of the rights that fell to it, or in favour of a king who should know no limit to the aspirations of his ambition or to the exercise of his revenge. The failure of the house of Lancaster, the tyranny of the house of York, the statecraft of Henry VII, the apparent extinction of the constitution under the dictatorship of Henry VIII, the political resurrection under

The discipline of three centuries more was required for a successful issue of the struggle.

Elizabeth, were all needed to prepare and equip England to cope successfully with the principles of Richard II, masked under legal, religious, philosophical embellishments in the theory of the Stewarts. Hence it is that in our short enumeration of the points at issue we are obliged to rest content with recording the claims of parliament rather than to pursue them to their absolute vindication: they were claimed under Edward III, they were won during the Rebellion, at the Restoration, or at the Revolution: some of them were never won at all in the sense in which they were first claimed; parliament does not at the present day elect the ministers, or obtain the royal assent to bills before granting supplies; but the practical responsibility of the ministers is not the less assured, and the crown cannot choose ministers unacceptable to the parliament, with the slightest probability of their continuing in office. If the development of the ministerial system had been the only point gained by the delay of the crisis for three centuries, from 1399 to 1688, England might perhaps have been content to accept the responsibility of becoming a republic in the fifteenth century. Had that been the case, the whole history of the nation, perhaps of Europe also, would have been changed in a way of which we can hardly conceive. Certainly the close of the fourteenth century was a moment at which monarchy might seem to be in extremis, France owning the rule of a madman, Germany nominally subject to a drunkard,—the victim, the tyrant, and the laughing-stock of his subjects,—and the apostolic see itself in dispute between two rival successions of popes. That the result was different may be attributed, for one at least out of several reasons, to the fact that the nations were not yet ready for self-government.

Progress of parliamentary institutions to be calculated by claims rather than by vindications.

298. The fourteenth century has other aspects besides that in which we have here viewed it, aspects which seem paradoxical until they are viewed in connexion with the general course of human history, in which the ebb and flow of the life of nations is seen to depend on higher laws, more general purposes, the guidance of a Higher Hand. Viewed as a period of constitutional growth it has much to attract the sympathies and to interest the student

Other aspects of the fourteenth century.

who is content laboriously to trace out the links of causes and results. In literary history likewise it has a very distinct and significant place; and it is scarcely second to any age in its importance as a time of germination in religious history. In these aspects it might seem to furnish sufficient and more than sufficient matters of attractive disquisition. Yet it is on the whole unattractive, and in England especially so: the political heroes are, as we have seen, men who for some cause or other seem neither to demand nor to deserve admiration; the literature with few exceptions owes its interest either to purely philological causes or to its connexion with a state of society and thought which repels more than it attracts; the religious history read impartially is chilling and unedifying; its literature on both sides is a compound of elaborate dialectics and indiscriminate invective, alike devoid of high spiritual aspirations and of definite human sympathies. The national character, although it must be allowed to have grown in strength, has not grown into a knowledge how to use its strength. The political bloodshed of the fourteenth century is the prelude to the internecine warfare of the fifteenth: personal vindictiveness becomes, far more than it has ever yet been, a characteristic of political history. Public and private morality seem to fall lower and lower: at court splendid extravagance and coarse indulgence are seen hand in hand; John of Gaunt, the first lord of the land, claims the crown of Castille in the right of his wife, and lives in adultery with one of her ladies; he is looked up to as the protector of a religious party, one of whose special claims to support lies in its assertion of a pure morality; his son, Henry Beaufort, soon to become a bishop, a crusader, and by and by a cardinal, is the father of an illegitimate daughter, whose mother is sister to the earl of Arundel and the archbishop of Canterbury. If we look lower down we are tempted to question whether the growth of religious thought and literary facility has as yet done more good or harm. Neither the lamentations nor the confessions of Gower, nor the sterner parables of Langland, nor the brighter pictures of Chaucer, nor the tracts and sermons of Wycliffe, reveal to us anything that shows the national

Its character is generally unattractive.

Decline in moral power.

Impressions made by the literature of the time.

character to be growing in the more precious qualities of truthfulness and tenderness. There is much misery and much indignation; much luxury and little sympathy. The lighter stories of Chaucer recall the novels of Boccaccio, not merely in their borrowed plot but in the tone which runs through them; vice taken for granted, revelry and indulgence accepted as the enjoyment and charm of life; if it be intended as satire it is a satire too far removed from sympathy for that which is better, too much impregnated with the spirit of that which it would deride. Edward III, celebrating his great feast on the institution of the order of the Garter in the midst of the Black Death, seems a typical illustration of this side of the life of the century. The disintegration of the older forms of society has been noted already as accounting for much of the political history of a period which notwithstanding is fruitful in result. There is no unity of public interest, no singleness of political aim, no heroism of self-sacrifice. The baronage is divided against itself, one part maintaining the popular liberties but retarding their progress by bitter personal antipathies, the other maintaining royal autocracy, and although less guilty as aggressors still more guilty by way of revenge. The clergy are neither intelligent enough to guide education nor strong enough to repress heresy; the heretics have neither skill to defend nor courage to die for their doctrines; the universities are ready to maintain liberty but not powerful enough to lead public opinion; the best prelates, even such as Courtenay and Wykeham, are conservative rather than progressive in their religious policy, and the lower type, which is represented by Arundel, seems to combine political liberality with religious intolerance in a way that resembles, though with different aspect and attitude, the policy of the later puritans.

Prevalence of luxury and misery.

General disintegration.

Decline in the clergy.

The transition is scarcely less marked in the region of art; in architecture the unmeaning symmetry of the Perpendicular style is an outgrowth but a decline from the graceful and affluent diversity of the Decorated. The change in the penmanship is analogous; the writing of the fourteenth century is coarse and blurred compared with the exquisite elegance of the thirteenth,

Changes in architecture and writing.

and yet even that is preferable to the vulgar neatness and deceptive regularity of the fifteenth. The chain of historical writers becomes slighter and slighter until it ceases altogether, except so far as the continuators of the Polychronicon preserve a broken and unimpressive series of isolated facts.

Decline of history.

It may seem strange that the training of the thirteenth century, the examples of the patriot barons, the policy of the constitutional king, organiser and legislator, should have had so lame results; that whilst constitutionally the age is one of progress, morally it should be one of decline, and intellectually one of blossom rather than fruit. But the historian has not yet arisen who can account on the principles of growth, or of reaction, or of alternation, for the tides in the affairs of men. How it was we can read in the pages of the annalists, the poets, the theologians: how it became so we can but guess; why it was suffered we can only understand when we see it overruled for good. It may be that the glories of the thirteenth century conceal the working of internal evils which are not new, but come into stronger relief when the brighter aspects fade away; and that the change of characters from Edward I to Edward II, Edward III and Richard II, does but take away the light that has dazzled the eye of the historian, and so reveals the hollowness and meanness that may have existed all along. It may be that the strength, the tension, the aspirations of the earlier produced the weakness, the relaxation, the grovelling degradation of the later. But it is perhaps still too early to draw a confident conclusion. Weak as is the fourteenth century, the fifteenth is weaker still; more futile, more bloody, more immoral; yet out of it emerges in spite of all, the truer and brighter day, the season of more general conscious life, higher longings, more forbearing, more sympathetic, purer, riper liberty.

These things are not to be explained by theories.

Index